BOSWELL'S LIFE OF JOHNSON

Edited by G. B. HILL
Revised by L. F. POWELL

JAMES BOSWELL
from the painting by SIR JOSHUA REYNOLDS, 1786
in the National Portrait Gallery

BOSWELL'S
LIFE OF JOHNSON

TOGETHER WITH BOSWELL'S JOURNAL OF A TOUR TO THE HEBRIDES
AND JOHNSON'S DIARY OF A JOURNEY INTO NORTH WALES

EDITED BY

GEORGE BIRKBECK HILL, D.C.L.

REVISED AND ENLARGED EDITION BY

L. F. POWELL

IN SIX VOLUMES

VOLUME V

**THE TOUR TO THE HEBRIDES
and
THE JOURNEY INTO NORTH WALES**

SECOND EDITION

OXFORD
AT THE CLARENDON PRESS
1964

Oxford University Press, Amen House, London E.C.4

GLASGOW   NEW YORK   TORONTO   MELBOURNE   WELLINGTON
BOMBAY   CALCUTTA   MADRAS   KARACHI   LAHORE   DACCA
CAPE TOWN   SALISBURY   NAIROBI   IBADAN   ACCRA
KUALA LUMPUR   HONG KONG

© *Oxford University Press 1964*

FIRST PUBLISHED 1950
SECOND EDITION 1964

PRINTED IN GREAT BRITAIN

PREFACE

THE original manuscripts of the two works of which this volume consists have been available to me and I have used them fully, each in a different way: Boswell's manuscript journal has served to illustrate and explain the printed book that he produced from it and Johnson's manuscript diary has provided an authentic text. Separate accounts of the two works and of the methods I have adopted in revising Dr. Hill's edition of them follow.

The Journal of a Tour to the Hebrides

The manuscript of Boswell's *Journal of a Tour to the Hebrides* was discovered at Malahide Castle, the Irish seat of Lord Talbot de Malahide, Boswell's great-great-grandson, in 1930 and acquired by Lt.-Col. Ralph Isham. It was described by Professor F. A. Pottle in 1931[1] and 1933[2] and edited in 1936 by Professor Pottle and Dr. C. H. Bennett.[3] The evidence supplied by this manuscript and other material at their command has enabled these scholars to explain the exact nature of the process by which Boswell transformed his original record into a printed book. The greater part of this record was compiled during the tour. Boswell and Johnson were together from 14 August to 22 November, and for most of the time Boswell kept his journal, actually from 18 August[4] to 26 October. Up to 22 October the journal was written at the time; the entries for 22 October to 26 October were written some years

---

[1] F. A. Pottle and Marion S. Pottle, *The Private Papers of James Boswell from Malahide Castle, A Catalogue*, 1931, No. 33.

[2] *The Papers of the Bibliographical Soc. of America*, vol. 27, pt. i, 1933, pp. 69-71.

[3] *Boswell's Journal of a Tour to the Hebrides with Samuel Johnson, LL.D.* 'Now First Published from the Original Manuscript. Prepared for the Press, with Preface and Notes by Frederick A. Pottle and Charles H. Bennett', London: William Heinemann, Ltd. 1936. The American edition was published simultaneously by the Viking Press of New York.

[4] Boswell made rough notes for the previous four days on loose sheets which have survived and been published, *Boswell Papers*, vi. 164, 175 ff. He did not, apparently, show them to Johnson, but he used them for his printed book. He did not begin to keep a 'regular full journal' till 21 August. The journal from 18 August to 11 October was written in three note-books; the entries for 12 October to 26 October were made on loose sheets.

later, in 1779, 1780, and 1782, apparently from rough notes made at the time.[1] This was the journal that Johnson, Sir William Forbes, Mrs. Thrale, and others read, and that Boswell, with Malone's help,[2] revised for the press. The revision was thorough. It can best be described in the words of Professor Pottle and Dr. Bennett: 'Indiscreet and indelicate matter was excised. Boswell's topographical observations were generally deleted, since Johnson had published a topographical account, and Boswell, with some justice, was sceptical as to his powers of "expressing visible objects". Many passages of personal reflection were dropped, because the book was to be an essay in Johnsonian biography, not an autobiography. In the latter half of the book the revision was dictated partly by considerations of space.... The revision was by no means confined to excision. Matter was transposed, matter was added, whole paragraphs were recast, and every sentence scanned for informal syntax and "inelegant" phraseology.'[3]

This elaborately revised journal, together with the newly composed portions at the beginning and end and the numerous footnotes, formed the copy that Boswell sent to the printer.[4] The first batch of copy was delivered on 2 May; the Dedication to Malone was written on 20 September; the book was published on 1 October 1785. Its success was immediate and the second edition, of which Malone was the virtual editor, was published on 22 December following;[5] in this edition Boswell added the useful table of contents, the Appendix, and numerous notes. The third edition, the last to appear in Boswell's lifetime and to receive his correction,

---

[1] It would appear from Boswell's remark under date 11 November, 'as I kept no Journal of any thing that passed after this morning' (*post*, 394), that he had kept a journal of some sort up to that date.

[2] Malone's help amounted to the closest collaboration. See *post*, p. 1, n. 5.

[3] *Boswell's Journal of a Tour to the Hebrides*, 1936, p. x.

[4] Dr. R. W. Chapman suggested in his edition, 1924, p. xvii, n. 1, that this was possible; Professor Pottle proves it by noticing that 'the compositor has marked the beginnings of press signatures throughout'. *The Private Papers of James Boswell*, 1931, No. 33. See also *The Papers of the Bibliographical Soc. of America*, vol. 27, pt. i, 1933, p. 71.

[5] Boswell, without his consent, acknowledged Malone's help: 'Mr. Malone ... was so kind as to superintend the press while I was in Scotland, and the first part of the second edition was printing.' *Ante*, iii. 323, n. 2. Malone's suggested corrections and improvements were made in his copy of the first edition. Dr. Chapman, who records them all in the notes to his edition, reports that 'Boswell made very few changes, merely verbal, except those which were suggested by Malone' (p. xix).

was published in October 1786; some notes and the map were added.

My editorial procedure has been the same as that followed for the *Life*: the original pagination of Dr. Hill's edition has been scrupulously retained, the text revised, and the commentary corrected and supplemented. I have adopted the third edition as the basis of the text,[1] collated it with the first and second editions, and when it is, in my opinion, incorrect, as it frequently is, restored the correct reading and recorded the variants in a critical note. My collation, which was made independently of Dr. Chapman's, confirms his judgement that 'the first edition has many readings which are indisputably right' (p. xix); the first edition is also greatly superior to the other editions in respect of punctuation and the like. To the readings of the editions I have added in the critical notes or elsewhere the readings of Boswell's original manuscript journal, which in many places supports the first edition and in others corrects a text corrupt or defective in all editions.[2] There are now no cruces in this text for Dr. Chapman to solve.

Dr. Hill's commentary does not reach the same high level of excellence as that with which he illustrated the *Life*: it is often inadequate and sometimes irrelevant or inaccurate. He made judicious and extensive use of Johnson's own account of his travels, as related in his letters to Mrs. Thrale and in his *Journey to the Western Islands*, and of Sir Walter Scott's notes, as printed by Croker or Lockhart; these were his chief sources on Scottish matters and personalities. Dr. Hill had little knowledge of Scotland in 1887, and he does not appear to have been in communication with the Scottish scholars and officials whom he met two years later, when, for the purposes of his *Footsteps of Dr. Johnson*,[3] he

---

[1] Dr. Hill nowhere states which edition he adopted. He prints Lord Pembroke's remark on Johnson's *bow-wow way* as a note (v. 18), a position to which it was first relegated in the fourth edition (1807), but he does not follow that edition in its correction of 'designed' (a misprint of the second and third editions) to 'designing' (v. 205), which he in fact suggested. He reproduced the title-page of the third edition and he probably used that edition, most of whose errors he leaves uncorrected. He occasionally consulted the first and second editions, but he made no systematic collation of them with the third. His text is not satisfactory.

[2] See especially *post*, v. 88, 89, 140.

[3] This work was published in 1890 and is primarily a picture-book, but it does contain some new and interesting material. Dr. Hill visited Scotland as a youth of seventeen in 1852, when he was in the Loch Lomond district, and twenty years later, when he stayed at

Preface

went over the ground covered by the travellers; he was, therefore, not in a position to include much first-hand information in his commentary. My additions to and corrections of this commentary have been considerable. Material has been abundant, even embarrassing in its richness. Apart from Boswell's original journal and the *Boswell Papers*, which are in a class by themselves, and the standard works of reference, the *Dictionary of National Biography*, Sir James Balfour Paul's *Scots Peerage*, G.E.C.'s *Complete Baronetage* and *Complete Peerage*, and Hew Scott's *Fasti Ecclesiæ Scoticanæ*, which are familiar to us, but were not available to Dr. Hill, my chief printed sources of information have been the journals and reports of other travellers, such as Pennant, of whom Johnson thought highly,[1] and David Henry, the publisher of the *Gentleman's Magazine*, to which he contributed terse descriptions of Scottish inns;[2] the various histories of the districts, counties, cities, towns, or universities which Johnson visited; family and clan histories, which have enabled me to identify and give biographical details of persons whom Johnson met or Boswell mentioned; and such collections of original material as the reminiscences and observations of John Ramsay of Ochtertyre (1736–1814),[3] the confidential report,[4] in the Whig interest, on the Scottish freeholders, giving an account of their circumstances, connections, and character; and the journals, narratives, and memoranda of the Jacobite Bishop Robert Forbes (1708–75).[5] All, or nearly all, of the numerous works quoted or referred to in my notes are in the National Library of Scotland,[6] and this library, together with the Signet Library, the Library of the University of Edinburgh, and the General Register House, has supplied me with valuable manuscript material. I may mention in

Braemar. *Footsteps of Dr. Johnson*, p. 254 and *Letters written by a Grandfather*, ed. Lucy Crump, 1903, p. 11.

[1] *Ante*, iii. 274; *post*, v. 221. Pennant made two journeys in Scotland, one in 1769, when he did not visit the Hebrides, the other in 1772, when he did. For the somewhat complicated bibliography of his published accounts of these journeys, *A Tour in Scotland; MDCCLXIX* and *A Tour in Scotland and Voyage to the Hebrides, 1772*, see my article 'The Tours of Thomas Pennant' in *The Library*, N.S., vol. xix, No. 2, 1938, pp. 135 ff.

[2] *Gent. Mag.* 1771, xli. 543 ff.

[3] Published by Alexander Allardyce under the title of *Scotland and Scotsmen in the Eighteenth Century*, 2 vols., 1888.

[4] *A view of the Political State of Scotland in 1788*, edited by Sir Charles Elphinstone Adam, 1887.

[5] *The Lyon in Mourning*, edited by Henry Paton (Scottish History Soc.), 3 vols., 1895–6.

[6] A number, chiefly of topographical or genealogical interest, are not in the British Museum or the Bodleian.

Preface

particular extracts from the Minutes of the Faculty of Advocates and the Senatus Minutes of the University of Edinburgh, which give details of the librarians of the Advocates' Library and the University Library respectively (v. 467, 469); the letters of Dr. John Macpherson of Sleat, which prove beyond a doubt that he revised and enlarged Kenneth Macaulay's *History of St. Kilda* (v. 506); a letter of Flora Macdonald, which shows that her husband was indeed 'embarrassed in his affairs' (v. 529); and Lady Grange's narrative of her abduction, which was misread by Sir Walter Scott (v. 539–40). Other manuscripts of Scottish interest in private hands have been placed at my service: the pathetic diary of Boswell's younger brother, John, by the late Dr. Alexander Boswell, the lineal descendant of Dr. John Boswell, Boswell's uncle (v. 464), and the lively memoirs of Lady Anne Barnard (*née* Lindsay), by the late Earl of Crawford and Balcarres (v. 576). Many Scottish friends and colleagues, to whom I have appealed when books failed me, have supplied me with much information; and, as I have followed in Johnson's footsteps and visited the places that he visited, I have been able to add a good deal to the commentary from ocular observation. The precise nature of this commentary will be seen from the ensuing paragraphs.

The number of anonymous or general descriptions of persons in the *Tour* is not so great proportionally as in the *Life*, which is of much wider scope: the respective totals are 70 and 511.[1] Croker[2] and Carruthers[3] successfully identified twenty-three of the persons whose names Boswell had concealed or suppressed. Napier,[4] with due acknowledgement, adopted most of Croker's identifications,

---

[1] See my article 'The Anonymous Designations in Boswell's Journal of a Tour to the Hebrides and their Identification', in *Edinburgh Bibliographical Society Transactions*, vol. ii, part 4, 1946, pp. 353 ff. The respective numbers there given are 64 and 414, but a closer scrutiny made during the compilation of the Table of Anonymous Persons (*post*, vi. 423 ff.) showed that these figures are too low.

[2] Croker was assisted by Sir Walter Scott, who made several false shots, but was right in suggesting that 'the young lady of quality', who paid Johnson one of the handsomest compliments that he ever received (v. 401), was 'probably one of the Ladies Lindsay, daughters of the Earl of Balcarres', and by the young but well-informed William Macpherson, a relation of Dr. John Macpherson of Sleat, who satisfied him that 'one of our company', who 'had hurt himself by too much study, particularly of infidel metaphysicians', was the Laird of Mackinnon (v. 168, 525).

[3] Robert Carruthers, who was editor of the *Inverness Courier* for fifty years, published his edition of the *Tour* in 1852.

[4] See *post*, v, p. xvi.

Preface

even those that were erroneous, ignored those made by Carruthers, and made none of his own. Dr. Hill added five new identifications, three of them involving Malone, but overlooked six made by the previous editors, Croker and Carruthers. Dr. Chapman, by the publication in his edition of Malone's notes to Boswell,[1] revealed that 'one of the club, who knew Mr. Vesey better than Dr. Johnson and I [Boswell]' was Malone himself (v. 108), that 'the lady on whom Johnson was very severe' at Dunvegan was Lady Macdonald, his hostess at Armadale (v. 231), that 'a certain baronet', who told Boswell that 'he never was happy in the country, till he was not on speaking terms with his neighbours', was Sir John Dalrymple, and that 'Lord ———', one of those neighbours who 'stuck long', was Lord Adam Gordon (v. 353, 560). I have been able, thanks largely to Boswell's original journal and other material that has been placed in my hands, to confirm a number of these identifications and to add to them considerably. The new identifications, which number twenty,[2] are not, it must be confessed, quite so exciting as those made in the *Life*, but some are of peculiar interest. 'A gentleman who published a Defence of my Journal' was, according to Boswell himself, one W. James, about whom I know nothing (v. 3; vi. 460–1). 'Another gentleman', who dined with Johnson and Boswell's other guests on the day after Johnson's arrival in Edinburgh, was Charles Hay, at the time an Advocate and later a Lord of Session, Lord Newton (v. 32). The Scottish Judge with whose argument on copyright Johnson did not agree, was Lord Gardenstone (v. 50, 474). 'A rapacious Chief would make a wilderness of his estate' looks innocent enough, but Boswell generalized the remark; Johnson meant Sir Alexander Macdonald in particular (v. 205): Sir Alexander is more openly described later as 'a rapacious Highland Chief' (v. 378), and his rapacity or parsimony is attacked on other occasions (v. 277, 279, 315). The 'two other gentlemen', who attended Boswell and Malcolm Macleod on their day-long tramp over very rugged ground in Raasay, were Donald Macleod, late tacksman of Canna, and John Macqueen, the Reverend Donald Macqueen's son (v. 168; vi. 462–3). The same Donald Macleod, 'an obliging serviceable man', who acted as the travellers' guide over the greater part of Skye, was 'our messenger', who found it

---

[1] See *ante*, v, p. vi, n. 5.
[2] Many are given in the edition of Boswell's original journal by Prof. F. A. Pottle and Dr. C. H. Bennett.

very difficult to procure cash for a bill; his name was suppressed, perhaps, because he got 'mortally drunk' at Portree and gave some of the money away (v. 254, 519). 'One of the candidates' for nomination in the Ayrshire election, who 'had artfully held himself out as a champion for the independency of the county against aristocratick influence', was Sir Adam Fergusson of Kilkerran, Boswell's political enemy (v. 354; vi. 464–5). 'A gentleman in company' at Inveraray, who, to avoid any appearance of servility to his political chief, the Duke of Argyll, 'whistled to show his independency', was Lt.-Col. Adam Livingstone, M.P. for Argyllshire (v. 358, 562). 'A very respectable Chieftain', who, 'when interrogated with the strictness of judicial inquiry . . . retracted what he had formerly asserted', was Sir Allan Maclean, the travellers' host at Inchkenneth (v. 390, 556). Malone may well have been, as Prof. Pottle and Dr. Bennett suggest, 'a learned friend', who doubted whether Hume's virtue had ever been severely tested (v. 31; vi. 460–1); he was, I am confident, 'one of the ablest commentators on Shakespeare, who knew much of Dr. Johnson' (v. 244, 542), and 'a friend for whose opinion I [Boswell] have great respect' (v. 246), descriptions which we know to be strictly true. The identity of the 'insular lady', whose health Johnson and Boswell drank in whisky, with Miss Isabel Macpherson, daughter of Dr. John Macpherson, is uncertain; Boswell, who was writing nine years after the event, only thought she was the lady; the silence of William Macpherson, Croker's correspondent, indicates the absence of any tradition on the subject in the family (v. 347). The names of some of the persons mentioned or described by Johnson in general terms were not known to Boswell; he did not, for instance, know that the 'old lawyer' who told Johnson, 'that after people had deliberated long, and thought of many for their executors, they settled at last by fixing on their relations', was, according to Mrs. Piozzi, Charles Scrase, her first husband's friend and legal adviser (v. 105, 499); that the uncle of Johnson, whose papers were in exact order on his death, was, in all probability, Dr. Joseph Ford (v. 316); and that 'the clergyman's widow', who caused so much trouble between Dr. Young and his son, was, in fact, a clergyman's daughter, Miss Mary Hallows, who survived long enough to read Johnson's vindication of her virtue and his not very flattering description of her character (v. 270, 548–9).

Preface

Johnson met a large number of persons on his journey through Scotland, and a much larger number are mentioned in Boswell's account of it; members of the nobility and landed gentry; Highland chiefs and lairds, their tacksmen, factors, and dependants; Lords of Session, Advocates, and other lawyers; scholars, university professors, and officials; Presbyterian and Episcopalian ministers; soldiers, doctors, and other professional men; ladies galore: their number is legion. Previous editors, notably Croker, who was aided by Sir Walter Scott, and Carruthers, identified some of these and gave interesting anecdotes of them, but the majority were left unnoted, even many who entertained the travellers in their houses. I have attempted a systematic identification of all of those not already sufficiently described by Dr. Hill; the description of the minor characters is necessarily brief and is sometimes confined to the Index; I hope and believe that no major character has been inadequately commemorated. The following may be regarded as representative of the above-mentioned groups: Dr. John Boswell, the biographer's uncle; Major John Brewse, a Royal Engineer of distinction; Dr. George Campbell, Principal of Marischal College, Aberdeen; the Dowager Lady Colville, Boswell's life-long friend; James Craig, the architect of the New Town, Edinburgh; George Dempster, M.P., an early promoter of Scottish industry; the Reverend John Dun, minister of Auchinleck; Alexander Montgomerie, 10th Earl of Eglinton, who took charge of Boswell on his 'elopement' to London, and his mother, Susanna, Lady Eglinton, who 'adopted' Johnson as her son; Lord Elibank, soldier and pamphleteer; James Hay (né Boyd), 15th Earl of Errol, who entertained Johnson at Slains Castle, and his brother Charles, the Jacobite; Francis Garden, Lord Gardenstone, the founder of Laurencekirk; Sir Alexander Gordon, of Lesmoir, Professor of Medicine at King's College, Aberdeen; Professor Thomas Gordon, Humanist at the same college, and his colleague at St. Paul's Episcopalian church, the Reverend James Riddoch, with whose wife Boswell had been in love; Lady Betty Hamilton, later Lady Derby; John Jeans, 'fossilist'; John Maclaurin, Lord Dreghorn, one of Boswell's closest friends; Dr. Charles Nisbet, minister of Montrose, who became the first President of Dickinson College, Carlisle, Pennsylvania; Robert Ord, Lord Chief Baron; Lt.-Col. John Pennington, later Lord Muncaster; James Robertson,

Preface

Librarian of the University of Edinburgh, with whose conversation Johnson was much pleased; William Robertson, Lord Monboddo's scholarly clerk and later Joint Deputy Keeper of the Records of Scotland; Alexander Trapaud, Resident Governor of Fort Augustus, and his more distinguished brother General Cyrus Trapaud, who has been overlooked by the editors of the *Dictionary of National Biography*; Dr. Alexander Webster, minister of the Tolbooth Church, Edinburgh, for forty-seven years, and a remarkably versatile man; and the Highlanders, most of whom were Hebrideans, Sir James Colquhoun, the Reverend John Macaulay and his younger brother Kenneth, Allan Macdonald of Kingsburgh (Flora's husband), Lachlan Mackinnon of Corrichatachin, Sir Allan Maclean, Donald Maclean ('young Coll'), Dr. Hector Maclean of Tobermory, John Maclean of Lochbuy, Macleod of Macleod (Norman, 20th Chief), Alexander Macleod of Muiravonside, Alexander Macleod of Ulinish, John Macleod of Raasay and his cousin Malcolm Macleod, Col. John Macleod of Talisker, the Reverend Neil Macleod of Mull, the Reverend Martin Macpherson of Sleat and his sister Isabel, Lauchlan MacQuarrie of Ulva, and the Reverend Donald Macqueen, reported to be 'the most intelligent man in Skye'.

The identification and description of the places visited by Johnson and Boswell is an important feature of this revision. I have, when it was necessary or desirable, written accounts of the churches, libraries, or public buildings that they saw, and of the mansions, houses, or inns in which they stayed. Some of the churches, many of the houses, and most of the inns no longer exist; their sites are generally known, and sometimes commemorated.[1]

Bibliographical problems are not so numerous as they are in the *Life*, but there are several of interest. I have identified and described a number of books and pamphlets that are not clearly named by Boswell and given more precise details of others than Dr. Hill was able to obtain. Among the books of which I have given an account or whose history I have investigated are: *The Muses Welcome to Prince James*, which Johnson adduced as evidence of Scottish learning (v. 57, 477); James Barclay's *An Examination of*

---

[1] Commemorative tablets mark the site of Boyd's Inn, the White Horse, Edinburgh (*post*, v. 21), and of the 'tolerable inn' at Oban (*post*, v. 559); there is also a tablet on the Laird of Lochbuy's house at Moy, Mull (*post*, v. 558).

Mr. Kenrick's Review of Mr. Johnson's Edition of Shakespeare, a very rare pamphlet of which Johnson did not think highly (v. 273, 549); Dr. Thomas Morell's translation and edition of Aeschylus, dedicated to, and highly recommended by, Garrick (v. 350, 560); *The History of St. Kilda*, published by the Reverend Kenneth Macaulay, but, as Boswell was informed,[1] and as I believe I have proved, written in part by Dr. John Macpherson of Sleat (v. 118, 505–7); Tom Cumming's *A Rational Inquiry concerning Prayer*, an anonymous and excessively rare pamphlet, which was not, as the Hon. Charles Boyd stated, a reply to Leechman but the treatise to which Leechman replied (v. 101, 497); John Wesley's *A Calm Address to our American Colonies*, which from the free use made by it of *Taxation no Tyranny* has some claim to inclusion in Johnsonian bibliography (v. 35, 466); and *A Sermon Preached at the Cathedral Church of St. Paul, Before the Sons of the Clergy, on Thursday the Second of May, 1745*, which, although ascribed on the title-page to Johnson's friend, the Hon. and Rev. Henry Hervey Aston, was, as I have shown, written by Johnson himself (v. 67, 483–4); of this addition to the canon of Johnson's works I have found only two copies.

New notes or supplements to existing notes have been added to the commentary on a great variety of other subjects. The following list of the more important of these will show their nature: Boswell's objection to the term 'Pretender' and the means he took to obtain royal permission to use a more gentlemanly designation (v. 185, 531); his controversy with his rival biographer, Mrs. Piozzi, over Mrs. Montagu's *Essay on Shakespear* (v. 245, 542); and his quarrel with Lord Macdonald, which nearly led to a duel (v. 415, 578); the precise details of his Dutch relations, the Van Sommelsdijks (v. 25, 463); the law cases on vicennial prescription of crime (v. 24, 87, 463) and copyright (v. 50, 474); the times of sitting of the Court of Session (v. 21, 462) and of holding church services in Edinburgh (v. 32, 464); communion tokens (v. 119, 507–8); the 'signed assurance' or Accession oath of the Hanoverian Sovereigns (v. 41, 467); the Scots Brigade in the Dutch service (v. 256, 544); Flora Macdonald's assistance to Prince Charles Edward (v. 187, 532–4); the history of Flora Macdonald and her husband in

---

[1] Boswell's informant was almost certainly the Rev. Martin Macpherson. Dr. John Macpherson's son. *R.E.S.*, xvi, 1940, p. 45.

Preface

America (v. 185, 529–31); Boswell's confusion of Macdonald of Clanranald, who was killed at Sheriffmuir, with Ranald Macdonald of Belfinlay, Skye, who was severely wounded at Culloden (v. 158, 520–1); Lady Grange's abduction and confinement in St. Kilda (v. 227, 539); the St. Kilda cough or 'boat-cold' (v. 278, 551); the monument to Smollett on the banks of the Leven, the epitaph for which was revised by Johnson (v. 366, 564); the Accession speech of George III (v. 204, 535–6); Warburton's vacillating relations with Theobald and Pope (v. 80, 490–1); Mickle's quarrel with Garrick over the rejection of his play, *Chateaubriant* (v. 349, 559);[1] Dr. Edward Young's estrangement from his only son (v. 270, 548); and Johnson's visit, or probable visit, to Capt. Joseph Knight, R.N., on board H.M.S. *Ramillies* in December 1770 (v. 514–15).

Johnson's Diary of a Journey into North Wales

The holograph manuscript of the diary that Johnson kept on his journey, with Mr. and Mrs. Thrale and their eldest daughter, Queeney, through the Midlands into North Wales was preserved by his residuary legatee, Frank Barber, and was, at some time before January 1813, acquired by the Reverend Henry Gostling White. From Mr. White's hands it passed successively to those of Richard Duppa and Dr. Samuel Butler, Headmaster of Shrewsbury School, and later Bishop of Lichfield; on Bishop Butler's death in 1839 it was purchased, with other of his manuscripts, by the British Museum.[2]

Duppa, with the valuable assistance of Mrs. Piozzi, published the diary in 1816;[3] Croker incorporated it in its chronological place

---

[1] Since writing my note on this subject I have had the privilege, through the kindness of Professor A. W. M. Ellis, of examining the Mickle papers in the possession of the Mickle family; they include, in addition to the correspondence with Boswell printed in the *Universal Magazine* and quoted by me, Mickle's copy of a letter, 26 Apr. '71, by Tom Warton to Garrick recommending the play to him, and I now think that 'the name at which Garrick would tremble' alluded to Tom Warton and not to Johnson, as I have suggested (v. 559). In this connexion it may be noted that two of the 'eminent critics' referred to by Boswell as having a good opinion of Mickle's play were, according to Boswell himself, 'both the Wartons' (v. 349, n. 1).

[2] See *post*, v. 427, n. 1 and *Catalogue of Additions to the MSS. in the British Museum, 1841–1845*, (1850), pp. 9, 32.

[3] *A Diary of a Journey into North Wales in the Year 1774;. by Samuel Johnson, LL.D. Edited, with illustrative notes, by R. Duppa, LL.B.* Most of the notes were derived from

xvi   *Preface*

in his editions of the *Life*;[1] and Napier included it in his fifth volume,[2] which also contained Boswell's *Journal of a Tour to the Hebrides*. Dr. Hill, who clearly did not know that the manuscript was available to him, followed the text of Croker's third edition,[3] but adopted Duppa's method of printing the entries, which corresponds generally to that of the manuscript. I have printed the manuscript as Johnson wrote it,[4] and preserved his orthography; I have, however, supplied, within brackets, words or parts of words that he inadvertently omitted, and, when I could do so with confidence, I have filled the blank spaces that he deliberately left for names that he did not know. The restoration of the passages omitted, together with the return to the original arrangement of the diary, has prevented me from maintaining throughout an exact correspondence with the pagination of Dr. Hill's edition; the difference, when it occurs, between the old pagination and the new is, however, not great.

I have revised the commentary on the same lines and to the same

information supplied by Mrs. Piozzi. Duppa's text is unsatisfactory. He silently omitted words or sentences that he thought unsuitable for the public eye or could not read; he arranged some of the entries under the wrong dates; and he misread on many occasions Johnson's somewhat difficult hand. The following are examples of his textual errors: 'no trees' for 'not tall trees' (p. 433, last line); 'patch' for 'path' (p. 434, l. 1); 'climbing' for 'tiring' (p. 436, l. 4); 'more' for 'mere' (p. 438, l. 21); 'paved' for 'paced' (p. 440, l. 12); 'Ruthin' for 'Ruthlan' (p. 442, l. 8); 'Washington' for 'Worthington' (p. 443, l. 14 foot); 'left' for 'lost' (p. 448, l. 6 foot); 'horrors' for 'horses' (p. 452, l. 13 foot); and 'Wheeler' for 'Hector' (p. 458, in four places).

[1] Croker in his second edition (1835, v. 193, n.) states that 'a collation of the original MS., kindly entrusted to Mr. Murray by its present proprietor, the Rev. Archdeacon Butler, of Shrewsbury, has supplied many corrections, and some omissions, in the text.' The collation was, however, very imperfect.

[2] Napier's only important contribution was a note on Bodvil, Mrs. Thrale's birthplace, from information supplied by Francis Turner Palgrave (1884, v. 391).

[3] Dr. Hill, in a note to his edition (1887, v. 427, n. 1), says that he has generally followed Croker's text; he does not specify which edition, but as he quotes the third edition in his notes and gives readings ('end' for 'foot', p. 430, last line, and 'across' for 'cross', p. 452, l. 12 foot) which occur in that edition alone, it is safe to assume that that was the edition he generally followed. That he did not rely solely on this edition is shown by his inclusion of the sentence 'The gallery one hundred and twenty feet long (all paved)' (p. 440, ll. 11, 12), which was omitted, by homoeoteleuton, in Croker's second edition and not restored in the third.

[4] Duppa distributed some of Johnson's 'Notes and Omissions' (p. 440) and 'Notes' (p. 461) to what he considered to be their appropriate places in the diary; those that he could not place, or thought unimportant, he omitted.

Preface

extent as I have revised that of the companion work. My chief source of information has been the diary, more fully written than Johnson's, kept by Mrs. Thrale on the tour;[1] with the aid of this and other material I have identified and described Johnson's several hosts, the people whom he met or mentioned, their houses, and the other places that he saw. Among the persons described are Johnson's or Dr. Taylor's Staffordshire and Derbyshire friends, Edward Walhouse Okeover of Okeover, the Gells of Hopton Hall, and the Dyotts of Freeford; Mrs. Thrale's relatives and friends, Sir Lynch Salusbury Cotton, her uncle, and Sir Robert, his son, Richard Lloyd, the boon companion of her father, Edwin, Lord Sandys of Ombersley, and William Henry Lyttelton, later Baron Westcote, of Little Hagley; and a number of Welsh squires, clerics, and notables, Hugh Griffith of Brynodol, John Griffiths of Cefn Amwlch, John Myddelton of Gwaynynog, the Reverend William Lloyd, headmaster of Beaumaris Grammar School, and the Reverend Robert Vanbrugh, headmaster of the King's School, Chester, Thomas Roberts, Registrar of Bangor, Dr. William Worthington of Llanrhaiadr, and Sir Thomas Wynn, later Baron Newborough. Among the more important places of which I have given an account are Bach-y-Graig, the Flintshire house of which Mrs. Thrale went to Wales to take possession; Bodvil Hall, Carnarvonshire, her birth-place and childhood's home; Combermere Abbey, Cheshire, and Llewenny Hall, Denbighshire, the seats of Sir Lynch Salusbury Cotton and his son, Sir Robert, respectively; Baron Hill, near Beaumaris, Anglesey; Brynodol, Carnarvonshire; Gwaynynog, Denbighshire, in the grounds of which Johnson is commemorated by an urn; Clynnog Fawr, Carnarvonshire, one of the most remarkable churches of North Wales; and Tremerchion, Flint, the church in which Mrs. Thrale, her second husband, Gabriel Piozzi, and her father, lie buried.

ACKNOWLEDGEMENTS

It remains for me to record my thanks to all those without whose help my work could not have been done.[2] I must in the first place express my great obligations to the Leverhulme Trustees for the

---

[1] Published in A. M. Broadley's *Dr. Johnson and Mrs. Thrale*, John Lane at the Bodley Head, 1910, a work in which Johnson's diary was reprinted.

[2] See *post*, vi, pp. vi and 423 for acknowledgement of help with the Index and the Table of Anonymous Persons.

grant of a Research Fellowship for the year 1936-7 and to the Curators of the Taylor Institution, Oxford, for enabling me to accept it by giving me leave of absence from official duties as their Librarian for the vacations of that year. Prolonged visits to Scotland were by their joint action made possible.

I am deeply indebted to various official bodies and private persons for permission to make use of documents or manuscripts in their charge or possession: to the Senatus of the University of Edinburgh, and the Faculty of Advocates, Edinburgh; to the Librarians of the National Library of Scotland, the Library of Edinburgh University, the Signet Library, Edinburgh, the John Rylands Library, Manchester, and the Bodleian Library; to the Director and Trustees of the Henry E. Huntington Library, San Marino, California; to the late Dr. Alexander Boswell, of Ashbourne; to the Marquis of Bristol; to Professor J. L. Clifford, of Columbia University; to the late Earl of Crawford and Balcarres; to Lt.-Col. Ralph Isham; to the late (sixth) Marquis of Lansdowne; and to the late Sir Randle Mainwaring, of Hafod y Coed, St. Asaph.

I acknowledge with gratitude the help given me by the following copyright books, from some of which I have quoted with considerable freedom: Sir Charles Elphinstone Adam's *View of the Political State of Scotland in the Last Century*, published by David Douglas, Edinburgh, 1887; Alexander Allardyce's *Scotland and Scotsmen in the Eighteenth Century*, published by William Blackwood and Sons, Edinburgh, 1888; A. M. Broadley's *Dr. Johnson and Mrs. Thrale*, published by John Lane at the Bodley Head, 1910; Henry Paton's *The Lyon in Mourning*, 1895-6, and W. B. Blaikie's *Itinerary of Prince Charles Edward Stuart*, 1897, both printed at the University Press, Edinburgh, by T. and A. Constable for the Scottish History Society; and Professor F. A. Pottle and Dr. C. H. Bennett's *Boswell's Journal of a Tour to the Hebrides*, published by William Heinemann, Ltd. 1936.[1] Books of special interest have been given or lent to me by friends or colleagues: the late R. B. Adam, Mr. R. A. Austen-Leigh, Miss

---

[1] Professor Pottle kindly sent me before the edition was published a typescript of the original manuscript, and it is from this typescript that many of the quotations in the footnotes, with the reference *MS.* or *MS*, *Journal*, are taken; in the more extensive commentary in Appendix D, which was compiled after 1936, the quotations are generally taken from the edition. I regret the lack of uniformity in citation.

K. C. Balderston, Miss O. B. Bertie, Dr. R. W. Chapman, Professor J. L. Clifford, the late Sir Charles Firth, the late Professor John Fraser, Dr. A. Mitchell Hunter, Professor E. L. McAdam, the late John B. Nicolson, of Raasay, the Reverend Donald MacKinnon, Colonel the Hon. Arthur C. Murray, Mr. E. Baillie Reynolds, and Mr. C. H. Wilkinson.

I have been compelled on very many occasions to appeal to colleagues and correspondents for help. My appeal was seldom made in vain, and I have to place on record my indebtedness to the following persons, who, with unfailing courtesy, supplied me with the information I needed: the late James R. Anderson, Librarian of Baillie's Institute, Glasgow; Dr. W. Angus, formerly Keeper of the Records of Scotland; Mr. R. Bain, Librarian of the Mitchell Library, Glasgow; Mr. C. W. Baty, formerly Headmaster of the King's School, Chester; the Reverend Charles S. Caldwell, formerly Rector of St. Paul's Episcopal Church, Aberdeen; Dr. John Campbell, late of the Tolbooth Church, Edinburgh; Mr. J. C. Cantley, Town Clerk of St. Andrews; Miss Irene V. Churchill, Librarian of Lambeth Palace; Mr. A. G. Cockburn, Town Clerk of Elgin; Mr. W. Crawford, Town Clerk of Hamilton; the late Howell Lloyd Davies, of Ruabon; the Reverend John Davies, formerly Vicar of Clynnog Fawr; the late John Grant, of Edinburgh; Mr. W. Forbes Gray, of Edinburgh; Mr. George Hayward, Librarian of Norwich Public Library; Miss Rosalind Hill, of Westfield College, a grand-daughter of Dr. Birkbeck Hill; the late T. Cann Hughes, of Lancaster; the late Right Reverend Sir David Hunter-Blair, O.S.B., Abbot of Fort Augustus; the late J. H. Jamieson, of Edinburgh; Mr. Stephen K. Jones, formerly Librarian of Dr. Williams's Library; Mr. Bennet Langton, of Langton, Spilsby, Lincolnshire; the late R. H. Lindsay, of the Register House, Edinburgh; the late Sir John E. Lloyd, of the University of North Wales, Bangor; Professor Paul Maas; the late Allan R. Macdonald, of Belfinlay, Skye; Mr. C. T. McInnes, Curator of Historical Records, the Register House, Edinburgh; Mr. Hector McKechnie, K.C., of Edinburgh; the Reverend Alexander MacKinnon, minister of Duirinish, Skye; the late Dr. Hector Maclean, minister of Strath, Skye; Flora, Mrs. MacLeod of MacLeod; Mr. Fred. T. Macleod, of Edinburgh; Dr. C. A. Malcolm, Librarian of the Signet Library; the late Reverend

Preface

William Metcalfe, minister of Cawdor, and his niece, Miss Mary Nelson; Mr. H. Minn, of Oxford; Mr. W. Fraser Mitchell, of Exeter College, Oxford; the Reverend A. Lowndes Moir; Professor Ernest Mossner, of the University of Texas; the Reverend Thomas M. Murchison, formerly minister of Glenelg; the late Sir Oswyn Murray, Secretary of the Admiralty; Mr. E. S. Murrell, of the London Library; Mr. J. B. Oldham, of Shrewsbury School; Mr. K. T. Parker, Keeper of the Department of Fine Art, Oxford; the late A. Ivor Pryce, Registrar of the Diocese of Bangor; the late Canon H. M. Ranken, Rector of Montrose; Dr. T. Richards, formerly Librarian of Bangor University; Mr. S. C. Roberts, Master of Pembroke College, Cambridge; the late Sir Humphry Rolleston; the late Kenneth Sanderson, W.S., of Edinburgh; Dr. L. W. Sharp, Librarian of the University Library, Edinburgh; Mr. D. Bonner Smith, Admiralty Librarian; the late John J. Smith, of St. Andrews; Major-General A. P. D. Telfer-Smollett, of Bonhill; Mr. Francis Thompson, the Librarian of Chatsworth; the Reverend W. R. Torvaney, Rector of St. James's, Aberdeen; the late A. S. White, Librarian of the War Office; and Professor H. G. Wright, of the University of North Wales, Bangor.

I owe something more than gratitude to personal friends and associates: to Dr. R. W. Chapman, the prime mover of all my Johnsonian studies and my constant support in their prosecution; to Dr. H. W. Meikle and Mr. William Beattie, of Edinburgh, and Dr. W. R. Cunningham, of Glasgow, whose familiarity with the Scottish scene has been my happy resource; to the Reverend Donald MacKinnon, formerly of Portree, Skye, and now of Kennoway, Fife, who has been my guide through the mazes of Highland family history; to Mr. A. L. Reade, of Blundellsands, whose rigorous methods of research are at once an example and an inspiration; to the late Dr. E. A. Sadler, of Ashbourne, whose knowledge of the district in which he lived and served for over fifty years was of the most intimate nature; to Mr. James Marshall Osborn, of Yale, who, at his own suggestion, introduced me to Scotland, and conveyed me to Skye by much the same route that Boswell took Johnson; and to Mr. Esmond de Beer, my frequent companion in the Hebrides, whose wide-ranging intellect has helped me to an extent that he himself probably does not realize.

The proofs of this volume have had the very great advantage of

Preface xxi

being read, in whole or in part, by Professor Edward Bensly, who died in 1939, Dr. R. W. Chapman, the Right Hon. Sir Frank Douglas MacKinnon, who died in 1946, Professor F. A. Pottle, Mr. Vernon Rendall, Professor D. Nichol Smith, and Mr. Leonard Whibley, who died in 1941. I am indebted to Dr. C. H. Bennett for a number of corrections, and Mr. Frederick Page has continued to give me his skilled assistance.

The frequency with which I have had to record the death of benefactors is a melancholy reminder of the length of time it has taken me to accomplish my task. When I began my work, over a quarter of a century ago, no one, least of all myself, foresaw that it would take so long; the delay in completing it is due to events beyond my control and to the state of the world.

OXFORD
16 *May* 1950

L. F. P.

PREFACE TO THE SECOND EDITION

THE falling out of print of this volume and the recovery and publication of material intimately connected with Boswell's *Tour to the Hebrides*, of which it chiefly consists, make a new edition of it imperative. This material, now at Yale, includes, *inter alia*, journal notes or author's copy for portions of the *Tour* for which Boswell kept no fully written journal, copy for additions to or revisions of the text, passages omitted or suppressed by Boswell, documents concerning the preparation of the copy or the printing of the book, and the actual proof-sheets of the first edition. It has been fully edited by Professor F. A. Pottle in a new edition of the *Tour* that he published in 1936 in collaboration with the late Dr. Charles H. Bennett.[1] This admirable edition has considerably

[1] *Boswell's Journal of a Tour to the Hebrides with Samuel Johnson, LL.D.* Ed. from the Original Manuscript by F. A. Pottle and C. H. Bennett. New Edition with Additional Notes by F. A. Pottle, New York (McGraw-Hill Book Co. [1962]). The English edition is published by W. Heinemann, Ltd. [1963].

Preface to the Second Edition

lightened my task, simple reference to it being often quite enough; but some new notes, chiefly corrections of notes in the first edition, were necessary and these I have written.[1]

The text has been submitted to further scrutiny and I have corrected it in several places:[2] one passage that has baffled previous editors is now explained,[3] and a reading that has always been doubtful is now certain.[4] The mystery of the date of Johnson's letter of thanks to the Duke of Argyll has been solved.[5]

The manuscript of Johnson's record of his journey into North Wales has been returned to the British Museum from its wartime sanctuary and I have been able to collate it with Duppa's text with my own eyes. I have preserved Johnson's punctuation, such as it is, and his spelling, but have generally adopted Duppa's division into paragraphs.[6]

This volume has been produced by photo-lithography and the pagination of the former edition, 1950, preserved, the new material,

---

[1] Examples are: (1) The identification of the author of *A Defence of Mr. Boswell's Journal* as W. James, later Sir Walter James James, and not R. James (v. 3, n. 2): (2) The identification of 'one Douglas', the author of 'a small account' of St. Andrews, as (Sir) William Douglas of Glenbervie, a Provost of the city, and not Francis Douglas, an Aberdeen bookseller and printer (v. 61, 479): (3) The identification of 'Mrs. Brooks', whose portrait was found 'by some strange chance in Sky', as Mrs. Brooke, an actress (v. 158, n. 3): (4) The sites of various buildings, houses, &c.—the Bishop's House at Elgin (v. 114, 502): the Episcopalian chapel at Inverness (v. 128, 510): the house at Armadale in which Sir Alexander Macdonald entertained the travellers (v. 147, n. 3): the parish church of Sleat (v. 151, n. 3): the ancient chapel at Auchinleck and the two predecessors of the modern mansion (v. 380 n. †): and the more precise identification of the site of the bank in Glenshiel on which Johnson rested and conceived the thought of his narrative (v. 141, n. 2).

Some supplementary notes, for which room could not be found on the pages to which they relate or in the Appendix D, are grouped together in Addenda to the latter. They are: (1) Johnson's reply to Lord Auchinleck which Boswell, out of filial piety, forbore to mention: (2) Johnson's baiting of Lady Dalrymple: (3) Boswell's fallibility as a textual critic.

[2] See v. 24, 135, 217, 289, 327, 359, 390.   [3] See v. 140, n. §.

[4] See v. 338. Whether the Rev. Neil MacLeod was 'the cleanest-headed man' or 'the clearest-headed man' in the Islands. The printer set 'clearest' as the catch-word on p. 423 of Boswell's book and as the first word of the following page. Boswell corrected both to 'cleanest'. Boswell's *Hebrides*, ed. Pottle and Bennett, 1962, p. 435.   [5] v. 363, n. *

[6] This diary has been included in Johnson's *Diaries, Prayers, and Annals*, ed. by E. L. McAdam, with Donald and Mary Hyde, 1958, and given an elaborate commentary.

Preface to the Second Edition

the corrections and revisions, replacing the old, the inaccurate or the inadequate. The reader may be assured that in the process of correction and revision truth has not been sacrificed to typography.

It remains for me to thank those who have helped me. My chief debt, and it is a large one, is to Professor F. A. Pottle, his University (Yale), and his publishers (McGraw-Hill Book Co.), for permission to make use of the material published in the new edition of Boswell's *Tour*. I have to acknowledge help courteously given me, not for the first time, by Dr. William Beattie, Librarian of the National Library of Scotland, Professor Donald Cornu of Seattle, Mr. Owen E. Holloway of the British Museum, Dr. and Mrs. Donald F. Hyde of Somerville, New Jersey, Mr. J. D. Fleeman of St. Andrews and Oxford, and the Rev. Dr. Donald MacKinnon of Kennoway, Fife. My last word must be one of deep gratitude to my friends Mr. and Mrs. Michael Sadler of Ashbourne for their hospitality, kindly shown me year by year, and to my fellow travellers in the Highlands and Hebrides, Dr. Esmond de Beer and his sisters, Miss Mary de Beer and Miss Dora H. de Beer, for their encouragement and their companionship.

OXFORD
24 *January* 1964

L. F. P.

ERRATA

Page 142, end of *n.* 2 of p. 141, *for* Ceannocroc *read* Ceanna-croc

Page 176, *n.* 2 l. 8, *for* had *read* has

Page 334, Critical notes: for ᶜ ᵈ *comma omitted* 3. read ᶜ *comma omitted* 3. ᵈ *comma omitted* 2, 3.

Page 544, l. 13 foot, *for* v. 161 note *read* v. 522

Page 565, *delete* l. 22.

Page 594, l. 4, *for* Llangwnodl *read* Llangwnadl

CONTENTS

VOLUME I

	PAGE
Preface to the New Edition	v
Acknowledgements	xix
Dr. Hill's Dedication to Jowett	xxix
Dr. Hill's Preface	xxxi
Title-page of the Third Edition	xlvii
Boswell's Dedication to Sir Joshua Reynolds	1
Advertisement to the First Edition	5
Advertisement to the Second Edition	10
Advertisement to the Third Edition	14
Chronological Catalogue of the Prose Works of Samuel Johnson, LL.D.	16
The Life of Samuel Johnson, LL.D. (18 Sept. 1709—Oct. 1765)	25–500

Appendixes:
- A. Johnson's Debates in Parliament . . . 501
- B. Johnson's Letters to his Mother and Miss Porter in 1759 . 512
- C. Johnson at Cambridge 517
- D. Johnson's Letter to Dr. Leland . . . 518
- E. Johnson's 'Engaging in Politicks with H———n' . 519
- F. Johnson's First Acquaintance with the Thrales and his serious Illness 520
- G. Additional Notes to the Whole Volume . . 522–56

VOLUME II

The Life of Samuel Johnson, LL.D. (1766—27 Mar. 1776) 1–475

Appendixes:
- A. Johnson's Sentiments towards his Fellow-subjects in America 476
- B. Additional Notes to the Whole Volume . . 478–543

VOLUME III

The Life of Samuel Johnson, LL.D. (28 Mar. 1776—17 Oct. 1780) 1–442

Appendixes:
- A. George Psalmanazar 443
- B. Johnson's Travels and Love of Travelling . . 449
- C. Election of Lord Mayors of London . . 460
- D. The Inmates of Johnson's House . . . 462
- E. Boswell's Letters of Acceptance of the Office of Secretary for Foreign Correspondence to the Royal Academy . 464
- F. Additional Notes to the Whole Volume . . 467–541

Contents

VOLUME IV

	PAGE
THE LIFE OF SAMUEL JOHNSON, LL.D. (1780—13 Dec. 1784)	1–430
APPENDIXES: A. Johnson's Altercation with Dr. Barnard on 'Improvement after the Age of 45'	431
B. Johnson and Priestley	434
C. Johnson's Ivy Lane Club	435
D. Johnson's Essex Head Club	436
E. Miss Burney's Account of Johnson's Last Days	439
F. Notes on Johnson's Will	440
G. Notes on Pages 407–8	445
H. The Portraits of Johnson	447
I. The Monuments of Johnson	464
J. Additional Notes to the Whole Volume	472
K. The Cancels in the First Edition	555–7

VOLUME V

JOURNAL OF A TOUR TO THE HEBRIDES WITH SAMUEL JOHNSON, LL.D.	
PREFACE (1950)	v
PREFACE TO THE SECOND EDITION (1964)	xxi
TITLE-PAGE OF THE THIRD EDITION	xxix
DEDICATION TO EDMOND MALONE, ESQ.	1
ADVERTISEMENT TO THE THIRD EDITION	3
CONTENTS	5
JOURNAL	13–416
APPENDIXES	
I. Letter from Dr. Blacklock	417
II. Verses of Sir Alexander Macdonald	419
Advertisement to the *Life*	421
A. Extracts from Warburton	423
B. Lord Houghton's Translation of Johnson's Ode written in Skye	424
C. Johnson's Use of the Word *big*	425
DIARY OF A JOURNEY INTO NORTH WALES IN THE YEAR 1774	427
APPENDIX (D) TO THE WHOLE VOLUME	462
ADDENDA	595–6

VOLUME VI

PREFACE (1950)	v
PREFACE TO THE SECOND EDITION (1964)	vii
INDEX	1–424
INDEX OF PERSONS MENTIONED ANONYMOUSLY	425
A TABLE OF ANONYMOUS PERSONS	431
A LIST OF THE WORKS QUOTED IN THE NOTES AND APPENDIXES	476
ERRATA	488–96

ILLUSTRATIONS

VOLUME I

SAMUEL JOHNSON, by SIR JOSHUA REYNOLDS, 1756. From the engraving by Heath, 1791 . . . . . . *Frontispiece*

FACSIMILE of BOSWELL'S REVISED PROOF of the *Life*, now (1964) in the possession of Mr. and Mrs. Donald F. Hyde . . *Facing page* 25

FACSIMILE of JOHNSON'S LETTER to WILLIAM STRAHAN, 20 Jan. 1759, in the possession of Harvard College . . . *Between pages* 340–1

VOLUME II

SAMUEL JOHNSON, from the painting by SIR JOSHUA REYNOLDS, 1769, in the Tate Gallery . . . . . . *Frontispiece*

FACSIMILE of JOHNSON's holograph copy of his letter to JAMES MACPHERSON, 20 Jan. 1775, now (1964) in the possession of the New York Public Library *Facing page* 298

SAMUEL JOHNSON, from the painting by JAMES BARRY, R.A., c. 1775, in the National Portrait Gallery . . . . *Facing page* 355

VOLUME III

SAMUEL JOHNSON, from the painting by SIR JOSHUA REYNOLDS, 1778, in the Tate Gallery . . . . . . *Frontispiece*

FACSIMILE of the ROUND ROBIN. From the engraving by H. Shepherd *Facing page* 83

SAMUEL JOHNSON, from the painting by JOHN OPIE, R.A., 1783, now (1964) in the possession of Mr. Arthur A. Houghton, Jr. . *Facing page* 245

VOLUME IV

SAMUEL JOHNSON, from the painting by SIR JOSHUA REYNOLDS, c. 1782–4, now (1964) in the possession of Miss Caroline Newton *Frontispiece*

FACSIMILES of JOHNSON's HANDWRITING at three periods of his life. From the engraving by H. Shepherd . . . *Facing page* 431

The MONUMENT of JOHNSON by JOHN BACON, R.A., in St. Paul's Cathedral *Facing page* 469

BUST of JOHNSON by JOSEPH NOLLEKENS, R.A. . . *Facing page* 555

VOLUME V

JAMES BOSWELL, from the painting by SIR JOSHUA REYNOLDS, 1786, in the National Portrait Gallery . . . . . *Frontispiece*

EDMOND MALONE, from the painting by SIR JOSHUA REYNOLDS, 1778, in the National Portrait Gallery . . . . *Facing page* 1

MAP of the TOUR through SCOTLAND and the HEBRIDES by Johnson and Boswell . . . . . . *Facing page* 5

FACSIMILE of JOHNSON's DIARY of the TOUR in WALES . *Facing page* 435

VOLUME VI

SAMUEL JOHNSON, from the painting by SIR JOSHUA REYNOLDS, c. 1775, now (1964) in the possession of Messrs. Courage and Barclay, Ltd.
Frontispiece

THE
JOURNAL
OF A TOUR TO THE
HEBRIDES,
WITH

SAMUEL JOHNSON, LL.D.

By *JAMES BOSWELL*, Esq.

CONTAINING

Some Poetical Pieces by Dr. JOHNSON, relative to the TOUR, and never before publifhed;

A Series of his Converfation, Literary Anecdotes, and Opinions of Men and Books:

WITH AN AUTHENTICK ACCOUNT OF

The Diftresses and Efcape of the GRANDSON of KING JAMES II. in the Year 1746.

THE THIRD EDITION, REVISED AND CORRECTED.

O! while along the ftream of time, thy name
Expanded flies, and gathers all its fame,
Say, fhall my little bark attendant fail,
Purfue the triumph and partake the gale? POPE.

[*Boswell's Motto and Crest.*]

LONDON:
PRINTED BY HENRY BALDWIN,
FOR CHARLES DILLY, IN THE POULTRY.
MDCCLXXXVI.

EDMOND MALONE
from the painting by SIR JOSHUA REYNOLDS, 1778
in the National Portrait Gallery

DEDICATION

TO

EDMOND MALONE, Esq.

MY DEAR SIR,

IN every narrative, whether historical or biographical, authenticity is of the utmost consequence [1]. Of this I have ever been so firmly persuaded, that I inscribed a former work [2] to that person who was the best judge of its truth. I need not tell you I mean General Paoli; who, after his great, though unsuccessful, efforts to preserve the liberties of his country, has found an honourable asylum in Britain, where he has now lived many years the object of Royal regard and private respect [3]; and whom I cannot name without expressing my very grateful sense of the uniform kindness which he has been pleased to shew me [4].

The friends of Doctor Johnson can best judge, from internal evidence, whether the numerous conversations which form the most valuable part of the ensuing pages, are correctly related. To them therefore I wish to appeal, for the accuracy of the portrait here exhibited to the world.

As one of those who were intimately acquainted with him, you have a title to this address. You have obligingly taken the trouble to peruse the original manuscript of this Tour, and can vouch for the strict fidelity of the present publication [5].

---

[1] See *ante*, ii. 434, note 1; iii. 209.

[2] His *Account of Corsica*, 1768.

[3] Walpole wrote on Nov. 6, 1769 (*Letters*, vii. 328):—' I found Paoli last week at court. The King and Queen both took great notice of him. He has just made a tour to Bath, Oxford, &c., and was everywhere received with much distinction.' See *ante*, ii. 71 ⟨and the *D.N.B.*, which is in error in stating that he was a member of The Club.⟩

[4] Boswell, when in London, was ' his constant guest'. *Ante*, iii. 35.

[5] ⟨Malone not only read the manuscript but gave Boswell very great aid in editing it; a large number of the alterations and corrections are in Malone's hand (see F. A. Pottle in *Papers of the Bibliogr. Soc. of America*, 1933, xxvii, pt. 2, p. 69). Boswell met Malone for the first time on 14 April 1781 (*ante*, iv. 91, note †) and subsequently at meetings of The Club, of which Malone became a member on 5 Feb. 1782 and treasurer in the same year (*Annals of The Club*, pp. 24–7: see also *ante*, iv. 326); they did not become intimate friends till the Spring of 1785, when Boswell came to London for the express purpose of preparing his *Tour* for publication. He arrived in London on 30 March and, after a month's dissipation, settled down to work with Malone at hand to help and advise him. On 29 April he dined with

Dedication

Your literary alliance with our much lamented friend, in consequence of having undertaken to render one of his labours more complete, by your edition of Shakspeare [6], a work which I am confident will not disappoint the expectations of the publick, gives you another claim. But I have a still more powerful inducement to prefix your name to this volume, as it gives me an opportunity of letting the world know that I enjoy the honour and happiness of your friendship; and of thus publickly testifying the sincere regard with which I am,

My dear Sir,
Your very faithful
And obedient servant,
JAMES BOSWELL.

LONDON,
20th September, 1785.

Malone and the next day went with Baldwin to Dilly's ' and fixed printing " Tour " ' ; on 2 May he delivered the first batch of copy. Throughout July, August, and September they met very frequently in Malone's house, where, during these months, the editing was actually done and to which the proofs were almost certainly sent. The following extracts from Boswell's journal show the closeness of their collaboration and Boswell's dependence on Malone : 2 July, ' Malone and I corrected all forenoon ' ; 11 July, ' The press had stopped a little for want of copy. Went to Malone and brought forward some ' ; 15 July, ' Went to Malone's and got a good deal done ' ; 26 July, ' The General [Paoli] . . . set me down at Malone's, where I was to dine. We revised some . . . Malone and I revised at night and sat till two in the morning ' ; 28 July, ' Went to Malone at two, . . . we had our quiet dinner most comfortably, and revised till six ' ; 11 Aug., ' Malone devoted the whole of this day to me, that we might get forward with my " Tour ". I breakfasted, dined, drank tea, and supt with him, and sat till near two in the morning. Yet we did not get a great deal winnowed, there was so very much chaff in that portion of it ' ; 17 Aug., ' Malone had promised me all the evening to revise. I went between 6 and 7, but was not very fit for the task. However, we went on till one in the morning ' ; 8 Sept., ' FINISHED REVISE with Malone at Baldwin's. Dined and supt Malone ' ; 16 Sept., ' An addition to my " Tour " (defending [my] faculty of writing conversations) occurred to me. So I staid in town and Malone and I laboured as usual ' ; 20 Sept., ' At night Malone's and found the end Sheet, etc., of my " Tour " ' ; 21 Sept., ' Went to Malone's and settled my title-page '. On 22 Sept. Boswell wrote with feeling : ' Dined at Malone's with the JURY on my " TOUR ", who applauded it much. . . . Drove to Dilly's at night, having bid a cordial adieu to my kind and elegant friend Malone.' *Boswell Papers*, xvi. 80 ff. Malone's attendance with Boswell at Baldwin's printing office is probably the basis of James Boswell Junior's story (*Gent. Mag.* 1813, i, p. 518), that their acquaintance began there.⟩

[6] Malone began his edition of *Shakespeare* in 1782 ; he brought it out in 1790. Prior's *Malone*, pp. 98, 166. ⟨Boswell notes in his journal, 27 July 1785, ' Malone was busy today with his Shakespeare. So I could not get any of his time ', and, 10 Aug. 1785, ' Malone was busy with his Shakespeare. So we did not SIT upon my " Tour ".' *Boswell Papers*, xvi. 113 and 118.⟩

ADVERTISEMENT
TO THE THIRD EDITION.

ANIMATED by the very favourable reception which two large impressions of this work have had [1], it has been my study to make it as perfect as I could in this edition, by correcting some inaccuracies which I discovered myself, and some which the kindness of friends or the scrutiny of adversaries pointed out. A few notes are added, of which the principal object is, to refute misrepresentation and calumny.

To the animadversions in the periodical Journals of criticism, and in the numerous publications to which my book has given rise, I have made no answer. Every work must stand or fall by its own merit. I cannot, however, omit this opportunity of returning thanks to a gentleman who published a Defence of my Journal [2], and has added to the favour by communicating his name to me in a very obliging letter.

It would be an idle waste of time to take any particular notice of the futile remarks, to many of which, a petty national resentment, unworthy of my countrymen, has probably given rise; remarks, which have been industriously circulated in the publick prints by shallow or envious cavillers, who have endeavoured to persuade the world that Dr. Johnson's character has been

---

[1] ⟨The 'Advertisement' to the second edition, dated 'London, 20th Dec. 1785' and signed 'J. B.', is as follows: 'By correcting the errours of the press in the former edition, and some inaccuracies for which the authour alone is answerable, and by supplying some additional notes, I have endeavoured to render this work more deserving of the very high honour which the publick has been pleased to shew it; the whole of the first impression having been sold in a few weeks.' For the various editions, etc., see Pottle,

Lit. Career of James Boswell, 112 ff.⟩

[2] ⟨*A Defence of Mr. Boswell's Journal; of a Tour to the Hebrides; in a Letter to the Author of the Remarks* signed *Verax*, was published in London in 1785. It was written by W. James, who in sending a copy to Boswell, 26 Dec. 1785, expressed dismay that it should have been ascribed to him (*Yale Boswell MS.* C 1586, kindly communicated by Prof. Pottle). Mr. James was probably identical with Sir Walter James James: see Index.⟩

Advertisement to the Third Edition

lessened by recording such various instances of his lively wit and acute judgment, on every topick that was presented to his mind. In the opinion of every person of taste and knowledge that I have conversed with, it has been greatly *heightened*; and I will venture to predict, that this specimen of the colloquial talents and extemporaneous effusions of my illustrious fellow-traveller will become still more valuable, when, by the lapse of time, he shall have become an *ancient* [1]; when all those who can now bear testimony to the transcendent powers of his mind, shall have passed away; and no other memorial [2] of this great and good man shall remain, but the following Journal, the other anecdotes and letters preserved by his friends, and those incomparable works, which have for many years been in the highest estimation, and will be read and admired as long as the English language shall be spoken or understood.

J. B.

LONDON, 15th Aug. 1786.

[1] ⟨' The poet, of whose works I have undertaken the revision, may now begin to assume the dignity of an ancient ', Johnson's *Preface to Shakespeare, Works,* v. 104.⟩

[2] ⟨It is strange that Boswell here ignores his own greater enterprise, which is often mentioned in the book, and is advertised at the end of it as *preparing for the press.* R.W.C. See also F. A. Pottle, *Literary Career of James Boswell,* 1929, p. 120.⟩

CONTENTS[1]

DEDICATION . . . . . Page 1
ADVERTISEMENT 3
INTRODUCTION. Character of Dr. Johnson. He arrives in Scotland 13 to 24
August 15. Sir W. Forbes. Practice of the law. Emigration. Dr. Beattie and Mr. Hume. Dr. Robertson. Mr. Burke's various and extraordinary talents. Question concerning genius. Whitfield and Wesley. Instructions to political parties. Dr. Johnson's opinion of Garrick as a tragedian 24
August 16. Ogden on Prayer. Aphoristick writing. Edinburgh surveyed. Character of Swift's works. Evil spirits and witchcraft. Lord Monboddo and the Ouran Outang . . . 38
August 17. Poetry and Dictionary-writing. Scepticism. Eternal necessity refuted. Lord Hailes's criticism on *The Vanity of human Wishes*. Mr. Maclaurin. Decision of the Judges in Scotland on literary property 46
August 18. Set out for the Hebrides. Sketch of the authour's character. Trade of Glasgow. Suicide. Inchkeith. Parliamentary knowledge. Influence of Peers. Popular clamours. Arrive at St. Andrews 51
August 19. Dr. Watson. Literature and patronage. Writing and conversation compared. Change of manners. The Union. Value of money. St. Andrews and John Knox. Retirement from the world. Dinner with the Professors. Question concerning sorrow and content. Instructions for composition. Dr. Johnson's method. Uncertainty of memory 58
August 20. Effect of prayer. Observance of Sunday. Professor Shaw. Transubstantiation. Literary property. Mr. Tyers's remark on Dr. Johnson. Arrive[a] at Montrose 68
August 21. Want of trees. Laurence Kirk. Dinner at Monboddo. Emigration. Homer. Biography and history compared. Decrease of learning. Causes of it. Promotion of bishops. Warburton. Lowth. Value of politeness. Dr. Johnson's sentiments concerning Lord Monboddo. Arrive at Aberdeen . . 73
August 22. Professor Thomas Gordon. Publick and private education. Sir Alexander Gordon. Trade of Aberdeen. Prescription of murder

[a] arrives 3

[1] ⟨The page-references are adjusted to this edition.⟩

Contents

in Scotland. Mystery of the Trinity. Satisfaction of Christ. Importance of old friendships 84

August 23. Dr. Johnson made a burgess of Aberdeen. Dinner at Sir Alexander Gordon's. Warburton's powers of invective. His *Doctrine of Grace*. Lock's verses. Fingal . . . 90

August 24. Goldsmith and Graham. Slains castle. Education of children. Buller of Buchan. Entails. Consequence of Peers. Sir Joshua Reynolds. Earl of Errol . . . 96

August 25. The advantage of being on good terms with relations. Nabobs. Feudal state of subordination. Dinner at Strichen. Life of country gentlemen. THE LITERARY CLUB . . 105

August 26. Lord Monboddo. Use and importance of wealth. Elgin. Macbeth's heath. Fores 110

August 27. Leonidas. Paul Whitehead. Derrick. Origin of Evil. Calder-manse. Reasonableness of ecclesiastical subscription. Family worship 116

August 28. Fort George. Sir Adolphus Oughton. Contest between Warburton and Lowth. Dinner at Sir Eyre Coote's. Arabs and English soldiers compared. The Stage. Mr. Garrick, Mrs. Cibber, Mrs. Pritchard, Mrs. Clive. Inverness . . . 122

August 29. Macbeth's Castle. Incorrectness of writers of Travels. Coinage of new words. Dr. Johnson's Dictionary . . 128

August 30. Dr. Johnson on horse-back. A Highland hut. Fort Augustus. Governour Trapaud 131

August 31. Anoch. Emigration. Goldsmith. Poets and soldiers compared. Life of a sailor. Landlord's daughter at Anoch 135

September 1. Glensheal. The Macraas. Dr. Johnson's anger at being left for a little while by the authour on a wild plain. Wretched inn at Glenelg 139

September 2. Dr. Johnson relents. Isle of Sky. Armidale . 147

September 3. Colonel Montgomery, now Earl of Eglintoune . 149

September 4. Ancient Highland Enthusiasm . . . 150

September 5. Sir James Macdonald's epitaph and last letters to his mother. Dr. Johnson's Latin ode on the Isle of Sky. Isaac Hawkins Browne 151

September 6. Corrichatachin. Highland hospitality and mirth. Dr. Johnson's Latin ode to Mrs. Thrale . . . 156

September 7. Uneasy state of dependence on the weather. State of those who live in the country. Dr. M'Pherson's Dissertations. Second Sight 158

September 8. Rev. Mr. Donald M'Queen. Mr. Malcolm M'Leod. Sail to Rasay. Fingal. Homer. Elegant and gay entertainment at Rasay 160

September 9. Antiquity of the family of Rasay. Cure of infidelity 167

Contents 7

September 10. Survey of the island of Rasay. Bentley. Mallet.
Hooke. Duchess of Marlborough 168
September 11. Heritable jurisdictions. Insular life. The Laird of
M'Cleod 176
September 12. Sail to Portree. Dr. Johnson's discourse on death.
Letters from Lord Elibank to Dr. Johnson and the authour. Dr.
Johnson's answer. Ride to Kingsburgh. Flora Macdonald 179
September 13. Distresses and escape of the grandson of King James II.
Arrive at Dunvegan   185
September 14. Importance of the chastity of women. Dr. Cadogan.
Whether the Practice of authours is necessary to enforce their Doctrines. Good humour acquirable 208
September 15. Sir George M'Kenzie. Mr. Burke's wit, knowledge, and
eloquence.   212
September 16. Dr. Johnson's hereditary melancholy. His minute
knowledge in various arts. Apology for the authour's ardour in
his pursuits. Dr. Johnson's imaginary seraglio. Polygamy. 214
September 17. Cunning. Whether great abilities are necessary to be
wicked. Temple of the Goddess Anaitis. Family portraits. Records not consulted by old English historians. Mr. Pennant's
Tours criticised 217
September 18. Ancient residence of a Highland Chief. Languages
the pedigree of nations. Laird of the Isle of Muck   . 222
September 19. Choice of a wife. Women an over-match for men.
Lady Grange in St. Kilda. Poetry of savages. French Literati.
Prize-fighting. French and English soldiers. Duelling . 226
September 20. Change of London manners. Laziness censured. Landed
and traded interest compared. Gratitude considered   . 230
September 21. Description of Dunvegan. Lord Lovat's Pyramid. Ride
to Ulinish. Phipps's Voyage to the North Pole .   . 232
September 22. Subterraneous house and vast cave in Ulinish. Swift's
Lord Orrery. Defects as well as virtues the proper subject of
biography, though the life be written by a friend. Studied conclusions of letters. Whether allowable in dying men to maintain
resentment to the last. Instructions for writing the lives of literary
men. Fingal denied to be genuine, and pleasantly ridiculed 236
September 23. Further disquisition concerning Fingal. Eminent men
disconcerted by a new mode of publick appearance. Garrick. Mrs.
Montague's Essay on Shakspeare. Persons of consequence watched
in London. Learning of the Scots from 1550 to 1650. The arts
of civil life little known in Scotland till the Union. Life of a sailor.
The folly of Peter the Great in working in a dock-yard. Arrive at
Talisker. Presbyterian clergy deficient in learning .   . 242

Contents

September 24. French hunting. Young Col. Dr. Birch. Dr. Percy. Lord Hailes. Historical impartiality. Whiggism unbecoming in a clergyman 253

September 25. Every island a prison. A Sky cottage. Return to Corrichatachin. Good fellowship carried to excess. . 255

September 26. Morning review of last night's intemperance. Old Kingsburgh's Jacobite song. Lady Margaret Macdonald adored in Sky. Different views of the same subject at different times. Self-deception 258

September 27. Dr. Johnson's popularity in the Isle of Sky. His good-humoured gaiety with a Highland lady . . . 260

September 28. Ancient Irish pride of family. Dr. Johnson on threshing and thatching. Dangerous to increase the price of labour. Arrive at Ostig. Dr. M'Pherson's Latin poetry . . 262

September 29. Reverend Mr. M'Pherson. Shenstone. Hammond. Sir Charles Hanbury Williams 266

September 30. Mr. Burke the first man every where. Very moderate talents requisite to make a figure in the House of Commons. Dr. Young. Dr. Dodridge. Increase of infidel writings since the accession of the Hanover family. Gradual impression made by Dr. Johnson. Particular minutes to be kept of our studies . 269

October 1. Dr. Johnson not answerable for all the words in his Dictionary. Attacks on authors useful to them. Return to Armidale 273

October 2. Old manners of great families in Wales. German courts. Goldsmith's love of talk. Emigration. Curious story of the people of Saint Kilda 275

October 3. Epictetus on the voyage of death. Sail for Mull. A storm. Driven into Col 279

October 4. Dr. Johnson's mode of living in the Temple. His curious appearance on a sheltie. Nature of sea-sickness. Burnet's History of his own Times. Difference between dedications and histories 284

October 5. People may come to do any thing by talking of it. The Reverend Mr. Hector Maclean. Bayle. Leibnitz and Clarke. Survey of Col. Insular life. Arrive at Breacacha. Dr. Johnson's powers of ridicule. 286

October 6. Heritable jurisdictions. The opinion of philosophers concerning happiness in a cottage, considered. Advice to landlords 292

October 7. Books the best solace in a state of confinement . 294

October 8. Pretended brother of Dr. Johnson. No redress for a man's name being affixed to a foolish work. Lady Sidney Beauclerk.

Contents

Carte's Life of the Duke of Ormond. Col's cabinet. Letters of the great Montrose. Present state of the island of Col. . 295
October 9. Dr. Johnson's avidity for a variety of books. Improbability of a Highland tradition. Dr. Johnson's delicacy of feeling . 302
October 10. Dependence of tenants on landlords . . 304
October 11. London and Pekin compared. Dr. Johnson's high opinion of the former 304
October 12. Return to Mr. M'Sweyn's. Other superstitions beside those connected with religion. Dr. Johnson disgusted with coarse manners. His peculiar habits 305
October 13. Bustle not necessary to dispatch. Oats the food not of the Scotch alone 307
October 14. Arrive in Mull. Addison's *Remarks on Italy.* Addison not much conversant with Italian literature. The French masters of the art of accommodating literature. Their *Ana.* Racine. Corneille. Moliere. Fenelon. Voltaire. Bossuet. Massillon. Bourdaloue. Virgil's description of the entrance into hell, compared to a printing-house 308
October 15. Erse poetry. Danger of a knowledge of musick. The propriety of settling our affairs so as to be always prepared for death. Religion and literary attainments not to be described to young persons as too hard. Reception of the travellers in their progress. Spence 314
October 16. Miss Maclean. Account of Mull. The value of an oak walking-stick in the Hebrides. Arrive at Mr. M'Quarrie's in Ulva. Captain Macleod. Second Sight. *Mercheta Mulierum,* and Borough-English. The grounds on which the sale of an estate may be set aside in a court of equity . . . 317
October 17. Arrive at Inchkenneth. Sir Allan Maclean and his daughters. None but theological books should be read on Sunday. Dr. Campbell. Dr. Johnson exhibited as a Highlander. Thoughts on drinking. Dr. Johnson's Latin verses on Inchkenneth 322
October 18. Young Col's various good qualities. No extraordinary talents requisite to success in trade. Dr. Solander. Mr. Burke. Dr. Johnson's intrepidity and presence of mind. Singular custom in the islands of Col and Otaheité. Further elogium on young Col. Credulity of a Frenchman in foreign countries . 327
October 19. Death of young Col. Dr. Johnson slow of belief without strong evidence. *La credulité des incredules.* Coast of Mull. Nun's Island. Past scenes pleasing in recollection. Land on Icolmkill 331
October 20. Sketch of the ruins of Icolmkill. Influence of solemn

Contents

scenes of piety. Feudal authority in the extreme. Return to
Mull 335
October 21. Pulteney. Pitt. Walpole. Mr. Wilkes. English and
Jewish history compared. Scotland composed of stone and water,
and a little earth. Turkish Spy. Dreary ride to Lochbuy. De-
scription of the laird 339
October 22. Uncommon breakfast offered to Dr. Johnson, and rejected.
Lochbuy's war-saddle. Sail to Oban . . . 342
October 23. Goldsmith's *Traveller*. Pope and Cowley compared.
Archibald Duke of Argyle. Arrive at Inveraray. Dr. Johnson
drinks some whisky, and assigns his reason. Letter from the
authour to Mr. Garrick. Mr. Garrick's answer . . 344
October 24. Specimen of Ogden on Prayer. Hervey's *Meditations*.
Dr. Johnson's Meditation on a Pudding. Country neighbours.
The authour's visit at the castle of Inveraray. Perverse opposition
to the influence of Peers in Ayrshire . . . 350
October 25. Dr. Johnson presented to the Duke of Argyle. Grandeur
of his grace's seat. The authour possesses himself in an embarrassing situation. Honourable Archibald Campbell on *a middle
state*. The old Lord Townshend. Question concerning luxury.
Nice trait of character. Good principles and bad practice . 355
October 26. A passage in Home's Douglas, and one in Juvenal, com-
pared. Neglect of religious buildings in Scotland. Arrive at Sir
James Colquhoun's 360
October 27. Dr. Johnson's letter to the Duke of Argyle. His grace's
answer. Lochlomond[a]. Dr. Johnson's sentiments on dress. Forms
of prayer considered. Arrive at Mr. Smollet's . . 363
October 28. Dr. Smollet's Epitaph. Dr. Johnson's wonderful memory.
His alacrity during the Tour. Arrive at Glasgow . . 366
October 29. Glasgow surveyed. Attention of the professors to Dr.
Johnson 369
October 30. Dinner at the Earl of Loudoun's. Character of that noble-
man. Arrive at Treesbank 371
October 31. Sir John Cunningham of Caprington . . 372
November 1. Rules for the distribution of charity. Castle of Dun-
donald. Countess of Eglintoune. Alexander Earl of Eglintoune 373
November 2. Arrive at Auchinleck. Character of Lord Auchinleck.
His idea of Dr. Johnson 375
November 3. Dr. Johnson's sentiments concerning the Highlands. Mr.
Harris of Salisbury 377
November 4. Auchinleck. Cattle without horns. Composure of mind
how far attainable 379

[a] Locklomond 2, 3, *but correctly spelled in the text* (p. 364), 1, 2, *though wrongly* 3

Contents

November 5. Dr. Johnson's high respect for the English clergy . 381
November 6. Lord Auchinleck and Dr. Johnson in collision . 382
November 7. Dr. Johnson's uniform piety. His dislike of presbyterian worship 384
November 8. Arrive at Hamilton 384
November 9. The Duke of Hamilton's house. Arrive at Edinburgh 385
November 10. Lord Elibank. Difference in political principles increased by opposition. Edinburgh Castle. Fingal. English credulity not less than Scottish. Second Sight. Garrick and Foote compared as companions. Moravian Missions and Methodism 385
November 11. History originally oral. Dr. Robertson's liberality of sentiment. Rebellion natural to man . . . 392

SUMMARY ACCOUNT of the manner in which Dr. Johnson spent his time from November 12 to November 21. Lord Mansfield. Mr. Richardson. The private life of an English Judge. Dr. Johnson's high opinion of Dr. Robertson and Dr. Blair. Letter from Dr. Blair to the authour. Officers of the army often ignorant of things belonging to their own profession. Academy for the deaf and dumb. A Scotch Highlander and an English sailor. Attacks on authours advantageous to them. Roslin Castle and Hawthornden. Dr. Johnson's Parody of Sir John Dalrymple's Memoirs. Arrive at Cranston. Dr. Johnson's departure for London. Letters from Lord Hailes and Mr. Dempster to the authour. Letter from the Laird of Rasay to the authour. The authour's answer. Dr. Johnson's Advertisement, acknowledging a mistake in his *Journey to the Western Islands*. His letter to the Laird of Rasay. Letter from Sir William Forbes to the authour. Conclusion . 394
Appendix 417

HE WAS OF AN ADMIRABLE PREGNANCY OF WIT, AND THAT PREGNANCY MUCH IMPROVED BY CONTINUAL STUDY FROM HIS CHILDHOOD; BY WHICH HE HAD GOTTEN SUCH A PROMPTNESS IN EXPRESSING HIS MIND, THAT HIS EXTEMPORAL SPEECHES WERE LITTLE INFERIOR TO HIS PREMEDITATED WRITINGS. MANY, NO DOUBT, HAD READ AS MUCH, AND PERHAPS MORE THAN HE; BUT SCARCE EVER ANY CONCOCTED HIS READING INTO JUDGEMENT AS HE DID [1].

BAKER'S CHRONICLE [ed. 1665, p. 449].

[1] ⟨Boswell found this passage at Corrichatachin on 27 Sept. 1773. In his original journal he wrote on 28 Sept.: 'Last night I shewed Corrichatachin in Baker's Chronicle two passages of King James VI's (or rather I's, as it is an english book) character that apply to Mr. J. His method of riding, and the accuracy of his extemporaneous discourse.'

Malone wrote in his copy of the first edition (now, 1964, in the Hyde collection): 'His great period of *study* was from the age of twelve to that of *eighteen*, as he told Mr. Langton, who gave me this information. E. M.' At the age of 54 Johnson said: 'I knew almost as much at eighteen as I do now.' *Ante*, i. 445.⟩

THE
JOURNAL
OF A
TOUR TO THE HEBRIDES,
WITH
SAMUEL JOHNSON, L.L.D.

DR. JOHNSON had for many years given me hopes that we should go together, and visit the Hebrides [1]. Martin's Account of those islands had impressed us with a notion that we might there contemplate a system of life almost totally different from what we had been accustomed to see ; and, to find simplicity and wildness, and all the circumstances of remote time or place, so near to our native great island, was an object within the reach of reasonable curiosity. Dr. Johnson has said in his ' Journey ' [2], ' that he scarcely remembered how the wish to visit the Hebrides was excited ; ' but he told me, in summer, 1763 [3], that his father put Martin's Account into his hands when he was very young, and that he was much pleased with it. We reckoned there would be some inconveniencies and hardships, and perhaps a little danger ; but these we were persuaded were magnified in the imagination of every body.

[1] See *ante*, i. 450, ii. 51 and 291.
[2] *A Journey to the Western Islands of Scotland*, 1924, p. 3.
[3] See *ante*, i. 450. ⟨Boswell's copy of the first edition of Martin Martin's *A Description of the Western Islands of Scotland*, 1703, is in the National Library of Scotland. It contains the following note in Boswell's hand : ' This very Book accompanied Mr. Samuel Johnson and me, in our Tour to the Hebrides in Autumn 1773. Mr. Johnson told me that he had read Martin when he was very young. Martin was a native of the Isle of Sky where a number of his relations still remain. His Book is a very im- perfect performance ; & he is erroneous as to many particulars, even some concerning his own Island. Yet as it is the only Book upon the subject, it is very generally known. I have seen a second edition of it. I cannot but have a kindness for him, notwithstanding his defects. James Boswell. 16 April 1774.' Dr. Chapman has collected the passages alluded to by Boswell or by Johnson, in an Appendix to his edition (1924, pp. 486–7). The second edition was published in 1716. For Martin see the *D.N.B.* He died on 9 Oct. 1718. *MS. 1389* (Nat. Libr. Scotl.), fol. 159.⟩

When I was at Ferney, in 1764, I mentioned our design to Voltaire. He looked at me, as if I had talked of going to the North Pole, and said, ' You do not insist on my accompanying you ? '—' No, sir.'—' Then I am very willing you should go.' † I was not afraid that our curious expedition would be prevented by such apprehensions ; but I doubted that it would not be possible to prevail on Dr. Johnson to relinquish, for some time, the felicity of a London life, which, to a man who can enjoy it with full intellectual relish, is apt to make existence in any narrower sphere seem insipid or irksome §. I doubted that he would not be willing to come down from his elevated state of philosophical dignity ; from a superiority of wisdom among the wise, and of learning among the learned ; and from flashing his wit upon minds bright enough to reflect it.

He had disappointed my expectations so long, that I began to despair ; but in spring, 1773, he talked of coming to Scotland that year with so much firmness, that I hoped he was at last in earnest. I knew that, if he were once launched from the metropolis, he would go forward very well ; and I got our common friends there to assist in setting him afloat. To Mrs. Thrale in particular, whose enchantment over him seldom failed, I was much obliged. It was, ' *I'll give thee a wind.*'—' *Thou art kind* [1].'—To *attract* him, we had invitations from the chiefs Macdonald and Macleod ; and, for additional aid, I wrote to Lord Elibank [2], Dr. William Robertson, and Dr. Beattie.

To Dr. Robertson, so far as my letter concerned the present subject, I wrote as follows :

' OUR friend, Mr. Samuel Johnson, is in great health and spirits ; and, I do think, has a serious resolution to visit Scotland this year. The more attraction, however, the better ; and therefore, though I know he will be happy to meet you there, it will forward the scheme, if, in your answer to this, you express yourself concerning it with that power of which you are so happily possessed, and which may be so directed as to operate strongly upon him.'

His answer to that part of my letter was quite as I could have wished. It was written with the address and persuasion of the historian of America.

† ⟨For Boswell's report made in 1764 see App. D, p. 462.⟩
§ ⟨See *ante*, iii. 378.⟩

[1] *Macbeth*, act i. sc. 3.
[2] See *ante*, iii. 24, and *post*, v. 385.

'WHEN I saw you last, you gave us some hopes that you might prevail with Mr. Johnson to make out that excursion to Scotland, with the expectation of which we have long flattered ourselves. If he could order matters so, as to pass some time in Edinburgh, about the close of the summer session, and then visit some of the Highland scenes, I am confident he would be pleased with the grand features of nature in many parts of this country : he will meet with many persons here who respect him, and some whom I am persuaded he will think not unworthy of his esteem. I wish he would make the experiment. He sometimes cracks his jokes upon us ; but he will find that we can distinguish between the stabs of malevolence, and *the rebukes of the righteous, which are like excellent oil* [1], *and break not the head* [2]. Offer my best compliments to him, and assure him that I shall be happy to have the satisfaction of seeing him under my roof.'

To Dr. Beattie I wrote, ' The chief intention of this letter is to inform you, that I now seriously believe Mr. Samuel Johnson will visit Scotland this year : but I wish that every power of attraction may be employed to secure our having so valuable an acquisition, and therefore I hope you will without delay write to me what I know you think, that I may read it to the mighty sage, with proper emphasis, before I leave London, which I must do soon. He talks of you with the same warmth that he did last year [3]. We are to see as much of Scotland as we can, in the months of August and September. We shall not be long of being at Marischal College [4]. He is particularly desirous of seeing some of the Western Islands.'

Dr. Beattie did better : *ipse venit*. He was, however, so polite as to wave his privilege of *nil mihi rescribas* [5], and wrote from Edinburgh, as follows :

[1] Our friend Edmund Burke, who by this time had received some pretty severe strokes from Dr. Johnson, on account of the unhappy difference in their politicks, upon my repeating this passage to him, exclaimed ' Oil of vitriol ! ' BOSWELL.
[2] *Psalms*, cxli. 5.
[3] ' We all love Beattie,' he had said. *Ante*, ii. 148.
[4] This, I find, is a Scotticism. I should have said, ' It will not be long before we shall be at Marischal College.' BOSWELL. In spite of this warning Sir Walter Scott fell into the same error. ' The light foot of Mordaunt Mertoun was not long of

bearing him to Jarlshof.' *Pirate*, ch. viii. CROKER, 1848. ⟨See also the Oxford Dictionary s.v. *Long* adv. 2, where Miss Seward is quoted (1799).⟩
[5] ' Nil mihi rescribas, at tamen ipse veni!' Ovid, *Heroides*, i. 2.
Boswell liked to display such classical learning as he had. When he visited Eton in 1789 he writes, ' I . . . was asked by Dr. Davies, the Head Master, to dine at the Fellows' table, and made a creditable figure. I certainly have the art of making the most of what I have. How should one who has had only a Scotch education be quite at home at Eton ? I had my

'YOUR very kind and agreeable favour of the 20th of April overtook me here yesterday, after having gone to Aberdeen, which place I left about a week ago. I am to set out this day for London, and hope to have the honour of paying my respects to Mr. Johnson and you, about a week or ten days hence. I shall then do what I can, to enforce the topick you mention; but at present I cannot enter upon it, as I am in a very great hurry; for I intend to begin my journey within an hour or two.'†

He was as good as his word, and threw some pleasing motives into the northern scale. But, indeed, Mr. Johnson loved all that he heard, from one whom he tells us, in his Lives of the Poets, Gray found 'a poet, a philosopher, and a good man [1].'

My Lord Elibank did not answer my letter to his lordship for some time. The reason will appear, when we come to the isle of Sky [2]. I shall then insert my letter §, with letters from his lordship, both to myself and Mr. Johnson. I beg it may be understood, that I insert my own letters, as I relate my own sayings, rather as keys to what is valuable belonging to others, than for their own sake.

Luckily Mr. Justice (now Sir Robert) Chambers [3], who was about to sail for the East-Indies, was going to take leave of his relations at Newcastle, and he conducted Dr. Johnson to that town. Mr. Scott, of University College, Oxford, (now Dr. Scott [4], of the Commons,) accompanied him from thence to Edinburgh. With such propitious convoys did he proceed to my native city. But, lest metaphor should make it be supposed he actually went by sea, I choose to mention that he travelled in post-chaises, of which the rapid motion was one of his most favourite amusements [5].

Dr. Samuel Johnson's character, religious, moral, political, and literary, nay his figure and manner, are, I believe, more generally known than those of almost any man; yet it may not be

classical quotations very ready.' *Letters*, No. 268, ii. 380.
† ⟨Beattie left Edinburgh on 1 May. See Margaret Forbes, *Beattie and his friends*, 1904, 75.⟩
[1] ⟨Gray visited Scotland in 1765 and met Beattie at Glamis Castle. See *Corres. Gray*, 1935, ii. 887 ff.⟩ Johnson writes (*Gray* 18):—' He naturally contracted a friendship with Dr. Beattie, whom he found a poet, a philosopher, and a good man.'
[2] *Post*, v. 181.

§ ⟨This letter, which Boswell failed to insert, is dated, from London, 22 April 1773. *Boswell Papers*, xviii. 349.⟩
[3] See *ante*, i. 274 ⟨and ii. 264⟩.
[4] Afterwards Lord Stowell. He, his brother Lord Eldon, and Chambers were all Newcastle men. Twiss, *Eldon*, 1844, i. 26. See *ante*, i. 462. ⟨See also R. Welford, *Men of Mark 'twixt Tyne and Tweed*, 1895, i. 511 ff. and iii. 360 ff.⟩
[5] See *ante*, ii. 453.

superfluous here to attempt a sketch of him. Let my readers
then remember that he was a sincere and zealous christian, of high-
church[a] of England and monarchical principles, which he would
not tamely suffer to be questioned; steady and inflexible in
maintaining the obligations of piety and virtue, both from a
regard to the order of society, and from a veneration for the
Great Source of all order; correct, nay stern in his taste; hard
to please, and easily offended, impetuous and irritable in his
temper, but of a most humane and benevolent heart; having a
mind stored with a vast and various collection of learning and
knowledge, which he communicated with peculiar perspicuity
and force, in rich and choice expression. He united a most
logical head with a most fertile imagination, which gave him an
extraordinary advantage in arguing; for he could reason close
or wide, as he saw best for the moment. He could, when he
chose it, be the greatest sophist that ever wielded a weapon in
the schools of declamation; but he indulged this only in conversation; for he owned he sometimes talked for victory [1]; he
was too conscientious to make errour permanent and pernicious,
by deliberately writing it. He was conscious of his superiority.
He loved praise when it was brought to him; but was too
proud to seek for it. He was somewhat susceptible of flattery [2].
His mind was so full of imagery, that he might have been
perpetually a poet. It has been often remarked, that in his
poetical pieces, which it is to be regretted are so few, because
so excellent, his style is easier than in his prose. There is
deception in this: it is not easier, but better suited to the
dignity of verse; as one may dance with grace, whose motions,
in ordinary walking,—in the common step, are awkward. He
had a constitutional melancholy, the clouds of which darkened
the brightness of his fancy, and gave a gloomy cast to his
whole course of thinking: yet, though grave and awful in
his deportment, when he thought it necessary or proper,—he
frequently indulged himself in pleasantry and sportive sallies.
He was prone to superstition, but not to credulity. Though his

[a] high-church 1, 2 : high church 3.

[1] See *ante*, iv. 111 ; ⟨*post*, v. 324⟩.
[2] Baretti, in a MS. note on *Piozzi
Letters*, i. 309, says :—' The most
unaccountable part of Johnson's
character was his total ignorance of
the character of his most familiar
acquaintance.' ⟨See *post*, v. 440,
n. 2.⟩

imagination might incline him to a belief of the marvellous, and the mysterious, his vigorous reason examined the evidence with jealousy. He had a loud voice, and a slow deliberate utterance, which no doubt gave some additional weight to the sterling metal of his conversation [1]. Lord Pembroke said once to me at Wilton, with a happy pleasantry, and some truth, that ' Dr. Johnson's sayings would not appear so extraordinary, were it not for his *bow-wow way :* ' but I admit the truth of this only on some occasions. The *Messiah*, played upon the *Canterbury organ*, is more sublime than when played upon an inferior instrument : but very slight musick will seem grand, when conveyed to the ear through that majestick medium. *While therefore Dr. Johnson's sayings are read, let his manner be taken along with them.* Let it however be observed, that the sayings themselves are generally great ; that, though he might be an ordinary composer at times, he was for the most part a Handel.—His person was large, robust, I may say approaching to the gigantick, and grown unwieldy from corpulency. His countenance was naturally of the cast of an ancient statue, but somewhat disfigured by the scars of that *evil*, which, it was formerly imagined, the *royal touch* [2] could cure. He was now in his sixty-fourth year, and was become a little dull of hearing.† His sight had always been somewhat weak ; yet, so much does mind govern, and even supply the deficiency of organs, that his perceptions were uncommonly quick and accurate [3]. His head, and sometimes also his body, shook with a kind of motion like the effect of a palsy : he appeared to be frequently disturbed by cramps, or convulsive contractions [4], of the nature of that distemper called *St. Vitus's* dance. He wore a full suit of plain brown clothes, with twisted-hair-buttons [5] of the same colour, a large bushy greyish wig, a

[1] See *ante*, ii. 326, 371, and iv. 236.
[2] See *ante*, i. 42.
† ⟨See *ante*, i. 500, n. 3.⟩
[3] See *ante*, i. 41, ⟨ii. 506, iv. 425.⟩
[4] Such they appeared to me ; but since the first edition, Sir Joshua Reynolds has observed to me, ' that Dr. Johnson's extraordinary gestures were only habits, in which he indulged himself at certain times. When in company, where he was not free, or when engaged earnestly in conversation, he never gave way to such habits, which proves that they were not involuntary.' I still however think, that these gestures were involuntary ; for surely had not that been the case, he would have restrained them in the publick streets. BOSWELL, ed. 2. See *ante*, i. 144.
[5] ⟨See App. D, p. 462.⟩

plain shirt, black worsted stockings, and silver buckles. Upon this tour, when journeying, he wore boots, and a very wide brown cloth great coat, with pockets which might have almost held the two volumes of his folio dictionary ; and he carried in his hand a large English oak stick. Let me not be censured for mentioning such minute particulars. Every thing relative to so great a man is worth observing. I remember Dr. Adam Smith, in his rhetorical lectures at Glasgow [1], told us he was glad to know that Milton wore latchets in his shoes, instead of buckles. When I mention the oak stick, it is but letting *Hercules* have his club ; and, by-and-by, my readers will find this stick will bud, and produce a good joke [2].

This imperfect sketch of ' the COMBINATION and the *form* [3] ' of that Wonderful Man, whom I venerated and loved while in this world, and after whom I gaze with humble hope, now that it has pleased ALMIGHTY GOD to call him to a better world, will serve to introduce to the fancy of my readers the capital object of the following journal, in the course of which I trust they will attain to a considerable degree of acquaintance with him.

His prejudice against Scotland [4] was announced almost as soon as he began to appear in the world of letters. In his *London*, a poem, are the following nervous lines [5] :

' For who would leave, unbrib'd, Hibernia's land ?
Or change the rocks of Scotland for the Strand ?
There none are swept by sudden fate away ;
But all, whom hunger spares, with age decay.'

[1] ⟨Adam Smith was elected Professor of Logic at Glasgow in Jan. 1751 and transferred to the Professorship of Moral Philosophy in Jan. 1752. Boswell, who attended his lectures in 1759, wrote in his Journal, 18 Oct. 1762 : ' I have a pleasure in hearing every story, tho' never so little, of so distinguished a Man [as Lord Marchmont]. I remember Smith took notice of this pleasure in his lectures upon Rhetoric, and said that he felt it when he read that Milton never wore buckles but strings in his shoes.' *Boswell Papers*, i. 107.⟩
[2] *Post*, v. 318.

[3] *Hamlet*, act iii. sc. 4, l. 60.
[4] See *ante*, iv. 169. Johnson is often reproached with his dislike of the Scotch, though much of it was assumed ; but no one blames Hume's dislike of the English, though it was deep and real. On Feb. 21, 1770, he wrote :—' Our Government has become a Chimera; and is too perfect in point of Liberty, for so vile a Beast as an Englishman, who is a Man, a bad Animal too, corrupted by above a Century of Licentiousness.' *Letters*, 1932, ii. 216.
[5] ⟨Lines 9–12. The punctuation is Boswell's.⟩

The truth is, like the ancient Greeks and Romans, he allowed himself to look upon all nations but his own as barbarians [1] : not only Hibernia, and Scotland, but Spain, Italy, and France, are attacked in the same poem. If he was particularly prejudiced against the Scots, it was because they were more in his way ; because he thought their success in England rather exceeded the due proportion of their real merit ; and because he could not but see in them that nationality which I believe no liberal-minded Scotsman will deny. He was indeed, if I may be allowed the phrase, at bottom much of a *John Bull* [2] ; much of a blunt *true-born* [a] *Englishman* [3]. There was a stratum of common clay under the rock of marble. He was voraciously fond of good eating [4] ; and he had a great deal of that quality called *humour*, which gives an oiliness and a gloss to every other quality.

I am, I flatter myself, completely a citizen of the world †.—In my travels through Holland, Germany, Switzerland, Italy, Corsica, France, I never felt myself from home ; and I sincerely love ' every kindred and tongue and people and nation [5].' I subscribe to what my late truly learned and philosophical friend Mr. Crosbie [6] said, that the English are better animals than the Scots ; they are nearer the sun ; their blood is richer, and more mellow : but when I humour any of them in an outrageous contempt of Scotland, I fairly own I treat them as children. And thus I have, at some moments, found myself obliged to treat even Dr. Johnson.

To Scotland however he ventured ; and he returned from it in great good humour, with his prejudices much lessened, and with very grateful feelings of the hospitality with which he was treated ; as is evident from that admirable work, his ' Journey to the Western Islands of Scotland,' which, to my utter astonishment, has been misapprehended, even to rancour, by many of my countrymen.

To have the company of Chambers and Scott, he delayed

[a] *true-born* 1, 2 : *true born* 3.

[1] See *ante*, iv. 15.
[2] The term *John Bull* came into the English language in 1712, when Dr. John Arbuthnot wrote *The History of John Bull*. ⟨See G. A. Aitken, *Arbuthnot*, 1892, p. 45.⟩
[3] Boswell in three other places so describes Johnson. See *ante*, i. 129, note 3.
[4] See *ante*, i. 467 ⟨and iii. 69⟩.
† ⟨See *ante*, ii. 306.⟩
[5] ' All nations, and kindreds, and people, and tongues.' *Rev.* vii. 9.
[6] See *ante*, ii. 376, n. 1.

his journey so long, that the court of session †, which rises on the eleventh of August, was broke up before he got to Edinburgh [1].

On Saturday the fourteenth of August, 1773, late in the evening, I received a note § from him, that he was arrived at Boyd's inn [2], at the head of the Canongate. I went to him directly. He embraced me cordially; and I exulted in the thought, that I now had him actually in Caledonia. Mr. Scott's amiable manners, and attachment to our *Socrates*, at once united me to him. He told me that, before I came in, the Doctor had unluckily had a bad specimen of Scottish cleanliness [3]. He

† ⟨See App. D, p. 462.⟩
[1] In Cockburn's *Life of Jeffrey*, 1852, i. 157, there is a description of Edinburgh, towards the close of the century, ' the last purely Scotch age that Scotland was destined to see. . . . Almost the whole official state, as settled at the union, survived; and all graced the capital, unconscious of the economical scythe which has since mowed it down. All our nobility had not then fled. . . . [The lawyers,] instead of disturbing good company by professional matter, . . . were remarkably free of this vulgarity; and being trained to take difference of opinion easily, and to conduct discussions with forbearance, were, without undue obtrusion, the most cheerful people that were to be met with. . . . Philosophy had become indigenous in the place, and all classes, even in their gayest hours, were proud of the presence of its cultivators. . . . And all this was still a Scotch scene. The whole country had not begun to be absorbed in the ocean of London. . . . According to the modern rate of travelling, the capitals of Scotland and of England were then about 2400 miles asunder. Edinburgh was still more distant in its style and habits. It had then its own independent tastes, and ideas, and pursuits.' Scotland at this time was distinguished by the liberality of mind of its leading clergymen, which was due, according to Dr. A. Carlyle (*Auto.*, p. 57), to the fact that the Professor of Theology under whom they had studied was ' dull, and Dutch, and prolix'. 'There was one advantage', he says, ' attending the lectures of a dull professor—viz., that he could form no school, and the students were left entirely to themselves, and naturally formed opinions far more liberal than those they got from the Professor.'

§ ⟨See *ante*, ii. 266, for the note, and *post*, App. D, p. 462.⟩

[2] ⟨The inn was at the corner of the Canongate and St. Mary's Wynd, now St. Mary's Street. It is described in *Gent. Mag.*, 1771, xli. 543 : ' White Horse, B[o]yde ; crouded and confused : The master lives in the stable, the mistress not equal to the business. You must not expect a breakfast here before nine o'clock.' Boyd let it in 1779 and it was demolished in 1867. A tablet on the building which now (1935) occupies its site has the inscription : ' Boyds Inn, at which Dr. Samuel Johnson arrived in Edinburgh, 14th August, 1773, on his memorable tour to the Hebrides, occupied the larger part of the site of this building.' See J. H. Jamieson in *The Book of the Old Edinburgh Club*, vol. xiv, p. 129.⟩

[3] Boswell, writing of Scotland in his *Hypochondriack*, No. 8, says :—' In the last age it was the common practice in the best families for all the company to eat milk, or pudding, or any other dish that is eat with a spoon, not by distributing the contents of the dish into small plates round the table, but by every person dipping his spoon into the large

then drank no fermented liquor. He asked to have his lemonade made sweeter; upon which the waiter, with his greasy fingers, lifted a lump of sugar, and put it into it. The Doctor, in indignation, threw it out of the window. Scott said, he was afraid he would have knocked the waiter down. Mr. Johnson told me, that such another trick was played him at the house of a lady in Paris [1]. He was to do me the honour to lodge under my roof. I regretted sincerely that I had not also a room for Mr. Scott. Mr. Johnson and I walked arm-in-arm up the High-street, to my house in James's court [2] : it was a dusky night : I could not prevent his being assailed by the evening effluvia of Edinburgh. I heard a late baronet, of some distinction in the political world in the beginning of the present reign, observe, that 'walking the streets of Edinburgh at night was pretty perilous, and a good deal odoriferous.' The peril is much abated, by the care which the magistrates have taken to enforce the city laws against throwing foul water from the windows [3] ; but, from the structure of the houses in the old town,

platter; and when the fashion of having a small plate for each guest was brought from the continent by a young gentleman returned from his travels, a good old inflexible neighbour in the country said, " he did not see any thing he had learnt, but to take his broth twice." Nay, in our own remembrance, the use of a carving knife was considered as a novelty; and a gentleman of ancient family and good literature used to rate his son, a friend of mine, for introducing such a foppish superfluity.'—*London Mag.* 1778, p. 198.

[1] See *ante*, ii. 403, and *Letters*, No. 326.

[2] Chambers says that James's Court, 'till the building of the New Town, was inhabited by a select set of gentlemen. . . . They kept a clerk to record their names and their proceedings, had a scavenger of their own, clubbed in many public measures, and had balls and assemblies among themselves.' *Trad. Edinburgh*, i. 219. ⟨The north-west property, in which Boswell had his rooms, was burnt down and rebuilt in 1857. R. T. Skinner, *Royal Mile*, 1928,

p. 14. Boswell's words of welcome to Johnson were :—' I'm glad to see you under my roof ', to which Johnson replied : ' And 'tis a very noble roof.' The next day Boswell recorded :—' Johnson said . . . , without any prompting at all, my drawing room was the pleasantest room he had ever been in.' *Boswell Papers*, vi. 176–7.⟩ Johnson wrote to Mrs. Thrale, 17 Aug. 1773 :—' Boswel has very handsome and spacious rooms level with the ground on one side of the house, and on the other four stories high.' *Letters*, No. 320. Dr. J. H. Burton says that Hume occupied them just before Boswell. He continues :— ' Of the first impression made on a stranger, at that period, when entering such a house, a vivid description is given by Sir Walter Scott in *Guy Mannering* ; and in Counsellor Pleydell's library, with its collection of books and the prospect from the window, we have probably an accurate picture of the room in which Hume spent his studious hours.' *Life of Hume*, ii. 137, 431. ⟨See App. D, p. 463.⟩

[3] The English servant-girl in

which consist of many stories, in each of which a different family lives, and there being no covered sewers, the odour still continues. A zealous Scotsman would have wished Mr. Johnson to be without one of his five senses upon this occasion. As we marched slowly along, he grumbled in my ear, ' I smell you in the dark [1] ! ' But he acknowledged that the breadth of the street, and the loftiness of the buildings on each side, made a noble appearance [2].

My wife had tea ready for him, which it is well known he delighted to drink at all hours, particularly when sitting up late, and of which his able defence against Mr. Jonas Hanway [3] should have obtained him a magnificent reward from the East-India Company. He shewed much complacency upon finding that the mistress of the house was so attentive to his singular habit ; and as no man could be more polite when he chose to be so, his address to her was most courteous and engaging ; and his conversation soon charmed her into a forgetfulness of his external appearance [4].

I did not begin to keep a regular full journal till some days after we had set out from Edinburgh ; but I have luckily

Humphry Clinker (letter of July 18), after describing how the filth is thus thrown out, says :—' The maid calls *Gardy loo* to the passengers, which signifies, *Lord have mercy upon you !* '

[1] Wesley, when at Edinburgh in May 1761, writes :—' How can it be suffered that all manner of filth should still be thrown even into this street [High Street] continually ? . . . How long shall the capital city of Scotland, yea, and the chief street of it, stink worse than a common sewer ? ' Wesley's *Journal*, iv. 452. Smollett in *Humphry Clinker* makes Matthew Bramble say (letter of July 18):—'The inhabitants [of Edinburgh] . . . are apt to imagine the disgust that we avow is little better than affectation.' ⟨Arnot describing Edinburgh in 1779 writes :—' No circum-stance can impress a stranger with a worse opinion of Edinburgh, than the first reception he meets in the city. The inns are mean buildings ; their apartments dirty and dismal.' *History of Edinburgh*, p. 352.⟩

[2] ' Most of their buildings are very mean, and the whole town bears some resemblance to the old part of Birmingham.' *Letters*, No. 320.

[3] See *ante*, i. 313.

[4] Miss Burney, describing her first sight of Johnson, says :—' Upon asking my father why he had not prepared us for such uncouth, untoward strangeness, he laughed heartily, and said he had entirely forgotten that the same impression had been, at first, made upon himself ; but had been lost even on the second interview.' *Memoirs of Dr. Burney*, ii. 91.

preserved a good many fragments † of his *Memorabilia* from his very first evening in Scotland.

We had, a little before this, had a trial for murder, in which the judges had allowed the lapse of twenty years since its commission as a plea in bar, in conformity with the doctrine of prescription in the *civil* law, which Scotland and several other countries in Europe have adopted. He at first disapproved of this; but then he thought there was something in it, if there had been for twenty years a neglect to prosecute a crime which was *known*. He would not allow that a murder, by not being *discovered* for twenty years, should escape punishment [1]. We talked of the ancient trial by duel. He did not think it so absurd as is generally supposed; ' For (said he) it was only allowed when the question was *in equilibrio*, as when one affirmed and another denied; and they had a notion that Providence would interfere in favour of him who was in the right. But as it was found that in a duel, he who was in the right had not a better chance than he who was in the wrong, therefore society instituted the present mode of trial, and gave the advantage to him who is in the right.'

We sat till near two in the morning, having chatted a good while after my wife left us. She had insisted, that to shew all respect to the Sage, she would give up our [a] own bed-chamber to him, and take a worse [2]. This I cannot but gratefully mention, as one of a thousand obligations which I owe her, since the great obligation of her being pleased to accept of me as her husband [3].

Sunday, 15th August. [4]

Mr. Scott came to breakfast, at which I introduced to Dr. Johnson, and him, my friend Sir William Forbes, now of Pit-

---

[a] our 1, 2 (*MS.*): her 3
† ⟨See *Boswell Papers*, vi. 175 ff., ix. 271 ff.⟩
[1] See *post*, v. 87 ⟨and App. D, p. 463.⟩
[2] See *ante*, iii. 216.
[3] Boswell writes, in his *Hypochondriack*, No. 43:—' Naturally somewhat singular, independent of any additions which affectation and vanity may perhaps have made, I resolved to have a more pleasing species of Marriage than common, and bargained with my bride, that I should not be bound to live with her longer than I really inclined; and that whenever I tired of her domestick society, I should be at liberty to give it up. Eleven years have elapsed, and I have never yet wished to take advantage of my stipulated privilege.' *London Mag.* 1781, p. 156. See *ante*, ii. 140, note 1.
[4] Sir Walter Scott was two years old this day. He was born in a

Sligo[1]; a man of whom too much good cannot be said; who, with distinguished abilities and application in his profession of a Banker, is at once a good companion, and a good christian; which I think is saying enough. Yet it is but justice to record, that once, when he was in a dangerous illness, he was watched with the anxious apprehension of a general calamity; day and night his house was beset with affectionate inquiries; and, upon his recovery, *Te deum* was the universal chorus from the *hearts* of his countrymen.

Mr. Johnson was pleased with my daughter Veronica,[2] then house at the head of the College Wynd. When Johnson and Boswell returned to Edinburgh Jeffrey was a baby there seventeen days old. Some seventeen or eighteen years later ' he had the honour of assisting to carry the biographer of Johnson, in a state of great intoxication, to bed. For this he was rewarded next morning by Mr. Boswell . . . clapping his head, and telling him that he was a very promising lad, and that " if you go on as you've begun, you may live to be a Bozzy yourself yet." ' Cockburn's *Jeffrey*, 1852, i. 33.

[1] He was one of Boswell's executors. *Ante*, iii. 301, note 1. It is to his *Life of Dr. Beattie* that Scott alludes in the Introduction to the fourth Canto of *Marmion* :—
 ' Scarce had lamented Forbes paid
 The tribute to his Minstrel's shade ;
 The tale of friendship scarce was told,
 Ere the narrator's heart was cold :
 Far may we search before we find
 A heart so manly and so kind ! '
⟨In some parts of Scotland, notably Aberdeenshire, *Forbes* is still (1935) a disyllable.

Lord Cockburn wrote severely of the ' old Edinburgh bankers ' : ' Respectable men they were ; but, without talent, general knowledge, or any liberal objects, they were the conspicuous sycophants of existing power.' His grandson excepts Sir William Forbes from this general condemnation. *Memorials*, ed. 1910, p. 238. See also *post*, v. 413.⟩

[2] The saint's name of *Veronica* was introduced into our family through my great grandmother Veronica, Countess of Kincardine, a Dutch lady of the noble house of Sommelsdyck, of which there is a full account in Bayle's Dictionary. The family had once a princely right in Surinam. The governour of that settlement was appointed by the States General, the town of Amsterdam, and Sommelsdyck. The States General have acquired Sommelsdyck's right ; but the family has still great dignity and opulence, and by intermarriages is connected with many other noble families. When I was at the Hague, I was received with all the affection of kindred. The present Sommelsdyck has an important charge in the Republick, and is as worthy a man as lives. He has honoured me with his correspondence for these twenty years. My great grandfather, the husband of Countess Veronica, was Alexander, Earl of Kincardine, that eminent *Royalist* whose character is given by Burnet in his *History of his own Times*. From him the blood of *Bruce* flows in my veins. Of such ancestry who would not be proud ? And, as *Nihil est, nisi hoc sciat alter*, is peculiarly true of genealogy, who would not be glad to seize a fair opportunity to let it be known ? BOSWELL, ed. 1. Boswell visited Holland in 1763. *Ante*, i. 473. Burnet says that the Earl ' was both the wisest and the worthiest man that belonged to his countrey, and fit for governing any affairs but his own ; which he by a wrong turn, and by his love for the

a child of about four months old. She had the appearance of listening to him. His motions seemed to her to be intended for her amusement; and when he stopped, she fluttered, and made a little infantine noise, and a kind of signal for him to begin again. She would be held close to him; which was a proof, from simple nature, that his figure was not horrid. Her fondness for him endeared her still more to me, and I declared she should have five hundred pounds of additional fortune [1].

We talked of the practice of the law. Sir William Forbes said, he thought an honest lawyer should never undertake a cause which he was satisfied was not a just one. 'Sir, (said Mr. Johnson,) a lawyer has no business with the justice or injustice of the cause which he undertakes, unless his client asks his opinion, and then he is bound to give it honestly. The justice or injustice of the cause is to be decided by the judge. Consider, Sir; what is the purpose of courts of justice? It is, that every man may have his cause fairly tried, by men appointed to try causes. A lawyer is not to tell what he knows to be a lie: he is not to produce what he knows to be a false deed; but he is not to usurp the province of the jury and of the judge, and determine what shall be the effect of evidence,—what shall be the result of legal argument. As it rarely happens that a man is fit to plead his own cause, lawyers are a class of the community, who, by study and experience, have acquired the art and power of arranging evidence, and of applying to the points at issue what the law has settled. A lawyer is to do for his client all that his client might fairly do for himself, if he could. If, by a superiority of attention, of knowledge, of skill, and a better method of communication, he has the advantage of his adversary, it is an advantage to which he is entitled. There

publick, neglected to his ruin. . . . His thoughts went slow, and his words came much slower: But a deep judgment appeared in every thing he said or did. . . . I may be perhaps inclined to carry his character too far; for he was the first man that entred into friendship with me.' Burnet's *History of his own Time*, 1724, i. 103. 'The ninth Earl succeeded as fifth Earl of Elgin and thus united the two dignities.' Burke's *Peerage*. Boswell's quotation is from Persius, *Satires*, i. 27 : ' Scire tuum nihil est, nisi te scire hoc sciat alter.' It is the motto to *The Spectator*, No. 379. ⟨For Boswell's Dutch relatives see App. D, p. 463.⟩

[1] ⟨Boswell provided this additional fortune by an unregistered deed, dated 3 March 1795. Veronica died before the grant was made. Boswell's *Hebrides*, ed. Pottle and Bennett, 1962, p. 407.⟩

must always be some advantage, on one side or other ; and it is better that advantage should be had by talents, than by chance. If lawyers were to undertake no causes till they were sure they were just, a man might be precluded altogether from a trial of his claim, though, were it judicially examined, it might be found a very just claim [1].'—This was sound practical doctrine, and rationally repressed a too refined scrupulosity [2] of conscience.

Emigration was at this time a common topick of discourse [3]. Dr. Johnson regretted it as hurtful to human happiness : ' For (said he) it spreads mankind,[a] which weakens the defence of a nation, and lessens the comfort of living. Men, thinly scattered, make a shift, but a bad shift, without many things. A smith is ten miles off : they'll do without a nail or a staple. A taylor is far from them : they'll botch their own clothes. It is being concentrated which produces high convenience [4].'

Sir William Forbes, Mr. Scott, and I, accompanied Mr. Johnson to the chapel [5], founded by Lord Chief Baron Smith, for the Service of the Church of England. The Reverend Mr. Carre, the senior clergyman, preached from these words, ' Because the Lord reigneth, let the earth be glad [6].'—I was sorry to think

[a] mankind, 1, 2 : mankind 3.

[1] See *ante*, ii. 47.
[2] See *ante*, iv. 5, n. 2; *post*, v. 62.
[3] See *ante*, iii. 231. Johnson (*Western Isl.*, 33) speaks of ' the general dissatisfaction, which is now driving the Highlanders into the other hemisphere.' This dissatisfaction chiefly arose from the fact that the chiefs were ' gradually degenerating from patriarchal rulers to rapacious landlords.' *Ib.* p. 81. ' That they [the people] may not fly from the increase of rent, I know not whether the general good does not require that the landlords be, for a time, restrained in their demands, and kept quiet by pensions proportionate to their loss . . . It affords a legislator little self-applause to consider, that where there was formerly an insurrection, there is now a wilderness.' *Ib.* p. 88. ' As the world has been let in upon them, they have heard of happier climates, and less arbitrary government.' *Ib.* p. 119.
[4] ' To a man that ranges the streets of London, where he is tempted to contrive wants for the pleasure of supplying them, a shop affords no image worthy of attention ; but in an Island, it turns the balance of existence between good and evil. To live in perpetual want of little things, is a state not indeed of torture, but of constant vexation. I have in Sky had some difficulty to find ink for a letter ; and if a woman breaks her needle, the work is at a stop.' *Ib.* p. 118.
[5] ⟨It was founded in 1722 and demolished in 1822. See Arnot's *Edinburgh*, 1779, p. 287, and Sir D. Wilson's *Memorials of Edinburgh*, 1891, ii. 61.⟩
[6] ' The Lord reigneth ; let the earth rejoice ; let the multitude of isles be glad thereof.' *Psalms*, xcvii. 1.

Mr. Johnson did not attend to the sermon, Mr. Carre's low voice not being strong enough to reach his hearing. A selection of Mr. Carre's sermons has, since his death, been published by Sir William Forbes [1], and the world has acknowledged their uncommon merit. I am well assured Lord Mansfield has pronounced them to be excellent.

Here I obtained a promise from Lord Chief Baron Orde [2], that he would dine at my house next day. I presented Mr. Johnson to his Lordship, who politely said to him, ' I have not the honour of knowing you ; but I hope for it, and to see you at my house. I am to wait on you to-morrow.' This respectable English judge will be long remembered in Scotland, where he built an elegant house, and lived in it magnificently. His own ample fortune, with the addition of his salary, enabled him to be splendidly hospitable. It may be fortunate for an individual amongst ourselves to be Lord Chief Baron ; and a most worthy man † now has the office ; but, in my opinion, it is better for Scotland in general, that some of our publick employments should be filled by gentlemen of distinction from the south side of the Tweed, as we have the benefit of promotion in England. Such an interchange would make a beneficial mixture of manners, and render our union more complete. Lord Chief Baron Orde was on good terms with us all, in a narrow country filled with jarring interests and keen parties ; and, though I well knew his opinion to be the same with my own, he kept himself aloof at a very critical period indeed, when the *Douglas cause* shook the sacred security of *birth-right* in Scotland to its foundation ; a cause, which had it happened before the Union, when there was no appeal to a British House of Lords, would have left the great fortress of honours and of property in ruins [3].

[1] ⟨Forbes gives a memoir of the Rev. George Carr, 1704–76, in his *Life of Beattie*, ii. 404–6. Carr's Sermons were first published, in three volumes, in 1777 ; the seventh edition appeared in 1796. Single sermons were published in 1744 and 1746.⟩

[2] ⟨Robert Ord was the son of John Ord, solicitor, and under-sheriff of Newcastle from 1685 to 1703. He inherited Hunstanworth and was M.P. for Morpeth from 1741 to 1755, when he was appointed Chief Baron ; he resigned in 1775 and died in 1778.

His house was No. 8 Queen Street. See R. Welford, *Men of Mark 'twixt Tyne and Tweed*, 1895, iii. 235, *Ret. Members of Parl.* ii. 90, 102, 114, Burke's *Landed Gentry*, 1886, p. 1390, and W. Harrison, *Mem. Edinb. Houses*, 1928, 127.⟩

† ⟨(Sir) James William Montgomery held the office from 1775 to 1801. See the *D.N.B.*⟩

[3] The House of Lords reversed the decision of the Court of Session in this cause. See *ante*, ii. 50, 230.

When we got home, Dr. Johnson desired to see my books. He took down Ogden's Sermons on Prayer [1], on which I set a very high value, having been much edified by them, and he retired with them to his room. He did not stay long, but soon joined us in the drawing-room. I presented to him Mr. Robert Arbuthnot, a relation of the celebrated Dr. Arbuthnot [2], and a man of literature and taste. To him we were obliged for a previous recommendation, which secured us a very agreeable reception at St. Andrews, and which Dr. Johnson, in his 'Journey,' ascribes to 'some invisible friend [3].'

Of Dr. Beattie, Mr. Johnson said, ' Sir, he has written like a man conscious of the truth, and feeling his own strength [4]. Treating your adversary with respect, is giving him an advantage to which he is not entitled [5]. The greatest part of men cannot judge of reasoning, and are impressed by character; so that, if you allow your adversary a respectable character, they will think, that though you differ from him, you may be in the wrong. Sir, treating your adversary with respect, is striking soft in a battle †. And as to Hume,—a man who has so much conceit as to tell all mankind that they have been bubbled [6] for ages, and he is the wise man who sees better than they,—a man who has so little scrupulosity as to venture to oppose those principles which have been thought necessary to human happiness,—is he to be surprised if another man comes and laughs at

[1] ⟨Dr. Samuel Ogden, 1716-78, schoolmaster, classical and oriental scholar, popular preacher, and Woodwardian Professor of Geology, published his *Sermons on the Efficacy of Prayer and Intercession*, at Cambridge, in 1770. Boswell 'preached' one of them in the ruined cathedral of Iona. *MS.Jrnl.*, 20 Oct. He mentions them so often that in the Collings-Rowlandson caricatures of the tour he is commonly represented as having them in his hand or pocket. See *ante*, iii. 248 ⟨and *post*, v. 88, 350⟩.

[2] ⟨Robert Arbuthnot, of Haddo, 1735-1803, was the great-grandson of Dr. John Arbuthnot's uncle Robert. He was an Edinburgh banker and Secretary to the Board of Trustees. See Aitken, *Life and Works of Arbuthnot*, 1892, 172, and *Scots Mag.* 1803,

p. 816.⟩ For Dr. Arbuthnot see *ante*, i. 425.
[3] 'We found, that by the interposition of some invisible friend, lodgings had been provided for us at the house of one of the professors, whose easy civility quickly made us forget that we were strangers.' *Western Islands*, p. 5.
[4] He is referring to Beattie's *Essay on Truth*. See *post*, v. 273, and *ante*, ii. 201.
[5] See *ante*, ii. 443, where Johnson again speaks of Hume.
† ⟨According to Boswell's original report Johnson said : ' Sir, 'tis like asking a man to strike soft in a battel.' *Boswell Papers*, vi. 178.⟩
[6] Johnson, in his *Dictionary*, calls bubble ' a cant word'.

him? If he is the great man he thinks himself, all this cannot hurt him: it is like throwing peas against a rock.' He added 'something much too rough,'† both as to Mr. Hume's head and heart, which I suppress. Violence is, in my opinion, not suitable to the Christian cause. Besides, I always lived on good terms with Mr. Hume, though I have frankly told him, I was not clear that it was right in me to keep company with him. ' But (said I) how much better are you than your books!' He was cheerful, obliging, and instructive; he was charitable to the poor; and many an agreeable hour have I passed with him [1]: I have preserved some entertaining and interesting memoirs of him, particularly when he knew himself to be dying, which I may some time or other communicate to the world [2]. I shall not, however, extol him so very highly as Dr. Adam Smith does, who says, in a letter to Mr. Strahan the Printer (not a confidential letter to his friend, but a letter which is published [3]

† ⟨' Something said of Chartres much too rough.' Pope, *Imit. Horace*, Bk. ii, *Sat.* i. 4. See App. D, p. 464, for Johnson's saying.⟩

[1] ⟨Boswell first met Hume in July 1758. Boswell's *Letters*, No. 1, i. 2. For his record of an agreeable hour with him on 4 Nov. 1762 see *Boswell Papers*, i. 126–9.⟩ He wrote to Temple in 1768 :—' David is really amiable. I allways regret to him his unlucky principles and he smiles at my faith. But I have a hope which he has not, or pretends not to have. So who has the best of it, my reverend friend?' *Letters*, No. 92, i. 160. Dr. A. Carlyle (*Auto*., pp. 275–6) says :—' Mr. Hume gave both elegant dinners and suppers, and the best claret, and ... he furnished the entertainment with the most instructive and pleasing conversation, for he assembled whosoever were most knowing and agreeable among either the laity or clergy. ... For innocent mirth and agreeable raillery I never knew his match.'

[2] ⟨Boswell preserved these memoirs in his archives; they have been published in the *Boswell Papers*, xii. 227–32.⟩

[3] This letter, though shattered by the sharp shot of Dr. Horne of Oxford's wit, in the character of ' One of the People called Christians', is still prefixed to Mr. Hume's excellent History of England, like a poor invalid on the piquet guard, or like a list of quack medicines sold by the same bookseller, by whom a work of whatever nature is published; for it has no connection with his *History*, let it have what it may with what are called his *Philosophical* Works. A worthy friend of mine in London was lately consulted by a lady of quality, of most distinguished merit, what was the best History of England for her son to read. My friend recommended Hume's. But, upon recollecting that its usher was a superlative panegyrick on one, who endeavoured to sap the credit of our holy religion, he revoked his recommendation. I am really sorry for

with all formality) : ' Upon the whole, I have always considered him, both in his life-time,[a] and since his death, as approaching as nearly to the idea of a perfectly wise and virtuous man as perhaps the nature of human frailty will permit.' Let Dr. Smith consider : Was not Mr. Hume blest with good health, good spirits, good friends, a competent and increasing fortune ? And had he not also a perpetual feast of fame [1] ? But, as a learned friend [2] has observed to me, 'What trials did he undergo, to prove the perfection of his virtue ? Did he ever experience any great instance of adversity ? '— When I read this sentence delivered by my old *Professor of Moral Philosophy*, I could not help exclaiming with the

[a] life-time, 1, 2 : life time 3

this ostentatious *alliance* ; because I admire ' The Theory of Moral Sentiments ', and value the greatest part of ' An Inquiry into the Nature and Causes of the Wealth of Nations'. Why should such a writer be so forgetful of human comfort, as to give any countenance to that dreary infidelity which would ' make us poor indeed ! ' [' makes me poor indeed.' *Othello*, iii. 3]. BOSWELL. Dr. Horne's book is entitled, *A Letter to Adam Smith LL.D. On the Life, Death, and Philosophy of his Friend David Hume Esq. By one of the People called Christians.* ⟨This pamphlet was originally published in 1777 ' at the Clarendon Press ' ; numerous editions appeared down to 1836 : it was included in Dr. Horne's *Works* published in 1818.⟩ Its chief wit is in the ' Advertisement.' ⟨For Adam Smith's letter see App. D, p. 464.⟩ The bookseller mentioned in this note was perhaps Francis Newbery, who succeeded his father, Goldsmith's publisher, as a dealer in quack medicines and books. C. Welsh, *A Bookseller of the Last Century*, pp. 22-3, 73.

[1] Hume says that his first work, his *Treatise of Human Nature*, ' fell dead-born from the Press.' Auto. in *Letters of Hume*, 1932, i. 2. His *Enquiry concerning Human Understanding* ' was entirely overlooked and neglected.' *Ib*. p. 3. His *Enquiry concerning the Principles of Morals* ' came unnoticed and unobserved into the World.' *Ib*. p. 4. The first volume of his *History of England* certainly met with numerous assailants ; but ' after the first Ebullitions of this Fury were over, what was still more mortifying, the Book seemed to sink into Oblivion. Mr. Millar told me,' he continues, ' that in a twelvemonth he sold only forty five Copies of it. . . . I was, . . . I confess, discouraged ; and had not the War been at that time breaking out between France and England, I had certainly retired to some provincial Town of the former Kingdom, have changed my Name, and never more have returned to my native Country.' *Ib*. p. 4. Only one of his works, his *Political Discourses*, was ' successful on the first Publication.' *Ibid*. By the time he was turned fifty, however, his books were selling very well, and he had become ' not only independant, but opulent.' *Ib*. p. 5. A few weeks before he died he wrote :— ' I see many Symptoms of my literary Reputation's breaking out at last with additional Lustre.' *Ib*. p. 7. ⟨See J. H. Burton, *Hume*, i. 399.⟩

[2] ⟨Probably Malone. Boswell's *Hebrides*, ed. Pottle and Bennett, p. 18.⟩

Psalmist, 'Surely I have now more understanding than my teachers [1]!'

While we were talking, there came a note to me from Dr. William Robertson.

'*Dear Sir*,

'I have been expecting every day to hear from you, of Dr. Johnson's arrival. Pray, what do you know about his motions? I long to take him by the hand. I write this from the college, where I have only this scrap of paper. Ever yours,

W. R.'

'*Sunday.*

It pleased me to find Dr. Robertson thus eager to meet Dr. Johnson. I was glad I could answer, that he was come: and I begged Dr. Robertson might be with us as soon as he could.

Sir William Forbes, Mr. Scott, Mr. Arbuthnot, and another gentleman † dined with us. 'Come, Dr. Johnson, (said I,) it is commonly thought that our veal in Scotland is not good. But here is some which I believe you will like.'—There was no catching him.—*Johnson*. 'Why, sir, what is commonly thought, I should take to be true. *Your* veal may be good; but that will only be an exception to the general opinion; not a proof against it.'

Dr. Robertson, according to the custom of Edinburgh at that time, dined in the interval between the forenoon and afternoon service, which was then later than now; § so we had not the pleasure of his company till dinner was over, when he came and drank wine with us. And then began some animated dialogue [2], of which here follows a pretty full note.

We talked of Mr. Burke.—Dr. Johnson said, he had great variety of knowledge, store of imagery, copiousness of language.— *Robertson*. 'He has wit too.'—*Johnson*. 'No, sir; he never succeeds there. 'Tis low; 'tis conceit. I used to say, Burke never once made a good joke [3]. What I most envy Burke for,

---

[1] *Psalms*, cxix. 99.
† ⟨Charles Hay, later Lord Newton. *Boswell Papers*, vi. 177. He and Boswell studied Erskine's *Institutes* together in 1774. *Ib*. ix. 185, 218, 223, 226–7.⟩
§ ⟨See App. D, p. 464.⟩
[2] We learn, *post*, v. 371, that Robertson was cautious in his talk,

though we see here that he had much more courage than the professors of Aberdeen or Glasgow. ⟨See *post*, v. 96.⟩
[3] This was one of the points upon which Dr. Johnson was strangely heterodox. For, surely, Mr. Burke, with his other remarkable qualities,

Edinburgh   *Sunday* 15 *August* 1773   33
is, his being constantly the same. He is never what we call
hum-drum ; never unwilling to begin to talk, nor in haste to

is also distinguished for his wit, and for wit of all kinds too; not merely that power of language which Pope chooses to denominate wit, (True wit is Nature to advantage drest ; What oft was thought, but ne'er so well exprest.) [*Ess. Crit.* l. 297.] but surprising allusions, brilliant sallies of vivacity, and pleasant conceits. His speeches in parliament are strewed with them. Take, for instance, the variety which he has given in his wide range, yet exact detail, when exhibiting his Reform Bill. And his conversation abounds in wit. Let me put down a specimen.—I told him, I had seen, at a *Blue-stocking* assembly, a number of ladies sitting round a worthy and tall friend of ours, listening to his literature. ' Ay, (said he) like maids round a May-pole.'—I told him, I had found out a perfect definition of human nature, as distinguished from the animal. An ancient philosopher said, Man was 'a two-legged animal without feathers,' upon which his rival Sage had a Cock plucked bare, and set him down in the school before all the disciples, as a ' Philosophick Man.' Dr. Franklin said, Man was ' a tool-making animal,' which is very well ; for no animal but man makes a thing, by means of which he can make another thing. But this applies to very few of the species. My definition of *Man* is, ' a Cooking Animal.' The beasts have memory, judgment, and all the faculties and passions of our mind, in a certain degree ; but no beast is a cook. The trick of the monkey using the cat's paw to roast a chestnut, is only a piece of shrewd malice in that *turpissima bestia*, which humbles us so sadly by its similarity to us. Man alone can dress a good dish ; and every man whatever is more or less a cook, in seasoning what he himself eats.[a]—Your definition is good, said Mr. Burke, and I now see the full force of the common proverb, ' There is *reason* in roasting of eggs.'—When Mr. Wilkes, in his days of tumultuous opposition, was borne upon the shoulders of the mob, Mr. Burke (as Mr. Wilkes told me himself, with classical admiration,) applied to him what *Horace* says of *Pindar*,

—— *numeris*que fertur

LEGE *solutis*. [*Odes*, iv. 2. 11.]

Sir Joshua Reynolds, who agrees with me entirely as to Mr. Burke's fertility of wit, said, that this was ' dignifying a pun.' He also observed, that he has often heard Burke say, in the course of an evening, ten good things, each of which would have served a noted wit (whom he named) to live upon for a twelvemonth.

I find, since the former edition, that some persons have objected to the instances which I have given of Mr. Burke's wit, as not doing justice to my very ingenious friend ; the specimens produced having, it is alledged, more of conceit than real wit, and being merely sportive sallies of the moment, not justifying the encomium which they think with me, he undoubtedly merits. I was well aware, how hazardous it was to exhibit particular instances of wit, which is of so airy and spiritual a nature as often to elude the hand that attempts to grasp it. The excellence and efficacy of a *bon mot* depend frequently so much on the occasion on which it is spoken, on the peculiar [b] manner of the speaker, on the person to [c] whom it is applied,

[a] eats. 1, 2 : eats 3.   [b] peculiar 2: particular 3.   [c] to 2: of 3.

2754·5   D

leave off.'—*Boswell.* 'Yet he can listen.'—*Johnson.* 'No; I cannot say he is good at that [1]. So desirous is he to talk, that, if one is speaking at this end of the table, he'll speak to somebody at the other end. Burke, sir, is such a man, that if you met him for the first time in a street [a] where you were stopped by a drove of oxen, and you and he stepped aside to take shelter but for five minutes, he'd talk to you in such a manner, that, when you parted, you would say, this is an extraordinary man [2]. Now, you may be long enough with me, without finding any thing extraordinary.' He said, he believed Burke was intended for the law; but either had not money enough to follow it, or had not diligence enough [3]. He said, he could not understand how a man could apply to one thing, and not to another. *Robertson* said, one man had more judgment,

[a] a street 1, 2 : the street 3.

the previous introduction, and a thousand minute particulars which cannot be easily enumerated, that it is always dangerous to detach a witty saying from the group to which it belongs, and to set it before the eye of the spectator, divested of those concomitant circumstances, which gave it animation, mellowness, and relief. I ventured, however, at all hazards, to put down the first instances that occurred to me, as proofs of Mr. Burke's lively and brilliant fancy; but am very sensible that his numerous friends could have suggested many of a superior quality. Indeed, the being in company with him, for a single day, is sufficient to shew that what I have asserted is well founded; and it was only necessary to have appealed to all who know him intimately, for a complete refutation of the heterodox opinion entertained by Dr. Johnson on this subject. *He* allowed Mr. Burke, as the reader will find hereafter [*post*, v. 213, 269], to be a man of consummate and unrivalled abilities in every light except that now under consideration; and the variety of his allusions, and splendour of his imagery, have made such an impression on *all the rest* of the world, that superficial observers are apt to overlook his other merits, and to suppose that *wit* is his chief and most prominent excellence; when in fact it is only one of the many talents that he possesses, which are so various and extraordinary, that it is very difficult to ascertain precisely the rank and value of each. BOSWELL.

For Malone's share in this note, see *ante*, iii. 323, note 2. For Burke's Economical Reform Bill, which was brought in on Feb. 11, 1780, see Prior's *Burke*, 1826, i. 380. For *Blue Stocking*, see *ante*, iv. 108. The 'tall friend of ours' was Langton (*ante*, i. 336). For Franklin's definition, see *ante*, iii. 245, and for Burke's classical pun, *ib.* p. 323. For Burke's 'talent of wit,' see *ante*, i. 453, iii. 323, iv. 276, and *post*, v. 213. ⟨For other notes on this note see App. D, p. 465.⟩

[1] See *ante*, iv. 27.
[2] ⟨See App. D, p. 465.⟩
[3] Prior (*Life of Burke*, 1826, i. 34) says that 'his destination, from an early period, was for the bar.' His name was entered at the Middle Temple in 1747, but he was never called.

another more imagination.—*Johnson*. 'No, sir ; it is only, one man has more mind than another. He may direct it differently ; he may, by accident, see the success of one kind of study, and take a desire to excel in it. I am persuaded that, had Sir Isaac Newton applied to poetry, he would have made a very fine epick poem. I could as easily apply to law † as to tragick poetry.'—*Boswell*. ' Yet, sir, you did apply to tragick poetry, not to law.'—*Johnson*. ' Because, sir, I had not money to study law. Sir, the man who has vigour, may walk to the east, just as well as to the west, if he happens to turn his head that way ¹.'—*Boswell*. ' But, sir, 'tis like walking up and down a hill ; one man will naturally do the one better than the other. A hare will run up a hill best, from her fore-legs being short ; a dog down.'—*Johnson*. ' Nay, sir ; that is from mechanical powers. If you make mind mechanical, you may argue in that manner. One mind is a vice, and holds fast ; there's a good memory. Another is a file ; and he is a disputant, a controversialist. Another is a razor ; and he is sarcastical.'—We talked of *Whitefield*. He said, he was at the same college with him ², and knew him *before he began to be better than other people* (smiling) ; that he believed he sincerely meant well, but had a mixture of politicks and ostentation : whereas *Wesley* thought of religion only ³.—*Robertson* said, Whitefield had strong natural eloquence, which, if cultivated,

† ⟨See App. D, p. 482.⟩
¹ See *ante*, ii. 437, note 2.
² ⟨The words ' with him ' were added by Boswell when he revised his Journal for publication. Whitefield and Johnson were not at Pembroke at the same time. See *ante*, i. 78, n. 2.⟩
³ That cannot be said now, after the flagrant part which Mr. *John Wesley* took against our American brethren, when, in his own name, he threw amongst his enthusiastick flock, the very individual combustibles of Dr. *Johnson's* ' Taxation no Tyranny ' ; and after the intolerant spirit which he manifested against our fellow-christians of the Roman Catholick Communion, for which that able champion, Father *O'Leary*, has

given him so hearty a drubbing. But I should think myself very unworthy, if I did not at the same time acknowledge Mr. John Wesley's merit, as a veteran ' Soldier of Jesus Christ ' [2 *Timothy*, ii. 3], who has, I do believe, ' turned ᵃ many from darkness into light, and from the power of *Satan* to the living GOD ' [*Acts*, xxvi. 18]. BOSWELL, ed. 1.
Wesley wrote on Nov. 11, 1775 (*Journal*, vi. 82), ' I made some additions to the *Calm Address to our American Colonies*. Need any one ask from what motive this was wrote ? Let him look round : England is in a flame !—a flame of malice and rage against the King, and almost all that are in authority

ᵃ ' turned 1 : turned 2, 3.

would have done great things.—*Johnson*. 'Why, sir, I take it, he was at the height of what his abilities could do, and was sensible of it. He had the ordinary advantages of education; but he chose to pursue that oratory which is for the mob [1].'— *Boswell*. 'He had great effect on the passions.'—*Johnson*. 'Why, sir, I don't think so. He could not represent a succession of pathetick images. He vociferated, and made an impression. *There*, again, was a mind like a hammer.'—Dr. Johnson now said, a certain eminent political friend of our's [2] was wrong, in his maxim of sticking to a certain set of *men* on all occasions. 'I can see that a man may do right to stick to a *party* (said he); that is to say, he is a *Whig*, or he is a *Tory*, and he thinks one of those parties upon the whole the best, and that,[a] to make it prevail, it must be generally supported, though, in particulars, it may be wrong. He takes its faggot of principles, in which there are fewer rotten sticks than in the other, though some rotten sticks to be sure; and they cannot well be separated. But, to bind one's self to one man, or one set of men, (who may be right to-day and wrong to-morrow,) without any general preference of system, I must disapprove [3].'

[a] that, 1: that 2, 3.

under him. I labour to put out this flame.' ⟨See *post*, App. D, p. 466.⟩ In his *Letter concerning the civil principles of Roman Catholics* published in Jan. 1780, he said:—' I insist upon it, That no government, not Roman catholic, ought to tolerate men of the Roman catholic persuasion.... They ought not to be tolerated by any government, Protestant, Mahometan, or Pagan.' To this the Rev. Arthur O'Leary replied with great wit and force, in a pamphlet entitled, *Remarks on the Rev. Mr. Wesley's Letters*. Dublin, 1780, vii. 274. Johnson wrote to Wesley on Feb. 6, 1776, 'I have thanks... to return you for the addition of your important suffrage to my argument on the American question. To have gained such a mind as yours may justly confirm me in my own opinion. What effect my paper has upon the publick, I know not; but I have no reason to be discouraged. The Lecturer was surely in the right, who, though he saw his audience slinking away, refused to quit the Chair, while Plato staid.' *Letters*, No. 451.

[1] ⟨' Whitefield's writings, of every kind, are certainly below mediocrity. They afford the measure of his knowledge and of his intellect, but not of his genius as a preacher.' Southey's *Wesley*, 1925, ii. 106.⟩ See *ante*, ii. 79.

[2] Burke. See ⟨*Boswell Papers*, vi. 179, facsimile⟩, *ante*, ii. 222, 285, note 3, and iii. 45.

[3] If due attention were paid to this observation, there would be more virtue, even in politicks. What Dr. Johnson justly condemned, has, I am sorry to say, greatly increased in the present reign. At the distance of four years from this conversation,

He told us of Cooke †, who translated Hesiod, and lived twenty years on a translation of Plautus, for which he was always taking subscriptions; and that he presented Foote to a Club, in the following singular manner : ' This is the nephew of the gentleman who was lately hung in chains for murdering his brother [1].'

In the evening I introduced to Mr. Johnson [2] two good friends

21st February 1777, My Lord Archbishop of York, in his ' sermon before the Society for the Propagation of the Gospel in Foreign Parts,' thus indignantly describes the then state of parties :
' Parties once had a *principle* belonging to them, absurd perhaps, and indefensible, but still carrying a notion of *duty*, by which honest minds might easily be caught.
' But they are now *combinations of individuals*, who, instead of being the sons and servants of the community, make a league for advancing their *private interests*. It is their business to hold high the notion of *political honour*. I believe and trust, it is not injurious to say, that such a bond is no better than that by which the lowest and wickedest combinations are held together; and that it denotes the last stage of political depravity.'
To find a thought, which just shewed itself to us from the mind of *Johnson*, thus appearing again at such a distance of time, and without any communication between them, enlarged to full growth in the mind of *Markham*, is a curious object of philosophical contemplation.—That two such great and luminous minds should have been so dark in one corner,—that *they* should have held it to be ' Wicked rebellion '[a] in the British subjects established in America, to resist the abject condition of holding all their property at the mercy of British subjects remaining at home, while their allegiance to our common Lord the King was to be

preserved inviolate,—is a striking proof to me, either that ' He who sitteth in Heaven' [*Psalms*, ii. 4], scorns the loftiness of human pride, —or that the evil spirit, whose personal existence I strongly believe, and even in this age am confirmed in that belief by a *Fell*, nay, by a *Hurd*, has more power than some choose to allow. BOSWELL, ed. 1.
It was Archbishop Markham to whom Johnson made the famous bow ; *ante*, iv. 198, n. 2. John Fell published in 1779 *Dæmoniacs ; an Enquiry into the Heathen and the Scripture Doctrine of Dæmons.* For Hurd see *ante*, iv. 290.
† ⟨See App. D, p. 466.⟩
[1] ⟨Foote's younger uncle Samuel Goodere, commander of H.M.S. *Ruby*, murdered his elder brother, Sir John Dineley Goodere, 19 Jan. 1741, mainly because he had cut the entail on his estates and expressed his intention of leaving them to one of the sons of his sister Eleanor, Foote's mother. Goodere was hanged 15 April 1741. Foote was ' prevailed upon ' to publish an account of the crime (*Memoirs of Sir J. D. Goodere*, etc., 1741) by the ' remonstrances that what came out under the name of so near a Relation . . . would have some weight.'⟩
[2] It may be observed, that I sometimes call my great friend, *Mr.* Johnson, sometimes *Dr.* Johnson ; though he had at this time a doctor's degree from Trinity College, Dublin. The University of Oxford afterwards conferred it upon him by a diploma, in very honourable terms. It was

[a] rebellion' 1, 2 : rebellion 3.

of mine, Mr. William Nairne, Advocate, and Mr. Hamilton of Sundrum †, my neighbour in the country, both of whom supped with us. I have preserved nothing of what passed, except that Dr. Johnson displayed another of his heterodox opinions,—a contempt of tragick acting ¹. He said, ' the action of all players in tragedy is bad. It should be a man's study to repress those signs of emotion and passion, as they are called.' He was of a directly contrary opinion to that of Fielding, in his *Tom Jones* ; who makes Partridge say, of Garrick, ' why, I could act as well as he myself. I am sure, if I had seen a ghost, I should have looked in the very same manner, and done just as he did ².' For, when I asked him, ' Would you not, sir, start as Mr. Garrick does, if you saw a ghost ? ' He answered, ' I hope not. If I did, I should frighten the ghost.'

Monday, 16th August.

Dr. William Robertson came to breakfast. We talked of *Ogden* on Prayer. Dr. Johnson said, ' The same arguments which are used against GOD's hearing prayer, will serve against his rewarding good, and punishing evil. He has resolved, he has declared, in the former case as in the latter.' He had last night looked into Lord Hailes's ' Remarks on the History of Scotland.' § Dr. Robertson and I said, it was a pity Lord Hailes did not write greater things. His lordship had not then published his ' Annals of Scotland ' ³.—*Johnson.* ' I remember I was once on a visit at the house of a lady for whom I had a high respect.

some time before I could bring myself to call him Doctor ; but, as he has been long known by that title, I shall give it to him in the rest of this Journal. BOSWELL, ed. 1. ⟨Boswell throughout his original Journal of the tour describes Johnson as ' Mr.'⟩ See *ante*, i. 488, note 3, and ii. 332, note 1.
† ⟨John Hamilton, 1739–1821. Burke's *Landed Gentry*, 1886, p. 821.⟩
¹ In *The Idler*, No. viii, Johnson has the following fling at tragedians. He had mentioned the terror struck into our soldiers by the Indian warcry, and he continues :—' I am of opinion, that, by a proper mixture of Asses, Bulls, Turkeys, Geese, and Tragedians, a noise might be procured equally horrid with the Warcry.' See *ante*, ii. 92.
² *Tom Jones*, bk. xvi. chap. 5. Mme. Necker in a letter to Garrick said :—' Nos acteurs se métamorphosent assez bien, mais Monsieur Garrick fait autre chose ; il nous métamorphose tous dans le caractère qu'il a revêtu ;... nous sommes remplis de terreur avec Hamlet,' &c. *Garrick Corres.* ii. 627.
§ ⟨Published in 1773. The book consists of nineteen short essays.⟩
³ See *ante*, i. 432, and ii. 278 ff.

There was a good deal of company in the room. When they were gone, I said to this lady, "What foolish talking have we had!"—"Yes, (said she,) but while they talked, you said nothing."—I was struck with the reproof. How much better is the man who does any thing that is innocent, than he who does nothing. Besides, I love anecdotes[1]. I fancy mankind may come, in time, to write all aphoristically, except in narrative; grow weary of preparation, and connection, and illustration, and all those arts by which a big book is made.—If a man is to wait till he weaves anecdotes into a system, we may be long in getting them, and get but few, in comparison of what we might get.'

Dr. Robertson said, the notions of *Eupham Macallan*, a fanatick woman, of whom Lord Hailes gives a sketch, were still prevalent among some of the Presbyterians; and therefore it was right in Lord Hailes, a man of known piety, to undeceive them.[2]

We walked out[3], that Dr. Johnson might see some of the things which we have to shew at Edinburgh. We went to the Parliament-House[4], where the Parliament of Scotland sat, and

---

[1] See *ante*, ii. 11.

[2] Euphan M'Cullan (not Eupham Macallan) is mentioned in Dalrymple's *Remarks on the History of Scotland*, p. 254. She maintained that 'she seldom ever prayed but she got a positive answer.' The minister of her parish was ill. 'She prayed, and *got an answer*, that for a year's time he should be spared; and after the year's end he fell sick again.' 'I went, said she, to pray yet again for his life; but *the Lord left me not an mouse's likeness* (a proverbial expression, meaning 'to reprove with such severity that the person reproved shrinks, and becomes abashed'), *and* said, 'Beast that thou art! shall I keep my servant in pain for thy sake?' And when I said, 'Lord, what then shall I do?' he answered me, *he was but a reed that I spoke through, and I will provide another reed to speak through*.' Dalrymple points out that it was a belief in these 'answers

from the Lord' that led John Balfour and his comrades to murder Archbishop Sharp.

[3] R. Chambers, in his *Traditions*, speaking of the time of Johnson's visit, says (i. 21), on the authority of 'a certain ancient native of Edinburgh, [that] people all knew each other by sight. The appearance of a new face upon the streets was at once remarked, and numbers busied themselves in finding out who and what the stranger was.'

[4] It was on this visit to the parliament-house, that Mr. Henry Erskine (brother of Lord Erskine), after being presented to Dr. Johnson by Mr. Boswell, and having made his bow, slipped a shilling into Boswell's hand, whispering that it was for the sight of his *bear*. WALTER SCOTT, 1831. ⟨For an account of the building of the Parliament House see R. K. Hannay and G. P. H. Watson in *The Book of the Old Edinburgh Club*, vol. xiii.⟩

40   *Monday* 16 *August* 1773   Edinburgh
where the *Ordinary Lords* of Session hold their courts ; and
to the New Session-House adjoining to it, where our Court of
Fifteen (the fourteen *Ordinaries,* with the Lord President at their
head,) sit as a court of Review. We went to the *Advocates'*
Library [1], of which Dr. Johnson took a cursory view, and then to
what is called the *Laigh* [2] (or under) Parliament-House, where
the records of Scotland, which has an universal security by
register, are deposited, till the great Register Office be finished.
I was pleased to behold Dr. Samuel Johnson rolling about in this
old magazine of antiquities. There was, by this time, a pretty
numerous circle of us attending upon him. Somebody talked of
happy moments for composition ; and how a man can write at one
time, and not at another.—' Nay (said Dr. Johnson) a man may
write at any time, if he will set himself *doggedly* [3] to it.'

I here began to indulge *old Scottish* [4] sentiments, and to express a warm regret, that, by our Union with *England,* we were
no more ;—our independent kingdom was lost [5].—*Johnson.*
' Sir, never talk of your independency, who could let your Queen
remain twenty years in captivity, and then be put to death,
without even a pretence of justice, without your ever attempting
to rescue her ; and such a Queen too ! as every man of any
gallantry of spirit would have sacrificed his life for.[6] '—Worthy
Mr. *James Kerr* [7], *Keeper of the Records.* ' Half our nation
was bribed by English money.'—*Johnson.* ' Sir, that is no
defence : that makes you worse.' Good *Mr. Brown* [8], *Keeper of*
the Advocates Library. 'We had better say nothing about

[1] ⟨This Library, founded in 1682 by Sir George Mackenzie and formally opened in 1689, was first established in a house in Parliament Close ; this house was burnt down in 1700, but the books were saved and transferred to the Laigh Parliament House, which they shared with the public records till the latter were removed to the Regi- ster House in 1789-90. The Faculty of Advocates presented the Library to the nation in 1925, when it became the National Library of Scotland. See *Libr. Assoc. Record,* 1927, 169 ff. For the Register House see *Book of the Old Edinburgh Club,* xvii. 146 ff.⟩

[2] ⟨See the Oxford Dictionary, s.v. *Laigh* adj.⟩

[3] This word is commonly used to signify *sullenly, gloomily* ; and in that sense alone it appears in Dr. Johnson's Dictionary. I suppose he meant by it, ' with an *obstinate reso- lution,* similar to that of a sullen man.' BOSWELL, ed. 3. ⟨Cf. *post,* v. 110.⟩
See *ante,* i. 332, for the influence of seasons on composition.

[4] Boswell, *post,* v. 374, writes of ' *old Scottish* enthusiasm,' again italicising these two words.

[5] See *ante,* iii. 410.

[6] See *ante,* i. 354.

[7] ⟨Joint Keeper, 1746-73 : see App. D, p. 466.⟩

[8] ⟨See App. D, p. 466.⟩

it.'—*Boswell.* ' You would have been glad, however, to have had us last war, sir, to fight your battles ! '—*Johnson.* ' We should have had you for the same price, though there had been no Union, as we might have had Swiss, or other troops. No, no, I shall agree to a separation. You have only to *go home.*'—Just as he had said this, I, to divert the subject, shewed him the signed assurances † of the three successive Kings of the Hanover family, to maintain the Presbyterian establishment in Scotland.— ' We'll give you that (said he) into the bargain.'

We next went to the great church of St. Giles, which has lost its original magnificence in the inside, by being divided into four places of Presbyterian worship [1]. ' Come, (said Dr. Johnson jocularly to Principal Robertson [2],) let me see what was once a church ! ' We entered that division which was formerly called the *New Church,* and of late the *High Church,* so well known by the eloquence of Dr. Hugh Blair. It is now very elegantly fitted up ; but it was then shamefully dirty [3]. Dr. Johnson said nothing

† ⟨See App. D, p. 467.⟩
[1] ⟨Arnot, writing in 1779, says : ' The chief of these divisions is called the *New Church.* It is formed out of the choir of St. Giles's. In it are the King's seat, those of the Lord Provost and magistrates, and of the judges of the court of session. . . . The central part is fitted up as a place of worship, for the accommodation of the citizens, and called the Old Church. The Tolbooth Church . . . occupies the south-west quarter . . . Haddow's-hole Church occupies the north-west part. . . . Besides these churches, the smaller apartments in this cathedral are appropriated to several purposes. The chief of them is fitted up for the General assembly. . . . In other parts of this church, the city-clerks of Edinburgh, and the kirk-session clerks, have their offices; and one of the rooms is used as the city-cartulary.' *Hist. Edinburgh,* pp. 269-70. William Chambers, 1800-83, the great publisher, when Lord Provost of Edinburgh, initiated a movement for the restoration of the cathedral to its original magnificence : this was completed in 1883. See W. Chambers, *Story of St. Giles' Church,* 1879. See also

Cockburn, *Life of Jeffrey,* i. 182.⟩
[2] I have hitherto called him Dr. William Robertson, to distinguish him from Dr. James Robertson, who is soon to make his appearance. But *Principal,* from his being the head of our college, is his usual designation, and is shorter; so I shall use it hereafter. BOSWELL. edd. 1, 2.

[3] The dirtiness of the Scotch churches is taken off in *The Tale of a Tub,* sect. xi :—' Neither was it possible for the united Rhetorick of Mankind to prevail with Jack to make himself clean again.' In *Humphry Clinker* (Matthew Bramble's letter of Aug. 8) we are told that ' the good people of Edinburgh no longer think dirt and cobwebs essential to the house of God.' Bp. Horne (*Memoirs,* 1799, p. 276) mentioning ' the maxim laid down in a neighbouring kingdom " That cleanliness is not essential to devotion",' continues, ' A church of England lady once offered to attend the kirk there, if she might be permitted to have the pew swept and lined. " The pew swept and lined ! " said Mess John's wife, " my husband would think it downright popery." '

42 *Monday* 16 *August* 1773   Edinburgh

at the time ; but when we came to the great door of the Royal Infirmary, where, upon a board, was this inscription, ' *Clean your feet !* ' he turned about slyly, and said, ' There is no occasion for putting this at the doors of your churches ! '

We then conducted him down the Post-house stairs, Parliament-close, and made him look up from the Cow-gate to the highest building in Edinburgh, (from which he had just descended,) being thirteen floors or stories from the ground upon the back elevation ; the front wall being built upon the edge of the hill, and the back wall rising from the bottom of the hill several stories before it comes to a level with the front wall. We proceeded to the College, with the Principal at our head. Dr. Adam Fergusson, whose ' Essay on the History of civil Society ' [1] gives him a respectable place in the ranks of literature, was with us. As the College buildings [2] are indeed very mean, the Principal said to Dr. Johnson, that he must give them the same epithet that a Jesuit did when shewing a poor college abroad : ' *Hæ miseriæ nostræ.*' Dr. Johnson was, however, much pleased with the library †, and with the conversation of Dr. James Robertson §, Professor of Oriental Languages, the Librarian. We talked of Kennicot's edition of the Hebrew Bible [3], and hoped it would be quite faithful.—*Johnson.* ' Sir, I know not any crime so great that a man could contrive to commit, as poisoning the sources of eternal truth.'

I pointed out to him where there formerly stood an old wall enclosing part of the college, which I remember bulged out in a threatening manner, and of which there was a common tradition similar to that concerning *Bacon's* Study [4] at Oxford, that it

[1] ⟨First published in 1767 ; the seventh edition appeared in 1814. Hume, from a specimen which he saw in 1759, formed a good opinion of this work, but when he read the whole in manuscript he changed his mind. Writing to Adam Smith, 11 Feb. 1766, he says : ' I have perus'd Ferguson's Papers more than once . . . I am sorry to say it, they have no-wise answer'd my Expectation. I do not think them fit to be given to the Public, neither on account of the Style nor the Reasoning ; the Form nor the Matter.' The book's success and the commendations of the great, which he was careful to report to Ferguson, did not affect his mature opinion. *Letters of Hume*, 1932, i. 304, 308, ii. 11, 120, 125, 133. Adam Ferguson was Professor of Moral Philosophy at Edinburgh, 1764–85 : see the *D.N.B.*⟩

[2] ⟨Proposals for their demolition and reconstruction were at this time before the University : see App. D, p. 467.⟩

† ⟨See App. D, p. 468.⟩

§ ⟨See App. D, pp. 468–9.⟩

[3] See *ante*, ii. 128.

[4] ⟨See App. D, pp. 469–70.⟩

Edinburgh   Monday 16 August 1773

would fall upon some very learned man [1]. It had some time before this been taken down, that the street might be widened, and a more convenient wall built. Dr. Johnson, glad of an opportunity to have a pleasant hit at Scottish learning, said, ' they have been afraid it never would fall.'

We shewed him the Royal Infirmary †, for which, and for every other exertion of generous publick spirit in his power, that noble-minded citizen of Edinburgh, George Drummond, will be ever held in honourable remembrance. And we were too proud not to carry him to the Abbey of Holyrood-house, that beautiful piece of architecture, but, alas ! that deserted mansion of royalty, which Hamilton of Bangour, in one of his elegant poems, calls

' A virtuous palace, where no monarch dwells [2].'

I was much entertained while Principal Robertson fluently harangued to Dr. Johnson, upon the spot, concerning scenes of his celebrated History of Scotland. We surveyed that part of the palace appropriated to the Duke of Hamilton, as Keeper, in which our beautiful Queen Mary lived, and in which David Rizzio was murdered ; and also the State Rooms. Dr. Johnson was a great reciter of all sorts of things serious or comical. I over-heard him repeating here, in a kind of muttering tone, a line of the old ballad, *Johnny Armstrong's Last Good-Night* :

' And ran him through the fair body [3] ! '

We returned to my house, where there met him, at dinner, the Duchess of Douglas [4], Sir Adolphus Oughton, Lord Chief Baron,

[1] See *ante*, iii. 357, and *post*, v. 438.
† ⟨See App. D, p. 470.⟩
[2] ' There where no statesman buys, no bishop sells ;
A virtuous palace, where no monarch dwells.'
An Epitaph. Hamilton's *Poems*, ed. 1760, p. 260. See *ante*, iii. 150, ⟨and *post*, v. 362⟩.
[3] The stanza from which he took this line is,
' But then rose up all Edinburgh, They rose up by thousands three ;
A cowardly Scot came John behind, And ran him through the fair body ! '   BOSWELL, ed. 1.
⟨See *Collection of Old Ballads*, 1723, i. 173.⟩

[4] ⟨Mrs. Sharpe says that she was one of Boswell's guests at ' a tea-party ' at this time. Her son, Charles Kirkpatrick Sharpe, relates : ' The doctor missed the rebuffs of Lady Margaret, who could be uncommonly vulgar, and my mother's most humorous recollections of the scene were the efforts of Boswell, as their go-between, to translate the unintelligible *gaucherie* of her ladyship into palatable commonplaces for his guest's ear.' See Sir Daniel Wilson, *Memorials of Edinb.*, 1891, i. 208.⟩ Johnson described the Duchess as ' an old Lady who talks broad Scotch with a paralytick voice, and is scarce understood by her own countrymen.' *Letters,*

Sir William Forbes, Principal Robertson, Mr. Cullen [1], advocate· Before dinner, he told us of a curious conversation between the famous George Faulkner [2] and him. George said that England had drained Ireland of fifty thousand pounds in specie, annually, for fifty years. ' How so, sir ! (said Dr. Johnson,) you must have a very great trade ? ' ' No trade.'—' Very rich mines ? ' ' No mines.'—' From whence, then, does all this money come ? ' ' Come ! why out of the blood and bowels of the poor people of Ireland ! '

He seemed to me to have an unaccountable prejudice against Swift [3] ; for I once took the liberty to ask him, if Swift had personally offended him, and he told me, he had not. He said to-day, ' Swift is clear, but he is shallow. In coarse humour, he is inferior to Arbuthnot [4] ; in delicate humour, he is inferior to Addison : So he is inferior to his contemporaries ; without putting him against the whole world. I doubt if the " Tale of a Tub " was his [5] : it has so much more thinking, more knowledge, more power, more colour, than any of the works which are indisputably his. If it was his, I shall only say, he was *impar sibi* [6].'

We gave him as good a dinner as we could. Our Scotch muir-fowl, or growse, were then abundant, and quite in season ;

No. 320. Dr. A. Carlyle (*Auto.*, p. 107) writes that in 1745 he heard her say :— ' I have sworn to be Duchess of Douglas, or never to mount a marriage-bed.' She married the Duke in 1758. ⟨See also C. K. Sharpe, *Letters*, 1888, i. 200, ii. 22; Sir W. Fraser, *Douglas Book*, 1885, i, p. lxxxv; and Sir James Balfour Paul's *Scots Peerage*, i. 211 and ix. 13.⟩

[1] See *ante*, ii. 154, note 1.

[2] ⟨The Dublin bookseller and printer (see *ante*, ii. 154). He was held in great esteem by Chesterfield, who writing to him, 1 July 1762, said : ' From my time down to the present, you have been in possession of governing the governors of Ireland, whenever you have thought fit to meddle with some business ; and if you had meddled more with some, it might perhaps have been better for them, and better for Ireland.' *Letters*, 1932, vi. 2394. See also *ib.* v. 2042, vi. 2909, and *post*, v. 130.⟩

[3] ' Dr. J[ohnso]n being one evening in company with some of the first-rate *literati* of the age *roundly* asserted in his *rough* way, that " Swift was a shallow fellow, a very shallow fellow." The ingenious Mr. Sh[erida]n . . . replied, warmly, but modestly, " Pardon me, Sir, for differing from you, but I always thought the dean a very *clear* writer." To this modest reply the following *laconic* answer was immediately vociferated : " All *shallows* are clear." ' *Town & Country Mag.*, Sept. 1769, p. 463. See *ante*, iv. 61.

[4] ' *The Memoirs of Scriblerus*,' says Johnson (*Pope*, 223), ' seem to be the production of Arbuthnot, with a few touches perhaps by Pope.' Swift also was concerned in it. Johnson goes on to shew why ' this joint production of three great writers has never obtained any notice from mankind.' Arbuthnot was the author of *John Bull*. See *ante*, i. 425 ⟨; v. 20, n. 2⟩.

[5] See *ante*, i. 452, and ii. 318.

[6] Horace, *Satires*, I. iii. 19.

Edinburgh   *Monday 16 August* 1773   45

and, so far as wisdom and wit can be aided by administering agreeable sensations to the palate, my wife took care that our great guest should not be deficient.

Sir Adolphus Oughton, then our Deputy Commander in Chief †, who was not only an excellent officer, but one of the most universal scholars I ever knew, had learned the Erse language, and expressed his belief in the authenticity of Ossian's Poetry [1]. Dr. Johnson took the opposite side of that perplexed question; and I was afraid the dispute would have run high between them. But Sir Adolphus, who had a very sweet temper, changed the discourse, grew playful, laughed at Lord Monboddo's [2] notion of men having tails, and called him a Judge[a] *à posteriori*, which amused Dr. Johnson; and thus hostilities were prevented.

At supper [3] we had Dr. Cullen, his son the advocate, Dr. Adam Fergusson, and Mr. Crosbie §, advocate. Witchcraft was introduced [4]. Mr. Crosbie said, he thought it the greatest blasphemy to suppose evil spirits counteracting the Deity, and raising storms, for instance, to destroy his creatures.—*Johnson.* 'Why, sir, if moral evil be consistent with the government of the Deity, why may not physical evil be also consistent with it? It is not more strange that there should be evil spirits, than evil men: evil unembodied spirits, than evil embodied spirits. And as to storms, we know there are such things; and it is no worse that evil spirits raise them, than that they rise.'—*Crosbie.* 'But it is not credible, that witches should have effected what they are said in stories to have done.'—*Johnson.* 'Sir, I am not defending their credibility. I am only saying, that your arguments are not good, and will not overturn the belief of witchcraft.—(Dr. Fergusson said to me, aside, 'He is right.')—And then, sir, you have all mankind, rude and civilized, agreeing in the belief of the agency of preternatural powers. You must take evidence: you must consider, that wise and great men have condemned witches to die [5].'—*Crosbie.* 'But an act of parliament put an

[a] Judge 1, 2: Judge, 3.

† ⟨This is apparently an unofficial title. Sir Adolphus was appointed Commander of the Forces in North Britain on 29 May 1778. See v. 142, n. 2.⟩
[1] See *ante*, i. 396, and ii. 298.
[2] See *ante*, ii. 74.
[3] 'At supper there was such a Conflux of company that I could scarcely support the tumult.' Johnson's *Letters*, No. 320.
§ ⟨See *ante*, ii. 376, n. 1.⟩
[4] See *ante* ⟨ii. 178⟩; iv. 17.
[5] Johnson was thinking of Sir Matthew Hale for one.

end to witchcraft ¹.'—*Johnson.* ' No, sir; witchcraft had ceased ; and therefore an act of parliament was passed to prevent persecution for what was not witchcraft. Why it ceased, we cannot tell, as we cannot tell the reason of many other things.'— Dr. Cullen, to keep up the gratification of mysterious disquisition, with the grave address for which he is remarkable in his companionable as in his professional hours, talked, in a very entertaining manner, of people walking and conversing in their sleep. I am very sorry I have no note of this. We talked of the *Ouran-Outang*, and of Lord Monboddo's thinking that he might be taught to speak. Dr. Johnson treated this with ridicule. Mr. Crosbie said, that Lord Monboddo believed the existence of every thing possible ; in short, that all which is in *posse* might be found in *esse*.—*Johnson.* ' But, sir, it is as possible that the *Ouran-Outang* does not speak, as that he speaks. However, I shall not contest the point. I should have thought it not possible to find a Monboddo ; yet *he* exists.'—I again mentioned the stage.—*Johnson.* ' The appearance of a player, with whom I have drunk tea, counteracts the imagination that he is the character he represents. Nay, you know, nobody imagines that he is the character he represents. They say, " See *Garrick !* how he looks to-night ! See how he'll clutch the dagger ! " That is the buz of the theatre ².'

Tuesday, 17*th August.*

Sir William Forbes came to breakfast, and brought with him

[1] ⟨' An Act against conjuration, witchcraft, and dealing with evil and wicked spirits ' of 1 James I, c. 12 (1604), which made witchcraft a capital offence, was repealed by the act of 9 Geo. II, c. 5 (1736). ' Folly and credulity, however, take an unconscionable time in dying, and even in 1733 Mr. [W.] Forbes, professor of law in Glasgow College, was unable to divest himself of a decaying conviction.' H. G. Graham, *Soc. Life in Scotl.*, 1901, p. 488. ' The last person who was brought to the stake in Scotland for the crime of witchcraft was condemned by Captain David Ross, ... sheriff-depute of Sutherland, 1722.' Arnot, *Criminal Trials*, 1785,

p. 367. The last execution for witchcraft in England took place at Exeter in 1684. C. L'Estrange Ewen, *Witch Hunting and Witch Trials*, 1929, p. 43.⟩

[2] A Dane wrote to Garrick from Copenhagen on Dec. 23, 1769 :— ' There is some of our retinue who, not understanding a word of your language, mimic your gesture and your action : so great an impression did it make upon their minds, the scene of daggers has been repeated in dumb show a hundred times, and those most ignorant of the English idiom can cry out with rapture, " A horse, a horse, my kingdom for a horse ! " ' *Garrick Corres.* i. 375. See *ante*, iv. 243.

Dr. Blacklock[1], whom he introduced to Dr. Johnson, who received him with a most humane complacency; 'Dear Dr. Blacklock, I am glad to see you!'—Blacklock seemed to be much surprized, when Dr. Johnson said, 'it was easier to him to write poetry than to compose his Dictionary[2]. His mind was less on the stretch in doing the one than the other. Besides; composing a Dictionary requires books and a desk: you can make a poem walking in the fields, or lying in bed.'—Dr. Blacklock spoke of scepticism in morals and religion, with apparent uneasiness, as if he wished for more certainty[3]. Dr. Johnson, who had thought it all over, and whose vigorous understanding was fortified by much experience, thus encouraged the blind Bard to apply to higher speculations what we all willingly submit to in common life: in short, he gave him more familiarly the able and fair reasoning of Butler's *Analogy*: 'Why, sir, the greatest concern we have in this world, the choice of our profession, must be determined without demonstrative reasoning. Human life is not yet so well known, as that we can have it. And take the case of a man who is ill. I call two physicians: they differ in opinion. I am not to lie down, and die between them: I must do something.'—The conversation then turned on Atheism; on that horrible book, *Système de la Nature*[4]; and on the supposition of an eternal necessity, without design, without a governing mind.—*Johnson*. 'If it were so, why has it ceased? Why don't we see men thus produced around us now? Why, at least, does it not keep pace, in some measure, with the progress of time? If it stops because there is now no

---

[1] See *ante*, i. 466.
[2] Johnson, in the preface to his *Dictionary* (¶ 72), after stating what he had at first planned, continues:—
'But these were the dreams of a poet doomed at last to wake a lexicographer.' See *ante*, i. 189, note 2, and iv. 219.
[3] See his letter on this subject in the APPENDIX. BOSWELL, ed. 3. *Post*, v. 417. ⟨For Hume's high opinion and active support of Blacklock see J. H. Burton's *Hume*, i. 385 ff., ii. 399, and Hume's *Letters*, ed. 1932.⟩
[4] By the Baron d'Holbach, 1770.

Voltaire (*Œuvres*, 1877, x. 172, note) describes this book as 'Une philippique contre Dieu.' He wrote to M. Saurin, 10 Nov. 1770:—'Ce maudit livre du *Système de la Nature* est un péché contre nature. Je vous sais bien bon gré de réprouver l'athéisme, et d'aimer ce vers: "Si Dieu n'existait pas, il faudrait l'inventer." Je suis rarement content de mes vers, mais j'avoue que j'ai une tendresse de père pour celui-là.' *Ib.* xlvii, 1882, 250. ⟨The line quoted is from *Épître à l'auteur du livre des trois imposteurs*. *Ib.* x. 403.⟩

need of it, then it is plain there is, and ever has been, an all-powerful intelligence. But stay! (said he, with one of his satyrick laughs [1].) Ha! ha! ha! I shall suppose Scotchmen made necessarily, and Englishmen by choice.'

At dinner this day, we had Sir Alexander Dick, whose amiable character, and ingenious and cultivated mind, are so generally known; (he was then on the verge of seventy, and is now (1785) eighty-one, with his faculties entire, his heart warm, and his temper gay † ;) Sir David Dalrymple Lord Hailes; Mr. Maclaurin [2], advocate; Dr. Gregory, who now worthily fills his father's medical chair [3]; and my uncle, Dr. Boswell. This was one of Dr. Johnson's best days. He was quite in his element. All was literature and taste, without any interruption. Lord Hailes, who is one of the best philologists in Great-Britain, who has written papers in the *World* [4], and a variety of other works in prose and in verse, both Latin and English, pleased him highly. He told him, he had discovered the Life of *Cheynel*, in the *Student* [5], to be his.—*Johnson.* ' No one else knows it.'—Dr. Johnson had, before this, dictated to me a law-paper, upon a question purely in the law of Scotland, concerning *vicious intromission* [6], that is to say, intermeddling with the effects of a deceased person, without a regular title; which formerly was understood to subject the intermeddler to payment of all the defunct's debts. The principle has of late been relaxed. Dr. Johnson's argument was, for a renewal of its strictness. The paper was printed, with additions by me, and given into the Court of Session. Lord Hailes knew Dr. Johnson's part not to be mine, and pointed out exactly where it began, and where it ended. Dr. Johnson said, ' It is much, now, that his lordship can distinguish so.'

---

[1] One of Garrick's correspondents, Mr. J. Sharp, speaks of ' the sneer of one of Johnson's ghastly smiles.' *Garrick Corres.* i. 334. ' Ghastly smile ' is borrowed from *Paradise Lost*, ii. 846.

† ⟨Boswell wrote of him in 1768: ' I don't believe there ever existed a man more continually amiable than Sir Alexr.' *Boswell Papers*, vii. 141. He died 10 Nov. 1785. See *ante*, iii. 102, 128; iv. 204, 261 ff.; *post*, v. 401; and *D.N.B.*⟩

[2] ⟨See *ante*, ii. 363, iii. 86, etc., and *D.N.B.* For his collaboration with Boswell in certain poems see Pottle, *Lit. Career Boswell*, pp. 271 ff.⟩

[3] Dr. John Gregory, Professor of Medicine in the University of Edinburgh, died on Feb. 10, 1773. It was his eldest son James who met Johnson.

[4] ⟨Numbers 140, 147, and 204. See A. Chalmers, *British Essayists*, 1802, xxvi, p. xlii.⟩

[5] See *ante*, i. 228.

[6] See *ante*, ii. 196 ff. ⟨and 496⟩.

Edinburgh   *Tuesday* 17 *August* 1773   49
In Dr. Johnson's *Vanity of Human Wishes*, there is the following passage:

'The teeming mother, anxious for her race,
Begs, for each birth, the fortune of a face:
Yet *Vane* could tell, what ills from beauty spring;
And *Sedley* curs'd the charms which pleas'd a king [1].'

Lord Hailes told him, he was mistaken in the instances he had given of unfortunate fair ones; for neither *Vane* nor *Sedley* had a title to that description. His Lordship has since been so obliging as to send me a note of this, for the communication of which I am sure my readers will thank me.

'The lines in the tenth Satire of Juvenal, according to my alteration, should have run thus:

" Yet *Shore* [2] could tell——;
And *Valiere* [3] curs'd——."

'The first was a penitent by compulsion, the second by sentiment; though the truth is, Mademoiselle de la Valière threw herself (but still from sentiment) in the King's way.

'Our friend chose *Vane* [4], who was far from being well-looked; and *Sedley*, who was so ugly, that Charles II. said, his brother had her by way of penance [5].'

Mr. Maclaurin's learning and talents † enabled him to do his part very well in' Dr. Johnson's company. He produced two epitaphs upon his father, the celebrated mathematician [6]. One

---

[1] In the original, *curs'd the Form that pleas'd a King*.
[2] Mistress of Edward IV. BOSWELL, ed. 1.
[3] Mistress of Louis XIV. BOSWELL, ed. 1.
Voltaire, speaking of the King and Mlle. de La Vallière, says:—'Il goûta avec elle le bonheur rare d'être aimé uniquement pour lui-même.' *Siècle de Louis XIV*, ch. 25. He describes her penitence in a fine passage. *Ib.* ch. 26.
[4] Malone, in a note on the *Life of Johnson*, ed. 5, 1807, i. 172, says that 'this lady was not the celebrated Lady Vane, whose memoirs were given to the publick by Dr. Smollett [in *Peregrine Pickle*], but Anne Vane, who was mistress to Frederick, Prince of Wales, and died in 1736, not long before Johnson settled in London.' ⟨See App. D, pp. 470–1.⟩
[5] Catharine Sedley, the mistress of James II, is described by Macaulay, *Hist. of Eng.*, ch. vi, ed. 1874, ii. 323.
† ⟨See App. D, pp. 471–2.⟩
[6] Dr. A. Carlyle (*Auto.*, p. 114) tells how in 1745 he found Professor Maclaurin 'busy on the walls on the south side of Edinburgh, endeavouring to make them more defensible.' He had even erected some small cannon. ⟨A. Henderson states (*Hist. Rebellion*, 1748, p. 11) that 'the worthy Mr. Maclaurin, the Archimedes of the Age, contributed to fix the Batteries'.⟩ See *ante*, iii. 15.

was in English, of which Dr. Johnson did not change one word. In the other, which was in Latin, he made several alterations. In place of the very words of *Virgil*, ' *Ubi luctus et pavor et plurima mortis imago* [1],' he wrote ' *Ubi luctus regnant et pavor.*' He introduced the word *prorsus* into the line ' *Mortalibus prorsus non absit solatium*,' and after ' *Hujus enim scripta evolve*,' he added ' *Mentemque tantarum rerum capacem corpori caduco superstitem crede ;* ' which is quite applicable to Dr. Johnson himself [2].

Mr. Murray, advocate, who married a niece † of Lord Mansfield's,[a] and is now one of the Judges of Scotland, by the title of Lord *Henderland*, sat with us a part of the evening ; but did not venture to say any thing, that I remember, though he is certainly possessed of talents which would have enabled him to have shewn himself to advantage, if too great anxiety had not prevented him.

At supper we had Dr. Alexander Webster §, who, though not learned, had such a knowledge of mankind, such a fund of information and entertainment, so clear a head and such accommodating manners, that Dr. Johnson found him a very agreeable companion.

When Dr. Johnson and I were left by ourselves, I read to him my notes of the Opinions of our Judges upon the Question [b] of Literary Property [3]. He did not like them ; and said, ' they make me think of your Judges not with that respect which I should wish to do.' To the argument of one of them, that there can be no property in blasphemy or nonsense, he answered, ' then your rotten sheep are mine !—By that rule, when a man's

[a] *comma omitted* 3.

[b] Question 1, 2 : questions 3.

[1] ' Crudelis ubique Luctus, ubique pavor et plurima mortis imago : '
' grim grief on every side, And fear on every side there is, and many-faced is death.'
Morris, Virgil *Æneids*, ii. 368.

[2] Mr. Maclaurin's epitaph, as engraved on a marble tombstone, in the Gray-Friars church-yard, Edinburgh :
Infra situs est
COLIN MACLAURIN,
Mathes. olim in Acad. Edin. Prof. Electus ipso Newtono suadente.
H. L. P. F.

Non ut nomini paterno consulat, Nam tali auxilio nil eget ;
Sed ut in hoc infelici campo
Ubi luctus regnant et pavor,
Mortalibus prorsus non absit solatium :
Hujus enim scripta evolve,
Mentemque tantarum rerum capacem
Corpori caduco superstitem crede.
BOSWELL, ed. 3. ⟨See App. D, p. 472.⟩
†, § ⟨See App. D, p. 472.⟩
[3] See *ante*, i. 437, and *post*, v. 72. ⟨Boswell published these Opinions: see App. D, p. 474.⟩

house falls into decay, he must lose it.'—I mentioned an argument of mine, that literary performances are not taxed. As Churchill says,

> 'No statesman yet has thought it worth his pains
> To tax our labours, or excise our brains [1];'

and therefore they are not property.—' Yet, (said he,) we hang a man for stealing a horse, and horses are not taxed.'—Mr. Pitt has since put an end to that argument [2].

Wednesday, 18th August.

On this day we set out from Edinburgh. We should gladly have had Mr. Scott to go with us; but he was obliged to return to England.—I have given a sketch of Dr. Johnson: my readers may wish to know a little of his fellow traveller [3]. Think,[a] then, of a gentleman of ancient blood, the pride of which was his predominant passion. He was then in his thirty-third year, and

[a] comma omitted 3

[1] 'What is't to us, if taxes rise or fall,
Thanks to our fortune *we* pay none at all.
. . . . . .
No statesman e'er will find it worth his pains
To tax our labours, and excise our brains.
Burthens like these vile earthly buildings bear,
No tribute's laid on *Castles* in the *Air*.'
Churchill's *Night*, lines 263 ff.

[2] Pitt, in 1784, laid a tax of ten shillings a year on every horse 'kept for the saddle, or to be put in carriages used solely for pleasure.' *Parl. Hist.* xxiv. 1028.

[3] In 1763 he published the following description of himself in *Letters between Erskine and Boswell*, p. 57. 'The author of the Ode to Tragedy, is a most excellent man: he is of an ancient family in the west of Scotland, upon which he values himself not a little. At his nativity there appeared omens of his future greatness. His parts are bright, and his education has been good. He has travelled in post-chaises, miles without number. He is fond of seeing much of the world. He eats of every good dish, especially apple-pie. He drinks old hock. He has a very fine temper. He is somewhat of an humourist, and a little tinctured with pride. He has a good manly countenance, and he owns himself to be amorous. He has infinite vivacity, yet is observed at times to have a melancholy cast. He is rather fat than lean, rather short than tall, rather young than old.' He is oddly enough described in Arrighi's *Histoire de Pascal Paoli*, 1843, i. 231, 'En traversant la Méditerranée sur de frêles navires pour venir s'asseoir au foyer de la nationalité corse, des hommes graves, tels que Boswel et Volney, obéissaient sans doute à un sentiment bien plus élevé, qu'au besoin vulgaire d'une puérile curiosité.' ⟨A. F. Tytler in his *Memoirs of Lord Kames* (1807, ii. 228) speaks of 'the sprightly fancy, and whimsical eccentricity of a Boswell'. For Fanny Burney's description of him see her *Diary*, v. 166, 307.⟩

Wednesday 18 August 1773 — Edinburgh

had been about four years happily married. His inclination was to be a soldier [1] ; but his father, a respectable [2] Judge, had pressed him into the profession of the law. He had travelled a good deal, and seen many varieties of human life. He had thought more than any body supposed, and had a pretty good stock of general learning and knowledge [3]. He had all Dr. Johnson's principles, with some degree of relaxation. He had rather too little, than too much prudence ; and, his imagination being lively, he often said things of which the effect was very different from the intention [4]. He resembled sometimes

' The best good man, with the worst natur'd muse [5].'

He cannot deny himself the vanity of finishing with the encomium of Dr. Johnson, whose friendly partiality to the companion of his Tour represents him as one, ' whose acuteness would help my inquiry, and whose gaiety of conversation, and civility of manners, are sufficient to counteract the inconveniences of travel, in countries less hospitable than we have passed [6].'

[1] See *ante*, i. 400. ⟨See App. D, p. 475.⟩

[2] For *respectable*, see *ante*, iii. 241, note 2.

[3] Boswell, in the last of his *Hypochondriacks*, says :—' I perceive that [my essays] are not so lively as I expected they would be. But they are more learned. And I beg I may not be charged with excessive arrogance, when I venture to say that they contain a considerable portion of original thinking.' *Lond. Mag.* Aug. 1783, p. 124.

[4] Burns, in *The Author's Earnest Cry and Prayer*, x, says :—
' But could I like MONTGOMERIES fight,
Or gab like BOSWELL.'
⟨Burns is not, as Prof. Pottle points out, speaking contemptuously. In 1788 he desired to be introduced to Boswell and wrote : ' As I had the honor of drawing my first breath almost in the same Parish with Mr. Boswell, my pride plumes itself on the connection.' *Boswell Papers*, xvii. 127.⟩

[5] ' For pointed Satyr I would Buckhurst choose,
The best Good Man, with the worst-natur'd Muse.'
Rochester's *Imit. Horace, Sat.* i. 10.

[6] *Journey Western Isl.*, p. 3. See *ante*, ii. 278, where he wrote to Boswell :—' I have endeavoured to do you some justice in the first paragraph [of the *Journey*].' The day before he started for Scotland he wrote to Dr. Taylor :—' Mr. Boswel an active lively fellow is to conduct me round the country.' *Letters*, No. 316. ' His inquisitiveness,' he said, ' is seconded by great activity.' *Western Isl.*, p. 10. Writing to Mrs. Thrale he says :—' Boswel will praise my resolution and perseverance ; and I shall in return celebrate his goodhumour and perpetual cheerfulness. . . . It is very convenient to travel with him, for there is no house where he is not received with kindness and respect.' *Letters*, No. 337. See also No. 968. He told Mrs. Knowles that ' Boswell was the best travelling

Edinburgh   *Wednesday 18 August 1773*   53

Dr. Johnson thought it unnecessary to put himself to the additional expence of bringing with him Francis Barber, his faithful black servant; so we were attended only by my man, Joseph Ritter, a Bohemian; a fine stately fellow above six feet high, who had been over a great part of Europe, and spoke many languages. He was the best servant I ever saw. Let not my readers disdain his introduction! For Dr. Johnson gave him this character: ' Sir, he is a civil man, and a wise man [1].'

From an erroneous apprehension of violence, Dr. Johnson had provided a pair of pistols, some gunpowder, and a quantity of bullets: but upon being assured we should run no risk of meeting any robbers, he left his arms and ammunition in an open drawer, of which he gave my wife the charge. He also left in that drawer one volume of a pretty full and curious Diary of his Life, of which I have a few fragments; but the book has been destroyed. I wish female curiosity had been strong enough to have had it all transcribed, which might easily have been done; and I should think the theft, being *pro bono publico*, might have been forgiven. But I may be wrong. My wife told me she never once looked into it [2].—She did not seem quite easy when we left her: but away we went!

Mr. Nairne, advocate, was to go with us as far as St. Andrews. It gives me pleasure that, by mentioning his *name*, I connect his title to the just and handsome compliment paid him by Dr. Johnson, in his book: ' A gentleman who could stay with us only long enough to make us know how much we lost by his leaving us [3].' When we came to Leith, I talked with perhaps

companion in the world.' *Ante*, iii. 294. Croker says (*Boswell*, 1831, iii. 110 n.) that he 'asked Lord Stowell in what estimation he found Boswell amongst his countrymen. " Generally liked as a good-natured jolly fellow," replied his lordship. " But was he *respected?* " " Why, I think he had about the proportion of *respect* that you might guess would be shown to a *jolly fellow.*" His lordship evidently thought that there was more *regard* than *respect*.'

[1] See *ante*, ii. 103, 411; ⟨iii. 216, and *post*, App. D, p. 475.⟩

[2] There were two quarto volumes of this Diary; perhaps one of them Johnson took with him. Boswell had ' accidentally seen them,' and 'had read a great deal in them,' as he owned to Johnson (*ante*, iv. 405), and moreover had, it should seem, copied from them (*ante*, i. 251). The ' few fragments ' he had received from Francis Barber (*ante*, i. 27).

[3] In the original ' how much we lost at separation.' *Western Isl.*, p. 3. ' Mr. William Nairne; afterwards Sir William, and a judge of the court of session, by the title . . . of Lord

too boasting an air, how pretty the Frith of Forth looked ; as indeed, after the prospect from Constantinople, of which I have been told, and that from Naples, which I have seen, I believe the view of that Frith and its environs, from the Castle-hill of Edinburgh, is the finest prospect in Europe. ' Ay, (said Dr. Johnson,) that is the state of the world. Water is the same every where.

Una est injusti cærula forma maris [1].'

I told him the port here was the mouth of the river or water of *Leith*. ' Not *Lethe*,' said Mr. Nairne.—' Why, sir, (said Dr. Johnson,) when a Scotchman sets out from this port for England, he forgets his native country.'—*Nairne*. ' I hope, sir, you will forget England here.'—*Johnson*. ' Then 'twill be still more *Lethe*.'—He observed of the Pier or Quay, ' you have no occasion for so large a one : your trade does not require it : but you are like a shopkeeper who takes a shop, not only for what he has to put into it, but that it may be believed he has a great deal to put into it.' It is very true, that there is now, comparatively, little trade upon the eastern coast of Scotland. The riches of Glasgow shew how much there is in the west ; and perhaps we shall find trade travel westward on a great scale, as well as a small.

We talked of a man's drowning himself.—*Johnson*. ' I should never think it time to make away with myself.'—I put the case of Eustace Budgell [2], who was accused of forging a will, and sunk himself in the Thames, before the trial of its authenticity came on. ' Suppose, sir, (said I,) that a man is absolutely sure, that, if he lives a few days longer, he shall be detected in a fraud, the consequence of which will be utter disgrace and expulsion from society.'—*Johnson*. ' Then, sir, let him go abroad to a distant country ; let him go to some place where he is *not* known. Don't let him go to the devil where he *is* known ! '

Dunsinnan. He was a man of scrupulous integrity. When sheriff depute of Perthshire, he found, upon reflection, that he had decided a poor man's case erroneously ; and as the only remedy, supplied the litigant privately with money to carry the suit to the supreme court, where his judgment was reversed. Sir William was of the old school of manners, somewhat formal, but punctiliously well bred.' SCOTT (Croker, 1831). ⟨See also *post*, App. D, p. 475.⟩

[1] Non illic urbes, non tu mirabere silvas :
Una est injusti cærula forma maris.
    Ovid. Amor. L. II. El. xi.
Nor groves nor towns the ruthless ocean shows ;
Unvaried still its azure surface flows. BOSWELL, ed. 2.

[2] See *ante*, ii. 229.

Inchkeith   *Wednesday* 18 *August* 1773

He then said, ' I see a number of people bare-footed here : I suppose you all went so before the Union. Boswell, your ancestors went so, when they had as much land as your family has now. Yet *Auchinleck* is the *Field of Stones :* there would be bad going bare-footed there. The *Lairds,* however, did it.'—I bought some *speldings,* fish (generally whitings) salted and dried in a particular manner, being dipped in the sea and dried in the sun, and eaten by the Scots by way of a relish. He had never seen them, though they are sold in London. I insisted on *scottifying* [1] his palate ; but he was very reluctant. With difficulty I prevailed with him to let a bit of one of them lie in his mouth. He did not like it.

In crossing the Frith, Dr. Johnson determined that we should land upon Inch Keith [2]. On approaching it, we first observed a high rocky shore. We coasted about, and put into a little bay on the North-west. We clambered up a very steep ascent, on which was very good grass, but rather a profusion of thistles. There were sixteen head of black cattle grazing upon the island. Lord Hailes observed to me, that Brantome † calls it *L'isle des Chevaux,* and that it was probably ' a *safer* stable ' than many others in his time. The fort [3], with an inscription on it, *Maria Re* 1564, is strongly built. Dr. Johnson examined it with much attention. He stalked like a giant among the luxuriant thistles and nettles. There are three wells in the island ; but we could not find one in the fort. There must probably have been one, though now filled up, as a garrison could not subsist without it. But I have dwelt too long on this little spot. Dr. Johnson afterwards bade me try to write a description of our discovering Inch Keith, in the usual style of travellers, describing fully every particular ; stating the grounds on which we concluded that it must have once been inhabited, and introducing many sage reflections ;

---

[1] My friend, General Campbell, Governour of Madras, tells me, that they make *speldings* in the East-Indies, particularly at Bombay, where they call them *Bombaloes* ᵃ. BOSWELL.

Johnson had told Boswell that he was ' the most *unscottified* of his countrymen.' *Ante,* ii. 242. ⟨Boswell's friend was Sir Archibald Campbell of Inverneil. See *ante,* iii. 58.⟩

[2] ' A small island, which neither of my companions had ever visited, though, lying within their view, it had all their lives solicited their notice.' Johnson's *Western Isl.,* p. 3.

† ⟨See App. D, p. 476.⟩

[3] The remains of the fort have been removed, to assist in constructing a very useful lighthouse upon the island. SCOTT, 1831.

⟨Inchkeith is once more a fortified place : its defences were erected in 1860 by the War Office.⟩

ᵃ Bombaloes 1, 2 : Bambaloes 3.

and we should see how a thing might be covered in words, so as to induce people to come and survey it. All that was told might be true, and yet in reality there might be nothing to see. He said, ' I'd have this island. I'd build a house, make a good landing-place, have a garden, and vines, and all sorts of trees. A rich man, of a hospitable turn, here, would have many visitors from Edinburgh.' When we had got into our boat again, he called to me, ' Come, now, pay a classical compliment to the island on quitting it.' I happened luckily, in allusion to the beautiful Queen Mary, whose name is upon the fort, to think of what Virgil makes Æneas say, on having left the country of his charming Dido :

Invitus, regina, tuo de littore cessi [1].

' Very well hit off ! ' said he.

We dined at Kinghorn †, and then got into a post-chaise [2]. Mr. Nairne and his servant, and Joseph, rode by us. We stopped at Cupar §, and drank tea. We talked of parliament ; and I said, I supposed very few of the members knew much of what was going on, as indeed very few gentlemen know much of their own private affairs.—*Johnson.* ' Why, sir, if a man is not of a sluggish mind, he may be his own steward. If he will look into his affairs, he will soon learn [3]. So it is as to publick affairs. There must always be a certain number of men of business in parliament.'—*Boswell.* ' But consider, sir ; what is the House of Commons ? Is not a great part of it chosen by peers ? Do you think, sir, they ought to have such an influence ? '— *Johnson.* ' Yes, sir. Influence must ever be in proportion to property ; and it is right it should [4].'—*Boswell.* ' But is there not reason to fear that the common people may be oppressed ? '—

---

[1] ' Unhappy queen !
Unwilling I forsook your friendly state.'
Dryden. [*Æneid*, vi. 460.] BOSWELL, ed. 2.

† ⟨See App. D, p. 476.⟩

[2] Dr. A. Carlyle (*Auto.*, p. 331) says of his journey to London in 1758 :—
' It is to be noted that we could get no four-wheeled chaise till we came to Durham, those conveyances being then only in their infancy. . . . Turn-

pike roads were only in their commencement in the north.' ' It affords a southern stranger,' wrote Johnson (*Western Islands*, p. 4), ' a new kind of pleasure to travel so commodiously without the interruption of toll-gates.'

§ ⟨The inn was kept by one Archibald. Boswell's *MS. Journal.*⟩

[3] See *ante*, iii. 265, for Lord Shelburne's statement on this subject.

[4] See *ante*, ii. 340, and iii. 205, note 4.

St. Andrews *Wednesday 18 August 1773* 57
Johnson. ' No, sir. Our great fear is from want of power in government. Such a storm of vulgar force has broke in.'—*Boswell.*—' It has only roared.'—*Johnson.* ' Sir, it has roared, till the Judges in Westminster-Hall have been afraid to pronounce sentence in opposition to the popular cry [1]. You are frightened by what is no longer dangerous, like Presbyterians by Popery.'—He then repeated a passage, I think, in Butler's *Remains*, which ends, ' and would cry, Fire ! Fire ! in Noah's flood [2].'

We had a dreary drive, in a dusky night, to St. Andrews, where we arrived late. We found a good supper at Glass's inn †, and Dr. Johnson revived agreeably. He said, ' the collection called " The Muses' Welcome to King James," § (first of England, and sixth of Scotland,) on his return to his native kingdom, shewed that there was then abundance of learning in Scotland ; and that the conceits in that collection, with which people find fault, were mere mode.' He added, ' we could not now entertain a sovereign so ; that Buchanan had spread the spirit of learning amongst us, but we had lost it during the civil wars [3].' He did

[1] See *ante*, iii. 46.
[2] The passage quoted by Dr. Johnson is in the *Character of the Assembly-man*, Butler's *Remains*, p. 232, edit. 1754.—' He preaches, indeed, both in season and out of season ; for he rails at Popery, when the land is almost lost in Presbytery ; and would cry [a] Fire ! Fire ! in Noah's flood.' ⟨See *post*, App. D, p. 476.⟩
There is reason to believe that this piece was not written by Butler, but by Sir John Birkenhead ; for Wood, in his *Athenæ Oxonienses*, Vol. II. p. 640, enumerates it among that gentleman's works, and gives the following account of it :
' *The Assembly-man* (or the character of an Assembly-man) written 1647, *Lond.* 1662-3, in three sheets in qu. The copy of it was taken from the author by those who said they could not rob, because all was theirs ; so excised what they liked not ; and so mangled and reformed it, that it was no character of an Assembly, but of themselves. At length, after

it had slept several years, the author published it, to avoid false copies. It is also reprinted in a book entit. *Wit and Loyalty revived*,[b] in a collection of some smart satyrs in verse and prose on the late times [b]. *Lond.* 1682, qu. said to be written by Abr. Cowley, Sir John Birkenhead, and Hudibras, alias Sam. Butler.'—For this information I am indebted to Mr. Reed, of Staple Inn. BOSWELL, ed. 1. This tract is in the *Harleian Misc.* ⟨For Birkenhead see *D.N.B.*⟩ †, § ⟨See App. D, pp. 476-7.⟩
[3] ' When a Scotsman was talking against Warburton, Johnson said he had more literature than had been imported from Scotland since the days of Buchanan. Upon his mentioning other eminent writers of the Scots,—These will not do, said Johnson, let us have some more of your northern lights, these are mere farthing candles.' Johnson's *Works* (1787), xi. 208. Dr. T. Campbell records (*Diary*, 5 Apr. p. 61) that at the dinner at Mr. Dilly's,

[a] cry out *original*.
[b] in . . . times *in italics in original as part of title.*

not allow the Latin Poetry of Pitcairne so much merit as has been usually attributed to it ; though he owned that one of his pieces, which he mentioned, but which I am sorry is not specified in my notes, was ' very well.' It is not improbable that it was the poem which Prior has so elegantly translated [1].

After supper, we made a *procession* to *Saint Leonard's College*, the landlord walking before us with a candle, and the waiter with a lantern. That college had some time before been dissolved ; and Dr. Watson, a professor here, (the historian of Philip II.) had purchased the ground, and what buildings remained †. When we entered his court, it seemed quite academical ; and we found in his house very comfortable and genteel accommodation [2].

Thursday, 19th August.
We rose much refreshed §. I had with me a map of Scotland, a Bible, which was given me by Lord Mountstuart when we were together in Italy [3], and Ogden's Sermons on Prayer.[a] Mr. Nairne introduced us to Dr. Watson, whom we found a well-informed man, of very amiable manners. Dr. Johnson, after they were acquainted, said, ' I take great delight in him.'—His daughter, a very pleasing young lady, made breakfast. Dr. Watson ob-

[a] Prayer. 1 : Prayer, 2, 3.

described *ante*, ii. 338, 'Dr. Johnson compared England and Scotland to two lions, the one saturated with his belly full, and the other prowling for prey.... He defied any one to produce a classical book, written in Scotland since Buchanan. Robertson, he said, used pretty words, but he liked Hume better, and neither of them would he allow to be more to Clarendon, than a rat to a cat. " A Scotch Surgeon ... may have more learning than an English one, and all Scotland could not muster learning enough for Louth's prelections." ' See *ante*, ii. 363, and iv. 185.

[1] The poem is entitled *Gualterus Danistonus ad Amicos*. It begins :—
' Dum studeo fungi fallentis munere vitæ.'
Which Prior imitates :—
' Studious the busy moments to deceive.'
Sir Walter Scott thought that the poem praised by Johnson was ' more likely the fine epitaph on John, Viscount of Dundee, translated by Dryden, and beginning *Ultime Scotorum !* ' Archibald Pitcairne, M.D., was born in 1652, and died in 1713.

[2] My Journal, from this day inclusive, was read by Dr. Johnson. BOSWELL, ed. 1. It was read by Johnson up to the second paragraph of Oct. 26. Boswell, it should seem, once at least shewed Johnson a part of the Journal from which he formed his *Life*. See *ante*, iii. 260, where he says :—' It delighted him, on a review, to find that his conversation teemed with point and imagery.' ⟨See *Essays and Studies*, xxiii, 1938, pp. 59–60.⟩
†, § ⟨See App. D, pp. 477–8.⟩
[3] See *ante*, ii. 20, note 4. ⟨Boswell travelled with Mountstuart from Rome to Milan in June and July, 1765 ; at Siena he endeavoured to steal his mistress, Porzia Sansedoni. See *Boswell Papers*, v. 3 ff., 32 ff., and 139 ff.⟩

served, that Glasgow University had fewer home-students, since trade increased, as learning was rather incompatible with it.—*Johnson.* ' Why, sir, as trade is now carried on by subordinate hands, men in trade have as much leisure as others ; and now learning itself is a trade. A man goes to a bookseller, and gets what he can. We have done with patronage [1]. In the infancy of learning, we find some great man praised for it. This diffused it among others. When it becomes general, an author leaves the great, and applies to the multitude.'—*Boswell.* ' It is a shame that authors are not now better patronized.'—*Johnson.* ' No, sir. If learning cannot support a man, if he must sit with his hands across till somebody feeds him, it is as to him a bad thing, and it is better as it is. With patronage, what flattery ! what falsehood ! While a man is in equilibrio, he throws truth among the multitude, and lets them take it as they please : in patronage, he must say what pleases his patron, and it is an equal chance whether that be truth or falsehood.'—*Watson.* ' But is not the case now, that, instead of flattering one person, we flatter the age ? '—*Johnson.* ' No, sir. The world always lets a man tell what he thinks, his own way. I wonder however, that so many people have written, who might have let it alone. That people should endeavour to excel in conversation, I do not wonder ; because in conversation praise is instantly reverberated [2].'

We talked of change of manners. Dr. Johnson observed, that our drinking less than our ancestors was owing to the change from ale to wine. ' I remember, (said he,) when all the *decent*

---

[1] Goldsmith, in his *Present State of Polite Learning*, published in 1759, says (ch. x) :—' When the great Somers was at the helm, patronage was fashionable among our nobility. . . . Since the days of a certain prime minister of inglorious memory [Sir Robert Walpole], the learned have been kept pretty much at a distance. . . . The author, when unpatronized by the Great, has naturally recourse to the bookseller. There cannot be, perhaps, imagined a combination more prejudicial to taste than this. It is the interest of the one to allow as little for writing, and of the other to write as much as possible ; accordingly, tedious compilations, and periodical magazines, are the result of their joint endeavours.'

[2] In the first number of *The Rambler*, Johnson shews how attractive to an author is the form of publication which he was himself then adopting :—' It heightens his alacrity to think in how many places he shall hear what he is now writing, read with ecstasies to morrow.'

people in Lichfield got drunk every night, and were not the worse thought of [1]. Ale was cheap, so you pressed strongly. When a man must bring a bottle of wine, he is not in such haste. Smoking has gone out. To be sure, it is a shocking thing, blowing smoke out of our mouths into other people's mouths, eyes, and noses, and having the same thing done to us. Yet I cannot account, why a thing which requires so little exertion, and yet preserves the mind from total vacuity, should have gone out [2]. Every man has something by which he calms himself : beating with his feet, or so [3]. I remember when people in England changed a shirt only once a week [4] : a Pandour †, when he gets a shirt, greases it to make it last. Formerly, good tradesmen had no fire but in the kitchen ; never in the parlour, except on Sunday. My father, who was a magistrate of Lichfield, lived thus. They never began to have a fire in the parlour, but on leaving off business, or some great revolution of their life.'—Dr. Watson said, the hall was as a kitchen, in old squires' houses.—*Johnson*. ' No, sir. The hall was for great occasions, and never was used for domestick refection [5].'—We talked

---

[1] Yet he said the inhabitants of Lichfield ' were the most sober, decent people in England.' *Ante*, ii. 463. ⟨The words ' in Lichfield ' were not in Boswell's MS. as written in 1773.⟩
[2] At the beginning of the eighteenth century, says Goldsmith ' smoking in the rooms [at Bath] was permitted.' When Nash became King of Bath he put it down. Goldsmith's *Life of Nash*, 1762, p. 24. ⟨See *post*, App. D, p. 478.⟩
[3] Dr. Johnson used to practice this himself very much. BOSWELL, ed. 1.
[4] In *The Tatler*, for May 24, 1709, we are told that ' Rural Esquires ... wear Shirts half a Week, and are drunk twice a Day.' In the year 1720, Fenton urged Gay ' to sell as much South Sea stock as would purchase an hundred a year for life, " which will make you sure of a clean shirt and a shoulder of mutton every day." ' Johnson's *Gay*, 14. In *Tristram Shandy*, ii. ch. 4, published in 1759, we read :—' It was in this year [about 1700] that my uncle began to break

in upon the daily regularity of a clean shirt.' In Richard Graves's *Spiritual Quixote*, published in 1773 (i. 51), Tugwell says to his master :—' Your Worship belike has been used to shift you twice a week.' Mrs. Piozzi (*Journey*, i. 105, date of 1789) says that she heard in Milan ' a travelled gentleman . . telling his auditors how all the men in London, *that were noble*, put on a clean shirt every day.' Johnson himself owned that he had ' no passion for clean linen.' *Ante*, i. 397.
† ⟨' Brutal Croatian soldier.' See *O.E.D.* s.v. *Pandour*.⟩
[5] Scott, in *Old Mortality*, vii, says :—' It was a universal custom in Scotland, that, when the family was at dinner, the outer-gate of the court-yard, if there was one, and if not, the door of the house itself, was always shut and locked.' In a note on this he says :—' The custom of keeping the door of a house or chateau locked during the time of dinner, probably arose from the family being

St. Andrews   *Thursday* 19 *August* 1773

of the Union, and what money it had brought into Scotland. Dr. Watson observed, that a little money formerly went as far as a great deal now.—*Johnson.* ' In speculation, it seems that a smaller quantity of money, equal in value to a larger quantity, if equally divided, should produce the same effect. But it is not so in reality. Many more conveniences and elegancies are enjoyed where money is plentiful, than where it is scarce. Perhaps a great familiarity with it, which arises from plenty, makes us more easily part with it.'

After what Dr. Johnson has [a] said of St. Andrews, which he had long wished to see, as our oldest university, and the seat of our Primate in the days of episcopacy, I can say little. Since the publication of Dr. Johnson's book, I find that he has been censured for not seeing here the ancient chapel of *St. Rule*, a curious piece of sacred architecture [1]. But this was neither his fault nor mine. We were both of us abundantly desirous of surveying such sort of antiquities : but neither of us knew of this. I am afraid the censure must fall on those who did not tell us of it. In every place, where there is any thing worthy of observation, there should be a short printed directory for strangers, such as we find in all the towns of Italy, and in some of the towns in England. I was told that there is a manuscript account of St. Andrews, by Martin, secretary to Archbishop Sharp [2] ; and that one Douglas † has published a small account of it. I inquired at a bookseller's, but could not get it. Dr. Johnson's veneration for the Hierarchy is well known [3]. There is no wonder then, that he was affected with a strong indignation, while he beheld the ruins of religious magnificence. I happened to ask where John Knox was buried. Dr. Johnson burst out, ' I hope in the high-way [4]. I have been looking at his reformations [5].'

[a] has 1 : had 2, 3.

anciently assembled in the hall at that meal, and liable to surprise.' ⟨See John Ramsay of Ochtertyre, *Scotl. and Scotsmen in 18th c.*, ii. 102, n.⟩

[1] ⟨This chapel, a simple oblong chamber, 26 ft. long by 20 ft. wide, with walls about 34 ft. high, was the original cathedral of St. Andrews. See Macgibbon and Ross, *Eccl. Archit. of Scotland*, 1896, i. 186 ff.⟩

[2] ⟨George Martine, 1635–1712 :

see App. D, p. 478.⟩
† ⟨See App. D, p. 479.⟩
[3] See *ante*, ii. 171, iv. 75, 197, 274.
[4] Knox *was* buried in a place which soon after became, and ever since has been, a *highway* ; namely, the old churchyard of St. Giles in Edinburgh. CHAMBERS (Croker, 1835).
[5] In *The Rambler*, No. 82, Johnson makes a virtuoso write :—' I

It was a very fine day. Dr. Johnson seemed quite wrapt up in the contemplation of the scenes which were now presented to him. He kept his hat off while he was upon any part of the ground where the cathedral had stood. He said well, that ' Knox had set on a mob, without knowing where it would end ; and that differing from a man in doctrine was no reason why you should pull his house about his ears.' As we walked in the cloisters, there was a solemn echo, while he talked loudly of a proper retirement from the world. Mr. Nairne said, he had an inclination to retire. I called Dr. Johnson's attention to this, that I might hear his opinion if it was right.—*Johnson.* ' Yes, when he has done his duty to society [1]. In general, as every man is obliged not only to " love GOD, but his neighbour as himself," he must bear his part in active life ; yet there are exceptions. Those who are exceedingly scrupulous, (which I do not approve, for I am no friend to scruples [2],) and find their scrupulosity [3] invincible, so that they are quite in the dark, and know not what they shall do,—or those who cannot resist temptations, and find they make themselves worse by being in the world, without making it better, may retire [4]. I never read of a hermit, but in imagination I kiss his feet ; never of a monastery, but I could fall on my knees, and kiss the pavement. But I think putting young people there, who know nothing of life, nothing of retirement, is dangerous and wicked [5].

often lamented that I was not one of that happy generation who demolished the convents and monasteries, and broke windows by law.' He had in 1754 ' viewed [the ruins of the abbies of Oseney and Rewley, near Oxford] with indignation.' *Ante*, i. 273. Smollett, in *Humphry Clinker* (Melford's letter of Aug. 8), describes St. Andrews as ' the skeleton of a venerable city.'

[1] ' Some talked of the right of society to the labour of individuals, and considered retirement as a desertion of duty. Others readily allowed, that there was a time when the claims of the publick were satisfied, and when a man might properly sequester himself, to review his life, and purify his heart.' *Rasselas*, ch. 22.

[2] See *ante*, ii. 421, 423.

[3] See *ante*, iv. 5, note 2, and v. 27.

[4] ' He that lives well in the world is better than he that lives well in a monastery. But, perhaps, every one is not able to stem the temptations of publick life ; and, if he cannot conquer, he may properly retreat.' *Rasselas*, ch. 47. See *ante*, ii. 435.

[5] ' A youthful passion for abstracted devotion should not be encouraged.' *Ante*, ii. 10. The hermit in *Rasselas* (ch. 21) says :—' The life of a solitary man will be certainly miserable, but not certainly devout.' In Johnson's *Works* (1787), xi. 203, we read that ' Johnson thought worse

St. Andrews   *Thursday* 19 *August* 1773   63
It is a saying as old as Hesiod,

Ἔργα νεῶν, βουλαῖτε μέσων, εὔχαιτε γερόντων[1].

That is a very noble line : not that young men should not pray, or old men not give counsel, but that every season of life has its proper duties. I have thought of retiring, and have talked of it to a friend † ; but I find my vocation is rather to active life.' I said, *some* young monks might be allowed, to shew that it is not age alone that can retire to pious solitude ; but he thought this would only shew that they could not resist temptation.

He wanted to mount the steeples, but it could not be done. There are no good inscriptions here. Bad Roman characters he naturally mistook for half Gothick, half Roman. One of the steeples, which he was told was in danger, he wished not to be taken down ; ' for, said he, it may fall on some of the posterity of John Knox ; and no great matter ! '—Dinner was mentioned.— *Johnson*. ' Ay, ay ; amidst all these sorrowful scenes, I have no objection to dinner [2].'

We went and looked at the castle, where Cardinal Beaton was murdered [3], and then visited Principal Murison at his college, where is a good library-room ; but the Principal was

of the vices of retirement than of those of society.' Southey (*Life of Wesley*, i. 32) writes of Wesley :— ' Some time before his return to the University, he had travelled many miles to see what is called " a serious man." This person said to him, " Sir, you wish to serve God and go to heaven. Remember, you cannot serve him alone : you must therefore *find* companions or *make* them : the Bible knows nothing of solitary religion." Wesley never forgot these words.'

[1] [*Ἔργα νέων, βουλαὶ δὲ μέσων, εὐχαὶ δὲ γερόντων*.
Hesiodi Fragmenta, Lipsiæ, 1840, p. 371.]
  Let youth in deeds, in counsel man engage ;
  Prayer is the proper duty of old age. ⟨Malone.⟩ BOSWELL, ed. 3.
† ⟨Perhaps Sir Joshua Reynolds : see *ante*, iv. 359.⟩

[2] One ' sorrowful scene ' Johnson was perhaps too late in the year to see. Wesley, who visited St. Andrews on May 27, 1776, during the vacation, writes (*Journal*, vi. 110) :— ' What is left of St. Leonard's College is only a heap of ruins. Two colleges remain. One of them has a tolerable square, but all the windows are broke, like those of a brothel. We were informed the students do this before they leave the college.' ⟨See App. D, pp. 479-80.⟩
[3] ' He was murdered by the ruffians of reformation, in the manner of which Knox has given what he himself calls a merry narrative.' Johnson's *Western Islands*, p. 6. In May 1546 the Cardinal had Wishart the Reformer burned at the stake, and at the end of the same month was himself murdered in revenge, by John Leslie.

abundantly vain of it, for he seriously said to Dr. Johnson, ' you have not such a one in England [1].'

The professors † entertained us with a very good dinner. Present: Murison, Shaw, Cooke, Hill, Haddo, Watson, Flint, Brown. I observed, that I wondered to see him eat so well, after viewing so many sorrowful scenes of ruined religious magnificence. ' Why, said he, I am not sorry, after seeing these gentlemen ; for they are not sorry.'—Murison said, all sorrow was bad, as it was murmuring against the dispensations of Providence.—*Johnson*. ' Sir, sorrow is inherent in humanity. As you cannot judge two and two to be either five, or three, but certainly four, so, when comparing a worse present state with a better which is past, you cannot but feel sorrow [2]. It is not cured by reason, but by the incursion of present objects, which wear out the past. You need not murmur, though you are sorry.'—*Murison*. ' But St. Paul says, "I have learnt, in whatever state I am, therewith to be content." '—*Johnson*. ' Sir, that relates to riches and poverty ; for we see St. Paul, when he had a thorn in the flesh, prayed earnestly to have it removed ; and then he could not be content.'—Murison, thus refuted, tried to be smart, and drank to Dr. Johnson, ' Long may you lecture ! '— Dr. Johnson afterwards, speaking of his not drinking wine, said, ' The Doctor spoke of *lecturing* (looking to him). I give all these lectures on water.'

He defended requiring subscription in those admitted to universities, thus : ' As all who come into the country must

---

[1] ⟨Boswell does not in his MS. Journal record Murison's remark ; perhaps he took it from Johnson, who⟩ says (*Western Isl.*, p. 7):—'.The doctor, by whom it was shewn, hoped to irritate or subdue my English vanity by telling me, that we had no such repository of books in England.' He wrote to Mrs. Thrale (*Letters*, No. 321) :—' For luminousness and elegance [it] may vie at least with the new edifice at Streatham.' ⟨See App. D, p. 480.⟩

† ⟨For these see App. D, pp. 480–1.⟩

[2] ' Sorrow is properly that state of the mind in which our desires are fixed upon the past, without looking forward to the future, an incessant wish that something were otherwise than it has been, a tormenting and harrassing want of some enjoyment or possession which we have lost, and which no endeavours can possibly regain.' *The Rambler*, No. 47. He wrote to Mrs. Thrale on the death of her son Harry :—' Do not indulge your sorrow, try to drive it away by either pleasure or pain ; for opposed to what you are feeling many pains will become pleasures.' *Letters*, No. 466.

obey the king, so all who come into an university must be of the church [1].'

And here I must do Dr. Johnson the justice to contradict a very absurd and ill-natured story, as to what passed at St. Andrews. It has been circulated, that, after grace was said in English, in the usual manner, he with the greatest marks of contempt, as if he had held it to be no grace in an university, would not sit down till he had said grace aloud in Latin. This would have been an insult indeed to the gentlemen who were entertaining us. But the truth was precisely thus. In the course of conversation at dinner, Dr. Johnson, in very good humour, said, ' I should have expected to have heard a Latin grace, among so many learned men : we had always a Latin grace at Oxford. I believe I can repeat it [2].' Which he did, as giving the learned men in one place a specimen of what was done by the learned men in another place.

We went and saw the church, in which is Archbishop Sharp's monument [3]. I was struck with the same kind of feelings with which the churches of Italy impressed me. I was much pleased to see Dr. Johnson actually in St. Andrews, of which we had talked so long. Professor Haddo was with us this afternoon, along with Dr. Watson. We looked at St. Salvador's College. The rooms for students seemed very commodious, and Dr. Johnson said, the chapel was the neatest place of worship he had seen. The key of the library could not be found ; for it seems Professor Hill, who was out of town, had taken it with him. Dr. Johnson told a joke he had heard of a monastery abroad, where the key of the library could never be found.

It was somewhat dispiriting, to see this ancient archiepiscopal city now sadly deserted [4]. We saw in one of its streets a

---

[1] See *ante*, ii. 151.
[2] The Pembroke College grace was written by Camden. It was as follows :—' Gratias tibi agimus, Deus misericors, pro acceptis a tua bonitate alimentis ; enixe comprecantes ut serenissimum nostrum Regem [Georgium], totam regiam familiam, populumque tuum universum tuta in pace semper custodias.' ⟨See D. Macleane, *Pembroke College*, 1897, 120.⟩
[3] ⟨The elaborate monument in Holy Trinity Church was erected by

Abp. Sharp's son, Sir W. Sharp of Scotscraig. It has a bas-relief representation of the murder of the Archbishop on Magus Muir, near St. Andrews, on 3 May 1679. Carruthers reports that when the tomb was repaired in 1849 it was found that the bones of the Archbishop had been removed.⟩
[4] ' One of its streets is now lost ; and in those that remain, there is the silence and solitude of inactive indigence and gloomy depopulation.

Thursday 19 August 1773   St. Andrews

remarkable proof of liberal toleration ; a nonjuring clergyman†, strutting about in his canonicals, with a jolly countenance and a round belly, like a well-fed monk.

We observed two occupations united in the same person, who had hung out two sign-posts. Upon one was, ' James Hood, White Iron Smith ' (*i.e.* Tin-plate Worker). Upon another, ' The Art of Fencing taught, by James Hood.'—Upon this last were painted some trees, and two men fencing, one of whom had hit the other in the eye, to shew his great dexterity ; so that the art was well taught.—*Johnson*. ' Were I studying here, I should go and take a lesson. I remember *Hope*, in his book on this art [1], says, " the Scotch are very good fencers." '

We returned to the inn, where we had been entertained at dinner, and drank tea in company with some of the Professors, of whose civilities I beg leave to add my humble and very grateful acknowledgement to the honourable testimony of Dr. Johnson, in his ' Journey ' [2].

We talked of composition, which was a favourite topick of Dr. Watson's, who first distinguished himself by lectures on rhetorick.—*Johnson*. ' I advised Chambers §, and would advise every young man beginning to compose, to do it as fast as he can, to get a habit of having his mind to start promptly ; it is so much more difficult to improve in speed than in accuracy [3].'— *Watson*. ' I own I am for much attention to accuracy in

. . . Saint Andrews seems to be a place eminently adapted to study and education. . . . The students however are represented as at this time not exceeding a hundred. . . . I saw no reason for imputing their paucity to the present professors.' Johnson's *Western Isl.*, pp. 6, 7. A student, he adds, of lower rank could get his board, lodging, and instruction for less than ten pounds for the seven months of residence. Stockdale says (*Memoirs*, 1809, i. 238) that ' in St. Andrews, in 1756, for a good bedchamber, coals, and the attendance of a servant, *I payed one shilling a week.*'

† ⟨See App. D, p. 482.⟩
[1] ⟨*The Scots Fencing Master*, by Sir William Hope, 1687. Hope says in his preface ' To the Reader ' : ' Our Scots play is, in my Opinion, far before any I ever saw abroad.'⟩

[2] ' In the whole time of our stay we were gratified by every mode of kindness, and entertained with all the elegance of lettered hospitality.' Johnson's *Western Isl.*, p. 5.

§ ⟨See App. D, p. 482.⟩

[3] Dugald Stewart (*Biogr. Mem. Adam Smith*, 1811, 107) writes :—' Mr. Smith observed to me, not long before his death, that after all his practice in writing, he composed as slowly, and with as great difficulty, as at first. He added, at the same time, that Mr. Hume had acquired so great a facility in this respect, that the last volumes of his *History* were printed from his original copy, with a few marginal corrections.' See *ante*, iii. 437 and iv. 12.

composing, lest one should get bad habits of doing it in a slovenly manner.'—*Johnson.* ' Why, sir, you are confounding *doing* inaccurately with the *necessity* of doing inaccurately. A man knows when his composition is inaccurate, and when he thinks fit he'll correct it. But, if a man is accustomed to compose slowly, and with difficulty, upon all occasions, there is danger that he may not compose at all, as we do not like to do that which is not done easily ; and, at any rate, more time is consumed in a small matter than ought to be.'—*Watson.* ' Dr. Hugh Blair has taken a week to compose a sermon.'—*Johnson.* ' Then, sir, that is for want of the habit of composing quickly, which I am insisting one should acquire.'—*Watson.* ' Blair was not composing all the week, but only such hours as he found himself disposed for composition.'—*Johnson.* ' Nay, sir, unless you tell me the time he took, you tell me nothing. If I say I took a week to walk a mile, and have had the gout five days, and been ill otherwise another day, I have taken but one day. I myself have composed about forty sermons [1]. I have begun a sermon after dinner, and sent it off by the post that night. I wrote forty-eight of the printed octavo pages of the Life of Savage at a sitting ; but then I sat up all night. I have also written six sheets in a day of translation from the French [2].'— *Boswell.* ' We have all observed how one man dresses himself slowly, and another fast.'—*Johnson.* ' Yes, sir; it is wonderful how much time some people will consume in dressing ; taking up a thing and looking at it, and laying it down, and taking it up again. Every one should get the habit of doing it quickly.

[1] Of these only twenty-five have been published in Johnson's *Works* (ix. 289–525.) See *ante*, iii. 19, note 3, 181, ⟨and 506–7⟩. Johnson wrote on April 20, 1778 :—' I have made sermons, perhaps as readily as formerly.' *Pr. and Med.* ¶ 127. ⟨Johnson wrote ' The Convict's Address ', a sermon delivered by Dr. Dodd. *Ante*, iii. 141. Mrs. Thrale in Dec. 1777 drew up what she describes as ' a Catalogue of such Writings as I *know* to be his ' : one of the items is ' Sermons for Strahan & Hervey. I know not how many.' *Thraliana*, ed. K. C. Balderston, 1942, i. 204. The Rev. George Strahan (*ante*, iv. 415) does not appear to have published any sermons. For a sermon published by the Rev. and Hon. Henry Hervey Aston, but written by Johnson, see App. D, p. 483.⟩

[2] ⟨This sentence does not appear in Boswell's MS. for this date and he may have taken it from his Journal of 3 June 1781 (*ante*, iv. 127), but whether he did so or not, there is no doubt that the translation there referred to is meant. See *ante*, iv. 494–6.⟩

I would say to a young divine, " Here is your text ; let me see how soon you can make a sermon." Then I'd say, " Let me see how much better you can make it." Thus I should see both his powers and his judgement.'

We all went to Dr. Watson's to supper. Miss Sharp, great grandchild of Archbishop Sharp, was there ; as was Mr. Craig, the ingenious architect of the new town of Edinburgh [1], and nephew of Thomson, to whom Dr. Johnson has since done so much justice, in his ' Lives of the Poets '.

We talked of memory, and its various modes.—*Johnson.* ' Memory will play strange tricks. One sometimes loses a single word. I once lost *fugaces* in the Ode *Posthume, Posthume* [2].' I mentioned to him, that a worthy gentleman † of my acquaintance actually forgot his own name.—*Johnson.* ' Sir, that was a morbid oblivion.'

Friday, 20th August.

Dr. Shaw, the professor of divinity, breakfasted with us. I took out my ' Ogden on Prayer ', and read some of it to the company. Dr. Johnson praised him. ' Abernethy [3], (said he,) allows only of a physical effect of prayer upon the mind, which may be produced many ways, as well as by prayer ; for instance, by meditation. Ogden goes farther. In truth, we have the consent of all nations for the efficacy of prayer, whether offered up by individuals, or by assemblies ; and Revelation has told us, it will be effectual.'—I said, ' Leechman seemed to incline to Abernethy's doctrine.' Dr. Watson observed, that Leechman meant to shew, that, even admitting no effect to be produced by prayer, respecting the Deity, it was useful to our own minds [4].

---

[1] ⟨For James Craig, see *post*, App. D, pp. 484-5.⟩ ' As far as I am acquainted with modern architecture, I am aware of no streets which, in simplicity and manliness of style, or general breadth and brightness of effect, equal those of the New Town of Edinburgh. But,' etc. Ruskin's *Lectures on Architecture and Painting*, p. 2.

[2] Horace, *Odes*, ii. 14. 1.

† ⟨See App. D, pp. 485-6.⟩

[3] John Abernethy, 1680-1740, Presbyterian divine. His works in 7 vols. 8vo were published in 1740-51.

[4] ⟨William Leechman was at this time Principal of Glasgow University. In 1743, when Minister of Beith, he published his famous sermon, *The Nature, Reasonableness, and Advantages of Prayer*, in which the Presbytery of Glasgow detected heresy ; the charge was not upheld by the Synod. Leechman's *Sermons*, 1789, i. 23 ff. Of this sermon⟩ Hume writes, 30 June 1743 :— ' First The Addressing of our virtuous Wishes & Desires to the Deity, since the Address has no Influence on him,

St. Andrews   *Friday 20 August* 1773   69

He had given only a part of his system : Dr. Johnson thought he should have given the whole.

Dr. Johnson enforced the strict observance of Sunday [1]. ' It should be different (he observed) from another day. People may walk, but not throw stones at birds. There may be relaxation, but there should be no levity [2].'

We went and saw Colonel Nairne's garden and grotto †. Here was a fine old plane tree. Unluckily the colonel said, there was but this and another large tree in the county. This assertion was an excellent cue for Dr. Johnson, who laughed enormously, calling to me to hear it. He had expatiated to me on the nakedness of that part of Scotland which he had seen. His ' Journey ' has been violently abused, for what he has said upon this subject. But let it be considered, that, when Dr. Johnson talks of trees, he means trees of good size, such as he was accustomed to see in England ; and of these there are certainly very few upon the *eastern coast* of Scotland. Besides, he said, that he meant to give only a map of the road ; and let any traveller observe how many trees, which deserve the name, he can see from the road from Berwick to Aberdeen [3]. Had Dr. Johnson

is only a kind of rhetorical Figure, in order to render these Wishes more ardent & passionate. This is Mr. Leechman's Doctrine. Now the Use of any figure of Speech can never be a Duty. Secondly this Figure, like most Figures of Rhetoric, has an evident Impropriety in it. For we can make use of no Expression or even Thought, in Prayers and Entreaties, which does not imply that these Prayers have an Influence. Thirdly. This Figure is very dangerous & leads directly & even unavoidably to Impiety & Blasphemy,' etc. *Letters of Hume*, 1932, i. 51. ⟨See *post*, v. 101, 370, and the *D.N.B.*⟩

[1] Nichols (*Lit. Anec.* ii. 555) records:—'During the whole time of my intimacy with Dr. Johnson, he rarely permitted me to depart without some sententious advice. . . . His words at parting were, " Take care of your eternal salvation. Remember to observe the Sabbath. Let it never be a day of business, nor wholly a day of dissipation." He concluded his solemn farewell with, " Let my words have their due weight. They are the words of a dying man." '

[2] See *ante*, ii. 72.

† ⟨See App. D, p. 486.⟩

[3] ' From the bank of the Tweed to St. Andrews I had never seen a single tree, which I did not believe to have grown up far within the present century. . . . The variety of sun and shade is here utterly unknown. . . . A tree might be a show in Scotland as a horse in Venice. At St. Andrews Mr. Boswell found only one, and recommended it to my notice ; I told him that it was rough and low, or looked as if I thought so. This, said he, is nothing to another a few miles off. I was still less delighted to hear that another tree

Friday 20 *August* 1773   St. Andrews–Leuchars
said, 'there are *no* trees' upon this line, he would have said what is colloquially true ; because, by no trees, in common speech, we mean few. When he is particular in counting, he may be attacked. I know not how Colonel Nairne came to say there were but *two* large trees in the county of Fife. I did not perceive that he smiled. There are certainly not a great many ; but I could have shewn him more than two at *Balmuto*, from whence my ancestors came, and which now belongs to a branch of my family [1].

The grotto was ingeniously constructed. In the front of it were petrified stocks of fir, plane, and some other tree. Dr. Johnson said, ' Scotland has no right to boast of this grotto ; it is owing to personal merit. I never denied personal merit to many of you.'—Professor Shaw said to me, as we walked, ' This is a wonderful man: he is master of every subject he handles.'— Dr. Watson allowed him a very strong understanding, but wondered at his total inattention to established manners, as he came from London.

I have not preserved, in my Journal, any of the conversation which passed between Dr. Johnson and Professor Shaw ; but I recollect Dr. Johnson said to me afterwards, ' I took much to Shaw.'

We left St. Andrews about noon, and some miles from it observing, at *Leuchars*, a church with an old tower, we stopped to look at it. The *manse*, as the parsonage-house is called in Scotland, was close by. I waited on the minister †, mentioned our names, and begged he would tell us what he knew about it. He was a very civil old man ; but could only inform us, that it was supposed to have stood eight hundred years. He told us, there was a colony of Danes in his parish [2] ; that they had

was not to be seen nearer. Nay, said a gentleman that stood by, I know but of this and that tree in the county.' Johnson's *Western Isl.*, p. 9. ' In all this journey [so far as Slains Castle] I had not . . . seen five trees fit for the Carpenter.' *Letters*, No. 323. See *ante*, ii. 301.

[1] ⟨John, the younger brother of Boswell's grandfather, bought the estate of Balmuto from his kinsman, Andrew, in 1722. His son was Claude Irvine Boswell, Lord Balmuto. *Burke's Landed Gentry*, 1937, p. 206.⟩

† ⟨See App. D, p. 486.⟩

[2] ' The Danish colony at Leuchars is a vain imagination concerning a certain fleet of Danes wrecked on Sheughy Dikes.' SCOTT (in Croker, 1831). ' The fishing people on that coast have, however, all the appearance of being a different race from the

Dundee–Arbroath *Friday 20 August* 1773

landed at a remote period of time, and still remained a distinct people. Dr. Johnson shrewdly inquired whether they had brought women with them. We were not satisfied as to this colony.

We saw, this day, Dundee and Aberbrothick, the last of which Dr. Johnson has celebrated in his ' Journey ' [1]. Upon the road we talked of the Roman Catholick faith. He mentioned (I think) Tillotson's argument against transubstantiation : ' That we are as sure we see bread and wine only, as that we read in the Bible the text on which that false doctrine is founded. We have only the evidence of our senses for both [2].' ' If, (he added,) GOD had never spoken figuratively, we might hold that he speaks literally, when he says, " This is my body [3]." '—*Boswell*. ' But what do you say, sir, to the ancient and continued tradition of the church upon this point ? '—*Johnson*. ' Tradition, sir, has no place, where the Scriptures are plain ; and tradition cannot persuade a man into a belief of transubstantiation. Able men, indeed, have *said* they believed it.'

This is an awful subject. I did not then press Dr. Johnson upon it ; nor shall I now enter upon a disquisition concerning the import of those words uttered by our Saviour [4], which had

---

inland population, and their dialect has many peculiarities.' LOCKHART (in Croker, 1835).

[1] ' I should scarcely have regretted my journey, had it afforded nothing more than the sight of Aberbrothick.' *Western Isl.*, p. 10.

[2] Johnson referred, I believe, to Tillotson's sermon on 1 Cor. iii. 15, in which the preacher says :—' Supposing the *Scripture* to be a *Divine Revelation*, and that these words (*This is My Body*) if they be in Scripture, must necessarily be taken in the strict and literal sense ; I ask now, what greater evidence any man has that these words (*This is My Body*) are in the Bible, than every man has that the Bread is not chang'd in the Sacrament ? Nay no man has so much; for we have only the evidence of *one* sense that these words are in the Bible, but that the Bread is not chang'd we have the concurring testimony of *several* of our senses.' *Works*, 1714, 123. ⟨See also Tillotson's sermon against transubstantiation, *ib.* 297–317, and *Boswell Papers*, vii. 19.⟩

[3] This also is Tillotson's argument. ' There is no more certain foundation for it [transubstantiation] in Scripture, than for our Saviour's being substantially changed into all those things which are said of him, as that he is a *rock*, a *vine*, a *door*, and a hundred other things.' *Works*, 1714, 122.

[4] *Then Jesus said unto them, verily, verily, I say unto you, except ye eat the flesh of the son of man, and drink his blood, ye have no life in you.* See St. John's Gospel, chap. vi. 53, and following verses. BOSWELL, ed. 3.

such an effect upon many of his disciples, that they ' went back, and walked no more with him.' The Catechism and solemn office for Communion, in the Church of England, maintain a mysterious belief in more than a mere commemoration of the death of Christ, by partaking of the elements of bread and wine.

Dr. Johnson put me in mind, that, at St. Andrews, I had defended my profession very well, when the question had again been started, Whether a lawyer might honestly engage with the first side that offers him a fee. ' Sir, (said I,) it was with your arguments against Sir William Forbes [1] : but it was much that I could wield the arms of Goliath [a].'

He said, our judges had not gone deep in the question concerning literary property. I mentioned Lord Monboddo's opinion, that if a man could get a work by heart, he might print it, as by such an act the mind is exercised.—*Johnson*. ' No, sir ; a man's repeating it no more makes it his property, than a man may sell a cow which he drives home.'—I said, printing an abridgement of a work was allowed, which was only cutting the horns and tail off the cow.—*Johnson*. ' No, sir ; 'tis making the cow have a calf [2].'

About eleven at night we arrived at Montrose. We found but a sorry inn, where I myself saw another waiter put a lump of sugar with his fingers into Dr. Johnson's lemonade, for which he called him ' Rascal ! ' It put me in great glee that our landlord was an Englishman. I rallied the Doctor upon this, and he grew quiet [3]. Both Sir John Hawkins's and Dr. Burney's History of Musick had then been advertised [4]. I asked if this was not unlucky : would not they hurt one another ?—*Johnson*. ' No, sir. They will do good to one another. Some will buy the one, some the other, and compare them ; and so a talk is made about a thing, and the books are sold.'

He was angry at me for proposing to carry lemons with us to Sky, that he might be sure to have his lemonade. ' Sir, (said

[a] Goliath 1 : Goliah 2, 3.

[1] See *ante*, v. 26.
[2] See *ante*, i. 140, note 5, v. 50, ⟨and App. D, p. 486.⟩
[3] Johnson, after saying that the inn was not so good as they expected, continues :—' But Mr. Bos-

well desired me to observe that the innkeeper was an Englishman, and I then defended him as well as I could.' *Western Isl.*, p. 11. ⟨See Boswell's *Hebrides*, 1962, p. 457.⟩
[4] ⟨See App. D, p. 487.⟩

he,) I do not wish to be thought that feeble man who cannot do without any thing. Sir, it is very bad manners to carry provisions to any man's house, as if he could not entertain you. To an inferior, it is oppressive ; to a superior, it is insolent.'

Having taken the liberty, this evening, to remark to Dr. Johnson, that he very often sat quite silent for a long time, even when in company with only a single friend, which I myself had sometimes sadly experienced, he smiled and said, ' It is true, sir [1]. Tom Tyers, (for so he familiarly called our ingenious friend, who, since his death, has paid a biographical tribute to his memory [2],) Tom Tyers described me the best. He once said to me, " Sir, you are like a ghost : you never speak till you are spoken to [3]." '

Saturday, 21st August.

Neither the Rev. Mr. Nisbet, the established minister, nor the Rev. Mr. Spooner, the episcopal minister, were in town [*]. Before breakfast, we went and saw the town-hall, where is a good dancing-room, and other rooms for tea-drinking. The appearance of the town from it is very well ; but many of the houses are built with their ends to the street, which looks awkward [†]. When we came down from it, I met Mr. Gleg§, a merchant here. He went with us to see the English chapel. It is situated on a pretty dry spot, and there is a fine walk to it. It is really an elegant building, both within and without. The organ is adorned with green and gold. Dr. Johnson gave a shilling extraordinary to the clerk, saying, ' He belongs to an honest church [4].' I put him in mind, that episcopals were but

---

[1] Johnson wrote to Mrs. Thrale on July 29, 1775 (*Letters*, No. 426) :— ' I hope I shall quickly come [to Streatham], and find you all well, and gay, and happy, and catch a little gayety and health, and happiness among you.' On this Baretti noted in his copy :—' That he never caught. He thought and mused at Streatham as he did habitually every where, and seldom or never minded what was doing about him.' On the margin of i. 315 Baretti has written :—' Johnson mused as much on the road to Paris as he did in his garret in London, as much at a French Opera, as in his room at Streatham.'

[2] *A Biographical Sketch of Dr. Samuel Johnson*, by Thomas Tyers, Esq. See *ante*, iii. 308 ⟨and 523.⟩

[3] This description of Dr. Johnson appears to have been borrowed from *Tom Jones*, Book xi. ch. ii. ' The other, who, like a ghost, only wanted to be spoke to, readily answered,' &c. BOSWELL. Ed. 3. ⟨See *ante*, iii. 307.⟩

[*], [†], [§] ⟨See App. D, pp. 487–8.⟩

[4] ' We .. went to view the English

74   *Saturday* 21 *August* 1773   Montrose
dissenters here ; they were only *tolerated*. ' Sir, (said he,) we are here, as Christians in Turkey.'—He afterwards went into an apothecary's shop, and ordered some medicine for himself, and wrote the prescription in technical characters. The boy took him for a physician [1].

I doubted much which road to take, whether to go by the coast, or by Laurence Kirk and Monboddo. I knew Lord Monboddo and Dr. Johnson did not love each other [2] : yet I was unwilling not to visit his lordship ; and was also curious to see them together [3]. I mentioned my doubts to Dr. Johnson, who said, he would go two miles out of his way to see Lord Monboddo [4]. I therefore sent Joseph forward, with the following note.

' *Montrose*, 21 *August.*
' *My dear Lord,*
    ' THUS far I am come with Mr. Samuel Johnson. We must be at Aberdeen to-night. I know you do not admire him so much as I do; but I cannot be in this country without making you a bow at your old place, as I do not know if I may again have an opportunity of seeing Monboddo. Besides, Mr. Johnson says, he would go two miles out of his way to see Lord Monboddo. I have sent forward my servant, that we may know if your lordship be at home.
        ' I am ever, my dear lord,
            ' Most sincerely yours,
                ' JAMES BOSWELL.'

As we travelled onwards from Montrose, we had the Grampian hills in our view, and some good land around us, but void of trees and hedges. Dr. Johnson has said ludicrously, in his chapel, and found a small church, clean to a degree unknown in any other part of Scotland.' *Western Isl.*, p. 11. ⟨See App. D, p. 488.⟩

[1] See *ante*, iii. 22.
[2] See *ante*, iv. 273, note 1. Yet Johnson says (*Western Isl.*, p. 11) :— ' The magnetism of Lord Monboddo's conversation easily drew us out of our way.'
[3] There were several points of similarity between them ; learning, clearness of head, precision of speech, and a love of research on many subjects which people in general do not investigate. Foote paid Lord Monboddo the compliment of saying, that he was ' an Elzevir edition of Johnson.' It has been shrewdly observed that Foote must have meant a diminutive, or *pocket* edition. BOSWELL.
⟨For the history of this note, which cost Boswell a cancel, see Dr. Chapman's edition, 1924, p. 466. See also *ante*, ii. 189, n. 1.⟩
[4] Lord Elibank (*post*, v. 181) said that he would go five hundred miles to see Dr. Johnson ; but Johnson never said more than he meant.

'Journey', that the *hedges* were of *stone*[1]; for, instead of the verdant *thorn* to refresh the eye, we found the bare *wall* or *dike* intersecting the prospect. He observed, that it was wonderful to see a country so divested, so denuded of trees.

We stopped at Laurence Kirk[2], where our great grammarian, Ruddiman[3], was once schoolmaster. We respectfully remembered that excellent man and eminent scholar, by whose labours a knowledge of the Latin language will be preserved in Scotland, if it shall be preserved at all. Lord Gardenston[4], one of our judges, collected money to raise a monument to him at this place, which I hope will be well executed[5]. I know my father gave five guineas towards it. Lord Gardenston is the proprietor of Laurence Kirk, and has encouraged the building of a manufacturing village, of which he is exceedingly fond, and has written a pamphlet upon it[6], as if he had founded Thebes; in which, however,[a] there are many useful precepts strongly expressed. The village seemed to be irregularly built, some of the houses being of clay, some of brick, and some of brick and stone. Dr. Johnson observed, they thatched well here.

I was a little acquainted with Mr. Forbes[7], the minister of the

a however, 1, 2: however 3.

[1] *Western Isl.*, p. 11. ⟨For *stone hedges*, see Boswell's *Letters*, No. 137, i. 216, and *O.E.D.* s.v. *Hedge sb.* 1 b.⟩ Of the road to Montrose Johnson remarks:—'When I had proceeded thus far, I had opportunities of observing what I had never heard, that there are many beggars in Scotland. In Edinburgh the proportion is, I think, not less than in London, and in the smaller places it is far greater than in English towns of the same extent. It must, however, be allowed that they are not importunate, nor clamorous. They solicit silently, or very modestly.' *Western Isl.*, p. 11. See *post*, v. 116, note 2.

[2] ⟨For an account of this village, which was erected into a burgh of barony in 1779, see W. R. Fraser's *History of Laurencekirk*, 1880.⟩

[3] See *ante*, i. 211. ⟨Ruddiman himself recorded that he was 'schoolmaster at Lawrence Kirk, during three years and a half, from April 1695 to October 1699.' G. Chalmers, *Life of Ruddiman*, p. 17 n. Here he met his patron, Pitcairne, who was 'detained by violence of weather' at the inn. *Ib.* p. 25.⟩

[4] ⟨Francis Garden, Lord Gardenstone, 1721–93, was a Whig and a patriot, a *bon vivant* and a free-thinker. See John Ramsay, of Ochtertyre, *Scotland and Scotsmen*, 1888, i. 369 ff., *Yale Univ. Library Gaz.*, 1928, ii, No. 3, p. 43, *post*, App. D, p. 489, and *D.N.B.*⟩

[5] G. Chalmers (*Life of Ruddiman*, p. 270) says:—'In May, 1790, Lord Gardenstone declared, "that he still intended to erect a proper monument, in his village, to the memory of the late learned, and worthy, Mr. Ruddiman."' In 1792 Gardenstone, in his *Miscellanies*, p. 257, attacked Ruddiman. 'It has of late become fashionable,' he wrote, 'to speak of Ruddiman in terms of the highest respect.' The monument was never raised. ⟨There is a tablet to his memory in the New Greyfriars Church, Edinburgh.⟩

[6] *Letter to the People of Laurencekirk*, 1780.

[7] ⟨See App. D, p. 489.⟩

Saturday 21 August 1773 Laurencekirk-parish. I sent to inform him that a gentleman desired to see him. He returned for answer, 'that he would not come to a stranger.' I then gave my name, and he came. I remonstrated to him for not coming to a stranger; and, by presenting him to Dr. Johnson, proved to him what a stranger might sometimes be. His Bible inculcates 'be not forgetful to entertain strangers,' and mentions the same motive [1]. He defended himself by saying, 'He had once come to a stranger who sent for him; and he found him " a *little-worth person!* " '

Dr. Johnson insisted on stopping at the inn †, as I told him that Lord Gardenston had furnished it with a collection of books, that travellers might have entertainment for the mind, as well as the body. He praised the design, but wished there had been more books, and those better chosen.

About a mile from Monboddo, where you turn off the road, Joseph was waiting to tell us my lord expected us to dinner. We drove over a wild moor. It rained, and the scene was somewhat dreary. Dr. Johnson repeated, with solemn emphasis, Macbeth's speech on meeting the witches §. As we travelled on, he told me, ' Sir, you got into our club by doing what a man can do [2]. Several of the members wished to keep you out. Burke told me, he doubted if you were fit for it: but, now you are in, none of them are sorry. Burke says, that you have so much good humour naturally, it is scarce a virtue [3].'—*Boswell.* 'They were afraid of you, sir, as it was you who proposed me.'—*Johnson.* ' Sir, they knew, that if they refused you, they'd probably never have got in another. I'd have kept them all out. Beauclerk was very earnest for you.'—*Boswell.* ' Beauclerk has a keenness of mind which is very uncommon.'—*Johnson.* ' Yes, sir; and every thing comes from him so easily. It

---

[1] ' Be not forgetful to entertain strangers : for thereby some have entertained angels unawares.' *Hebrews*, xiii. 2.
† ⟨See App. D, pp. 489–90.⟩
§ ⟨See *post*, v. 115.⟩
[2] This, I find, is considered as obscure. I suppose Dr. Johnson meant, that I assiduously and earnestly recommended myself to some of the members, as in a canvass for an election into parliament. BOSWELL, ed. 2. See *ante*, ii. 235

⟨Mr. V. Rendall suggests that Johnson is referring, with slight sarcasm, to *Macbeth*, I. vii. 46 : ' I dare do all that may become a man.'⟩
[3] Goldsmith in *Retaliation*, a few months later, wrote of William Burke :—
' Would you ask for his merits?
    alas! he had none;
What was good was spontaneous,
    his faults were his own.'
See *ante*, iii. 362, note 2.

appears to me that I labour, when I say a good thing.'—Boswell. ' You are loud, sir ; but it is not an effort of mind [1].'

Monboddo is a wretched place, wild and naked, with a poor old house ; though, if I recollect right, there are two turrets which mark an old baron's residence. Lord Monboddo received us at his gate most courteously ; pointed to the Douglas arms upon his house, and told us that his great-grandmother was of that family †. ' In such houses (said he,) our ancestors lived, who were better men than we.'—' No, no, my lord (said Dr. Johnson). We are as strong as they, and a great deal wiser [2].'—This was an assault upon one of Lord Monboddo's capital dogmas, and I was afraid there would have been a violent altercation in the very close, before we got into the house. But his lordship is distinguished not only for ' ancient metaphysicks,' but for ancient *politesse*, ' *la vieille cour*,' and he made no reply [3].

His lordship was drest in a rustick suit, and wore a little round hat ; he told us, we now saw him as *Farmer Burnet* [4], and

[1] See *ante*, iii. 260, 390, 425, ⟨537⟩.
† ⟨See App. D, p. 490.⟩
[2] Hannah More (*Memoirs*, 1836, i. 201) wrote of Monboddo in 1782 :—' He is such an extravagant adorer of the ancients, that he scarcely allows the English language to be capable of any excellence, still less the French. . . . He said we moderns were entirely degenerated. I asked in what ? " In every thing," was his answer. . . . He advocates slavery upon principle. I asked him how he could vindicate such an enormity. He owned it was because Plutarch justified it. . . . He is so wedded to system that, as Lord Barrington said to me the other day, rather than sacrifice his favourite opinion, that men were born with tails, he would be contented to wear one himself.'
[3] Scott, in a note on *Guy Mannering*, ed. 1829, ii. 267, writes of Monboddo :—' The conversation of the excellent old man, his high, gentleman-like, chivalrous spirit, the learning and wit with which he defended his fanciful paradoxes, the kind and liberal spirit of his hospitality,

must render these *noctes cœnæque* dear to all who, like the author, (though then young) had the honour of sitting at his board.' ⟨In his anonymously published *Antient Metaphysics*, six volumes quarto, 1779–99, Monboddo sought ' to revive antient Theism, particularly the theism of Plato and Aristotle ' (i. Introd. p. 1).⟩

[4] Lord Cockburn, writing of the title that Jeffrey took when he was raised to the Bench in 1834, said :—' The Scotch Judges are styled *Lords* ; a title to which long usage has associated feelings of reverence in the minds of the people, who could not now be soon made to respect or understand *Mr. Justice*. During its strongly feudalised condition, the landholders of Scotland, who were almost the sole judges, were really known only by the names of their estates. It was an insult, and in some parts of the country it is so still, to call a laird by his personal, instead of his territorial, title. . . . But this assumption of two names, one official and one personal, and being addressed by the one and

we should have his family dinner, a farmer's dinner. He said, 'I should not have forgiven Mr. Boswell, had he not brought you here, Dr. Johnson.' He produced a very long stalk of corn, as a specimen of his crop, and said, ' You see here the *lætas segetes* [1]:' he added, that *Virgil* seemed to be as enthusiastick a farmer as he [2], and was certainly a practical one.—*Johnson*. ' It does not always follow, my lord, that a man who has written a good poem on an art, has practised it. Philip Miller told me, that in Philips's CYDER, a poem, all the precepts were just, and indeed better than in books written for the purpose of instructing ; yet Philips had never made cyder [3].'

I started the subject of emigration [4].—*Johnson*. ' To a man of mere animal life, you can urge no argument against going to America, but that it will be some time before he will get the earth to produce. But a man of any intellectual enjoyment will not easily go and immerse himself and his posterity for ages in barbarism.'

He and my lord spoke highly of Homer.—*Johnson*. ' He had all the learning of his age. The shield of Achilles shews a nation in war, a nation in peace ; harvest-sport[a], nay stealing [5].'—

[a] harvest-sport 2 : harvest sport 1, 3.

subscribing by the other, is wearing out, and will soon disappear entirely.' Cockburn's *Jeffrey*, 1852, i. 365. See *post*, v. 111, note 1.

[1] *Georgics*, i. 1.

[2] Walter Scott used to tell an instance of Lord Monboddo's agricultural enthusiasm, that returning home one night after an absence (I think) on circuit, he went out with a candle to look at a field of turnips, then a novelty in Scotland. CROKER, ed. 1848.

[3] Johnson says the same in his *Life of John Philips*, 15, and adds :—' This I was told by Miller, the great gardener and botanist, whose experience was, that " there were many books written on the same subject in prose, which do not contain so much truth as that poem." ' Miller is mentioned, Sept. 1753, in Walpole's *Letters*, iii. 186 :—' There is extreme taste in the park [Hagley] : the seats are not the best, but there is not one absurdity. There is a ruined castle, built by Miller, that would get him his freedom, even of Strawberry : it has the true rust of the Barons' Wars.'

[4] See *ante*, v. 27.

[5] My note of this is much too short. *Brevis esse laboro, obscurus fio*. Yet as I have resolved that *the very Journal which Dr. Johnson read*, shall be presented to the publick, I will not expand the text in any considerable degree, though I may occasionally supply a word to complete the sense, as I fill up the blanks of abbreviation in the writing ; neither of which can be said to change the genuine Journal. One of the best criticks of our age conjectures that the imperfect passage above has probably been as follows : ' In his book we have an accurate display of a nation in war, and a nation in peace ; the peasant

Monboddo. 'Ay, and what we (looking to me) would call a parliament-house scene [1]; a cause pleaded.'—*Johnson.* 'That is part of the life of a nation in peace. And there are in Homer such characters of heroes, and combinations of qualities of heroes, that the united powers of mankind ever since have not produced any but what are to be found there.'—*Monboddo.* 'Yet no character is described.'—*Johnson.* 'No; they all develope themselves. Agamemnon is always a gentleman-like character; he has always Βασιλικον τι. That the ancients held so, is plain from this; that Euripides, in his Hecuba, makes him the person to interpose [2].'—*Monboddo.* 'The history of manners is the most valuable. I never set a high value on any other history.'—*Johnson.* 'Nor I; and therefore I esteem biography, as giving us what comes near to ourselves, what we can turn to use [3].'—*Boswell.* 'But in the course of general history, we find manners. In wars, we see the dispositions of people, their degrees of humanity, and other particulars.'—*Johnson.* 'Yes; but then you must take all the facts to get this; and it is but a little you get.'—*Monboddo.* 'And it is that little which

is delineated as truly as the general; nay, even harvest-sport, and the modes of ancient theft are described.' BOSWELL, ed. 1.
⟨Boswell's quotation is from Horace, *Ars Poet.* l. 25. For the relationship of the printed text to Boswell's original manuscript see the Preface to this revised edition (pp. v, vi). 'One of the best criticks' was, as Dr. Hill conjectured, Malone. See also *post*, v. 360.⟩

[1] It was in the Parliament-house that 'the ordinary Lords of Session,' the Scotch Judges, that is to say, held their courts. *Ante*, v. 39.

[2] Dr. Johnson modestly said, he had not read Homer so much as he wished he had done. But this conversation shews how well he was acquainted with the Mœonian bard; and he has shewn it still more in his criticism upon Pope's Homer, in his Life of that Poet. My excellent friend, Mr. Langton, told me, he was once present at a dispute between Dr. Johnson and Mr. Burke, on the comparative merits of Homer and Virgil, which was carried on with extraordinary abilities on both sides. Dr. Johnson maintained the superiority of Homer. BOSWELL, ed. 1. See *ante*, iii. 193, and iv. 218.

[3] Johnson ten years earlier told Boswell that he loved most 'the biographical part of literature.' *Ante*, i. 425. Goldsmith said of biography:—'It furnishes us with an opportunity of giving advice freely, and without offence.... Counsels..., as well as compliments, are best conveyed in an indirect and oblique manner; and this renders biography, as well as fable, a most convenient vehicle for instruction. An ingenious gentleman was asked what was the best lesson for youth? He answered, "The life of a good man." Being again asked what was the next best, he replied, "The life of a bad one."' *Works*, 1886, v. 65.

makes history valuable.' Bravo! thought I; they agree like two brothers.—*Monboddo*. 'I am sorry, Dr. Johnson, you were not longer at Edinburgh, to receive the homage of our men of learning.'—*Johnson*. 'My lord, I received great respect and great kindness.'—*Boswell*. 'He goes back to Edinburgh after our tour.'—We talked of the decrease of learning in Scotland, and of the 'Muses' Welcome [1]'.—*Johnson*. 'Learning is much decreased in England, in my remembrance [2].'— *Monboddo*. 'You, sir, have lived to see its decrease in England, I its extinction in Scotland.' However, I brought him to confess that the High School of Edinburgh did well.—*Johnson*. 'Learning has decreased in England, because learning will not do so much for a man as formerly. There are other ways of getting preferment. Few bishops are now made for their learning. To be a bishop, a man must be learned in a learned age,—factious in a factious age; but always of eminence [3]. Warburton is an exception; though his learning alone did not raise him. He was first an antagonist to Pope, and helped Theobald to publish his Shakspeare; but, seeing Pope the rising man,—when Crousaz attacked his "Essay on Man", for some faults which it has, and some which it has not, Warburton defended it in the Review of that time [4]. This brought him acquainted with Pope, and he gained his friendship. Pope introduced him to Allen, Allen married him to his niece: so, by Allen's interest and his own, he was made a bishop [5]. But then his learning

---

[1] See *ante*, v. 57.

[2] Ten years later he said:— 'There is now a great deal more learning in the world than there was formerly; for it is universally diffused.' *Ante*, iv. 217. Windham (*Diary*, p. 17) records 'Johnson's opinion that I could not name above five of my college acquaintants who read Latin with sufficient ease to make it pleasurable.'

[3] See *ante*, ii. 352.

[4] 'Warburton, whatever was his motive, undertook without solicitation to rescue Pope from the talons of Crousaz, by freeing him from the imputation of favouring fatality or rejecting revelation, and from month to month continued a vindication of the *Essay on Man* in the literary journal of that time, called the *Republick of Letters*.' Johnson's *Pope*, 189. Pope wrote to Warburton of the *Essay on Man*:—'You understand my work better than I do myself.' Pope's *Works*, 1886, ix. 211. ⟨See App. A and D, pp. 423 and 490–1.⟩

[5] See *ante*, ii. 37, note 1, and Pope's *Works*, ix. 220. Allen was Ralph Allen of Prior Park near Bath, to whom Fielding dedicated *Amelia*, and who is said to have been the original

was the *sine qua non:* He knew how to make the most of it; but I do not find by any dishonest means.'—*Monboddo.* 'He is a great man.'—*Johnson.* 'Yes; he has great knowledge,— great power of mind. Hardly any man brings greater variety of learning to bear upon his point [1].'—*Monboddo.* 'He is one of the greatest lights of your church.'—*Johnson.* 'Why, we are not so sure of his being very friendly to us [2]. He blazes, if you will, but that is not always the steadiest light.—Lowth† is another bishop who has risen by his learning.'

Dr. Johnson examined young Arthur §, Lord Monboddo's son, in Latin. He answered very well; upon which he said, with complacency, 'Get you gone! When King James comes back [3], you shall be in the "Muses' Welcome!"'—My lord and Dr. Johnson disputed a little, whether the Savage or the London Shopkeeper had the best existence; his lordship, as usual, preferring the Savage.—My lord was extremely hospitable, and I saw both Dr. Johnson and him liking each other better every hour.

Dr. Johnson having retired for a short time, his lordship spoke of his conversation as I could have wished. Dr. Johnson had said, 'I have done greater feats with my knife than this;' though he had eaten a very hearty dinner.—My lord, who affects or believes he follows an abstemious system, seemed struck with

---

of Allworthy in *Tom Jones.* ⟨See W. L. Cross, *Fielding,* 1918, ii. 162.⟩ It was he of whom Pope wrote :—
   'Let low-born Allen, with an awkward Shame,
   Do good by stealth and blush to find it Fame.'
      Epilogue to the Satires, i. 135.
Low-born in later editions was changed to *humble.* Warburton not only married his niece, but, on his death, became in her right owner of Prior Park.

[1] Mark Pattison (*Satires of Pope,* p. 158) points out Warburton's 'want of penetration in that subject [metaphysics] which he considered more peculiarly his own'. Warburton said of 'the late Mr. [Andrew] Baxter', that 'a few pages of his reasoning have not only more sense and substance than all the elegant discourses of Dr. Berkley, but infinitely better entitle him to the character of a great genius.'

[2] It is of Warburton that Churchill wrote in *The Duellist* (iii. 197-202) :—
   'To prove his Faith, which all admit
   Is at least equal to his Wit,
   And make himself a Man of note,
   He in defence of Scripture wrote;
   So long he wrote, and long about it,
   That e'en Believers 'gan to doubt it.'
† ⟨See *ante,* v. 57, n. 3.⟩
§ ⟨Born 1763, died 1774. *The Family of Burnett of Leys,* New Spalding Club, 1901, p. 146.⟩
[3] I find, some doubt has been entertained concerning Dr. Johnson's meaning here. It is to be supposed that he meant, 'when a king shall again be entertained in Scotland'. BOSWELL. Ed. 2.
⟨One of the addresses with which the King was welcomed in 1617 was delivered by a boy (see App. D, p. 477.)⟩

Dr. Johnson's manner of living. I had a particular satisfaction in being under the roof of Monboddo, my lord being my father's old friend, and having been always very good to me. We were cordial together. He asked Dr. Johnson and me to stay all night. When I said we *must* be at Aberdeen, he replied, ' Well, I am like the Romans : I shall say to you, " Happy to come ;— happy to depart ! " ' He thanked Dr. Johnson for his visit.— *Johnson.* ' I little thought, when I had the honour to meet your lordship in London, that I should see you at Monboddo.' After dinner, as the ladies [1] were going away, Dr. Johnson would stand up. He insisted that politeness was of great consequence in society. ' It is, (said he,) fictitious benevolence [2]. It supplies the place of it amongst those who see each other only in publick, or but little. Depend upon it, the want of it never fails to produce something disagreeable to one or other. I have always applied to good breeding, what Addison in his *Cato* [3] says of honour :

" Honour's a sacred tie ; the law of Kings ;
The noble mind's distinguishing perfection,
That aids and strengthens Virtue where it meets her,
And imitates her actions where she is not." '

When he took up his large oak stick, he said, ' My lord, that's *Homerick* [4] ; ' thus pleasantly alluding to his lordship's favourite writer.

Gory, my lord's black servant, was sent as our guide, to conduct us to the high road. The circumstance of each of them having a black servant was another point of similarity between Johnson and Monboddo. I observed how curious it was to see

---

[1] ⟨Boswell writes in his MS. Journal : ' We found at Monboddo, Mrs. Farquharson, & her two daughters, & the Parish minister's widow.' Mrs. Farquharson was Lord Monboddo's mother-in-law.⟩

[2] In the *Rambler*, No. 98, entitled *The Necessity of Cultivating Politeness*, Johnson says :—' The universal axiom in which all complaisance is included, and from which flow all the formalities which custom has established in civilised nations, is, *That no man should give any preference to himself.*'

[3] Act ii. sc. 5, ed. 1713, sig. E 3.

[4] Perhaps he was referring to Polyphemus's club, which was
' Of height and bulk so vast,
The largest ship might claim it for a mast.'
        Pope's *Odyssey*, ix. 382.
Or to Agamemnon's sceptre :—
' Which never more shall Leaves or Blossoms bear.'
        Iliad, i. 310.

an African in the north of Scotland, with little or no difference of manners from those of the natives. Dr. Johnson laughed to see Gory and Joseph riding together most cordially. ' Those two fellows, (said he,) one from Africa, the other from Bohemia, seem quite at home.'—He was much pleased with Lord Monboddo to-day. He said, he would have pardoned him for a few paradoxes, when he found he had so much that was good : but that, from his appearance in London, he thought him all paradox ; which would not do. He observed, that his lordship had talked no paradoxes to-day. ' And as to the savage and the London shopkeeper, (said he,) I don't know but I might have taken the side of the savage equally, had any body else taken the side of the shopkeeper [1].'—He had said to my lord, in opposition to the value of the savage's courage, that it was owing to his limited power of thinking, and repeated Pope's verses, in which ' Macedonia's madman ' is introduced, and the conclusion is,

' Yet ne'er looks forward farther than his nose [2].'

I objected to the last phrase, as being low.—*Johnson.* ' Sir, it is intended to be low : it is satire. The expression is debased, to debase the character.'

When Gory was about to part from us, Dr. Johnson called to him, ' Mr. Gory, give me leave to ask you a question ! are you baptised ? ' Gory told him he was,—and confirmed by the Bishop of Durham. He then gave him a shilling.

We had tedious driving this afternoon, and were somewhat drowsy. Last night I was afraid Dr. Johnson was beginning to faint in his resolution ; for he said, ' If we must ride much, we shall not go ; and there's an end on't.'—To-day, when he talked

[1] ' We agreed pretty well, only we differed in adjusting the claims of merit between a Shopkeeper of London, and a Savage of the American wildernesses. Our opinions were, I think, maintained on both sides without full conviction ; Monbodo declared boldly for the Savage, and I perhaps for that reason sided with the Citizen.' *Letters*, No. 321.

[2] ' Heroes are much the same, the point's agreed,

From Macedonia's madman to the Swede ;
The whole strange purpose of their lives, to find,
Or make, an enemy of all mankind !
Not one looks backward, onward still he goes,
Yet ne'er looks forward farther than his nose.'
Essay on Man, iv. 219-24.

of *Sky* with spirit, I said, ' Why, sir, you seemed to me to despond yesterday. You are a delicate Londoner ;—you are a maccaroni [1] ; you can't ride.' *Johnson.* ' Sir, I shall ride better than you. I was only afraid I should not find a horse able to carry me.'—I hoped then there would be no fear of getting through our wild Tour.

We came to Aberdeen at half an hour past eleven. The New Inn †, we were told, was full. This was comfortless. The waiter, however, asked, if one of our names was Boswell, and brought me a letter left at the inn : it was from Mr. Thrale, enclosing one to Dr. Johnson [2]. Finding who I was, we were told they would contrive to lodge us by putting us for a night into a room with two beds. The waiter said to me in the broad strong Aberdeenshire dialect, ' I thought I knew you, by your likeness to your father.'— My father puts up at the New Inn, when on his circuit. Little was said to-night. I was to sleep in a little press-bed in Dr. Johnson's room. I had it wheeled out into the dining-room, and there I lay very well.

Sunday, 22d August.

I sent a message to Professor Thomas Gordon, who came and breakfasted with us. He had secured seats for us at the English chapel §. We found a respectable congregation, and an admirable organ, well played by Mr. Tait.

We walked down to the shore. Dr. Johnson laughed to hear that Cromwell's soldiers taught the Aberdeen people to make shoes and stockings, and to plant cabbages [3]. He asked, if

---

[1] *Maccaroni* is not in Johnson's *Dictionary*. Walpole (*Letters*, v. 450) on Feb. 6, 1764, mentions 'the Maccaroni Club, (which is composed of all the travelled young men who wear long curls and spying-glasses).' On the following Dec. 16 he says :—' The Maccaroni Club . . . has quite absorbed Arthur's, for you know old fools will hobble after young ones.' *Ibid.* vi. 157.

† ⟨Now destroyed. See F. Douglas, *E. Coast of Scotl.*, 1782, p. 90.⟩

[2] ' We came late to Aberdeen, where I found my dear Mistress's Letter, and learned that all our little people, were happily recovered of the Measles. Every part of your letter was pleasing.' *Letters*, No. 321.

§ ⟨See App. D, pp. 491 ff.⟩

[3] See *ante*, ii. 455. ' They taught us,' said one of the professors, ' to raise cabbage and make shoes. How they lived without shoes may yet be seen, but in the passage through villages, it seems to him that surveys their gardens, that when they had not cabbage they had nothing.' *Letters*, No. 321. Johnson in the same letter says that ' New

Sunday 22 August 1773

weaving the plaids [1] was ever a domestick art in the Highlands, like spinning or knitting. They could not inform him here. But he conjectured probably, that where people lived so remote from each other, it was likely to be a domestick art ; as we see it was among the ancients, from Penelope.—I was sensible to-day, to an extraordinary degree, of Dr. Johnson's excellent English pronunciation. I cannot account for its striking me more now than any other day : but it was as if new to me ; and I listened to every sentence which he spoke, as to a musical composition.—Professor Gordon gave him an account of the plan of education † in his college. Dr. Johnson said, it was similar to that at Oxford.—Waller the poet's great grandson § was studying here. Dr. Johnson wondered that a man should send his son so far off, when there were so many good schools in England [2]. He said, ' At a great school there is all the splendour and illumination of many minds ; the radiance of all is concentrated in each, or at least reflected upon each. But we must own that neither a dull boy, nor an idle boy, will do so well at a great school as at a private one. For at a great school there are always boys enough to do well easily, who are sufficient to keep up the credit of the school ; and after whipping being tried to no purpose, the dull or idle boys are left at the end of a class, having the appearance of going through the course, but learning nothing at all [3]. Such boys may do good at a private school, where constant attention is paid to them, and they are watched. So that the question of publick or private education is not properly a general one ; but whether one or the other is best for *my son*.'

Aberdeen is . . built almost wholly of that Granite which is used for the new pavement in London.'
[1] ' In Aberdeen I first saw the women in plaids.' *Letters*, No. 321.
† ⟨See App. D, p. 493.⟩
§ ⟨Great-great-grandson : see App. D, p. 493.⟩
[2] Seven years later Mackintosh, on entering King's College, found there the son of Johnson's old friend, ' the learned Dr. Charles Burney, finishing his term at Aberdeen.' Among his fellow-students were also some English Dissenters, among them Robert Hall. Mackintosh's *Life*, i. 10, 13. In Forbes's *Life of Beattie* (i. 294) is a letter by Beattie, dated Oct. 15, 1773, in which the English and Scotch Universities are compared. Colman, in his *Random Records*, ii. 85, gives an account of his life at Aberdeen as a student.
[3] Lord Bolingbroke (*Study Hist.*, iii.) in 1735 speaks of ' the little care that is taken in the training up our youth,' and adds, ' surely it is impossible to take less.' See *ante*, ii. 407, and iii. 12.

Sunday 22 *August* 1773   Aberdeen

We were told the present Mr. Waller † was a plain country gentleman ; and his son would be such another. I observed, a family could not expect a poet but in a hundred generations.— ' Nay, (said Dr. Johnson,) not one family in a hundred can expect a poet in a hundred generations.' He then repeated Dryden's celebrated lines §,

' Three poets in three distant ages born,' &c.

and a part of a Latin translation of it done at Oxford [1] : he did not then say by whom.

He received a card from Sir Alexander Gordon *, who had been his acquaintance twenty years ago in London, and who, ' if forgiven for not answering a line from him,' would come in the afternoon. Dr. Johnson rejoiced to hear of him, and begged he would come and dine with us. I was much pleased to see the kindness with which Dr. Johnson received his old friend Sir Alexander [2] ; a gentleman of good family, *Lismore*, but who had not the estate. The King's College here made him Professor of Medicine, which affords him a decent subsistence. He told us that the value of the stockings exported from Aberdeen was, in peace, a hundred thousand pounds ; and amounted, in time of war, to one hundred and seventy thousand pounds. Dr. Johnson asked, What made the difference ? Here we had a proof of the comparative sagacity of the two professors. Sir Alexander answered, ' Because there is more occasion for them in war.' Professor Thomas Gordon answered, ' Because the Germans, who are our great rivals in the manufacture of stockings, are other-

† ⟨See App. D, p. 493.⟩
§ ⟨' Under Mr. Milton's Picture, before his Paradise Lost.'⟩
[1]   *London,* 2*d May,* 1778.
Dr. Johnson acknowledged that he was himself the authour of the translation above alluded to, and dictated it to me as follows :
    Quos laudet vates Graius Romanus
        et Anglus
    Tres tria temporibus secla dedere
        suis.
    Sublime ingenium Graius ; Romanus habebat
    Carmen grande sonans ; Anglus utrumque tulit.

Nil majus Natura capit : clarare priores
Quæ potuere duos tertius unus habet. BOSWELL, ed. 1.
⟨Boswell suspected on 22 Aug. 1773 that Johnson was the translator. In his original Journal for that date he adds ' perhaps his own. I must ask.'⟩
* ⟨See App. D, p. 493.⟩
[2] ' We were on both sides glad of the interview, having not seen nor perhaps thought on one another for many years. But we had no emulation, nor had either of us risen to the other's envy, and our old kindness was easily renewed.' *Letters*, No. 321.

wise employed in time of war.—*Johnson.* ' Sir, you have given a very good solution.' †

At dinner, Dr. Johnson ate several plate-fulls of Scotch broth, with barley and peas in it, and seemed very fond of the dish. I said, ' You never ate it before.'—*Johnson.* ' No, sir ; but I don't care how soon I eat it again [1].'—My cousin, Miss Dallas, formerly of Inverness, was married to Mr. Riddoch, one of the ministers of the English chapel here §. He was ill, and confined to his room ; but she sent us a kind invitation to tea, which we all accepted. She was the same lively, sensible, cheerful woman, as ever. Dr. Johnson here threw out some jokes against Scotland. He said, ' You go first to Aberdeen ; then to *Enbru* (the Scottish pronunciation of Edinburgh) ; then to Newcastle, to be polished by the colliers ; then to York ; then to London.' And he laid hold of a little girl, Stuart Dallas *, niece to Mrs. Riddoch, and, representing himself as a giant, said, he would take her with him ! telling her, in a hollow voice, that he lived in a cave, and had a bed in the rock, and she should have a little bed cut opposite to it !

He thus treated the point, as to prescription of murder in Scotland [2]. ' A jury in England would make allowance for deficiencies of evidence, on account of lapse of time : but a general rule that a crime should not be punished, or tried for the purpose of punishment, after twenty years, is bad : It is cant to talk of the King's advocate delaying a prosecution from malice. How unlikely is it the King's advocate should have malice against persons who commit murder, or should even know them at all.—If the son of the murdered man should kill the murderer who got off merely by prescription, I would help him to make his escape ; though, were I upon his jury, I would not acquit him. I would not advise him to commit such an act. On the contrary, I would bid him submit to the determination of society, because a man is bound to submit to the inconveniences of it, as he enjoys the good : but the young man, though politically wrong, would not be morally wrong.

† ⟨The Peninsular War ruined the manufacture. W. Kennedy, *Hist. of Aberdeen*, 1818, ii. 199. Cf. *ante*, iii. 242.⟩

[1] Johnson wrote on Sept. 30 :— ' Barley broth is a constant dish, and is made well in every house. A stranger if he is prudent, will secure his share for it is not certain that he will be able to eat any thing else.' *Letters*, No. 329 (ed. Chapman), i. 371.

§, * ⟨See App. D, p. 494.⟩

[2] See *ante*, v. 24.

He would have to say, " Here I am amongst barbarians, who not only refuse to do justice, but encourage the greatest of all crimes. I am therefore in a state of nature : for, so far as there is no law, it is a state of nature : and consequently, upon the eternal and immutable law of justice, which requires that he who sheds man's blood should have his blood shed [1], I will stab the murderer of my father." '

We went to our inn, and sat quietly. Dr. Johnson borrowed, at Mr. Riddoch's, a volume of *Massillon's* Discourses on the Psalms : but I found he read little in it. Ogden too he sometimes took up, and glanced at ; but threw it down again. I then entered upon religious conversation. Never did I see him in a better frame : calm, gentle, wise, holy.—I said, ' Would not the same objection hold against the Trinity as against Transubstantiation ? '—' Yes, (said he,) if you take three and one in the same sense. If you do so, to be sure you cannot believe it : but the three persons in the Godhead are Three in one sense, and One in another. We cannot tell how ; and that is the mystery ! '

I spoke of the satisfaction of Christ. He said his notion was, that it did not atone for the sins of the world ; but, by satisfying divine justice, by shewing that no less than the Son of God suffered for sin, it shewed to men and innumerable created beings, the heinousness of it, and therefore rendered it unnecessary for divine vengeance to be exercised against sinners, as it otherwise must have been ; that in this way it might operate even in favour of those who had never heard of it : as to those who did hear of it, the effect it should produce would be repentance and piety, by impressing upon the mind a just notion of sin : that original sin was the propensity to evil, which no doubt was occasioned by the fall. He presented this solemn subject in a new light to me [2], and rendered much more rational and clear the doctrine of what our Saviour has done for us ;—as it removed the notion of imputed righteousness in[3] co-operating ; whereas by

---

[1] *Genesis*, ix. 6.

[2] My worthy, intelligent, and candid friend, Dr. Kippis, informs me, that several divines have thus explained the mediation of our Saviour. What Dr. Johnson now delivered, was but a temporary opinion ; for he afterwards was fully convinced of the *propitiatory sacrifice*, as I shall shew at large in my future work, THE LIFE OF SAMUEL JOHNSON, L.L.D. BOSWELL, ed. 1. For Johnson on the propitiatory sacrifice, see *ante*, iv. 124.

[3] ⟨The text is defective here : Boswell's MS. reads in addition : ' the usual sense, and the difficulty of our righteousness '.⟩

this view, Christ has done all already that he had to do, or is ever to do, for mankind, by making his great satisfaction; the consequences of which will affect each individual according to the particular conduct of each. I would illustrate this by saying, that Christ's satisfaction resembles a sun placed to shew light to men, so that it depends upon themselves whether they will walk the right way or not, which they could not have done without that sun, '*the sun of righteousness*[1].' There is, however, more in it than merely giving light [a],—*a light to lighten the Gentiles*[2]: for we are told, there is *healing under his wings*[3]. Dr. Johnson said to me, 'Richard Baxter commends a treatise by Grotius, *De Satisfactione Christi* †. I have never read it: but I intend to read it; and you may read it.' I remarked, upon the principle now laid down, we might explain the difficult and seemingly hard text, 'They that believe shall be saved; and they that believe not shall be damned[4]:' They that believe shall have such an impression made upon their minds, as will make them act so that they may be accepted by GOD.

We talked of one of our friends[5] taking ill, for a length of time, a hasty expression of Dr. Johnson's to him, on his attempting to prosecute a subject that had a reference to religion, beyond the bounds within which the Doctor thought such topicks should be confined in a mixed company.—*Johnson.* 'What is to become of society, if a friendship of twenty years is to be broken off for such a cause?' As Bacon says,

'Who then to frail mortality shall trust,
But limns the water, or but writes in dust[6].'

I said, he should write expressly in support of Christianity; for that, although a reverence for it shines through his works in several places, that is not enough. 'You know, (said I,) what Grotius has done, and what Addison has done[7].—You[b] should do also.' He replied, 'I hope I shall.'

[a] light, 2: light 1: light. 3.   [b] done.—You 1, 2, 3: *read* done, you
(*as in orig. Journal*).

[1] *Malachi*, iv. 2. [2] *St. Luke*, ii. 32.
[3] 'Healing *in* his wings,' *Malachi*, iv. 2.
† ⟨See App. D, p. 494.⟩
[4] 'He that believeth and is baptised shall be saved; but he that believeth not shall be damned.' *St. Mark*, xvi. 16.
[5] ⟨Langton, according to Boswell's Journal, ed. F. A. Pottle and C. Bennett, p. 64. The incident occurred on 7 May 1773. See *ante*, ii. 254, 265, 282, 292.⟩
[6] ⟨First printed and ascribed to Bacon in Farnaby, *Flor. Epigr. Græc.*, 1629, p. 10. The quotation was almost certainly made by Johnson.⟩. See Spedding's *Bacon*, vii. 271.
[7] ⟨In his *Evidences of the Christian*

Monday, 23d August.

Principal Campbell, Sir Alexander Gordon, Professor Gordon, and Professor Ross, visited us in the morning, as did Dr. Gerard, who had come six miles from the country on purpose. We went and saw the Marischal College [1], and at one o'clock we waited on the magistrates in the town-hall, as they had invited us in order to present Dr. Johnson with the freedom of the town, which Provost Jopp did with a very good grace. Dr. Johnson was much pleased with this mark of attention, and received it very politely. There was a pretty numerous company assembled. It was striking to hear all of them drinking ' Dr. Johnson ! Dr. Johnson ! ' in the town-hall of Aberdeen, and then to see him with his burgess-ticket, or diploma [2], in his hat,

Religion, first published in *Works*, 1721.⟩ ' Addison now returned to his vocation, and began to plan literary occupations for his future life. He purposed a tragedy on the death of Socrates. . . . He engaged in a nobler work, a defence of the Christian religion, of which part was published after his death.' Johnson's *Life of Addison*, 87, 88.

[1] Dr. Beattie was so kindly entertained in England, that he had not yet returned home. BOSWELL, ed. 1. Beattie was staying in London till his pension got settled. Early in July he had been told that he was to have a pension of £200 a year (*ante*, ii. 264, note 2). It was not till Aug. 20 that it was conferred. On July 9, he, in company with Sir Joshua Reynolds, received the degree of LL.D. at Oxford. On Aug. 24, he had a long interview with the King: 'He asked,' Beattie records, ' whether we had any good preachers at Aberdeen ? I said, " yes," and named Campbell and Gerard, with whose names, however, I did not find that he was acquainted.' It was this same summer that Reynolds painted him in the ' allegorical picture, representing the triumph of truth over scepticism and infidelity ' (*post*, v. 273, n. 4). Forbes's *Beattie*, i. 265, 272, 290. ⟨The picture is now in the Court Room at Marischal College.⟩

[2] Dr. Johnson's burgess-ticket was in these words :
' Aberdoniæ, vigesimo tertio die mensis Augusti, anno Domini millesimo septingentesimo septuagesimo tertio, in presentia honorabilium virorum, Jacobi Jopp, armigeri, præpositi, Adami Duff, Gulielmi Young, Georgii Marr, et Gulielmi Forbes, Balivorum, Gulielmi Rainie Decani guildæ, et Joannis Nicoll Thesaurarii dicti burgi.
' Quo die vir generosus et doctrina clarus, Samuel Johnson, L.L.D. receptus et admissus fuit in municipes et fratres guildæ præfati burgi de Aberdeen. In deditissimi amoris et affectus ac eximiæ observantiæ tesseram, quibus dicti Magistratus eum amplectuntur. Extractum per me, ALEX. CARNEGIE.' BOSWELL. ⟨Boswell entered this in his original Jrnl. under date 12 Sept. 1773.⟩ ' I was presented with the freedom of the city, not in a gold box but in good Latin. Let me pay Scotland one just praise. There was no officer gaping for a fee ; this could have been said of no city on the English side of the Tweed.' *Letters*, No. 322. Baretti, in a MS. note on this passage, says :—' Throughout England nothing is done for nothing. Stop a

which he wore as he walked along the street, according to the usual custom.—It gave me great satisfaction to observe the regard, and indeed fondness too, which every body here had for my father.

While Sir Alexander Gordon conducted Dr. Johnson to old Aberdeen, Professor Gordon and I called on Mr. Riddoch, whom I found to be a grave worthy clergyman. He observed, that, whatever might be said of Dr. Johnson while he was alive, he would, after he was dead, be looked upon by the world with regard and astonishment, on account of his Dictionary.

Professor Gordon and I walked over to the Old College, which Dr. Johnson had seen by this time. I stepped into the chapel, and looked at the tomb of the founder, Archbishop Elphinston [1], of whom I shall have occasion to write in my History of James IV. of Scotland, the patron of my family [2].

moment to look at the rusticks mowing a field, and they will presently quit their work to come to you, and ask something to drink.' Aberdeen conferred its freedom so liberally about this time that it is surprising that Boswell was passed over. George Colman the younger, when a youth of eighteen, was sent to King's College. He says in his worthless *Random Records*, ii. 99 :—' I had scarcely been a week in Old Aberdeen, when the Lord Provost of the New Town invited me to drink wine with him, one evening, in the Town Hall ; there I found a numerous company assembled. . . . The object of this meeting was soon declared to me by the Lord Provost, who drank my health, and presented me with the Freedom of the City.' Two of his English fellow-students, of a little older standing, had, he said, received the same honour. His statement seemed to me incredible ; but by the politeness of the Town-clerk, Mr. W. Gordon, I have found out that in the main it is correct. Colman, with one of the two, was admitted as an Honorary Burgess on Oct. 8, 1781, being described as *vir generosus* ; the other had been admitted earlier. ⟨Lord Auchinleck was made an honorary

burgess of the Old Town in 1759. See A. M. Munro, *Records of Old Aberdeen*, 1899, i, p. 287.⟩

[1] ⟨William Elphinstone, Bishop of Aberdeen, 1431–1514. He was buried in the college chapel beneath the first step of the high altar. For the university, of which Hector Boece (*ante*, iv. 265, n. 2) was the first Principal, see Rashdall, *Universities of Europe in the Middle Ages*, ed. Powicke and Emden, ii. 318–20.⟩

[2] ⟨Boswell mentions in the *Life* and *Tour* the following other works as projected or in course of compilation by him :—

1. A complete edition of Johnson's poems. *Ante*, i. 16 n. and iv. 375 n. 2.
2. A work maintaining the merits of Addison's poetry. *Ante*, i. 225 n. 2.
3. A dictionary of words peculiar to Scotland. *Ante*, ii. 91.
4. A work upon the antiquities of Scotland. *Ib.* p. 92.
5. A history of Sweden. *Ib.* p. 156.
6. A life of Ruddiman. *Ib.* p. 216.
7. An account of a tour to the Isle of Man. *Ante*, iii. 80.
8. An edition of Walton's *Lives*. *Ib.* p. 107.
9. A history of the Civil War in Great Britain in 1745 and 1746. *Ib.* p. 162. See also *ib.* p. 414.

Monday 23 August 1773   Aberdeen

We dined at Sir Alexander Gordon's. The Provost, Professor Ross, Professor Dunbar, Professor Thomas Gordon, were there. After dinner came in Dr. Gerard, Professor Leslie [1], Professor Macleod. We had had [a] little or no conversation in the morning; now we were but barren. The professors seemed afraid to speak [2].

Dr. Gerard told us that an eminent printer [3] was very intimate with Warburton.—*Johnson.* ' Why, sir, he has printed some of his works, and perhaps bought the property of some of them. The intimacy is such as one of the professors here may have with one of the carpenters who is repairing the college.'— ' But, (said Gerard,) I saw a letter from him to this printer, in which he says, that the one half of the clergy of the church of Scotland are fanaticks, and the other half infidels.'—*Johnson.* ' Warburton has accustomed himself to write letters just as he speaks, without thinking any more of what he throws out [4].

[a] had had 1 (*and orig. Jrnl.*): had 2, 3.

10. An edition of the autobiography of Sir Robert Sibbald. *Ib.* pp. 227 and 515.
11. An account of his own travels upon the continent. *Ib.* p. 300.
12. A collection of feudal tenures and charters of Scotland. *Ib.* p. 414, n. 3. See also ii. 202.
13. Memoirs of Hume. *Ante*, v. 30.
14. A poetical letter to Johnson on his return from Scotland. *Post*, v. 139.
For a number of other works projected by Boswell, see F. A. Pottle, *Literary Career of Boswell*, pp. 301–9.⟩
Thomas Boswell received from James IV. the estate of Auchinleck. *Ante*, ii. 413. See *post*, v. 379.

[1] Mackintosh says, *Life*, i. 9 :—' In October, 1780, I was admitted into the Greek class, then taught by Mr. Leslie, who did not aspire beyond teaching us the first rudiments of the language.'

[2] ' Boswell was very angry that the Aberdeen professors would not talk.' *Letters*, No. 322. Dr. Robertson and Dr. Blair, whom Boswell, five years earlier, invited to meet Johnson at supper, ' with an excess of prudence . . . hardly opened their lips ' (*ante*, ii. 63). At Glasgow the professors did not dare to talk much (*post*, v. 371). On another occasion when Johnson came in, the company ' were all as quiet as a school upon the entrance of the head-master.' *Ante*, iii. 332. ⟨For the Professors see App. D, p. 495.⟩

[3] ⟨Strahan's name is given in Boswell's original Journal. Beattie writes in his Journal, 4 June 1773 : ' On my way home I called for Mr. Strachan. He entertained me with a large parcel of Bishop Warburton's letters which he put into my hand. . . . There are excellent strokes in some of them. Speaking of the Church of Scotland he says : " It is just now divided into two parties, one of which, in the extreme, is made up of sober pagans, and the other of wild fanatics ".' Margaret Forbes, *Beattie and his friends*, 1904, p. 80. See also Hume's *Letters*, 1932, ii. 244. Strahan printed for Andrew Millar Warburton's Fast-day sermon, 1756 (*teste* R. A. Austen-Leigh), and he may have printed other works of his.⟩

[4] An instance of this is given in Johnson's *Pope*, 186.

When I read Warburton first, and observed his force, and his contempt of mankind, I thought he had driven the world before him; but I soon found that was not the case; for Warburton, by extending his abuse, rendered it ineffectual [1].'

He told me, when we were by ourselves, that he thought it very wrong in the printer, to shew Warburton's letter, as it was raising a body of enemies against him. He thought it foolish in Warburton to write so to the printer; and added, ' Sir, the worst way of being intimate, is by scribbling.' He called Warburton's ' Doctrine of Grace ' [2] a poor performance, and so he said was Wesley's Answer [3]. ' Warburton, he observed, had laid himself very open. In particular, he was weak enough to say, that, in some disorders of the imagination, people had spoken with tongues, had spoken languages which they never knew before; a thing as absurd as to say, that, in some disorders of the imagination, people had been known to fly.'

I talked of the difference of genius, to try if I could engage Gerard in a disquisition with Dr. Johnson †; but I did not succeed. I mentioned, as a curious fact, that Locke had written verses.—*Johnson.* ' I know of none, sir, but a kind of exercise prefixed to Dr. Sydenham's Works [4], in which he has some conceits about the dropsy, in which water and burning are united and how Dr. Sydenham removed fire by drawing off water, contrary to the usual practice, which is to extinguish fire by

---

[1] ' Goldsmith ridiculously asserted that Warburton was a weak writer.... "Warburton (said Johnson) *may* be absurd; but he will *never* be weak; he flounders well." ' Stockdale's *Memoirs*, ii. 64. See Appendix A.

[2] *The Doctrine of Grace; or, The Office and Operations of the Holy Spirit vindicated from the Insults of Infidelity, and the Abuses of Fanaticism*, 1762.

[3] *A Letter to the Bishop of Gloucester, occasioned by his Tract on the Office and Operations of the Holy Spirit*, by John Wesley, 1763.

† ⟨See App. D, pp. 495-6.⟩

[4] Malone records :—' I could not find from Mr. Walpole that his father read any other book but Sydenham in his retirement.' To his admiration of Sydenham his death was attributed; for it led him to treat himself wrongly when he was suffering from the stone. Prior's *Malone*, p. 387. Johnson wrote a *Life of Sydenham* ⟨*ante,* i. 153⟩. In it he ridicules the notion that ' a man, eminent for integrity, practised medicine by chance, and grew wise only by murder.' *Works,* vi. 409.

bringing water upon it.—I am not sure that there is a word of all this ; but it is such kind of talk [1].'

[1] All this, as Dr. Johnson suspected at the time, was the immediate invention of his own lively imagination ; for there is not one word of it in Mr. Locke's complimentary performance. My readers will, I have no doubt, like to be satisfied, by comparing them ; and, at any rate, it may entertain them to read verses composed by our great metaphysician, when a Bachelor in Physick.

AUCTORI, IN TRACTATUM EJUS DE FEBRIBUS.

Febriles æstus, victumque ardoribus
   orbem
  Flevit, non tantis par Medicina
   malis.
Nam post mille artes, medicæ tenta-
   mina curæ,
  Ardet adhuc Febris ; nec velit arte
   regi.
Præda sumus flammis ; solum hoc
   speramus ab igne,
  Ut restet paucus, quem capit urna,
   cinis.
Dum quærit medicus febris caussam-
   que, modumque,
  Flammarum & tenebras, & sine
   luce faces ;
Quas tractat patitur flammas, & febre
   calescens,
  Corruit ipse suis victima rapta
   focis.
Qui tardos potuit morbos, artusque
   trementes,
  Sistere, febrili se videt igne rapi.
Sic faber exesos fulsit tibicine
   muros ;
  Dum trahit antiquas lenta ruina
   domos.
Sed si flamma vorax miseras in-
   cenderit ædes,
  Unica flagrantes tunc sepelire
   salus.
Fit fuga, tectonicas nemo tunc in-
   vocat artes ;

Cum perit artificis non minus usta
   domus.
Se tandem SYDENHAM *febrisque*
   Scholæque furori
Opponens, morbi quærit, & artis
   opem.
Non temere incusat tectæ putredinis [a]
   ignes ;
  Nec fictus, febres qui fovet, humor
   erit.
Non bilem ille movet, nulla hic pitu-
   ita ; Salutis
  Quæ spes, si fallax ardeat intus
   aqua ?
Nec doctas magno rixas ostentat
   hiatu,
  Quîs ipsis major febribus ardor
   inest.
Innocuas placide corpus jubet urere
   flammas,
  Et justo rapidos temperat igne
   focos.
Quid febrim exstinguat, varius quid
   postulat usus,
  Solari ægrotos, qua potes arte,
   docet.
Hactenus ipsa suum timuit Natura
   calorem,
  Dum sæpe incerto, quo calet, igne
   perit :
Dum reparat tacitos male provida
   sanguinis ignes,
  Prælusit busto, fit calor iste rogus.
Jam secura suas foveant præcordia
   flammas,
  Quem Natura negat, dat Medicina
   modum.
Nec solum faciles compescit san-
   guinis æstus,
  Dum dubia est inter spemque
   metumque salus ;
Sed fatale malum domuit, quodque
   astra malignum
  Credimus, iratam vel genuisse
   Stygem.
Extorsit Lachesi *cultros, Pestique*
   venenum

[a] *putredinis* 1 (and Locke): *putedinis* 2, 3.

Aberdeen *Monday 23 August 1773* 95

We spoke of Fingal [1]. Dr. Johnson said calmly, ' If the poems were really translated, they were certainly first written down. Let Mr. Macpherson deposite the manuscript in one of the colleges at Aberdeen, where there are people who can judge ; and, if the professors certify the authenticity, then there will be an end of the controversy. If he does not take this obvious and easy method, he gives the best reason to doubt ; considering too, how much is against it *à priori*.'

We sauntered after dinner in Sir Alexander's garden †, and saw his little grotto, which is hung with pieces of poetry written in a fair hand. It was agreeable to observe the contentment and kindness of this quiet, benevolent man. Professor Macleod § was brother to Macleod of Talisker, and brother-in-law to the Laird of Col. He gave me a letter to young Col. I was weary of this day, and began to think wishfully of being again in motion. I was uneasy to think myself too fastidious, whilst I fancied Dr. Johnson quite satisfied. But he owned to me that he was fatigued and teased by Sir Alexander's doing too much to entertain him. I said, it was all kindness.—*Johnson*. ' True, sir ; but sensation is sensation.'—*Boswell*. ' It is so : we feel pain equally from the surgeon's probe, as from the sword of the foe.'

We visited two booksellers' shops, and could not find Arthur Johnston's Poems [2]. We went and sat near an hour at Mr. Riddoch's. He could not tell distinctly how much education at the

Abstulit, & tantos non sinit esse metus.
Quis tandem arte nova domitam mitescere Pestem
Credat, & antiquas ponere posse minas ?
Post tot mille neces, cumulataque funera busto,
Victa jacet, parvo vulnere, dira Lues.
Ætheriæ quanquam spargunt contagia flammæ,
Quicquid inest istis ignibus, ignis erit.
Delapsæ cœlo flammæ licet acrius urant,
Has gelida exstingui non nisi morte putas ?

Tu meliora paras victrix Medicina ; tuusque,
Pestis quæ superat cuncta, triumphus erit [a].
Vive liber, victis febrilibus ignibus ; unus
Te simul & mundum qui manet, ignis erit.
J. LOCK, A.M. Ex Aede Christi, Oxon. BOSWELL, ed. I. ⟨See App. D, p. 496.⟩

[1] See *ante*, ii. 126, 292, 298, ⟨510 ff.⟩
†, § ⟨See App. D, pp. 493-4, 496.⟩
[2] ' One of its ornaments [i.e. of Marischal College] is the picture of Arthur Johnston, who was principal of the college, and who holds among the Latin poets of Scotland the next

[a] *erit* 1 (and Locke) : *eris* 2, 3.

college here costs [1], which disgusted Dr. Johnson. I had pledged myself that we should go to the inn, and not stay supper. They pressed us, but he was resolute. I saw Mr. Riddoch did not please him. He said to me, afterwards, ' Sir, he has no vigour in his talk.' But my friend should have considered that he himself was not in good humour; so that it was not easy to talk to his satisfaction.—We sat contentedly at our inn. He then became merry, and observed how little we had either heard or said at Aberdeen: That the Aberdonians had not started a single *mawkin* (the Scottish word for hare) for us to pursue [2].

Tuesday, 24th August.

We set out about eight in the morning, and breakfasted at Ellon. The landlady said to me, ' Is not this the great Doctor that is going about through the country ? '—I said, ' Yes.'—' Ay, (said she,) we heard of him. I made an errand into the room on purpose to see him. There's something great in his appearance: it is a pleasure to have such a man in one's house; a man who does so much good. If I had thought of it, I would have shewn him a child of mine, who has had a lump on his throat for some time.'—' But, (said I,) he is not a doctor of physick.'— ' Is he an oculist ? ' said the landlord.—' No, (said I,) he is only a very learned man.'—*Landlord.* ' They say he is the greatest man in England, except Lord Mansfield [3].'—Dr. Johnson was highly entertained with this, and I do think he was pleased too.

place to the elegant Buchanan.' Johnson's *Western Isl.*, 1924, p. 14. Pope, attacking Benson, who ' endeavoured to raise himself to Fame by erecting monuments ' to Milton, and by printing editions of Johnston's version of the *Psalms*, introduces the Scotch Poet in the *Dunciad* :—
  ' On two unequal crutches propt he came,
  Milton's on this, on that one Johnston's name.'
      Dunciad, bk. iv. l. 111.
Johnson wrote to Boswell for a copy of Johnston's *Poemata omnia* (*ante*, iii. 104) and for his likeness (*ante*, iv. 265).

[1] ' Education is here of the same price as at St. Andrews only the session is but from the first of November to the first of April ' [five months instead of seven]. *Letters*, No. 321. In his *Western Isl.*, p. 15, Johnson by mistake gives eight months to the St. Andrews session. On p. 7 he gives it rightly as seven.

[2] Beattie, as an Aberdeen professor, was grieved at this saying when he read the book. ' Why is it recorded ? ' he asked. ' For no reason that I can imagine, unless it be in order to return evil for good.' Forbes's *Beattie*, ii. 178.

[3] See *ante*, ii. 336, and iii. 209.

Slains Castle   *Tuesday 24 August* 1773

He said, ' I like the exception : to have called me the greatest man in England, would have been an unmeaning compliment : but the exception marked that the praise was in earnest ; and, in *Scotland*, the exception must be *Lord Mansfield*, or—*Sir John Pringle* [1].'

He told me a good story of Dr. Goldsmith. Graham, who wrote ' Telemachus, a Masque [2] ', was sitting one night with him and Dr. Johnson, and was half drunk. He rattled away to Dr. Johnson : ' You are a clever fellow, to be sure ; but you cannot write an essay like Addison, or verses like the *Rape of the Lock.*' At last he said [3], ' *Doctor*, I should be happy to see you at Eaton [4].'—' I shall be glad to wait on you,' answered Goldsmith.—' No, (said Graham,) 'tis not you I mean, Dr. *Minor;* 'tis Doctor *Major*, there.'—Goldsmith was excessively hurt by this. He afterwards spoke of it himself. ' Graham, (said he,) is a fellow to make one commit suicide.'

We had received a polite invitation to Slains castle. We arrived there just at three o'clock, as the bell for dinner was ringing. Though, from its being just on the North-east Ocean, no trees will grow here, Lord Errol has done all that can be done. He has cultivated his fields so as to bear rich crops of every kind, and he has made an excellent kitchen-garden, with a hot-house. I had never seen any of the family : but there had been a card of invitation written by the honourable Charles Boyd, the earl's brother [5]. We were conducted into the house,

[1] See *ante*, iii. 65, and *post*, v. 376.
[2] See *ante*, i. 411. Johnson, no doubt, was reminded of this story by his desire to get this book. Later on (*ante*, iii. 104) he asked Boswell ' to be vigilant and get him Graham's " Telemachus." '
[3] I am sure I have related this story exactly as Dr. Johnson told it to me ; but a friend who has often heard him tell it, informs me that he usually introduced a circumstance which ought not to be omitted. ' At last, sir, Graham, having now got to about the pitch of looking at one man, and talking to another, said Doctor, &c.' ' What effect (Dr. Johnson used to add) this had on Goldsmith, who was as irascible as a hornet, may be easily conceived.' BOSWELL. Ed. 2.
[4] Graham was an assistant at Eton College.
[5] It was to Johnson that the invitation was due. ' When I was at the English Church in Aberdeen, I happened to be espied by Lady Di. Middleton whom I had sometime seen in London. She told what she had seen to Mr. Boyd, Lord Errol's Brother, who wrote us an invitation to Lord Errol's house.' *Letters*, No. 322. ⟨For the Hon. Charles Boyd, see *post*, App. D, p. 497.⟩

and at the dining-room door were met by that gentleman, whom both of us at first took to be Lord Errol; but he soon corrected our mistake. My lord was gone to dine in the neighbourhood, at an entertainment given by Mr. Irvine of Drum †. Lady Errol received us politely, and was very attentive to us during the time of dinner. There was nobody at table but her ladyship, Mr. Boyd, and some of the children, their governour and governess. Mr. Boyd put Dr. Johnson in mind of having dined with him at Cumming the Quaker's [1], along with a Mr. Hall and Miss Williams [2] : this was a bond of connection between them. For me, Mr. Boyd's acquaintance with my father was enough. After dinner, Lady Errol favoured us with a sight of her young family, whom she made stand up in a row. There were six daughters and two sons. It was a very pleasing sight.

Dr. Johnson proposed our setting out. Mr. Boyd said, he hoped we would stay all night; his brother would be at home in the evening, and would be very sorry if he missed us. Mr. Boyd was called out of the room. I was very desirous to stay in so comfortable a house, and I wished to see Lord Errol.

---

† ⟨See App. D, p. 496.⟩

[1] 'In 1745, my friend, Tom Cumming, the Quaker, said, he would not fight, but he would drive an ammunition cart.' *Ante*, iv. 212. Smollett (*Continuation of Compl. Hist. of Eng.*, 1760, ii. 271 ff.) describes how, in 1758, the conquest of Senegal was due to this 'sensible Quaker,' 'this honest Quaker,' as he calls him, who not only conceived the project, but 'was concerned as a principal director and promoter of the expedition.... If it was the first military scheme of any Quaker, let it be remembered it was also the first successful expedition of this war, and one of the first that was ever carried on according to the pacific system of the Quakers, without the loss of a drop of blood on either side.' If there was no bloodshed, it was by good luck, for 'a regular engagement was warmly maintained on both sides.' It was a Quaker, then, who led the van in the long line of conquests which have made Chatham's name so famous. ⟨See also *Annual Register*, 1758, p. 75, and E. C. Martin, *British West African Settlements*, 1927, p. 57.⟩ Mrs. Piozzi, writing of newspaper abuse, says (*Anecd.*, p. 185 : John. Misc. i. 274) that Johnson once told her 'that Cummyns the famous Quaker, whose friendship he valued very highly, fell a sacrifice to their insults, having declared on his deathbed to Dr. Johnson, that the pain of an anonymous letter, written in some of the common prints of the day, fastened on his heart, and threw him into the slow fever of which he died.' Mr. Seward records (*Anec*. iii. 384) :— 'Mr. Cummins, the celebrated American Quaker, said of Mr. Pitt (Lord Chatham) :—" The first time I come to Mr. Pitt upon any business, I find him extremely ignorant; the second time I come to him, I find him completely informed upon it."' ⟨See App. D, pp. 496–7, for Tom Cumming.⟩

[2] See *ante*, i. 232. ⟨Mr. Hall was perhaps John Wesley's brother-in-law. *Ante*, iv. 92, n. 3. He died in 1776.⟩

Dr. Johnson, however, was right in resolving to go, if we were not asked again, as it is best to err on the safe side in such cases, and to be sure that one is quite welcome. To my great joy, when Mr. Boyd returned, he told Dr. Johnson that it was Lady Errol who had called him out, and said that she would never let Dr. Johnson into the house again, if he went away that night ; and that she had ordered the coach, to carry us to view a great curiosity on the coast, after which we should see the house. We cheerfully agreed.

Mr. Boyd was engaged, in 1745-6, on the same side with many unfortunate mistaken noblemen and gentlemen. He escaped, and lay concealed for a year in the island of Arran, the ancient territory of the Boyds. He then went to France, and was about twenty years on the continent. He married a French Lady, and now lived very comfortably at Aberdeen, and was much at Slains castle. He entertained us with great civility. He had a pompousness or formal plenitude in his conversation, which I did not dislike. Dr. Johnson said, ' there was too much elaboration in his talk.' It gave me pleasure to see him, a steady branch of the family, setting forth all its advantages with much zeal. He told us that Lady Errol was one of the most pious and sensible women in the island ; had a good head, and as good a heart. He said, she did. not use force or fear in educating her children.—*Johnson*. ' Sir, she is wrong [1] ; I would rather have the rod to be the general terror to all, to make them learn, than tell a child, if you do thus or thus, you will be more esteemed than your brothers or sisters. The rod produces an effect which terminates in itself. A child is afraid of being whipped, and gets his task, and there's an end on't ; whereas, by exciting emulation, and comparisons of superiority, you lay the foundation of lasting mischief ; you make brothers and sisters hate each other [2].'

During Mr. Boyd's stay in Arran, he had found a chest of medical books, left by a surgeon there, and had read them till he acquired some skill in physick, in consequence of which he is often consulted by the poor. There were several here waiting for him as patients. We walked round the house till stopped by a cut made by the influx of the sea. The house is built quite

[1] See *ante*, i. 46.
[2] 〈' Men have a foolish manner . . . in creating and breeding an Emulation between Brothers, during Childhood, which many times sorteth to Discord, when they are Men ; And disturbeth Families.' Bacon, *Essays, Of Parents and Children.*〉

upon the shore; the windows look upon the main ocean, and the King of Denmark is Lord Errol's nearest neighbour on the north-east [1].

We got immediately into the coach, and drove to *Dunbui*, a rock near the shore, quite covered with sea-fowls; then to a circular bason of large extent, surrounded with tremendous rocks. On the quarter next the sea, there is a high arch in the rock, which the force of the tempest has driven out. This place is called *Buchan's Buller*, or the *Buller* of *Buchan*, and the country people call it the *Pot*. Mr. Boyd said it was so called from the French *Bouloir*. It may be more simply traced from *Boiler* in our own language [2]. We walked round this monstrous cauldron. In some places, the rock is very narrow; and on each side there is a sea deep enough for a man of war to ride in; so that it is somewhat horrid to move along. However, there is earth and grass upon the rock, and a kind of road marked out by the print of feet; so that one makes it out pretty safely: yet it alarmed me to see Dr. Johnson striding irregularly along [3]. He insisted on taking a boat, and sailing into the Pot. We did so. He was stout, and wonderfully alert. The Buchanmen all shewing their teeth, and speaking with that strange sharp accent which distinguishes them, was to me a matter of curiosity. He was not sensible of the difference of pronunciation in the South and North of Scotland, which I wondered at.

As the entry into the *Buller* is so narrow that oars cannot be used as you go in, the method taken is, to row very hard when you come near it, and give the boat such a rapidity of motion that it glides in. Dr. Johnson observed what an effect this scene would have had, were we entering into an unknown place. There are caves of considerable depth; I think, one on each side. The boatmen had never entered either of them far enough to know the size. Mr. Boyd told us that it is customary for the

---

[1] 'From the windows the eye wanders over the sea that separates Scotland from Norway, and when the winds beat with violence must enjoy all the terrifick grandeur of the tempestuous ocean. I would not for my amusement wish for a storm; but as storms, whether wished or not, will sometimes happen, I may say, without violation of humanity, that I should willingly look out upon them from Slanes Castle.' *Western Isl.*, p. 16.

[2] ⟨See Sir W. A. Craigie's *Dict. of the Older Scottish Tongue*, s.v. *Buller*.⟩

[3] ⟨'The edge of the Buller is not wide, and to those that walk round, appears very narrow. . . . We however went round, and were glad when the circuit was completed.' *Western Isl.*, p. 17.⟩

Slains Castle   *Tuesday 24 August 1773*

company at Peterhead-well, to make parties, and come and dine in one of the caves here.

He told us, that, as Slains is at a considerable distance from Aberdeen, Lord Errol, who has a very large family, resolved to have a surgeon of his own. With this view he educated one of his tenants'[a] sons, who is now settled in a very neat house and farm just by, which we saw from the road. By the salary which the earl allows him, and the practice which he has had, he is in very easy circumstances. He had kept an exact account of all that had been laid out on his education, and he came to his lordship one day, and told him that he had arrived at a much higher situation than ever he expected ; that he was now able to repay what his lordship had advanced, and begged he would accept of it. The earl was pleased with the generous gratitude and genteel offer of the man ; but refused it.—Mr. Boyd also told us, Cumming the Quaker first began to distinguish himself, by writing against Dr. Leechman on Prayer [1], to prove it unnecessary, as GOD knows best what should be, and will order it without our asking :—the old hackneyed objection.

When we returned to the house we found coffee and tea in the drawing-room. Lady Errol was not there, being, as I supposed, engaged with her young family. There is a bow-window fronting the sea. Dr. Johnson repeated the ode, *Jam satis terris* [2], while Mr. Boyd was with his patients. He spoke well in favour of entails [3], to preserve lines of men whom mankind are accustomed to reverence. His opinion was,[b] that so much land should be entailed as that families should never fall into contempt, and as much left free as to give them all the advantages of property in case of any emergency. ' If (said he,) the nobility are suffered to sink into indigence [4], they of course become corrupt ; they are ready to do whatever the king chooses ; therefore it is fit they should be kept from becoming poor, unless it is fixed that when they fall below a certain

[a] tenants' 1, 2 : tenant's 3.   [b] *comma omitted* 3.

[1] ⟨See App. D, p. 497.⟩
[2] Horace. *Odes*, i. 2.
[3] See *ante*, ii. 428.
[4] Sir Walter Scott wrote in 1814 :—
' Imprudence, or ill fortune as fatal as the sands of Belhelvie [shifting sands that had swallowed up a whole parish], has swallowed up the estate of Errol, excepting this dreary mansion-house and a farm or two adjoining.' Lockhart's *Scott*, 1837, iii. 139.

102   *Tuesday 24 August* 1773   Slains Castle

standard of wealth they shall lose their peerages [1]. We know the House of Peers have made noble stands, when the House of Commons durst not. The two last years of a parliament [a] they dare not contradict the populace [2].'

This room is ornamented with a number of fine prints, and with a whole length picture of Lord Errol, by Sir Joshua Reynolds. This led Dr. Johnson and me to talk of our amiable and elegant friend, whose panegyrick he concluded by saying, ' Sir Joshua Reynolds, sir, is the most invulnerable man I know ; the man with whom if you should quarrel, you would find the most difficulty how to abuse [3].'

Dr. Johnson observed, the situation here was the noblest he had ever seen,—better than Mount Edgecumbe, reckoned the first in England ; because, at Mount Edgecumbe [4], the sea is bounded by land on the other side, and, though there is there the grandeur of a fleet, there is also the impression of there being a dock-yard, the circumstances of which are not agreeable. At Slains is an excellent old house [5]. The noble owner has built of brick, along the square in the inside, a gallery, both on the first and second story, the house being no higher ; so that he has always a dry walk ; and the rooms, to which formerly there was no approach but through each other, have now all separate entries from the gallery, which is hung with Hogarth's works, and other prints. We went and sat a while in the library. There is a valuable and[b] numerous collection. It was chiefly made

[a] a parliament 1, 2 : parliament 3.   [b] and *omitted* 2, 3.

[1] See *ante*, ii. 421, note 1.
[2] Since the accession of George I. only one parliament had had so few as five sessions, and it was dissolved before its time by his death. One had six sessions, six seven sessions, (including the one that was now sitting,) and one eight. There was therefore so little dread of a sudden dissolution that for five years of each parliament the members durst ' contradict the populace.'
[3] To Miss Burney Johnson once said :—' Sir Joshua Reynolds possesses the largest share of inoffensiveness of any man that I know.' *Memoirs of Dr. Burney*, i. 343. ' Once at Mr. Thrale's, when Reynolds left the room, Johnson observed,—" There goes a man not to be spoiled by prosperity." ' Northcote's *Reynolds*, i. 82. Burke wrote of him :—' He had a strong turn for humour, and well saw the weak sides of things. He enjoyed every circumstance of his good fortune, and had no affectation on that subject. And I do not know a fault or weakness of his that he did not convert into something that bordered on a virtue, instead of pushing it to the confines of a vice.' Leslie and Taylor's *Reynolds*, ii. 638.
[4] ⟨He visited Mount Edgecumbe in 1762. Leslie and Taylor's *Reynolds*, i. 215.⟩   [5] ⟨See App. D, p. 498.⟩

Slains Castle   *Tuesday 24 August 1773*

by Mr. Falconer †, husband to the late Countess of Errol in her own right. This earl has added a good many modern books. About nine the Earl came home. Captain Gordon of Park § was with him. His lordship put Dr. Johnson in mind of their having dined together in London, along with Mr. Beauclerk. I was exceedingly pleased with Lord Errol. His dignified person and agreeable countenance, with the most unaffected affability, give me high satisfaction. From perhaps a weakness, or, as I rather hope, more fancy and warmth of feeling than is quite reasonable, my mind is ever impressed with admiration for persons of high birth, and I could, with the most perfect honesty, expatiate on Lord Errol's good qualities; but he stands in no need of my praise. His agreeable manners and softness of address prevented that constraint which the idea of his being Lord High Constable of Scotland [1] might otherwise have occasioned. He talked very easily and sensibly with his learned guest. I observed that Dr. Johnson, though he shewed that respect to his lordship, which, from principle, he always does to high rank, yet, when they came to argument, maintained that manliness which becomes the force and vigour of his understanding. To shew external deference to our superiors, is proper: to seem to yield to them in opinion, is meanness [2].

†, § ⟨See App. D, p. 498.⟩
[1] Walpole, describing the coronation of George III, writes, 24 Sept. 1761 :—' One there was...the noblest figure I ever saw, the High-Constable of Scotland, Lord Errol—as one saw him in a space capable of containing him, one admired him. At the wedding, dressed in tissue, he looked like one of the Giants in Guildhall, new gilt. It added to the energy of his person, that one considered him acting so considerable a part in that very Hall, where so few years ago one saw his father, Lord Kilmarnock, condemned to the block.' *Letters*, v. 112. ⟨Gray, describing the same scene, says :—' Of the Men doubtless the noblest and most striking figure was the Earl of Errol.' *Letters*, No. 345.⟩ Beattie says :— ' He often put me in mind of an ancient hero ; and I remember Dr.

Johnson was positive, that he resembled Homer's character of Sarpedon.' Sir W. Forbes, *Life*, 1806, ii. 351. Mrs. Piozzi says :—' The earl of Errol, dressed in his robes at the coronation . . . and Mrs. Siddons in the character of Murphy's Euphrasia, were the noblest specimens of the human race I ever saw.' *Synonymy*, i. 43. He sprang from a race of rebels. ' He united in his person,' says Sir W. Forbes, ' the four earldoms of Erroll, Kilmarnock, Linlithgow, and Callander.' The last two were attainted in 1715, and Kilmarnock in 1746. *Life Beattie*, 1806, ii. 350. ⟨For the Erroll family, see App. D, p. 498.⟩
[2] Lord Chesterfield, in his letters to his son [ii. 105], complains of one who argued in an indiscriminate manner with men of all ranks. Probably the noble lord had felt

The earl said grace, both before and after supper, with much decency. He told us a story of a man who was executed at Perth, some years ago, for murdering a woman who was with child by him, and a former child he had by her. His hand was cut off : he was then pulled up ; but the rope broke, and he was forced to lie an hour on the ground, till another rope was brought from Perth, the execution being in a wood at some distance,—at the place where the murders were committed. '*There*, (said my lord,) *I see the hand of Providence.*'—I was really happy here. I saw in this nobleman the best dispositions and best principles ; and I saw him, *in my mind's eye* [1], to be the representative of the ancient Boyds of Kilmarnock. I was afraid he might have urged drinking, as, I believe, he used formerly to do ;[a] but he drank port and water out of a large glass himself, and let us do as we pleased [2]. He went with us to our

[a] do; 1: do, 2, 3.

with some uneasiness what it was to encounter stronger abilities than his own. If a peer will engage at foils with his inferior in station, he must expect that his inferior in station will avail himself of every advantage ; otherwise it is not a fair trial of strength and skill. The same will hold in a contest of reason, or of wit. —A certain king entered the lists of genius with *Voltaire*. The consequence was, that, though the king had great and brilliant talents, Voltaire had such a superiority that his majesty could not bear it ; and the poet was dismissed, or escaped, from that court.—In the reign of James I. of England, Crichton, Lord Sanquhar, a peer of Scotland, from a vain ambition to excel a fencing-master in his own art, played at rapier and dagger with him. The fencing-master, whose fame and bread were at stake, put out one of his lordship's eyes. Exasperated at this, Lord Sanquhar hired ruffians, and had the fencing-master assassinated ; for which his lordship was capitally tried, condemned, and hanged. Not being a peer of England, he was tried by the name of Robert Crichton, Esq. ; but he was admitted to be a baron of three hundred years standing.—See the State Trials ; and the History of England by Hume, who applauds the impartial justice executed upon a man of high rank. BOSWELL, ed. 1. The ' stronger abilities ' that Chesterfield encountered were Johnson's. Boswell thought wrongly that it was of Johnson that his Lordship complained in his letters to his son. *Ante*, i. 267, note 2. ' A certain King ' was Frederick the Great. *Ante*, i. 434. The fencing-master was murdered in his own house in London, five years after Sanquhar (or Sanquire) had lost his eye. Bacon, who was Solicitor-General, said :—' Certainly the circumstance of time is heavy unto you ; it is now five years since this unfortunate man Turner, be it upon accident or despight, gave the provocation, which was the seed of your malice.' *State Trials*, 1735, vii. 89, and Hume's *History of Gt. Brit.* 1754, i. 45. ⟨See also G. L. Craik, *Romance of Peerage*, iii. 334 ff.⟩

[1] *Hamlet*, act i. sc. 2.

[2] ⟨Lord Erroll was not, as Dr. Hill thought, the Scotch Lord, ' celebrated for hard drinking ', mentioned *ante*, iii. 170 and 503.⟩

rooms at night; said, he took the visit very kindly; and told me, my father and he were very old acquaintance;—that I now knew the way to Slains, and he hoped to see me there again.

I had a most elegant room; but there was a fire in it which blazed; and the sea, to which my windows looked, roared; and the pillows were made of the feathers of some sea-fowl, which had to me a disagreeable smell: so that, by all these causes, I was kept awake a good while. I saw, in imagination, Lord Errol's father, Lord Kilmarnock [1], (who was beheaded on Tower-hill in 1746,) and I was somewhat dreary. But the thought did not last long, and I fell asleep.

Wednesday, 25th August.
We got up between seven and eight, and found Mr. Boyd in the dining-room, with tea and coffee before him, to give us breakfast. We were in an admirable humour. Lady Errol had given each of us a copy of an ode [2] by Beattie, on the birth of her son, Lord Hay. Mr. Boyd asked Dr. Johnson, how he liked it. Dr. Johnson, who did not admire it, got off very well, by taking it out, and reading the second and third stanzas of it with much melody. This, without his saying a word, pleased Mr. Boyd. He observed, however, to Dr. Johnson, that the expression as to the family of Errol,

'A thousand years have seen it shine,'

compared with what went before, was an anti-climax, and that it would have been better

Ages have seen, &c.

Dr. Johnson said, 'So great a number as a thousand is better. *Dolus latet in universalibus* [3]. Ages might be only two ages.'— He talked of the advantage of keeping up the connections of relationship, which produce much kindness. 'Every man (said he,) who comes into the world, has need of friends. If he has to get them for himself, half his life is spent, before his merit is known. Relations are a man's ready friends, who support him. When a man is in real distress, he flies into the arms of his relations. An old lawyer [4], who had much experience in making wills, told me, that after people had deliberated long,

[1] 'Pity'd by gentle minds Kilmarnock died.' *Ante*, i. 180.
[2], [3] ⟨See App. D, pp. 498–9.⟩
[4] ⟨Mr. Scrase: see App. D, p. 499.⟩

and thought of many for their executors, they settled at last by fixing on their relations. This shews the universality of the principle.'[a]

I regretted the decay of respect for men of family, and that a Nabob now would carry an election from them.—*Johnson.* 'Why, sir, the Nabob will carry it by means of his wealth, in a country where money is highly valued, as it must be where nothing can be had without money; but, if it comes to personal preference, the man of family will always carry it [1]. There is generally a *scoundrelism* about a low man [2].'—Mr. Boyd said, that was a good *ism.*

I said, I believed mankind were happier in the ancient feudal state [3] of subordination, than they are in the modern state of independency.—*Johnson.* 'To be sure, the *Chief* was: but we must think of the number of individuals. That *they* were less happy, seems plain; for that state from which all escape as soon as they can, and to which none return after they have left it, must be less happy; and this is the case with the state of dependance on a chief or great man.'

I mentioned the happiness of the French in their subordination, by the reciprocal benevolence and attachment between the great and those in lower ranks [b] [4].—Mr. Boyd gave us an instance

[a] *quotation-mark omitted* 3.   [b] ranks 1 (*and MS.*): rank 2, 3.

[1] Scott describes the talk that he had in 1814 near Slains Castle with an old fisherman. ' The old man says Slains is now inhabited by a Mr. Bowles, who comes so far from the southward that naebody kens whare he comes frae. " Was he frae the Indies? "—" Na; he did not think he came that road. He was far frae the southland. Naebody ever heard the name of the place; but he had brought more guid out o' Peterhead than a' the Lords he had seen in Slains, and he had seen three."' Lockhart's *Scott*, iii. 140. The first of the three was Johnson's host.

[2] See *ante*, ii. 153, and iii. 1, note 2.

[3] Smollett, in *Humphry Clinker* (Letter of Sept. 6), writing of the Highlanders and their chiefs, says:—

'The original attachment... is founded on something prior to the *feudal system*, about which the writers of this age have made such a pother, as if it was a new discovery, like the *Copernican system*. . . . For my part, I expect to see the use of trunk-hose and buttered ale ascribed to the influence of the *feudal system*.' See *ante*, ii. 177.

[4] Mme. Riccoboni wrote to Garrick on May 3, 1769:—' Vous conviendrez que les nobles sont peu ménagés par vos auteurs: le sot, le fat, ou le malhonnête homme mêlé dans l'intrigue est presque toujours un lord.' *Garrick Corres.*, ii. 561. Dr. J. Moore (*View of Society in France*, i. 31) writing in 1779 says:—' I am convinced there is no country in Europe where royal favour, high birth, and

Strichen *Wednesday 25 August 1773*

of their gentlemanly spirit. An old *Chevalier de Malthe*, of ancient *noblesse*, but in low circumstances, was in a coffee-house at Paris, where was *Julien* †, the great Manufacturer at the Gobelins, of the fine tapestry, so much distinguished both for the figures and the *colours*. The chevalier's carriage was very old. Says Julien, with a plebeian insolence, ' I think, sir, you had better have your carriage new painted.' The chevalier looked at him with indignant contempt, and answered, ' Well, sir, you may take it home and *dye* it ! '—All the coffee-house rejoiced at Julien's confusion.

We set out about nine. Dr. Johnson was curious to see one of those structures which northern antiquarians call a Druid's temple. I had a recollection of one at Strichen,[a] which I had seen fifteen years ago ; so we went four miles out of our road, after passing Old Deer, and went thither. Mr. Fraser, the proprietor, was at home, and shewed it to us. But I had augmented it in my mind ; for all that remains is two stones set up on end, with a long one laid upon them, as was usual,[b] and one stone at a little distance from them. That stone was the capital one of the circle which surrounded what now remains. Mr. Fraser was very hospitable [1]. There was a fair at Strichen ; and he had

[a] Strichen, 1, 2 : Strichen ; 3.   [b] *comma omitted* 3.

the military profession, could be allowed such privileges as they have in France, and where there would be so few instances of their producing rough and brutal behaviour to inferiors.' Mrs. Piozzi, writing in 1784, said :—' The French are really a contented race of mortals ;—precluded almost from possibility of adventure, the low Parisian leads a gentle humble life, nor envies that greatness he never can obtain.' *Journey through France*, 1789, i. 13.
† ⟨See App. D, p. 500.⟩
[1] He is the worthy son of a worthy father, the late Lord Strichen, one of our judges, to whose kind notice I was much obliged. Lord Strichen was a man not only honest, but highly generous ; for,[a] after his succession to the family estate, he paid a large sum of debts contracted by his predecessor, which he was not under any obligation to pay. Let me here, for the credit of *Ayrshire*, my own county, record a noble instance of liberal honesty in *William Hutchison*, drover, in Lanehead, *Kyle*, who formerly obtained a full discharge from his creditors upon a composition of his debts ; but,[b] upon being restored to good circumstances, invited his creditors last winter to a dinner, without telling the reason, and paid them their full sums, principal and interest. They presented him with a piece of plate, with an inscription to commemorate this extraordinary instance of true worth ; which should make some people in Scotland blush, while, though mean themselves, they strut about under the protection of great alliance, conscious of the wretchedness of numbers who have lost by them, to whom they never think of making reparation, but in-

[a], [b] *comma omitted* 3.

several of his neighbours from it at dinner. One of them, Dr. Fraser, who had been in the army, remembered to have seen Dr. Johnson at a lecture on experimental philosophy, at Lichfield. The Doctor recollected being at the lecture ; and he was surprised to find here somebody who knew him.

Mr. Fraser sent a servant to conduct us by a short passage into the high-road. I observed to Dr. Johnson, that I had a most disagreeable notion of the life of country gentlemen ; that I left Mr. Fraser just now, as one leaves a prisoner in a jail.— Dr. Johnson said, that I was right in thinking them unhappy ; for that they had not enough to keep their minds in motion [1].

I started a thought this afternoon which amused us a great part of the way. ' If, (said I,) our club should come and set up in St. Andrews, as a college, to teach all that each of us can, in the several departments of learning and taste, we should rebuild the city : we should draw a wonderful concourse of students.'—Dr. Johnson entered fully into the spirit of this project. We immediately fell to distributing the offices. I was to teach Civil and Scotch law [2] ; Burke, politicks and eloquence ; Garrick, the art of publick speaking ; Langton was to be our Grecian [3], Colman our Latin professor [4] ; Nugent to teach physick [5] ; Lord Charlemont, modern history [6] ; Beauclerk,[a] natural philosophy [7] ; Vesey, Irish antiquities, or Celtick learning [8] ; Jones, Oriental learning [9] ; Gold-

[a] *comma omitted* 3.

dulge themselves and their families in most unsuitable expence. BOSWELL, ed. 1. ⟨See App. D, p. 500.⟩

[1] See *ante*, ii. 194 ; iii. 353 ; iv. 338.

[2] Malone says that ' Lord Auchinleck told him [Boswell] one day, that it would cost him more trouble to hide his ignorance', in the Scotch and English law, 'than to shew his knowledge. This Mr. Boswell owned he had found to be true.' *European Magazine*, June, 1798, p. 376.

[3] See *ante*, iv. 8, note 3, iv. 20, ⟨and *post*, App. D, p. 501.⟩

[4] See *ante*, iv. 18.   [5] See *ante*, i. 477.

[6] ⟨Charlemont appears to have compiled a history of Italian poetry. See Hardy's *Charlemont*, pp. 153, 422, and R. Marshall's *Italy in Eng. Lit.*, p. 135.⟩

[7] See *ante*, i. 250, and ii. 378, note 1.

[8] Since the first edition, it has been suggested by one of the club, who knew Mr. Vesey better than Dr. Johnson and I, that we did not assign him a proper place ; for he was quite unskilled in Irish antiquities and Celtick learning, but might with propriety have been made professor of architecture, which he understood well, and has left a very good specimen of his knowledge and taste in that art, by an elegant house built on a plan of his own formation, at Lucan, a few miles from Dublin. BOSWELL. ⟨This note first appears in ed. 2.   ' One of the club ' is Dr. Barnard. Letter to Boswell, 14 Aug. 1785 (*Yale Boswell MS. C 86*).⟩

[9] Sir William Jones, who died at the age of forty-seven, had ' studied

smith, poetry and ancient history; Chamier, commercial politicks [1]; Reynolds, painting, and the arts which have beauty for their object; Chambers, the law of England [2]. Dr. Johnson at first said, ' I'll trust theology to nobody but myself.' But, upon due consideration, that Percy is a clergyman, it was agreed that Percy should teach practical divinity and British antiquities; Dr. Johnson himself, logick, metaphysicks [3], and scholastick divinity. In this manner did we amuse ourselves;—each suggesting, and each varying or adding, till the whole was adjusted. Dr. Johnson said, we only wanted a mathematician since Dyer [4] died, who was a very good one; but as to every thing else, we should have a very capital university [5].

We got at night to Banff. I sent Joseph on to *Duff-house*: but Earl Fife was not at home, which I regretted much, as we should have had a very elegant reception from his lordship. We found here but an indifferent inn [6]. Dr. Johnson wrote a long

eight languages critically, eight less perfectly, but all intelligible with a dictionary, and twelve least perfectly, but all attainable.' Teignmouth's *Life of Sir W. Jones*, ed. 1804, p. 376, note. See *ante*, iv. 69, note 2.
[1] See *ante*, i. 478.   [2] See *ante*, v. 16.
[3] Mackintosh in his *Life*, ii. 166, says:—' From the refinements of abstruse speculation Johnson was withheld, partly perhaps by that repugnance to such subtleties which much experience often inspires, and partly also by a secret dread that they might disturb those prejudices in which his mind had found repose from the agitations of doubt.'
[4] See *ante*, iv. 11, note 1.
[5] Our club, originally at the Turk's Head, Gerrard-street, then at Prince's, Sackville-street, now at Baxter's, [a] Dover-street, which at Mr. Garrick's funeral acquired a *name* for the first time, and was called THE LITERARY CLUB, was instituted in 1764, and now consists of thirty-five members. It has, since 1773, been greatly augmented; and though Dr. Johnson with justice observed, that, by losing Goldsmith, Garrick, Nu-

gent, Chamier, Beauclerk, we had lost what would make an eminent club, yet when I mention, as an accession, Mr. Fox, Dr. George Fordyce, Sir Charles Bunbury, Lord Ossory, Mr. Gibbon, Dr. Adam Smith, Mr. R. B. Sheridan, the Bishops of Kilaloe and St. Asaph, Dean Marlay, Mr. Steevens, Mr. Dunning, Sir Joseph Banks, Dr. Scott of the Commons, Earl Spencer, Mr. Windham of Norfolk, Lord Elliott, Mr. Malone, Dr. Joseph Warton, the Rev. Mr. [b] Thomas Warton, Lord Lucan, Mr. Burke junior, Lord Palmerston, Dr. Burney, Sir William Hamilton, and Dr. Warren, it will be acknowledged that we might establish a second university of high reputation. BOSWELL, ed. 1, slightly revised, ed. 2.
Sir William Jones wrote in 1780 (*Life*, p. 193):—' Of our club I will only say, that there is no branch of human knowledge, on which some of our members are not capable of giving information.' ⟨The history of THE CLUB has been written: see *Annals of The Club*, 1914. See also *ante*, i. 477.⟩
[6] Here, unluckily, the windows had

[a] *comma omitted* 3.   [b] Mr. *omitted* 2, 3.

letter to Mrs. Thrale. I wondered to see him write so much so easily. He verified his own doctrine,[a] that 'a man may always write when he will set himself *doggedly* to it [1].'

Thursday, 26th August.

We got a fresh chaise here, a very good one, and very good horses. We breakfasted at Cullen. They set down dried haddocks broiled, along with our tea. I ate one; but Dr. Johnson was disgusted by the sight of them, so they were removed [2]. Cullen has a comfortable appearance, though but a very small town, and the houses mostly poor buildings.

I called on Mr. Robertson, who has the charge of Lord Findlater's affairs, and was formerly Lord Monboddo's clerk, was three times in France with him, and translated Condamine's Account of the Savage Girl, to which his lordship wrote a preface, containing several remarks of his own [3]. Robertson said, he did not believe so much as his lordship did; that it was plain to him, the girl confounded what she imagined with what

[a] *comma omitted* 3.

no pullies; and Dr. Johnson, who was constantly eager for fresh air, had much struggling to get one of them kept open. Thus he had a notion impressed upon him, that this wretched defect was general in Scotland; in consequence of which he has erroneously enlarged upon it in his 'Journey'. I regretted that he did not allow me to read over his book before it was printed. I should have changed very little; but I should have suggested an alteration in a few places where he has laid himself open to be attacked. I hope I should have prevailed with him to omit or soften his assertion, that 'a Scotsman must be a sturdy moralist, who does not prefer Scotland to truth,'—for I really think it is not founded; and it is harshly said. BOSWELL, ed. 1.

⟨Johnson gives his 'diminutive observations' on Scottish windows under 'Bamff' in his *Journey to the Western Islands* (1924), p. 19. Boswell in the 'Remarks' which he sent to Johnson on his book says: 'You are certainly mistaken as to the windows in Scotland seldom having weights and pullies. Allmost all the houses in Ed[r.] and all the good houses

that I can recollect have them.' R. B. Adam Library, 1929, vol. ii. He makes no comment on Johnson's 'assertion'. (See *ante*, ii. 311). For the inn see App. D, p. 501.⟩

[1] See *ante*, v. 40.

[2] A protest may be entered on the part of most Scotsmen against the doctor's taste in this particular. A Finnon haddock dried over the smoke of the sea-weed, and sprinkled with salt water during the process, acquires a relish of a very peculiar and delicate flavour, inimitable on any other coast than that of Aberdeenshire. Some of our Edinburgh philosophers tried to produce their equal in vain. I was one of a party at a dinner, where the philosophical haddocks were placed in competition with the genuine Finnon-fish. These were served round without distinction whence they came; but only one gentleman, out of twelve present, espoused the cause of philosophy. SCOTT, 1831.

⟨The fish served up to the travellers at Cullen was the common dried haddock. CARRUTHERS, 1852.⟩

[3] ⟨See App. D, p. 501.⟩

she remembered : that, besides, she perceived Condamine and Lord Monboddo forming theories, and she adapted her story to them.

Dr. Johnson said, ' It is a pity to see Lord Monboddo publish such notions as he has done ; a man of sense, and of so much elegant learning. There would be little in a fool doing it ; we should only laugh ; but when a wise man does it, we are sorry. Other people have strange notions ; but they conceal them. If they have tails, they hide them ; but Monboddo is as jealous of his tail as a squirrel.'—I shall here put down some more remarks of Dr. Johnson's on Lord Monboddo, which were not made exactly at this time, but come in well from connection. He said, he did not approve of a judge's calling himself *Farmer* Burnett [1], and going about with a little round hat [2]. He laughed heartily at his lordship's saying he was an *enthusiastical* farmer ; ' for, (said he,) what can he do in farming by his *enthusiasm?* ' Here, however, I think Dr. Johnson mistaken. He who wishes to be successful, or happy, ought to be enthusiastical, that is to say, very keen in all the occupations or diversions of life. An ordinary gentleman-farmer will be satisfied with looking at his fields once or twice a day : an enthusiastical farmer will be constantly employed on them ;—will have his mind earnestly engaged ; will talk perpetually of them. But Dr. Johnson has much of the *nil admirari* [3] in smaller concerns. That survey of life which gave birth to his *Vanity of Human Wishes* early sobered his mind. Besides, so great a mind as his cannot be moved by inferior objects : an elephant does not run and skip like lesser animals.

Mr. Robertson sent a servant with us, to shew us through Lord

---

[1] It is the custom in Scotland for the judges of the Court of Session to have the title of *lords*, from their estates ; thus Mr. Burnett is Lord *Monboddo*, as Mr. Home was Lord *Kames*. There is something a little aukward in this ; for they are denominated in deeds by their *names*, with the addition of ' one of the Senators of the College of Justice ; ' and subscribe their christian and surname, as *James Burnett, Henry Home*, even in judicial acts. BOSWELL, ed. 1. See *ante*, v. 77, note 4.

[2] See *ante*, ii. 344, where Johnson says :—' A Judge may be a farmer ; but he is not to geld his own pigs.'

[3] ' Not to admire, is all the Art I know,
To make men happy, and to keep them so.'
Pope *Imit. Horace*, Epistles, i. vi. 1.

Cullen-Findlater's wood, by which our way was shortened, and we saw some part of his domain, which is indeed admirably laid out. Dr. Johnson did not choose to walk through it. He always said, that he was not come to Scotland to see fine places, of which there were enough in England ; but wild objects,——mountains, ——water-falls,——peculiar manners ; in short, things which he had not seen before. I have a notion that he at no time has had much taste for rural beauties. I have myself very little [1].

Dr. Johnson said, there was nothing more contemptible than a country gentleman living beyond his income, and every year growing poorer and poorer [2]. He spoke strongly of the influence which a man has by being rich. 'A man, (said he,) who keeps his money, has in reality more use from it, than he can have by spending it.' I observed that this looked very like a paradox ; but he explained it thus : 'If it were certain that a man would keep his money locked up for ever, to be sure he would have no influence ; but, as so many want money, and he has the power of giving it, and they know not but by gaining his favour they may obtain it, the rich man will always have the greatest influence. He again who lavishes his money, is laughed at as foolish, and in a great degree with justice, considering how much is spent from vanity. Even those who partake of a man's hospitality, have but a transient kindness for him. If he has not the command of money, people know he cannot help them, if he would ; whereas the rich man always can, if he will, and for the chance of that, will have much weight.'—*Boswell*. 'But philosophers and satirists have all treated a miser as contemptible.'—*Johnson*. 'He is so philosophically ; but not in the practice of life [3].'—*Boswell*. 'Let me see now :—I do not know the instances of misers in England, so as to examine into their influence.'—*Johnson*. 'We have had few misers in England.'—*Boswell*. 'There was Lowther [4].'—*Johnson*. 'Why,

[1] See *ante*, i. 461.
[2] See *ante*, iv. 152.
[3] See *ante*, iii. 322.
[4] In the *Gent. Mag.*, Jan. 1755, p. 42, among the deaths is entered 'Sir James Lowther, Bart., member for Cumberland, reckoned the richest commoner in Great Britain, and worth above a million.' According to Lord Shelburne, Lord Sunderland, who had been advised 'to nominate Lowther one of his Treasury, on account of his great property,' appointed him to call on him. After waiting for some time he rang to ask whether he had come. 'The servants answered that nobody had called ; upon his repeating the inquiry the

–Elgin *Thursday 26 August* 1773 113
sir, Lowther, by keeping his money, had the command of the county, which the family has now lost, by spending it 1.[a] I take it, he lent a great deal ; and that is the way to have influence, and yet preserve one's wealth. A man may lend his money upon very good security, and yet have his debtor much under his power.'—*Boswell*. ' No doubt, sir. He can always distress him for the money ; as no man borrows, who is able to pay on demand quite conveniently.'

We dined at Elgin, and saw the noble ruins of the cathedral. Though it rained much, Dr. Johnson examined them with a most patient attention. He could not here feel any abhorrence

[a] it. 1 : it, 2, 3.

servants said that there was an old man, somewhat wet, sitting by the fireside in the hall, who they supposed had some petition to deliver to his Lordship. When he went out, it proved to be Sir James Lowther. Lord Sunderland desired him to be sent about his business, saying that no such mean fellow should sit at his Treasury.' Fitzmaurice's *Shelburne*, 1912, i. 26.

[1] I do not know what was at this time the state of the parliamentary interest of the ancient family of Lowther ; a family before the Conquest : but all the nation knows it to be very extensive at present. A due mixture of severity and kindness, œconomy and munificence, characterises its present Representative. BOSWELL, ed. 1. Boswell, most unhappily not clearly seeing where his own genius lay, too often sought to obtain fame and position by the favour of some great man. For some years he courted in a very gross manner ' the present Representative,' the first Earl of Lonsdale, who treated him with great brutality. ⟨For Boswell's relations with Lonsdale, see *Boswell Papers*, vols. xvii and xviii.⟩ In the *Ann. Reg.* 1771, p. 56, it is shewn how by this bad man ' the whole county of Cumberland was thrown into a state of the greatest terror and confusion ; 400 ejectments were served in one day.' Dr. A. Carlyle (*Auto.* p. 418) says that he was ' more detested than any man alive, as a shameless political sharper, a domestic bashaw, and an intolerable tyrant over his tenants and dependents.' Lord Albemarle (*Memoirs of Rockingham*, 1852, ii. 70) describes the ' bad Lord Lonsdale '. ' He exacted a serf-like submission from his poor and abject dependents. He professed a thorough contempt for modern refinements. Grass grew in the neglected approaches to his mansion. . . . Awe and silence pervaded the inhabitants [of Penrith] when the gloomy despot traversed their streets. He might have been taken for a Judge Jefferies, about to open a royal commission to try them as state criminals. . . . In some years of his life, he resisted the payment of all bills.' Among his creditors was Wordsworth's father, ' who died leaving the poet and four other helpless children.' ⟨Lord Lonsdale left instructions in his will that his just debts should be paid. The Wordsworths claimed a total sum of £10,388, and received £8,500, in instalments, the last in 1804. Wordsworth's *Letters*, ed. E. de Selincourt, p. 3, n. 1.⟩ See also De Quincey's *Works*, 1862, ii. 151 ff.

at the Scottish reformers [1], for he had been told by Lord Hailes, that it was destroyed before the Reformation, by the Lord of Badenoch [2], who had a quarrel with the bishop. The bishop's house †, and those of the other clergy, which are still pretty entire, do not seem to have been proportioned to the magnificence of the cathedral, which has been of great extent, and had very fine carved work. The ground within the walls of the cathedral is employed as a burying-place. The family of Gordon have their vault here ; but it has nothing grand.

We passed Gordon Castle [3] this forenoon, which has a princely appearance. Fochabers, the neighbouring village, is a poor place, many of the houses being ruinous ; but it is remarkable,

[1] 'Let us not,' he says, 'make too much haste to despise our neighbours. Our own cathedrals are mouldering by unregarded dilapidation. It seems to be part of the despicable philosophy of the time to despise monuments of sacred magnificence.' ⟨Johnson substituted the last two sentences for a more precise censure : see App. D, p. 502.⟩

[2] NOTE, by Lord *Hailes*.

'The cathedral of Elgin was burnt by the Lord of Badenoch, because the Bishop of Moray had pronounced an award not to his liking. The indemnification that the see obtained, was, that the Lord of Badenoch stood for three days bare-footed at the great gate of the cathedral. The story is in the Chartulary of Elgin.' BOSWELL, ed. 1.

⟨Elgin cathedral was burnt by Alexander Stewart, Earl of Buchan, and son of Robert II, on 7 June 1390. The Chartulary tells the story, but it makes no specific mention of the 'indemnification' for the outrage ; it does, however, record the Earl's 'absolution', and it is this, perhaps, to which Lord Hailes refers. This occurs in a document printed by Cosmo Innes (Adv. MS.34. 4. 10, f. lxii), which is undated, but was written in the first quarter of the 15th century. It is in the following terms : 'Post hec [the burning of the Cathedral, etc.] idem dominus Alexander Senes-calli ex speciali commissione domini Alexandri Burr episcopi fuit absolutus per dominum Walterum Trayle episcopum Sancti Andree in presencia domini Regis ... et multorum aliorum apud Perth ante fores ecclesie fratrum predicatorum et postea ante magnum altare a sentencia excommunicacionis sub conditione quod satisfaceret indilate ecclesie Moraviensi et quod mitteret ad Papam pro absolucione obtinenda aliter reincideret pristinam excommunicacionis sentenciam ipso facto.' *Regist. Episc. Moraviensis*, 1837, pp. 381–2. There is no evidence that either the Earl or the ecclesiastical authorities took any further steps in the matter. Robert III, his brother, made annual payments, 1391–97, of £20 towards the rebuilding of the cathedral (*Exchequer Rolls Scotl.* iii. 276, 316, 348, 376, 403, and 430), but he himself apparently made no reparation. Cf. Hume Brown, *Hist. Scotland*, 1911, i. 159. See App. D, p. 502, for the subsequent history of the cathedral.⟩

† ⟨See App. D, p. 502.⟩

[3] I am not sure whether the duke was at home. But, not having the honour of being much known to his grace, I could not have presumed to enter his castle, though to introduce even so celebrated a stranger. We were at any rate in a hurry to get forward to the wildness which we came to see. Perhaps, if this noble family

they have in general orchards well stored with apple-trees [1]. Elgin has what in England are called piazzas, that run in many places on each side of the street. It must have been a much better place formerly. Probably it had piazzas all along the town, as I have seen at Bologna. I approved much of such structures in a town, on account of their conveniency in wet weather. Dr. Johnson disapproved of them, ' because (said he) it makes the under story of a house very dark, which greatly over-balances the conveniency, when it is considered how small a part of the year it rains; how few are usually in the street at such times; that many who are might as well be at home; and the little that people suffer, supposing them to be as much wet as they commonly are in walking a street.'

We fared but ill at our inn here; and Dr. Johnson said, this was the first time he had seen a dinner in Scotland that he could not eat [2].

In the afternoon, we drove over the very heath where Macbeth met the witches, according to tradition [3]. Dr. Johnson again [4] solemnly repeated—

> ' How far is't called to Fores ? What are these,
> So wither'd, and so wild in their attire ?
> That look not like the inhabitants o' the earth,
> And yet are on't ? '

He repeated a good deal more of *Macbeth*. His recitation [5] was grand and affecting, and, as Sir Joshua Reynolds has observed

---

had still preserved that sequestered magnificence which they maintained when catholicks, corresponding with the Grand Duke of Tuscany, we might have been induced to have procured proper letters of introduction, and devoted some time to the contemplation of venerable superstitious state. BOSWELL, ed. 1. ⟨See App. D, p. 503.⟩

[1] ' In the way we saw for the first time some houses with fruit trees about them. The improvements of the Scotch are for immediate profit, they do not yet think it worth while to plant what will not produce something to be eaten or sold in a very little time.' Johnson's *Letters*, No. 323.

[2] ⟨See App. D, pp. 503–4.⟩

[3] ⟨It was in fact the next morning, as Johnson states, that the travellers ' entered upon the road, on which Macbeth heard the fatal prediction'. *Western Isl.*, p. 22. See *post*, App. D, p. 504.⟩   [4] See *ante*, v. 76.

[5] Murphy (*Life*, p. 145) says that ' his manner of reciting verses . . . was wonderfully impressive.' According to Mrs. Piozzi (*Anec.* p. 302 : John. Misc. i. 347), ' whoever once heard him repeat an ode of Horace, would be long before they could endure to hear it repeated by another.'

to me, had no more tone than it should have : it was the better for it. He then parodied the *All-hail* of the witches to Macbeth, addressing himself to me. I had purchased some land called *Dalblair* † ; and, as in Scotland it is customary to distinguish landed men by the name of their estates, I had thus two titles, *Dalblair* and Young *Auchinleck*. So my friend, in imitation of

' All hail Macbeth ! hail to thee, Thane of Cawdor ! '

condescended to amuse himself with uttering

' All hail Dalblair ! hail to thee, Laird of Auchinleck [1] ! '

We got to Fores [2] at night, and found an admirable inn §, in which Dr. Johnson was pleased to meet with a landlord who styled himself ' Wine-Cooper, from LONDON.'

Friday, 27th August.

It was dark when we came to Fores last night ; so we did not see what is called King Duncan's monument [3].—I shall now mark some gleanings of Dr. Johnson's conversation. I spoke of *Leonidas* [4], and said there were some good passages in it.— *Johnson.* 'Why, you must *seek* for them.'—He said, Paul Whitehead's *Manners* [5] was a poor performance.—Speaking of

---

† ⟨Boswell bought Dalblair, in the vale of Glenmuir on the eastern border of Auchinleck parish, in 1767. *Ante*, iii. 207.⟩

[1] ⟨*Auchinlèck* was in Boswell's time, and for long after, pronounced *Affléck*; this pronunciation is still (1935) known and occasionally used ; but the name is generally pronounced as it is written. See *ante*, ii. 413, note 1.⟩

[2] At this stage of his journey Johnson recorded :—' There are . . more beggars than I have ever seen in England ; they beg, if not silently, yet very modestly.' *Letters*, No. 323. See *ante*, v. 75, note 1.

§ ⟨' Found an admirable house kept by Lawson [?], wine-cooper, from London '. Boswell's *Hebrides*, ed. Pottle and Bennett, 1936, p. 84. In 1771 the chief inn, the Crown, was kept by ' a gay looking landlady and a lame cuckold-like landlord ', whose name was Brodie. *Gent. Mag.*, Dec. 1771, xli. 544.⟩

[3] Duncan's monument; a huge column on the roadside near Fores, more than twenty feet high, erected in commemoration of the final retreat of the Danes from Scotland, and properly called Swene's Stone. SCOTT, 1831. ⟨See G. Bain, *Nairn-shire*, p. 45.⟩

[4] ⟨By Richard Glover: see App. D pp. 504-5.⟩

[5] See *ante*, i. 125.

Derrick, he told me 'he had a kindness for him, and had often said, that if his letters had been written by one of a more established name, they would have been thought very pretty letters [1].'

This morning I introduced the subject of the origin of evil [2].—*Johnson.* 'Moral evil is occasioned by free will, which implies choice between good and evil. With all the evil that there is, there is no man but would rather be a free agent, than a mere machine without the evil; and what is best for each individual, must be best for the whole. If a man would rather be the machine, I cannot argue with him. He is a different being from me.'—*Boswell.* 'A man, as a machine, may have agreeable sensations; for instance, he may have pleasure in musick.'—*Johnson.* 'No, sir, he cannot have pleasure in musick; at least no power of producing musick; for he who can produce musick may let it alone: he who can play upon a fiddle may break it: such a man is not a machine.' This reasoning satisfied me. It is certain, there cannot be a free agent, unless there is the power of being evil as well as good. We must take the inherent possibilities of things into consideration, in our reasonings or conjectures concerning the works of GOD.

We came to Nairn to breakfast †. Though a county town and a royal burgh, it is a miserable place. Over the room where we sat, a girl was spinning wool with a great wheel, and singing an Erse song [3]: 'I'll warrant you, (said Dr. Johnson,) one of the songs of Ossian.' He then repeated these lines:

'Verse sweetens toil, however rude the sound.
All at her work the village maiden sings;
Nor, while she turns the giddy wheel around,
Revolves the sad vicissitude of things [4].'

---

[1] See *ante*, i. 456, and *post*, v. 240.
[2] See *ante*, ii. 82; *post*, v. 366.
† ⟨Perhaps the travellers stopped at 'The Horse', or 'The White Horse', in Harbour Street, which was kept by one Clark, who took 'every method to give satisfaction'. *Gent. Mag.*, Dec. 1771, xli. 544.⟩
[3] ⟨Of Nairn James VI boasted to his English courtiers that it was 'sae lang, that the folk at the tae end couldna understand the tongue spoken at the tother'. G. and P. Anderson,

Guide to Highlands, 1861, p. 358. 'Here', writes Johnson (*Western Isl.*, p. 22), 'I first saw peat fires, and first heard the Erse language.' In 1800 the town was still regarded as the linguistic boundary. *Rep. S.P.C.K.* (*Scotl.*), App., 1800, p. 15. Gaelic is generally not understood, and still less spoken, there to-day (1939).⟩

[4] 'Verse softens Toil, however rude the Sound;
She feels no biting Pang the while she sings;

118   *Friday 27 August* 1773   Nairn–

I thought I had heard these lines before.—*Johnson.* ' I fancy not, sir ; for they are in a detached poem, the name of which I do not remember, written by one Giffard, a parson.'

I expected Mr. Kenneth M'Aulay [1], the minister of Calder, who published the history of St. Kilda [2], a book which Dr. Johnson liked, would have met us here, as I had written to him from Aberdeen. But I received a letter from him, telling me that

Nor, as she turns the giddy Wheel around,
Revolves the sad Vicissitude of things.'
Contemplation. London : Printed for R. Dodsley in Pall-mall; and sold by M. Cooper, at the Globe in Paternoster-Row. MDCCLIII. ⟨There is a copy in the British Museum : 11630 e. 18.⟩ The author's name is not on the title-page. Mr. Nichols (*Lit. Illus.* v. 183) says that the author was the Rev. Richard Gifford of Balliol College, Oxford. He adds that ' Mr. Gifford frequently mentioned to him with much satisfaction the circumstance that Johnson quoted the poem in his *Dictionary.*' It was there very likely that Boswell had seen the lines. ⟨In Boswell's original Journal the reading is ' seen ', not ' heard '.⟩ They are quoted under *wheel* sb. 5 :—
' Verse sweetens care, however rude the sound,
All at her work the village maiden sings ;
Nor as she turns the giddy wheel around,
Revolves the sad vicissitudes of things.'   ' *Giffard.*'
Contemplation, which was published two years after Gray's *Elegy*, was suggested by it. The rising, not the parting day, is described. The following verse precedes the one quoted by Johnson :—
' Ev'n from the straw-roof'd Cot the Note of Joy

Flows full and frequent, as the Village-Fair,
Whose little Wants the busy Hour employ,
Chanting some rural Ditty sooths her Care.'
Bacon, in his essay ' Of Vicissitude of Things ' (*Essays*, 1625, p. 339), says :—' It is not good, to looke too long vpon these turning Wheeles of Vicissitude, lest we become Giddy.' This may have suggested Gifford's last two lines. *Reflections on a Grave, &c.* (*ante*, ii. 26), has a line borrowed from this poem :—
' These all the hapless state of mortals show,
The sad vicissitude of things below.'
Cowper, *Table Talk*, Hope, 488, writes of
' The sweet vicissitudes of day and night.'
The following elegant version of these lines by Mr. A. T. Barton, Fellow and Tutor of Johnson's own College, will please the classical reader :—
Musa levat duros, quamvis rudis ore, labores ;
Inter opus cantat rustica Pyrrha suum ;
Nec meminit, secura rotam dum versat euntem,
Non aliter nostris sortibus ire vices.

[1] He was the brother of the Rev. John M'Aulay (*post*, v. 355), the grandfather of Lord Macaulay. ⟨See App. D, pp. 505–7.⟩

[2] See *ante*, ii. 51.

he could not leave home, as he was to administer the sacrament the following Sunday, and earnestly requesting to see us at his manse. 'We'll go,' said Dr. Johnson; which we accordingly did. Mrs. M'Aulay received us, and told us her husband was in the church distributing tokens [1]. We arrived between twelve and one o'clock, and it was near three before he came to us.

Dr. Johnson thanked him for his book, and said 'it was a very pretty piece of topography.' M'Aulay did not seem much to mind the compliment. From his conversation, Dr. Johnson was persuaded that he had not written the book which goes under his name. I myself always suspected so; and I have been told it was written by the learned Dr. John M'Pherson of Sky [2], from the materials collected by M'Aulay. Dr. Johnson said privately to me, 'There is a combination in it of which M'Aulay is not capable [3].' However, he was exceedingly hospitable; and, as he obligingly promised us a route for our Tour through the Western Isles, we agreed to stay with him all night.

After dinner, we walked to the old castle of Calder, (pronounced Cawder) the Thane of Cawdor's seat. I was sorry that my friend, this 'prosperous gentleman [4],' was not there. The old tower must be of great antiquity [5]. There is a drawbridge,—what has been a moat,—and an ancient court. There is a hawthorn-tree, which rises like a wooden pillar through the rooms of the castle; for, by a strange conceit, the walls have been built round it. The thickness of the walls, the small

[1] In Scotland, there is a great deal of preparation before administering the sacrament. The minister of the parish examines the people as to their fitness, and to those of whom he approves gives little pieces of tin, stamped with the name of the parish, as *tokens*, which they must produce before receiving it. This is a species of priestly power, and sometimes may be abused. I remember a lawsuit brought by a person against his parish minister, for refusing him admission to that sacred ordinance. BOSWELL, ed. 1. ⟨See App. D, p. 507.⟩

[2] See *post*, v. 159, 206, 265.
[3] Mr. Trevelyan (*Life of Macaulay*, ch. i) says:—'Johnson pronounced that Mr. Macaulay was not competent to have written the book that went by his name; a decision which, to those who happen to have read the work, will give a very poor notion of my ancestor's abilities.' ⟨See App. D, pp. 505–7.⟩
[4]   'The thane of Cawdor lives,
   A prosperous gentleman.'
         Macbeth, act i. sc. 3.
⟨See App. D, p. 508.⟩
[5] ⟨See App. D, p. 508.⟩

slaunting windows, and a great iron door at the entrance on the second story as you ascend the stairs, all indicate the rude times in which this castle was erected. There were here some large venerable trees.

I was afraid of a quarrel between Dr. Johnson and Mr. M'Aulay, who talked slightingly of the lower English clergy. The Doctor gave him a frowning look, and said, ' This is a day of novelties : I have seen old trees in Scotland, and I have heard the English clergy treated with disrespect [1].'

I dreaded that a whole evening at Calder-manse would be heavy; however, Mr. Grant [2], an intelligent and well-bred minister in the neighbourhood, was there, and assisted us by his conversation. Dr. Johnson, talking of hereditary occupations in the Highlands, said, ' There is no harm in such a custom as this ; but it is wrong to enforce it, and oblige a man to be a taylor or a smith, because his father has been one.' This custom, however, is not peculiar to our Highlands ; it is well known that in India a similar practice prevails.

Mr. M'Aulay began a rhapsody against creeds and confessions. Dr. Johnson shewed, that ' what he called *imposition*, was only a voluntary declaration of agreement in certain articles of faith, which a church has a right to require, just as any other society can insist on certain rules being observed by it's members. Nobody is compelled to be of the church, as nobody is compelled to enter into a society.'—This was a very clear and just view of the subject : but, M'Aulay could not be driven out of his track. Dr. Johnson said, ' Sir, you are a *bigot to laxness*.'

Mr. M'Aulay and I laid the map of Scotland before us ; and he pointed out a route for us from Inverness, by Fort Augustus, to Glenelg, Sky, Mull, Icolmkill, Lorn, and Inveraray, which I wrote down. As my father was to begin the northern circuit about the 18th of September, it was necessary for us either to make our tour with great expedition, so as to get to Auchinleck before he set out, or to protract it, so as not to be there till his return, which would be about the 10th of October. By M'Aulay's calculation, we were not to land in Lorn till the 20th of September. I thought that the interruptions by bad days, or by occasional excursions, might make it ten days later ; and I

---

[1] See *post*, v. 382. ⟨Boswell in his original Journal adds : ' He did not perceive that honest Kenneth was not to be minded.' Ed. Pottle and Bennett, 1936, p. 87.⟩

[2] ⟨See App. D, p. 509.⟩

thought too, that we might perhaps go to Benbecula, and visit Clanranald, which would take a week of itself.

Dr. Johnson went up with Mr. Grant to the library, which consisted of a tolerable collection ; but the Doctor thought it rather a lady's library, with some Latin books in it by chance, than the library of a clergyman. It had only two of the Latin fathers, and one of the Greek fathers in Latin. I doubted whether Dr. Johnson would be present at a Presbyterian prayer. I told Mr. M'Aulay so, and said that the Doctor might sit in the library while we were at family worship. Mr. M'Aulay said, he would omit it, rather than give Dr. Johnson offence : but I would by no means agree that an excess of politeness, even to so great a man, should prevent what I esteem as one of the best pious regulations. I know nothing more beneficial, more comfortable, more agreeable, than that the little societies of each family should regularly assemble, and unite in praise and prayer to our heavenly Father, from whom we daily receive so much good, and may hope for more in a higher state of existence. I mentioned to Dr. Johnson the over-delicate scrupulosity of our host. He said, he had no objection to hear the prayer. This was a pleasing surprise to me ; for he refused to go and hear Principal Robertson [1] preach. ' I will hear him, (said he,) if he will get up into a tree and preach ; but I will not give a sanction, by my presence, to a Presbyterian assembly [2].'

Mr. Grant having prayed, Dr. Johnson said, his prayer was a very good one ; but objected to his not having introduced the Lord's Prayer [3]. He told us, that an Italian of some note in London said once to him, ' We have in our service a prayer called the *Pater Noster*, which is a very fine composition. I wonder who is the author of it.'—A singular instance of ignorance in a man of some literature and general inquiry [4] !

---

[1] The historian. *Ante*, v. 41. ⟨It was evidently on 15 Aug. that Johnson refused to hear him preach. *Ib.* 32.⟩
[2] See *ante*, iii. 336, and *post*, v. 384.
[3] See *post*, v. 365.
[4] Baretti was the Italian. Boswell disliked him (*ante*, ii. 98 note). Baretti complained to Malone that ' the story as told gave an unfair representation of him.' He had, he said, ' observed to Johnson that the petition *lead us not into temptation* ought rather to be addressed to the tempter of mankind than a benevolent Creator. . . . " Pray, sir," said Johnson, " do you know who was the author of the Lord's Prayer ? " Baretti (who did not wish to get into any serious dispute, and who

Saturday, 28th August.

Dr. Johnson had brought a Sallust with him in his pocket from Edinburgh. He gave it last night to Mr. M'Aulay's son, a smart young lad about eleven years old. Dr. Johnson had given an account of the education at Oxford, in all its gradations. The advantage of being a servitor to a youth of little fortune struck Mrs. M'Aulay much [1]. I observed it aloud. Dr. Johnson very handsomely and kindly said, that, if they would send their boy to him, when he was ready for the university, he would get him made a servitor, and perhaps would do more for him. He could not promise to do more; but would undertake for the servitorship [2].

I should have mentioned that Mr. White [3], a Welchman, who has been many years factor (*i.e.* steward) on the estate of Calder, drank tea with us last night, upon getting a note from Mr. M'Aulay, and[a] asked us to his house. We had not time to accept of

[a] and *before* asked 1, 2 (*MS. Journal*) : *before* upon 3.

appears to be an Infidel), by way of putting an end to the conversation, only replied :—" Oh, sir, you know by *our* religion (Roman Catholic), we are not permitted to read the Scriptures. You can't therefore expect an answer."' Prior's *Malone*, p. 399. Sir Joshua Reynolds, on hearing this from Malone, said :— 'This turn which Baretti now gives to the matter was an after-thought; for he once said to me myself, " There are various opinions about the writer of that prayer; some give it to St. Augustine, some to St. Chrysostom, &c. What is your opinion?"' *Ib.* p. 394. Mrs. Piozzi says that she heard Baretti ' tell Evans [the Rector of Southwark] the story of Dives and Lazarus as the subject of a poem he once had composed in the Milanese dialect, expecting great credit for his powers of invention.' Hayward's *Piozzi* (ed. 1), ii. 348.

[1] Goldsmith (*Present State of Polite Learning*, chap. 13) thus wrote of servitorships : ' Sure pride itself has dictated to the fellows of our colleges the absurd passion of being attended at meals, and on other public occasions, by those poor men, who, willing to be scholars, come in upon some charitable foundation. It implies a contradiction, for men to be at once learning the *liberal* arts, and at the same time treated as *slaves*; at once studying freedom, and practising servitude.' Yet a young man like Whitefield was willing enough to be a servitor. He had been a waiter in his mother's inn. See *Dr. Johnson : His Friends & his Critics*, p. 27.

[2] Dr. Johnson did not neglect what he had undertaken. By his interest with the Rev. Dr. Adams, master of Pembroke College, Oxford, where he was educated for some time, he obtained a servitorship for young M'Aulay. But it seems he had other views; and I believe went abroad. BOSWELL, ed. 1. See *ante*, ii. 380 ⟨and *post*, App. D, p. 505⟩.

[3] ⟨See App. D, p. 509.⟩

his invitation. He gave us a letter of introduction to Mr. Ferne †, master of stores at Fort George. He shewed it to me. It recommended 'two celebrated gentlemen ; no less than Dr. Johnson, *author of his Dictionary*,—and Mr. Boswell, known at Edinburgh by the name of Paoli.'—He said, he hoped I had no objection to what he had written ; if I had, he would alter it. I thought it was a pity to check his effusions, and acquiesced ; taking care, however, to seal the letter, that it might not appear that I had read it.

A conversation took place, about saying grace at breakfast (as we do in Scotland) as well as at dinner and supper ; in which Dr. Johnson said, ' It is enough if we have stated seasons of prayer ; no matter when [1]. A man may as well pray when he mounts his horse, or a woman when she milks her cow, (which Mr. Grant told us is done in the Highlands,) as at meals ; and custom is to be followed [2].'

We proceeded to Fort George §. When we came into the square, I sent a soldier with the letter to Mr. Ferne. He came to us immediately, and along with him came Major *Brewse* of the Engineers, pronounced *Bruce*. He said he believed it was originally the same Norman name with Bruce. That he had dined at a house in London, where were three Bruces, one of the Irish line, one of the Scottish line, and himself of the English line. He said he was shewn it in the Herald's office spelt fourteen different ways [3]. I told him the different spellings of

† ⟨Various ' imprests ' or advances were paid to George Fern from the Office of Ordnance in 1772 and 1773 (W.O. 54/133 in P.R.O.).⟩
[1] ' I once drank tea,' writes Lamb, ' in company with two Methodist divines of different persuasions. . . . Before the first cup was handed round, one of these reverend gentlemen put it to the other, with all due solemnity, whether he chose to *say any thing*. It seems it is the custom with some sectaries to put up a short prayer before this meal also. His reverend brother did not at first quite apprehend him, but upon an explanation, with little less importance he made answer, that it was not a custom known in his church.' *Elia, Grace before Meat*.

[2] He could not bear to have it thought that, in any instance whatever, the Scots are more pious than the English. I think grace as proper at breakfast as at any other meal. It is the pleasantest meal we have. Dr. Johnson has allowed the peculiar merit of breakfast in Scotland. BOSWELL, ed. 1.
' If an epicure could remove by a wish, in quest of sensual gratifications, wherever he had supped he would breakfast in Scotland.' Johnson's *Western Isl.*, p. 50.
§ ⟨See App. D, p. 509.⟩
[3] Bruce, the Abyssinian traveller, found in the annals of that region a king named *Brus*, which he chooses to consider the genuine orthography of the name. This circumstance

my name [1]. Dr. Johnson observed, that there had been great disputes about the spelling of Shakspear's name; at last it was thought it would be settled by looking at the original copy of his will; but, upon examining it, he was found to have written it himself no less than three different ways †.

Mr. Ferne and Major Brewse first carried us to wait on Sir Eyre Coote [2], whose regiment, the 37th, was lying here, and who then commanded the fort. He asked us to dine with him, which we agreed to do.

Before dinner we examined the fort. The Major explained the fortification to us, and Mr. Ferne gave us an account of the stores. Dr. Johnson talked of the proportions of charcoal and salt-petre in making gunpowder, of granulating it, and of giving it a gloss [3]. He made a very good figure upon these topicks. He said to me afterwards, that 'he had talked *ostentatiously* [4].'—We reposed ourselves a little in Mr. Ferne's house. He had every thing in neat order as in England; and a tolerable collection of books. I looked into Pennant's Tour in Scotland. He says little of this fort; but that 'the barracks, &c. form several streets [5].' This is aggrandising. Mr. Ferne observed, if he had said they form a square, with a row of buildings before it, he would have given a juster description. Dr. Johnson remarked, 'how seldom descriptions correspond with realities; and the reason is, that people do not write them till some time after, and then their imagination has added circumstances.'

We talked of Sir Adolphus Oughton [6]. The Major said, he knew a great deal for a military man.—*Johnson*. 'Sir, you

occasioned some mirth at the court of Gondar. SCOTT, 1831. ⟨For Major Brewse see App. D, p. 509.⟩

[1] See *ante*, ii. 169, note 2, ⟨iii. 439, 540⟩. Johnson, so far as I have observed, spelt the name *Boswel*. ⟨Lord Auchinleck invariably spelt it so.⟩

† ⟨See App. D, pp. 509–10.⟩

[2] ⟨Sir Eyre Coote, 1726–83. As an ensign in the 27th Foot he saved the King's Colour at Falkirk, an act which was misunderstood and for which he was broke by court martial. He led a division at Plassey, 1757, commanded at the two battles of Wandewash, 1759–60, and captured Pondicherry, 1761. He was ap-

pointed Commander-in-Chief in India in 1777 and repeatedly defeated Hyder Ali in 1780. See *D.N.B.* and Col. H. C. Wylly, *Life of Coote*, 1922.⟩

[3] See *ante*, iii. 361.

[4] Reynolds wrote of Johnson:—'He sometimes, it must be confessed, covered his ignorance by generals rather than appear ignorant.' Leslie and Taylor's *Reynolds*, ii. 457.

[5] 'The barracks are very handsome, and form several regular and good streets.' Pennant's *Tour Scotl.* *1769*, 1771, p. 136.

[6] ⟨Boswell notes, 10 Dec. 1774, 'Sir Adolphus allways inspirits me.' *Boswell Papers*, x. 64. See *ante*, v. 45; *post*, v. 272, and 394.⟩

will find few men, of any profession, who know more. Sir Adolphus is a very extraordinary man; a man of boundless curiosity and unwearied diligence.'

I know not how the Major contrived to introduce the contest between Warburton and Lowth.—*Johnson.* ' Warburton kept his temper all along, while Lowth was in a passion. Lowth published some of Warburton's letters. Warburton drew *him* on to write some very abusive letters, and then asked his leave to publish them; which he knew Lowth could not refuse, after what *he* had done. So that Warburton contrived that he should publish, apparently with Lowth's consent, what could not but shew Lowth in a disadvantageous light [1].'

At three the drum beat for dinner. I, for a little while, fancied myself a military man, and it pleased me. We went to Sir Eyre Coote's, at the governour's house, and found him a most gentleman-like man. His lady is a very agreeable woman, with an uncommonly mild and sweet tone of voice. There was a pretty large company: Mr. Ferne, Major Brewse, and several officers. Sir Eyre had come from the East-Indies by land, through the Desarts of Arabia. He told us, the Arabs could live five days without victuals, and subsist for three weeks on nothing else but the blood of their camels, who could lose so much of it as would suffice for that time, without being exhausted. He highly praised the virtue of the Arabs; their fidelity, if they undertook to conduct any person; and said, they would sacrifice their lives rather than let him be robbed. Dr. Johnson, who is always for maintaining the superiority of civilized over uncivilized men [2], said, ' Why, sir, I can see no superiour virtue in this. A serjeant and twelve men, who are my guard, will die, rather than that I shall be robbed.'—Colonel Pennington [3], of the 37th regiment, took up the argument with a good deal of spirit and ingenuity.—*Pennington.* ' But the soldiers

---

[1] Here Dr. Johnson gave us part of a conversation held between a Great Personage and him, in the library at the Queen's Palace, in the course of which this contest was considered. I have been at great pains to get that conversation as perfectly preserved as possible. It may perhaps at some future time be given to the publick. BOSWELL, edd. 1, 2. For ' a Great Personage ' see *ante,* i. 219. ⟨The conversation was first published separately. See *ante,* ii. 34 note.⟩

[2] See *ante,* ii. 73, 228, 248; iii. 49; and iv. 308–9.

[3] ⟨See App. D, p. 510.⟩

are compelled to this, by fear of punishment.'—*Johnson.* ' Well, sir, the Arabs are compelled by the fear of infamy.'—*Pennington.* ' The soldiers have the same fear of infamy, and the fear of punishment besides ; so have less virtue ; because they act less voluntarily.'—Lady Coote observed very well, that it ought to be known if there was not, among the Arabs, some punishment for not being faithful on such occasions.

We talked of the stage. I observed, that we had not now such a company of actors as in the last age ; Wilks [1], Booth [2], &c. &c.—*Johnson.* ' You think so, because there is one who excels all the rest so much : you compare them with Garrick, and see the deficiency. Garrick's great distinction is his universality [3]. He can represent all modes of life, but that of an easy fine-bred gentleman [4].'—*Pennington.* ' He should give over playing young parts.'—*Johnson.* ' He does not take them now ; but he does not leave off those which he has been used to play, because he does them better than any one else can do them. If you had generations of actors, if they swarmed like bees, the young ones might drive off the old. Mrs. Cibber [5], I think, got more reputation than she deserved, as she had a great sameness ; though her expression was undoubtedly very fine †. Mrs. Clive [6] was the best player I ever saw. Mrs. Pritchard [7] was a very good one ; but she had something affected in her manner : I imagine she had some player of the former age in her eye, which occasioned it.'

---

[1] See *ante*, i. 167, note 1.

[2] Booth acted Cato, and Wilks Juba, when Addison's *Cato* was brought out. Pope told Spence that ' Lord Bolingbroke's carrying his friends to the house, and presenting Booth with a purse of guineas, for so well representing the character of a person " who rather chose to die than be a general for life," . . . carried the success of the play much beyond what they ever expected.' Spence's *Anec.*, 1858, p. 35. Bolingbroke alluded to the Duke of Marlborough. Pope in his *Imitations of Horace*, Bk. 2, Epist. i. 123, introduces ' wellmouth'd Booth.'

[3] See *ante*, iii. 35, and iv. 243.

[4] ' Garrick used to tell, that Johnson said of an actor, who played Sir Harry Wildair at Lichfield, " There is a courtly vivacity about the fellow ; " when in fact, according to Garrick's account, " he was the most vulgar ruffian that ever went upon *boards*." ' *Ante*, ii. 465.

[5] Mrs. Cibber was the sister of Dr. Arne the musical composer, and the wife of Theophilus Cibber, Colley Cibber's son. She died in 1766, and was buried in the cloisters of Westminster Abbey. Baker's *Biog. Dram.*, 1782, i. 85–6. ⟨See also *D.N.B.*⟩

† ⟨' Though she had something very fine.' Boswell's *Hebrides*, ed. Pottle and Bennett, 1936, p. 93.⟩

[6] See *ante*, iv. 7 and 243.

[7] See *ante*, i. 197 ; ii. 348 ; iv. 243.

Fort George   *Saturday 28 August* 1773

Colonel Pennington said, Garrick sometimes failed in emphasis [1] ; as for instance, in *Hamlet*,

    I will speak *daggers* to her ; but use *none* [2].

instead of

    I will *speak* daggers to her ; but *use* none.

We had a dinner of two complete courses, variety of wines, and the regimental band of musick playing in the square, before the windows, after it. I enjoyed this day much. We were quite easy and cheerful. Dr. Johnson said, ' I shall always remember this fort with gratitude.' I could not help being struck with some admiration, at finding upon this barren sandy point, such buildings,—such a dinner,—such company : it was like enchantment. Dr. Johnson, on the other hand, said to me more rationally, that ' it did not strike *him* as any thing extraordinary ; because he knew, here was a large sum of money expended in building a fort ; here was a regiment. If there had been less than what we found, it would have surprized him.' *He* looked coolly and deliberately through all the gradations : my warm imagination jumped from the barren sands to the splendid dinner and brilliant company, to borrow the expression of an absurd poet,

          ' Without ands or ifs,
    I leapt from off the sands upon the cliffs.'

The whole scene gave me a strong impression of the power and excellence of human art.

We left the fort between six and seven o'clock. Sir Eyre Coote, Colonel Pennington, and several more, accompanied us down stairs, and saw us into our chaise. There could not be greater attention paid to any visitors. Sir Eyre spoke of the hardships which Dr. Johnson had before him.—*Boswell.* ' Considering what he has said of us, we must make him feel something rough in Scotland.'—Sir Eyre said to him, ' You must change your name, sir.'—*Boswell.* ' Ay, to Dr. M'Gregor [3].'

---

[1] Johnson had set him to repeat the ninth commandment, and had with great glee put him right in the emphasis. *Ante*, i. 168.

[2] Act iii. sc. 2.

[3] ⟨The reference is to the famous Act of 3 April 1603 by which it was ordained that ' the name of mcgregoure sulde be altogidder abolisched And þat the haill persounes of thatt clan suld renunce thair name and tak thame sum vther name And

Sunday 29 August 1773 — Inverness

We got safely to Inverness, and put up at Mackenzie's inn †. Mr. Keith, the collector of Excise here, my old acquaintance at Ayr, who had seen us at the Fort, visited us in the evening, and engaged us to dine with him next day, promising to breakfast with us, and take us to the English chapel; so that we were at once commodiously arranged.

Not finding a letter here that I expected, I felt a momentary impatience to be at home. Transient clouds darkened my imagination, and in those clouds I saw events from which I shrunk; but a sentence or two of the *Rambler's* conversation gave me firmness, and I considered that I was upon an expedition for which I had wished for years, and the recollection of which would be a treasure to me for life.

Sunday, 29th August.

Mr. Keith breakfasted with us. Dr. Johnson expatiated rather too strongly upon the benefits derived to Scotland from the Union [1], and the bad state of our people before it. I am entertained with his copious exaggeration upon that subject; but I am uneasy when people are by, who do not know him as well as I do, and may be apt to think him narrow-minded [2]. I therefore diverted the subject.

The English chapel §, to which we went this morning, was but mean. The altar was a bare fir table, with a coarse stool for kneeling on, covered with a piece of thick sail-cloth doubled, by way of cushion. The congregation was small. Mr. Tait, the clergyman, read prayers very well, though with much of the Scotch accent. He preached on '*Love your Enemies* [3].' It was remarkable that, when talking of the connections amongst men, he said, that some connected themselves with men of distinguished talents, and since they could not equal them, tried to deck themselves with their merit, by being their companions.

---

that They nor nane of thair posteritie suld call þame selffis gregor or mᶜgregoure thairefter.' *Acts Parl. Scotl.*, 1816, iv. 550. See *Lives of Poets, Mallet,* 2.⟩

† ⟨Described in *Gent. Mag.*, 1771, xli. 544. ' Horns, Mrs. Mackenzie; dirty and ill managed.' Boswell adds in his original Journal: ' The inn was dirty and ill-furnished. The entertainment pretty good.' Ed. Pottle and Bennett, 1936, p. 95. See App. D, p. 510.⟩

[1] See *ante*, iii. 410.

[2] It is remarkable that Dr. Johnson read this gentle remonstrance, and took no notice of it to me. Boswell, ed. 1. See *post*, v. 307, n. 2.

§ ⟨See App. D, p. 510.⟩

[3] St. Matthew, v. 44.

Inverness *Sunday 29 August* 1773

The sentence was to this purpose. It had an odd coincidence with what might be said of my connecting myself with Dr. Johnson [1].

After church, we walked down to the Quay. We then went to Macbeth's castle [2]. I had a romantick satisfaction in seeing Dr. Johnson actually in it. It perfectly corresponds with Shakspeare's description, which Sir Joshua Reynolds has so happily illustrated, in one of his notes on our immortal poet [3] :

'This castle hath a pleasant seat : the air
Nimbly and sweetly recommends itself
Unto our gentle sense,' &c.[4]

Just as we came out of it, a raven perched on one of the chimney-tops, and croaked. Then I repeated

'————The raven himself is hoarse,
That croaks the fatal enterance of Duncan
Under my battlements [5].'

---

[1] It is odd that Boswell did not suspect the parson, who, no doubt, had learnt the evening before from Mr. Keith that the two travellers would be present at his sermon. Northcote (*Life of Reynolds*, ii. 283) says that one day at Sir Joshua's dinner-table, when his host praised Malone very highly for his laborious edition of *Shakespeare*, he (Northcote) 'rather hastily replied, "What a very despicable creature must that man be who thus devotes himself, and makes another man his God ;" when Boswell, who sat at my elbow, and was not in my thoughts at the time, cried out immediately, "Oh! Sir Joshua, then that is me!"'

[2] Johnson (*Western Isl.*, p. 23) more cautiously says :—' Here is a castle, called the castle of Macbeth.' ⟨See App. D, p. 511.⟩

[3] 'This short dialogue between Duncan and Banquo, whilst they are approaching the gates of Macbeth's castle, has always appeared to me a striking instance of what in painting is termed *repose*. Their conversation very naturally turns upon the beauty of its situation, and the pleasantness of the air ; and Banquo, observing the martlets' nests in every recess of the cornice, remarks, that where those birds most breed and haunt, the air is delicate. The subject of this quiet and easy conversation gives that repose so necessary to the mind after the tumultuous bustle of the preceding scenes, and perfectly contrasts the scene of horror that immediately succeeds. It seems as if Shakspeare asked himself, What is a prince likely to say to his attendants on such an occasion? Whereas the modern writers seem, on the contrary, to be always searching for new thoughts, such as would never occur to men in the situation which is represented.—This also is frequently the practice of Homer, who from the midst of battles and horrors, relieves and refreshes the mind of the reader, by introducing some quiet rural image, or picture of familiar domestick life.' Malone's *Suppl. to Shakspeare*, 1780, i. 152. ⟨Reynolds adapted this note from his eighth *Discourse* (1779). For other notes by Reynolds see Hilles, *Lit. Career Reynolds*, 1936, 27 ff. and 98 ff.⟩

[4] Act i. sc. 6.
[5] Act i. sc. 5.

We dined at Mr. Keith's. Mrs. Keith was rather too attentive to Dr. Johnson, asking him many questions about his drinking only water. He repressed that observation, by saying to me, 'You may remember that Lady Errol took no notice of this.'

Dr. Johnson has the happy art (for which I have heard my father praise the old Earl of Aberdeen) of instructing himself, by making every man he meets tell him something of what he knows best. He led Keith to talk to him of the Excise in Scotland, and, in the course of conversation, mentioned that his friend Mr. Thrale, the great brewer, paid twenty thousand pounds a year to the revenue; and that he had four casks, each of which holds sixteen hundred barrels,—above a thousand hogsheads.

After this there was little conversation that deserves to be remembered. I shall therefore here again glean what I have omitted on former days. Dr. Gerrard, at Aberdeen, told us, that when he was in Wales, he was shewn a valley inhabited by Danes, who still retain their own language, and are quite a distinct people. Dr. Johnson thought it could not be true, or all the kingdom must have heard of it. He said to me, as we travelled, 'these people, sir, that Gerrard talks of, may have somewhat of a *peregrinity* in their dialect, which relation has augmented to a different language.' I asked him if *peregrinity* was an English word: he [a] laughed, and said, 'No.' I told him this was the second time that I had heard him coin a word [1]. When Foote broke his leg, I observed that it would make him fitter for taking off George Faulkner as Peter Paragraph [2], poor George having a wooden leg. Dr. Johnson at that time said, 'George will rejoice at the *depeditation* of Foote;' and when I challenged that word, laughed, and owned he had made it; [b] and added that he had not made above three or four in his Dictionary [3].

[a] word? He 1 : word : he 2, 3.   [b] it; 1, 2: it, 3.

[1] Boswell forgets *scoundrelism*, ante, v. 106, which Johnson ⟨was the first to use. *Peregrinity* in the sense of 'foreignness', 'outlandishness', is recorded as early as 1591. See the Oxford Dictionary.⟩

[2] See *ante*, ii. 154, note 3. Peter Paragraph is one of the characters in Foote's comedy of *The Orators*.

[3] When upon the subject of this *peregrinity*, he told me some particulars concerning the compilation of his Dictionary, and concerning his throwing off Lord Chesterfield's patronage, of which very erroneous accounts have been circulated. These particulars, with others which he afterwards gave me,—as also his celebrated letter to Lord Chesterfield, which he dictated to me,—I reserve for his 'LIFE'. BOSWELL, ed. 1. See *ante*, i. 221, 261.

Inverness–Lock Ness *Monday* 30 *August* 1773

Having conducted Dr. Johnson to our inn, I begged permission to leave him for a little, that I might run about and pay some short visits to several good people of Inverness. He said to me, ' You have all the old-fashioned principles, good and bad.'—I acknowledge I have. That of attention to relations in the remotest degree, or to worthy persons [a] in every state whom I have once known, I inherit from my father. It gave me much satisfaction to hear every body at Inverness speak of him with uncommon regard.—Mr. Keith and Mr. Grant, whom we had seen at Mr. M'Aulay's, supped with us at the inn †. We had roasted kid, which Dr. Johnson had never tasted before. He relished it much.

Monday, 30th August.

This day we were to begin our *equitation*, as I said; for *I* would needs make a word too. It is remarkable, that my noble, and to me most constant friend, the Earl of Pembroke [1], (who, if there is too much ease on my part, will be pleased [b] to pardon what his benevolent, gay, social intercourse, and lively correspondence, have insensibly produced,) has since hit upon the very same word. The title of the first edition of his lordship's very useful book was, in simple terms, 'A Method of breaking Horses,[c] and teaching Soldiers to ride.' The title of the second edition is, ' MILITARY EQUITATION [2].'

We might have taken a chaise to Fort Augustus; but, had we not hired horses at Inverness, we should not have found them afterwards: so we resolved to begin here to ride. We had three horses, for Dr. Johnson, myself, and Joseph, and one which carried our portmanteaus, and two Highlanders who walked along with us, John Hay and Lauchlan Vass, whom Dr. Johnson has remembered with credit in his JOURNEY [3], though he has omitted their names. Dr. Johnson rode very well.

[a] persons 1, 2 : persons, 3.   [b] will be pleased 1 : will be pleased 2 : will please 3.   [c] Horses, 1, 2 : Horses 3.

† ⟨See App. D, p. 511.⟩
[1] See *ante*, ii. 326, 371, and v. 18.
[2] It is the third edition, published in 1778, that first bears this title. The first edition was published in 1761, and the second in 1762. ⟨There was a fourth edition in 1793. The word ' equitation ' was not new : see O.E.D. See also *Ann. Reg.*, 1771,

ii, Account of Books, 263.⟩
[3] ' One of them was a man of great liveliness and activity, of whom his companion said, that he would tire any horse in Inverness. Both of them were civil and ready-handed. Civility seems part of the national character of Highlanders.' *Western Isl.*, p. 25. ⟨See also *Letters*, No. 323.⟩

Monday 30 August 1773   Loch Ness

About three miles beyond Inverness, we saw, just by the road, a very complete specimen of what is called a Druid's temple. There was a double circle, one of very large, the other of smaller stones. Dr. Johnson justly observed, that, ' to go and see one druidical temple is only to see that it is nothing, for there is neither art nor power in it; and seeing one is quite enough.'

It was a delightful day. Lochness, and the road upon the side of it, shaded with birch trees, and the hills above it, pleased us much. The scene was as sequestered and agreeably wild as could be desired, and for a time engrossed all our attention [1].

To see Dr. Johnson in any new situation is always an interesting object to me; and, as I saw him now for the first time on horseback, jaunting about at his ease in quest of pleasure and novelty, the very different occupations of his former laborious life, his admirable productions, his *London*, his *Rambler*, &c. &c. immediately presented themselves to my mind, and the contrast made a strong impression on my imagination.

When we had advanced a good way by the side of Lochness, I perceived a little hut, with an old-looking woman at the door of it.[2] I thought here might be a scene that would amuse Dr. Johnson; so I mentioned it to him. ' Let's go in,' said he. We dismounted, and we and our guides entered the hut. It was a wretched little hovel of earth only, I think, and for a window had only a small hole, which was stopped with a piece of turf, that was taken out occasionally to let in light. In the middle of the room or space which we entered, was a fire of peat, the smoke going out at a hole in the roof. She had a pot upon it, with goat's flesh, boiling. There was at one end under the same roof, but divided by a kind of partition made of wattles, a pen or fold in which we saw a good many kids.

Dr. Johnson was curious to know where she slept. I asked one of the guides, who questioned her in Erse. She answered

---

[1] ' The way was very pleasant. The rock out of which the road was cut was covered with Birch trees, fern and heath. The Lake below was beating its bank by a gentle wind. . . . In one part of the way we had trees on both sides, for perhaps half a mile. Such a length of Shade perhaps Scotland cannot show in any other place.' *Letters*, No. 323. The travellers must have passed close by the cottage where James Mackintosh was living, a child of seven.

[2] ⟨The site is marked by a stone.⟩

with a tone of emotion, saying, (as he told us,) she was afraid we wanted to go to bed to her. This *coquetry*, or whatever it may be called, of so wretched a being, was truly ludicrous. Dr. Johnson and I afterwards were merry upon it. I said, it was he who alarmed the poor woman's virtue.—' No, sir, (said he,) she'll say, " there came a wicked young fellow, a wild dog, who I believe would have ravished me, had there not been with him a grave old gentleman, who repressed him : but when he gets out of the sight of his tutor, I'll warrant you he'll spare no woman he meets, young or old." '—' No, sir, (I replied,) she'll say, " There was a terrible ruffian who would have forced me, had it not been for a civil decent young man,[a]† who, I take it, was an angel sent from heaven to protect me." '

Dr. Johnson would not hurt her delicacy, by insisting on ' seeing her bed-chamber,' like *Archer* in the *Beaux Stratagem* [1]. But my curiosity was more ardent ; I lighted a piece of paper, and went into the place where the bed was. There was a little partition of wicker, rather more neatly done than that for the fold, and close by the wall was a kind of bedstead of wood with heath upon it by way of bed ; at the foot of which I saw some sort of blankets or covering rolled up in a heap. The woman's name was Fraser ; so was her husband's. He was a man of eighty. Mr. Fraser of Balnain § allows him to live in this hut, and keep sixty goats, for taking care of his woods, where he then was. They had five children, the eldest only thirteen. Two were gone to Inverness to buy meal [2] ; the rest were looking after the goats. This contented family had four stacks of barley, twenty-four sheaves in each. They had a few fowls. We were informed that they lived all the spring without meal, upon milk and curds and whey alone. What they get for their goats, kids, and fowls, maintains them during the rest of the year.

[a] man, 1, 2 : man 3.

† ⟨' A gentle, mild-looking youth ' in Boswell's *Hebrides*, ed. Pottle and Bennett, 1936, p. 106.⟩

[1] Boswell refers, I think, to a passage in act iv. sc. 1 of Farquhar's comedy, where Archer says to Mrs. Sullen :—' I can't at this Distance, Madam, distinguish the Figures of the Embroidery.' This passage is copied by Goldsmith in *She Stoops to Conquer*, act iii.

§ ⟨William Fraser, W.S., 1703–75. See Alex. Mackenzie, *Hist. Frasers*, 1896, pp. 552, 557, and Sir C. Fraser-Mackintosh, *Letters of Two Centuries*.⟩

[2] Johnson (*Western Isl.*, p. 28) gives a long account of this woman. 'Meal she considered as expensive food, and told us, that in Spring, when the goats gave milk, the children could live without it.'

She asked us to sit down and take a dram. I saw one chair. She said,ᵃ she was as happy as any woman in Scotland. She could hardly speak any English,ᵇ except a few detached words. Dr. Johnson was pleased at seeing, for the first time, such a state of human life. She asked for snuff. It is her luxury, and she uses a great deal. We had none; but gave her sixpence a piece. She then brought out her whisky bottle. I tasted it; as did Joseph and our guides: so I gave her sixpence more. She sent us away with many prayers in Erse.

We dined at a littleᶜ publick house called the *General's* Hut ¹, from General Wade, who was lodged there when he commanded in the North. Near it is the meanest parish Kirk † I ever saw. It is a shame it should be on a high road. After dinner, we passed through a good deal of mountainous country. I had known Mr. Trapaud §, the deputy governour of Fort Augustus, twelve years ago, at a circuit at Inverness, where my father was judge. I sent forward one of our guides, and Joseph, with a card to him, that he might know Dr. Johnson and I were coming up, leaving it to him to invite us or not ². It was dark when we arrived. The inn was wretched. Government ought to build one, or give the resident governour an additional salary; as,ᵈ in the present state of things, he must necessarily be put to a great expence in entertaining travellers. Joseph announced to us, when we alighted, that the governour waited for us at the gate of the fort. We walked to it. He met us, and with much civility conducted us to his house. It was comfortable to find ourselves in a well-built little square, and a neatly furnished house, in good company, and with a good supper before us; in short, with all the conveniencies of civilized life in the midst of rude mountains. Mrs. Trapaud, and the governour's daughter, and her husband, Captain Newmarsh ³, were all most obliging and polite. The governour had excellent animal spirits, the conversation of a

ᵃ, ᵇ *comma omitted* 3.   ᶜ little *omitted* 3.   ᵈ *comma omitted* 3.

¹ ⟨Johnson's description is more accurate; he says it is 'so called because it was the temporary abode of Wade, while he superintended the works upon the road. It is now a house of entertainment for passengers, and we found it not ill stocked with provisions'. *Western Isl.*, p. 29. Its exact position is shown by a map reproduced by Dr. Hill. *Footsteps*, p. 150. Dr. T. Garnett reports a change of site, to one 'very near' its original position, but not of name. *Tour Highlands*, 1800, i. 322. See also Johnson's *Letters*, No. 323.⟩
†, § ⟨See App. D, pp. 511-12.⟩
² 'Mr. Boswell, who, between his father's merit and his own, is sure of reception wherever he comes, sent a servant before,' &c. Johnson's *Western Isl.*, pp. 29-30.
³ ⟨See App. D, p. 512.⟩

Fort Augustus–Anoch Tuesday 31 August 1773

soldier, and somewhat of a Frenchman, to which his extraction entitles him. He is brother to General Cyrus Trapaud. We passed a very agreeable evening [1].

Tuesday, 31st August.

The governour has a very good garden. We looked at it, and at all[a] the rest of the fort, which is but small, and may be commanded from a variety of hills around. We also looked at the galley or sloop belonging to the fort, which sails upon the Loch, and brings what is wanted for the garrison. Captains Urie and Darippe, of the 15th regiment of foot, breakfasted with us. They had served in America, and entertained Dr. Johnson much with an account of the Indians [2]. He said, he could make a very pretty book out of them, were he to stay there. Governour Trapaud was much struck with Dr. Johnson. 'I like to hear him, (said he,) it is so majestick. I should be glad to hear him speak in your court.'—He pressed us to stay dinner; but I considered that we had a rude road before us, which we could more easily encounter in the morning, and that it was hard to say when we might get up, were we to sit down to good entertainment, in good company: I therefore begged the governour would excuse us.—Here,[b] too, I had another very pleasing proof how much my father is regarded. The governour expressed the highest respect for him, and bade me tell him, that, if he would come that way on the Northern circuit, he would do him all the honours of the garrison.

Between twelve and one we set out, and travelled eleven miles, through a wild country, till we came to a house in Glenmorison, called *Anoch*, kept by a M'Queen [3]. Our landlord was

[a] all *omitted* 3. [b] comma *omitted* 2, 3.

[1] On April 6, 1777, Johnson noted down: 'I passed the night in such sweet uninterrupted sleep, as I have not known since I slept at Fort Augustus.' *Pr. and Med.* ¶ 121. On Nov. 21, 1778, he wrote to Boswell: 'The best night that I have had these twenty years was at Fort-Augustus.' *Ante*, iii. 369.

[2] See *ante*, iii. 246. ⟨The captains were Lewis Ourry and Isaac Augustus D'Aripé: see App. D, p. 513.⟩

[3] *A* M'Queen is a Highland mode of expression. An Englishman would say *one* M'Queen. But where there are *clans* or *tribes* of men, distinguished by *patronymick* surnames, the individuals of each are considered as if they were of different species, at least as much as nations are distinguished; so that a *M'Queen*, a *M'Donald*, a *M'Lean*, is said, as we say a Frenchman, an Italian, a Spaniard. BOSWELL, ed. 1.

a sensible fellow : he had learnt his grammar [1], and Dr. Johnson justly observed, that 'a man is the better for that as long as he lives.' There were some books here : a Treatise against Drunkenness, translated from the French ; a volume of the Spectator ; a volume of Prideaux's Connection †, and Cyrus's Travels [2]. M'Queen said he had more volumes ; and his pride seemed to be much piqued that we were surprised at his having books.

Near to this place we had passed a party of soldiers, under a serjeant's command, at work upon the road. We gave them two shillings to drink. They came to our inn, and made merry in the barn. We went and paid them a visit, Dr. Johnson saying, ' Come, let's go and give 'em another shilling a-piece.' We did so ; and he was saluted ' MY LORD ' by all of them. He is really generous, loves influence, and has the way of gaining it. He said, ' I am quite feudal, sir.' Here I agree with him. I said, I regretted I was not the head of a clan ; however, though not possessed of such an hereditary advantage, I would always endeavour to make my tenants follow me. I could not be a *patriarchal* chief, but I would be a *feudal* chief.

The poor soldiers got too much liquor. Some of them fought, and left blood upon the spot, and cursed whisky next morning. The house here was built of thick turfs, and thatched with thinner turfs and heath. It had three rooms in length, and a little room which projected. Where we sat, the side-walls were *wainscotted*, as Dr. Johnson said, with wicker, very neatly plaited. Our landlord had made the whole with his own hands.

After dinner, M'Queen sat by us a while, and talked with us. He said, all the Laird of Glenmorison's people would bleed for

---

[1] ' I praised the propriety of his language, and was answered that I need not wonder, for he had learned it by grammar. By subsequent opportunities of observation, I found that my host's diction had nothing peculiar. Those Highlanders that can speak English, commonly speak it well, with few of the words, and little of the tone by which a Scotchman is distinguished. . . . By their Lowland neighbours they would not willingly be taught ; for they have long considered them as a mean and degenerate race.' *Western Isl.*, p. 31. He wrote to Mrs. Thrale : ' This man's conversation we were glad of while we staid. He had been *out*, as they call it, in forty five, and still retained his old opinions.' *Letters*, No. 326. ⟨For MacQueen see *post*, App. D, p. 514.⟩

† ⟨*The Old and New Testament Connected in the History of the Jews and Neighbouring Nations*. By H. Prideaux, Dean of Norwich, first published in 1716-18, in two volumes octavo.⟩

[2] By the Chevalier Ramsay ⟨1727. The English translation was published in the same year and ran into nine editions by 1763.⟩

him, if they were well used; but that seventy men had gone out of the Glen to America. That he himself intended to go next year; for that the rent of his farm, which twenty years ago was only five pounds, was now raised to twenty pounds. That he could pay ten pounds, and live; but no more [1].—Dr. Johnson said, he wished M'Queen laird of Glenmorison, and the laird to go to America. M'Queen very generously answered, he should be sorry for it; for the laird could not shift for himself in America as he could do.

I talked of the officers whom we had left to-day; how much service they had seen, and how little they got for it, even of fame.—*Johnson.* ' Sir, a soldier gets as little as any man can get.'—*Boswell.* ' Goldsmith has acquired more fame than all the officers last war, who were not Generals [2].'—*Johnson.* ' Why, sir, you will find ten thousand fit to do what they did, before you find one who does what Goldsmith has done. You must consider, that a thing is valued according to its rarity. A pebble that paves the street is in itself more useful than the diamond upon a lady's finger.'—I wish our friend Goldsmith had heard this [3].

I yesterday expressed my wonder that John Hay, one of our guides, who had been pressed aboard a man of war, did not choose to continue in it longer than nine months, after which time he got off.—*Johnson.* ' Why, sir, no man will be a sailor, who has contrivance enough to get himself into a jail; for, being in a ship is being in a jail, with the chance of being drowned [4].'

[1] ' From him we first heard of the general dissatisfaction, which is now driving the Highlanders into the other hemisphere; and when I asked him whether they would stay at home, if they were well treated, he answered with indignation, that no man willingly left his native country.' *Western Isl.*, p. 33. See *ante*, v. 27. ⟨See *post*, App. D, p. 514.⟩

[2] ' The chief glory of every people arises from its authors.' *Pref. to Dictionary*, ¶ 92.

[3] Four years later, three years after Goldsmith's death, Johnson ' observed in Lord Scarsdale's dressing-room Goldsmith's *Animated Nature*; and said, " Here's our friend ! The poor Doctor would have been happy to hear of this." ' *Ante*, iii. 162.

[4] See *ante*, i. 348 and ii. 438, and *post*, v. 249. ⟨Cf. Burton, *Anat.* II. iii. 4 ' What is a ship but a prison'.⟩ Mackintosh says : ' Johnson's idea, that a ship was a prison, with the danger of drowning, is taken from Endymion Porter's *Consolation to Howell*, on his imprisonment in the *Fleet*, and was originally suggested by the pun.' *Life of Mackintosh*, ii. 83. The passage to which he refers is found in Howell's letter of Jan. 2, 1646 (book ii. letter 39), in which he writes to Porter :—' You go on to prefer my captivity in this *Fleet* to that of a Voyager at Sea, in regard that he is

Tuesday 31 August 1773

We had tea in the afternoon, and our landlord's daughter, a modest civil girl, very neatly drest, made it for us. She told us, she had been a year at Inverness, and learnt reading and writing, sewing, knotting [1], working lace, and pastry. Dr. Johnson made her a present of a book which he had bought at Inverness [2].

The room had some deals laid across the joists, as a kind of ceiling. There were two beds in the room, and a woman's gown was hung on a rope to make a curtain of separation between them. Joseph had sheets, which my wife had sent with us, laid on them. We had much hesitation, whether to

---

subject to storms and springing of Leaks, to Pirates and Picaroons, with other casualties.' ⟨See App. D, p. 514.⟩

[1] See *ante*, iii. 242.

[2] This book has given rise to much inquiry, which has ended in ludicrous surprise. Several ladies, wishing to learn the kind of reading which the great and good Dr. Johnson esteemed most fit for a young woman, desired to know what book he had selected for this Highland nymph. 'They never adverted, (said he,) that I had no *choice* in the matter. I have said that I presented her with a book which I *happened* to have about me.'—And what was this book?—My readers, prepare your features for merriment. It was *Cocker's Arithmetick!*— Wherever this was mentioned, there was a loud laugh, at which Dr. Johnson, when present, used sometimes to be a little angry. One day, when we were dining at General Oglethorpe's, where we had many a valuable day, I ventured to interrogate him, ' But, sir, is it not somewhat singular that you should *happen* to have *Cocker's Arithmetick* about you on your journey? What made you buy such a book at Inverness?'—He gave me a very sufficient answer. 'Why, sir, if you are to have but one book with you upon a journey, let it be a book of science. When you have read through a book of entertainment, you know it, and it can do no more for you; but a book of science is inexhaustible.' BOSWELL, ed. 1.

⟨The day was 10 April 1775 when Mrs. Oglethorpe ' plagued ' Johnson about his gift. *Boswell Papers*, x. 202-3. For Miss MacQueen see *post*, p. 514.⟩

Johnson thus mentions his gift: 'I presented her with a book, which I happened to have about me, and should not be pleased to think that she forgets me.' *Western Isl.*, p. 32. ⟨The first edition of *Cocker's Arithmetick* was published in 1678.⟩ Though Johnson says that 'a book of science is inexhaustible,' yet in *The Rambler*, No. 154, he asserts that 'the principles of arithmetick and geometry may be comprehended by a close attention in a few days.' Mrs. Piozzi says (*Anec.* p. 77: John. Misc. i. 200) that ' when Mr. Johnson felt his fancy ... disordered, his constant recurrence was to the study of arithmetic; and one day that he was totally confined to his chamber, and I enquired what he had been doing to divert himself; he shewed me a calculation which I could scarce be made to understand, so vast was the plan of it ...: no other indeed than that the national debt, computing it at one hundred and eighty millions sterling, would, if converted into silver, serve to make a meridian of that metal, I forget how broad, for the globe of the whole earth.' See *ante*, iii. 207, and iv. 171, n. 3. ⟨Cocker was one of the works that Johnson recommended to Queeney Thrale in her study of arithmetic. *Letters*, No. 839.1.⟩

Anoch undress, or lie down with our clothes on. I said at last, ' I'll plunge in ! There will be less harbour for vermin about me, when I am stripped ! '—Dr. Johnson said, he was like one hesitating whether to go into the cold bath. At last he resolved too. I observed, he might serve a campaign.—*Johnson.* ' I could do all that can be done by patience : whether I should have strength enough, I know not.'—He was in excellent humour. To see the Rambler as I saw him to-night, was really an amusement. I yesterday told him, I was thinking of writing a poetical letter to him, *on his return from Scotland*, in the stile of Swift's humorous epistle in the character of Mary Gulliver to her husband, Captain Lemuel Gulliver, on his return to England from the country of the *Houyhnhnms :*

> ' At early morn I to the market haste,
> Studious in ev'ry thing to please thy taste.
> A curious *fowl* and *sparagrass* I chose ;
> (For I remember you were fond of those :)
> Three shillings cost the first, the last sev'n groats ;
> Sullen you turn from both, and call for OATS [1]. '

He laughed, and asked in whose name I would write it. I said, in Mrs. Thrale's. He was angry. ' Sir, if you have any sense of decency or delicacy, you won't do that ! '—*Boswell.* ' Then let it be in Cole's, the landlord of the *Mitre tavern ;* where we have so often sat together.'—*Johnson.* ' Ay, that may do.'

After we had offered up our private devotions, and had chatted a little from our beds, Dr. Johnson said, ' GOD bless us both, for Jesus Christ's sake ! Good night ! '—I pronounced ' Amen.'—He fell asleep immediately. I was not so fortunate for a long time. I fancied myself bit by innumerable vermin under the clothes ; and that a spider was travelling from the *wainscot* towards my mouth. At last I fell into insensibility.

Wednesday, 1st September.

I awaked very early. I began to imagine that the landlord, being about to emigrate, might murder us to get our money, and lay it upon the soldiers in the barn. Such groundless fears will arise in the mind, before it has resumed its vigour after sleep !

---

[1] ⟨The epistle is Pope's. It was first printed in *Several Copies of* *Verses on Occasion of Mr. Gulliver's Travels*, 1727.⟩

Dr. Johnson had had the same kind of ideas; for he told me afterwards, that he considered so many soldiers, having seen us, would be witnesses, should any harm be done, and that circumstance, I suppose, he considered as a security [1]. When I got up, I found him sound asleep in his miserable *stye*, as I may call it, with a coloured handkerchief tied round his head. With difficulty could I awaken him. It reminded me of Henry the Fourth's fine soliloquy on sleep; for there was here as *uneasy a pallet* [2] as the poet's imagination could possibly conceive.

A *red-coat* of the 15th regiment, whether officer, or only serjeant, I could not be sure, came to the house, in his way to the mountains to shoot deer, which it seems the Laird of Glenmorison does not hinder any body to do. Few, indeed, can do them harm. We had him to breakfast with us. We got away about eight. M'Queen walked some miles to give us a convoy. He had, in 1745, joined the Highland army at Fort Augustus, and continued in it till after the battle of Culloden. As he narrated the particulars of that ill-advised, but brave attempt, I could not refrain from tears †. There is a certain association of ideas in my mind upon that subject, by which I am strongly affected. The very Highland names, or the sound of a bagpipe, will stir my blood, and fill me with a mixture of melancholy and respect for courage; with pity for an § unfortunate and superstitious regard for antiquity, and thoughtless inclination for war; in short, with a crowd of sensations with which sober rationality has nothing to do.

We passed through Glensheal, with prodigious mountains on each side. We saw where the battle was fought in the year 1719 [3]. Dr. Johnson owned he was now in a scene of as wild nature

---

[1] 'We told [the soldiers] how kindly we had been treated at the garrison, and as we were enjoying the benefit of their labours, begged leave to shew our gratitude by a small present.... They had the true military impatience of coin in their pockets, and had marched at least six miles to find the first place where liquor could be bought. Having never been before in a place so wild and unfrequented, I was glad of their arrival, because I knew that we had made them friends, and to gain still more of their good will, we went to them, where they were carousing in the barn, and added something to our former gift.' *Western Isl.*, pp. 30-2.

[2] 'Why rather, sleep, liest thou in smoky cribs, Upon uneasy pallets stretching thee,' &c.
   2 *Hen. IV*, act iii. sc. 1.

† ⟨Edition 1, which follows the original MS., reads 'I several times burst into tears'.⟩

§ ⟨Boswell's MS. reads 'the', but Boswell and Malone directed the printer to read as here printed. Ed. 1 has a comma after 'unfortunate'.⟩

[3] ⟨See App. D, p. 516.⟩

Glenshiel *Wednesday 1 September* 1773

as he could see; but he corrected me sometimes in my inaccurate observations.—' There, (said I,) is a mountain like a cone.'— *Johnson.* ' No, sir. It would be called so in a book; and when a man comes to look at it, he sees it is not so. It is indeed pointed at the top; but one side of it is larger than the other [1].'—Another mountain I called immense.—*Johnson.* ' No; it is no more than a considerable protuberance.'

We came to a rich green valley, comparatively speaking, and stopped a while to let our horses rest and eat grass [2]. We soon afterwards came to Auchnasheal, a kind of rural village, a number of cottages being built together, as we saw all along in the Highlands. We passed many miles this day without seeing a house, but only little summer-huts, called *shielings*. Evan Campbell, servant to Mr. Murchison, factor to the Laird of Macleod in Glenelg, ran along with us to-day. He was a very

[1] Boswell mentions this *ante*, i. 41, as a proof of Johnson's ' perceptive quickness.'

[2] Dr. Johnson, in his *Journey*, thus beautifully describes his situation here : ' I sat down on a bank, such as a writer of romance might have delighted to feign. I had, indeed, no trees to whisper over my head; but a clear rivulet streamed at my feet. The day was calm, the air soft, and all was rudeness, silence, and solitude. Before me, and on either side, were high hills, which, by hindering the eye from ranging, forced the mind to find entertainment for itself. Whether I spent the hour well, I know not; for here I first conceived the thought of this narration.'—The *Critical Reviewers*, with a spirit and expression worthy of the subject, say,—' We congratulate the publick on the event with which this quotation concludes, and are fully persuaded that the hour in which the entertaining traveller conceived this narrative will be considered, by every reader of taste, as a fortunate event in the annals of literature. Were it suitable to the task in which we are at present engaged, to indulge ourselves in a poetical flight, we would invoke the winds of the Caledonian mountains to blow for ever, with their softest breezes, on the bank where our author reclined, and request of Flora, that it might be perpetually adorned with the gayest and most fragrant productions of the year.' BOSWELL, ed. 1. ⟨Johnson, resuming his narrative, writes : ' We . . . continued our journey along the side of a lough. . . . The lough at last ended in a river broad and shallow. . . . Beyond it is a valley called *Glensheals*. . . . Here we found a village called *Auknasheals*.' *Western Isl.*, p. 36. His description to Mrs. Thrale is similar : ' In about an hour we remounted, and persued our journey. The lake by which we had travelled for some time ended in a river, which we passed by a bridge and came to another Glen with a collection of huts, called Auknasheals.' *Letters*, No. 326. It will be seen, therefore, as was first pointed out by the Rev. A. Matheson, that Boswell's description is misleading. Hill's *Footsteps*, p. 156. The travellers passed through Glenshiel after the halt and not before it. Mr. J. D. Fleeman claims to have identified the spot where this halt was made : he writes (*T.L.S.* 29 Sept. 1961, p. 645) : ' The only narrow valley along this part of the route lies just east of the

obliging fellow. At Auchnasheal, we sat down on a green turf-seat at the end of a house; they brought us out two wooden dishes of milk, which we tasted. One of them was frothed like a syllabub. I saw a woman preparing it with such a stick as is used for chocolate, and in the same manner. We had a considerable circle about us, men, women and children, all M'Craas, Lord Seaforth's people. Not one of them could speak English. I observed to Dr. Johnson, it was much the same as being with a tribe of Indians.—*Johnson.* ' Yes, sir ; but not so terrifying [1].' I gave all who chose it, snuff and tobacco. Governour Trapaud had made us buy a quantity at Fort Augustus, and put them up in small parcels. I also gave each person a bit of wheat bread, which they had never tasted before. I then gave a penny apiece to each child. I told Dr. Johnson of this ; upon which he called to Joseph and our guides, for change for a shilling, and declared that he would distribute among the children. Upon this being announced in Erse, there was a great stir ; not only did some children come running down from neighbouring huts, but I observed one black-haired man, who had been with us all along, had gone off, and returned, bringing a very young child. My fellow traveller then ordered the children to be drawn up in a row ; and he dealt about his copper, and made them and their parents all happy. The poor M'Craas, whatever may be their present state, were of considerable estimation in the year 1715, when there was a line in a song,

And aw the brave M'Craas are coming [2].

small Loch Lundie, which is about half-way along the northern side of Loch Cluanie. It is 16½ miles from Fort Augustus, 4½ miles west of Ceannocroc Bridge and about 6 miles east of the Cluanie Inn.'⟩

[1] ' The villagers gathered about us in considerable numbers, I believe without any evil intention, but with a very savage wildness of aspect and manner.' *Western Isl.*, p. 37.

[2] The M'Craas, or Macraes, were since that time brought into the king's army, by the late Lord Seaforth. When they lay in Edinburgh castle in 1778, and were ordered to embark for Jersey, they, with a number of other men in the regiment, for different reasons, but especially an apprehension that they were to be sold to the East-India Company, though enlisted not to be sent out of Great-Britain without their own consent, made a determined mutiny, and encamped upon the lofty mountain, *Arthur's seat*, where they remained three days and three nights ; bidding defiance to all the force in Scotland. At last they came down, and embarked peaceably, having obtained formal articles of capitulation, signed by Sir Adolphus Oughton, commander in chief, General Skene, deputy commander, the Duke of Buccleugh, and the Earl of Dunmore, which quieted them. Since

There was great diversity in the faces of the circle around us: Some were as black and wild in their appearance as any American savages whatever. One woman was as comely almost as the figure of Sappho, as we see it painted. We asked the old woman, the mistress of the house where we had the milk, (which,[2] by the bye, Dr. Johnson told me, for I did not observe it myself, was built not of turf, but of stone,) what we should pay. She said, what we pleased. One of our guides asked her, in Erse, if a shilling was enough. She said, 'Yes.' But some of the men bade her ask more [1]. This vexed me; because it shewed a desire to impose upon strangers, as they knew that even a shilling was high payment. The woman, however, honestly persisted in her first price; so I gave her half a crown.— Thus we had one good scene of life uncommon to us. The people were very much pleased, gave us many blessings, and said they had not had such a day since the old Laird of Macleod's time.

Dr. Johnson was much refreshed by this repast. He was pleased when I told him he would make a good Chief. He said, 'Were I a chief, I would dress my servants better than myself, and knock a fellow down if he looked saucy to a Macdonald in rags: but I would not treat men as brutes. I would let them know why all of my clan were to have attention paid to them. I would tell my upper servants why, and make them tell the others.'

[a] *comma omitted 3.*

[2] the secession of the Commons of Rome to the *Mons Sacer*, a more spirited exertion has not been made. I gave great attention to it from first to last, and have drawn up a particular account of it. Those brave fellows have since served their country effectually at Jersey, and also in the East-Indies, to which, after being better informed, they voluntarily agreed to go. BOSWELL, ed. 1. ⟨For Boswell's account see App. D, p. 516.⟩
The line which Boswell quotes is from *The Chevalier's Muster Roll*:—
'The laird of M'Intosh is coming, M'Crabie & M'Donald's coming, M'Kenzie & M'Pherson's coming, And the wild M'Craw's coming.
Little wat ye wha's coming, Donald Gun and a's coming.'
Hogg's *Jacobite Relics*, 1819, i. 152. ⟨In another song '*Will ye go to Sherriffmuir*' they are called 'the bauld M'Craws'. *Ibid.* 150.⟩. Walpole (*Letters*, x. 408), writing on May 9, 1779, tells how on May 1 'the French had attempted to land [on Jersey], but Lord Seaforth's new-raised regiment of seven hundred Highlanders, assisted by some militia and some artillery, made a brave stand and repelled the intruders.'

[1] 'One of the men advised her, with the cunning that clowns never can be without, to ask more but she said that a shilling was enough. We gave her half a crown and she offered part of it again.' *Letters*, No. 326.

We rode on well [1], till we came to the high mountain called the Rattakin, by which time both Dr. Johnson and the horses were a good deal fatigued. It is a terrible steep to climb, notwithstanding the road is formed slanting along it; however, we made it out. On the top of it we met Captain M'Leod of Balmenoch [2] (a Dutch officer who had come from Sky) riding with his sword slung across him. He asked, 'Is this Mr. Boswell?' which was a proof that we were expected. Going down the hill on the other side was no easy task. As Dr. Johnson was a great weight, the two guides agreed that he should ride the horses alternately. Hay's were the two best, and the Doctor would not ride but upon one or other of them, a black or a brown. But, as Hay complained much,[a] after ascending the *Rattakin*, the Doctor was prevailed with to mount one of Vass's greys. As he rode upon it down hill, it did not go well; and he grumbled. I walked on a little before, but was excessively entertained with the method taken to keep him in good humour. Hay led the horse's head, talking to Dr. Johnson as much as he could; and (having heard him, in the forenoon, express a pastoral pleasure on seeing the goats browzing) just when the Doctor was uttering his displeasure, the fellow cried, with a very Highland accent, 'See, such pretty goats!' Then he whistled, *whu!* and made them jump.—Little did he conceive what Dr. Johnson was. Here now was a common ignorant Highland clown imagining that he could divert, as one does a child,—*Dr. Samuel Johnson!*—The ludicrousness, absurdity, and extraordinary contrast between what the fellow fancied, and the reality, was truly comick.

It grew dusky; and we had a very tedious ride for what was called five miles; but I am sure would measure ten. We had no conversation. I was riding forward to the inn at Glenelg, on the shore opposite to Sky, that I might take proper measures, before Dr. Johnson, who was now advancing in dreary [b] silence, Hay leading his horse, should arrive. Vass also walked by the side of his horse, and Joseph followed behind: as therefore he

---

[a] *comma omitted* 3. [b] *weary Boswell's MS.*

[1] Of this part of the journey Johnson wrote :—'We ... had very little entertainment as we travelled either for the eye or ear. There are, I fancy, no singing birds in the Highlands.' *Letters*, No. 326.

[2] ⟨Perhaps Capt., later Major, John Macleod, a descendant of Tormod Macleod, 3rd of Glendale. See A. Mackenzie, *Hist. Macleods*, p. 208.⟩

was thus attended, and seemed to be in deep meditation, I thought there could be no harm in leaving him for a little while. He called me back with a tremendous shout, and was really in a passion with me for leaving him. I told him my intentions, but he was not satisfied, and said, ' Do you know, I should as soon have thought of picking a pocket, as doing so.'—*Boswell.* ' I am diverted with you, sir.'—*Johnson.* ' Sir, I could never be diverted with incivility. Doing such a thing, makes one lose confidence in him who has done it, as one cannot tell what he may do next.'—His extraordinary warmth confounded me so much, that I justified myself but lamely to him ; yet my intentions were not improper. I wished to get on, to see how we were to be lodged, and how we were to get a boat ; all which I thought I could best settle myself, without his having any trouble. To apply his great mind to minute particulars, is wrong : it is like taking an immense balance, such as is kept on quays for weighing cargoes of ships,—to weigh a guinea. I knew I had neat little scales, which would do better ; and that his attention to every thing which falls in his way, and his uncommon desire to be always in the right, would make him weigh, if he knew of the particulars : it was right therefore for me to weigh them, and let him have them only in effect. I however continued to ride by him, finding he wished I should do so.

As we passed the barracks at Bernéra †, I looked at them wishfully, as soldiers have always every thing in the best order : but there was only a serjeant and a few men there. We came on to the inn § at Glenelg. There was no provender for our horses ; so they were sent to grass, with a man to watch them. A maid shewed us up stairs into a room damp and dirty, with bare walls, a variety of bad smells, a coarse black greasy fir table, and forms of the same kind ; and out of a wretched bed started a fellow from his sleep, like Edgar in King Lear [1], ' Poor Tom's a cold [2].'

†, § ⟨See App. D, pp. 516–17.⟩
[1] Act iii. sc. 4.
[2] It is amusing to observe the different images which this being presented to Dr. Johnson and me. The Doctor, in his JOURNEY, com-
pares him to a *Cyclops.* BOSWELL, ed. 1.
' Out of one of the beds, on which we were to repose, started up, at our entrance, a man black as a Cyclops from the forge.' *Western Isl.*, p. 43. Johnson wrote to Mrs. Thrale :—

This inn was furnished with not a single article that we could either eat or drink [1]; but Mr. Murchison †, factor to the Laird of Macleod in Glenelg, sent us a bottle of rum and some sugar, with a polite message, to acquaint us, that he was very sorry that he did not hear of us till we had passed his house, otherwise he should have insisted on our sleeping there that night; and that, if he were not obliged to set out for Inverness early next morning, he would have waited upon us.—Such extraordinary attention from this gentleman, to entire strangers, deserves the most honourable commemoration.

Our bad accommodation here made me uneasy, and almost fretful. Dr. Johnson was calm. I said, he was so from vanity.—*Johnson.* ' No, sir, it is from philosophy.'—It pleased me to see that the *Rambler* could practise so well his own lessons.

I resumed the subject of my leaving him on the road, and endeavoured to defend it better. He was still violent upon that head, and said, ' Sir, had you gone on, I was thinking that I should have returned with you to Edinburgh, and then have parted from you, and never spoken to you more.'

I sent for fresh hay, with which we made beds for ourselves, each in a room equally miserable. Like Wolfe, we had a ' *choice of difficulties* [2].' Dr. Johnson made things easier by comparison. At M'Queen's, last night, he observed, that few were so well

' When we were taken up stairs, a dirty fellow bounced out of the bed where one of us was to lie. Boswel blustered, but nothing could be got.' *Letters*, No. 326. Macaulay in his review of Croker (*Lit. Essays*, 1923, p. 246) says :—' It is clear that Johnson himself did not think in the dialect in which he wrote. The expressions which came first to his tongue were simple, energetic, and picturesque. When he wrote for publication, he did his sentences out of English into Johnsonese. His letters from the Hebrides to Mrs. Thrale are the original of that work of which the Journey to the Hebrides is the translation; and it is amusing to compare the two versions.' Macaulay thereupon quotes these two passages. See *ante*, iv. 237.

[1] ' We had a lemon and a piece of bread, which supplied me with my supper.' *Letters*, No. 326. Goldsmith, who in his student days had been in Scotland, thus writes of a Scotch inn :—' Vile entertainment is served up, complained of and sent down·; up comes worse, and that also is changed, and every change makes our wretched cheer more unsavoury.' *Present State of Polite Learning*, ch. 12.

† ⟨See App. D, p. 517.⟩

[2] General Wolfe, in his despatch from head-quarters on Sept. 2, 1759, eleven days before his death, wrote :— ' In this situation, there is such a choice of difficulties, that I own myself at a loss how to determine.' *Ann. Reg.* 1759, p. 246.

lodged in a ship. To-night he said, we were better than if we had been upon the hill. He lay down buttoned up in his great coat. I had my sheets spread on the hay, and my clothes and great coat laid over me, by way of blankets †.

Thursday, 2d September.

I had slept ill. Dr. Johnson's anger had affected me much. I considered that, without any bad intention, I might suddenly forfeit his friendship; and was impatient to see him this morning. I told him how uneasy he had made me, by what he had said, and reminded him of his own remark at Aberdeen, upon old friendships being hastily broken off. He owned, he had spoken to me in passion; that he would not have done what he threatened; and that, if he had, he should have been ten times worse than I; that forming intimacies, would indeed be ' limning the water [1],' were they liable to such sudden dissolution; and he added, ' Let's think no more on't.'—*Boswell.* ' Well then, sir, I shall be easy. Remember, I am to have fair warning in case of any quarrel. You are never to spring a mine upon me. It was absurd in me to believe you.'—*Johnson.* 'You deserved about as much, as to believe me from night to morning.'

After breakfast, we got into a boat for Sky. It rained much when we set off, but cleared up as we advanced. One of the boatmen, who spoke English, said, that a mile at land was two miles at sea. I then observed, that from Glenelg to Armidale in Sky, which was our present course, and is called twelve, was only six miles: but this he could not understand. ' Well, (said Dr. Johnson,) never talk to me of the native good sense of the Highlanders. Here is a fellow who calls one mile two, and yet cannot comprehend that twelve such imaginary miles make in truth but six.'

We reached the shore of Armidale before one o'clock. Sir Alexander M'Donald came down to receive us. He and his lady, (formerly Miss Bosville of Yorkshire [2],) were then in a house [3] built by a tenant at this place, which is in the district of Slate, the family mansion here having been burned in Sir Donald Macdonald's time.

† ⟨See Johnson's *Letters*, No. 326.⟩
[1] See *ante*, v. 89.
[2] See *ante*, ii. 169, n. 2 ⟨and iii. 540⟩.
[3] ⟨Armadale Castle is on, or approximately on, the site of this house: see *post*, v, p. 517.⟩

Thursday 2 September 1773 Skye: Armadale

¹ The most ancient seat of the chief of the Macdonalds in the isle of Sky was at Duntulm, where there are the remains of a stately castle ². The principal residence of the family is now at Mugstot, at which there is a considerable building ³. Sir Alexander and lady Macdonald had come to Armidale in their way to Edinburgh, where it was necessary for them to be soon after this time ⁴.

¹ Boswell, in a note that he added to the second edition (see *post*, v. 415, note 4), says that he has omitted ' a few observations . . . the publication of which might perhaps be considered as passing the bounds of a strict decorum.' In the first edition (p. 165) the three paragraphs beginning ' The most ancient seat ', ' Armidale is situated ', ' Sir Alexander Macdonald ', were as follows :— ' Instead of finding the head of the Macdonalds surrounded with his clan, and a festive entertainment, we had a small company, and cannot boast of our cheer. The particulars are minuted in my Journal, but I shall not trouble the publick with them. I shall mention but one characteristick circumstance. My shrewd and hearty friend, Sir Thomas (Wentworth) Blacket, Lady Macdonald's uncle, who had preceded us in a visit to this chief, upon being asked by him, if the punch-bowl then upon the table was not a very handsome one, replied, " Yes,—if it were full."

' Sir Alexander Macdonald having been an Eton Scholar, Dr. Johnson had formed an opinion of him which was much diminished when he beheld him in the isle of Sky, where we heard heavy complaints of rents racked, and the people driven to emigration. Dr. Johnson said, " It grieves me to see the chief of a great clan appear to such disadvantage. This gentleman has talents, nay some learning ; but he is totally unfit for this situation. Sir, the Highland chiefs should not be allowed to go farther south than Aberdeen. A strong-minded man, like his brother Sir James, may be improved by an English education ; but in general, they will be tamed into insignificance."

' I meditated an escape from this house the very next day ; but Dr. Johnson resolved that we should weather it out till Monday.' Johnson wrote to Mrs. Thrale, 21 Sept. 1773 :—' We saw the Isle of Skie before us darkening the horizon with its rocky coast. A boat was procured, and we launched into one of the Straits of the Atlantick Ocean. We had a passage of about twelve miles to the point where Sir Alexander resided, having come from his Seat in the midland part, to a small house on the shore, as we believe, that he might with less reproach entertain us meanly. If he aspired to meanness his retrograde ambition was completely gratified . . . Boswel was very angry, and reproached him with his improper parsimony.' *Letters*, No. 326. On 3 Nov. he wrote :—' I have done thinking of Sir Alexander, whom we now call Sir Sawney, he has disgusted all mankind by injudicious parsimony, and given occasion to so many stories, that Boswel has some thoughts of collecting them, and making a novel of his life.' *Ib*. No. 337. See also *Ib*. No. 324 and *post*, v. 315. The last of the Collings–Rowlandson caricatures ('*Picturesque Beauties of Boswell*', 1786) of Boswell's *Journal* is entitled *Revising for the Second Edition*. Macdonald is represented as seizing Boswell by the throat and pointing with his stick to the *Journal* that lies open at pages 168, 169. On the ground lie pages 165, 167, torn out. Boswell, in an agony of fear, is begging for mercy. ⟨See *post*, App. D, p. 578.⟩
², ³ ⟨See App. D, p. 517.⟩
⁴ ⟨Their eldest son, Alexander Wentworth, was born 9 Dec. 1773.⟩

Armidale is situated on a pretty bay of the narrow sea, which flows between the main land of Scotland and the Isle of Sky. In front there is a grand prospect of the rude mountains of Moidart and Knoidart [1]. Behind are hills gently rising and covered with a finer verdure than I expected to see in this climate, and the scene is enlivened by a number of little clear brooks.

Sir Alexander Macdonald having been an Eton scholar [2], and being a gentleman of talents, Dr. Johnson had been very well pleased with him in London [3]. But my fellow-traveller and I were now full of the old Highland spirit, and were dissatisfied at hearing of racked rents and emigration; and finding a chief not surrounded by his clan. Dr. Johnson said, ' Sir, the Highland chiefs should not be allowed to go farther south than Aberdeen. A strong-minded man, like Sir James Macdonald [4], may be improved by an English education; but in general, they will be tamed into insignificance.'

We found here Mr. Janes † of Aberdeenshire, a naturalist. Janes said he had been at Dr. Johnson's, in London, with Ferguson the astronomer [5].—*Johnson.* ' It is strange that, in such distant places, I should meet with any one who knows me. I should have thought I might hide myself in Sky.'

Friday, 3d September.

This day proving wet, we should have passed our time very uncomfortably, had we not found in the house two chests of books, which we eagerly ransacked. After dinner, when I alone was left at table with the few Highland gentlemen who were of the company, having talked with very high respect of Sir James Macdonald, they were all so much affected as to shed tears. One of them was Mr. Donald Macdonald [6], who had been lieutenant of grenadiers in the Highland regiment, raised by Colonel Montgomery, now Earl of Eglintoune [7], in the war

[1] ' Here, in Badenoch, here, in Lochaber anon, in Lochiel, in Knoydart, Moydart, Morrer, Ardgower, and Ardnamurchan, Here I see him and here : I see him ; anon I lose him ! '
  Clough's *Bothie*, iv. 15–17.
[2] See his Latin verses addressed to Dr. Johnson, in the APPENDIX.

BOSWELL, ed. 3. *Post,* v. 419 ⟨and 579⟩.
[3] See *ante*, ii. 157.
[4] See *ante*, i. 449.
† ⟨For Mr. Janes or Jeans see App. D, p. 517.⟩
[5] See *ante*, ii. 99.
[6] ⟨See App. D, p. 518.⟩
[7] ⟨See *ante*, iii. 170, n. 2, and 503.⟩

before last; one of those regiments which the late Lord Chatham prided himself in having brought from 'the mountains of the North [1]:' by doing which he contributed to extinguish in the Highlands the remains of disaffection to the present Royal Family. From this gentleman's conversation, I first learnt how very popular his Colonel was among the Highlanders; of which I had such continued proofs, during the whole course of my Tour, that on my return I could not help telling the noble Earl himself, that I did not before know how great a man he was.

We were advised by some persons here to visit Rasay, in our way to Dunvegan, the seat of the Laird of Macleod. Being informed that the Rev. Mr. Donald M'Queen † was the most intelligent man in Sky, and having been favoured with a letter of introduction to him, by the learned Sir James Foulis §, I sent it to him by an express, and requested he would meet us at Rasay; and at the same time enclosed a letter to the Laird of Macleod, informing him that we intended in a few days to have the honour of waiting on him at Dunvegan.

Dr. Johnson this day endeavoured to obtain some knowledge of the state of the country; but complained that he could get no distinct information about any thing, from those with whom he conversed [2].

Saturday, 4th September.

My endeavours to rouse the English-bred Chieftain [3], in whose

---

[1] See *ante*, iii. 198, note 1.
† ⟨See *post*, v. 161 and 522.⟩
§ ⟨See *post*, v. 242 and App. D, p. 518.⟩
[2] 'Such is the laxity of Highland conversation, that the inquirer is kept in continual suspense, and by a kind of intellectual retrogradation, knows less as he hears more.' *Western Isl.*, p. 45. 'They are not much accustomed to be interrogated by others; and seem never to have thought upon interrogating themselves; so that if they do not know what they tell to be true, they likewise do not distinctly perceive it to be false. Mr. Boswell was very diligent in his inquiries; and the result of his investigations was, that the answer to the second question was commonly such as nullified the answer to the first.' *Ib.* p. 106.

[3] Mr. Carruthers, in his edition, 1852, of Boswell's *Hebrides*, says (p. xiv):—'The new management and high rents took the tacksmen by surprise. They were indignant at the treatment they received, and, selling off their stock, in disgust and despair, they emigrated to America. In the twenty years from 1772 to 1792, sixteen vessels with emigrants sailed from the western shores of Inverness-shire and Ross-shire, containing about 6,400 persons, who carried with them, in specie, at least £38,400. A desperate effort was made by the tacksmen on the estate of Lord

Skye : Armadale *Sunday 5 September* 1773

house we were, to the feudal and patriarchal feelings, proving ineffectual, Dr. Johnson this morning tried to bring him to our way of thinking.—*Johnson.* ' Were I in your place, sir, in seven years I would make this an independant island. I would roast oxen whole, and hang out a flag as a signal to the Macdonalds to come and get beef and whisky.'—Sir Alexander was still starting difficulties.—*Johnson.* ' Nay, sir ; if you are born to object, I have done with you. Sir, I would have a magazine of arms.'—*Sir Alexander.* ' They would rust.'— *Johnson.* ' Let there be men to keep them clean. Your ancestors did not use to let their arms rust [1].'

We attempted in vain to communicate to him a portion of our enthusiasm. He bore with so polite a good-nature our warm, and what some might call Gothick, expostulations, on this subject, that I should not forgive myself, were I to record all that Dr. Johnson's ardour led him to say [2].—This day was little better than a blank.

Sunday, 5th September.

I walked to the parish church of Slate, which is a very poor one[3]. There are no church bells in the island. I was told there were once some ; what has become of them, I could not learn. The minister not being at home, there was no service. I went into the church, and saw the monument of Sir James Macdonald, which was elegantly executed at Rome, and has the following inscription, written by his friend, George Lord Lyttelton :

To the memory
Of Sir JAMES MACDONALD, Bart.
Who in the flower of youth,
Had attained to so eminent a degree of knowledge
In Mathematics, Philosophy, Languages,

Macdonald. . . They bound themselves by a solemn oath . . . not to offer for any farm that might become vacant, believing that they would thus repress competition and continue low rents. The combination failed of its object, but it appeared so formidable in the eyes of the " English-bred chieftain," that he retreated precipitately from Skye and never afterwards returned.'

[1] Dr. Johnson seems to have

forgotten that a Highlander going armed at this period incurred the penalty of serving as a common soldier for the first, and of transportation beyond sea for a second offence. And as for ' calling out his clan,' twelve Highlanders and a bagpipe made a rebellion. Scott, 1831.

[2] ⟨See *Hebrides*, ed. Pottle and Bennett, 1936, p. 117, for Johnson's sayings.⟩

[3] ⟨A ruin since 1876, when the

Sunday 5 September 1773   Skye : Armadale
And in every other branch of useful and polite learning,
As few have [a] acquired in a long life
Wholly devoted to study :
Yet to this erudition he joined
What can rarely be found with it,
Great talents for business,
Great propriety of behaviour,
Great politeness of manners !
His eloquence was sweet, correct, and flowing ;
His memory vast and exact ;
His judgement strong and acute ;
All which endowments, united
With the most amiable temper
And every private virtue,
Procured him, not only in his own country,
But also from foreign nations,
The highest marks of esteem.
In the year of our Lord
1766 [1],
The 25th of his life,
After a long and extremely painful illness,
Which he supported with admirable patience and fortitude,
He died at Rome,
Where, notwithstanding the difference of religion,
Such extraordinary honours were paid to his memory,
As had never graced that of any other British subject [b],
Since the death of Sir Philip Sydney.
The fame he left behind him is the best consolation
To his afflicted family,
And to his countrymen in this isle,
For whose benefit he had planned
Many useful improvements,
Which his fruitful genius suggested,
And his active spirit promoted,
Under the sober direction
Of a clear and enlightened understanding.
Reader, bewail our loss,
And that of all Britain.

[a] have ever *Epitaph*.   [b] subject in any foreign land, *Epitaph*.
[1] ⟨He died on 26 July.⟩
present church near by, into which   was removed, was built.⟩
Sir James Macdonald's   monument

Skye : Armadale *Sunday 5 September 1773* 153
In testimony of her love,
And as the best return she can make
To her departed son,
For the constant tenderness and affection
Which, even to his last moments,
He shewed for her,
His much afflicted mother,
The LADY MARGARET MACDONALD,
Daughter to the EARL of EGLINTOUNE,
Erected this Monument,
A.D. 1768 [1].'

[1] This extraordinary young man, whom I had the pleasure of knowing intimately, having been deeply regretted by his country, the most minute particulars concerning him must be interesting to many. I shall therefore insert his two last letters to his mother, Lady Margaret Macdonald, which her ladyship has been pleased to communicate to me.

'*Rome, July* 9th, 1766.
'MY DEAR MOTHER,
'YESTERDAY's post brought me your answer to the first letter in which I acquainted you of my illness. Your tenderness and concern upon that account are the same I have always experienced, and to which I have often owed my life. Indeed it never was in so great danger as it has been lately ; and though it would have been a very great comfort to me to have had you near me, yet perhaps I ought to rejoice, on your account, that you had not the pain of such a spectacle. I have been now a week in Rome, and wish I could continue to give you the same good accounts of my recovery as I did in my last : but I must own that, for three days past, I have been in a very weak and miserable state, which however seems to give no uneasiness to my physician. My stomach has been greatly out of order, without any visible cause ; and the palpitation does not decrease. I am told that my stomach will soon recover its tone, and that the palpitation must cease in time. So I am willing to believe ; and with this hope support the little remains of spirits which I can be supposed to have, on the forty-seventh day of such an illness. Do not imagine I have relapsed ;—I only recover slower than I expected. If my letter is shorter than usual, the cause of it is a dose of physick, which has weakened me so much to-day, that I am not able to write a long letter. I will make up for it next post, and remain always
'Your most sincerely affectionate son,
'J. MACDONALD.'

He grew gradually worse ; and on the night before his death he wrote as follows, from Frescati :
'MY DEAR MOTHER,
'THOUGH I did not mean to deceive you in my last letter from Rome, yet certainly you would have very little reason to conclude of the very great and constant danger I have gone through ever since that time. My life, which is still almost entirely desperate, did not at that time appear to me so, otherwise I should have represented, in its true colours, a fact which acquires very little horror by that means, and comes with redoubled force by deception. There is no circumstance of danger and pain of which I have not had the

Dr. Johnson said, the inscription should have been in Latin, as every thing intended to be universal and permanent, should be [1].

This being a beautiful day, my spirits were cheered by the mere effect of climate. I had felt a return of spleen during my stay at Armidale, and had it not been that I had Dr. Johnson to contemplate, I should have sunk into dejection; but his firmness supported me. I looked at him, as a man whose head is turning giddy at sea looks at a rock, or any fixed object. I wondered at his tranquillity. He said, ' Sir, when a man retires into an island, he is to turn his thoughts intirely on [a] another world. He has done with this.'—*Boswell*. ' It appears to me, sir, to be very difficult to unite a due attention to this world, and that which is to come; for, if we engage eagerly in the affairs of life, we are apt to be totally forgetful of a future state; and, on the other hand, a steady contemplation of the awful concerns of eternity renders all objects here so insignificant, as to make us indifferent and negligent about them.'— *Johnson*. ' Sir, Dr. Cheyne has laid down a rule to himself on this subject, which should be imprinted on every mind : " *To neglect nothing to secure my eternal peace, more than if I had been certified I should die within the day : nor to mind any thing that my secular obligations and duties demanded of me, less than if I had been ensured to live fifty years more* [2]." '

I must here observe, that though Dr. Johnson appeared now to be philosophically calm, yet his genius did not shine forth as in companies, where I have listened to him with admiration. The vigour of his mind was, however, sufficiently manifested, by

[a] on 1, 2 (*MS.*) : to 3.

experience, for a continued series of above a fortnight ; during which time I have settled my affairs, after my death, with as much distinctness as the hurry and the nature of the thing could admit of. In case of the worst, the Abbé Grant will be my executor in this part of the world, and Mr. Mackenzie in Scotland, where my object has been to make you and my younger brother as independent of the eldest as possible.' BOSWELL, ed. 1.

Walpole (*Letters*, xi. 76), 11 Dec. 1779, thus mentions this ' younger brother ', Sir Archibald Macdonald, 1747–1826 :—' Macdonald . . . abused Lord North in very gross, yet too applicable terms, and next day pleaded he had been drunk, recanted, and was all admiration and esteem for his Lordship's talents and virtues.' ⟨The ' eldest ' brother, Sir Alexander, resented the publication of this letter : see *Boswell Papers*, xvi. p. 243. Lady Margaret was the daughter of the ninth Earl of Eglinton : she died 30 March 1799. W. Fraser, *Memorials of the Montgomeries*, 1859, i. 106.⟩

[1] See *ante*, iii. 85, and *post*, v. 366.
[2] Cheyne's *English Malady*, ed. 1733, p. 334.

Skye: Armadale *Sunday 5 September* 1773

his discovering no symptoms of feeble relaxation in the dull, ' weary, flat ,[a] and unprofitable [1] ' state in which we now were placed.

I am inclined to think that it was on this day he composed the following Ode upon the *Isle of Sky*, which a few days afterwards † he shewed me at Rasay :

O D A.

Ponti profundis clausa recessibus,
Strepens procellis, rupibus obsita,
Quam grata defesso virentem
Skia sinum nebulosa pandis.

His cura, credo, sedibus exulat ;
His blanda certe pax habitat locis :
Non ira, non mœror quietis
Insidias meditatur horis.

At non cavata rupe latescere,
Menti nec ægræ montibus aviis
Prodest vagari, nec frementes
E scopulo numerare fluctus.

Humana virtus non sibi sufficit,
Datur nec æquum cuique animum sibi
Parare posse, ut Stoicorum
Secta crepet nimis alta fallax.

Exæstuantis pectoris impetum,
Rex summe, solus tu regis arbiter,
Mentisque, te tollente, surgunt,
Te recidunt moderante fluctus [2].

a flat, 1, 2 : flat 3.

[1] ' Weary, stale, flat, and unprofitable.' *Hamlet*, act i. sc. 2. See *ante*, iii. 350.
† ⟨On 9 Sept. Boswell wrote in his original Journal:
' Mr. Johnson showed me today two odes which he had written in Skye. One of them was to Mrs Thrale . . . . I asked it from him. He said " I'd as soon give you my ears ".' He allowed Boswell to copy the other, i.e. this ode, on 20 Sept. Ed. Pottle and Bennett, pp. 136, 193-4.⟩
[2] VARIOUS READINGS.
Line 2. In the manuscript, Dr. Johnson, instead of *rupibus obsita*, had written *imbribus uvida*, and *uvida nubibus*, but struck them both out.
Lines 15 and 16. Instead of these two lines, he had written, but afterwards struck out, the following :
Parare posse, utcunque jactet
Grandiloquus nimis alta Zeno.
BOSWELL, ed. 1.
In Johnson's *Works*, 1787, xi. 394, these lines are given with some variations, which perhaps are in part due to Mr. Langton, who, we are told (*ante*, iv. 384), edited some, if not indeed all, of Johnson's Latin poems. ⟨A translation of this ode will be found in *Scots Mag.*, 1799, p. 261.⟩

Monday 6 September 1773   Skye: Corrichatachin

After supper, Dr. Johnson told us, that Isaac Hawkins Browne drank freely for thirty years, and that he wrote his poem, *De Animi Immortalitate*, in some of the last of these years [1].—I listened to this with the eagerness of one, who, conscious of being himself fond of wine, is glad to hear that a man of so much genius and good thinking as Browne had the same propensity [2].

Monday, 6th September.

We set out, accompanied by Mr. Donald M'Leod (late of Canna) † as our guide. We rode for some time along the district of Slate, near the shore. The houses in general are made of turf, covered with grass. The country seemed well peopled. We came into the district of Strath, and passed along a wild moorish tract of land till we arrived at the shore. There we found good verdure, and some curious whin-rocks, or collections of stones like the ruins of the foundations of old buildings. We saw also three *Cairns* of considerable size.

About a mile beyond Broadfoot §, is Corrichatachin, a farm of Sir Alexander Macdonald's, possessed by Mr. M'Kinnon [3],

---

[1] Cowper wrote to S. Rose on May 20, 1789 :—' Browne was an entertaining companion when he had drunk his bottle, but not before ; this proved a snare to him, and he would sometimes drink too much.' Southey's *Cowper*, vi. 237. His *De Animi Immortalitate* was published in 1754. He died in 1760, aged fifty-four. See *ante*, ii. 339 ⟨and Hayward's *Piozzi*, ed. 1, i. 152⟩.

[2] Boswell, in No. 30 of his *Hypochondriack* (*ante*, iv. 179) says :—' I do fairly acknowledge that I love Drinking ; that I have a constitutional inclination to indulge in fermented liquors, and that if it were not for the restraints of reason and religion, I am afraid I should be as constant a votary of Bacchus as any man. . . . Drinking is in reality an occupation which employs a considerable portion of the time of many people ; and to conduct it in the most rational and agreeable manner is one of the great arts of living.... Were we so framed that it were possible by perpetual supplies of wine to keep ourselves for ever gay and happy, there could be no doubt that Drinking would be the *summum bonum*, the *chief good*, to find out which philosophers have been so variously busied. . . . But we know from humiliating experience that men cannot be kept long in a state of elevated intoxication.'

† ⟨See *post*, v. 260, 272 and App. D, pp. 518–19.⟩

§ ⟨Broadford.⟩

[3] That my readers may have my narrative in the style of the country through which I am travelling, it is proper to inform them, that the chief of a clan is denominated by his *surname* alone, as M'Leod, M'Kinnon, M'Intosh. To prefix *Mr*. to it would be a degradation from *the* M'Leod, &c. My old friend, the Laird of M'Farlane, the great antiquary, took it highly amiss, when General Wade called him *Mr*.[a] M'Farlane. Dr. Johnson said, he could not bring

[a] *Mr*. 1, 2 : Mr. 3.

Skye : Corrichatachin *Monday 6 September* 1773   157
who received us with a hearty welcome, as did his wife, who was what we call in Scotland a *lady-like* woman. Mr. Pennant†, in the course of his tour to the Hebrides, passed two nights at this gentleman's house. On its being mentioned, that a present had here been made to him of a curious specimen of Highland antiquity, Dr. Johnson said, ' Sir, it was more than he deserved : the dog is a Whig[a] [1].'

We here enjoyed the comfort of a table plentifully furnished [2], the satisfaction of which was heightened by a numerous and cheerful company ; and we for the first time had a specimen of the joyous social manners of the inhabitants of the Highlands. They talked in their own ancient language, with fluent vivacity, and sung many Erse songs with such spirit, that, though Dr. Johnson was treated with the greatest respect and attention, there were moments in which he seemed to be forgotten. For myself, though but a *Lowlander*, having picked up a few words of the language, I presumed to mingle in their mirth; and joined in the chorusses with as much glee as any of the company. Dr. Johnson,[b] being fatigued with his journey, retired early to his chamber, where he composed the following Ode, addressed to Mrs. Thrale [3] :

[a] Whig 1 : whig 2, 3.   [b] Johnson, 1: Johnson 2, 3.

himself to use this mode of address ; it seemed to him to be too familiar, as it is the way in which, in all other places, intimates or inferiors are addressed. When the chiefs have *titles*, they are denominated by them, as *Sir James Grant, Sir Allan M'Lean.* The other Highland gentlemen, of landed property, are denominated by their *estates*, as *Rasay, Boisdale* ; and the wives of all of them have the title of *ladies*. The *tacksmen*, or principal tenants, are named by their farms, as *Kingsburgh, Corrichatachin* ; and their wives are called the *mistress* of Kingsburgh, the *mistress* of Corrichatachin.—Having given this explanation, I am at liberty to use that mode of speech which generally prevails in the Highlands and the Hebrides. BOSWELL, ed. 1.
† ⟨See App. D, p. 519.⟩
[1] See *ante*, iii. 275.
[2] Boswell implies that Sir A. Mac-

donald's table had not been furnished plentifully. Johnson wrote, 21 Sept. :—' At night we came to a tenant's house of the first rank of tenants where we were entertained better than [at] the Landlords.' *Letters*, No. 326. ⟨For the fare and the company see App. D, p. 519.⟩
[3] ' Little did I once think,' he wrote to her the same day, ' of seeing this region of obscurity, and little did you once expect a salutation from this verge of European Life. I have now the pleasure of going where nobody goes, and seeing what nobody sees.' *Letters*, No. 323. ' About fourteen years since, I landed in Sky, with a party of friends, and had the curiosity to ask what was the first idea on every one's mind at landing. All answered separately that it was this Ode.' SCOTT, 1831. ⟨For Johnson's refusal to allow Boswell to copy this ode, see *ante*, v. 155 note †.⟩

Tuesday 7 September 1773   Skye: Corrichatachin

ODA.

Permeo terras, ubi nuda rupes
Saxeas miscet nebulis ruinas,
Torva ubi rident steriles coloni
    Rura labores.
Pervagor gentes, hominum ferorum
Vita ubi nullo decorata cultu
Squallet informis, tugurique fumis
    Fœda latescit.
Inter erroris salebrosa longi,
Inter ignotæ strepitus loquelæ,
Quot modis mecum, quid agat, requiro,
    Thralia dulcis?
Seu viri curas pia nupta mulcet,
Seu fovet mater sobolem benigna,
Sive cum libris novitate pascit [a]
    Sedula mentem;
Sit memor nostri, fideique merces,
Stet fides constans, meritoque blandum
Thraliæ discant resonare nomen
    Littora Skiæ.

Scriptum in Skiá, Sept. 6, 1773[1].

Tuesday, 7th September.

Dr. Johnson was much pleased with his entertainment here. There were many good books in the house: Hector Boethius in Latin; Cave's Lives of the Fathers; Baker's Chronicle; Jeremy Collier's Church History; Dr. Johnson's small Dictionary; Craufurd's Officers of State, and several more [2]:—a mezzotinto of Mrs. Brooks the actress (by some strange chance in Sky [3]); and also a print of Macdonald of Clanranald [4], with a Latin

[a] *pascet* 1, 2, 3: *pascit* holograph MS.

[1] See *post*, App. B, v. 424.
[2] 'I never was in any house of the Islands, where I did not find books in more languages than one, if I staid long enough to want them, except one from which the family was removed.' *Western Isl.*, p. 48. He is speaking of 'the higher rank of the Hebridians,' for on p. 58 he says:—'The greater part of the Islanders make no use of books.'
[3] ⟨'Mrs. Brooks' was the wife of James Brooke, journalist, whom she left to go on the stage, first at Edinburgh and then at Norwich. She died in London in 1782. There are three different mezzotints of 'Mrs Brooks', after the painting by T. Worlidge, the original of which John Taylor, who knew her and her family intimately, asserted was owned by Mrs. Brooke's elder daughter. See J. Taylor, *Records*, 1832, i. 31 ff. For the portraits see Chaloner Smith, *Brit. Mezzotinto Portr.*, ii. 649, iii. 1011, 1337, and F. O'Donoghue, *Catal. Engr. Brit. Portr.*, i. 251.⟩
[4] ⟨See App. D, p. 520.⟩

Skye : Corrichatachin *Tuesday 7 September* 1773
inscription about the cruelties after the battle of Culloden, which will never be forgotten.

It was a very wet stormy day ; we were therefore obliged to remain here, it being impossible to cross the sea to Rasay.

I employed a part of the forenoon in writing this Journal. The rest of it was somewhat dreary, from the gloominess of the weather, and the uncertain state which we were in, as we could not tell but it might clear up every hour. Nothing is more painful to the mind than a state of suspence, especially when it depends upon the weather, concerning which there can be so little calculation. As Dr. Johnson said of our weariness on the Monday at Aberdeen, ' Sensation is sensation [1] : ' Corrichatachin, which was last night a hospitable house, was, in my mind, changed to-day into a prison. After dinner,[a] I read some of Dr. Macpherson's Dissertations on the Ancient Caledonians [2]. I was disgusted by the unsatisfactory conjectures as to antiquity, before the days of record. I was happy when tea came. Such, I take it, is the state of those who live in the country. Meals are wished for from the cravings of vacuity of mind, as well as from the desire of eating. I was hurt to find even such a temporary feebleness, and that I was so far from being that robust wise man who is sufficient for his own happiness. I felt a kind of lethargy of indolence. I did not exert myself to get Dr. Johnson to talk, that I might not have the labour of writing down his conversation.—He enquired here, if there were any remains of the second sight [3]. Mr. M'Pherson, Minister of Slate, said, he was *resolved* not to believe it, because it was founded on no principle [4].—*Johnson*. ' There are many things then, which we are sure are true, that you will not believe. What principle is there, why a loadstone attracts iron ? why an egg produces a chicken by heat ? why a tree grows upwards, when the natural tendency of all things is downwards ? Sir, it depends upon the degree of evidence that you have.'—Young Mr. M'Kinnon

[a] dinner, 1 : dinner 2, 3.

[1] See *ante*, v. 95.
[2] See v. 119, 206, 265 ⟨and App. D, p. 546.⟩
[3] Sir Walter Scott, when in Skye in 1814, wrote :—' We learn that most of the Highland superstitions, even that of the second-sight, are still in force.' Lockhart's *Scott*, 1837, iii. 228. See *ante*, ii. 10, 318.
[4] Of him Johnson wrote :—' One of the Ministers honestly told me, that he came to Sky with a resolution not to believe it.' *Western Isl.*, p. 99. ⟨See *post*, v. 265, 267.⟩

mentioned one M'Kenzie, who is still alive, who had often fainted in his presence, and when he recovered, mentioned visions which had been presented to him. He told Mr. M'Kinnon, that at such a place he should meet a funeral, and that such and such people would be the bearers, naming four ; and three weeks afterwards he saw what M'Kenzie had predicted. The naming the very spot in a country where a funeral comes a long way, and the very people as bearers, when there are so many out of whom a choice may be made, seems extraordinary. We should have sent for M'Kenzie, had we not been informed that he could speak no English. Besides, the facts were not related with sufficient accuracy.

Mrs. M'Kinnon, who is a daughter of old Kingsburgh, told us that her father was one day riding in Sky, and some women, who were at work in a field on the side of the road, said to him, they had heard two *taiscks*, (that is, two voices of persons about to die [1],) and what was remarkable, one of them was an *English taisck*, which they never heard before. When he returned, he at that very place met two funerals, and one of them was that of a woman who had come from the main land, and could speak only English. This, she remarked, made a great impression upon her father.

How all the people here were lodged, I know not †. It was partly done by separating man and wife, and putting a number of men in one room, and of women in another.

Wednesday, 8th September.

When I waked, the rain was much heavier than yesterday ; but the wind had abated. By breakfast, the day was better, and in a little while it was calm and clear. I felt my spirits much elated. The propriety of the expression, ' *the sunshine of the breast* [2],' now struck me with peculiar force ; for the brilliant rays penetrated into my very soul. We were all in better humour than before. Mrs. M'Kinnon, with unaffected hospitality and politeness, expressed her happiness in having such

[1] ' By the term *Second Sight*, seems to be meant a mode of seeing, superadded to that which Nature generally bestows. In the *Earse* it is called *Taisch* ; which signifies likewise a spectre, or a vision.' Johnson's *Western Isl.*, p. 98.
† ⟨See App. D, p. 521.⟩
[2] Gray's *Ode on a Distant Prospect of Eton College*, l. 44.

Skye : Corrichatachin *Wednesday 8 September* 1773

company in her house, and appeared to understand and relish Dr. Johnson's conversation, as indeed all the company seemed to do. When I knew she was old Kingsburgh's daughter, I did not wonder at the good appearance which she made.

She talked as if her husband and family would emigrate, rather than be oppressed by their landlord †; and said, ' how agreeable would it be, if these gentlemen should come in upon us when we are in America.'—Somebody observed that Sir Alexander Macdonald was always frightened at sea.—*Johnson.* ' *He* is frightened at sea ; and his tenants are frightened when he comes to land.'

We resolved to set out directly after breakfast. We had about two miles to ride to the sea-side, and there we expected to get one of the boats belonging to the fleet of bounty [1] herring-busses then on the coast, or at least a good country fishing-boat. But while we were preparing to set out, there arrived a man with the following card from the Reverend Mr. Donald M'Queen :

' Mr. M'Queen's compliments to Mr. Boswell, and begs leave to acquaint him that, fearing the want of a proper boat, as much as the rain of yesterday, might have caused a stop, he is now at Skianwden with Macgillichallum's [2] carriage, to convey him and Dr. Johnson to Rasay, where they will meet with a most hearty welcome, and where Macleod, being on a visit, now attends their motions.'

Wednesday forenoon [a].

This card was most agreeable ; it was a prologue to that hospitable and truly polite reception which we found at Rasay. In a little while arrived Mr. Donald M'Queen [3] himself ; a decent minister, an elderly man with his own black hair, courteous, and rather slow of speech, but candid, sensible and well informed, nay learned. Along with him came, as our pilot, a gentleman whom I had a great desire to see, Mr. Malcolm Macleod [4], one of the Rasay family, celebrated in the year 1745-6. He was now sixty-two years of age, hale, and well proportioned,—with a manly countenance, tanned by the weather, yet having a

[a] *forenoon* 1 (*MS.*) : *afternoon* 2, 3.

† ⟨Sir Alexander Macdonald. Boswell's *Hebrides*, ed. Pottle and Bennett, 1936, p. 125.⟩
[1] A bounty of thirty shillings a ton was at this time given to the owners of busses for the encouragement of the white herring fishery. Adam

Smith (*W. N.*, iv. 5) shows how mischievous was its effect.
[2] The Highland expression for Laird of Rasay. BOSWELL, ed. 1. ⟨For his ' carriage ' see App. D, p. 522.⟩
[3], [4] ⟨See App. D, pp. 522-3.⟩

ruddiness in his cheeks, over a great part of which his rough beard extended.—His eye was quick and lively, yet his look was not fierce, but he appeared at once firm and good-humoured. He wore a pair of brogues [1],—Tartan hose which came up only near to his knees, and left them bare,—a purple camblet kilt [2],—a black waistcoat,—a short green cloth coat bound with gold cord,—a yellowish bushy wig,—a large blue bonnet with a gold thread button. I never saw a figure that gave a more perfect representation of a Highland gentleman. I wished much to have a picture of him just as he was. I found him frank and *polite*, in the true sense of the word.

The good family at Corrichatachin said, they hoped to see us on our return. We rode down to the shore; but Malcolm walked with graceful agility.

We got into Rasay's *carriage*, which was a good strong open boat made in Norway. The wind had now risen pretty high, and was against us; but we had four stout rowers, particularly a Macleod, a robust, black-haired fellow, half naked, and bareheaded, something between a wild Indian and an English tar. Dr. Johnson sat high on the stern, like a magnificent Triton. Malcolm sung an Erse song, the chorus of which was '*Hatyin foam foam eri*,' with words of his own [3]. The tune resembled '*Owr the muir amang the heather*.' † The boatmen and Mr. M'Queen chorused, and all went well. At length Malcolm himself took an oar, and rowed vigorously. We sailed along the coast of Scalpa, a rugged island, about four miles in length. Dr. Johnson proposed that he and I should buy it, and found a good school, and an episcopal church, (Malcolm [4] said, he would come to it,) and have a printing-press, where he would print all the Erse that could be found.

Here I was strongly struck with our long-projected scheme of

[1] 'In Sky I first observed the use of Brogues, a kind of artless shoes, stitched with thongs so loosely, that though they defend the foot from stones, they do not exclude water.' *Western Isl.*, p. 44.
[2] To evade the law against the tartan dress, the Highlanders used to dye their variegated plaids and kilts into blue, green, or any single colour. SCOTT, 1831.
[3] See *post*, v. 290.
† ⟨See App. D, p. 523.⟩
[4] The Highlanders were all well inclined to the episcopalian form, *proviso* that the right *king* was prayed for. I suppose Malcolm meant to say, 'I will come to your church because you are *honest* folk;' viz. *Jacobites*. SCOTT, 1831.

visiting the Hebrides being realized [1]. I called to him, 'We are contending with seas;' which I think were the words of one of his letters to me [2]. 'Not much,' said he; and though the wind made the sea lash considerably upon us, he was not discomposed. After we were out of the shelter of Scalpa, and in the sound between it and Rasay, which extended about a league, the wind made the sea very rough [3]. I did not like it.—*Johnson*. 'This now is the Atlantick. If I should tell at a tea-table in London, that I have crossed the Atlantick in an open boat, how they'd shudder, and what a fool they'd think me to expose myself to such danger![a]' He then repeated Horace's ode,

Otium Divos rogat in patenti
Prensus Ægæo ———————[4]

In the confusion and hurry of this boisterous sail, Dr. Johnson's spurs, of which Joseph had charge, were carried over-board into the sea, and lost [5]. This was the first misfortune that had befallen us. Dr. Johnson was a little angry at first, observing that 'there was something wild in letting a pair of spurs be carried into the sea out of a boat;' but then he remarked, 'that, as Janes [6] the naturalist had said upon losing his pocket-book, it was rather an inconvenience than a loss.' He told us, he now recollected that he dreamt the night before, that he put his staff into a river, and chanced to let it go, and it was carried down the stream and lost. 'So now you see, (said he,) that I have lost my spurs; and this story is better than many of those which we have concerning second sight and dreams.' Mr. M'Queen said he did not believe the second sight; that he never met with any well attested instances; and if he should, he should impute them to chance; because all who pretend to that quality often

[a] danger! 1: danger? 2, 3.

[1] See *ante*, i. 450, and ii. 291.
[2] Perhaps he was thinking of Johnson's letter of June 20, 1771 (*ante*, ii. 140), where he says:—' I hope the time will come when we may try our powers both with cliffs and water.'
[3] 'The wind blew enough to give the boat a kind of dancing agitation.' *Letters*, No. 326. 'The water was calm, and the rowers were vigorous; so that our passage was quick and pleasant.' *Western Isl.*, p. 52.
[4] ' Caught in the wild Ægean seas, The sailor bends to heaven for ease.'
FRANCIS. Horace, 2 *Odes*, xvi. 1.
[5] See *ante*, iv. 408 note.
[6] ⟨See *ante*, v. 149 and App. D, p. 517.⟩

fail in their predictions, though they take a great scope, and sometimes interpret literally, sometimes figuratively, so as to suit the events. He told us, that, since he came to be minister of the parish where he now is, the belief of witchcraft, or charms, was very common, insomuch that he had many prosecutions before his *session* (the parochial ecclesiastical court) against women, for having by these means carried off the milk from people's cows. He disregarded them; and there is not now the least vestige of that superstition. He preached against it; and in order to give a strong proof to the people that there was nothing in it, he said from the pulpit, that every woman in the parish was welcome to take the milk from his cows, provided she did not touch them [1].

Dr. Johnson asked him as to Fingal. He said he could repeat some passages in the original; that he heard his grandfather had a copy of it; but that he could not affirm that Ossian composed all that poem as it is now published. This came pretty much to what Dr. Johnson has [a] maintained [2]; though he goes farther, and contends that it is no better than such an epick poem as he could make from the song of Robin Hood [3]; that is to say, that, except a few passages, there is nothing truly ancient but the names and some vague traditions. Mr. M'Queen alledged that Homer was made up of detached fragments. Dr. Johnson denied this; observing, that it had been one work originally, and that you could not put a book of the Iliad out of its place; and he believed the same might be said of the Odyssey.

The approach to Rasay was very pleasing. We saw before us a beautiful bay, well defended by a rocky coast; a good family mansion; a fine verdure about it,—with a considerable number of trees;—and beyond it hills and mountains in gradation of

[a] has 1: had 2, 3.

[1] Such spells are still believed in. A lady of property in Mull, a friend of mine, had a few years since much difficulty in rescuing from the superstitious fury of the people an old woman, who used a *charm* to injure her neighbour's cattle. It is now in my possession, and consists of feathers, parings of nails, hair, and such like trash, wrapt in a lump of clay. SCOTT, 1831.

[2] Sir Walter Scott, writing in Skye in 1814, says:—'Macleod and Mr. Suter have both heard a tacksman of Macleod's ... recite the celebrated Address to the Sun; and another person ... repeat the description of Cuchullin's car. But all agree as to the gross infidelity of Macpherson as a translator and editor.' Lockhart's *Scott*, 1837, iii. 230.

[3] See *post*, v. 389.

wildness. Our boatmen sung with great spirit. Dr. Johnson observed, that naval musick was very ancient. As we came near the shore, the singing of our rowers was succeeded by that of reapers, who were busy at work, and who seemed to shout as much as to sing, while they worked with a bounding activity [1]. Just as we landed, I observed a cross, or rather the ruins of one, upon a rock, which had to me a pleasing vestige of religion. I perceived a large company coming out from the house. We met them as we walked up. There were Rasay himself; his brother Dr. Macleod; his nephew the Laird of M'Kinnon; the Laird of Macleod; Colonel Macleod of Talisker, an officer in the Dutch service, a very genteel man, and a faithful branch of the family; Mr. Macleod of Muiravenside, best known by the name of Sandie Macleod, who was long in exile on account of the part which he took in 1745; and several other persons †. We were welcomed upon the green, and conducted into the house, where we were introduced to Lady Rasay, who was surrounded by a numerous family, consisting of three sons and ten daughters. The laird of Rasay is a sensible, polite, and most hospitable gentleman. I was told that his island of Rasay, and that of Rona, (from which the eldest son of the family has his title,) and a considerable extent of land which he has in Sky, do not altogether yield him a very large revenue [2]: and yet he lives in great splendour; and so far is he from distressing his people, that, in the present rage for emigration, not a man has left his estate.

It was past six o'clock when we arrived. Some excellent

---

[1] 'The women reaped the corn, and the men bound up the sheaves. The strokes of the sickle were timed by the modulation of the harvest song, in which all their voices were united.' *Western Isl.*, p. 56.

† ⟨For the various Macleods and the 'other persons' see App. D, pp. 523-5.⟩

[2] 'The money which he raises by rent from all his dominions, which contain at least fifty thousand acres, is not believed to exceed two hundred and fifty pounds; but as he keeps a large farm in his own hands, he sells every year great numbers of cattle...: The Wine circulates vigorously, and the Tea, Chocolate, and Coffee, however they are got, are always at hand.' *Letters*, No. 326. 'Of Wine and punch they are very liberal, for they get them cheap, but as there is no custom house on the Island, they can hardly be considered as Smugglers.' *Ib.* No. 329. 'Their trade is unconstrained; they pay no customs, for there is no officer to demand them; whatever therefore is made dear only by impost, is obtained here at an easy rate.' *Western Isl.*, p. 50.

brandy was served round immediately, according to the custom of the Highlands, where a dram is generally taken every day. They call it a *scalch* [1]. On a side-board was placed for us, who had come off the sea, a substantial dinner, and a variety of wines. Then we had coffee and tea. I observed in the room several elegantly-bound books, and other marks of improved life. Soon afterwards a fidler appeared, and a little ball began. Rasay himself danced with as much spirit as any man, and Malcolm bounded like a roe. Sandie Macleod, who has at times an excessive flow of spirits, and had it now, was, in his days of absconding, known by the name of *M'Cruslick* [2], which it seems was the designation of a kind of wild man in the Highlands, something between Proteus and Don Quixotte; and so he was called here. He made much jovial noise. Dr. Johnson was so delighted with this scene, that he said, ' I know not how we shall get away.' It entertained me to observe him sitting by, while we danced, sometimes in deep meditation,—sometimes smiling complacently,—sometimes looking upon Hooke's Roman History,—and sometimes talking a little, amidst the noise of the ball, to Mr. Donald M'Queen, who anxiously gathered knowledge from him. He was pleased with M'Queen, and said to me, ' This is a critical man, sir. There must be great vigour of mind to make him cultivate learning so much in the isle of Sky, where he might do without it. It is wonderful how many of the new publications he has. There must be a snatch of every opportunity.' Mr. M'Queen told me that his brother (who is the fourth generation of the family following each other as ministers of the parish of Snizort,) and he joined together, and

---

[1] ⟨Boswell's k's and h's are indistinguishable and he may have written ' scalck ': the Gaelic is *sgàilc*.⟩ ' No man is so abstemious as to refuse the morning dram, which they call a *skalk*.' *Western Isl.*, p. 49.

[2] Alexander Macleod, of Muiravenside, advocate, became extremely obnoxious to government by his zealous personal efforts to engage his chief, Macleod, and Macdonald of Sky, in the Chevalier's attempt of 1745. Had he succeeded, it would have added one-third at least to the jacobite army. Boswell has oddly described *M'Cruslick*, the being whose name was conferred upon this gentleman, as something between Proteus and Don Quixote. It is the name of a species of satyr, or *esprit follet*, a sort of mountain Puck or hobgoblin, seen among the wilds and mountains, as the old Highlanders believed, sometimes mirthful, sometimes mischievous. Alexander Macleod's precarious mode of life, and variable spirits, occasioned the *soubriquet*. SCOTT, 1831. ⟨See App. D, p. 525.⟩

bought from time to time such books as had reputation. Soon after we came in, a black cock and grey hen, which had been shot, were shewn, with their feathers on, to Dr. Johnson, who had never seen that species of bird before. We had a company of thirty at supper; and all was good humour and gaiety, without intemperance.

Thursday, 9th September.

At breakfast this morning, among a profusion of other things, there were oat-cakes, made of what is called *graddaned* meal, this is, meal made of grain separated from the husks, and toasted by fire, instead of being threshed and kiln-dried.—This seems to be bad management, as so much fodder is consumed by it†. Mr. M'Queen however defended it, by saying, that it is doing the thing much quicker, as one operation effects what is otherwise done by two. His chief reason however was, that the servants in Sky are, according to him, a faithless pack, and steal what they can; so that much is saved by the corn passing but once through their hands, as at each time they pilfer some. It appears to me, that the gradaning is a strong proof of the laziness of the Highlanders, who will rather make fire act for them, at the expence of fodder, than labour themselves. There was also, what I cannot help disliking at breakfast, cheese: it is the custom over all the Highlands to have it; and it often smells very strong, and poisons to a certain degree the elegance of an Indian repast [1]. The day was showery; however, Rasay and I took a walk, and had some cordial conversation. I conceived a more than ordinary regard for this worthy gentleman. His family has possessed this island above four hundred years [2]. It is the remains of the estate of Macleod of Lewis, whom he represents.—When we returned, Dr. Johnson walked with us to see the old chapel. He was in fine spirits. He said, ' This is truly the patriarchal life: this is what we came to find.'

† ⟨In the process of making it the straw was burnt. See *Trans. Gaelic Soc. of Inverness*, 1918, xviii. 116.⟩
[1] Johnson also complained of the cheese. ' In the islands .., they do what I found it not very easy to endure. They pollute the tea-table by plates piled with large slices of cheshire cheese, which mingles its less grateful odours with the fragrance of the tea.' *Western Isl.*, p. 50.
[2] ' The estate has not, during four hundred years, gained or lost a single acre.' *Ib.*, p. 53.

After dinner, M'Cruslick, Malcolm, and I, went out with guns, to try if we could find any black-cock ; but we had no sport, owing to a heavy rain. I saw here what is called a Danish fort. Our evening was passed as last night was. One of our company [1], I was told, had hurt himself by too much study, particularly of infidel metaphysicians, of which he gave a proof, on second sight being mentioned. He immediately retailed some of the fallacious arguments of Voltaire and Hume against miracles in general. Infidelity in a Highland gentleman appeared to me peculiarly offensive. I was sorry for him, as he had otherwise a good character. I told Dr. Johnson that he had studied himself into infidelity.—*Johnson.* ' Then he must study himself out of it again. That is the way. Drinking largely will sober him again [2].'

Friday, 10th September.

Having resolved to explore the island of Rasay, which could be done only on foot, I last night obtained my fellow-traveller's permission to leave him for a day, he being unable to take so hardy a walk. Old Mr. Malcolm M'Leod [3], who had obligingly promised to accompany me, was at my bedside between five and six. I sprang up immediately, and he and I, attended by two other gentlemen, traversed the country during the whole of this day. Though we had passed over not less than four-and-twenty miles of very rugged ground, and had a Highland dance on the top of *Dun Can*, the highest mountain in the island, we returned in the evening not at all fatigued, and piqued ourselves at not being outdone at the nightly ball by our less active friends, who had remained at home.

My survey of Rasay did not furnish much which can interest my readers ; I shall therefore put into as short a compass as I can, the observations upon it, which I find registered in my journal. It is about fifteen English miles long, and four broad. On the south side is the laird's family seat, situated on a pleasing low spot. The old tower of three stories, mentioned by Martin [4], was taken down soon after 1746, and a modern house supplies its place. There are very good grass-fields and corn-lands about it, well dressed. I observed, however, hardly

---

[1] ⟨The Laird of MacKinnon: see App. D, p. 525.⟩
[2] ⟨' Then shallow draughts intoxicate the brain,
And drinking largely sobers us again.'
Pope, *Essay on Criticism*, 218.⟩
[3] ⟨See App. D, p. 523.⟩
[4] ⟨*Western Isl.*, 1703, p. 164.⟩

any inclosures, except a good garden plentifully stocked with vegetables, and strawberries, raspberries, currants, &c.

On one of the rocks just where we landed, which are not high, there is rudely carved a square, with a crucifix in the middle. Here, it is said, the Lairds of Rasay, in old times, used to offer up their devotions. I could not approach the spot, without a grateful recollection of the event commemorated by this symbol.

A little from the shore, westward, is a kind of subterraneous house. There has been a natural fissure, or separation of the rock, running towards the sea, which has been roofed over with long stones, and above them turf has been laid. In that place the inhabitants used to keep their oars. There are a number of trees near the house, which grow well ; some of them of a pretty good size. They are mostly plane and ash. A little to the west of the house is an old ruinous chapel, unroofed, which never has been very curious. We here saw some human bones of an uncommon size. There was a heel-bone, in particular, which Dr. Macleod said was such, that,[a] if the foot was in proportion, it must have been twenty-seven inches long. Dr. Johnson would not look at the bones. He started back from them with a striking appearance of horror [1]. Mr. M'Queen told us, it was formerly much the custom, in these isles, to have human bones lying above ground, especially in the windows of churches. On the south of the chapel is the family burying-place. Above the door, on the east end of it, is a small bust or image of the Virgin Mary, carved upon a stone which makes part of the wall. There is no church upon the island. It is annexed to one of the parishes of Sky ; and the minister comes and preaches either in Rasay's house, or some other house, on certain Sundays. I could not but value the family seat more, for having even the ruins of a chapel close to it. There was something comfortable in the thought of being so near a piece of consecrated ground [2].

[a] that, 1, 2 : that 3.

[1] Lord Stowell told me, that on the road from Newcastle to Berwick, Dr. Johnson and he passed a cottage, at the entrance of which were set up two of those great bones of the whale, which are not unfrequently seen in maritime districts. Johnson expressed great horror at the sight of these bones ; and called the people, who could use such relics of mortality as an ornament, mere savages. CROKER, 1831. ⟨Some of these bones are still, 1939, at Raasay.⟩

[2] In like manner Boswell wrote :—

Dr. Johnson said, ' I look with reverence upon every place that has been set apart for religion ; ' and he kept off his hat while he was within the walls of the chapel [1].

The eight crosses, which Martin [2] mentions as pyramids for deceased ladies, stood in a semicircular line, which contained within it the chapel. They marked out the boundaries of the sacred territory within which an asylum was to be had. One of them, which we observed upon our landing, made the first point of the semicircle. There are few of them now remaining. A good way farther north, there is a row of buildings about four feet high : they run from the shore on the east along the top of a pretty high eminence, and so down to the shore on the west, in much the same direction with the crosses. Rasay took them to be the marks for the asylum ; but Malcolm thought them to be false sentinels, a common deception, of which instances occur in Martin [3], to make invaders imagine an island better guarded. Mr. Donald M'Queen, justly in my opinion, supposed the crosses which form the inner circle to be the church's land-marks.

The south end of the island is much covered with large stones or rocky strata. The laird has enclosed and planted part of it with firs, and he shewed me a considerable space marked out for additional plantations.

Dun Can is a mountain three computed miles from the laird's house. The ascent to it is by consecutive risings, if that expression may be used when vallies intervene, so that there is but a short rise at once ; but it is certainly very high above the sea. The palm of altitude is disputed for by the people of Rasay and those of Sky ; the former contending for Dun Can,

' It is divinely cheering to me to think that there is a Cathedral so near Auchinleck [as Carlisle].' *Ante*, iii. 416.

[1] ' It is not only in Raasay that the chapel is unroofed and useless ; through the few islands which we visited, we neither saw nor heard of any house of prayer, except in Sky, that was not in ruins. The malignant influence of Calvinism has blasted ceremony and decency together ... It has been, for many years, popular to talk of the lazy devotion of the Romish clergy ; over the sleepy laziness of men that erected churches, we may indulge our superiority with a new triumph, by comparing it with the fervid activity of those who suffer them to fall.' Johnson's *Western Isl.*, p. 58. He wrote to Mrs. Thrale :—' By the active zeal of Protestant devotion, almost all [the chapels] have sunk into ruin.' *Letters*, No. 329.

[2] ⟨*Western Isl.*, 1703, p. 164.⟩
[3] ⟨*Ibid.*, p. 59.⟩

the latter for the mountains in Sky, over against it. We went up the east side of Dun Can pretty easily. It is mostly rocks all around, the points of which hem the summit of it. Sailors, to whom it is [a] a good object as they pass along, call it Rasay's cap. Before we reached this mountain, we passed by two lakes. Of the first, Malcolm told me a strange fabulous tradition. He said, there was a wild beast in it, a sea-horse, which came and devoured a man's daughter; upon which the man lighted a great fire, and had a sow roasted at it, the smell of which attracted the monster. In the fire was put a spit. The man lay concealed behind a low wall of loose stones, and he had an avenue formed for the monster, with two rows of large flat stones, which extended from the fire over the summit of the hill, till it reached the side of the loch. The monster came, and the man with the red-hot spit destroyed it. Malcolm shewed me the little hiding-place, and the rows of stones. He did not laugh when he told this story. I recollect having seen in the Scots Magazine, several years ago, a poem upon a similar tale, perhaps the same, translated from the Erse, or Irish, called *Albin and the Daughter of Mey* †.

There is a large tract of land, possessed as a common, in Rasay. They have no regulations as to the number of cattle. Every man puts upon it as many as he chooses. From Dun Can northward, till you reach the other end of the island, there is much good natural pasture unincumbered by stones. We passed over a spot, which is appropriated for the exercising ground. In 1745, a hundred fighting men were reviewed here, as Malcolm told me, who was one of the officers that led them to the field [1]. They returned home all but about fourteen. What a princely thing is it to be able to furnish such a band! Rasay has the true spirit of a chief. He is, without exaggeration, a father to his people.

There is plenty of lime-stone in the island, a great quarry of free-stone, and some natural woods, but none of any age, as they cut the trees for common country uses. The lakes, of which there are many, are well stocked with trout. Malcolm

[a] is 1 (*MS.*) : was 2, 3.

† ⟨See App. D, p. 525.⟩
[1] 'Not many years ago,' writes Johnson, 'the late Laird led out one hundred men upon a military expedition.' *Western Isl.*, p. 57. What the expedition was he is careful not to state.

catched one of four-and-twenty pounds weight in the loch next to Dun Can, which, by the way, is certainly a Danish name, as most names of places in these islands are.

The old castle, in which the family of Rasay formerly resided, is situated upon a rock very near the sea. The rock is not one mass of stone, but a concretion of pebbles and earth, so firm that it does not appear to have mouldered. In this remnant of antiquity I found nothing worthy of being noticed, except a certain accommodation rarely to be found at the modern houses of Scotland, and which Dr. Johnson and I sought for in vain at the Laird of Rasay's new-built mansion, where nothing else was wanting †. I took the liberty to tell the Laird it was a shame there should be such a deficiency in civilized times. He acknowledged the justice of the remark. But perhaps some generations may pass before the want is supplied. Dr. Johnson observed to me, how quietly people will endure an evil, which they might at any time very easily remedy; and mentioned as an instance, that the present family of Rasay had possessed the island for more than four hundred years, and never made a commodious landing place, though a few men with pickaxes might have cut an ascent of stairs out of any part of the rock in a week's time [1].

The north end of Rasay is as rocky as the south end. From it I saw the little isle of Fladda, belonging to Rasay, all fine green ground;—and Rona, which is of so rocky a soil that it appears to be a pavement. I was told however that it has a great deal of grass, in the interstices. The Laird has it all in his own hands. At this end of the island of Rasay is a cave in a striking situation. It is in a recess of a great cleft, a good way up from the sea. Before it the ocean roars, being dashed against monstrous broken rocks; grand and aweful *propugnacula*. On the right hand of it is a longitudinal cave, very low at the entrance, but higher as you advance. The sea having scooped it out, it seems strange and unaccountable that the

† ⟨See App. D, p. 526.⟩
[1] 'I considered this rugged ascent as the consequence of a form of life inured to hardships, and therefore not studious of nice accommodations. But I know not whether, for many ages, it was not considered as a part of military policy, to keep the country not easily accessible. The rocks are natural fortifications.' *Western Isl.*, p. 52. ⟨See App. D, p. 526, for Raasay House.⟩

interior part, where the water must have operated with less force, should be loftier than that which is more immediately exposed to its violence. The roof of it is all covered with a kind of petrifications formed by drops, which perpetually distil from it. The first cave has been a place of much safety.—I find a great difficulty in describing visible objects [1]. I must own too that the old castle and cave, like many other things, of which one hears much, did not answer my expectations. People are every where apt to magnify the curiosities of their country.

This island has abundance of black cattle, sheep, and goats; —a good many horses, which are used for ploughing, carrying out dung, and other works of husbandry. I believe the people never ride. There are indeed no roads through the island, unless a few detached beaten tracks deserve that name. Most of the houses are upon the shore ; so that all the people have little boats, and catch fish. There is great plenty of potatoes here. There are black-cock in extraordinary abundance, moorfowl, plover,[a] and wild pigeons, which seemed to me to be the same as we have in pigeon-houses, in their state of nature. Rasay has no pigeon-house. There are no hares nor rabbits in the island, nor was there ever known to be a fox [2], till last year, when one was landed on it by some malicious person, without whose aid he could not have got thither, as that animal is known to be a very bad swimmer. He has done much mischief.† There is a great deal of fish caught in the sea around [b] Rasay ; it is a place where one may live in plenty, and even in luxury. There are no deer ; but Rasay told us he would get some.

They reckon it rains nine months in the year in this island, owing to its being directly opposite to the western [3] coast of Sky, where the watery clouds are broken by high mountains. The hills here, and indeed all the heathy grounds in general,

[a] plover, 1, 2: plover 3.   [b] around 1 (*MS*.) : round 2, 3.

[1] See *post*, v. 219.
[2] In Skye a price was set 'upon the heads of foxes, which, as the number was diminished, has been gradually raised, from three shillings and sixpence to a guinea, a sum so great in this part of the world, that, in a short time, Sky may be as free from foxes, as England from wolves. The fund for these rewards is a tax of sixpence in the pound, imposed by the farmers on themselves, and said to be paid with great willingness.' *Western Isl.*, p. 55.
† 〈' Mr. J. said they should set a trap for him.' Boswell's *Hebrides*, ed. Pottle and Bennett, 1936, p. 149.〉
[3] Boswell means that the *eastern* coast of Sky is *westward* of Rasay. CROKER, 1848.

abound with the sweet-smelling plant which the Highlanders call *gaul* †, and (I think) with dwarf juniper in many places. There is enough of turf, which is their fuel, and it is thought there is a mine of coal.—Such are the observations which I made upon the island of Rasay, upon comparing it with the description given by Martin, whose book we had with us.

There has been an ancient league between the families of Macdonald and Rasay. Whenever the head of either family dies, his sword is given to the head of the other. The present Rasay has the late Sir James Macdonald's sword. Old Rasay joined the Highland army in 1745, but prudently guarded against a forfeiture, by previously conveying his estate to the present gentleman, his eldest son [1]. On that occasion, Sir Alexander, father of the late Sir James Macdonald, was very friendly to his neighbour. ' Don't be afraid, Rasay, said he ; I'll use all my interest to keep you safe ; and if your estate should be taken, I'll buy it for the family.'—And he would have done it.

Let me now gather some gold dust,—some more fragments of Dr. Johnson's conversation, without regard to order of time. He said, ' he thought very highly of Bentley ; that no man now went so far in the kinds of learning that he cultivated [2] ; that the many attacks on him were owing to envy, and to a desire of being known, by being in competition with such a man ; that it was safe to attack him, because he never answered his opponents, but let them die away [3]. It was attacking a man who would not beat them, because his beating them would make them live the longer. And he was right not to answer ; for, in his hazardous method of writing, he could not but be often enough wrong ; so it was better to leave things to their general appearance, than own himself to have erred in particulars.'—He said, ' Mallet was the prettiest drest puppet about town [4], and

---

† ⟨See App. D, p. 526.⟩
[1] ' The prince was hidden in his distress two nights at Raarsa, and the king's troops burnt the whole country, and killed some of the Cattle. You may guess at the opinions that prevail in this country, they are however content with fighting for their king, they do not drink for him ; we had no foolish healths.'

Johnson's *Letters*, No. 327.
[2] See *ante*, iv. 217, where he said :—' You have, perhaps, no man who knows as much Greek and Latin as Bentley.'
[3] See *ante*, ii. 61, and *post*, v. 273.
[4] ⟨Mrs. Mallet appears to have been responsible for her husband's clothes. Davies, *Life Garrick*, ch. 32, 1808, ii. 46. Boswell wrote ' poppet '.⟩

always kept good company [1]. That, from his way of talking, he saw, and always said, that he had not written any part of the Life of the Duke of Marlborough, though perhaps he intended to do it at some time, in which case he was not culpable in taking the pension [2]. That he imagined the Duchess furnished the materials for her Apology, which Hooke wrote, and Hooke furnished the words and the order, and all that in which the art of writing consists. That the duchess had not superior parts, but was a bold frontless woman, who knew how to make the most of her opportunities in life. That Hooke got a *large* sum of money for writing her Apology [3]. That he wondered Hooke should have been weak enough to insert so profligate a maxim, as that to tell another's secret to one's friend, is no breach of confidence [4] ; though perhaps Hooke, who was a virtuous man [5],

[1] See *ante*, i. 268, note 1.
[2] Steele had had the Duke of Marlborough's papers, and ' in some of his exigencies put them in pawn. They then remained with the old dutchess, who in her will assigned the task to Glover and Mallet, with a reward of a thousand pounds, and a prohibition to insert any verses. Glover rejected, I suppose, with disdain, the legacy, and devolved the whole work upon Mallet; who had from the late duke of Marlborough a pension to promote his industry, and who talked of the discoveries which he made; but left not, when he died, any historical labours behind him.' Johnson's *Life of Mallet*, 14. The Duchess died in 1744 and Mallet in 1765. For more than twenty years he thus imposed more or less successfully on the world. About the year 1751 he played on Garrick's vanity. ' Mallet, in a familiar conversation with Garrick, discoursing of the diligence which he was then exerting upon the *Life of Marlborough*, let him know that in the series of great men, quickly to be exhibited, he should *find a nich* for the hero of the theatre. Garrick professed to wonder by what artifice he could be introduced ; but Mallet let him know, that, by a dexterous anticipation, he should fix him in a conspicuous place. " Mr. Mallet," says Garrick, in his gratitude of exultation, " have you left off to write for the stage ? " Mallet then confessed that he had a drama in his hands. Garrick promised to act it ; and *Alfred* was produced.' *Ib.* 13. See *ante*, iii. 386. ⟨Hume in 1762 said that Mallet had given him to understand that his work was ' ready for the Press '. *Letters*, 1932, i. 370. On Mallet's death the papers were offered to, and refused by, Hume, *ib.* ii. 6 ; fifty years later they were used by Coxe for his *Memoirs of John Duke of Marlborough*, 1818.⟩
[3] According to Dr. Warton (*Essay on Pope*, 1782, ii. 145) he received £5000. ' Old Marlborough,' wrote Walpole in March, 1742 (*Letters*, i. 191), ' has at last published her Memoirs ; they are digested by one Hooke, who wrote a Roman history ; but from her materials, which are so womanish, that I am sure the man might sooner have made a gown and petticoat with them.' ⟨The work, which is said to have been taken down from the Duchess's lips, was entitled *An Account of the Conduct of the Dowager Duchess of Marlborough, from her first coming to Court to the year 1710.*⟩
[4] See *ante*, i. 153.
[5] ' Hooke,' says Dr. Warton (*Essay on Pope*, 1782, ii. 145), ' was a Mystic, and a Quietist, and a warm disciple of Fenelon. It was he who brought a Catholic priest to take Pope's confession on his death-bed.'

as his *History* shews, and did not wish her well, though he wrote her Apology, might see its ill tendency, and yet insert it at her desire. He was acting only ministerially.'—I apprehend, however, that Hooke was bound to give his best advice. I speak as a lawyer. Though I have had clients whose causes I could not, as a private man, approve ; yet, if I undertook them, I would not do any thing that might be prejudicial to them, even at their desire, without warning them of their danger.

Saturday, 11th September.

It was a storm of wind and rain ; so we could not set out. I wrote some of this Journal, and talked awhile with Dr. Johnson in his room, and passed the day, I cannot well say how, but very pleasantly. I was here amused to find Mr. Cumberland's comedy of the *Fashionable Lover* [1], in which he has very well drawn a Highland character, Colin M'Cleod, of the same name with the family under whose roof we now were. Dr. Johnson was much pleased with the Laird of Macleod, who is indeed a most promising youth, and with a noble spirit struggles with difficulties, and endeavours to preserve his people. He has been left with an incumbrance of forty thousand pounds debt, and annuities to the amount of thirteen hundred pounds a year. Dr. Johnson said, ' If he gets the better of all this, he'll be a hero ; and I hope he will [2]. I have not met with a young man who

[1] See Cumberland's *Memoirs*, p. 254.

[2] Croker, 1831, says that ' though he had sold a great tract of land in Harris, he left at his death, in 1801, the original debt of £50,000 increased to £70,000.' When Johnson visited Macleod at Dunvegan, he wrote to Mrs. Thrale :—' Here though poor Macleod had been left by his Grandfather overwhelmed with debts, we had another exhibition of feudal hospitality. There were two Stags in the house, and venison came to the table every day in its various forms. Macleod, besides his Estate in Skie, larger, I suppose than some English Counties, is Proprietor of nine inhabited Islands ; and of his Islands uninhabited I doubt if he very exactly knows the number. I told him that he was a mighty monarch. Such dominions fill an Englishman with envious wonder, but when he surveys the naked mountain and treads the quaking moor, and wanders over wide regions of gloomy barrenness his wonder may continue, but his envy ceases. The unprofitableness of these vast domains can be conceived only by the means of positive instances. The Heir of Col an Island not far distant has lately told me how wealthy he should be if he could let Rum another of his Islands, for twopence halfpenny an acre ; and Macleod has an estate which the Surveyor reports to contain eighty thousand acres, rented at six

had more desire to learn, or who has learnt more. I have seen nobody that I wish more to do a kindness to than Macleod.'—Such was the honourable elogium, on this young chieftain, pronounced by an accurate observer, whose praise was never lightly bestowed.

There is neither justice of peace, nor constable,[a] in Rasay. Sky has Mr. M'Cleod of Ulinish †, who is the sheriff substitute, and no other justice of peace. The want of the execution of justice is much felt among the islanders. Macleod very sensibly observed, that taking away the heritable jurisdictions [1] had not been of such service in the islands, as was imagined. They had not authority enough in lieu of them. What could formerly have been settled at once, must now either take much time and trouble, or be neglected. Dr. Johnson said, ' A country is in a bad state, which is governed only by laws ; because a thousand things occur for which laws cannot provide, and where authority ought to interpose. Now destroying the authority of the chiefs set the people loose. It did not pretend to bring any positive good, but only to cure some evil ; and I am not well enough acquainted with the country to know what degree of evil the heritable jurisdictions occasioned [2].'—I maintained hardly any ; because the chiefs generally acted right, for their own sakes.

[a] constable, 1, 2: constable 3.

hundred pounds a year.' *Letters*, No. 329. ⟨See also App. D, pp. 526–8.⟩

† ⟨See *post*, v. 235 and App. D, p. 541.⟩

[1] They were abolished by an act passed in 1747 ⟨20 Geo. II, c. 43⟩, being ' reckoned among the principal sources of those rebellions that had been excited since the revolution. In the Highlands, they certainly kept the common people in subjection to their chiefs. . . . By this act these mountaineers were legally emancipated from slavery : but as the tenants enjoyed no leases, and were at all times liable to be ejected from their farms, they still depended on the pleasure of their lords, notwithstanding this interposition of the legislature, which granted a valuable consideration in money to every nobleman and petty baron, who was thus deprived of one part of his inheritance.' Smollett's *England*, 1758, iv. 686. See *post*, v. 343.

[2] ' I doubt not but that since the regular judges have made their circuits through the whole country, right has been every where more wisely, and more equally distributed ; the complaint is, that litigation is grown troublesome, and that the magistrates are too few, and therefore often too remote for general convenience. . . . In all greater questions . . . there is now happily an end to all fear or hope from malice or from favour. The roads are secure in those places through which, forty years ago, no traveller could pass without a convoy . . . . No scheme of policy has, in any country, yet brought the rich and poor on equal terms into courts of judicature. Perhaps experience, improving on experience,

Dr. Johnson was now wishing to move. There was not enough of intellectual entertainment for him, after he had satisfied his curiosity, which he did, by asking questions, till he had exhausted the island; and where there was so numerous a company, mostly young people, there was such a flow of familiar talk, so much noise, and so much singing and dancing, that little opportunity was left for his energetick conversation [1]. He seemed sensible of this; for when I told him how happy they were at having him there, he said, ' Yet we have not been able to entertain them much.'—I was fretted, from irritability of nerves, by M'Cruslick's too obstreperous mirth. I complained of it to my friend, observing we should be better if he was gone.—' No, sir (said he). He puts something into our society, and takes nothing out of it.'—Dr. Johnson, however, had several opportunities of instructing the company; but I am sorry to say, that I did not pay sufficient attention to what passed, as his discourse now turned chiefly on mechanicks, agriculture, and such subjects, rather than on science and wit.—Last night Lady Rasay shewed him the operation of *wawking* cloth, that is, thickening it in the same manner as is done by a mill. Here it is performed by women, who kneel upon the ground, and rub it with both their hands, singing an Erse song all the time. He was asking questions while they were performing this operation, and, amidst their loud and wild howl, his voice was heard even in the room above [2].

They dance here every night. The queen of our ball was the eldest Miss Macleod, of Rasay, an elegant well-bred woman, and celebrated for her beauty over all those regions, by the name of Miss Flora Rasay [3]. There seemed to be no jealousy, no dismay in time effect it.' *Western Isl.*, p. 84.

[1] He described Rasay as ' the seat of plenty, civility, and cheerfulness.' *Letters*, No. 329. ⟨On 10 Sept. 1773, he said of it to Boswell : ' If one had a mind to retire for study for a summer, it would be a fine place.' Boswell's *Hebrides*, ed. Pottle and Bennett, p. 149.⟩

[2] ' We heard the women singing as they *waulked* the cloth by rubbing it with their hands and feet, and screaming all the while in a sort of chorus. At a distance, the sound was wild and sweet enough, but rather discordant when you approached too near the performers.' Lockhart's *Scott*, 1837, iii. 230.

[3] She had been some time at Edinburgh, to which she again went, and was married to my worthy neighbour, Colonel Mure Campbell, now Earl of Loudoun; but she died soon afterwards, leaving one daughter. BOSWELL, ed. 1.

' Miss Flora Macleod is a celebrated

content among them ; and the gaiety of the scene was such, that I for a moment doubted whether unhappiness had any place in Rasay. But my delusion was soon dispelled, by recollecting the following lines of my fellow-traveller :

> ' Yet hope not life from pain or danger free,
> Or think the doom of man revers'd for thee [1] ! '

Sunday, 12th September.

It was a beautiful day, and although we did not approve of travelling on Sunday, we resolved to set out, as we were in an island from whence one must take occasion as it serves. Macleod and Talisker sailed in a boat of Rasay's for Sconser, to take the shortest way to Dunvegan. M'Cruslick went with them to Sconser, from whence he was to go to Slate, and so to the main land. We were resolved to pay a visit at Kingsburgh, and see the celebrated Miss Flora Macdonald, who is married to the present Mr. Macdonald of Kingsburgh ; so took that road, though not so near. All the family, but Lady Rasay, walked down to the shore to see us depart. Rasay himself went with us in a large boat, with eight oars, built in his island [2] ; as did Mr. Malcolm M'Cleod, Mr. Donald M'Queen, Dr. Macleod, and some others. We had a most pleasant sail between Rasay and Sky ; and passed by a cave, where Martin [3] says fowls were caught by lighting fire in the mouth of it. Malcolm remembers this. But it is not now practised, as few fowls come into it.

We spoke of Death. Dr. Johnson on this subject observed, that the boastings of some men, as to dying easily, were idle

Beauty, has been admired at Edinburgh, dresses her head very high, and has manners so Ladylike, that I wish her headdress was lower.' *Letters,* No. 327. See *ante,* iii. 118.

[1] ' Yet hope not Life from *Grief* or Danger free,
Nor think the Doom of Man revers'd for thee.'
The Vanity of Human Wishes.

[2] ' Raarsay accompanied us in his six-oar'd boat, which he said was his coach and six. It is indeed the vehicle in which the Ladies take the air, and pay their visits, but they have

taken very little care for accommodations. There is no way in or out of the boat for a woman, but by being carried, and in the boat, thus dignified with a pompous name, there is no seat, but an occasional bundle of straw.' *Letters,* No. 329. In describing the distance of one family from another, Johnson writes :—' Visits last several days, and are commonly paid by water ; yet I never saw a boat furnished with benches.' Johnson's *Western Isl.,* p. 93.

[3] ⟨Martin's *Western Isl.,* 1703, p. 151.⟩

talk [1], proceeding from partial views. I mentioned Hawthornden's Cypress-grove, where it is said that the world is a mere show; and that it is unreasonable for a man to wish to continue in the show-room, after he has seen it. Let him go cheerfully out, and give place to other spectators [2].—*Johnson.* 'Yes, sir, if he is sure he is to be well, after he goes out of it. But if he is to grow blind after he goes out of the show-room, and never to see any thing again; or if he does not know whither he is to go next, a man will not go cheerfully out of a show-room. No wise man will be contented to die, if he thinks he is to go into a state of punishment. Nay, no wise man will be contented to die, if he thinks he is to fall into annihilation: for however unhappy any man's existence may be, he yet would rather have it, than not exist at all [3]. No; there is no rational principle by which a man can die contented, but a trust in the mercy of GOD, through the merits of Jesus Christ.'—This short sermon, delivered with an earnest tone, in a boat upon the sea, which was perfectly calm, on a day appropriated to religious worship, while every one listened with an air of satisfaction, had a most pleasing effect upon my mind.

Pursuing the same train of serious reflection, he added, that it seemed certain that happiness could not be found in this life, because so many had tried to find it, in such a variety of ways, and had not found it.

We reached the harbour of Portree, in Sky, which is a large and good one. There was lying in it a vessel to carry off the emigrants, called the *Nestor*. It made a short settlement of the differences between a chief and his clan:

'——————— *Nestor* componere lites
Inter Peleiden festinat & inter Atriden.[4]'

We approached her, and she hoisted her colours. Dr. Johnson

---

[1] See *ante*, ii. 106, and iii. 154.

[2] 'They which forewent vs did leaue a Roome for vs, and should wee grieue to doe the same to these which should come after vs? who beeing admitted to see the exquisite Rarities of some Antiquaries Cabinet is grieued, all viewed, to haue the Courtaine drawn, and giue place to new Pilgrimes?' *Flowres of Sion*, etc., by William Drummond of Hawthorne-denne, ed. 1630, p. 68.

[3] See *ante*, iii. 153, 295.

[4] 'While hoary Nestor, by experience wise,
To reconcile the angry monarch tries.'
FRANCIS. Horace, 1 *Epis.* ii. 11.

Skye : Portree *Sunday* 12 *September* 1773

and Mr. M'Queen remained in the boat : Rasay and I, and the rest, went on board of her. She was a very pretty vessel, and, as we were told, the largest in Clyde. Mr. Harrison, the captain, shewed her to us. The cabin was commodious, and even elegant. There was a little library, finely bound. *Portree* has its name from King James the Fifth having landed there in his tour through the Western Isles, *Ree* in Erse being King, as *Re* is in Italian ; so it is *Port-Royal*. There was here a tolerable inn †. On our landing, I had the pleasure of finding a letter from home ; and there were also letters to Dr. Johnson and me from Lord Elibank [1], which had been sent after us from Edinburgh. —His lordship's letter to me was as follows :

' *Dear Boswell*,
 ' I flew to Edinburgh the moment I heard of Mr. Johnson's arrival ; but so defective was my intelligence, that I came too late.
 ' It is but justice to believe, that I could never forgive myself, nor deserve to be forgiven by others, if I was to fail in any mark of respect to that very great genius.—I hold him in the highest veneration ; for that very reason I was resolved to take no share in the merit, perhaps guilt, of enticing him to honour this country with a visit.—I could not persuade myself there was any thing in Scotland worthy to have a summer of Samuel Johnson bestowed on it ; but since he has done us that compliment, for heaven's sake inform me of your motions. I will attend them most religiously ; and though I should regret to let Mr. Johnson go a mile out of his way on my account, old as I am [2], I shall be glad to go five hundred miles to enjoy a day of his company. Have the charity to send a council-post [3] with intelligence ; the post does not suit us in the country.—At any rate write to me. I will attend you in the north, when I shall know where to find you.
 ' I am,
  ' My dear Boswell,
   ' Your sincerely
    ' Obedient humble servant,
     ' ELIBANK.'
' *August* 21*st*, 1773.'

† ⟨' We found here a very good half-finished inn, kept by James Macdonald, who is going to America.' Boswell's *Hebrides*, ed. Pottle and Bennett, p. 156.⟩ [1] See *ante*, v. 16.
[2] Lord Elibank died Aug. 3, 1778, aged 75. *Gent. Mag.* 1778, xlviii. p. 391.
[3] A term in Scotland for a special messenger, such as was formerly sent with dispatches by the lords of the council. BOSWELL, ed. 1.

The letter to Dr. Johnson was in these words :

'*Dear Sir*,

' I was to have kissed your hands at Edinburgh, the moment I heard of you ; but you was gone.

' I hope my friend Boswell will inform me of your motions. It will be cruel to deprive me an instant of the honour of attending you. As I value you more than any King in Christendom, I will perform that duty with infinitely greater alacrity than any courtier. I can contribute but little to your entertainment ; but, my sincere esteem for you gives me some title to the opportunity of expressing it.

' I dare say you are by this time sensible that things are pretty much the same, as when Buchanan complained of being born *solo et seculo inerudito* †. Let me hear of you ; and be persuaded that none of your admirers is more sincerely devoted to you, than,

' Dear Sir,
' Your most obedient,
' And most humble servant,
' ELIBANK.'

Dr. Johnson, on the following Tuesday, answered for both of us, thus :

' MY LORD,

' ON the rugged shore of Skie, I had the honour of your Lordship's letter, and can with great truth declare, that no place is so gloomy but that it would be cheered by such a testimony of regard, from a mind so well qualified to estimate characters, and to deal out approbation in its due proportions. If I have more than my share, it is your Lordship's fault ; for I have always reverenced your judgement [a] too much, to exalt myself in your presence by any false pretensions.

' Mr. Boswell and I are at present at the disposal of the winds, and therefore cannot fix the time at which we shall have the honour of seeing your lordship. But we should either of us think ourselves injured by the supposition that we would miss your lordship's conversation, when we could enjoy it ; for I have often declared[b] that I never met you without going away a wiser man [1].

' I am, my Lord,
' Your lordship's most obedient
' And most humble servant,
' SAM. JOHNSON.'

' *Skie, Sept.* 14, 1773.'

[a] judgement 1, 2 (*orig.*) : judgment 3.   [b] declared, 1 : declared 2, 3 (*orig.*).
† ⟨*Iambon Liber*, i. 7 : see App. D, nothing *conclusive* in his talk.' *Ante*, p. 528.⟩   iii. 57.
[1] Yet he said of him :—' There is

At Portree, Mr. Donald M'Queen went to church and officiated in Erse, and then came to dinner. Dr. Johnson and I resolved that we should treat the company, so I played the landlord, or master of the feast, having previously ordered Joseph to pay the bill.

Sir James Macdonald intended to have built a village here, which would have done great good. A village is like a heart to a country. It produces a perpetual circulation, and gives the people an opportunity to make profit of many little articles, which would otherwise be in a good measure lost. We had here a dinner, *et præterea nihil*. Dr. Johnson did not talk. When we were about to depart, we found that Rasay had been beforehand with us, and that all was paid : I would fain have contested this matter with him, but seeing him resolved, I declined it. We parted with cordial embraces from him and worthy Malcolm. In the evening Dr. Johnson and I remounted our horses †, accompanied by Mr. M'Queen and Dr. Macleod. It rained very hard. We rode what they call six miles, upon Rasay's lands in Sky, to Dr. Macleod's house §. On the road Dr. Johnson appeared to be somewhat out of spirits. When I talked of our meeting Lord Elibank, he said, ' I cannot be with him much. I long to be again in civilized life ; but can stay but a short while ; ' (he meant at Edinburgh). He said, ' let us go to Dunvegan to-morrow.'— ' Yes, (said I,) if it is not a deluge.'—' At any rate,' he replied.— This shewed a kind of fretful impatience ; nor was it to be wondered at, considering our disagreeable ride. I feared he would give up Mull and Icolmkill, for he said something of his apprehensions of being detained by bad weather in going to Mull and *Iona*. However I hoped well. We had a dish of tea at Dr. Macleod's, who had a pretty good house, where was his brother, a half-pay officer. His lady was a polite, agreeable woman. Dr. Johnson said, he was glad to see that he was so well married, for he had an esteem for physicians [1]. The doctor accompanied us to Kingsburgh, which is called a mile farther ; but the computation of Sky has no connection whatever with real distance [2].

† ⟨They were Sir Alexander Macdonald's : see App. D, p. 528.⟩
§ ⟨See App. D, p. 528.⟩
[1] ' I believe every man has found in physicians great liberality and dignity of sentiment, very prompt effusion of beneficence, and willingness to exert a lucrative art where there is no hope of lucre.' Johnson's *Life of Garth*, 3. See *ante*, iv. 263.
[2] Johnson says (*Western Isl.*, p. 144) that when the military road was made

Sunday 12 September 1773   Skye : Kingsburgh

I was highly pleased to see Dr. Johnson safely arrived at Kingsburgh, and received by the hospitable Mr. Macdonald, who, with a most respectful attention, supported him into the house †. Kingsburgh was completely the figure of a gallant Highlander,—exhibiting ' the graceful mien,[a] and manly looks [1],' which our popular Scotch song has justly attributed to that character. He had his Tartan plaid thrown about him, a large blue bonnet with a knot of black ribband like a cockade, a brown short coat of a kind of duffil, a Tartan waistcoat with gold buttons and gold button-holes, a bluish philibeg, and Tartan hose. He had jet black hair tied behind, and was a large stately man, with a steady sensible countenance.

There was a comfortable parlour with a good fire, and a dram went round. By and by supper was served, at which there appeared the lady of the house, the celebrated Miss Flora Macdonald. She is a little woman, of a genteel appearance, and uncommonly mild and well-bred [2]. To see Dr. Samuel Johnson, the great champion of the English Tories, salute Miss Flora Macdonald in the isle of Sky, was a striking sight ; for though somewhat congenial in their notions, it was very improbable they should meet here.

Miss Flora Macdonald (for so I shall call her) told me, she heard upon the main land, as she was returning home about a fortnight before, that Mr. Boswell was coming to Sky, and one Mr. Johnson, a young English buck [3], with him. He was

[a] mien, 1 : mien 2, 3.

through Glencroe, ' stones were placed to mark the distances, which the inhabitants have taken away, resolved, they said, *to have no new miles.*'
† ⟨See App. D, p. 529.⟩
[1] ' The lawland lads think they are fine,
But O they're vain and idly gawdy.
How much unlike that graceful mien,
And manly look of my highland laddie.'
From ' *The Highland Laddie,* written long since by Allan Ramsay, and now sung at Ranelagh and all the other Gardens ; often fondly encore'd, and sometimes ridiculously hiss'd.' *Gent. Mag.* 1750, July, xx. p. 325.

[2] ' She . . . is of a pleasing person and elegant behaviour. She told me that she thought herself honoured by my visit, and I am sure that whatever regard she bestowed on me, was liberally repaid.' *Letters,* No. 329. In his *Western Isl.* (p. 60), Johnson speaks of Flora Macdonald, as ' a name that will be mentioned in history, and if courage and fidelity be virtues, mentioned with honour.' ⟨See App. D, pp. 529 ff.⟩
[3] This word, which meant much the same as *fop* or *dandy,* is found in Bk. x. ch. 2 of Fielding's *Amelia* (published in 1751) :—' A large Assembly of young Fellows, whom they call Bucks.' Less than forty years ago, in the neighbourhood of London,

Skye: Kingsburgh *Monday* 13 *September* 1773

highly entertained with this fancy. Giving an account of the afternoon which we passed at *Anock* [a], he said, 'I, being a *buck*, had miss [1] in to make tea.'—He was rather quiescent to-night, and went early to bed. I was in a cordial humour, and promoted a cheerful glass. The punch was excellent. Honest Mr. M'Queen observed that I was in high glee, 'my *governour* [2] being gone to bed.' Yet in reality my heart was grieved, when I recollected that Kingsburgh was embarrassed in his affairs, and intended to go to America [3]. However, nothing but what was good was present, and I pleased myself in thinking that so spirited a man would be well every where. I slept in the same room with Dr. Johnson. Each had a neat bed, with Tartan curtains, in an upper chamber.

Monday, 13*th September.*

The room where we lay was a celebrated one. Dr. Johnson's bed was the very bed in which the grandson of the unfortunate King James the Second [4] lay, on one of the nights after the

[a] read *Anoch*.

it was, I remember, still commonly applied by the village lads to the boys of a boarding-school. ⟨See *O.E.D.* s.v. *Buck sb.*[1] 2 b.⟩

[1] This word was at this time often used in a loose sense, though Johnson could not have so used it. Thus Walpole, writing on May 16, 1759 (*Letters*, iv. 267), tells a story of the little Prince Frederick. 'T'other day as he was with the Prince of Wales, Kitty Fisher passed by, and the child named her—the Prince, to try him, asked who that was?—"Why, a Miss."—" A Miss," said the P. of W., " why, are not all girls Misses ? "— " Oh ! but a particular sort of Miss— a Miss that sells oranges."' Cunningham in a note (1880, iii. 227) on this says :—' Orange-girls at theatres were invariably courtezans.' ⟨See *O.E.D.* s.v. *Miss sb.*[2] 1. Boswell's *MS*. reads after ' tea ', ' or some such expression about McQueen's daughter '.⟩

[2] *Governor* was the term commonly given to a tutor, especially a travelling tutor. Thus Peregrine

[a] *the* 1: the 2, 3.

Pickle was sent first to Winchester and afterwards abroad 'under the immediate care and inspection of a governor.' *Peregrine Pickle*, ch. [xvii] xv. ⟨See *O.E.D.*, s.v. *Governor*, 6.⟩

[3] ⟨The Macdonalds emigrated in August 1774 and settled in North Carolina. Flora returned to Scotland in 1779 and her husband in 1784. See App. D, pp. 529 ff.⟩

[4] I do not call him *the Prince of Wales,* or *the Prince,* because I am quite satisfied that the right which the *House of Stuart* had to the throne is extinguished. I do not call him *the*[a] *Pretender,* because it appears to me as an insult to one who is still alive, and, I suppose, thinks very differently. It may be a parliamentary expression ; but it is not a gentlemanly expression. I *know*, and I exult in having it in my power to tell, that THE ONLY PERSON in the world who is intitled to be offended at this delicacy, " thinks [b] and feels as I do " ; and has liberality of mind and generosity of sentiment enough to

[b] " thinks 1, 2: thinks 3.

Monday 13 September 1773 Skye: Kingsburgh failure of his rash attempt in 1745–6, while he was eluding the pursuit of the emissaries of government, which had offered thirty thousand pounds as a reward for apprehending him. To see Dr. Samuel Johnson lying in that bed, in the isle of Sky, in the house of Miss Flora Macdonald, struck me with such a group of ideas as it is not easy for words to describe, as they passed through the mind. He smiled, and said, ' I have had no ambitious thoughts in it [1].'—The room was decorated with a great variety of maps and prints. Among others, was Hogarth's print of Wilkes grinning, with the cap of liberty on a pole by him. That too was a curious circumstance in the scene this morning; such a contrast was Wilkes to the above group. It reminded me of Sir William Chambers's Account of Oriental Gardening [2], in which we are told all odd, strange, ugly, and even terrible objects, are introduced, for the sake of variety; a wild extravagance of taste which is so well ridiculed in the celebrated Epistle to him [3]. The following lines of that poem immediately occurred to me:

> ' Here too, O king of vengeance! in thy fane,
> Tremendous Wilkes shall rattle his gold chain [4].'

Upon the table in our room I found in the morning a slip of

approve of my tenderness for what even *has been* Blood-Royal. That he is *a prince* by *courtesy*, cannot be denied; because his mother was the daughter of Sobiesky, king of Poland. I shall, therefore, *on that account alone*, distinguish him by the name of *Prince Charles Edward*. BOSWELL, ed. 1.

To have called him the *Pretender* in the presence of Flora Macdonald would have been hazardous. In her old age, ' such is said to have been the virulence of [the Jacobite] spirit in her composition, that she would have struck any man with her fist, who presumed, in her hearing, to call Charles by his ordinary epithet *the Pretender*.' Chambers's *Rebellion in Scotland*, ii. 330. ⟨See App. D, p. 531.⟩

[1] This, perhaps, was said in allusion to some lines ascribed to *Pope*, on his lying, at John Duke of Argyle's, at Adderbury, in the same bed in which Wilmot, Earl of Rochester, had slept:
' With no poetick ardour fir'd,
  I press the bed where Wilmot lay;
That here he liv'd, or here expir'd,
  Begets no numbers, grave or gay.'   BOSWELL, ed. 1.
⟨In l. 2 of the quotation the original reads ' press'd ', in l. 3, ' lov'd '.⟩

[2] See *ante*, iv. 60, 187.

[3] See *ante*, iv. 113 and 315.

[4] ' This was written while Mr Wilkes was Sheriff of London, and when it was to be feared that he would rattle his chain a year longer as Lord Mayor.' Mason's note to *Heroic Epistle*, lines 87–8. By ' here ' the poet means *at Tyburn*.

Skye *Monday* 13 *September* 1773

paper, on which Dr. Johnson had written with his pencil these words: 'Quantum cedat virtutibus aurum [1].' What he meant by writing them I could not tell [2]. He had caught cold a day or two ago, and the rain yesterday having made it worse, he was become very deaf. At breakfast he said, he would have given a good deal rather than not have lain in that bed. I owned he was the lucky man; and observed, that without doubt it had been contrived between Mrs. Macdonald and him. She seemed to acquiesce; adding, ' You know young *bucks* are always favourites of the ladies.' He spoke of Prince Charles being here, and asked Mrs. Macdonald, ' *Who* was with him ? We were told, madam, in England, there was one Miss Flora Macdonald with him.'—She said, ' they were very right;' and perceiving Dr. Johnson's curiosity, though he had delicacy enough not to question her, very obligingly entertained him with a recital of the particulars which she herself knew of that escape, which does so much honour to the humanity, fidelity, and generosity, of the Highlanders. Dr. Johnson listened to her with placid attention, and said, ' All this should be written down [3].'

From what she told us, and from what I was told by others personally concerned, and from a paper of information which Rasay was so good as to send me, at my desire, I have compiled the following abstract, which, as it contains some curious anecdotes, will, I imagine,[a] not be uninteresting to my readers, and even, perhaps, be of some use to future historians [4].

Prince Charles Edward, after the battle of Culloden, was conveyed to what is called the *Long Island* [5], where he lay for some time concealed. But intelligence having been obtained where he was, and a number of troops having come in quest of him, it

[a] imagine 1, 2, 3.

[1] With virtue weigh'd, what worthless trash is gold! BOSWELL, ed. 2.
[2] Since the first edition of this book, an ingenious friend has observed to me, that Dr. Johnson had probably been thinking on the reward which was offered by government for the apprehension of the grandson of King James II., and that he meant by these words to express his admiration of the Highlanders, whose fidelity and attachment had resisted the golden temptation that had been held out to them. BOSWELL, ed. 2.
[3] ⟨' She said Bishop Forbes at Leith had it.' Boswell's *Hebrides*, ed. Pottle and Bennett, p. 162. Flora's narrative is in *The Lyon in Mourning*, i. 296 ff. See also Home, *Hist. of the '45*, pp. 373–6.⟩
[4] ⟨See App. D, pp. 532 ff.⟩
[5] ⟨*i.e.* the Outer Hebrides.⟩

became absolutely necessary for him to quit that country without delay. Miss Flora Macdonald, then a young lady, animated by what she thought the sacred principle of loyalty, offered, with the magnanimity of a Heroine, to accompany him in an open boat to Sky, though the coast they were to quit was guarded by ships. He dressed himself in women's clothes, and passed as her supposed maid, by the name of Betty Bourke, an Irish girl. They got off undiscovered, though several shots were fired to bring them to, and landed at Mugstot, the seat of Sir Alexander Macdonald. Sir Alexander was then at Fort Augustus, with the Duke of Cumberland ; but his lady was at home. Prince Charles took his post upon a hill near the house. Flora Macdonald waited on Lady Margaret [1], and acquainted her of the enterprise in which she was engaged. Her ladyship, whose active benevolence was ever seconded by superior talents, shewed a perfect presence of mind, and readiness of invention, and at once settled that Prince Charles should be conducted to old Rasay, who was himself concealed with some select friends. The plan was instantly communicated to Kingsburgh, who was dispatched to the hill to inform the Wanderer, and carry him refreshments. When Kingsburgh approached, he started up, and advanced, holding a large knotted stick, and in appearance ready to knock him down, till he said, 'I am Macdonald of Kingsburgh, come to serve your highness.' The Wanderer answered, 'It is well,' and was satisfied with the plan.

Flora Macdonald dined with Lady Margaret, at whose table there sat an officer [2] of the army, stationed here with a party of soldiers, to watch for Prince Charles in case of his flying to the isle of Sky. She afterwards often laughed in good humour with this gentleman, on her having so well deceived him.

After dinner, Flora Macdonald on horseback, and her sup-

[1] On the subject of Lady Margaret Macdonald, it is impossible to omit an anecdote which does much honour to Frederick, Prince of Wales. By some chance Lady Margaret had been presented to the princess, who, when she learnt what share she had taken in the Chevalier's escape, hastened to excuse herself to the prince, and explain to him that she was not aware that Lady Margaret was the person who had harboured the fugitive. The prince's answer was noble : ' And would *you* not have done the same, madam, had he come to you, as to her, in distress and danger ? I hope—I am sure you would ! ' SCOTT, 1831.

[2] ⟨See App. D, pp. 534-5.⟩

posed maid and Kingsburgh, with a servant carrying some linen, all on foot, proceeded towards that gentleman's house. Upon the road was a small rivulet which they were obliged to cross. The Wanderer, forgetting his assumed sex, that his clothes might not be wet, held them up a great deal too high. Kingsburgh mentioned this to him, observing, it might make a discovery. He said, he would be more careful for the future. He was as good as his word ; for the next brook they crossed, he did not hold up his clothes at all, but let them float upon the water. He was very awkward in his female dress. His size was so large, and his strides so great, that some women whom they met reported that they had seen a very big woman, who looked like a man in woman's clothes, and that perhaps it was (as they expressed themselves) the *Prince*, after whom so much search was making.

At Kingsburgh he met with a most cordial reception ; seemed gay at supper, and after it indulged himself in a cheerful glass with his worthy host. As he had not had his clothes off for a long time, the comfort of a good bed was highly relished by him, and he slept soundly till next day at one o'clock.

The mistress of Corrichatachin told me [1], that in the forenoon she went into her father's room, who was also in bed, and suggested to him her apprehensions that a party of the military might come up, and that his guest and he had better not remain here too long. Her father said, ' Let the poor man repose himself after his fatigues ; and as for me, I care not, though they take off this old grey head ten or eleven years sooner than I should die in the course of nature.' He then wrapped himself in the bed-clothes, and again fell fast asleep.

On the afternoon of that day, the Wanderer, still in the same dress, set out for Portree, with Flora Macdonald and a man servant. His shoes being very bad, Kingsburgh provided him with a new pair, and taking up the old ones, said, ' I will faithfully keep them till you are safely settled at St. James's. I will then introduce myself by shaking them at you, to put you in mind of your night's entertainment and protection under my roof.'—He smiled, and said, ' Be as good as your word ! '—Kingsburgh kept the shoes as long as he lived. After his death, a zealous Jacobite gentleman gave twenty guineas for them.

[1] ⟨8 Sept. 1773. Boswell's *Hebrides*, ed. Pottle and Bennett, 1936, p. 125.⟩

Old Mrs. Macdonald, after her guest had left the house, took the sheets in which he had lain, folded them carefully, and charged her daughter that they should be kept unwashed, and that, when she died, her body should be wrapped in them as a winding sheet. Her will was religiously observed.

Upon the road to Portree, Prince Charles changed his dress, and put on man's clothes again; a tartan short coat and waistcoat, with philibeg and short hose, a plaid, and a wig and bonnet.

Mr. Donald M'Donald, called Donald Roy, had been sent express to the present Rasay, then the young laird, who was at that time at his sister's house, about three miles from Portree, attending his brother, Dr. Macleod, who was recovering of a wound he had received at the battle of Culloden. Mr. M'Donald communicated to young Rasay the plan of conveying the Wanderer to where old Rasay was; but was told that old Rasay had fled to Knoidart, a part of Glengary's estate. There was then a dilemma what should be done. Donald Roy proposed that he should conduct the Wanderer to the main land; but young Rasay thought it too dangerous at that time, and said it would be better to conceal him in the island of Rasay, till old Rasay could be informed where he was, and give his advice what was best. But the difficulty was, how to get him to Rasay. They could not trust a Portree crew, and all the Rasay boats had been destroyed, or carried off by the military, except two belonging to Malcolm M'Leod, which he had concealed somewhere.

Dr. Macleod being informed of this difficulty, said he would risk his life once more for Prince Charles; and it having occurred, that there was a little boat upon a fresh-water lake in the neighbourhood, young Rasay and Dr. Macleod, with the help of some women, brought it to the sea, by extraordinary exertion, across a Highland mile of land, one half of which was bog, and the other a steep precipice.

These gallant brothers, with the assistance of one little boy, rowed the small boat to Rasay, where they were to endeavour to find Captain M'Leod, as Malcolm was then called, and get one of his good boats, with which they might return to Portree, and receive the Wanderer; or, in case of not finding him, they were to make the small boat serve, though the danger was considerable.

Fortunately, on their first landing, they found their cousin Malcolm, who, with the utmost alacrity, got ready one of his boats, with two strong men, John M'Kenzie, and Donald M'Friar. Malcolm, being the oldest man, and most cautious, said, that as young Rasay had not hitherto appeared in the unfortunate business, he ought not to run any risk; but that Dr. Macleod and himself, who were already publickly engaged, should go on this expedition. Young Rasay answered, with an oath, that he would go, at the risk of his life and fortune.—' In GOD's name then (said Malcolm) let us proceed.' The two boatmen, however, now stopped short, till they should be informed of their destination; and M'Kenzie declared he would not move an oar till he knew where they were going. Upon which they were both sworn to secrecy; and the business being imparted to them, they were eager to put off to sea without loss of time. The boat soon landed about half a mile from the inn at Portree.

All this was negotiated before the Wanderer got forward to Portree. Malcolm M'Leod, and M'Friar, were dispatched to look for him. In a short time he appeared, and went into the publick house. Here Donald Roy, whom he had seen at Mugstot, received him, and informed him of what had been concerted. He wanted silver for a guinea, but the landlord had only thirteen shillings. He was going to accept of this for his guinea; but Donald Roy very judiciously observed, that it would discover him to be some great man; so he desisted. He slipped out of the house, leaving his fair protectress, whom he never again saw; and Malcolm M'Leod was presented to him by Donald Roy, as a captain in his army. Young Rasay and Dr. Macleod had waited, in impatient anxiety, in the boat. When he came, their names were announced to him. He would not permit the usual ceremonies of respect, but saluted them as his equals.

Donald Roy staid in Sky, to be in readiness to get intelligence, and give an alarm in case the troops should discover the retreat to Rasay; and Prince Charles was then conveyed in a boat to that island in the night. He slept a little upon the passage, and they landed about day-break. There was some difficulty in accommodating him with a lodging, as almost all the houses in the island had been burnt by the soldiery. They repaired to a little hut, which some shepherds had lately built, and having prepared it as well as they could, and made a bed of heath for the stranger, they kindled a fire, and partook of some provisions which had been sent with him from Kingsburgh. It was observed, that he would not taste wheat-bread, or brandy, while oat-bread and whisky lasted ; ' for these, said he, are my own country bread and drink.'—This was very engaging to the Highlanders.

Young Rasay being the only person of the company that durst appear with safety, he went in quest of something fresh for them to eat ; but though he was amidst his own cows, sheep, and goats, he could not venture to take any of them for fear of a discovery, but was obliged to supply himself by stealth. He therefore caught a kid, and brought it to the hut in his plaid, and it was killed and drest, and furnished them a meal which they relished much. The distressed Wanderer, whose health was now a good deal impaired by hunger, fatigue, and watching, slept a long time, but seemed to be frequently disturbed. Malcolm told me he would start from broken slumbers, and speak to himself in different languages, French, Italian, and English. I must however acknowledge, that it is highly probable that my worthy friend Malcolm did not know precisely the difference between French and Italian. One of his expressions in English was, ' O GOD ! poor Scotland ! '

While they were in the hut, M'Kenzie and M'Friar, the two boatmen, were placed as sentinels upon different eminences ; and one day an incident happened, which must not be omitted. There was a man wandering about the island, selling tobacco. Nobody knew him, and he was suspected to be a spy. M'Kenzie came running to the hut, and told that this suspected person was approaching. Upon which the three gentlemen, young Rasay, Dr. Macleod, and Malcolm, held a council of war upon him, and were unanimously of opinion that he should be instantly [a] put to death. Prince Charles, at once assuming a grave and even severe countenance, said, ' GOD forbid that we should take away a man's life, who may be innocent, while

[a] should be instantly 1 : should instantly be 2, 3.

we can preserve our own.' The gentlemen however persisted in their resolution, while he as strenuously continued to take the merciful side. John M'Kenzie, who sat watching at the door of the hut, and overheard the debate, said in Erse, ' Well, well ; he must be shot. You are the king, but we are the parliament, and will do what we choose.'—Prince Charles, seeing the gentlemen smile, asked what the man had said, and being told it in English, he observed that he was a clever fellow, and, notwithstanding the perilous situation in which he was, laughed loud and heartily. Luckily the unknown person did not perceive that there were people in the hut, at least did not come to it, but walked on past it, unknowing of his risk. It was afterwards found out that he was one of the Highland army, who was himself in danger. Had he come to them, they were resolved to dispatch him ; for, as Malcolm said to me, ' We could not keep him with us, and we durst not let him go. In such a situation, I would have shot my brother, if I had not been sure of him.'—John M'Kenzie was at Rasay's house, when we were there [1]. About eighteen years before, he hurt one of his legs when dancing, and being obliged to have it cut off, he now was going about with a wooden leg. The story of his being a *member of parliament* is not yet forgotten. I took him out a little way from the house, gave him a shilling to drink Rasay's health, and led him into a detail of the particulars which I have just related.—With less foundation, some writers have traced the idea of a parliament, and of the British constitution, in rude and early times. I was curious to know if he had really heard, or understood, any thing of that subject, which, had he been a greater man, would probably have been eagerly maintained. ' Why, John, (said I,) did you think the king should be controuled by a parliament ? '—He answered, ' I thought, sir, there were many voices against one.'

The conversation then turning on the times, the Wanderer said, that, to be sure, the life he had led of late was a very hard one ; but he would rather live in the way he now did, for ten years, than fall into the hands of his enemies. The gentlemen asked him, what he thought his enemies would do with him,

[1] This old Scottish *member of parliament*, I am informed, is still living (1785). BOSWELL, ed. 2.

should he have the misfortune to fall into their hands. He said, he did not believe they would dare to take his life publickly, but he dreaded being privately destroyed by poison or assassination.—He was very particular in his inquiries about the wound which Dr. Macleod had received at the battle of Culloden, from a ball which entered at one shoulder, and went cross to the other. The doctor happened still to have on the coat which he wore on that occasion. He mentioned, that he himself had his horse shot under him at Culloden ; that the ball hit the horse about two inches from his knee, and made him so unruly that he was obliged to change him for another. He threw out some reflections on the conduct of the disastrous affair at Culloden, saying, however, that perhaps it was rash in him to do so.—I am now convinced that his suspicions were groundless ; for I have had a good deal of conversation upon the subject with my very worthy and ingenious friend, Mr. Andrew Lumisden, who was under secretary to Prince Charles, and afterwards principal secretary to his father at Rome, who, he assured me, was perfectly satisfied both of the abilities and honour of the generals who commanded the Highland army on that occasion. Mr. Lumisden has written an account of the three battles in 1745–6, at once accurate and classical [1]. Talking of the different Highland corps, the gentlemen who were present wished to have his opinion which were the best soldiers. He said, he did not like comparisons among those corps : they were all best.

He told his conductors, he did not think it advisable to remain long in any one place ; and that he expected a French ship to come for him to Lochbroom, among the Mackenzies. It then was proposed to carry him in one of Malcolm's boats to Lochbroom, though the distance was fifteen leagues coastwise. But he thought this would be too dangerous, and desired that at any rate they might first endeavour to obtain intelligence. Upon which young Rasay wrote to his friend, Mr. M'Kenzie of Applecross, but received an answer, that there was no appearance of any French ship.

It was therefore resolved that they should return to Sky,

[1] ⟨Lumisden's ' A short account of the battles of Preston, Falkirk, and Culloden ; by a Gentleman who was in these actions ' was written for John Home (ante, iii. 162, n. 5). It was printed by Dr. W. B. Blaikie in his Origins of the '45 (Sc. Hist. Soc. 1916), pp. 403–19 : see Introd., pp. lxxxiv ff. The manuscript is now in the National Library of Scotland. For Lumisden see ante, ii. 401, n. 2, op. cit. supra, and D.N.B.⟩

which they did, and landed in Strath, where they reposed in a cow-house belonging to Mr. Niccolson of Scorbreck. The sea was very rough, and the boat took in a good deal of water. The Wanderer asked if there was danger, as he was not used to such a vessel. Upon being told there was not, he sung an Erse song with much vivacity. He had by this time acquired a good deal of the Erse language.

Young Rasay was now dispatched to where Donald Roy was, that they might get all the intelligence they could; and the Wanderer, with much earnestness, charged Dr. Macleod to have a boat ready, at a certain place about seven miles off, as he said he intended it should carry him upon a matter of great consequence; and gave the doctor a case, containing a silver spoon, knife, and fork, saying, ' keep you that till I see you,' which the doctor understood to be two days from that time. But all these orders were only blinds; for he had another plan in his head, but wisely thought it safest to trust his secrets to no more persons than was absolutely necessary. Having then desired Malcolm to walk with him a little way from the house, he soon opened his mind, saying, ' I deliver myself to you. Conduct me to the Laird of M'Kinnon's country.'—Malcolm objected that it was very dangerous, as so many parties of soldiers were in motion. He answered, ' There is nothing now to be done without danger.'—He then said, that Malcolm must be the master, and he the servant; so he took the bag, in which his linen was put up, and carried it on his shoulder; and observing that his waistcoat, which was of scarlet tartan, with a gold twist button, was finer than Malcolm's, which was of a plain ordinary tartan, he put on Malcolm's waistcoat, and gave him his; remarking at the same time, that it did not look well that the servant should be better dressed than the master.

Malcolm, though an excellent walker, found himself excelled by Prince Charles, who told him, he should not much mind the parties that were looking for him, were he once but a musquet shot from them; but that he was somewhat afraid of the Highlanders who were against him. He was well used to walking in Italy, in pursuit of game; and he was even now so keen a sportsman, that, having observed some partridges, he was going to take a shot; but Malcolm cautioned him against it, observing that the firing might be heard by the tenders [1] who were hovering upon the coast.

As they proceeded through the mountains, taking many a circuit to avoid any houses, Malcolm, to try his resolution, asked him what they should do, should they fall in with a party of soldiers : he answered, ' Fight,[a] to be sure ! '—Having asked Malcolm if he should be known in his present dress, and Malcolm having replied he would, he said, ' Then I'll blacken my face with powder.'—' That, said Malcolm, would discover you at once.'—' Then, said he, I must be put in the greatest dishabille possible.' So he pulled off his wig, tied a handkerchief round his head, and put his night-cap over it, tore the ruffles from his shirt, took the buckles out of his shoes, and made Malcolm fasten them with strings ; but still Malcolm thought he would be known. ' I have so odd a face, (said he) that no man ever saw me but he would know me again [2].'

He seemed unwilling to give credit to the horrid narrative of men being massacred in cold blood, after victory had declared for the army commanded by the Duke of Cumberland. He could not allow himself to think that a general could be so barbarous [3].

[a] Fight, 1 : Fight 2, 3.

[1] ⟨This word is first entered in the fourth edition, 1773, of Johnson's *Dictionary*.⟩

[2] Dr. A. Carlyle (*Auto.*, p. 153) describes him in 1745 as ' a good-looking man, of about five feet ten inches ; his hair was dark red, and his eyes black. His features were regular, his visage long, much sunburnt and freckled, and his countenance thoughtful and melancholy.' When the Pretender was in London in 1750, ' he came one evening,' writes Dr. W. King (*Anec.* p. 199), ' to my lodgings and drank tea with me : my servant, after he was gone, said to me, " that he thought my new visitor very like Prince Charles." " Why," said I, " have you ever seen Prince Charles ? " " No, Sir," replied the fellow, " but this gentleman, whoever he may be, exactly resembles the busts which are sold in Red-lion-street, and are said to be the busts of Prince Charles." The truth is, these busts were taken in plaster of Paris from his face. He has an handsome face and good eyes.'

[3] Sir Walter Scott, writing of his childhood, mentions ' the stories told in my hearing of the cruelties . . . after the battle of Culloden. One or two of our own distant relations had fallen, . . . and I remember detesting the name of Cumberland with more than infant hatred.' Lockhart's *Scott*, i. 18. ' I was,' writes Dr. A. Carlyle (*Auto.* p. 190), ' in the coffee-house with Smollett when the news of the battle of Culloden arrived, and when London all over was in a perfect uproar of joy.' On coming out into the street, ' Smollett,' he continues, ' cautioned me against speaking a

Skye   *Monday* 13 *September* 1773   197

When they came within two miles of M'Kinnon's house, Malcolm asked if he chose to see the laird. ' No, (said he) by no means. I know M'Kinnon to be as good and as honest a man as any in the world, but he is not fit for my purpose at present. You must conduct me to some other house ; but let it be a gentleman's house.'—Malcolm then determined that they should go to the house of his brother-in-law, Mr. John M'Kinnon, and from thence be conveyed to the main land of Scotland, and claim the assistance of Macdonald of Scothouse. The Wanderer at first objected to this, because Scothouse was cousin to a person of whom he had suspicions. But he acquiesced in Malcolm's opinion.

When they were near Mr. John M'Kinnon's house, they met a man of the name of Ross, who had been a private soldier in the Highland army. He fixed his eyes steadily on the Wanderer in his disguise, and having at once recognized him, he clapped his hands, and exclaimed, ' Alas ! is this the case ? ' Finding that there was now a discovery, Malcolm asked ' What's to be done ? ' ' Swear him to secrecy,' answered Prince Charles. Upon which Malcolm drew his dirk, and on the naked blade[a] made him take a solemn oath, that he would say nothing of his having seen the Wanderer, till his escape should be made publick.

Malcolm's sister, whose house they reached pretty early in the morning, asked him who the person was that was along with him. He said,[b] it was one Lewis Caw, from Crieff, who being a fugitive like himself, for the same reason, he had engaged him as his servant, but that he had fallen sick. ' Poor man ! (said she) I pity him. At the same time my heart warms to a man of his appearance.'—Her husband was gone a little way from home ; but was expected every minute to return. She set down to her brother a plentiful Highland breakfast.

[a] blade 1, 2 : blade, 3.   [b] said, 1, 2 : said 3.

word, lest the mob should discover my country and become insolent, " for John Bull," says he, " is as haughty and valiant to-night as he was abject and cowardly on the Black Wednesday when the Highlanders were at Derby." . . . I saw not Smollett again for some time after, when he showed . . . me his manuscript of his *Tears of Scotland*.

. . . Smollett, though a Tory, was not a Jacobite, but he had the feelings of a Scotch gentleman on the reported cruelties that were said to be exercised after the battle of Culloden.' See *ante*, ii. 374, for the madman ' beating his straw, supposing it to be the Duke of Cumberland, whom he was punishing for his cruelties in Scotland, in 1746.'

Prince Charles acted the servant very well, sitting at a respectful distance, with his bonnet off. Malcolm then said to him, ' Mr. Caw, you have as much need of this as I have ; there is enough for us both : you had better draw nearer and share with me.'— Upon which he rose, made a profound bow, sat down at table with his supposed master, and eat very heartily. After this there came in an old woman, who, after the mode of ancient hospitality, brought warm water, and washed Malcolm's feet. He desired her to wash the feet of the poor man who attended him. She at first seemed averse to this, from pride, as thinking him beneath her, and in the periphrastick language of the Highlanders and the Irish, said warmly, ' Though I wash your father's son's feet, why should I wash his father's son's feet ? '—She was however persuaded to do it.

They then went to bed, and slept for some time ; and when Malcolm awaked, he was told that Mr. John M'Kinnon, his brother-in-law, was in sight. He sprang out to talk to him before he should see Prince Charles. After saluting him, Malcolm, pointing to the sea, said, ' What, John, if the prince should be prisoner on board one of those tenders ? '—' GOD forbid ! ' replied John.—' What if we had him here ? ' said Malcolm.—' I wish we had,' answered John ; ' we should take care of him.'—' Well, John, said Malcolm, he is in your house.'—John, in a transport of joy, wanted to run directly in, and pay his obeisance ; but Malcolm stopped him, saying, ' Now is your time to behave well, and do nothing that can discover him.'—John composed himself, and having sent away all his servants upon different errands, he was introduced into the presence of his guest, and was then desired to go and get ready a boat lying near his house, which, though but a small leaky one, they resolved to take, rather than go to the Laird of M'Kinnon. John M'Kinnon, however, thought otherwise ; and upon his return told them, that his Chief and Lady M'Kinnon were coming in the laird's boat. Prince Charles said to his trusty Malcolm, ' I am sorry for this, but must make the best of it.'—M'Kinnon then walked up from the shore, and did homage to the Wanderer. His lady waited in a cave, to which they all repaired, and were entertained with cold meat and wine.—Mr. Malcolm M'Leod being now superseded by the Laird of M'Kinnon, desired leave to return, which was granted him, and Prince Charles wrote a short note, which he subscribed *James Thompson*, informing his friends that he had got away from Sky, and thanking them for their kindness ; and he desired this might be speedily conveyed to young Rasay and Dr. Macleod, that they might not wait longer in expectation of seeing him again. He bade a cordial adieu to Malcolm, and insisted on his accepting of a silver stock-buckle, and ten guineas from his purse, though, as Malcolm told me, it did not appear to contain above forty. Malcolm at first begged to be excused, saying, that he had a few guineas at his service ; but Prince Charles answered, ' You will have need of money. I shall get enough when I come upon the main land.'

The Laird of M'Kinnon then conveyed him to the opposite coast of Knoidart. Old Rasay, to whom intelligence had been sent, was crossing at the same time to Sky ; but as they did not know of each other, and each had apprehensions, the two boats kept aloof.

These are the particulars which I have collected concerning the extraordinary concealment and escapes of Prince Charles, in the Hebrides. He was often in imminent danger [1]. The troops traced him from the Long Island, across Sky, to Portree, but there lost him.

Here I stop,—having received no farther authentick information of his fatigues and perils before he escaped to France.— Kings and subjects may both take a lesson of moderation from the melancholy fate of the House of Stuart ; that Kings may not suffer degradation and exile, and subjects may not be harrassed by the evils of a disputed succession.

Let me close the scene on that unfortunate House with the elegant and pathetick reflections of *Voltaire*, in his *Histoire Generale*.—

' Que les hommes privés (says that brilliant writer, speaking of Prince Charles) qui se croyent malheureux, jettent les yeux sur ce prince et ses ancêtres [2].'

[1] ' He was obliged to trust his life to the fidelity of above fifty individuals, and many of these were in the lowest paths of fortune. They knew that a price of thirty thousand pounds was set upon his head.' Smollett's *Hist. of England*, 1758, iv. 675. . ⟨See also Pennant's *Voy*.

Hebrides 1772, 1774, p. 346, and John Ramsay of Ochtertyre's *Scotl. & Scotsmen*, 1888, ii. 494.⟩

[2] ' Que les hommes privés, qui se plaignent de leurs petites infortunes, jettent les yeux sur ce prince et sur ses ancêtres ! ' *Siècle de Louis XV*, ch. 25.

In another place he thus sums up the sad story of the family in general :—

'Il n'y a aucun exemple dans l'histoire d'une maison si longtems infortunée. Le premier des Rois d'Écosse, ses aïeux[a], qui eut le nom de *Jacques*, après avoir été dix-huit ans prisonnier en Angleterre, mourut assassiné, avec sa femme, par la main de ses sujets. *Jacques* II, son fils, fut tué à vingt-neuf ans en combattant contre les Anglois. *Jacques* III, mis en[b] prison par son peuple, fut tué ensuite par les révoltés, dans une bataille. *Jacques* IV. périt dans un combat qu'il perdit. *Marie Stuart*, sa petite-fille, chassée de son trône, fugitive en Angleterre, ayant langui dix-huit ans en prison, se vit condamnée à mort par des juges Anglais, et eut la tête tranchée. *Charles* I, petit-fils de *Marie*, Roi d'Écosse et d'Angleterre, vendu par les Écossois, et jugé à mort par les Anglais, mourut sur un échaffaut dans la place publique. *Jacques*, son fils, septième du nom, et deuxième en Angleterre, fut chassé de ses trois royaumes ; et pour comble de malheur on contesta à son fils jusqu'à[c] sa naissance. Ce[d] fils ne tenta de remonter sur le trône de ses[e] pères, que pour faire périr ses amis par des bourreaux ; et nous avons vu le Prince *Charles Édouard*, réunissant en vain les vertus de ses pères [1] et le courage du Roi *Jean Sobieski*, son ayeul maternel, exécuter les exploits et essuyer les malheurs les plus incroyables. Si quelque chose justifie ceux qui croyent une fatalité à laquelle rien ne peut se soustraire, c'est cette suite continuelle de malheurs qui a persécuté la maison de *Stuart*, pendant plus de trois-cents années [2].'

The gallant Malcolm was apprehended in about ten days after they separated, put aboard a ship and carried prisoner to London[3]. He said, the prisoners in general were very ill

[a] ses aïeux omitted.   [b] en I : un 2, 3.   [c] jusqu'à omitted.   [d] Le 1, 2, 3.
[e] ses 1 : ces 2, 3.

[1] 'I never heard him express any noble or benevolent sentiments, ... or discover any sorrow or compassion for the misfortunes of so many worthy men who had suffered in his cause. But the most odious part of his character is his love of money, a vice which I do not remember to have been imputed by our historians to any of his ancestors, and is the certain index of a base and little mind.... I have known this gentleman, with 2000 Louis d'ors in his strong box, pretend he was in great distress, and borrow money from a lady in Paris, who was not in affluent circumstances.' Dr. W. King's *Anec.* p. 201. 'Lord Marischal,' writes Hume, 'had a very bad opinion of this unfortunate prince ; and thought there was no vice so mean or atrocious of which he was not capable ; of which he gave me several instances.' *Letters*, 1932, ii. 273.

[2] *Siècle de Louis XIV*, ch. 15. The accentuation of this passage, which was very incorrect as quoted by Boswell, I have corrected. ⟨Queen Jane was wounded, not killed.⟩

[3] ⟨See App. D, p. 535.⟩

treated in their passage; but there were soldiers on board who lived well, and sometimes invited him to share with them: that he had the good fortune not to be thrown into jail, but was confined in the house of a messenger, of the name of Dick. To his astonishment, only one witness could be found against him, though he had been so openly engaged; and therefore, for want of sufficient evidence, he was set at liberty. He added, that he thought himself in such danger, that he would gladly have compounded for banishment [1]. Yet, he said, 'he should never be so ready for death as he then was [2].'—There is philosophical truth in this. A man will meet death much more firmly at one time than another. The enthusiasm even of a mistaken principle warms the mind, and sets it above the fear of death; which in our cooler moments, if we really think of it, cannot but be terrible, or at least very awful.

Miss Flora Macdonald being then also in London, under the protection of Lady Primrose [3], that lady provided a post-chaise to convey her to Scotland, and desired she might choose any friend she pleased to accompany her. She chose Malcolm. 'So (said he, with a triumphant air) I went to London to be hanged, and returned in a post-chaise with Miss Flora Macdonald.'

Mr. Macleod of Muiravenside, whom we saw at Rasay, assured us that Prince Charles was in London in 1759 [4], and that there was

[1] By banishment he meant, I conjecture, transportation as a convict-slave to the American plantations.

[2] Wesley in his *Journal* ⟨6 and 12 Feb. 1740: ed. Curnock, 1911, ii. 335-6⟩ seemed from this consideration almost to regret a reprieve that came to a penitent convict.

[3] Hume describes how in 1753 (? 1750) the Pretender, on his secret visit to London, 'came to the house of a lady (who I imagined to be Lady Primrose)... without giving her any preparatory information; and entered the room, when she had a pretty large company with her, and was herself playing at cards. He was announced by the servant under another name. She thought the cards would have dropped from her hands on seeing him. But she had presence enough of mind... to call him by the name he assumed.' *Letters*, 1932, ii. 272. Croker (*Boswell*, 1848, p. 331, n. 4) prints an autograph letter from Flora Macdonald which shows that Lady Primrose in 1751 had lodged £627 in a friend's hands for her behoof, and that she had in view to add more.

[4] ⟨Dr. Macleod confirmed this statement and gave more details:— 'The present Royal Family were all to have been seized and put aboard a ship; he was to have been in London; a number of persons of great consequence, among which was the Lord Mayor.. were in the plot,... the Prince Regent would have issued writs and called a Parliament.' Boswell's *Hebrides*, ed. Pottle and Bennett, 1936, p. 162.⟩ From what

then a plan in agitation for restoring his family. Dr. Johnson could scarcely credit this story, and said, ' There[a] could be no probable plan at that time. Such an attempt could not have succeeded, unless the King of Prussia had stopped the army in Germany ; for both the army and the fleet would, even without orders, have fought for the King, to whom they had engaged themselves.'

Having related so many particulars concerning the grandson of the unfortunate King James the Second ; having given due praise to fidelity and generous attachment, which, however erroneous the judgement may be, are honourable for the heart ; I must do the Highlanders the justice to attest, that I found every where amongst them a high opinion of the virtues of the King now upon the throne, and an honest disposition to be faithful subjects to his majesty, whose family has possessed the sovereignty of this country so long, that a change, even for the abdicated family, would now hurt the best feelings of all his subjects.

The *abstract* point of *right* would involve us in a discussion of remote and perplexed questions ; and after all, we should have no clear principle of decision. That establishment, which, from political necessity, took place in 1688, by a breach in the succession of our kings, and which, whatever benefits may have accrued from it, certainly gave a shock to our monarchy [1],—the able and constitutional Blackstone wisely rests on the solid footing of authority.—' Our ancestors having most indisputably a competent jurisdiction to decide this great and important question, and having, in fact, decided it, it is now become our duty, at this distance of time, to acquiesce in their determination [2].'

Mr. Paley, the present Archdeacon of Carlisle, in his *Principles of Moral and Political Philosophy*, having, with much clearness of argument, shewn the duty of submission to civil government

[a] ' There 1, 2 : there 3.

Johnson goes on to say it is clear that George II. was in Germany at the time of the Prince's secret visit. He was there the greater part of 1750, but not in 1753 or 1759. In 1750, moreover, the great army of the King of Prussia ' overawed Hanover.' Smollett's *Continuation of Hist. Eng.*, 1760, i. 84. This explains what Johnson says about the King of Prussia stopping the army in Germany. ⟨There is adequate evidence for Prince Charles's secret visit to London in 1750. See *ante*, i. 279, note 5. Conclusive evidence for later visits is lacking.⟩

[1] See *ante*, iv. 165, 170–1.

[2] COMMENTARIES on the Laws of England, Book I. chap. 3. ⟨1765, p. 205.⟩ BOSWELL, ed. 1.

to be founded neither on an indefeasible *jus divinum*, nor on *compact*, but on *expediency*, lays down this rational position :—

' Irregularity in the first foundation of a state, or subsequent violence, fraud, or injustice, in getting possession of the supreme power, are not sufficient reasons for resistance, after the government is once peaceably settled. No subject of the *British* empire conceives himself engaged to vindicate the justice of the *Norman* claim or conquest, or apprehends that his duty in any manner depends upon that controversy. So likewise, if the house of *Lancaster*, or even the posterity of *Cromwell*, had been at this day seated upon the throne of *England*, we should have been as little concerned to enquire how the founder of the family came there ¹.'

¹ B. VI. chap. 3. Since I have quoted Mr. Archdeacon Paley upon one subject, I cannot but transcribe, from his excellent work, a distinguished passage in support of the Christian Revelation.—After shewing, in decent but strong terms, the unfairness of the *indirect* attempts of modern infidels to unsettle and perplex religious principles, and particularly the irony, banter, and sneer, of one whom he politely calls ' an eloquent historian,' the archdeacon thus expresses himself :

' Seriousness is not constraint of thought ; nor levity, freedom. Every mind which wishes the advancement of truth and knowledge, in the most important of all human researches, must abhor this licentiousness, as violating no less the laws of reasoning than the rights of decency. There is but one description of men to whose principles it ought to be tolerable.[a] I mean that class of reasoners who can see *little* in christianity, even supposing it to be true. To such adversaries we address this reflection.—Had *Jesus Christ* delivered no other declaration than the following, " The hour is coming in the which all that are in the graves shall hear his voice, and shall come forth,—they that have done well [b] unto the resurrection of life, and they that have done evil unto the resurrection of damnation," [*St. John* v. 25] he had pronounced a message of inestimable importance, and well worthy of that splendid apparatus of prophecy and miracles with which his mission was introduced and attested :—a message in which the wisest of mankind would rejoice to find an answer to their doubts, and rest to their inquiries. It is idle to say that a future state had been discovered already.—It had been discovered as the Copernican System was ;—it was one guess amongst many. He alone discovers who *proves ;* and no man can prove this point but the teacher who testifies by miracles that his doctrine comes from GOD.'—Book V. chap. 9 [pp. 397-8].

If infidelity be disingenuously dispersed in every shape that is likely to allure, surprise, or beguile the imagination,—in a fable, a tale, a novel, a poem,—in books of travels, of philosophy, of natural history,— as Mr. Paley has well observed,— I hope it is fair in me thus to meet such poison with an unexpected antidote, which I cannot doubt will be found powerful. BOSWELL, ed. 1. The 'eloquent historian' was Gibbon. See Paley's *Principles*, v. ix, 1785, p. 395. ⟨The punctuation of the quotation given in this note is Boswell's.⟩

[a] tolerable, *Paley.*

[b] good, *Paley.*

In conformity with this doctrine, I myself, though fully persuaded that the House of *Stuart* had originally no right to the crown of *Scotland*; for that *Baliol*, and not *Bruce*, was the lawful heir; should yet have thought it very culpable to have rebelled, on that account, against Charles the First, or even a prince of that house much nearer the time, in order to assert the claim of the posterity of Baliol.

However convinced I am of the justice of that principle, which holds allegiance and protection to be reciprocal, I do however acknowledge, thàt I am not satisfied with the cold sentiment which would confine the exertions of the subject within the strict line of duty. I would have every breast animated with the *fervour* of loyalty [1]; with that generous attachment which delights in doing somewhat more than is required, and makes 'service perfect freedom [2].' And, therefore, as our most gracious Sovereign, on his accession to the throne, gloried in being *born a Briton* [3]; so, in my more private sphere, *Ego me nunc* denique natum, *gratulor* [4]. I am happy that a disputed succession no longer distracts our minds; and that a monarchy, established by law, is now so sanctioned by time, that we can fully indulge those feelings of loyalty which I am ambitious to excite. They are feelings which have ever actuated the inhabitants of the Highlands and the Hebrides. The plant of loyalty is there in full vigour, and the Brunswick graft now flourishes like a native shoot. To that spirited race of people I may with propriety apply the elegant lines of a modern poet, on the 'facile temper of the beauteous sex [5]:'

> 'Like birds new-caught, who flutter for a time,
> And struggle with captivity in vain;
> But by-and-by they rest,[a] they smooth their plumes,
> And to *new masters* sing their former notes [6].'

[a] rest; *original*.

[1] In *The Life of Johnson* (*ante*, iii. 113), Boswell quotes these words, without shewing that they are his own; but italicises not 'fervour', but 'loyalty'.

[2] 'Whose service is perfect freedom.' *Book of Common Prayer*.

[3] See *ante*, i. 353, n. 1 ⟨and *post*, App. D, pp. 535–6⟩.

[4] Ovid, *Ars Amatoria*, iii. 121.

[5] 'This facile temper of the beauteous sex
Great Agamemnon, brave Pelides, prov'd.'
These two lines follow the four which Boswell quotes. *Agis*, act iv.

[6] *Agis*, a tragedy, by John Home. BOSWELL, ed. 1. ⟨Published in 1758.⟩

Surely such notes are much better than the querulous growlings of suspicious Whigs and discontented Republicans.

Kingsburgh conducted us in his boat, across one of the lochs, as they call them, or arms of the sea, which flow in upon all the coasts of Sky,—to a mile beyond a place called *Grishinish*.[a] Our horses had been sent round by land to meet us. By this sail we saved eight † miles of bad riding. Dr. Johnson said, ' When we take into the computation what we have saved, and what we have gained, by this agreeable sail, it is a great deal.' He observed, ' it is very disagreeable riding in Sky. The way is so narrow, one only at a time can travel, so it is quite unsocial; and you cannot indulge in meditation by yourself, because you must be always attending to the steps which your horse takes.' —This was a just and clear description of its inconveniencies.

The topick of emigration being again introduced [1], Dr. Johnson said, that ' a rapacious Chief would make a wilderness of his estate.' Mr. Donald M'Queen told us, that the oppression, which then made so much noise, was owing to landlords listening to bad advice in the letting of their lands ; that interested and designing [2] people flattered them with golden dreams of much higher rents than could reasonably be paid ; and that some of the gentlemen *tacksmen* [3], or upper tenants, were themselves in part the occasion of the mischief, by over-rating the farms of others. That many of the *tacksmen*, rather than comply with exorbitant demands, had gone off to America, and impoverished the country, by draining it of its wealth ; and that their places were filled by a number of poor people, who had lived under them, properly speaking, as servants, paid by a certain proportion of the produce of the lands, though called sub-tenants. I observed, that if the men of substance were once banished from a Highland estate, it might probably be greatly reduced in its

[a] *read* Grishornish.

† ⟨Carruthers points out that the distance actually saved was about seventeen miles.⟩
[1] See *ante*, v. 27. ⟨According to Boswell's *MS*. Johnson said merely ' Sir Alexander would make ', &c.⟩
[2] ⟨Misprinted ' designed ', 2 and 3.⟩
[3] ' Next in dignity to the Laird is the Tacksman ; a large taker or lease-holder of land, of which he keeps part, as a domain, in his own hand, and lets part to under tenants. The Tacksman is necessarily a man capable of securing to the Laird the whole rent, and is commonly a collateral relation.' *Western Isl.*, p. 78.

value ; for one bad year might ruin a set of poor tenants, and men of any property would not settle in such a country, unless from the temptation of getting land extremely cheap ; for an inhabitant of any good county in Britain had better go to America than to the Highlands or the Hebrides. Here therefore was a consideration that ought to induce a Chief to act a more liberal part, from a mere motive of interest, independent of the lofty and honourable principle of keeping a clan together, to be in readiness to serve his king. I added, that I could not help thinking a little arbitrary power in the sovereign, to control the bad policy and greediness of the Chiefs, might sometimes be of service. In France a Chief would not be permitted to force a number of the king's subjects out of the country.—Dr. Johnson concurred with me, observing, that ' were an oppressive chieftain a subject of the French king, he would probably be admonished by a *letter* [1].'

During our sail, Dr. Johnson asked about the use of the dirk, with which he imagined the Highlanders cut their meat. He was told, they had a knife and fork besides, to eat with. He asked, how did the women do ? and was answered, some of them had a knife and fork too ; but in general the men, when they had cut their meat, handed their knives and forks to the women, and they themselves eat with their fingers. The old tutor of Macdonald always eat fish with his fingers, alledging that a knife and fork gave it a bad taste. I took the liberty to observe to Dr. Johnson, that he did so. ' Yes, said he ; but it is because I am short-sighted, and afraid of bones, for which reason I am not fond of eating many kinds of fish, because I must use my fingers †.'

Dr. M'Pherson's *Dissertations on Scottish Antiquities*, which he had looked at when at Corrichatachin [2], being mentioned, he remarked, that ' you might read half an hour, and ask yourself what you had been reading : there were so many words to so little matter, that there was no getting through the book.'

As soon as we reached the shore, we took leave of Kingsburgh, and mounted our horses. We passed through a wild moor, in many places so soft that we were obliged to walk, which was very fatiguing to Dr. Johnson. Once he had advanced on horseback to a very bad step. There was a steep

---

[1] No doubt a *lettre de cachet*. CROKER, 1831.

† ⟨See App. D, p. 536.⟩
[2] *Ante*, v. 159, and *post*, v. 265.

Skye : Dunvegan *Monday* 13 *September* 1773

declivity on his left, to which he was so near, that there was not room for him to dismount in the usual way. He tried to alight on the other side, as if he had been a *young buck* † indeed, but in the attempt he fell at his length upon the ground ; from which, however, he got up immediately without being hurt. During this dreary ride, we were sometimes relieved by a view of branches of the sea, that universal medium of connection amongst mankind. A guide, who had been sent with us from Kingsburgh, explored the way (much in the same manner as, I suppose, is pursued in the wilds of America,) by observing certain marks known only to the inhabitants. We arrived at Dunvegan late in the afternoon. The great size of the castle, which is partly old and partly new, and is built upon a rock close to the sea, while the land around it presents nothing but wild, moorish, hilly, and craggy appearances, gave a rude magnificence to the scene. Having dismounted, we ascended a flight of steps, which was made by the late Macleod, for the accommodation of persons coming to him by land, there formerly being, for security, no other access to the castle but from the sea ; so that visitors who came by the land were under the necessity of getting into a boat, and sailed [a] round to the only place where it could be approached. We were introduced into a stately dining-room, and received by Lady Macleod, mother of the laird, who, with his friend Talisker, having been detained on the road, did not arrive till some time after us.

We found the lady of the house a very polite and sensible woman, who had lived for some time in London, and had there been in Dr. Johnson's company §. After we had dined, we repaired to the drawing-room, where some of the young ladies of the family, with their mother, were at tea [1]. This room had formerly been the bed-chamber of Sir Roderick Macleod, one of the old Lairds ; and he chose it, because, behind it, there was a considerable cascade [2], the sound of which disposed him to

[a] *? read* sailing.

† ⟨See *ante*, v. 184, 185, 187.⟩
§ ⟨At the house of her connexion, Captain David Brodie. Boswell's *Hebrides*, ed. Pottle and Bennett, 1936, p. 166.⟩
[1] Lady Macleod, who had repeatedly helped Dr. Johnson to sixteen dishes, or upwards, of tea, asked him if a small bason would not save him trouble, and be more agreeable.

"I wonder, madam," answered he roughly,"why all the ladies ask me such impertinent questions ? It is to save yourselves trouble, madam, and not me.' The lady was silent, and went on with her task.' John Knox's *Tour through the Highlands*, 1787, p. 143.
[2] ' In the garden—or rather the orchard which was formerly the

Tuesday 14 September 1773   Skye: Dunvegan
sleep. Above his bed was this inscription : ' Sir Rorie M'Leod of Dunvegan, Knight. GOD send good rest ! '—Rorie is the contraction of Roderick. He was called Rorie *More*, that is, great Rorie, not from his size, but from his spirit.—Our entertainment here was in so elegant a style, and reminded my fellow-traveller so much of England, that he became quite joyous. He laughed, and said, ' Boswell, we came in at the wrong end of this island.'—' Sir, (said I,) it was best to keep this for the last.' —He answered, ' I would have it both first and last.'

Tuesday, 14th September.

Dr. Johnson said in the morning, ' Is not this a fine lady [1] ? ' There was not a word now of his ' impatience to be in civilized life [2] ; '—though indeed I should beg pardon,—he found it here. We had slept well, and lain long. After breakfast we surveyed the castle, and the garden. Mr. Bethune [3], the parish minister,— Magnus M'Leod of Claggan, brother to Talisker, and M'Leod of Bay, two substantial gentlemen [4] of the clan, dined with us. We had admirable venison, generous wine ; in a word, all that a good table has. This was really the hall of a chief. Lady M'Leod had been much obliged to my father, who had settled by arbitration a variety of perplexed claims between her and her relation, the Laird of Brodie, which she now repaid by particular attention to me.—M'Leod started the subject of making women do penance in the church for fornication.— *Johnson.* ' It is right, sir. Infamy is attached to the crime,

garden—is a pretty cascade, divided into two branches, and called Rorie More's Nurse, because he loved to be lulled to sleep by the sound of it.' Lockhart's *Scott*, 1837, iii. 227.

[1] It has been said that she expressed considerable dissatisfaction at Dr. Johnson's rude behaviour at Dunvegan. Her grandson, the present Macleod, assures me that it was not so : ' they were all,' he says emphatically, ' *delighted* with him.' CROKER, 1831. Mr. Croker refers, I think, to a letter, 30 Jan. 1829, from Sir Walter Scott, published in the *Croker Corres.* ii. 33. Scott writes :—' When wind-bound at Dunvegan, Johnson's temper became most execrable, and beyond all endurance, save that of his guide. The Highlanders, who are very courteous in their way, held him in great contempt for his want of breeding, but had an idea at the same time there was something respectable about him, they could not tell what, and long spoke of him as the Sassenach *mohr* or large Saxon.'

[2] ' I long to be again in civilized life.' *Ante*, v. 183.

[3, 4] ⟨See App. D, pp. 536–7.⟩

by universal opinion, as soon as it is known. I would not be the man who would discover it, if I alone knew it, for a woman may reform; nor would I commend a parson who divulges a woman's first offence; but being once divulged, it ought to be infamous. Consider, of what importance to society the chastity of women is. Upon that all the property in the world depends [1]. We hang a thief for stealing a sheep; but the unchastity of a woman transfers sheep, and farm and all, from the right owner. I have much more reverence for a common prostitute than for a woman who conceals her guilt. The prostitute is known. She cannot deceive: she cannot bring a strumpet into the arms of an honest man, without his knowledge.'—*Boswell.* ' There is, however, a great difference between the licentiousness of a single woman, and that of a married woman.'—*Johnson.* ' Yes, sir; there is a great difference between stealing a shilling, and stealing a thousand pounds; between simply taking a man's purse, and murdering him first, and then taking it. But when one begins to be vicious, it is easy to go on. Where single women are licentious, you rarely find faithful married women.'—*Boswell.* ' And yet we are told that in some nations in India, the distinction is strictly observed.'—*Johnson.* ' Nay, don't give us India. That puts me in mind of Montesquieu, who is really a fellow of genius too in many respects; whenever he wants to support a strange opinion, he quotes you the practice of Japan or of some other distant country, of which he knows nothing. To support polygamy, he tells you of the island of Formosa, where there are ten women born for one man [2]. He had but to suppose another island, where there are ten men born for one woman, and so make a marriage between them [3].'

[1] See *ante,* iii. 406.
[2] Johnson refers, I think, to a passage in *L'Esprit des Lois,* Book xvi. chap. 4, where Montesquieu says :—' J'avoue que si ce que les Relations nous disent étoit vrai qu'à Bantam il y a dix femmes pour un homme, ce seroit un cas bien particulier de la polygamie. Dans tout ceci je ne justifie pas les usages, mais j'en rens les raisons.'
[3] What my friend treated as so wild a supposition, has actually happened in the Western islands of Scotland, if we may believe Martin, who tells it of the islands of Col and Tyr-yi, and says that it is proved by the parish registers. BOSWELL, ed. 1. ' The Isle of Coll produces more Boys than Girls, and the Isle of Tyr-iy more Girls than Boys; as if Nature intended both these Isles for mutual Alliances, without being at the trouble of going to the adjacent Isles or Continent to be matched. The Parish Book in which the number of the

Tuesday 14 September 1773 Skye: Dunvegan

At supper, Lady Macleod mentioned Dr. Cadogan's book on the gout [1].—*Johnson.* 'It is a good book in general, but a foolish one in particulars. It is good in general, as recommending temperance and exercise, and cheerfulness. In that respect it is only Dr. Cheyne's book † told in a new way; and there should come out such a book every thirty years, dressed in the mode of the times. It is foolish, in maintaining that the gout is not hereditary, and that one fit of it, when gone, is like a fever when gone.'—Lady Macleod objected that the authour does not practice what he teaches [2].—*Johnson.* 'I cannot help that, madam. That does not make his book the worse. People are influenced more by what a man says, if his practice is suitable to it,—because they are blockheads. The more intellectual people are, the readier will they attend to what a man tells them. If it is just, they will follow it, be his practice what it will. No man practises so well as he writes. I have, all my life long, been lying till noon [3]; yet I tell all young men, and tell them with great sincerity, that nobody who does not rise early will ever do any good. Only consider! You read a book; you are convinced by it; you do not know the authour. Suppose you afterwards know him, and find that he does not practice what he teaches; are you to give up your former conviction? At this rate you would be kept in a state of equilibrium, when

Baptized is to be seen, confirms this observation.' Martin's *Western Islands*, p. 271. ⟨This curious parish-book no longer exists, and we need hardly say the modern registers give no countenance to the supposition. CARRUTHERS, 1852.⟩
[1] *A Dissertation on the Gout*, by W. Cadogan, M.D., 1771. It went through nine editions in its first year.
† ⟨*The English Malady.* See *ante*, iii. 27.⟩
[2] This was a general reflection against Dr. Cadogan, when his very popular book was first published. It was said, that whatever precepts he might give to others, he himself indulged freely in the bottle. But I have since had the pleasure of becoming acquainted with him, and, if his own testimony may be believed, (and I have never heard it impeached,) his course of life has been conformable to his doctrine. BOSWELL,

ed. 1. ⟨See also Johnson's admission to Mrs. Thrale that he had 'not been sufficiently diligent to practise' that which he had endeavoured to teach. *Letters*, No. 748. For his defence of the 'vicious moralist' see *Rambler*, No. 77.⟩
[3] 'April 7, 1765. I purpose to rise at eight because though I shall not yet rise early it will be much earlier than I now rise, for I often lye till two.' *Pr. and Med.* ¶ 54. 'Sept. 18, 1771. My nocturnal complaints grow less troublesome towards morning, and I am tempted to repair the deficiencies of the night. I think however to try to rise every day by eight, and to combat indolence as I shall obtain strength.' *Ib.* ¶ 91. 'April 14, 1775. As my life has from my earliest years been wasted in a morning bed my purpose is from Easter day to rise early, not later than eight.' *Ib.* ¶ 110.

Skye : Dunvegan *Tuesday* 14 *September* 1773

reading every book, till you knew how the authour practised [1].' —' But, said Lady M'Leod, you would think better of Dr. Cadogan, if he acted according to his principles.'—*Johnson.* 'Why, madam, to be sure, a man who acts in the face of light, is worse than a man who does not know so much ; yet I think no man should be the worse thought of for publishing good principles. There is something noble in publishing truth, though it condemns one's self [2].'—I expressed some surprize at Cadogan's recommending good humour, as if it were quite in our own power to attain it.—*Johnson.* ' Why, sir, a man grows better humoured as he grows older. He improves by experience. When young, he thinks himself of great consequence, and every thing of importance. As he advances in life, he learns to think himself of no consequence, and little things of little importance ; and so he becomes more patient, and better pleased. All goodhumour and complaisance are acquired. Naturally a child seizes directly what it sees, and thinks of pleasing itself only. By degrees, it is taught to please others, and to prefer others ; and that this will ultimately produce the greatest happiness. If a man is not convinced of that, he never will practice it. Common language speaks the truth as to this : we say, a person is well-*bred*[a]. As it is said, that all material motion is primarily in a right line, and is never *per circuitum*, never in another form, unless by some particular cause ; so it may be said intellectual motion is.'—Lady M'Leod asked, if no man was naturally good ?—*Johnson.* ' No, madam, no more than a wolf.'—*Boswell.* ' Nor no woman, sir ? ' *Johnson.* ' No, sir [3].'—Lady M'Leod started at this, saying, in a low voice, ' This is worse than Swift.'

M'Leod of Ulinish had come in the afternoon. We were a jovial company at supper. The Laird, surrounded by so many of his clan, was to me a pleasing sight. They listened

[a] well-*bred* 1 : well *bred* 2, 3.

[1] See *post*, v. 359.
[2] See *ante*, iv. 396.
[3] Miss Mulso (Mrs. Chapone) wrote in 1753 :—' I had the assurance to dispute with Mr. Johnson on the subject of human malignity, and wondered to hear a man who by his actions shews so much benevolence, maintain that the human heart is naturally malevolent, and that all the benevolence we see in the few who are good, is acquired by reason and religion.' Mrs. Chapone's *Posthumous Works*, 1807, i. p. 73. See *post*, v. 214.

Wednesday 15 *September* 1773 Skye : Dunvegan
with wonder and pleasure, while Dr. Johnson harangued. I am
vexed that I cannot take down his full strain of eloquence.

Wednesday, 15*th September.*

The gentlemen of the clan went away early in the morning to
the harbour of Lochbracadale †, to take leave of some of their friends
who were going to America. It was a very wet day. We looked
at Rorie More's horn §, which is a large cow's horn, with the mouth
of it ornamented with silver curiously carved. It holds rather
more than a bottle and a half. Every Laird of M'Leod, it is
said, must, as a proof of his manhood, drink it off full of claret,
without laying it down.—From Rorie More many of the branches
of the family are descended ; in particular, the Talisker branch ;
so that his name is much talked of. We also saw his bow,
which hardly any man now can bend, and his *Glaymore,* which
was wielded with both hands, and is of a prodigious size. We
saw here some old pieces of iron armour, immensely heavy.
The broad-sword now used, though called the *Glaymore,* (*i.e.* the
great sword,) is much smaller than that used in Rorie More's
time. There is hardly a target now to be found in the Highlands. After the disarming act [1], they made them serve as covers
to their butter-milk barrels ; a kind of change, like beating spears
into pruning-hooks [2].

Sir George Mackenzie's Works (the folio edition) happened to
lie in a window in the dining room. I asked Dr. Johnson to
look at the *Characteres Advocatorum.* He allowed him power
of mind, and that he understood very well what he tells [3] ; but
said, that there was too much declamation, and that the Latin
was not correct. He found fault with *appropinquabant* [4], in the
character of Gilmour. I tried him with the opposition between
gloria and *palma,* in the comparison between Gilmour and

† ⟨' Lochbradale ' in error, 1, 2, 3.⟩
§ ⟨See *post,* v. 320 and App. D,
p. 537.⟩
[1] This act was passed in 1746.
[2] *Isaiah,* ii. 4.
[3] Sir Walter Scott, after mentioning Lord Orford's (Horace Walpole)
History of His Own Time, continues :—' The Memoirs of our Scots
Sir George Mackenzie are of the
same class—both immersed in little

political detail, and the struggling
skirmish of party, seem to have lost
sight of the great progressive movements of human affairs.' Lockhart's
Scott, 1837, v. 163.
[4] ' Illum Jura potius ponere, quam
de Jure respondere dixisses ; eique
appropinquabant Clientes tanquam
Judici, potius quam Advocato.' Mackenzie's *Works,* ed. 1716, vol. i. part
2, p. 7.

Skye : Dunvegan   *Wednesday* 15 *September* 1773   213
Nisbet, which Lord Hailes, in his Catalogue of the Lords of Session, thinks difficult to be understood †. The words are, '*penes illum gloria, penes hunc palma* [1].' §—In a short Account of the Kirk of Scotland, which I published some years ago, I applied these words to the two contending parties, and explained them thus : ' The popular party has most eloquence ; Dr. Robertson's party most influence.'—I was very desirous to hear Dr. Johnson's explication.—*Johnson.* ' I see no difficulty. Gilmour was admired for his parts ; Nisbet carried his cause by his skill in law. *Palma* is victory.'—I observed, that the character of Nicholson, in this book, resembled that of Burke : for it is said, in one place, ' *in omnes lusos* [a] *& jocos se sæpe resolvebat* [2] ; ' and, in another, ' *sed accipitris more e conspectu aliquando astantium sublimi se protrahens volatu, in prædam miro impetu descendebat* 3.'—*Johnson.* ' No, sir ; I never heard Burke make a good joke in my life 4.'—*Boswell.* ' But, sir, you will allow he is a hawk.'—Dr. Johnson, thinking that I meant this of his joking, said, ' No, sir, he is not the hawk there. He is the beetle in the mire 5.'—I still adhered to my metaphor,—' But he *soars* as the hawk.'—*Johnson.* ' Yes, sir ; but he catches nothing.'—M'Leod asked, what is the particular excellence of Burke's eloquence ?—*Johnson.* ' Copiousness and fertility of allusion ; a power of diversifying his matter, by placing it in various relations. Burke has great information, and great command of language ; though, in my opinion, it has not in every respect the highest elegance.' —*Boswell.* ' Do you think, sir, that Burke has read Cicero much ? ' —*Johnson.* ' I don't believe it, sir. Burke has great knowledge,

[a] read *lusus.*

† ⟨See App. D, p. 537.⟩
[1] ' Opposuit ei Providentia Nisbetum : qui summâ doctrinâ, consummataque eloquentiâ causas agebat, ut Justitiæ scalæ in æquilibrio essent ; nimia tamen arte semper utens, artem suam suspectam reddebat. Quoties ergo conflixerunt, penes Gilmorum gloria, penes Nisbetum palma fuit ; quoniam in hoc plus artis & cultus, in illo naturæ & virium.' Mackenzie's *Works,* 1716, vol. i, part 2, p. 7.
§ ⟨See App. D, p. 537.⟩
[2] He often indulged himself in every species of pleasantry and wit.

BOSWELL, ed. 2.
3 But like the hawk, having soared with a lofty flight to a height which the eye could not reach, he was wont to swoop upon his quarry with wonderful rapidity. BOSWELL, ed. 2. The two Latin quotations are part of the same paragraph, and are not even separated by a word. *Ib.* p. 6.
4 See *ante,* i. 453 ; iii. 323 ; iv. 276 ; and v. 32.
5 Some years later he said that ' when Burke lets himself down to jocularity, he is in the kennel.' *Ante,* iv. 276.

great fluency of words, and great promptness of ideas, so that he can speak with great illustration on any subject that comes before him. He is neither like Cicero, nor like Demosthenes [1], nor like any one else, but speaks as well as he can.'

In the 65th page of the first volume of Sir George Mackenzie, Dr. Johnson pointed out a paragraph beginning with *Aristotle*, and told me there was an error in the text, which he bade me try to discover. I was lucky enough to hit it at once. As the passage is printed, it is said that the devil answers *even* in *engines*. I corrected it to—*ever* in *ænigmas*†. 'Sir, (said he,) you are a good critick. This would have been a great thing to do in the text of an ancient authour.'

Thursday, 16th September.

Last night much care was taken of Dr. Johnson, who was still distressed by his cold. He had hitherto most strangely slept without a night-cap. Miss M'Leod made him a large flannel one, and he was prevailed with to drink a little brandy when he was going to bed. He has great virtue, in not drinking wine or any fermented liquor, because, as he acknowledged to us, he could not do it in moderation [2].—Lady M'Leod would hardly believe him, and said, ' I am sure, sir, you would not carry it too far.'—*Johnson*. ' Nay, madam, it carried me. I took the opportunity of a long illness to leave it off. It was then prescribed to me not to drink wine ; and having broken off the habit, I have never returned to it [3].'

In the argument on Tuesday night, about natural goodness, Dr. Johnson denied that any child was better than another, but by difference of instruction ; though, in consequence of greater attention being paid to instruction by one child than another, and of a variety of imperceptible causes, such as instruction being counteracted by servants, a notion was conceived, that of two children, equally well educated, one was naturally much worse than another. He owned, this morning, that one might have a greater aptitude to learn than another, and that we

---

[1] Cicero and Demosthenes, no doubt, were brought in by the passage about Nicholson. Mackenzie continues :—' Hic primus nos a Syllogismorum servitute manumisit, & Aristotelem Demostheni potius, quam Ciceroni forum concedere coegit.' *Works*, 1716, vol. i, part 2, p. 6.
† ⟨See App. D, p. 538.⟩
[2] See *ante*, ii. 435 and iv. 149, note 3.
[3] See *ante*, i. 103.

inherit dispositions from our parents [1]. 'I inherited, (said he,) a vile melancholy from my father, which has made me mad all my life, at least not sober [2].'—Lady M'Leod wondered he should tell this.—' Madam, (said I,) he knows that with that madness he is superior to other men.'

I have often been astonished with what exactness and perspicuity he will explain the process of any art. He this morning explained to us all the operation of coining, and, at night, all the operation of brewing, so very clearly, that Mr. M'Queen said, when he heard the first, he thought he had been bred in the Mint; when he heard the second, that he had been bred a brewer.

I was elated by the thought of having been able to entice such a man to this remote part of the world. A ludicrous, yet just,[a] image presented itself to my mind, which I expressed to the company. I compared myself to a dog who has got hold of a large piece of meat, and runs away with it to a corner, where he may devour it in peace, without any fear of others taking it from him. 'In London, Reynolds, Beauclerk, and all of them, are contending who shall enjoy Dr. Johnson's conversation. We are feasting upon it, undisturbed, at Dunvegan.'

It was still a storm of wind and rain. Dr. Johnson however walked out with M'Leod, and saw Rorie More's cascade in full perfection. Colonel M'Leod, instead of being all life and gaiety, as I have seen him, was at present grave, and somewhat depressed by his anxious concern about M'Leod's affairs, and by finding some gentlemen of the clan by no means disposed to act a generous or affectionate part to their Chief in his distress, but bargaining with him as with a stranger. However, he was agreeable and polite, and Dr. Johnson said, he was a very pleasing man.—My fellow-traveller and I talked of going to Sweden [3]; and, while we were settling our plan, I expressed a pleasure in the prospect of seeing the king.—*Johnson.* 'I doubt, sir, if he would speak to us.'—Colonel M'Leod said, 'I am sure Mr. Boswell would speak to *him*.' But, seeing me

[a] just, 1, 2: just 3.

[1] See *ante*, ii. 436. [2] See *ante*, i. 65.
[3] ⟨' Mr. Johnson said he would go to Sweden with me'. Boswell's *Hebrides*, ed. Pottle and Bennett, 1936, p. 175.⟩ On Sept. 13, 1777, Johnson wrote:—' Boswell shrinks from the Baltick expedition, which I think is the best scheme in our power.' *Letters*, No. 545. See *ante*, iii. 134, note 1.

a little disconcerted by his remark, he politely added, ' and with great propriety.'—Here let me offer a short defence of that propensity in my disposition, to which this gentleman alluded. It has procured me much happiness. I hope it does not deserve so hard a name as either forwardness or impudence. If I know myself, it is nothing more than an eagerness to share the society of men distinguished either by their rank or their talents, and a diligence to attain what I desire [1]. If a man is praised for seeking knowledge, though mountains and seas are in his way, may he not be pardoned, whose ardour, in the pursuit of the same object, leads him to encounter difficulties as great, though of a different kind ?

After the ladies were gone from table, we talked of the Highlanders not having sheets ; and this led us to consider the advantage of wearing linen.—*Johnson.* ' All animal substances are less cleanly than vegetables. Wool, of which flannel is made, is an animal substance ; flannel therefore is not so cleanly as linen. I remember I used to think tar dirty ; but when I knew it to be only a preparation of the juice of the pine, I thought so no longer. It is not disagreeable to have the gum that oozes from a plumb-tree upon your fingers, because it is vegetable ; but if you have any candle-grease, any tallow upon your fingers, you are uneasy till you rub it off.—I have often thought, that, if I kept a seraglio, the ladies should all wear linen gowns,—or cotton ;—I mean stuffs made of vegetable substances. I would have no silk ; you cannot tell when it is clean : It will be very nasty before it is perceived to be so. Linen detects its own dirtiness.'

To hear the grave Dr. Samuel Johnson, ' that majestick teacher of moral and religious wisdom †,' while sitting solemn in an armchair in the Isle of Sky, talk, *ex cathedra*, of his keeping a seraglio [2], and acknowledge that the supposition had *often* been in his thoughts, struck me so forcibly with ludicrous contrast, that I could not but laugh immoderately. He was too proud to submit, even for a moment, to be the object of ridicule, and instantly retaliated with such keen sarcastick wit, and such a variety of degrading images [3], of every one of which I was the object, that, though I can bear such attacks as well as most

---

[1] See *ante*, ii. 59, note 1.
† ⟨See *ante*, i. 201.⟩
[2] See *ante*, iii. 368.
[3] ⟨See App. D, p. 538.⟩

Skye : Dunvegan *Friday* 17 *September* 1773

men, I yet found myself so much the sport of all the company, that I would gladly expunge from my mind every trace of this severe retort.

Talking of our friend Langton's house † in Lincolnshire, he said, ' the old house of the family was burnt. A temporary building was erected in its room ; and to this[a] they have been always adding as the family increased. It is like a shirt made for a man when he was a child, and enlarged always as he grows older.'

We talked to-night of Luther's allowing the Landgrave of Hesse two wives, and that it was with the consent of the wife to whom he was first married.—*Johnson*. ' There was no harm in this, so far as she was only[b] concerned, because *volenti non fit injuria*. But it was an offence against the general order of society, and against the law of the Gospel, by which one man and one woman are to be united. No man can have two wives, but by preventing somebody else from having one.'

Friday, 17th September.

After dinner yesterday, we had a conversation upon cunning. M'Leod said that he was not afraid of cunning people ; but would let them play their tricks about him like monkeys. ' But, (said I,) they'll scratch ; ' and Mr. M'Queen added, ' they'll invent new tricks, as soon as you find out what they do.'—*Johnson*. ' Cunning has effect from the credulity of others, rather than from the abilities of those who are cunning. It requires no extraordinary talents to lie and deceive [1].'—This led us to consider whether it did not require great abilities to be very wicked. —*Johnson*. ' It requires great abilities to have the *power* of being very wicked ; but not to *be* very wicked. A man who has the power, which great abilities procure him, may use it well or ill ;

---

[a] this 1, 2 : this day 3.   [b] she only was *MS*.

† ⟨See App. D, pp. 538-9.⟩

[1] ' Every man wishes to be wise, and they who cannot be wise are almost always cunning . . .: nor is caution ever so necessary as with associates or opponents of feeble minds.' *The Idler*, No. 92. In a letter to Dr. Taylor Johnson says :— ' To help the ignorant commonly requires much patience, for the ignorant are always trying to be cunning.' *Letters*, No. 807. Churchill, in *The Journey*, lines 97-98, says :—
' 'Gainst Fools be guarded ; 'tis a certain rule,
Wits are safe things, there's danger in a Fool.'

and it requires more abilities to use it well, than to use it ill. Wickedness is always easier than virtue; for it takes the short cut to every thing. It is much easier to steal a hundred pounds, than to get it by labour, or any other way. Consider only what act of wickedness requires great abilities to commit it, when once the person who is to do it has the power; for *there* is the distinction. It requires great abilities to conquer an army, but none to massacre it after it is conquered.'

The weather this day was rather better than any that we had since we came to Dunvegan. Mr. M'Queen had often mentioned a curious piece of antiquity near this, which he called a temple of the Goddess *Anaitis*. Having often talked of going to see it, he and I set out after breakfast, attended by his servant, a fellow quite like a savage. I must observe here, that in Sky there seems to be much idleness; for men and boys follow you, as colts follow passengers upon a road. The usual figure of a Sky-boy, is a *lown* with bare legs and feet, a dirty *kilt*, ragged coat and waistcoat, a bare head, and a stick in his hand, which, I suppose, is partly to help the lazy rogue to walk, partly to serve as a kind of a defensive weapon. We walked what is called two miles, but is probably four, from the castle, till we came to the sacred place. The country around is a black dreary moor on all sides, except to the sea-coast, towards which there is a view through a valley; and the farm of *Bay* shews some good land. The place itself is green ground, being well drained, by means of a deep glen on each side, in both of which there runs a rivulet with a good quantity of water, forming several cascades, which make a considerable appearance and sound. The first thing we came to was an earthen mound, or dyke, extending from the one precipice to the other. A little farther on, was a strong stone-wall, not high, but very thick, extending in the same manner. On the outside of it were the ruins of two houses, one on each side of the entry or gate to it. The wall is built all along of uncemented stones, but of so large a size as to make a very firm and durable rampart. It has been built all about the consecrated ground, except where the precipice is steep enough to form an enclosure of itself. The sacred spot contains more than two acres. There are within it the ruins of many houses, none of them large,—a *cairn*,—and many graves

Skye: Dunvegan *Friday* 17 *September* 1773

marked by clusters of stones. Mr. M'Queen insisted that the ruin of a small building, standing east and west, was actually the temple of the Goddess *Anaitis*, where her statue was kept, and from whence processions were made to wash it in one of the brooks. There is, it must be owned, a hollow road visible for a good way from the entrance; but Mr. M'Queen, with the keen eye of an antiquary, traced it much farther than I could perceive it. There is not above a foot and a half in height of the walls now remaining; and the whole extent of the building was never, I imagine, greater than an ordinary Highland house. Mr. M'Queen has collected a great deal of learning on the subject of the temple of *Anaitis*; and I had endeavoured, in my journal, to state such particulars as might give some idea of it, and of the surrounding scenery; but,[a] from the great difficulty of describing visible objects [1], I found my account so unsatisfactory, that my readers would probably have exclaimed

'And write about it, *Goddess*, and about it [2];'

and therefore I have omitted it.

When we got home, and were again at table with Dr. Johnson, we first talked of portraits. He agreed in thinking them valuable in families. I wished to know which he preferred, fine portraits, or those of which the merit was resemblance.—*Johnson*. 'Sir, their chief excellence is in [b] being like.'—*Boswell*. 'Are you of that opinion as to the portraits of ancestors, whom one has never seen?'—*Johnson*. 'It then becomes of more consequence that they should be like; and I would have them in the dress of the times, which makes a piece of history. One should like to see how *Rorie More* looked. Truth, sir, is of the greatest value in these things [3].'—Mr. M'Queen observed, that if you think it of

---

[a] but, 1, 2 : but 3. [b] in 1, 2 (*MS.*) : *omitted* 3.

[1] See *ante*, v. 173.

[2] 'For thee we dim the eyes, and stuff the head
With all such reading as was never read :
For thee explain a thing till all men doubt it,
And write about it, Goddess, and about it.'
    The Dunciad, iv. 249–52.

[3] 'Genius is chiefly exerted in historical pictures, and the art of the Painter of Portraits is often lost in the obscurity of his subject. But it is in Painting as in Life; what is greatest is not always best. I should grieve to see Reynolds transfer to Heroes and to Goddesses, to empty Splendor and to airy Fiction, that art which is now employed in

no consequence whether portraits are like, if they are but well painted, you may be indifferent whether a piece of history is true or not, if well told.

Dr. Johnson said at breakfast to-day, ' that it was but of late that historians bestowed pains and attention in consulting records, to attain to accuracy [1]. Bacon, in writing his History of Henry VII., does not seem to have consulted any, but to have just taken what he found in other histories, and blended it with what he learnt by tradition.' He agreed with me that there should be a chronicle kept in every considerable family, to preserve the characters and transactions of successive generations.

After dinner I started the subject of the temple of *Anaitis*. Mr. M'Queen had laid stress on the name given to the place by the country people,—*Ainnit* ; and added, ' I knew not what to make of this piece of antiquity, till I met with the *Anaitidis delubrum* in Lydia, mentioned by Pausanias and the elder Pliny.' —Dr. Johnson, with his usual acuteness, examined Mr. M'Queen as to the meaning of the word *Ainnit*, in Erse ; and it proved to be a *water-place*, or a place near water, ' which, said Mr. M'Queen, agrees with all the descriptions of the temples of that goddess, which were situated near rivers, that there might be water to wash the statue.'—*Johnson*. ' Nay, sir, the argument from the name is gone. The name is exhausted by what we see. We have no occasion to go to a distance for what we can pick up under our feet. Had it been an accidental name, the similarity between it and *Anaitis* might have had something in it ; but it turns out to be a mere physiological name.'—Macleod said, Mr. M'Queen's knowledge of etymology had destroyed his conjecture.—*Johnson*. ' Yes, sir ; Mr. M'Queen is like the eagle mentioned by Waller, who was shot with an arrow feathered

diffusing friendship, in reviving tenderness, in quickening the affections of the absent, and continuing the presence of the dead.' *The Idler*, No. 45.

[1] Southey wrote thirty years later : ' I find daily more and more reason to wonder at the miserable ignorance of English historians, and to grieve with a sort of despondency, at seeing how much that has been laid up among the stores of knowledge, has been neglected and utterly forgotten.' Southey's *Life*, ii. 264. On another occasion he said of Robertson :—' To write his introduction to *Charles V*, without reading these *Laws* [the *Laws* of Alonso the Wise], is one of the thousand and one omissions for which he ought to be called rogue, as long as his volumes last.' *Ib.* p. 318.

Skye : Dunvegan *Friday* 17 *September* 1773

from his own wing ¹.'—Mr. M'Queen would not, however, give up his conjecture.—*Johnson*. 'You have one possibility for you, and all possibilities against you. It is possible it may be the temple of *Anaitis*. But it is also possible that it may be a fortification ;—or it may be a place of Christian worship, as the first Christians often chose remote and wild places, to make an impression on the mind :—or, if it was a heathen temple, it may have been built near a river, for the purpose of lustration ; and there is such a multitude of divinities, to whom it may have been dedicated, that the chance of its being a temple of *Anaitis* is hardly any thing. It is like throwing a grain of sand upon the sea-shore to-day, and thinking you may find it to-morrow. No, sir, this temple, like many an ill-built edifice, tumbles down before it is roofed in.'—In his triumph over the reverend antiquarian, he indulged himself in a *conceit ;* for, some vestige of the *altar* of the goddess being much insisted on in support of the hypothesis, he said, ' Mr. M'Queen is fighting *pro* aris *et focis* †.'

It was wonderful how well time passed in a remote castle, and in dreary weather. After supper, we talked of Pennant. It was objected that he was superficial. Dr. Johnson defended him warmly ². He said, ' Pennant has greater variety of enquiry than almost any man, and has told us more than perhaps one in ten thousand could have done, in the time that he took. He has not said what he was to tell ; so you cannot find fault with him, for what he has not told. If a man comes to look for fishes, you cannot blame him if he does not attend to fowls.' —' But, said Colonel M'Leod, he mentions the unreasonable rise of rents in the Highlands, and says, " the gentlemen are for emptying the bag, without filling it ³ ; " for that is the phrase

---

¹ ' That Eagles fate and mine are one,
Which, on the shaft that made him die,
Espi'd a feather of his own,
Wherewith hee wont to soare so high.'
    To a Lady Singing a Song, etc.
† ⟨Cicero, De Nat. Deorum, iii. 40, 94.⟩
² See *ante*, iii. 271. ⟨Pennant describes this defence as ' a tender hug '. *Of London,* 1790, p. 200.⟩

³ ' In England there may be reason for raising the rents, (in a certain degree) where the value of lands is encreased by accession of commerce, . . . but here (contrary to all policy) the great men begin at the wrong end, with squeezing the bag, before they have helped the poor tenant to fill it, by the introduction of manufactures.' Pennant's *Tour in Scotland 1769,* ed. 1771, p. 180.

he uses. Why does he not tell how to fill it?'—*Johnson*. ' Sir, there is no end of negative criticism. He tells what he observes, and as much as he chooses. If he tells what is not true, you may find fault with him; but, though he tells that the land is not well cultivated, he is not obliged to tell how it may be well cultivated. If I tell that many of the Highlanders go barefooted, I am not obliged to tell how they may get shoes. Pennant tells a fact. He need go no farther, except he pleases. He exhausts nothing; and no subject whatever has yet been exhausted. But Pennant has surely told a great deal. Here is a man six feet high, and you are angry because he is not seven.'—Notwithstanding this eloquent *Oratio pro Pennantio*, which they who have read this gentleman's *Tours*, and recollect the *Savage* and the *Shopkeeper* at *Monboddo* [1], will probably impute to the spirit of contradiction, I still think that he had better have given more attention to fewer things, than have thrown together such a number of imperfect accounts.

Saturday, 18th September.

Before breakfast, Dr. Johnson came up to my room, to forbid me to mention that this was his birth-day; but I told him I had done it already; at which he was displeased [2]; I suppose from wishing to have nothing particular done on his account. Lady M'Leod and I got into a warm dispute. She wanted to build a house upon a farm which she has taken, about five miles from the castle, and to make gardens and other ornaments there; all of which I approved of; but insisted that the seat of the family should always be upon the rock of Dunvegan.—*Johnson*. ' Ay, in time we'll build all round this rock. You may make a very good house at the farm; but it must not be such as to tempt the Laird of M'Leod to go thither to reside. Most of the great families in England have a secondary residence, which is called

---

[1] Boswell refers, not to a passage in *Pennant*, but to Johnson's admission that in his dispute with Monboddo, ' he might have taken the side of the savage, had any body else taken the side of the shopkeeper.' *Ante*, v. 83.

[2] ' Boswel, with some of his troublesome kindness, has informed this family, and reminded me that the eighteenth of September is my birthday. The return of my Birthday, if I remember it, fills me with thoughts which it seems to be the general care of humanity to escape.' *Letters*, No. 326. ⟨On 24 Sept. Johnson wrote:—' On last Saturday was my sixty fourth birthday. I might perhaps have forgotten it had not Boswel told me of it, and, what pleased me less, told the family at Dunvegan.' *Pr. and Med.* ¶ 104.⟩ See *ante*, iii. 157.

Skye : Dunvegan *Saturday* 18 *September* 1773

a jointure-house : let the new house be of that kind.'—The lady insisted that the rock was very inconvenient ; that there was no place near it where a good garden could be made ; that it must always be a rude place ; that it was a *Herculean* labour to make a dinner here.—I was vexed to find the alloy of modern refinement in a lady who had so much old family spirit.—' Madam, (said I,) if once you quit this rock, there is no knowing where you may settle, You move five miles first ;—then to St. Andrews, as the late Laird did ;—then to Edinburgh ;—and so on,[1] till you end at Hampstead, or in France. No, no ; keep to the rock : it is the very jewel of the estate. It looks as if it had been let down from heaven by the four corners, to be the residence of a Chief. Have all the comforts and conveniencies of life upon it, but never leave Rorie More's cascade.'—' But, (said she,) is it not enough if we keep it ? Must we never have more convenience than Rorie More had ? He had his beef brought to dinner in one basket, and his bread in another. Why not as well be Rorie More all over, as live upon his rock ? And should not we tire, in looking perpetually on this rock ? It is very well for you, who have a fine place, and every thing easy, to talk thus, and think of chaining honest folks to a rock. You would not live upon it yourself.'— 'Yes, madam, (said I,) I would live upon it, were I Laird of M'Leod, and should be unhappy if I were not upon it.'—*Johnson*. (with a strong voice, and most determined manner,) ' Madam, rather than quit the old rock, Boswell would live in the pit ; he would make his bed in the dungeon.'—I felt a degree of elation, at finding my resolute feudal enthusiasm thus confirmed by such a sanction. The lady was puzzled a little. She still returned to her pretty farm,—rich ground,—fine garden.— ' Madam, (said Dr. Johnson,) were they in Asia[2], I would not leave the rock.'—My opinion on this subject is still the same. An ancient family residence ought to be a primary object ; and though the situation of Dunvegan be such that little can be done here in gardening, or pleasure-ground, yet, in addition to the veneration acquired by the lapse of time, it has many circumstances of natural grandeur, suited to the seat of a Highland Chief : it has the sea,—islands,—rocks,—hills,—a noble cascade ; and when the family is again in opulence, something may be done by art.

[1] ⟨on, 1, 2 : on 3.⟩   [2] ⟨Cf. *ante*, ii. 195.⟩

Saturday 18 September 1773   Skye: Dunvegan

Mr. Donald M'Queen went away to-day, in order to preach at Bracadale next day. We were so comfortably situated at Dunvegan, that Dr. Johnson could hardly be moved from it. I proposed to him that we should leave it on Monday. 'No, sir, (said he,) I will not go before Wednesday. I will have some more of this good [1].'—However, as the weather was at this season so bad, and so very uncertain, and we had a great deal to do yet, Mr. M'Queen and I prevailed with him to agree to set out on Monday, if the day should be good. Mr. M'Queen,[a] though it was inconvenient for him to be absent from his harvest, engaged to wait on Monday at Ulinish for us. When he was going away, Dr. Johnson said, 'I shall ever retain a great regard for you [2];' then asked him if he had the *Rambler*.—Mr. M'Queen said, 'No; but my brother has it.'—*Johnson*. 'Have you the *Idler*?'— *M'Queen*. 'No, sir.'—*Johnson*. 'Then I will order one for you at Edinburgh, which you will keep in remembrance of me.'—Mr. M'Queen was much pleased with this. He expressed to me, in the strongest terms, his admiration of Dr. Johnson's wonderful knowledge, and every other quality for which he is distinguished. I asked Mr. M'Queen, if he was satisfied with being a minister in Sky. He said he was; but he owned that his forefathers having been so long there, and his having been born there, made a chief ingredient in forming his contentment. I should have mentioned, that,[b] on our left hand, between Portree and Dr. Macleod's house, Mr. M'Queen told me there had been a college of the Knights Templars; that tradition said so; and that there was a ruin remaining of their church, which had been burnt: but I confess Dr. Johnson has weakened my belief in remote tradition. In the dispute about *Anaitis*, Mr. M'Queen said, Asia Minor was peopled by Scythians, and, as they were the ancestors of the Celts, the same religion might be in Asia Minor and Sky.— *Johnson*. 'Alas! sir, what can a nation that has not letters tell of its original. I have always difficulty to be patient when

[a] M'Queen, 1, 2 : M'Queen 3.   [b] that, 1, 2 : that 3.

[1] 'At Dunvegan I had tasted lotus, and was in danger of forgetting that I was ever to depart, till Mr. Boswell sagely reproached me with my sluggishness and softness.' Johnson's *Western Isl.*, p. 63.

[2] Johnson wrote of the ministers :—

'I saw not one in the Islands, whom I had reason to think either deficient in learning, or irregular in life; but found several with whom I could not converse without wishing, as my respect increased, that they had not been Presbyterians.' *Ib.* p. 95.

I hear authours gravely quoted, as giving accounts of savage nations, which accounts they had from the savages themselves. What can the M'Craas[1] tell about themselves a thousand years ago? There is no tracing the connection of ancient nations, but by language; and therefore I am always sorry when any language is lost, because languages are the pedigree of nations[2]. If you find the same language in distant countries, you may be sure that the inhabitants of each have been the same people; that is to say, if you find the languages a good deal the same; for a word here and there being the same, will not do. Thus Butler, in his *Hudibras*, remembering that *Penguin*, in the Straits of Magellan, signifies a bird with a white head, and that the same word has, in Wales, the signification of a white-headed wench, (*pen* head, and *guin* white,) by way of ridicule, concludes that the people of those Straits are Welch[3].'

A young gentleman of the name of M'Lean, nephew to the Laird of the isle of Muck, came this morning; and, just as we sat down to dinner, came the Laird of the isle of Muck himself, his lady, sister to Talisker, two other ladies their relations, and a daughter of the late M'Leod of Hamer, who wrote a treatise on the second sight, under the designation of *Theophilus Insulanus*[4]. It was somewhat droll to hear this Laird called by his title. *Muck* would have sounded ill; so he was called *Isle of Muck*, which went off with great readiness. The name, as now written, is unseemly, but is not so bad in the original Erse, which is *Mouach*, signifying the Sows' Island. Buchanan calls it *Insula Porcorum*. It is so called from its form. Some call it Isle of *Monk*. The Laird[5] insists that this is the proper name. It was formerly church-land belonging to Icolmkill, and

---

[1] See *ante*, v. 142.
[2] See *ante*, ii. 28.
[3] ' So Horses they affirm to be Mere Engines made by Geometry,
And were invented first from Engins,
As Indian Britans were from Penguins.'
Hudibras, part i. canto 2, line 57. ⟨Butler's own note on these lines is:— 'The American Indians call a great Bird they have, with a white head a *Penguin*; which signify's the same thing in the Brittish Tongue: From whence (with other words of the same kind) some Authors have indeavour'd to prove, That the Americans are originally deriv'd from the Brittains.' See also Selden's note in Drayton's *Polyolbion*, ix, p. 148.⟩
[4] Published in Edinburgh in 1763.
[5] ⟨He died 14 Nov. 1780 and the notice of his death in the *Scots Mag.*, xlii. 618, reads: ' In the Isle of Sky, Hector Maclean, Esq; of the Isle of Monk.'⟩

a hermit lived in it. It is two miles long, and about three quarters of a mile broad. The Laird said, he had seven score of souls upon it. Last year he had eighty persons inoculated, mostly children, but some of them eighteen years of age. He agreed with a surgeon [a] to come and do it, at half a crown a head.—It is very fertile in corn, of which they export some; and its coasts abound in fish. A taylor comes there six times in a year. They get a good blacksmith from the isle of Egg.

Sunday, 19th September.

It was rather worse weather than any that we had yet. At breakfast Dr. Johnson said, ' Some cunning men choose fools for their wives, thinking to manage them, but they always fail. There is a spaniel fool and a mule fool. The spaniel fool may be made to do by beating. The mule fool will neither do by words nor [b] blows; and the spaniel fool often turns mule at last: and suppose a fool to be made do pretty well, you must have the continual trouble of making her do. Depend upon it, no woman is the worse for sense and knowledge [1].'—Whether afterwards he meant merely to say a polite thing, or to give his opinion, I could not be sure; but he added, ' Men know that women are an over-match for them, and therefore they choose the weakest or most ignorant. If they did not think so, they never could be afraid of women knowing as much as themselves [2].'—In justice to the sex, I think it but candid to acknowledge, that, in a subsequent conversation, he told me that he was serious in what he had said.

He came to my room this morning before breakfast, to read my Journal, which he has done all along. He often before said, ' I take great delight in reading it.' To-day he said, ' You improve: it grows better and better.'—I observed, there was a danger of my getting a habit of writing in a slovenly manner.—' Sir, said he, it is not written in a slovenly manner.

[a] a surgeon 1 (*MS.*): the surgeon 2, 3.   [b] nor 1 (*MS.*): or 2, 3.

[1] See *ante*, ii. 76. ' He [Johnson] used to say, that in all family-disputes the odds were in favour of the husband, from his superior knowledge of life and manners.' Johnson's *Works* (1787), xi. 210.

[2] He wrote to Dr. Taylor, 18 Aug. 1763:—' Nature has given women so much power that the law has very wisely given them little.' *Letters*, No. 157.

It might be printed, were the subject fit for printing¹.'—While Mr. Beaton † preached to us in the dining-room, Dr. Johnson sat in his own room, where I saw lying before him a volume of Lord Bacon's works, the *Decay of Christian Piety* ††, Monboddo's *Origin of Language* §, and Sterne's Sermons ².—He asked me to-day, how it happened that we were so little together: I told him, my Journal took up much time. Yet, on reflection, it appeared strange to me, that although I will run from one end of London to another, to pass an hour with him, I should omit to seize any spare time to be in his company, when I am settled in the same house with him. But my Journal is really a task of much time and labour, and he forbids me to contract it.

I omitted to mention, in its place, that Dr. Johnson told Mr. M'Queen that he had found the belief of the second sight universal in Sky, except among the clergy, who seemed determined against it. I took the liberty to observe to Mr. M'Queen, that the clergy were actuated by a kind of vanity. 'The world, (say they,) takes us to be credulous men in a remote corner. We'll shew them that we are more enlightened than they think.' The worthy man said, that his disbelief of it was from his not finding sufficient evidence; but I could perceive that he was prejudiced against it ³.

After dinner to-day, we talked of the extraordinary fact of Lady Grange's being sent to St. Kilda, and confined there for several years, without any means of relief ⁴. Dr. Johnson said,

¹ As I have faithfully recorded so many minute particulars, I hope I shall be pardoned for inserting so flattering an encomium on what is now offered to the publick. BOSWELL, edd. 1, 2.

† ⟨Beaton and Bethune are spellings of the same name and are pronounced alike in Scotland. Boswell means Mr. Bethune, the parish minister: see *ante*, v. 208.⟩

†† ⟨*The Causes of the Decay of Christian Piety*, 1667. The title-page states that it is 'written by the Author of the Whole Duty of Man', who is said to have been Richard Allestree.⟩

§ ⟨See *ante*, ii. 74 and 259.⟩

² See *ante*, iv. 109, note 1.

³ 'The Islanders of all degrees, whether of rank or understanding, universally admit it, except the Ministers, who universally deny it, and are suspected to deny it, in consequence of a system, against conviction.' Johnson's *Western Isl.*, p. 99.

⁴ The true story of this lady, which happened in this century, is as frightfully romantick as if it had been the fiction of a gloomy fancy. She was the wife of one of the Lords of Session in Scotland, a man of the very first blood of his country. For some mysterious reasons, which have never been discovered, she was seized and carried off in the dark, she knew not by whom, and by nightly journies was conveyed to the Highland shores, from whence she was transported by sea to the remote rock of

Sunday 19 September 1773   Skye : Dunvegan

if M'Leod would let it be known that he had such a place for naughty ladies, he might make it a very profitable island.—We had, in the course of our tour, heard of St. Kilda poetry. Dr. Johnson observed, ' it must be very poor, because they have very few images.'—*Boswell.* ' There may be a poetical genius shewn

St. Kilda, where she remained, amongst its few wild inhabitants, a forlorn prisoner, but had a constant supply of provisions, and a woman to wait on her. No inquiry was made after her, till she at last found means to convey a letter to a confidential friend, by the daughter of a Catechist, who concealed it in a clue of yarn. Information being thus obtained at Edinburgh, a ship was sent to bring her off ; but intelligence of this being received, she was conveyed to M'Leod's island of Herries, where she died.

In *Carstares's State Papers,* we find an authentick narrative of Connor, a catholick priest, who turned protestant, being seized by some of Lord Seaforth's people, and detained prisoner in the island of Herries several years ; he was fed with bread and water, and lodged in a house where he was exposed to the rains and cold. Sir James Ogilvy writes (June 18, 1667 [1697]), that the Lord Chancellor, the Lord Advocate, and himself, were to meet next day, to take effectual methods to have this redressed. Connor was then still detained. P. 310.—This shews what private oppression might in the last century be practised in the Hebrides.

In the same collection the Earl of Argyle gives a picturesque account of an embassy from *the great M'Neil of Barra,* as that insular Chief used to be denominated :—' I received a letter yesterday from M'Neil of Barra, who lives very far off, sent by a gentleman in all formality, offering his service, which had made you laugh to see his entry. His style of his letter runs as if he were of another kingdom.'—P. 643. BOSWELL, ed. 1. ⟨In *State-Papers and Letters addressed to William Carstares,* published by J. McCormack, 1784, the priest's name is given as Conn, and the date of Ogilvy's letter as June 18, 1697 : the date of the Earl of Argyle's account is Sept. 15, 1700, and it occurs on p. 648.⟩

Sir Walter Scott says :—' I have seen Lady Grange's Journal. She had become privy to some of the jacobite intrigues, in which her husband, Lord Grange (brother of the Earl of Mar, and a lord of session), and his family were engaged. Being on indifferent terms with her husband, she is said to have thrown out hints that she knew as much as would cost him his life. The judge probably thought with Mrs. Peachum, that it is rather an awkward state of domestic affairs, when the wife has it in her power to hang the husband. Lady Grange was the more to be dreaded, as she came of a vindictive race, being the grandchild [according to Mr. Chambers, the child] of that Chiesley of Dalry, who assassinated Sir George Lockhart, the lord president. Many persons of importance in the Highlands were concerned in removing her testimony. The notorious Lovat, with a party of his men, were the direct agents in carrying her off ; and St. Kilda, belonging then to Macleod, was selected as the place of confinement. The name by which she was spoken or written of was *Corpach,* an ominous distinction, corresponding to what is called *subject* in the lecture-room of an anatomist, or *shot* in the slang of the Westport murderers' [Burke and Hare]. Sir Walter adds that ' it was said of M'Neil of Barra, that when he dined, his bagpipes blew a particular strain, intimating that all the world might go to dinner.' Croker's *Boswell,* 1831, ii. 451 n. ⟨See *post,* App. D, pp. 539–40, for Lady Grange.⟩

in combining these, and in making poetry of them.'—*Johnson*.
'Sir, a man cannot make fire but in proportion as he has fuel. He cannot coin guineas but in proportion as he has gold.'—At tea he talked of his intending to go to Italy in 1775. M'Leod said, he would like Paris better.—*Johnson*. 'No, sir; there are none of the French literati now alive, to visit whom I would cross a sea. I can find in Buffon's book all that he can say [1].'

After supper he said, 'I am sorry that prize-fighting is gone out [2]; every art should be preserved, and the art of defence is surely important. It is absurd that our soldiers should have swords, and not be taught the use of them. Prize-fighting made people accustomed not to be alarmed at seeing their own blood, or feeling a little pain from a wound. I think the heavy *glaymore* was an ill-contrived weapon. A man could only strike once with it. It employed both his hands, and he must of course be soon fatigued with wielding it; so that if his antagonist could only keep playing a while, he was sure of him. I would fight with a dirk against Rorie More's sword. I could ward off a blow with a dirk, and then run in upon my enemy. When within that heavy sword, I have him; he is quite helpless, and I could stab him at my leisure, like a calf.—It is thought by sensible military men, that the English do not enough avail themselves of their superior strength of body against the French; for that must always have a great advantage in pushing with bayonets. I have heard an officer say, that if women could be made to stand, they would do as well as men in a mere interchange of bullets from a distance: but, if a body of men should

---

[1] I doubt the justice of my fellow-traveller's remark concerning the French literati, many of whom, I am told, have considerable merit in conversation, as well as in their writings. That of Monsieur de Buffon, in particular, I am well assured is highly instructive and entertaining. BOSWELL, ed. 1. See *ante*, iii. 253.

[2] Walpole, writing of 1758, says:—'Prize-fighting, in which we had horridly resembled the most barbarous and most polite nations, was suppressed by the Legislature.' *Memoirs of the Reign of George II*, iii. 99. According to Mrs. Piozzi (*Anec.* p. 5: John. Misc. i. 149), Johnson said that his 'father's brother, Andrew, kept the ring in Smithfield (where they wrestled and boxed) for a whole year, and never was thrown or conquered.' 'Mr. Johnson was,' she continues, 'very conversant in the art of attack and defence by boxing.' She had heard him descant upon it 'much to the admiration of those who had no expectation of his skill in such matters.'

come close up to them, then to be sure they must be overcome; now, (said he,) in the same manner the weaker-bodied French must be overcome by our strong soldiers.'

The subject of duelling was introduced [1].—*Johnson*. ' There is no case in England where one or other of the combatants *must* die : if you have overcome your adversary by disarming him, that is sufficient, though you should not kill him; your honour, or the honour of your family, is restored, as much as it can be by a duel. It is cowardly to force your antagonist to renew the combat, when you know that you have the advantage of him by superior skill. You might just as well go and cut his throat while he is asleep in his bed. When a duel begins, it is supposed there may be an equality; because it is not always skill that prevails. It depends much on presence of mind; nay on accidents. The wind may be in a man's face. He may fall. Many such things may decide the superiority.—A man is sufficiently punished, by being called out, and subjected to the risk that is in a duel.'—But on my suggesting that the injured person is equally subjected to risk, he fairly owned he could not explain the rationality of duelling.

Monday, 20th September.

When I awaked, the storm was higher still. It abated about nine, and the sun shone; but it rained again very soon, and it was not a day for travelling. At breakfast, Dr. Johnson told us, ' there was once a pretty good tavern † in Catharine-street in the Strand, where very good company met in an evening, and each man called for his own half-pint of wine, or gill, if he pleased; they were frugal men, and nobody paid but for what he himself drank. The house furnished no supper; but a woman attended with mutton-pies, which any body might purchase. I was introduced to this company by Cumming the Quaker [2], and used to go there sometimes when I drank wine. In the last age, when my mother lived in London, there were two sets of people, those who gave the wall, and those who took it; the peaceable and the quarrelsome. When I returned to Lichfield, after having been in London, my mother asked me whether I was one of those who gave the wall, or those who took it. Now, it is fixed that

[1] See *ante*, ii. 179, 226, and iv. 211.   † ⟨Cf. *ante*, i. 103.⟩   [2] See *ante*, v. 98.

every man keeps to the right; or, if one is taking the wall, another yields it, and it is never a dispute ¹.'—He was very severe on a lady †, whose name was mentioned. He said, he would have her sent ᵃ to St. Kilda. That she was as bad as negative badness could be, and stood in the way of what was good : that insipid beauty would not go a great way ; and that such a woman might be cut out of a cabbage, if there was a skilful artificer.

M'Leod was too late in coming to breakfast. Dr. Johnson said, laziness was worse than the tooth-ach.—*Boswell*. ' I cannot agree with you, sir ; a bason of cold water, or a horse-whip, will cure laziness.'—*Johnson*. ' No, sir ; it will only put off the fit ; it will not cure the disease. I have been trying to cure my laziness all my life, and could not do it.'—*Boswell*. ' But if a man does in a shorter time what might be the labour of a life, there is nothing to be said against him.'—*Johnson* (perceiving at once that I alluded to him and his Dictionary). ' Suppose that flattery to be true, the consequence would be, that the world would have no right to censure a man ; but that will not justify him to himself ².'

After breakfast, he said to me, ' A Highland Chief should now endeavour to do every thing to raise his rents, by means of the industry of his people. Formerly, it was right for him to have his house full of idle fellows ; they were his defenders, his servants, his dependants, his friends. Now they may be better employed. The system of things is now so much altered, that the family cannot have influence but by riches, because it has no longer the power of ancient feudal times. An individual of a family may have it ; but it cannot now belong to a family, unless you could have a perpetuity of men with the same views.³ M'Leod has four times the land that the Duke of Bedford has. I think, with his spirit, he may in time make himself the greatest man in the king's dominions ; for land may always be improved to a certain degree. I would never have any man sell land, to throw money into the funds, as is often done, or to try any other species of trade. Depend upon it, this rage of trade will destroy itself. You and I shall not see it ; but the time will

ᵃ have her sent 1 (*MS.*) : have sent her 2, 3.

¹ See *ante*, i. 110.
† ⟨Lady Macdonald. Boswell's *Hebrides*, ed. Pottle and Bennett, p. 192.⟩
² See *ante*, i. 398, and ii. 15, 35, 441.

³ ⟨Johnson added : ' One man like Sir Alexander destroys what twenty ancestors have gained.' Boswell's *Hebrides*, ed. Pottle and Bennett, p. 193.⟩

Tuesday 21 September 1773 Skye: Dunvegan

come when there will be an end of it. Trade is like gaming. If a whole company are gamesters, play must cease; for there is nothing to be won. When all nations are traders, there is nothing to be gained by trade [1], and it will stop first where it is brought to the greatest perfection. Then the proprietors of land only will be the great men.'—I observed, it was hard that M'Leod should find ingratitude in so many of his people. —*Johnson.* ' Sir, gratitude is a fruit of great cultivation; you do not find it among gross people.'—I doubt of this. Nature seems to have implanted gratitude in all living creatures [2]. The lion, mentioned by Aulus Gellius, had it [3]. It appears to me that culture, which brings luxury and selfishness with it, has a tendency rather to weaken than promote this affection.

Dr. Johnson said this morning, when talking of our setting out, that he was in the state in which Lord Bacon represents kings. He desired the end, but did not like the means [4]. He wished much to get home, but was unwilling to travel in Sky. —' You are like kings too in this, sir, (said I,) that you must act under the direction of others †.'

Tuesday, 21st September.

The uncertainty of our present situation having prevented me from receiving any letters from home for some time, I could not help being uneasy. Dr. Johnson had an advantage over me, in this respect, he having no wife or child to occasion anxious apprehensions in his mind [5].—It was a good morning; so we

---

[1] Gibbon, thirteen years later, writing to Lord Sheffield about the commercial treaty with France, said (*Misc. Works*, ii. 399):—' I hope both nations are gainers; since otherwise it cannot be lasting; and such double mutual gain is surely possible in fair trade, though it could not easily happen in the mischievous amusements of war and gaming.'

[2] Johnson (*Savage*, 148), writing of gratitude and resentment, says: —' Though there are few who will practise a laborious virtue, there will never be wanting multitudes that will indulge an easy vice.'

[3] Aul. Gellius, Lib. v. c. xiv. BOSWELL, ed. 3.

[4] ' The difficulties in Princes Businesse, are many and great; But the greatest difficulty, is often in their owne Minds. For it is common with Princes, (saith Tacitus) to will Contradictories, *Sunt plerumque Regum voluntates vehementes, et inter se contrariæ*. For it is the Solœcisme of Power, to thinke to Command the End, and yet not to endure the Meane.' Bacon's *Essays*, No. xix (*of Empire*).

† ⟨On the next page of his Journal Boswell says: ' I must observe that Mr. J. read all my Journal to the foot of the preceding page, and said to me, " It is a very pretty Journal ".'⟩

[5] Yet Johnson wrote to Mrs. Thrale on Sept. 30 :—' I am now no

Skye: Dunvegan *Tuesday* 21 *September* 1773

resolved to set out. But, before quitting this castle, where we have been so well entertained, let me give a short description of it.

Along the edge of the rock, there are the remains of a wall, which is now covered with ivy. A square court is formed by buildings of different ages, particularly some towers, said to be of great antiquity; and at one place there is a row of false cannon of stone [1]. There is a very large unfinished pile, four stories high, which we were told was here when *Leod*, the first of this family, came from the Isle of Man, married the heiress of the M'Crails, the ancient possessors of Dunvegan, and afterwards acquired by conquest as much land as he had got by marriage. He surpassed the house of Austria; for he was *felix* both *bella gerere* et *nubere* [2]. John *Breck* M'Leod, the grandfather of the late laird, began to repair the castle, or rather to complete it: but he did not live to finish his undertaking [3]. Not

longer pleased with the delay, you can hear from me but seldom, and I cannot at all hear from you. It comes into my mind, that some evil may happen.' *Letters*, No. 329. On Oct. 15 he wrote to Mr. Thrale:— 'Having for many weeks had no letter, my longings are very great to be informed how all things are at home, as you and mistress allow me to call it ... I beg to have my thoughts set at rest by a letter from you or my mistress.' *Ib.* No. 330. See *ante*, iii. 4.

[1] Sir Walter Scott thus describes Dunvegan in 1814:—' The whole castle occupies a precipitous mass of rock overhanging the lake, divided by two or three islands in that place, which form a snug little harbour under the walls. There is a courtyard looking out upon the sea, protected by a battery, at least a succession of embrasures, for only two guns are pointed, and these unfit for service. The ancient entrance rose up a flight of steps cut in the rock, and passed into this court-yard through a portal, but this is now demolished. You land under the castle, and, walking round, find yourself in front of it.

This was originally inaccessible, for a brook coming down on the one side, a chasm of the rocks on the other, and a ditch in front, made it impervious. But the late Macleod built a bridge over the stream, and the present laird is executing an entrance suitable to the character of this remarkable fortalice, by making a portal between two advanced towers and an outer court, from which he proposes to throw a draw-bridge over to the high rock in front of the castle.' Lockhart's *Scott*, iii. 226. ⟨The 'false cannon' are really gargoyles.⟩

[2] ' Bella gerant alii! tu, felix Austria, nube!
    Nam quae Mars aliis, dat tibi regna Venus!'
⟨See Büchmann, *Geflügelte Worte*, 1920, p. 399, and W. F. H. King, *Classical Quotations*, 1904, p. 28.⟩

[3] Johnson says of this castle:— ' It is so nearly entire, that it might have easily been made habitable, were there not an ominous tradition in the family, that the owner shall not long outlive the reparation. The grandfather of the present Laird, in defiance of prediction, began the work, but desisted in a little time,

doubting, however, that he should do it, he, like those who have had their epitaphs written before they died, ordered the following inscription, composed by the minister of the parish, to be cut upon a broad stone above one of the lower windows, where it still remains to celebrate what was not done, and to serve as a memento of the uncertainty of life, and the presumption of man :

'Joannes Macleod Beganoduni Dominus gentis suæ Philarchus [1], Durinesiæ Haraiæ Vaternesiæ, &c. Baro D. Floræ Macdonald matrimoniali vinculo conjugatus turrem hanc Beganodunensem proavorum habitaculum longe vetustissimum diu penitus labefectatam Anno æræ vulgaris MDCLXXXVI instauravit.

> 'Quem stabilire juvat proavorum tecta vetusta,
> Omne scelus fugiat, justitiamque colat.
> Vertit in aerias turres magalia virtus,
> Inque casas humiles tecta superba nefas.'

M'Leod and Talisker accompanied us. We passed by the parish church of *Durinish*. The church-yard is not enclosed, but a pretty murmuring brook runs along one side of it. In it is a pyramid erected to the memory of Thomas Lord Lovat, by his son Lord Simon, who suffered on Tower-hill [2]. It is of freestone, and, I suppose, about thirty [3] feet high. There is an inscription on a piece of white marble inserted in it, which I suspect to have been the composition of Lord Lovat himself, being much in his pompous style :

'This pyramid was erected by SIMON LORD FRASER of LOVAT, in honour of LORD THOMAS his Father, a Peer of Scotland, and Chief of the great and ancient Clan of the FRASERS. Being attacked for his birthright by the family of ATHOLL, then in power and favour with KING WILLIAM, yet, by the valour and fidelity of his clan, and the assistance of the CAMPBELLS, the old friends and allies of his family, he defended his birthright with such greatness and fermety of soul, and such valour and activity, that he was an honour to his name, and a [a] good pattern to all brave Chiefs of clans. He died in the month of May, 1699, in the

[a] *a not in the inscription.*

and applied his money to worse uses.' *Western Isl.*, p. 60.

[1] Macaulay (*Literary Essays*, 1923, 215) ends a lively piece of criticism on Mr. Croker by saying :—' It requires no Bentley or Casaubon to perceive that Philarchus is merely a false spelling for Phylarchus, the chief of a tribe.'
[2] See *ante*, i. 180.
[3] ⟨Twenty-five.⟩

Skye: Ulinish *Tuesday 21 September 1773*

63d year of his age, in Dunvegan, the house of the LAIRD of MAC LEOD, whose sister he had married : by whom he had the above SIMON LORD FRASER, and several other children. And, for the great love he bore to the family of MAC LEOD, he desired to be buried near his wife's relations, in the place where two of her uncles lay. And his son LORD SIMON, to shew to posterity his great affection for his mother's kindred, the brave MAC LEODS, chooses rather to leave his father's bones with them, than carry them to his own burial-place, near Lovat.'

I have preserved this inscription [1], though of no great value, thinking it characteristical of a man who has made some noise in the world. Dr. Johnson said, it was poor stuff, such as Lord Lovat's butler might have written.

I observed, in this church-yard, a parcel of people assembled at a funeral, before the grave was dug. The coffin, with the corpse in it, was placed on the ground, while the people alternately assisted in making a grave. One man, at a little distance, was busy cutting a long turf for it, with the crooked spade which is used in Sky ; a very aukward instrument. The iron part of it is like a plough-coulter. It has a rude tree for a handle, in which a wooden pin is placed for the foot to press upon. A traveller might, without further enquiry, have set this down as the mode of burying in Sky. I was told, however, that the usual way is to have a grave previously dug †.

I observed to-day, that the common way of carrying home their grain here is in loads on horseback. They have also a few sleds, or *cars*, as we call them in Ayrshire, clumsily made, and rarely used [2].

We got to Ulinish about six o'clock, and found a very good farm-house, of two stories. Mr. M'Leod of Ulinish [3], the sheriff-substitute of the island, was a plain honest gentleman, a good deal like an English justice of peace ; not much given to talk,

[1] Scott wrote in 1814 :—'The monument is now nearly ruinous, and the inscription has fallen down.' Lockhart's *Scott*, iii. 230. ⟨The pyramid has been repaired and now, 1936, shows no sign of falling down.⟩

† ⟨See App. D, p. 540.⟩

[2] ' Wheel carriages they have none, but make a frame of timber, which is drawn by one horse with the two points behind pressing on the ground.

On this they sometimes drag home their sheaves, but often convey them home in a kind of open panier, or frame of sticks upon the horse's back.' Johnson's *Western Isl.*, p. 72. 'The young Laird [of Col] has attempted what no Islander perhaps ever thought on. He has begun a road capable of a wheel-carriage. He has carried it about a mile.' *Ib.* p. 118.

[3] ⟨See App. D, p. 541.⟩

Wednesday 22 September 1773 Skye: Ulinish

but sufficiently sagacious, and somewhat droll. His daughter, though she was never out of Sky, was a very well-bred woman. —Our reverend friend, Mr. Donald M'Queen, kept his appointment, and met us here.

Talking of Phipps's voyage to the North Pole, Dr. Johnson observed, that it ' was conjectured that our former navigators have kept too near land, and so have found the sea frozen far north, because the land hinders the free motion of the tide ; but, in the wide ocean, where the waves tumble at their full convenience, it is imagined that the frost does not take effect [1].'

Wednesday, 22d September.

In the morning I walked out, and saw a ship, the Margaret of Clyde, pass by with a number of emigrants on board. It was a melancholy sight.—After breakfast, we went to see what was called a subterraneous house, about a short[a] mile off. It was upon the side of a rising-ground. It was discovered by a fox's having taken up his abode in it, and in chacing him, they dug into it. It was very narrow and low, and seemed about forty feet in length. Near it, we found the foundations of several small huts, built of stone.—Mr. M'Queen, who is always for making every thing as ancient as possible, boasted that it was the dwelling of some of the first inhabitants of the island, and observed, what a curiosity it was to find here a specimen of the houses of the *Aborigines*, which he believed could be found no where else ; and it was plain that they lived without fire.—Dr. Johnson remarked, that they who made this were not in the rudest state ; for that it was more difficult to make *it* than to build a house ; therefore certainly those who made it were in possession of houses, and had this only as a hiding-place.—It appeared to me, that the vestiges of houses, just by it, confirmed Dr. Johnson's opinion.

From an old tower, near this place, is an extensive view of Loch-Braccadil, and, at a distance, of the isles of Barra and South Uist ; and on the land-side, the *Cuillin*, a prodigious range of mountains, capped with rocky pinnacles in a strange variety

[a] short 1, 2 (*MS.*) : omitted 3.

[1] ⟨The object of Capt. Constantine Phipps's voyage, April–Sept. 1773, was the discovery of a northern passage to India. He found the ice north of Spitzbergen impenetrable. See his account, *A Voyage towards the North Pole*, 1774. Nelson was a midshipman on one of his two ships.⟩

Skye : Ulinish *Wednesday 22 September* 1773

of shapes. They resemble the mountains near Corté in Corsica, of which there is a very good print. They make part of a great range for deer, which, though entirely devoid of trees, is in these countries called a *forest*.

In the afternoon, Ulinish carried us in his boat to an island possessed by him, where we saw an immense cave, much more deserving the title of *antrum immane*[1] than that of the Sybil described by Virgil, which I likewise have visited. It is one hundred and eighty feet long, about thirty feet broad, and at least thirty feet high. This cave, we were told, had a remarkable echo ; but we found none[2]. They said it was owing to the great rains having made it damp. Such are the excuses by which the exaggeration of Highland narratives is palliated. —There is a plentiful garden at Ulinish, (a great rarity in Sky,) and several trees ; and near the house is a hill, which has an Erse name, signifying ' *the hill of strife*,' where, Mr. M'Queen informed us, justice was of old administered. It is like the *mons placiti* of *Scone*, or those hills which are called *laws*[3], such as Kelly *law*, North-Berwick *law*, and several others. It is singular that this spot should happen now to be the sheriff's residence.

We had a very cheerful evening, and Dr. Johnson talked a good deal on the subject of literature.—Speaking of the noble family of Boyle, he said, that all the Lord Orrerys, till the present, had been writers. The first wrote several plays[4] ; the

[1] *Æneid*, vi. 11.
[2] ' In the afternoon an interval of calm sunshine courted us out to see a cave on the shore famous for its echo. When we went into the boat one of our companions was asked in Earse by the boatmen who they were that came with him, he gave us characters, I suppose to our advantage, and was asked in the spirit of the highlands, whether I could recite a long series of Ancestors. The Boatmen said, as I heard afterwards, that they perceived the cry of an English Ghost, this, Boswell says disturbed him. . . . There was no echo, such is the fidelity of report.' *Letters*, No. 329. 〈' It was not Ulinish's boatmen, but those who rowed us from Sconser on Saturday 25 Septr. who asked about your genealogy ', remarked Boswell of Johnson's *Western Isl.*: see ed. 1924, pp. 66 and 456.〉

[3] 〈*Law* is the northern representative of O.E. *hláw*, *hlǽw*, Low, a hill, especially one more or less round or conical ; it frequently occurs as the second element in place-names. See the Oxford Dictionary (*Low* sb.[1]) and Mawer, *Chief Elements used in English Place-names*, 1924, p. 37.〉

[4] Pepys often mentions them. At first he praises them highly, but of one of the later ones—*Tryphon*—he writes :—' The play, though admirable, yet no pleasure almost in it, because just the very same design, and words, and sense, and plot, as every one of his plays have, any one of which alone would be held admirable, whereas so many of the same

238   *Wednesday 22 September* 1773   Skye : Ulinish
second [1] was Bentley's antagonist ; the third [2] wrote the Life of Swift, and several other things ; his son Hamilton † wrote some papers in the *Adventurer* and *World*. He told us, he was well acquainted with Swift's Lord Orrery. He said, he was a feeble-minded man ; that, on the publication of Dr. Delany's *Remarks* on his book, he was so much alarmed that he was afraid to read them. Dr. Johnson comforted him, by telling him they were both in the right ; that Delany had seen most of the good side of Swift,—Lord Orrery most of the bad.—M'Leod asked, if it was not wrong in Orrery to expose the defects of a man with whom he lived in intimacy.—*Johnson*. ' Why no, sir, after the man is dead ; for then it is done historically [3].' He added, ' If Lord Orrery had been rich, he would have been a very liberal patron. His conversation was like his writings, neat and elegant, but without strength. He grasped at more than his abilities could reach ; tried to pass for a better talker, a better writer, and a better thinker, than he was [4]. There was a quarrel between him and his father, in which his father was to blame ; because it arose from the son's not allowing his wife to keep company with his father's mistress. The old lord shewed his resentment in his will [5],—leaving his library from his son, and assigning, as his reason, that he could not make use of it.'

I mentioned the affectation of Orrery, in ending all his letters on the Life of Swift in studied varieties of phrase [6], and never

design and fancy do but dull one another.' Pepys's *Diary*, 8 Dec. 1668.

[1] The second and third earls are passed over by Johnson. It was the fourth earl who, as Charles Boyle, had been Bentley's antagonist. See Macaulay's *Life of Atterbury* ⟨and Monk's *Bentley*, i. 64, ii. 172⟩.

[2] The fifth earl, John. See *ante*, i. 185, and iii. 249. ⟨He received a pension of £800 a year from the secret service funds from 1756 to 1762. Namier, *Structure of Politics*, 1926, i. 275.⟩

† ⟨See App. D, p. 541.⟩

[3] See *ante*, i. 9, and iii. 155.

[4] See *ante*, ii. 129, and iii. 183.

[5] The young lord was married on the 8th May, 1728, and the father's will is dated the 6th Nov. following. ' Having,' says the testator, ' never observed that my son hath showed much taste or inclination, either for the entertainment or knowledge which study and learning afford, I give and' bequeath all my books and mathematical instruments [with certain exceptions] to Christchurch College, in Oxford.' CROKER, 1831.

[6] His *Life of Swift* is written in the form of *Letters to his Son, the Hon. Hamilton Boyle*. The fifteenth Letter (p. 131), in which he finishes his criticism of *Gulliver's Travels*, affords a good instance of this ' studied variety of phrase.' ' I may finish my letter,' he writes, ' especially as the conclusion of it naturally turns my thoughts from Yahoos, to one of the

Skye: Ulinish *Wednesday 22 September* 1773

in the common mode of '*I am*, &c.'[a] an observation which I remember to have been made several years ago by old Mr. Sheridan. This species of affectation in writing, as a foreign lady of distinguished talents once remarked to me, is almost peculiar to the English. I took up a volume of Dryden, containing the *Conquest of Granada*, and several other plays, of which all the dedications had such studied conclusions. Dr. Johnson said, such conclusions were more elegant, and, in addressing persons of high rank, (as when Dryden dedicated to the Duke of York [1],) they were likewise more respectful. I agreed that *there* it was much better : it was making his escape from the Royal presence with a genteel sudden timidity, in place of having the resolution to stand still, and make a formal bow.

Lord Orrery's unkind treatment of his son in his will, led us to talk of the dispositions a man should have when dying. I said, I did not see why a man should act differently with respect to those of whom he thought ill when in health, merely because he was dying.—*Johnson.* ' I should not scruple to speak against a party, when dying ; but should not do it against an individual. —It is told of Sixtus Quintus, that on his death-bed, in the intervals of his last pangs, he signed death-warrants [2].'—Mr. M'Queen said, he should not do so ; he would have more

[a] '*I am*, &c.' 1 : '*I am*', &c. 2, 3.

dearest pledges I have upon earth, yourself : to whom I am a most
  ' Affectionate Father
    ' ORRERY.'

See *ante*, i. 275-284, for Johnson's letters to Thomas Warton, many of which end ' in studied varieties of phrase.'

[1] *The Conquest of Granada* was dedicated to the Duke of York. The conclusion is as follows :—' If at any time Almanzor fulfils the parts of personal Vallour and of conduct, of a Souldier, and of a General ; or, if I could yet give him a Character more advantagious than what he has ; of the most unshaken friend, the greatest of Subjects, and the best of Masters, I shou'd then draw all the world, a true resemblance of your worth and vertues ; at least as farr as they are capable of being copied, by the mean abilities of
  ' Sir,
    ' Your Royal Highnesse's
      ' Most humble and most
        'obedient Servant
          ' J. DRYDEN.'

[2] On the day of his coronation he was asked to pardon four young men who had broken the law against carrying arms. ' So long as I live,' replied Sixtus, ' every criminal must die.' ' Sixtus was inexorable in individual cases ; he adhered to his laws with a rigour that amounted to cruelty, while, in the framing of general rules, we find him mild, yielding and placable.' Ranke's *Popes*, ed. 1866, i. 307, 311.

tenderness of heart.—*Johnson.* ' I believe I should not either; but Mr. M'Queen and I are cowards [1]. It would not be from tenderness of heart; for the heart is as tender when a man is in health as when he is sick, though his resolution may be stronger [2]. Sixtus Quintus was a sovereign as well as a priest; and, if the criminals deserved death, he was doing his duty to the last. You would not think a judge died ill, who should be carried off by an apoplectick fit while pronouncing sentence of death. Consider a class of men whose business it is to distribute death :—soldiers, who die scattering bullets.—Nobody thinks they die ill on that account.'

Talking of Biography, he said, he did not think that the life of any literary man in England had been well written [3]. Beside the common incidents of life, it should tell us his studies, his mode of living, the means by which he attained to excellence, and his opinion of his own works. He told us, he had sent Derrick to Dryden's relations, to gather materials for his Life [4]; and he believed Derrick had got all that he himself should have got; but it was nothing. He added, he had a kindness for Derrick [5], and was sorry he was dead.

His notion as to the poems published by Mr. M'Pherson, as the works of Ossian, was not shaken here. Mr. M'Queen always evaded the point of authenticity, saying only that Mr. M'Pherson's pieces fell far short of those he knew in Erse, which were said to be Ossian's.—*Johnson.* ' I hope they do. I am not disputing that you may have poetry of great merit; but that M'Pherson's is not a translation from ancient poetry. You do not believe it. I say before you, you do not believe it, though you are very willing that the world should believe it.'—Mr. M'Queen made no answer to this [6].—Dr. Johnson proceeded

---

[1] See *ante*, iii. 239, where he discusses the question of shooting a highwayman.

[2] In *The Rambler*, No. 78, he says :—' I believe men may be generally observed to grow less tender as they advance in age.'

[3] He passed over his own *Life of Savage*.

[4] ⟨Derrick expressed his disappointment at his failure to obtain materials. Dryden's *Misc. Works*, 1760, i, p. ix.⟩

[5] See *ante*, i. 456 and v. 117.

[6] ' I asked a very learned Minister in Sky, who had used all arts to make me believe the genuineness of the book, whether at last he believed it himself? but he would not answer. He wished me to be deceived, for the honour of his country; but would not directly and formally deceive me. Yet has this man's testi-

Skye : Ulinish *Wednesday 22 September 1773* 241
' I look upon M'Pherson's *Fingal* to be as gross an imposition as ever the world was troubled with. Had it been really an ancient work, a true specimen how men thought at that time, it would have been a curiosity of the first rate. As a modern production, it is nothing.'—He said, he could never get the meaning of an *Erse* song explained to him [1]. They told him, the chorus was generally unmeaning. ' I take it, (said he,) Erse songs are like a song which I remember : it was composed in Queen Elizabeth's time, on the Earl of Essex ; and the burthen was

" Radaratoo, radarate, radara tadara tandore." '

' But surely, said Mr. M'Queen, there were words to it, which had meaning.'—*Johnson*. ' Why, yes, sir ; I recollect a stanza, and you shall have it :

" O ! then bespoke the prentices all,
Living in London, both proper and tall,
For Essex's sake they would fight all.
Radaratoo, radarate, radara, tadara, tandore [2]." '

When Mr. M'Queen began again to expatiate on the beauty of Ossian's poetry, Dr. Johnson entered into no further controversy, but, with a pleasant smile, only cried, ' Ay, ay ; *Radaratoo radarate.*'

mony been publickly produced, as of one that held Fingal to be the work of Ossian.' *Western Isl.*, p. 107. ⟨Macqueen told Blair, 17 April 1764, that he had ' a just esteem' for Macpherson's ' genius ' and that there was ' a foundation in the ancient songs for every part of his work '. *Highland Soc. Rep.*, 1805, App., p. 36.⟩

[1] A young lady had sung to him an Erse song. He asked her, ' What is it about ? I question, if she conceived that I did not understand it. For the entertainment of the company, said she. But, Madam, what is the meaning of it ? It is a love song. This was all the intelligence that I could obtain, nor have I ever been able to procure the translation of a line of Erse.' *Letters*, No. 327. See *post*, v. 318.

[2] This droll quotation, I have since found, was from a song in honour of the Earl of Essex, called ' *Queen Elizabeth's Champion*,' which is preserved in a collection of Old Ballads, in three volumes, published in London in different years, between 1720 and 1730. The full verse is as follows :

' Oh ! then bespoke the prentices all,
Living in London, both proper and tall,
In a kind letter sent straight to the Queen,
For Essex's sake they would fight all.
Raderer too, tandaro te,
Raderer, tandorer, tan do re.'
BOSWELL, ed. 1.
⟨A Collection of Old Ballads first appeared, in three vols., in 1723-25. See A. E. Case, *Eng. Poet. Misc.*, No. 326. Ambrose Philips is sometimes stated to have been the compiler.⟩

Thursday 23d September

I took *Fingal* down to the parlour in the morning, and tried a test proposed by Mr. Roderick M'Leod †, son to Ulinish. Mr. M'Queen had said he had some of the poem in the original. I desired him to mention any passage in the printed book, of which he could repeat the original. He pointed out one in page 50 of the quarto edition, and read the Erse, while Mr. Roderick M'Leod and I looked on the English ;—and Mr. M'Leod said, that it was pretty like what Mr. M'Queen had recited. But when Mr. M'Queen read a description of Cuchullin's sword in Erse, together with a translation of it in English verse, by Sir James Foulis, Mr. M'Leod said, that was much more like than Mr. M'Pherson's translation of the former passage. Mr. M'Queen then repeated in Erse a description of one of the horses in Cuchullin's car. Mr. M'Leod said, Mr. M'Pherson's English was nothing like it.

When Dr. Johnson came down, I told him that I had now obtained some evidence concerning Fingal ; for that Mr. M'Queen had repeated a passage in the original Erse, which Mr. M'Pherson's translation was pretty like ; and reminded him that he himself had once said, he did not require Mr. M'Pherson's Ossian to be more like the original than Pope's Homer.—*Johnson.* ' Well, sir, this is just what I always maintained. He has found names, and stories, and phrases, nay passages in old songs, and with them has blended his own compositions, and so made what he gives to the world as the translation of an ancient poem.'—If this was the case, I observed, it was wrong to publish it as a poem in six books.—*Johnson.* ' Yes, sir ; and to ascribe it to a time too when the Highlanders knew nothing of *books*, and nothing of *six ;*—or perhaps were got the length of counting six. We have been told, by Condamine, of a nation that could count no more than four [1]. This should be told to Monboddo ;

---

† ⟨He became a lieutenant in the army and was killed in America. A. Mackenzie, *Hist. Macleods*, 1889, p. 276.⟩

[1] Condamine describes a tribe called the Tameos, on the north side of the river Tiger in S. America, who have a word for *three.* ' Happily for those who have transactions with them, their arithmetic goes no farther. .. The Brazilian tongue ... is equally barren ; the people who speak it, where more than three is to be expressed, are obliged to use the Portuguese.' Pinkerton's *Voy.*, 1813, xiv. 225.

it would help him. There is as much charity in helping a man down-hill, as in helping him up-hill.'—*Boswell*. ' I don't think there is as much charity.'—*Johnson*. ' Yes, sir, if his *tendency* be downwards. Till he is at the bottom, he flounders ; get him once there, and he is quiet. Swift tells, that Stella had a trick, which she learned from Addison, of encouraging a man in absurdity, instead of endeavouring to extricate him [1].'

Mr. M'Queen's answers to the inquiries concerning Ossian were so unsatisfactory, that I could not help observing, that, were he examined in a court of justice, he would find himself under a necessity of being more explicit.—*Johnson*. ' Sir, he has told Blair a little too much, which is published [2] ; and he sticks to it. He is so much at the head of things here, that he has never been accustomed to be closely examined ; and so he goes on quite smoothly.'—*Boswell*. ' He has never had any body to work [3] him.'—*Johnson*. ' No, sir ; and a man is seldom disposed to work himself ; though he ought to work himself, to be sure.'—Mr. M'Queen made no reply [4].

Having talked of the strictness with which witnesses are examined in courts of justice, Dr. Johnson told us, that Garrick, though accustomed to face multitudes, when produced as a witness in Westminster-hall, was so disconcerted by a new mode of publick appearance, that he could not understand what was asked [5]. It was a cause where an actor claimed a *free benefit* ;

---

[1] ' It was Addison's practice when he found any man invincibly wrong to flatter his opinions by acquiescence, and sink him yet deeper in absurdity. This artifice of mischief was admired by Stella ; and Swift seems to approve her admiration.' Johnson's *Addison*, 120. Swift, in his ' character ' of Mrs. Johnson (Stella), says :—' Whether this proceeded from her easiness in general, or from her indifference to persons, or from her despair of mending them, or from the same practice which she much liked in Mr. Addison, I cannot determine ; but when she saw any of the company very warm in a wrong opinion, she was more inclined to confirm them in it than oppose them. The excuse she commonly gave, when her friends asked the reason, was, that it prevented noise, and saved time.' Swift's *Prose Works*, 1907, xi. 136.

[2] In the Appendix to Blair's *Critical Dissertation on the Poems of Ossian* Macqueen is mentioned as one of his authorities for his statement. ⟨Boswell, writing 27 March 1768, says : 'He [Johnson] was very hard on poor Dr. Blair, whom he holds wonderfully cheap for having written ' this *Dissertation. Boswell Papers*, vii. 176.⟩

[3] See *ante*, iv. 261, note 3 ad fin.

[4] I think it but justice to say, that I believe Dr. Johnson meant to ascribe Mr. M'Queen's conduct to inaccuracy and enthusiasm, and did not mean any severe imputation against him. BOSWELL, ed. 1.

[5] In Baretti's trial (*ante*, ii. 97, note 1) he seems to have given his evidence clearly. What he had to say, however, was not much.

Thursday 23 September 1773 Skye: Ulinish

that is to say, a benefit without paying the expence of the house; but the meaning of the term was disputed. Garrick was asked, 'Sir, have you a free benefit?'—'Yes.'—'Upon what terms have you it?'—'Upon—the terms—of—a free benefit.' —He was dismissed as one from whom no information could be obtained.—Dr. Johnson is often too hard on our friend Mr. Garrick. When I asked him, why he did not mention him in the Preface to his Shakspeare [1], he said, 'Garrick has been liberally paid for any thing he has done for Shakspeare. If I should praise him, I should much more praise the nation who paid him. He has not made Shakspeare better known [2]; he

---

[1] ⟨Boswell questioned Johnson about this omission 'going from Forres to Nairn': see App. D, p. 541, where Johnson's unedited answer is given. See also *ante*, ii. 92.⟩

[2] It has been triumphantly asked, 'Had not the plays of Shakspeare lain dormant for many years before the appearance of Mr. Garrick? Did he not exhibit the most excellent of them frequently for thirty years together, and render them extremely popular by his own inimitable performance?' He undoubtedly did. But Dr. Johnson's assertion has been misunderstood. Knowing as well as the objectors what has been just stated, he must necessarily have meant, that 'Mr. Garrick did not as *a critic* make Shakspeare better known; he did not *illustrate* any one *passage* in any of his plays by acuteness of disquisition, or sagacity of conjecture:' and what had been done with any degree of excellence in *that* way was the proper and immediate subject of his preface. I may add in support of this explanation the following anecdote, related to me by one of the ablest commentators on Shakspeare, who knew much of Dr. Johnson: 'Now I have quitted the theatre, cries Garrick, I will sit down and read Shakspeare.' ''Tis time you should, exclaimed Johnson, for I much doubt if you ever examined one of his plays from the first scene to the last.' BOSWELL,

ed. 3. According to Davies (*Life of Garrick*, ch. xi) during the twenty years' management of Drury Lane by Booth, Wilks and Cibber (about 1712–1732) not more than eight or nine of Shakspeare's plays were acted, whereas Garrick annually gave the public seventeen or eighteen. *Romeo and Juliet* had lain neglected near 80 years, when in 1748–9 Garrick brought it out, or rather a hash of it. 'Otway made some alteration in the catastrophe, which Mr. Garrick greatly improved, by the addition of a scene, which was written with a spirit not unworthy of Shakespeare himself.' Murphy (*Life of Garrick*, p. 100), writing of this alteration, says:—'The catastrophe, as it now stands, is the most affecting in the whole compass of the drama.' Davies says, ch. iii, that shortly before Garrick's time 'a taste for Shakespeare had been revived, by the encouragement of the most distinguished persons of both sexes; but more especially by the ladies, who formed themselves into a society, under the title of The Shakespeare Club. They bespoke, every week, some favourite play of this great writer.' This revival was shown in the increasing number of readers of Shakespeare. It was in 1741 that Garrick began to act. In the previous sixteen years there had been published four editions of Pope's *Shakespeare* and two of Theobald's. In

Skye: Ulinish *Thursday 23 September 1773* 245
cannot illustrate Shakspeare: So I have reasons enough against mentioning him, were reasons necessary. There should be reasons *for* it.'—I spoke of Mrs. Montague's very high praises of Garrick [1].—*Johnson.* ' Sir, it is fit she should say so much, and I should say nothing. Reynolds is fond of her book, and I wonder at it ; for neither I, nor Beauclerk, nor Mrs. Thrale, could get through it [2].'

the next ten years were published five editions of Hanmer's *Shakespeare*, and two of Warburton's, besides Johnson's *Observations on Macbeth.*

[1] In her *Essay on Shakespear*, p. 15. See *ante*, ii. 88.

[2] No man has less inclination to controversy than I have, particularly with a lady. But as I have claimed, and am conscious of being entitled to, credit, for the strictest fidelity, my respect for the publick obliges me to take notice of an insinuation which tends to impeach it.

Mrs. Piozzi (late Mrs. Thrale), to her "Anecdotes of Dr. Johnson", added the following postscript :
' *Naples, Feb.* 10, 1786.
' Since the foregoing went to the press, having seen a passage from Mr. Boswell's "Tour to the Hebrides", in which it is said, that *I could not get through Mrs. Montague's " Essay on Shakspeare,"* I do not delay a moment to declare, that, on the contrary, I have always commended it myself, and heard it commended by every one else ; and few things would give me more concern than to be thought incapable of tasting, or unwilling to testify my opinion of its excellence.'

It is remarkable that this postscript is so expressed, as not to point out the person who said that Mrs. Thrale could not get through Mrs. Montague's book ; and therefore I think it necessary to remind Mrs. Piozzi, that the assertion concerning her was Dr. Johnson's, and not mine. The second observation that I shall make on this postscript is, that it does not deny the fact asserted, though I must acknowledge from the praise it bestows on Mrs. Montague's book, it may have been designed to convey that meaning.

What Mrs. Thrale's opinion is or was, or what she may or may not have said to Dr. Johnson concerning Mrs. Montague's book, it is not necessary for me to enquire. It is only incumbent on me to ascertain what Dr. Johnson said to me. I shall therefore confine myself to a very short state of the fact.

The unfavourable opinion of Mrs. Montague's book, which Dr. Johnson is here reported to have given, is known to have been that which he uniformly expressed, as many of his friends well remember. So much for the authenticity of the paragraph, as far as it relates to his own sentiments. The words containing the assertion, to which Mrs. Piozzi objects, are printed from my manuscript Journal, and were taken down at the time. The Journal was read by Dr. Johnson, who pointed out some inaccuracies, which I corrected, but did not mention any inaccuracy in the paragraph in question : and what is still more material, and very flattering to me, a considerable part of my Journal, containing this paragraph, *was read several years ago by Mrs. Thrale herself* [see *ante*, ii. 383], who had it for some time in her possession, and returned it to me, without intimating that Dr. Johnson had mistaken her sentiments.

When the first edition of my Journal

246 *Thursday 23 September* 1773   Skye : Ulinish

Last night Dr. Johnson gave us an account of the whole process of tanning,—and of the nature of milk, and the various operations upon it, as making whey, &c. His variety of information is surprizing [1] ; and it gives one much satisfaction to find such a man bestowing his attention on the useful arts of life. Ulinish was much struck with his knowledge ; and said, ' He is a great orator, sir ; it is musick to hear this man speak.' —A strange thought struck me, to try if he knew any thing of an art, or whatever it should be called, which is no doubt very useful in life, but which lies far out of the way of a philosopher and poet ; I mean the trade of a butcher. I enticed him into the subject, by connecting it with the various researches into the manners and customs of uncivilized nations, that have been made by our late navigators to [a] the South Seas.—I began with observing, that Mr. (now Sir Joseph) Banks tells us, that the art of slaughtering animals was not known in Otaheite, for, instead of bleeding to death their dogs, (a common food with them,) they

[a] to 1 : into 2, 3.

was passing through the press, it occurred to me, that a peculiar delicacy was necessary to be observed in reporting the opinion of one literary lady concerning the performance of another ; and I had such scruples on that head, that in the proof sheet I struck out the name of Mrs. Thrale from the above paragraph, and two or three hundred copies of my book were actually printed and published without it ; of these Sir Joshua Reynolds's copy happened to be one. But while the sheet was working off, a friend, for whose opinion I have great respect, suggested that I had no right to deprive Mrs. Thrale of the high honour which Dr. Johnson had done her, by stating her opinion along with that of Mr. Beauclerk, as coinciding with, and, as it were, sanctioning his own. The observation appeared to me so weighty and conclusive, that I hastened to the printing-house, and, as a piece of justice, restored Mrs. Thrale to that place from which a too scrupulous delicacy had excluded her.

On this simple state of facts I shall make no observation whatever. BOSWELL, ed. 3. ⟨Boswell noted, 15 Apr. 1786, ' Break[fasted] Malone. Courtenay came, concerted my Answer to Mrs. Piozzi.' *Boswell Papers*, xvi. 184–5. This ' answer ', which is the foregoing note, was printed in *The Gazetteer*, 17 April, and *The Public Advertiser*, 18 April, and reprinted in *Gent. Mag.*, April 1786, lvi. 285. It contained, after Mrs. Piozzi's Postscript, the following paragraph, which was not appropriate to the *Tour* : ' I might perhaps with propriety have waited till I should have an opportunity of answering this Postscript in a future publication ; but, being sensible that impressions once made are not easily effaced, I think it better thus early to ascertain a fact which seems to be denied.'

The friend who suggested the restoration of Mrs. Thrale's name was John Courtenay (Boswell's letters to Malone 27 Oct. 1785 and 31 Mar. 1786. *Yale MSS.* L. 921 and 934). No copy has been discovered without it. For Mrs. Piozzi's Postscript see App. D, p. 542.⟩

[1] See *ante*, v. 215, for his knowledge of coining and brewing, and *post*, v. 263, for his knowledge of threshing and thatching. Now and then, no doubt, ' he talked *ostentatiously*,' as he had at Fort George about gunpowder (*ante*, v. 124).

strangle them. This he told me himself ; and I supposed that their hogs were killed in the same way. Dr. Johnson said, ' This must be owing to their not having knives,—though they have sharp stones with which they can cut a carcase in pieces tolerably.' By degrees, he shewed that he knew something even of butchery. ' Different animals (said he) are killed differently. An ox is knocked down, and a calf stunned ; but a sheep has its throat cut, without any thing being done to stupify it. The butchers have no view to the ease of the animals, but only to make them quiet, for their own safety and convenience. A sheep can give them little trouble.—Hales [1] is of opinion, that every animal should be blooded, without having any blow given to it, because it bleeds better.'—*Boswell.* ' That would be cruel.'—*Johnson.* ' No, sir ; there is not much pain, if the jugular vein be properly cut.'—Pursuing the subject, he said, the kennels of Southwark ran with blood two or three days in the week ; that he was afraid there were slaughter-houses in more streets in London than one supposes ; (speaking with a kind of horrour of butchering ;) and yet,[a] he added, ' any of us would kill a cow, rather than not have beef.'—I said,[b] we *could* not.—' Yes, (said he,) any one may. The business of a butcher is a trade indeed, that is to say, there is an apprenticeship served to it ; but it may be learnt in a month [2].'

I mentioned a club in London, at the Boar's Head in Eastcheap, the very tavern [3] where Falstaff and his joyous companions met ; the members of which all assume Shakspeare's characters. One is Falstaff, another Prince Henry, another Bardolph, and so on.—*Johnson.* ' Don't be of it, sir. Now that you have a name, you must be careful to avoid many things, not bad in themselves, but which will lessen your character [4]. This every man who has a name must observe. A man who is not publickly known may

[a] and, yet 1, 2 3.   [b] said, 1 : said 2, 3.

[1] ⟨Stephen Hales, 1677-1761, whose important experiments on the blood and blood-vessels of animals are described in his *Statical Essays,* vol. ii, 1733. See also *D.N.B.*⟩

[2] Evidence was given at the Tichborne Trial to shew that it takes some years to learn the trade.

[3] Not the very tavern, which was burned down in the great fire. P. CUNNINGHAM. ⟨The house rebuilt on the original site had a stone sign of a *boar's head*, with the date of 1668, let into the wall. CROKER, 1848.⟩

[4] I do not see why I might not have been of this club without lessening my character. But Dr. Johnson's caution against supposing one's self concealed in London, may be very useful to prevent some people from doing many things, not only foolish, but criminal. BOSWELL, ed. 1.

live in London as he pleases, without any notice being taken of him; but it is wonderful how a person of any consequence is watched. There was a member of parliament, who wanted to prepare himself to speak on a question that was to come on in the House; and he and I were to talk it over together. He did not wish it should be known that he talked with me; so he would not let me come to his house, but came to mine. Some time after he had made his speech in the house, Mrs. Cholmondeley [1], a very airy [2] lady, told me, " Well, you could make nothing of him ! " naming the gentleman ; which was a proof that he was watched.—I had once some business to do for government, and I went to Lord North's. Precaution was taken that it should not be known. It was dark before I went ; yet a few days after I was told, " Well, you have been with Lord North." That the door of the prime minister should be watched, is not strange ; but that a member of parliament should be watched, or that my door should be watched, is wonderful.'

We set out this morning,[a] on our way to Talisker, in Ulinish's boat, having taken leave of him and his family. Mr. Donald M'Queen still favoured us with his company, for which we were much obliged to him. As we sailed along Dr. Johnson got into one of his fits of railing at the Scots. He owned that they had been a very learned nation for a hundred years, from about 1550 to about 1650; but that they afforded the only instance of a people among whom the arts of civil life did not advance in proportion with learning ; that they had hardly any trade, any money, or any elegance, before the Union ; that it was strange that, with all the advantages possessed by other nations, they had not any of those conveniencies and embellishments which are the fruit of industry, till they came in contact with a civilized people. ' We have taught you, (said he,) and we'll do the same in time to all barbarous nations,—to the Cherokees,—and at last to the Ouran-Outangs ;' laughing with as much glee as if Monboddo had been present.—*Boswell.* ' We had wine before the Union.'—*Johnson.* ' No, sir ; you had some weak stuff, the refuse of France, which would not make you drunk.'—*Boswell.* ' I assure you, sir, there was a great deal of drunkenness.'

[a] morning, 1, 2 : morning 3.
[1] See *ante*, iii. 318. [2] Johnson defines *airy* as *gay, sprightly, full of mirth,* &c.

Skye: Ulinish *Thursday 23 September* 1773

—*Johnson.* ' No, sir ; there were people who died of dropsies, which they contracted in trying to get drunk [1].'

I must here glean some of his conversation at Ulinish, which I have omitted. He repeated his remark, that a man in a ship was worse than a man in a jail [2]. ' The man in a jail, (said he,) has more room, better food, and commonly better company, and is in safety.'—' Ay ; but, (said Mr. M'Queen,) the man in the ship has the pleasing hope of getting to shore.'—*Johnson.* ' Sir, I am not talking of a man's getting to shore ; but of a man while he is in a ship : and then, I say, he is worse than a man while he is in a jail. A man in a jail *may* have the " *pleasing hope* " of getting out. A man confined for only a limited time, actually *has* it.'—M'Leod mentioned his schemes for carrying on fisheries with spirit, and that he would wish to understand the construction of boats. I suggested that he might go to a dock-yard and work, as Peter the Great did.—*Johnson.* ' Nay, sir, he need not work. Peter the Great had not the sense to see that the mere mechanical work may be done by any body, and that there is the same art in constructing a vessel, whether the boards are well or ill wrought. Sir Christopher Wren might as well have served his time to a bricklayer, and first, indeed, to a brick-maker.'

There is a beautiful little island in the Loch of Dunvegan, called *Isa*. M'Leod said, he would give it to Dr. Johnson, on condition of his residing on it three months in the year ; nay one month. Dr. Johnson was highly amused with the fancy. I have seen him please himself with little things, even with mere ideas like the present. He talked a great deal of this island ;—how he would build a house there,—how he would fortify it,—how he would have cannon,—how he would plant,— how he would sally out, and *take* the isle of Muck ;—and then he laughed with uncommon glee, and could hardly leave off. I have seen him do so at a small matter that struck him, and was a sport to no one else [3]. Mr. Langton told me, that one night he did so while the company [4] were all grave about him :— only Garrick, in his significant smart manner, darting his eyes

---

[1] ' A man would be drowned by claret before it made him drunk.' *Ante*, iii. 381.

[2] *Ante*, v. 137. [3] See *ante*, ii. 261.
[4] ⟨At The Club. Boswell's *Hebrides*, ed. Pottle and Bennett, p. 212.⟩

around, exclaimed, '*Very* jocose, to be sure!' †—M'Leod encouraged the fancy of Dr. Johnson's becoming owner of an island; told him, that it was the practice in this country to name every man by his lands; and begged leave to drink to him in that mode: '*Island Isa,* your health!'—Ulinish, Talisker, Mr. M'Queen, and I, all joined in our different manners, while Dr. Johnson bowed to each, with much good humour.

We had good weather, and a fine sail this day. The shore was varied with hills, and rocks, and corn-fields, and bushes, which are here dignified with the name of natural *wood*. We landed near the house of Ferneley, a farm possessed by another gentleman of the name of M'Leod §, who, expecting our arrival, was waiting on the shore, with a horse for Dr. Johnson. The rest of us walked.—At dinner, I expressed to M'Leod the joy which I had in seeing him on such cordial terms with his clan. 'Government (said he) has deprived us of our ancient power; but it cannot deprive us of our domestick satisfactions. I would rather drink punch in one of their houses, (meaning the houses of his people,) than be enabled,^a by their hardships, to have claret in my own ¹.'—This should be the sentiment of every Chieftain. All that he can get by raising his rents, is more luxury in his own house. Is it not better to share the profits of his estate, to a certain degree, with his kinsmen, and thus have both social intercourse and patriarchal influence?

We had a very good ride, for about three miles, to Talisker, where Colonel M'Leod introduced us to his lady. We found here Mr. Donald M'Lean², the young Laird of *Col,* (nephew to Talisker,) to whom I delivered the letter with which I had

^a enabled, 1 : enabled 2, 3.

†, § ⟨See App. D, pp. 542–3.⟩

¹ Lord Chesterfield wrote in 1747 (*Misc. Works,* ii. 465) :—' Drinking is a most beastly vice in every country, but it is really a ruinous one to Ireland : nine gentlemen in ten in Ireland are impoverished by the great quantity of claret, which from mistaken notions of hospitality and dignity, they think it necessary should be drunk in their houses ; this expence leaves them no room to improve their estates, by proper indulgence upon proper conditions to their tenants, who must pay them to the full, and upon the very day, that they may pay their wine merchants.' In 1754 he wrote (*ib.* p. 561) :—' If it would but please God, by his lightning, to blast all the vines in the world, and by his thunder to turn all the wines now in Ireland sour, as I most sincerely wish he would, Ireland would enjoy a degree of quiet and plenty that it has never yet known.'

² ⟨See App. D, p. 543.⟩

been favoured by his uncle, Professor M'Leod, at Aberdeen [1]. He was a little lively young man. We found he had been a good deal in England, studying farming, and was resolved to improve the value of his father's lands, without oppressing his tenants, or losing the ancient Highland fashions.

Talisker is a better place than one commonly finds in Sky. It is situated in a rich bottom. Before it is a wide expanse of sea, on each hand of which are immense rocks; and, at some distance in the sea, there are three columnal rocks rising to sharp points. The billows break with prodigious force and noise on the coast of Talisker [2]. There are here a good many well-grown trees. Talisker is an extensive farm. The possessor of it has, for several generations, been the next heir to M'Leod, as there has been but one son always in that family. The court before the house is most injudiciously paved with the round blueish-grey pebbles which are found upon the sea-shore; so that you walk as if upon cannon-balls driven into the ground.

After supper, I talked of the assiduity of the Scottish clergy, in visiting and privately instructing their parishioners, and observed how much in this they excelled the English clergy. Dr. Johnson would not let this pass. He tried to turn it off, by saying, ' There are different ways of instructing. Our clergy pray and preach.'—M'Leod and I pressed the subject, upon which he grew warm, and broke forth : ' I do not believe your people are better instructed. If they are, it is the blind leading the blind; for your clergy are not instructed themselves.' Thinking he had gone a little too far, he checked himself, and added, ' When I talk of the ignorance of your clergy, I talk of them as a body : I do not mean that there are not individuals who are learned (looking at Mr. M'Queen [3]). I suppose there

[1] See *ante*, v. 95 ⟨and App. D, p. 496.⟩

[2] 'The sea being broken by the multitude of islands, does not roar with so much noise, nor beat the shore with such foamy violence, as I have remarked on the coast of Sussex. Though, while I was in the Hebrides, the wind was extremely turbulent, I never saw very high billows.' John-son's *Western Isl.*, p. 62.

[3] Johnson about this time thus wrote of Mr. M'Queen to Mrs. Thrale :—' You find that all the Islanders even in these recesses of life are not barbarians. One of the Ministers who has adhered to us almost all the time is an excellent Scholar.' *Letters*, No. 329.

are such among the clergy in Muscovy. The clergy of England have produced the most valuable books in support of religion, both in theory and practice. What have your clergy done, since you sunk into presbyterianism? Can you name one book of any value, on a religious subject, written by them [1]?'
—We were silent.—' I'll help you. Forbes † wrote very well; but I believe he wrote before episcopacy was quite extinguished.' —And then pausing a little, he said, ' Yes, you have Wishart AGAINST Repentance [2].'—*Boswell.* ' But, sir, we are not contending for the superior learning of our clergy, but for their superior assiduity.'—He bore us down again, with thundering against their ignorance, and said to me, ' I see you have not been well taught; for you have not charity.'—He had been in some measure forced into this warmth, by the exulting air which I assumed; for, when he began, he said, ' Since you *will* drive the nail!'—He again thought of good Mr. M'Queen, and, taking him by the hand, said, ' Sir, I did not mean any disrespect to you [3].'

Here I must observe, that he conquered by deserting his ground, and not meeting the argument as I had put it. The assiduity of the Scottish clergy is certainly greater than that of the English. His taking up the topick of their not having so much learning, was, though ingenious, yet a fallacy in logick.

---

[1] See *post*, v. 383.

† ⟨Perhaps, as Carruthers suggests, John Forbes, 1592–1648, Professor of Divinity at King's College, Aberdeen. His *Works* were published in 1702–3.⟩

[2] This was a dexterous mode of description, for the purpose of his argument; for what he alluded to was, a Sermon published by the learned Dr. William Wishart, formerly principal of the college at Edinburgh, to warn men *against* confiding in a death-bed *repentance*, of the inefficacy of which he entertained notions very different from those of Dr. Johnson. BOSWELL, ed. I. ⟨The reference is to Wishart's discourse, 'An Essay on the Indispensible Necessity of a Holy and Good Life', first published in *Discourses on Several Subjects,* 1753.⟩

[3] The Rev. Dr. A. Carlyle (*Auto.* p. 441) thus writes of the English clergy whom he met at Harrogate in 1763:—' I had never seen so many together before, and between this and the following year I was able to form a true judgment of them. They are, in general—I mean the lower order—divided into bucks and prigs; of which the first, though inconceivably ignorant, and sometimes indecent in their morals, yet I held them to be most tolerable, because they were unassuming, and had no other affectation but that of behaving themselves like gentlemen. The other division of them, the prigs, are truly not to be endured, for they are but half learned, are ignorant of the world, narrow-minded, pedantic, and overbearing. And now and then you meet with a *rara avis* who is accomplished and agreeable, a man of the world without licentiousness, of learning without pedantry, and pious without sanctimony; but this *is* a *rara avis.*'

Skye : Talisker *Friday 24 September* 1773

It was as if there should be a dispute whether a man's hair is well dressed, and Dr. Johnson should say, ' Sir, his hair cannot be well dressed ; for he has a dirty shirt. No man who has not clean linen has his hair well dressed.'—When some days † afterwards he read this passage, he said, ' No, sir ; I did not say that a man's hair could not be well dressed because he has not clean linen, but because he is bald.'

He used one argument against the Scottish clergy being learned, which I doubt was not good :[a] ' As we believe a man dead till we know that he is alive ; so we believe men ignorant till we know that they are learned.' Now our maxim in law is, to presume a man alive, till we know he is dead. However, indeed, it may be answered, that we must first know he has lived ; and that we have never known the learning of the Scottish clergy. Mr. M'Queen, though he was of opinion that Dr. Johnson had deserted the point really in dispute, was much pleased with what he said, and owned to me, he thought it very just ; and Mrs. M'Leod was so much captivated by his eloquence, that she told me ' I was a good advocate for a bad cause.'

Friday, 24th September.

This was a good day. Dr. Johnson told us, at breakfast, that he rode harder at a fox-chace[b] than any body [1]. ' The English (said he) are the only nation who ride hard a-hunting. A Frenchman goes out upon a managed [2] horse, and capers in the field, and no more thinks of leaping a hedge than of mounting a breach. Lord Powerscourt laid a wager, in France, that he would ride a great many miles in a certain short time. The French academicians set to work, and calculated that, from the resistance of the air, it was impossible. His lordship however performed it.'

Our money being nearly exhausted, we sent a bill for thirty pounds, drawn on Sir William Forbes and Co.[3] to Lochbracca-

---

[a] good : 1 : good, 2, 3.   [b] fox-chace 1, 2 : fox chace 3.

† ⟨On 3 October at Armadale. Boswell's *Hebrides*, ed. Pottle and Bennett, 1936, p. 245.
[1] See *ante*, i. 446, note 1.
[2] Johnson defines *manage* in this sense *to train a horse to graceful action*, and quotes Young :—' They vault from hunters to the manag'd steed.'
[3] ⟨For the history of Sir William Forbes, James Hunter, & Co., originally Messrs. Coutts & Co., see W. Graham, *The One Pound Note*, 1912, pp. 72 ff., and A. W. Kerr, *Hist. of Banking in Scotland*, 1926, pp. 50 ff.⟩

Friday 24 September 1773

Skye: Talisker

dale, but our messenger † found it very difficult to procure cash for it; at length, however, he got us value from the master of a vessel which was to carry away some emigrants. There is a great scarcity of specie in Sky [1]. Mr. M'Queen said,[a] he had the utmost difficulty to pay his servants' wages, or to pay for any little thing which he has to buy. The rents are paid in bills [2], which the drovers give. The people consume a vast deal of snuff and tobacco, for which they must pay ready money; and pedlars[b], who come about selling goods, as there is not a shop in the island, carry away the cash. If there were encouragement given to fisheries and manufactures, there might be a circulation of money introduced. I got one-and-twenty shillings in silver at Portree, which was thought a wonderful store.

Talisker, Mr. M'Queen, and I, walked out, and looked at no less than fifteen different water-falls near the house, in the space of about a quarter of a mile [3]. We also saw Cuchullin's [c] well, said to have been the favourite spring of that ancient hero. I drank of it. The water is admirable [4]. On the shore are many stones full of crystallizations in the heart.

Though our obliging friend, Mr. M'Lean, was but the young laird, he had the title of *Col* constantly given him. After dinner he and I walked to the top of Prieshwell, a very high rocky hill, from whence there is a view of Barra,—the Long Island,—Bernera,—the Loch of Dunvegan,—part of Rum—part of Rasay, and a vast deal of the isle of Sky. Col, though he had come into Sky with intention [d] to be at Dunvegan, and pass a considerable time in the island, most politely resolved first to conduct us to Mull, and then to return to Sky. This was a very

---

[a] said, 1: said 2, 3. Cuchillin's 2, 3. [b] pedlars 1: pedlers 2, 3. [c] Cuchullin's 1: Cuchillin's 2, 3. [d] intention 1: an intention 2, 3.

† ⟨Donald MacLeod, who got drunk and gave some of the cash away: see App. D, pp. 518–19.⟩

[1] This scarcity of cash still exists on the islands, in several of which five-shilling notes are necessarily issued to have some circulating medium. If you insist on having change, you must purchase something at a shop. WALTER SCOTT, 1831.

[2] 'The payment of rent in kind has been so long disused in England, that it is totally forgotten. It was practised very lately in the Hebrides, and probably still continues, not only in St. Kilda, where money is not yet known, but in others of the smaller and remoter Islands.' Johnson's *Western Isl.*, p. 103.

[3] 'A place where the imagination is more amused cannot easily be found. The Mountains about it are of great height, with waterfalls succeeding one another so fast, that as one ceases to be heard another begins.' *Letters*, No. 329.

[4] ⟨Talisker would drink no other. CARRUTHERS, 1852.⟩

fortunate circumstance; for he planned an expedition for us of more variety than merely going to Mull. He proposed we should see the islands of *Egg*, *Muck*, *Col*, and *Tyr-yi*. In all these islands he could shew us every thing worth seeing; and in Mull he said he should be as if at home, his father having lands there, and he a farm.

Dr. Johnson did not talk much to-day, but seemed intent in listening to the schemes of future excursion, planned by *Col*. Dr. Birch [1], however, being mentioned, he said, he had more anecdotes than any man. I said, Percy had a great many; that he flowed with them, like one of the brooks here.—*Johnson*. ' If Percy is like one of the brooks here, Birch was like the river Thames. Birch excelled Percy in that, as much as Percy excels Goldsmith.'—I mentioned Lord Hailes as a man of anecdote. He was not pleased with him, for publishing only such memorials and letters as were unfavourable for the Stuart family [2]. ' If, (said he,) a man fairly warns you, " I am to give all the ill; do you find the good; " he may: but if the object which he professes be to give a view of a reign, let him tell all the truth. I would tell truth of the two Georges, or of that scoundrel, king William [3].—Granger's Biographical History [4] is full of curious anecdote, but might have been better done. The dog is a Whig. I do not like much to see a Whig in any dress; but I hate to see a Whig in a parson's gown [5].'

Saturday, 25th September.

It was resolved that we should set out, in order to return to Slate, to be in readiness to take boat whenever there should

[1] See *ante*, i. 159.

[2] Johnson seems to be speaking of Hailes's two books *Memorials and Letters Relating to the History of Britain in the Reign of James I*, 1762, and of *Charles I*, 1766. ⟨Hailes also published *The Secret Correspondence of Sir R. Cecil with James I*, 1766.⟩

[3] See *ante*, ii. 341.

[4] See *ante*, iii. 91 ⟨and 484⟩.

[5] ' In all Ages of the World, Priests have been Enemies to Liberty, and 'tis certain, that this steady Conduct of theirs must have been founded on fixt Reasons of Interest and Ambition. Liberty of Thinking, and of expressing our Thoughts, is always fatal to Priestly Power, and to those pious Frauds, on which it is commonly founded. . . . Hence it must happen, that in such a Government as that of Britain, that the establish'd Clergy, while Things are in their natural Situation, will always be of the *Court*-Party; as, on the contrary, Dissenters of all Kinds will be of the *Country*-Party.' Hume's *Essays, Parties of Great-Britain*, 1748, p. 91.

256 *Saturday 25 September 1773* Skye: Talisker
be a fair wind. Dr. Johnson remained in his chamber writing a letter, and it was long before we could get him into motion. He did not come to breakfast, but had it sent to him. When he had finished his letter, it was twelve o'clock, and we should have set out at ten. When I went up to him, he said to me, ' Do you remember a song which begins,

" Every island is a prison [1]
Strongly guarded by the sea ;
Kings and princes, for that reason,
Pris'ners are, as well as we. [a] " '

I suppose he had been thinking of our confined situation [2]. He would fain have gone in a boat from hence, instead of riding back to Slate. A scheme for it was proposed. He said, ' We'll not be driven tamely from it : '—but it proved impracticable.

We took leave of M'Leod and Talisker, from whom we parted with regret. Talisker, having been bred to physick, had a tincture of scholarship in his conversation, which pleased Dr. Johnson, and he had some very good books ; and being a colonel in the Dutch service [3], he and his lady, in consequence of having lived abroad, had introduced the ease and politeness of the continent into this rude region.

Young *Col* was now our leader. Mr. M'Queen was to accompany us half a day more. We stopped at a little hut, where we saw an old woman grinding with the *quern*, the ancient Highland instrument, which it is said was used by the Romans, but which, being very slow in its operation, is almost entirely gone into disuse.

The walls of the cottages in Sky, instead of being one compacted mass of stones, are often formed by two exterior surfaces

[a] we. 1, 2, 3: we? *MS.*

[1] The song begins :—
' Welcome, welcome, brother debtor,
  To this poor, but merry place,
  Where no bailiff, dun, nor setter,
    Dare to shew his frightful face.'
⟨It is printed in *The Charmer*, 1749, p. 269, which Johnson read at Capt. MacLean's in Coll, *post*, v. 313. According to Ritson (*Sel. Collect. Engl. Songs*, 1783, Corrections and Addit. Notes), it was written ' by Mr. Coffey '.⟩ See *ante*, iii. 269.

[2] ⟨The letter that he wrote to Mrs. Thrale is dated 24 Sept. He says⟩ :—
' I am still in Skie. Do you remember the Song ?
  Ev'ry Island is a prison,
  Strongly guarded by the Sea.
We have at one time no boat, and at another may have too much wind.' *Letters*, No. 327.

[3] ⟨See App. D, p. 544.⟩

of stone, filled up with earth in the middle, which makes them very warm. The roof is generally bad. They are thatched, sometimes with straw, sometimes with heath, sometimes with fern. The thatch is secured by ropes of straw, or of heath ; and, to fix the ropes, there is a stone tied to the end of each. These stones hang round the bottom of the roof, and make it look like a lady's hair in papers ; but I should think that, when there is wind, they would come down, and knock people on the head.

We dined at the inn at Sconser [1], where I had the pleasure to find a letter from my wife. Here we parted from our learned companion, Mr. Donald M'Queen. Dr. Johnson took leave of him very affectionately, saying, ' Dear sir, do not forget me ! '—We settled, that he should write an account of the Isle of Sky [2], which Dr. Johnson promised to revise. He said, Mr. M'Queen should tell all that he could ; distinguishing what he himself knew, what was traditional, and what conjectural.

We sent our horses round a point of land, that we might shun some very bad road ; and resolved to go forward by sea. It was seven o'clock when we got into our boat. We had many showers, and it soon grew pretty dark. Dr. Johnson sat silent and patient. Once he said, as he looked on the black coast of Sky,—black, as being composed of rocks seen in the dusk,—' This is very solemn.' Our boatmen were rude singers, and seemed so like wild Indians, that a very little imagination was necessary to give one an impression of being upon an American river. We landed at *Strolimus*, from whence we got a guide to walk before us, for two miles, to *Corrichatachin*. Not being able to procure a horse for our baggage, I took one portmanteau before me, and Joseph another. We had but a single star to light us on our way. It was about eleven when we arrived. We were most hospitably received by the master and mistress [3], who were just going to bed, but, with unaffected ready kindness, made a good fire, and at twelve o'clock at night had supper on the table.

James Macdonald, of *Knockow*, Kingsburgh's brother, whom we had seen at Kingsburgh, was there. He shewed me a bond granted by the late Sir James Macdonald, to old Kingsburgh, the preamble of which does so much honour to the feelings of

---

[1] ⟨The landlord, James Macdonald, had married Mr. M'Queen's daughter. Boswell's *Hebrides*, ed. Pottle and Bennett, 1936, p. 221. See App. D, p. 544.⟩

[2] ⟨See App. D, p. 544.⟩
[3] ⟨For Mr. and Mrs. MacKinnon see *ante*, v. 156, and *post*, App. D, pp. 519–20.⟩

that much-lamented gentleman, that I thought it worth transcribing. It was as follows :

' I, Sir James Macdonald, of Macdonald, Baronet, now, after arriving at my perfect age, from the friendship I bear to Alexander Macdonald of Kingsburgh, and in return for the long and faithful services done and performed by him to my deceased father, and to myself during my minority, when he was one of my Tutors and Curators ; being resolved, now that the said Alexander Macdonald is advanced in years, to contribute my endeavours for making his old age placid and comfortable,'—therefore he grants him an annuity of fifty pounds sterling.

Dr. Johnson went to bed soon. When one bowl of punch was finished, I rose, and was near the door, in my way up stairs to bed ; but Corrichatachin said, it was the first time Col had been in his house, and he should have his bowl ;—and would not I join in drinking it ? The heartiness of my honest landlord, and the desire of doing social honour to our very obliging conductor, induced me to sit down again. *Col's* bowl was finished ; and by that time we were well warmed. A third bowl was soon made, and that too was finished. We were cordial, and merry to a high degree ; but of what passed I have no recollection, with any accuracy. I remember calling *Corrichatachin* by the familiar appellation of *Corri*, which his friends do [1]. A fourth bowl was made, by which time Col, and young M'Kinnon, Corrichatachin's son, slipped away to bed. I continued a little with *Corri* and *Knockow* ; but at last I left them. It was near five in the morning when I got to bed.

Sunday, 26th September.

I awaked at noon, with a severe head-ach. I was much vexed that I should have been guilty of such a riot, and afraid of a reproof from Dr. Johnson. I thought it very inconsistent with that conduct which I ought to maintain, while the companion of the *Rambler*. About one he came into my room, and accosted me, ' What, drunk yet ? '—His tone of voice was not that of severe upbraiding ; so I was relieved a little.—' Sir, (said I,) they kept me up.'—He answered, ' No, you kept them up, you drunken dog : '—This he said with good-humoured English pleasantry. Soon afterwards, Corrichatachin, Col, and other

[1] ⟨This is now the universal practice ; Corrichatachin has, both in speech and writing, been commuted into Corry. CARRUTHERS, 1852.⟩

Skye: Corrichatachin *Sunday 26 Sept.* 1773

friends assembled round my bed. *Corri* had a brandy-bottle and glass with him, and insisted I should take a dram.—' Ay, said Dr. Johnson, fill him drunk again. Do it in the morning, that we may laugh at him all day. It is a poor thing for a fellow to get drunk at night, and sculk to bed, and let his friends have no sport.'—Finding him thus jocular, I became quite easy; and when I offered to get up, he very good-naturedly said, ' You need be in no such hurry now [1].'—I took my host's advice, and drank some brandy, which I found an effectual cure for my head-ach. When I rose, I went into Dr. Johnson's room, and taking up Mrs. M'Kinnon's Prayer-book, I opened it at the twentieth Sunday after Trinity, in the epistle for which I read, ' And be not drunk with wine, wherein there is excess [2].' Some would have taken this as a divine interposition.

Mrs. M'Kinnon told us at dinner, that old Kingsburgh, her father, was examined at Mugstot, by General Campbell [3], as to the particulars of the dress of the person who had come to his house in woman's clothes, along with Miss Flora M'Donald; as the General had received intelligence of that disguise. The particulars were taken down in writing, that it might be seen how far they agreed with the dress of the *Irish girl* who went with Miss Flora from the Long Island. Kingsburgh, she said, had but one song, which he always sung when he was merry over a glass. She dictated the words to me, which are foolish enough:

[1] My ingenuously relating this occasional instance of intemperance has I find been made the subject both of serious criticism and ludicrous banter. With the banterers I shall not trouble myself, but I wonder that those who pretend to the appellation of serious criticks should not have had sagacity enough to perceive that here, as in every other part of the present work, my principal object was to delineate Dr. Johnson's manners and character. In justice to him I would not omit an anecdote, which, though in some degree to my own disadvantage, exhibits in so strong a light the indulgence and good humour with which he could treat those excesses in his friends, of which he highly disapproved.

In some other instances, the criticks have been equally wrong as to the true motive of my recording particulars, the objections to which I saw as clearly as they. But it would be an endless task for an authour to point out upon every occasion the precise object he has in view. Contenting himself with the approbation of readers of discernment and taste, he ought not to complain that some are found who cannot or will not understand him. BOSWELL, ed. 3. ⟨Peter Pindar was one of the banterers, see *post*, v. 415 n. 4 and App. D, p. 544.⟩

[2] In the original, ' wherein is excess.'

[3] ⟨See App. D, p. 544.⟩

Monday 27 Sept. 1773   Skye : Corrichatachin

> Green sleeves [1] and pudding pies,
> Tell me where my mistress lies,
> And I'll be with her before she rise,
> Fiddle and aw' together.
> May our affairs abroad succeed,
> And may our king come home with speed,
> And all pretenders shake for dread,
> And let *his* health go round.
> To all our injured friends in need,
> This side and beyond the Tweed !—
> Let all pretenders shake for dread,
> And let *his* health go round.
> Green sleeves, &c.

While the examination was going on, the present Talisker, who was there as one of M'Leod's militia, could not resist the pleasantry of asking Kingsburgh, in allusion to his only song, ' Had she *green sleeves?* ' Kingsburgh gave him no answer. Lady Margaret M'Donald was very angry at Talisker for joking on such a serious occasion, as Kingsburgh was really in danger of his life †.—Mrs. M'Kinnon added that Lady Margaret was quite adored in Sky. That when she travelled through the island, the people ran in crowds before her, and took the stones off the road, lest her horse should stumble and she be hurt [2]. Her husband, Sir Alexander, is also remembered with great regard. We were told that every week a hogshead of claret was drunk at his table.

This was another day of wind and rain ; but good cheer and good society helped to beguile the time. I felt myself comfortable enough in the afternoon. I then thought that my last night's riot was no more than such a social excess as may happen without much moral blame ; and recollected that some physicians maintained, that a fever produced by it was, upon the whole, good for health : so different are our reflections on the same subject, at different periods ; and such the excuses with which we palliate what we know to be wrong.

Monday, 27th September.

Mr. Donald M'Leod [3], our original guide, who had parted from us at Dunvegan, joined us again to-day. The weather was still

---

[1] See Chappell's *Popular Music of the Olden Time*, i. 231.
† ⟨See App. D, p. 545.⟩
[2] See *ante*, iii. 383.
[3] ⟨See *ante*, v. 156, and *post*, App. D. pp. 518–19.⟩

so bad that we could not travel. I found a closet here, with a good many books, beside those that were lying about. Dr. Johnson told me, he found a library in his room at Talisker; and observed, that it was one of the remarkable things of Sky, that there were so many books in it.

Though we had here great abundance of provisions, it is remarkable that Corrichatachin has literally no garden: not even a turnip, a carrot or a cabbage.—After dinner, we talked of the crooked spade used in Sky, already described †, and they maintained that it was better than the usual garden-spade, and that there was an art in tossing it, by which those who were accustomed to it could work very easily with it.—' Nay, (said Dr. Johnson,) it may be useful in land where there are many stones to raise; but it certainly is not a good instrument for digging good land. A man may toss it, to be sure; but he will toss a light spade much better: its weight makes it an incumbrance. A man *may* dig any land with it; but he has no occasion for such a weight in digging good land. You may take a field-piece to shoot sparrows; but all the sparrows you can bring home will not be worth the charge.'—He was quite social and easy amongst them; and, though he drank no fermented liquor, toasted Highland beauties with great readiness. His conviviality engaged them so much, that they seemed eager to shew their attention to him, and vied with each other in crying out, with a strong Celtick pronunciation, ' Toctor Shonson, Toctor Shonson, your health!'

This evening one of our married ladies, a lively pretty little woman, good-humouredly sat down upon Dr. Johnson's knee, and, being encouraged by some of the company, put her hands round his neck, and kissed him.—' Do it again, (said he,) and let us see who will tire first.'—He kept her on his knee some time, while he and she drank tea. He was now like a *buck* [1] indeed. All the company were much entertained to find him so easy and pleasant. To me it was highly comick, to see the grave philosopher,—the Rambler,—toying with a Highland beauty [2]!——But what could he do? He must have been surly,

† ⟨*Ante*, v. 235.⟩
[1] See *ante*, v. 184.
[2] See *ante*, ii. 120, where he took upon his knee a young woman who came to consult him on the subject of Methodism. ⟨The Highland lady was the wife of Dr. Alexander Macdonald of Gillen: see App. D, p. 545.⟩

and weak too, had he not behaved as he did. He would have been laughed at, and not more respected, though less loved.

He read to-night, to himself, as he sat in company, a great deal of my Journal, and said to me, ' The more I read of this, I think the more highly of you [1].'—The gentlemen sat a long time at their punch, after he and I had retired to our chambers. The manner in which they were attended struck me as singular :— The bell being broken, a smart lad lay on a table in the corner of the room, ready to spring up and bring the kettle, whenever it was wanted. They continued drinking, and singing Erse songs, till near five in the morning, when they all came into my room, where some of them had beds. Unluckily for me, they found a bottle of punch in a corner, which they drank ; and Corrichatachin went for another, which they also drank. They made many apologies for disturbing me. I told them, that, having been kept awake by their mirth, I had once thoughts of getting up, and joining them again. Honest Corrichatachin said, ' To have had you done so, I would have given a cow.'

Tuesday, 28th September.

The weather was worse than yesterday. I felt as if imprisoned. Dr. Johnson said, it was irksome to be detained thus: yet he seemed to have less uneasiness, or more patience, than I had. What made our situation worse here was, that we had no rooms that we could command ; for the good people had no notion that a man could have any occasion but for a mere sleeping-place ; so, during the day, the bed-chambers were common to all the house. Servants eat in Dr. Johnson's ; and mine was a kind of general rendezvous of all under the roof, children and dogs not excepted. As the gentlemen occupied the parlour, the ladies had no place to sit in, during the day, but Dr. Johnson's room [2]. I had always some quiet time for writing in it, before he was up ; and, by degrees, I accustomed the ladies to let me sit in it after breakfast, at my Journal, without minding me.

Dr. Johnson was this morning for going to see as many islands as we could ; not recollecting the uncertainty of the season, which might detain us in one place for many weeks. He said to me, ' I have more the spirit of adventure than you.'

[1] ⟨Boswell queried ' Are you in earnest ? ' Said he, ' It is true, whether I am in earnest or no. ' Boswell's *Hebrides*, ed. Pottle and Bennett, 1936, p. 226.⟩
[2] ⟨See Johnson's *Letters*, No. 329.⟩

—For my part, I was anxious to get to Mull, from whence we might almost any day reach the main land.

Dr. Johnson mentioned, that the few ancient Irish gentlemen yet remaining have the highest pride of family; that Mr. Sandford, a friend of his, whose mother was Irish, told him, that O'Hara (who was true Irish, both by father and mother) and he, and Mr. Ponsonby, son to the Earl of Besborough, the greatest man of the three, but of an English family, went to see one of those ancient Irish, and that he distinguished them thus: ' O'Hara, you are welcome ! Mr. Sandford, your mother's son is welcome ! Mr. Ponsonby, you may sit down †.'

He talked both of threshing and thatching. He said, it was very difficult to determine how to agree with a thresher. ' If you pay him by the day's wages, he will thresh no more than he pleases; though, to be sure, the negligence of a thresher is more easily detected than that of most labourers, because he must always make a sound while he works. If you pay him by the piece, by the quantity of grain which he produces, he will thresh only while the grain comes freely, and, though he leaves a good deal in the ear, it is not worth while to thresh the straw over again; nor can you fix him to do it sufficiently, because it is so difficult to prove how much less a man threshes than he ought to do. Here then is a dilemma: but, for my part, I would engage him by the day; I would rather trust his idleness than his fraud.' He said, a roof thatched with Lincolnshire reeds would last seventy years, as he was informed when in that county; and that he told this in London to a great thatcher, who said, he believed it might be true.—Such are the pains that Dr. Johnson takes to get the best information on every subject [1].

He proceeded: ' It is difficult for a farmer in England to find day-labourers, because the lowest manufacturers can always get more than a day-labourer. It is of no consequence how high the wages of manufacturers are; but it would be of very bad consequence to raise the wages of those who procure the immediate necessaries of life, for that would raise the price of provisions. Here then is a problem for politicians. It is not reasonable that the most useful body of men should be the

† ⟨See App. D, p. 545, for another version of this anecdote.⟩
[1] See *ante*, v. 215, 246.

worst paid; yet it does not appear how it can be ordered otherwise. It were to be wished, that a mode for its being otherwise were found out. In the mean time, it is better to give temporary assistance by charitable contributions to poor labourers, at times when provisions are high, than to raise their wages; because, if wages are once raised, they will never get down again [1].'

Happily the weather cleared up between one and two o'clock, and we got ready to depart; but our kind host and hostess would not let us go without taking a *snatch*, as they called it; which was in truth a very good dinner. While the punch went round, Dr. Johnson kept a close whispering conference with Mrs. M'Kinnon, which, however, was loud enough to let us hear that the subject of it was the particulars of Prince Charles's escape. The company were entertained and pleased to observe it. Upon that subject, there was something congenial between the soul of Dr. Samuel Johnson, and that of an isle of Sky farmer's wife. It is curious to see people, how far so ever removed from each other in the general system of their lives, come close together on a particular point which is common to each. We were merry with Corrichatachin, on Dr. Johnson's whispering with his wife. She, perceiving this, humourously cried, ' I am in love with him. What is it to live and not to love?' Upon her saying something, which I did not hear, or cannot recollect, he seized her hand eagerly, and kissed it.

As we were going, the Scottish phrase of ' *honest man !* ' which is an expression of kindness and regard, was again and again applied by the company to Dr. Johnson. I was also treated with much civility; and I must take some merit from my assiduous attention to him, and from my contriving that he shall be easy wherever he goes, that he shall not be asked twice to eat or drink any thing, (which always disgusts him,[2]) that he shall be provided with water at his meals, and many such little things, which, if not attended to, would fret him. I also may be allowed to claim some merit in leading the conversation: I do not mean leading, as in an orchestra, by playing the first fiddle; but leading as one does in examining a witness,—starting topicks, and making him pursue them. He appears to me like a great

---

[1] See *ante*, iv. 176.   [2] ⟨See App. D, p. 545.⟩

mill, into which a subject is thrown to be ground. It requires, indeed, fertile minds to furnish materials for this mill. I regret whenever I see it unemployed ; but sometimes I feel myself quite barren, and have [a] nothing to throw in.—I know not if this mill be a good figure ; though Pope makes his mind a mill for turning verses [1].

We set out about four. Young Corrichatachin went with us. We had a fine evening, and arrived in good time at *Ostig*, the residence of Mr. Martin M'Pherson, minister of Slate. It is a pretty good house, built by his father, upon a farm near the church. We were received here with much kindness by Mr. and Mrs. M'Pherson, and his sister, Miss M'Pherson, who pleased Dr. Johnson much, by singing Erse songs, and playing on the guittar. He afterwards sent her a present of his *Rasselas*. In his bed-chamber was a press stored with books, Greek, Latin, French, and English, most of which had belonged to the father of our host, the learned Dr. M'Pherson ; who, though his *Dissertations* have been mentioned in a former page [2] as unsatisfactory, was a man of distinguished talents †. Dr. Johnson looked at a Latin paraphrase of the song of Moses, written by him, and published in the *Scots Magazine* for 1747, and said, ' It does him honour ; he has a great deal of Latin, and good Latin.'—Dr. M'Pherson published also in the same magazine §, June 1739, an original Latin ode, which he wrote from the isle of Barra, where he was minister for some years. It is very poetical, and exhibits a striking proof how much all things depend upon comparison : for Barra, it seems, appeared to him so much worse than Sky, his *natale solum* [3], that he languished for its ' blessed mountains,' and thought himself buried alive amongst barbarians where he was—My readers will probably not be displeased to have a specimen of this ode :

> ' Hei mihi ! quantos patior dolores,
> Dum procul specto juga ter beata ;
> Dum feræ Barræ steriles arenas
>   Solus oberro.

[a] have 1 (*MS.*): having 2, 3.

[1] ' If ev'ry wheel of that unweary'd Mill
That turn'd ten thousand verses, now stands still.'
Imitations of Horace, 2 *Epis*. ii. 78.
[2] *Ante*, v. 206.

† ⟨See App. D, pp. 546–7, for the Macphersons.⟩
§ ⟨Vol. 1, p. 273.⟩
[3] ' Nescio qua natale solum dulcedine cunctos
Ducit.'—Ovid, *Ex Ponto*, i. 3. 35.

'Ingemo, indignor, crucior, quod inter
Barbaros Thulen lateam colentes ;
Torpeo languens, morior sepultus,
Carcere cœco.'

After wishing for wings to fly over to his dear country, which was in his view, from what he calls *Thule*, as being the most western isle of Scotland, except St. Kilda ; after describing the pleasures of society, and the miseries of solitude, he at last, with becoming propriety, has recourse to the only sure relief of thinking men,—*Sursum corda*,[1]—the hope of a better world, and disposes his mind to resignation :

'Interim fiat, tua, rex, voluntas :
Erigor sursum quoties subit spes
Certa migrandi Solymam supernam,
Numinis aulam.'

He concludes in a noble strain of orthodox piety :

'Vita tum demum vocitanda vita est,
Tum licet gratos socios habere,
Seraphim et sanctos TRIADEM verendam
Concelebrantes.'

Wednesday, 29th September [2].

After a very good sleep, I rose more refreshed than I had

[1] Lift up your hearts.
[2] ⟨There is preserved at Dunvegan the following letter written to Macleod the day before : it was first printed by Croker, 1831.⟩

'DEAR SIR,

'We are now on the margin of the Sea, waiting for a boat and a wind. Boswel grows impatient, but the kind treatment which I find wherever I go, makes me leave with some heaviness of heart an Island which I am not very likely to see again. Having now gone as far as horses can carry us, we thankfully return them. My Steed will, I hope, be received with kindness ; he has born me, heavy as I am, over ground both rough and steep with great fidelity, and for the use of him, as for your other favours, I hope you will believe me thankful, and willing, at whatever distance we may be placed, to show my sense of your kindness by any offices of friendship that may fall within my power.

'Lady Macleod and the young Ladies have by their hospitality and politeness made an impression on my mind which will not easily be effaced. Be pleased to tell them that I remember them with great tenderness and great respect.

'I am, Sir, Your most obliged and most humble servant,
              'SAM: JOHNSON.

'We passed two days at Talisker very happily, both by the pleasantness of the place, and elegance of our reception.'

'Ostig, Sept. 28. 1773.'

been for some nights. We were now at but a little distance from the shore, and saw the sea from our windows, which made our voyage seem nearer. Mr. M'Pherson's manners and address pleased us much. He appeared to be a man of such intelligence and taste as to be sensible of the extraordinary powers of his illustrious guest. He said to me, ' Dr. Johnson is an honour to mankind; and, if the expression may be used, is an honour to religion.'

Col, who had gone yesterday to pay a visit at Camuscross, joined us this morning at breakfast. Some other gentlemen also came to enjoy the entertainment of Dr. Johnson's conversation.—The day was windy and rainy, so that we had just seized a happy interval for our journey last night. We had good entertainment here, better accommodation than at Corrichatachin, and time enough to ourselves. The hours slipped along imperceptibly. We talked of Shenstone. Dr. Johnson said, he was a good layer-out of land [1], but would not allow him to approach excellence as a poet [†]. He said, he believed he had tried to read all his Love Pastorals, but did not get through them. I repeated the stanza,

> She gazed [a] as I slowly withdrew ;
> My path I could hardly discern ;
> So sweetly she bade me adieu,
> I thought that she bade me return [2].

He said, ' That seems to be pretty.' I observed that Shenstone, from his short maxims in prose, appeared to have some power of thinking ; but Dr. Johnson would not allow him that merit [3].

[a] gaz'd, *Pastoral Ballad*, pt. 1, stanza 5.

[1] Johnson (*Shenstone*, 10), after describing how Shenstone laid out the Leasowes, continues :—' Whether to plant a walk in undulating curves, and to place a bench at every turn where there is an object to catch the view ; to make water run where it will be heard, and to stagnate where it will be seen ; to leave intervals where the eye will be pleased, and to thicken the plantation where there is something to be hidden, demands any great powers of mind, I will not enquire : perhaps a sullen and surly speculator may think such performances rather the sport than the business of human reason.'

[†] ⟨See *ante*, i, App. G, p. 555.⟩

[2] Johnson quotes this and the two preceding stanzas as ' passages, to which if any mind denies its sympathy, it has no acquaintance with love or nature.' *Shenstone*, 26.

[3] ' His mind was not very comprehensive, nor his curiosity active ; he had no value for those parts of knowledge which he had not himself cultivated.' *Ib.* 17.

He agreed, however, with Shenstone, that it was wrong in the brother of one of his correspondents to burn his letters [1]; 'for, (said he,) Shenstone was a man whose correspondence was an honour.'—He was this afternoon full of critical severity, and dealt about his censures on all sides.† He said, Hammond's Love Elegies were poor things [2]. He spoke contemptuously of our lively and elegant, though too licentious, Lyrick bard, Hanbury Williams, and said, 'he had no fame, but from boys who drank with him [3].'

While he was in this mood, I was unfortunate enough, simply perhaps, but I could not help thinking, undeservedly, to come within 'the whiff and wind of his fell sword [4].' I asked him, if he had ever been accustomed to wear a night-cap [5]. He said 'No.' I asked, if it was best not to wear one.—*Johnson.* 'Sir, I had this custom by chance; and perhaps no man shall ever know whether it is best to sleep with or without a night-cap.' —Soon afterwards he was laughing at some deficiency in the Highlands, and said, 'One might as well go without shoes and stockings.'—Thinking to have a little hit at his own deficiency, I ventured to add,——' or without a night-cap, sir.' But I had better have been silent; for he retorted directly. 'I do not see the connection there (laughing). Nobody before was ever foolish enough to ask whether it was best to wear a night-cap or not. This comes of being a little wrong-headed.'—He carried the

---

[1] In the Preface to vol. iii. of Shenstone's *Works*, ed. 1769, a quotation is given (p. vii) from one of the poet's letters in which he complains of this burning. He writes :—' I look upon my Letters as some of my *chef-d'œuvres.*' On p. 340, after mentioning *Rasselas*, he continues :— ' Did I tell you I had a letter from Johnson, inclosing Vernon's *Parish-clerk* ? ' ⟨It was John Whistler who destroyed Shenstone's letters to his brother Anthony.⟩

† ⟨One of the victims was Garrick : see App. D, p. 548.⟩

[2] ' The truth is these elegies have neither passion, nature, nor manners. Where there is fiction, there is no passion : he that describes himself as a shepherd, and his Neæra or Delia as a shepherdess, and talks of goats and lambs, feels no passion. He that courts his mistress with Roman imagery deserves to lose her ; for she may with good reason suspect his sincerity.' Johnson's *Hammond*, 6. See *ante*, iv. 17.

[3] ⟨Johnson, according to Boswell's *Hebrides* (1936, p. 233), called him ' a wretched Scribbler '.⟩ His lines on Pulteney still deserve some fame :—
' Leave a blank here and there in each page,
To enrol the fair deeds of his youth !
When you mention the acts of his age,
Leave a blank for his honour and truth ! '
From *The Statesman*, H. C. Williams's *Odes*, p. 47. ⟨See the Earl of Ilchester and Mrs. Langford-Brooke's *Life* (1928).⟩

[4] *Hamlet*, act ii. sc. 2.

[5] ⟨See *ante*, i. 250.⟩

Skye: Ostaig *Thursday 30 September* 1773

company along with him: and yet the truth is, that if he had always worn a night-cap, as is the common practice, and found the Highlanders did not wear one, he would have wondered at their barbarity; so that my hit was fair enough.

Thursday, 30th September.

There was as great a storm of wind and rain as I have almost ever seen, which necessarily confined us to the house; but we were fully compensated by Dr. Johnson's conversation. He said, he did not grudge Burke's being the first man in the House of Commons, for he was the first man every where; but he grudged that a fellow who makes no figure in company, and has a mind as narrow as the neck of a vinegar cruet, should make a figure in the House of Commons, merely by having the knowledge of a few forms, and being furnished with a little occasional information [1]. He told us, the first time he saw Dr. Young was at the house of Mr. Richardson, the author of *Clarissa*. He was sent for, that the doctor might read to him his *Conjectures on original Composition* [2], which he did, and Dr. Johnson made his remarks; and he was surprized to find Young receive as novelties, what he thought very common maxims. He said, he believed Young was not a great scholar, nor had studied regularly the art of writing [3]; that there were

[1] He did not mention the name of any particular person; but those who are conversant with the political world will probably recollect more persons than one to whom this observation may be applied. BOSWELL, ed. 1. Croker thinks that Lord North was meant. For his ministry Johnson certainly came to have a great contempt (*ante*, iv. 139). If Johnson was thinking of him, he differed widely in opinion from Gibbon, who describes North as 'a consummate master of debate, who could wield, with equal dexterity, the arms of reason and of ridicule.' Gibbon's *Memoirs*, 1900, p. 192.

[2] ⟨*Conjectures on Original Composition; in a Letter to the Author of Sir Charles Grandison*, published in May 1759. Richardson, to whom Young had submitted the manuscript, wrote to him soon after its publication 24 May:—' Mr. Johnson is much pleased with it: he made a few observations on some passages, which I encouraged him to commit to paper, and which he promised to do, and send to you.' Young replied the next day:—' I shall not send a copy till I have the pleasure of Mr. Johnson's letter on the points he spoke of to you; and please to let him know that I impatiently wait for it.' Richardson did as he was bid, but from an undated note of Young it appears that Johnson's remarks never reached him:—' It was very kind in you to send to Mr. Johnson's; and unfortunate to me that you sent in vain.' See *Modern Philology*, xxii. 403-4.⟩

[3] ' His [Young's] plan seems to

very fine things in his *Night Thoughts*[1], though you could not find twenty lines together without some extravagance. He repeated two passages from his *Love of Fame*,—the characters of Brunetta[2] and Stella[3], which he praised highly. He said Young pressed him much to come to Wellwyn. He always intended it, but never went[4]. He was sorry when Young died. The cause of quarrel between Young and his son, he told us, was, that his son insisted Young should turn away a clergyman's

have started in his mind at the present moment, and his thoughts appear the effects of chance, sometimes adverse, and sometimes lucky, with very little operation of judgement. . . . His verses are formed by no certain model; for he is no more like himself in his different productions than he is like others. He seems never to have studied prosody, nor to have had any direction but from his own ear. But, with all his defects, he was a man of genius and a poet.' Johnson's *Young*, 154 and 168. Mrs. Piozzi (*Synonymy*, ii. 371) tells why 'Dr. Johnson despised Young's quantity of common knowledge as comparatively small. 'Twas only because speaking once upon the subject of metrical composition, [he] seemed totally ignorant of what are called . . . rhopalick verses.'

[1] He had said this before. *Ante*, ii. 96.

[2] ' Brunetta's wise in actions great, and rare ;
But scorns on trifles to bestow her care.
Thus ev'ry hour Brunetta is to blame,
Because th' occasion is beneath her aim.
Think nought a trifle, though it small appear ;
Small sands the mountains, moments make the year ;
And trifles life. Your care to trifles give,

Or you may die, before you truly live.'
Love of Fame, Satire vi. 201 ff.
Johnson often taught that life is made up of trifles. See *ante*, i. 433.

[3] ' But hold, she cries, lampooner ! have a care ;
Must I want common sense, because I'm fair ?
O no : see Stella ; her eyes shine as bright,
As if her tongue was never in the right ;
And yet what real learning, judgment, fire !
She seems inspir'd, and can herself inspire :
How then (if malice rul'd not all the fair)
Could Daphne publish, and could she forbear ?
We grant that beauty is no bar to sense,
Nor is't a sanction for impertinence.'
Love of Fame, Satire v. 145 ff.

[4] Johnson called on Young's son at Welwyn in June, 1781. *Ante*, iv. 120 ⟨and 493⟩. Croft, in his *Life of Young* (Johnson's *Young*, 132), says that ' Young and his housekeeper were ridiculed, with more ill-nature than wit, in a kind of novel published by Kidgell in 1755, called *The Card*, under the names of Dr. Elwes and Mrs. Fusby.' ⟨See App. D, p. 548.⟩

widow, who lived with him, and who, having acquired great influence over the father, was saucy to the son. Dr. Johnson said, she could not conceal her resentment at him, for saying to Young, that 'an old man should not resign himself to the management of any body.'—I asked him, if there was any improper connection between them.—'No, sir, no more than between two statues.—He was past fourscore, and she a very coarse woman. She read to him, and, I suppose, made his coffee, and frothed his chocolate, and did such things as an old man wishes to have done for him.'

Dr. Dodridge being mentioned, he observed that 'he was author of one of the finest epigrams in the English language. It is in Orton's Life of him [1]. The subject is his family-motto, —*Dum vivimus, vivamus*; which, in its primary signification, is, to be sure, not very suitable to a Christian divine; but he paraphrased it thus:

> " Live, while you live, the *epicure* would say,
> And seize the pleasures of the present day.
> Live, while you live, the sacred *preacher* cries,
> And give to GOD each moment as it flies.
> Lord, in my views let both united be;
> I live in *pleasure*, when I live to *thee*." '

I asked,[a] if it was not strange that government should permit so many infidel writings to pass without censure.—*Johnson*. 'Sir, it is mighty foolish. It is for want of knowing their own power. The present family on the throne came to the crown against the will of nine tenths of the people [2]. Whether those nine tenths were right or wrong, it is not our business now to inquire. But such being the situation of the royal family, they were glad to encourage all who would be their friends. Now you know every bad man is a Whig [3]; every man who has loose notions. The church was all against this family. They were, as I say, glad to encourage any friends; and therefore, since their accession, there is no instance of any man being kept back on account of his bad principles; and hence this inundation

[a] asked, 1: asked 2, 3.

[1] *Memoirs of Philip Doddridge* [By Job Orton], 1766, p. 171.
[2] So late as 1783 he said 'this Hanoverian family is *isolée* here.' *Ante*, iv. 165.
[3] ⟨See *ante*, i. 431.⟩

of impiety [1].' I observed that Mr. Hume, some of whose writings were very unfavourable to religion, was, however, a Tory.—*Johnson*. ' Sir, Hume is a Tory by chance [2], as being a Scotchman ; but not upon a principle of duty ; for he has no principle. If he is any thing, he is a Hobbist.'

There was something not quite serene in his humour to-night, after supper ; for he spoke of hastening away to London, without stopping much at Edinburgh. I reminded him, that he had General Oughton and many others to see.—*Johnson*. ' Nay, I shall neither go in jest, nor stay in jest. I shall do what is fit.'—*Boswell*. ' Ay, sir, but all I desire is, that you will let me tell you when it is fit.'—*Johnson*. ' Sir, I shall not consult you.'—*Boswell*. ' If you are to run away from us, as soon as you get loose, we will keep you confined in an island.' He was, however, on the whole, very good company. Mr. Donald M'Leod expressed very well the gradual impression made by Dr. Johnson on those who are so fortunate as to obtain his acquaintance. ' When you see him first, you are struck with awful reverence ; —then you admire him ;—and then you love him cordially.'

I read this evening some part of Voltaire's History of the War in 1741 [3], and of Lord Kames against Hereditary Indefeasible Right †. This is a very slight circumstance, with which I should not trouble my reader, but for the sake of observing, that every man should keep minutes of whatever he reads. Every circumstance of his studies should be recorded ; what books he has consulted ; how much of them he has read ; at what times ; how often the same authors ; and what opinions he formed of them, at different periods of his life.—Such an account would much illustrate the history of his mind [4].

[1] Cf. *ante*, ii. 81 : ' Sir, this gloom of infidelity, I hope, is only a transient cloud.'

[2] Boswell has recorded this saying, *ante*, iv. 194. ⟨He repeated it to Hume when he was dying. *Boswell Papers*, xii. 231.⟩

[3] ⟨Voltaire's *Hist. de la guerre de 1741* was first published in 1756 and there was an English version in the same year. *Gent. Mag.*, Dec. 1755, p. 574. For the history of this work and its close connexion with Voltaire's *Essai sur les mœurs* and his *Précis du Siècle de Louis XV*, see *Œuvres*, 1878, xv, pp. 145 ff.⟩

† ⟨' The hereditary and indefeasible Right of Kings ', printed as an Appendix to *Essays upon several Subjects*, 1747.⟩

[4] Boswell is here merely repeating Johnson's words, who on April 11 of this year, advising him to keep a journal, had said, ' The great thing to be recorded is the state of your own mind.' *Ante*, ii. 217.

Skye : Ostaig   *Friday 1 October 1773*   273

Friday, 1st October.

I shewed to Dr. Johnson verses in a magazine, on his Dictionary, composed of uncommon words taken from it:
'Little of *Anthropopathy* [1] has he,' &c.
He read a few of them, and said, ' I am not answerable for all the words in my Dictionary.'—I told him, that Garrick kept a book of all who had either praised or abused him.—On the subject of his own reputation, he said, ' Now that I see it has been so current a topick, I wish I had done so too ; but it could not well be done now, as so many things are scattered in news-papers.'—He said he was angry at a boy of Oxford, who wrote in his defence against Kenrick ; because it was doing him hurt to answer Kenrick. He was told afterwards, the boy was to come to him to ask a favour. He first thought to treat him rudely, on account of his meddling in that business ; but then he considered, he had meant to do him all the service in his power, and he took another resolution ; he told him he would do what he could for him, and did so ; and the boy was satisfied. He said, he did not know how his pamphlet was done, as he had read very little of it. The boy made a good figure at Oxford, but died [2]. He remarked, that attacks on authors did them much service. ' A man who tells me my play is very bad, is less my enemy than he who lets it die in silence. A man, whose business it is to be talked of, is much helped by being attacked [3].'
—Garrick, I observed, had been often so helped.—*Johnson.* ' Yes, sir ; though Garrick had more opportunities than almost any man, to keep the publick in mind of him, by exhibiting himself to such numbers, he would not have had so much reputation, had he not been so much attacked. Every attack produces a defence ; and so attention is engaged. There is no sport in mere praise, when people are all of a mind.'—*Boswell.* ' Then Hume is not the worse for Beattie's attack [4] ?'—*Johnson.* ' He

---

[1] ⟨Johnson entered this word in the fourth edition of his *Dictionary*. The verses are by John Maclaurin (*ante*, ii. 363, v. 48) and are included in his *Works* (1798, i. 29).⟩

[2] ⟨The boy was James Barclay : see *ante*, i. 498, 556, and *post*, App. D, pp. 549-50.⟩

[3] See *ante*, ii. 61, 335 ; iii. 375, and *post*, v. 400.

[4] Beattie had attacked Hume in his *Essay on Truth* (*ante*, ii. 201 and v. 29). Reynolds this autumn had painted Beattie in his gown of an Oxford Doctor of Civil Law, with his *Essay* under his arm. ' The angel of Truth is going before him, and beating down the Vices, Envy,

2754·5   T

is, because Beattie has confuted him. I do not say, but that there may be some attacks which will hurt an author. Though Hume suffered from Beattie, he was the better for other attacks.' (He certainly could not include in that number those of Dr. Adams [1], and Mr. Tytler [2].)—*Boswell.* ' Goldsmith is the better for attacks.'—*Johnson.* ' Yes, sir ; but he does not think so yet. When Goldsmith and I published, each of us something, at the same time [3], we were given to understand that we might review each other. Goldsmith was for accepting the offer. I said, No ; set Reviewers at defiance.—It was said to old Bentley, upon the attacks against him, " Why, they'll write you down." " No, sir, he replied ; depend upon it, no man was ever written down but by himself [4]." ' He observed to me afterwards, that the advantages

Falsehood, &c. which are represented by a group of figures falling at his approach, and the principal head in this group is made an exact likeness of Voltaire. When Dr. Goldsmith saw this picture, he was very indignant at it, saying :—" It very ill becomes a man of your eminence and character, Sir Joshua, to condescend to be a mean flatterer, or to wish to degrade so high a genius as Voltaire before so mean a writer as Dr. Beattie ; for Dr. Beattie and his book together will, in the space of ten years, not be known ever to have been in existence, but your allegorical picture, and the fame of Voltaire will live for ever to your disgrace as a flatterer." ' Northcote's *Reynolds*, i. 300. Another of the figures was commonly said to be a portrait of Hume ; but Forbes (*Life of Beattie*, i. 275, note) says he had reason to believe that Sir Joshua had no thought either of Hume or Voltaire. ⟨There is no resemblance to either Hume or Voltaire in the heads of the figures.⟩ Beattie's *Essay* is so much a thing of the past that Dr. J. H. Burton does not, I believe, take the trouble ever to mention it in his *Life of Hume*. Burns did not hold with Goldsmith, for he took Beattie's side :—
 ' Hence, sweet harmonious BEATTIE sung
 His " Minstrel lays " ;
 Or tore, with noble ardour stung,
 The *Sceptic's* bays.'
 (*The Vision*, duan ii.)
[1] See *ante*, ii. 441.

[2] William Tytler published in 1760 an *An historical and critical Enquiry into the Evidence . . . against Mary Queen of Scots* [etc.]. It was reviewed by Johnson. *Ante*, i. 354.
[3] Johnson's *Rasselas* was published on the 19th, and Goldsmith's *Polite Learning* on the 2nd, of April, 1759. I do not find that they published any other works at the same time. If these are the works meant, we have a proof that the two writers knew each other earlier than was otherwise known. ⟨See App. D, p. 550.⟩
[4] ⟨Thomas Bentley, replying to Pope's ridicule of his uncle in *Sober Advice from Horace*, writes (*A Letter to Mr. Pope*, 1735, p. 14) : ' Let me advise you as a Friend . . , don't hurt your self by your own Writings ; have it always before your Eyes, That no Man is demolished but by himself.' See G. Sherburn, *Early Life of Pope*, 1935, p. 265. Perhaps the nephew intentionally quoted his uncle's saying.⟩ Warburton in a note to *Imit. Hor., Epist. to Augustus*, l. 104, writes of Bentley : ' for however he might sometime mistake his fort, he was never the dupe of the Public judgment. Of which a learned Prelate, now living, gave me this instance : He accidentally met Bentley in the days of Phalaris; and after having complimented him on that noble piece of Criticism (the *Answer* to the Oxford writers) he bad him not be discouraged at this run upon him: for tho' they had got the laughers on their side, yet mere wit and raillery could

authours derived from attacks, were chiefly in subjects of taste, where you cannot confute, as so much may be said on either side [1].—He told me he did not know who was the authour of the *Adventures of a Guinea* [2], but that the bookseller had sent the first volume to him in manuscript, to have his opinion if it should be printed ; and he thought it should.

The weather being now somewhat better, Mr. James M'Donald, factor to Sir Alexander M'Donald in Slate, insisted that all the company at Ostig should go to the house at Armidale, which Sir Alexander had left, having gone with his lady to Edinburgh, and be his guests, till we had an opportunity of sailing to Mull. We accordingly got there to dinner ; and passed our day very cheerfully, being no less than fourteen in number.

Saturday, 2d *October.*

Dr. Johnson said, that ' a Chief and his Lady should make their house like a court. They should have a certain number of the gentlemen's daughters to receive their education in the family, to learn pastry and such things from the housekeeper,

[1] However advantageous attacks may be, the feelings with which they are regarded by authors are better not long hold out against a work of so much merit. To which the other replied, " Indeed, Dr. S. I am in no pain about the matter. For I hold it as certain, that no man was ever written out of reputation, but by himself." ' Pope's *Works*, 1751 (large 8° ed.), iv. 159. ' Against personal abuse,' says Hawkins (*Life*, p. 348), ' Johnson was ever armed, by a reflection, that I have heard him utter : " Alas ! reputation would be of little worth, were it in the power of every concealed enemy to deprive us of it." ' He wrote to Baretti :—' A man of genius has been seldom ruined but by himself.' *Ante*, i. 381. ⟨Boswell reports, 22 Dec. 1785, that Mason ' said he was very angry that he was not attacked by Johnson in my *Tour*. " It looks," said he, " as if one was nobody." ' *Boswell Papers*, xvi. 149.⟩ See *ante*, ii. 61 note 4, and v. 174.

described by Fielding when he says :—' Nor shall we conclude the Injury done this Way to be very slight, when we consider a Book as the Author's Offspring, and indeed as the Child of his Brain. The Reader who hath suffered his Muse to continue hitherto in a Virgin State, can have but a very inadequate Idea of this Kind of paternal Fondness. To such we may parody the tender Exclamation of Macduff, " Alas ! Thou hast written no Book." ' *Tom Jones*, bk. xi. ch. 1.

[2] It is strange that Johnson should not have known that the *Adventures of a Guinea* was written by a namesake of his own, Charles Johnson. Being disqualified for the bar, which was his profession, by a supervening deafness, he went to India, and made some fortune, and died there about 1800. SCOTT, 1831. ⟨*Chrysal, or the Adventures of a Guinea* was published anonymously in four volumes, 1760–5. The author's name was Charles Johnstone.⟩

and manners from my lady. That was the way in the great families in Wales; at Lady Salisbury's [1], Mrs. Thrale's grandmother, and at Lady Philips's [2]. I distinguish the families by the ladies, as I speak of what was properly their province. There were always six young ladies at Sir John Philips's: when one was married, her place was filled up. There was a large school-room, where they learnt needle-work and other things.' —I observed, that, at some courts in Germany, there were academies for the pages, who are the sons of gentlemen, and receive their education without any expence to their parents. Dr. Johnson said, that manners were best learnt at those courts. 'You are admitted with great facility to the prince's company, and yet must treat him with much respect. At a great court, you are at such a distance that you get no good.'—I said, 'Very true: a man sees the court of Versailles, as if he saw it on a theatre.' —He said, ' The best book that ever was written upon good breeding, *Il Corteggiano*, by Castiglione [3], grew up at the little court of Urbino, and you should read it.'—I am glad always to have his opinion of books. At Mr. M'Pherson's, he commended *Whitby's Commentary* [4], and said, he had heard him called rather lax; but

[1] ⟨Lady Hester Salusbury Cotton.⟩
[2] Walpole in 1745 described his cousin Sir John Philips, of Picton Castle, Pembrokeshire, as 'a distinguished Jacobite'. *Letters*, ii. 153. See also *ib.* 241. He thus mentions Lady Philipps in 1788 when she was 'very aged.' 'They have a favourite black, who has lived with them a great many years, and is remarkably sensible. To amuse Lady Philipps under a long illness, they had read to her the account of the Pelew Islands. Somebody happened to say we were sending . . . a ship thither; the black, who was in the room, exclaimed, " Then there is an end of their happiness!" What a satire on Europe!' *Ib.* xiv. 95. Lady Philipps was known to Johnson through Miss Williams, to whom, as Lady Knight stated (*European Mag.*, Oct. 1799, p. 225), she made a small yearly allowance. ⟨For Sir John Philipps see *post*, App. D, p. 550.⟩
[3] 'To teach the minuter decencies and inferior duties, to regulate the practice of daily conversation, to correct those depravities which are rather ridiculous than criminal, and remove those grievances which, if they produce no lasting calamities, impress hourly vexation, was first attempted by Casa in his book of *Manners*, and Castiglione in his *Courtier*, two books yet celebrated in Italy for purity and elegance.' Johnson's *Addison*, 37. ⟨*Il libro del Corteggiano* was first published at Venice in 1528: it was translated into English by Sir Thomas Hoby in 1561.⟩
[4] Burnet (*History of His Own Time*, i. 674) mentions Daniel Whitby among 'the persons who both managed and directed the controversial war' against Popery towards the end of Charles II's reign. 'Popery,' he says, ' was never so well understood by the Nation, as it came to be upon this occasion.' Whitby's *Paraphrase and Commentary on the New Testament* was first published in two folio volumes in 1703.

he did not perceive it. He had looked at a novel, called *The Man of the World* [1], at Rasay, but thought there was nothing in it. He said to-day, while reading my Journal, ' This will be a great treasure to us some years hence.'

Talking of a very penurious gentleman of our acquaintance [2], he observed, that he exceeded *L'Avare* in the play [3]. I concurred with him, and remarked that he would do well, if introduced in one of Foote's farces ; that the best way to get it done, would be to bring Foote to be entertained at his house for a week, and then it would be *facit indignatio* [4].—*Johnson.* ' Sir, I wish he had him. I, who have eaten his bread, will not give him to him ; but I should be glad he came honestly by him †.'

He said, he was angry at Thrale, for sitting at General Oglethorpe's without speaking. He censured a man for degrading himself to a non-entity. I observed, that Goldsmith was on the other extreme ; for he spoke at all ventures [5].—*Johnson.* ' Yes, sir ; Goldsmith, rather than not speak, will talk of what he knows himself to be ignorant, which can only end in exposing him.'—' I wonder, (said I,) if he feels that he exposes himself. If he was with two taylors '—' Or with two founders, (said Dr. Johnson, interrupting me,) he would fall a talking on the method of making cannon, though both of them would soon see that he did not know what metal a cannon is made of.'—We were very social and merry in his room this forenoon. In the evening the company danced as usual. We performed, with much activity, a dance which, I suppose, the emigration from Sky has occasioned. They call it *America*. Each of the couples, after the common *involutions* and *evolutions*, successively whirls round in a circle, till all are in motion ; and the dance seems intended to shew how emigration catches, till a whole neighbourhood is set afloat.—Mrs. M'Kinnon told me, that last year when a ship

---

[1] By Henry Mackenzie, the author of *The Man of Feeling. Ante*, i. 360. It had been published anonymously in February of this year. ⟨Johnson met Mackenzie in Edinburgh: see H. W. Thompson's *A Scottish Man of Feeling*, 1931, p. 140.⟩

[2] Sir A. Macdonald. *Ante*, v. 148. See *post*, v. 315.

[3] Molière's play of *L'Avare*.

[4] '. . . facit indignatio versum.'
Juvenal, *Sat.* i. 79.
† ⟨Johnson then ' took off My Lady : " Thomson, some wine and water," with her mouth full ; adding, " People are generally taught to empty their mouths of meat before they call for drink. She wants to be whipped in a nursery ".' Boswell's *Hebrides*, ed. Pottle and Bennett, p. 242.⟩

[5] See *ante*, iii. 252.

sailed from Portree for America, the people on shore were almost distracted when they saw their relations go off; they lay down on the ground, tumbled, and tore the grass with their teeth.—This year there was not a tear shed. The people on shore seemed to think that they would soon follow. This indifference is a mortal sign for the country.

We danced to-night to the musick of the bagpipe, which made us beat the ground with prodigious force. I thought it better to endeavour to conciliate the kindness of the people of Sky, by joining heartily in their amusements, than to play the abstract scholar †. I looked on this Tour to the Hebrides as a copartnership between Dr. Johnson and me. Each was to do all he could to promote its success; and I have some reason to flatter myself, that my gayer exertions were of service to us. Dr. Johnson's immense fund of knowledge and wit was a wonderful source of admiration and delight to them; but they had it only at times; and they required to have the intervals agreeably filled up, and even little elucidations of his learned text. I was also fortunate enough frequently to draw him forth to talk, when he would otherwise have been silent. The fountain was at times locked up, till I opened the spring.—It was curious to hear the Hebridians, when any dispute happened while he was out of the room, saying, ' Stay till Dr. Johnson comes: say that to *him !* '

Yesterday Dr. Johnson said, ' I cannot but laugh, to think of myself roving among the Hebrides at sixty [1]. I wonder where I shall rove at fourscore [2] !'—This evening he disputed the truth of what is said, as to the people of St. Kilda catching cold whenever strangers come. ' How can there (said he) be a physical effect without a physical cause [3] ?'—He added, laughing, ' the arrival of a ship full of strangers would kill them; for, if one stranger gives them one cold, two strangers must give them two colds; and so in proportion.'—I wondered to hear him ridicule this, as he had praised M'Aulay for putting it in his book: saying, that it was manly in him to tell a fact, however strange, if he himself believed it [4]. He said, the evidence was not

† ⟨Boswell confesses in his Journal: ' I do not like dancing. But I force myself to it, when it promotes social happiness, as in the country, where it is as much one of the means towards that end as dinner; so I danced a reel to-night.' Op. cit., p. 243.⟩
[1] He was sixty-four.
[2] ⟨See *post*, v. 333.⟩
[3] See *ante*, ii. 51 ⟨,482, and *post* v, App. D, p. 551.⟩
[4] See *ante*, ii. 150.

adequate to the improbability of the thing; that if a physician, rather disposed to be incredulous, should go to St. Kilda, and report the fact, then he would begin to look about him. They said, it was annually proved by M'Leod's steward, on whose arrival all the inhabitants caught cold. He jocularly remarked, ' the steward always comes to demand something from them ; and so they fall a coughing. I suppose the people in Sky all take a cold, when —— (naming a certain person [1]) comes.'—They said, he came only in summer.—*Johnson.* ' That is out of tenderness to you. Bad weather and he, at the same time, would be too much.'

Sunday, 3d October.

Joseph reported that the wind was still against us. Dr. Johnson said, ' A wind, or not a wind ? that is the question [2] ; ' for he can amuse himself at times with a little play of words, or rather of [a] sentences. I remember when he turned his cup at Aberbrothick, where we drank tea, he muttered, *Claudite jam rivos, pueri* [3]. I must again and again apologize to fastidious readers, for recording such minute particulars. They prove the scrupulous fidelity of my Journal. Dr. Johnson said it was a very exact picture of a portion of his life.

While we were chatting in the indolent stile of men who were to stay here all this day at least, we were suddenly roused by [b] being told that the wind was fair, that a little fleet of herring-busses was passing by for Mull, and that Mr. Simpson's vessel was about to sail. Hugh M'Donald, the skipper, came to us, and was impatient that we should get ready, which we soon did. Dr. Johnson, with composure and solemnity, repeated the observation of Epictetus [4], that, ' as man has the voyage of death before him,—whatever may be his employment, he should be ready at the master's call ; and an old man should never be far from the shore, lest he should not be able to get himself ready.' He rode, and I and the other gentlemen walked, about an English mile to the shore, where the vessel lay. Dr. Johnson said, he should never forget Sky, and returned thanks for all

[a] of *omitted* 2, 3.   [b] by 1 : at 2, 3.

[1] Sir Alexander Macdonald.
[2] ' To be or not to be : that is the question.' *Hamlet,* act iii. sc. 1.
[3] Virgil, *Eclogues,* iii. 111. ⟨The practice of turning the tea-cup upside down as a sign that one had had enough tea was not extinct in Ireland at the end of the nineteenth century. *N. & Q.,* 7th ser., 1891, xii. 273.⟩
[4] ⟨*Enchiridion,* ch. vii. See Gennadius in *Johnson Club Papers,* 1st series, 1899, p. 47, note.⟩

civilities. We were carried to the vessel in a small boat which she had, and we set sail very briskly about one o'clock. I was much pleased with the motion for many hours. Dr. Johnson grew sick, and retired under cover, as it rained a good deal. I kept above, that I might have fresh air, and finding myself not affected by the motion of the vessel, I exulted in being a stout seaman, while Dr. Johnson was quite in a state of annihilation. But I was soon humbled; for after imagining that I could go with ease to America or the East-Indies, I became very sick, but kept above board, though it rained hard.

As we had been detained so long in Sky by bad weather, we gave up the scheme that Col had planned for us of visiting several islands, and contented ourselves with the prospect of seeing Mull, and Icolmkill and Inchkenneth, which lie near to it.

Mr. Simpson was sanguine in his hopes for awhile, the wind being fair for us. He said, he would land us at Icolmkill that night. But when the wind failed, it was resolved we should make for the sound of Mull, and land in the harbour of Tobermorie. We kept near the five herring vessels for some time; but afterwards four of them got before us, and one little wherry fell behind us. When we got in full view of the point of Ardnamurchan, the wind changed, and was directly against our getting into the sound. We were then obliged to tack, and get forward in that tedious manner. As we advanced, the storm grew greater, and the sea very rough. Col then began to talk of making for Egg, or Canna, or his own island. Our skipper said, he would get us into the Sound. Having struggled for this a good while in vain, he said, he would push forward till we were near the land of Mull, where we might cast anchor, and lie till the morning; for although, before this, there had been a good moon, and I had pretty distinctly seen not only the land of Mull, but up the Sound, and the country of Morven as at one end of it, the night was now grown very dark. Our crew consisted of one M'Donald, our skipper, and two sailors, one of whom had but one eye; Mr. Simpson himself, Col, and Hugh M'Donald his servant, all helped. Simpson said, he would willingly go for Col, if young Col or his servant would undertake to pilot us to a harbour; but, as the island is low land, it was dangerous to run upon it in the dark. Col and his servant appeared a little dubious. The scheme of running for Canna seemed then to be embraced ; but Canna was ten leagues off, all out of our way ; and they were afraid to attempt the harbour of Egg. All these different plans were successively in agitation. The old skipper still tried to make for the land of Mull ; but then it was considered that there was no place there where we could anchor in safety. Much time was lost in striving against the storm. At last it became so rough, and threatened to be so much worse, that Col and his servant took more courage, and said they would undertake to hit one of the harbours in Col.—' Then let us run for it in GOD'S name,' said the skipper ; and instantly we turned towards it. The little wherry which had fallen behind us, had hard work. The master begged that, if we made for Col, we should put out a light to him. Accordingly one of the sailors waved a glowing peat for some time. The various difficulties that were started, gave me a good deal of apprehension, from which I was relieved, when I found we were to run for a harbour before the wind. But my relief was but of short duration ; for I soon heard that our sails were very bad, and were in danger of being torn in pieces, in which case we should be driven upon the rocky shore of Col. It was very dark, and there was a heavy and incessant rain. The sparks of the burning peat flew so much about, that I dreaded the vessel might take fire. Then, as Col was a sportsman, and had powder on board, I figured that we might be blown up. Simpson and he appeared a little frightened, which made me more so ; and the perpetual talking, or rather shouting, which was carried on in Erse, alarmed me still more. A man is always suspicious of what is saying in an unknown tongue ; and, if fear be his passion at the time, he grows more afraid. Our vessel often lay so much on one side, that I trembled lest she should be overset, and indeed they told me afterwards, that they had run her sometimes to within an inch of the water, so anxious were they to make what haste they could before the night should be worse. I now saw what I never saw before, a prodigious sea, with immense billows coming upon a vessel, so as that it seemed hardly possible to escape. There was something grandly horrible in the sight. I am glad I have seen it once. Amidst all these terrifying circumstances, I endeavoured to compose my mind. It was not easy to do it; for all the stories that I had heard of the dangerous sailing among the Hebrides, which is proverbial [1], came full upon my recollection. When I thought of those who were dearest to me, and would suffer severely, should I be lost, I upbraided myself, as not having a sufficient cause for putting myself in such danger. Piety afforded me comfort; yet I was disturbed by the objections that have been made against a particular providence, and by the arguments of those who maintain that it is in vain to hope that the petitions of an individual, or even of congregations, can have any influence with the Deity; objections which have been often made, and which Dr. Hawkesworth has lately revived, in his Preface to the Voyages to the South Seas [2]; but Dr. Ogden's excellent doctrine on the efficacy of intercession prevailed.

It was half an hour after eleven before we set ourselves in the course for Col. As I saw them all busy doing something, I asked Col, with much earnestness, what I could do. He, with a happy readiness, put into my hand a rope, which was fixed to the top of one of the masts, and told me to hold it till he bade me pull. If I had considered the matter, I might have seen that this could not be of the least service; but his object was to keep me out of the way of those who were busy working the vessel, and at the same time to divert my fear, by employing me, and making me think that I was of use. Thus did I stand firm to my post, while the wind and rain beat upon me, always expecting a call to pull my rope.

---

[1] 'The stormy Hebrides.' Milton's *Lycidas*, l. 156.

[2] Boswell was thinking of the passage (p. xxi) in which Hawkesworth tells how one of Captain Cook's ships was saved by the wind falling. 'If,' he writes, 'it was a natural event, providence is out of the question, at least we can with no more propriety say that providentially the wind ceased, than that providentially the sun rose in the morning. If it was not,' &c. The attacks made on Hawkesworth in the newspapers for this passage 'affected him so much that, from low spirits he was seized with a nervous fever, which on account of the high living he had indulged in had the more power on him; and he is supposed to have put an end to his life by intentionally taking an immoderate dose of opium.' Prior's *Malone*, p. 441. Mme D'Arblay says that these attacks shortened his life. *Memoirs of Dr. Burney*, i. 278. He died on Nov. 17 of this year. See *ante*, ii. 247 ⟨and A. Chalmers, *Brit. Essayists*, 1802, xxiii, pp. xxii ff.⟩.

The man with one eye steered ; old M'Donald, and Col and his servant, lay upon the fore-castle, looking sharp out for the harbour. It was necessary to carry much *cloth*, as they termed it, that is to say, much sail, in order to keep the vessel off the shore of Col. This made violent plunging in a rough sea. At last they spied the harbour of Lochiern †, and Col cried, ' Thank GOD, we are safe ! ' We ran up till we were opposite to it, and soon afterwards we got into it, and cast anchor.

Dr. Johnson had all this time been quiet and unconcerned. He had lain down on one of the beds, and having got free from sickness, was satisfied. The truth is, he knew nothing of the danger we were in [1] : but, fearless and unconcerned, might have said, in the words which he has chosen for the motto to his *Rambler*,

Quo me cunque rapit tempestas, deferor hospes [2].

Once, during the doubtful consultations, he asked whither we were going ; and upon being told that it was not certain whether to Mull or Col, he cried, ' Col for my money ! '—I now went down, with Col and Mr. Simpson, to visit him. He was lying in philosophick tranquillity, with a greyhound of Col's at his back, keeping him warm. Col is quite the *Juvenis qui gaudet canibus* [3]. He had, when we left Talisker, two greyhounds, two

[1] ' After having been detained by storms many days at Sky, we left it, as we thought, with a fair wind But a violent gust which Bos had a great mind to call a tempest, forced us into Coll.' *Letters*, No. 331. ' The wind . . . blew against us, in a short time, with such violence, that we, being no seasoned sailors, were willing to call it a tempest. . . . The master knew not well whither to go ; and our difficulties might perhaps have filled a very pathetick page, had not Mr. Maclean of Col . . . piloted us safe into his own harbour.' *Western Isl.*, p. 108. Sir Walter Scott says, ' Their risque, in a sea full of islands, was very considerable. Indeed the whole expedition was highly perilous, considering the season of the year, the precarious chance of getting sea- worthy boats, and the ignorance of the Hebrideans, who, notwithstanding the opportunities, I may say the *necessities* of their situation, are very careless and unskilful sailors.' Croker's *Boswell*, 1831, ii. 509, n. 1.

[2] For as the tempest drives, I shape my way. FRANCIS. [Horace, *Epistles*, i. 1. 15.] BOSWELL.

[3] ' Imberbus juvenis, tandem custode remoto,
Gaudet equis canibusque, et aprici gramine campi.'
' The youth, whose will no froward tutor bounds,
Joys in the sunny field, his horse and hounds.'
FRANCIS. Horace, *Ars Poet.* l. 161.
† ⟨Loch Eatharna. Boswell's *Hebrides*, ed. Pottle and Bennett, 1962, p. 476.⟩

terriers, a pointer, and a large Newfoundland water-dog. He lost one of his terriers by the road, but had still five dogs with him. I was very ill, and very desirous to get to shore. When I was told that we could not land that night, as the storm had now increased, I looked so miserably, as Col afterwards informed me, that what Shakspeare has made the Frenchman say of the English soldiers, when scantily dieted, ' *Piteous they will look, like drowned mice* [1] *!* ' might, I believe, have been well applied to me. There was in the harbour, before us, a Campbell-town vessel, the Betty, Kenneth Morison master, taking in kelp, and bound for Ireland. We sent our boat to beg beds for two gentlemen, and that the master would send his boat, which was larger than ours. He accordingly did so, and Col and I were accommodated in his vessel till the morning.

Monday, 4th October.

About eight o'clock we went in the boat to Mr. Simpson's vessel, and took in Dr. Johnson. He was quite well, though he had tasted nothing but a dish of tea since Saturday night. On our expressing some surprise at this, he said, that, ' when he lodged in the Temple, and had no regular system of life, he had fasted for two days at a time, during which he had gone about visiting, though not at the hours of dinner or supper ; that he had drunk tea, but eaten no bread ; that this was no intentional fasting, but happened just in the course of a literary life [2].'

There was a little miserable publick-house close upon the shore, to which we should have gone, had we landed last night : but this morning Col resolved to take us directly to the house of Captain Lauchlan M'Lean, a descendant of his family, who had acquired a fortune in the East-Indies, and taken a farm in Col [3]. We had about an English mile to go to it. Col and Joseph, and some others, ran to some little horses, called here *Shelties*, that were running wild on a heath, and catched one of them. We had a saddle with us, which was clapped upon it, and a straw-halter was put on its head. Dr. Johnson was then mounted, and

---

[1] 1 *Henry VI*, act i. sc. 2.
[2] See *ante*, i. 469, and iii. 306.
[3] Johnson describes him as ' a gentleman who has lived some time in the East Indies ; but having dethroned no Nabob, is not too rich to settle in his own country.' *Western Isl.*, p. 109. ⟨For his house see App. D, p. 551. He resigned from the army in 1766 and died 25 Dec. 1802. Dixon Wecter in *P.M.L.A.* liii. 1938, p. 1116.⟩

Joseph very slowly and gravely led the horse. I said to Dr. Johnson, ' I wish, sir, *the club* saw you in this attitude [1].'

It was a very heavy rain, and I was wet to the skin. Captain M'Lean had but a poor temporary house, or rather hut ; however, it was a very good haven to us. There was a blazing peat-fire, and Mrs. M'Lean, daughter of the minister of the parish, got us tea. I felt still the motion of the sea. Dr. Johnson said, it was not imagination, but a continuation of motion in [a] the fluids, like that of the sea itself after the storm is over.

There were some books on the board which served as a chimney-piece. Dr. Johnson took up *Burnet's History of his own Times* [2]. He said, ' The first part of it is one of the most entertaining books in the English language ; it is quite dramatick : while he went about every where, saw every where, and heard every where. By the first part, I mean so far as it appears that Burnet himself was actually engaged in what he has told ; and this may be easily distinguished.' Captain M'Lean censured Burnet, for his high praise of Lauderdale in a dedication [3], when he shews him in his history to have been so bad a man.—*Johnson.* ' I do not myself think that a man should say in a dedication what he could not say in a history. However, allowance should be made ; for there is a great difference. The known style of a dedication is flattery : it professes to flatter. There is the same difference between what a man

[a] not in imagination, but a continuation of motion on 2, 3.

[1] This curious exhibition may perhaps remind some of my readers of the ludicrous lines, made, during Sir Robert Walpole's administration, on Mr. George (afterwards Lord) Littelton, though the figures of the two personages must be allowed to be very different :

' But who is this astride the pony ;
So long, so lean, so lank, so bony ?
Dat be de great orátor, Little-tony.' BOSWELL, ed. 1.

⟨This is the sixth verse of the ten forming the letterpress of the well-known caricature called *The Motion* published on 21 Feb. 1741 : The exact words are :—

' Who's dat who ride astride de Poney,
So long, so lank, so lean, and bony ?
O he be de great Orator *Little-Toney.*'

See *Catal. Prints and Drawings in British Mus.*, 1877, iii. i. 369, and T. Wright, *Engl. and the House of Hanover*, 1848, i. 178 ff.⟩

[2] See *ante*, ii. 213.

[3] In 1673 Burnet, who was then Professor of Theology in Glasgow, dedicated to Lauderdale *A Vindication of the Authority, &c., of the Church and State of Scotland.* In it he writes of the Duke's ' noble character ', and ' more lasting and inward characters of his princely mind.'

says in a dedication, and what he says in a history, as between a lawyer's pleading a cause, and reporting it.'

The day passed away pleasantly enough. The wind became fair for Mull in the evening, and Mr. Simpson resolved to sail next morning : but having been thrown into the island of Col, we were unwilling to leave it unexamined, especially as we considered that the Campbell-town vessel would sail for Mull in a day or two, and therefore we determined to stay.

Tuesday, 5th October.

I rose, and wrote my Journal till about nine ; and then went to Dr. Johnson, who sat up in bed and talked and laughed. I said, it was curious to look back ten years, to the time when we first thought of visiting the Hebrides [1]. How distant and improbable the scheme then appeared ! Yet here we were actually among them.—' Sir, (said he,) people may come to do any thing almost, by talking of it. I really believe, I could talk myself into building a house upon island Isa [2], though I should probably never come back again to see it. I could easily persuade Reynolds to do it ; and there would be no great sin in persuading him to do it. ˋSir, he would reason thus : " What will it cost me to be there once in two or three summers ?—Why, perhaps, five hundred pounds ; and what is that, in comparison of having a fine retreat, to which a man can go, or to which he can send a friend ? " He would never find out that he may have this within twenty miles of London.—Then I would tell him, that he may marry one of the Miss M'Leods, a lady of great family.—Sir, it is surprising how people will go to a distance for what they may have at home. I knew a lady [3] who came up from Lincolnshire to Knightsbridge with one of her daughters, and gave five guineas a week for a lodging and a warm bath ; that is, mere warm water. *That*, you know, could not be had in *Lincolnshire !* She said, it was made either too hot or too cold there.'

After breakfast, Dr. Johnson and I, and Joseph, mounted horses, and Col and the captain walked with us about a short mile across the island. We paid a visit to the Reverend Mr. Hector M'Lean. His parish consists of the islands of Col and

[1] See *ante*, i. 450.
[2] See *ante*, v. 250.
[3] ⟨According to Boswell's Journal (ed. Pottle and Bennett, p. 255) Mrs. Langton, who was, no doubt, Bennet Langton's mother. Johnson asks, 25 April 1780, ' Can warm water be had only at Bath, as steam was to be found only at Knightsbridge ? ' *Letters*, No. 662.⟩

Tyr-yi. He was about seventy-seven years of age, a decent ecclesiastick, dressed in a full suit of black clothes, and a black wig. He appeared like a Dutch pastor, or one of the assembly of divines at Westminster. Dr. Johnson observed to me afterwards, ' that he was a fine old man, and was as well-dressed, and had as much dignity in his appearance as the dean of a cathedral.' We were told, that he had a valuable library, though but poor accommodation for it, being obliged to keep his books in large chests. It was curious to see him and Dr. Johnson together. Neither of them heard very distinctly ; so each of them talked in his own way, and at the same time. Mr. M'Lean said, he had a confutation of Bayle, by Leibnitz.—*Johnson.* ' A confutation of Bayle, sir ! What part of Bayle do you mean ? The greatest part of his writings is not confutable : it is historical and critical.'— Mr. M'Lean said, ' the irreligious part ; ' and proceeded to talk of Leibnitz's controversy with Clarke, calling Leibnitz a great man.—*Johnson.* ' Why, sir, Leibnitz persisted in affirming that Newton called space *sensorium numinis*, notwithstanding he was corrected, and desired to observe that Newton's words were QUASI *sensorium numinis* [1]. No, sir ; Leibnitz was as paltry a fellow as I know. Out of respect to Queen Caroline, who patronised him, Clarke treated him too well [2].'

During the time that Dr. Johnson was thus going on, the old

[1] ' Others have considered infinite Space as the Receptacle, or rather the Habitation of the Almighty : But the noblest and most exalted Way of considering this infinite Space, is that of Sir Isaac Newton, who calls it the *Sensorium* of the Godhead. Brutes and Men have their *Sensoriola*, or little *Sensoriums*, by which they apprehend the Presence, and perceive the Actions, of a few Objects that lie contiguous to them. Their Knowledge and Observation turn within a very narrow Circle. But as God Almighty cannot but perceive and know every Thing in which he resides, infinite Space gives Room to infinite Knowledge, and is, as it were, an Organ to Omniscience.' Addison, *The Spectator*, No. 565.

[2] ' Le célèbre philosophe Leibnitz . . . attaqua ces expressions du philosophe anglais dans une lettre qu'il écrivit, en 1715, à la feue reine d'Angleterre, épouse de George second ; cette princesse, digne d'être en commerce avec Leibnitz et Newton, engagea une dispute réglée par lettres entre les deux parties. Mais Newton, ennemi de toute dispute, et avare de son temps, laissa le docteur Clarke, son disciple en physique, et pour le moins son égal en métaphysique, entrer pour lui dans la lice. La dispute roula sur presque toutes les idées métaphysiques de Newton : et c'est peut-être le plus beau monument que nous ayons des combats littéraires.' Voltaire's *Œuvres*, 1879, xxii. 408.

minister was standing with his back to the fire, cresting up erect, pulling down the front of his periwig, and talking what a great man Leibnitz was. To give an idea of the scene, would require a page with two columns ; but it ought rather to be represented by two good players. The old gentleman said, Clarke was very wicked, for going so much into the Arian system [1]. ' I will not say he was wicked, said Dr. Johnson ; he might be mistaken.'—*M'Lean.* ' He was wicked, to shut his eyes against the Scriptures ; and worthy men in England have since confuted him to all intents and purposes.'—*Johnson.* ' I know not *who* has confuted him to *all intents and purposes.*'—Here again there was a double talking, each continuing to maintain his own argument, without hearing exactly what the other said.

I regretted that Dr. Johnson did not practice the art of accommodating himself to different sorts of people. Had he been softer with this venerable old man, we might have had more conversation ; but his forcible spirit, and impetuosity of manner, may be said to spare neither sex nor age. I have seen even Mrs. Thrale stunned ; but I have often maintained, that it is better he should retain his own manner [2]. Pliability of address I conceive to be inconsistent with that majestick power of mind which he possesses, and which produces such noble effects. A lofty oak will not bend like a supple willow.

He told me afterwards, he liked firmness in an old man, and was pleased to see Mr. M'Lean so orthodox. ' At his age, it is too late for a man to be asking himself questions as to his belief [3].'

We rode to the northern part of the island, where we saw the

---

[1] See *ante*, iii. 248.

[2] See *ante*, iv. 295, where Boswell asked Johnson ' if he would not have done more good if he had been more gentle.' JOHNSON. ' No, Sir ; I have done more good as I am. Obscenity and Impiety have always been repressed in my company.'

[3] ' Mr. Maclean has the reputation of great learning : he is seventy-seven years old, but not infirm, with a look of venerable dignity, excelling what I remember in any other man. His conversation was not unsuitable to his appearance. I lost some of his good-will, by treating a heretical writer with more regard than, in his opinion, a heretick could deserve. I honoured his orthodoxy, and did not much censure his asperity. A man who has settled his opinions, does not love to have the tranquillity of his conviction disturbed ; and at seventy-seven it is time to be in earnest.' Johnson's *Western Isl.*, p. 109. ⟨Mr. MacLean was born in 1696, ordained in 1733, and died in 1775. Hew Scott, *Fasti Eccl. Scot.*, 1923, iv. 108.⟩

ruins of a church or chapel [1]. We then proceeded to a place called Grissipol, or the rough Pool.

At Grissipol we found a good farm-house †, belonging to the Laird of Col, and possessed by Mr. M'Sweyn. On the beach here there is a singular variety of curious stones. I picked up one very like a small cucumber. By the by, Dr. Johnson told me, that Gay's line in the *Beggar's Opera*, ' As men should serve a cucumber [2],' &c. has no waggish meaning, with reference to men flinging away cucumbers as too *cooling*, which some have thought ; for it has been a common saying of physicians in England, that a cucumber should be well sliced, and dressed with pepper and vinegar, and then thrown out, as good for nothing.—Mr. M'Sweyn's predecessors had been in Sky from a very remote period, upon the estate belonging to M'Leod ; probably before M'Leod had it. The name is certainly Norwegian, from *Sueno*, King of Norway. The present Mr. M'Sweyn left Sky upon the late M'Leod's raising his rents. He then got this farm from Col.

He appeared to be near fourscore ; but looked as fresh, and was as strong,[a] as a man of fifty. His son Hugh looked older ; and, as Dr. Johnson observed, had more the manners of an old man than he. I had often heard of such instances, but never saw one before. Mrs. M'Sweyn was a decent old gentlewoman. She was dressed in tartan, and could speak nothing but Erse. She said, she had[b] taught Sir James M'Donald Erse, and would teach me soon. I could now sing a verse of the

[a] strong, 1, 2 : strong 3.

[b] had 1 (*MS.*) : omitted 2, 3.

[1] ' Mr. Maclean has no publick edifice for the exercise of his ministry ; and can officiate to no greater number, than a room can contain ; and the room of a hut is not very large . . . The want of churches is not the only impediment to piety : there is likewise a want of Ministers. A parish often contains more Islands than one . . . All the provision made by the present ecclesiastical constitution, for the inhabitants of about a hundred square miles, is a prayer and sermon in a little room, once in three weeks.' Johnson's *Western Isl.*, p. 110.

† ⟨Now, 1936, a ruin.⟩

[2] ' Our Polly is a sad Slut! nor heeds what we have taught her.
I wonder any man alive will ever rear a daughter!
For she must have both hoods and gowns, and hoops to swell her pride,
With Scarfs and Stays, and Gloves and Lace ; and she will have Men beside ;
And when she's drest with care and cost, all-tempting, fine and gay,
As men should serve a Cowcumber, she flings herself away.'
Act 1, sc. viii. ⟨See App. D, p. 552.⟩

song *Hatyin foam'eri* [1], made in honour of Allan, the famous Captain of Clanranald, who fell at Sherrif-muir [2]; whose servant, who lay on the field watching his master's dead body, being asked next day who that was, answered, 'He was a man yesterday.'

We were entertained here with a primitive heartiness †. Whisky was served round in a shell, according to the ancient Highland custom. Dr. Johnson would not partake of it; but, being desirous to do honour to the modes ' of other times,' drank some water out of the shell.

In the forenoon Dr. Johnson said, 'it would require great resignation to live in one of these islands.'—*Boswell*. 'I don't know, sir; I have felt myself at times in a state of almost mere physical existence, satisfied to eat, drink, and sleep, and walk about, and enjoy my own thoughts; and I can figure a continuation of this.'—*Johnson*. 'Ay, sir; but if you were shut up here, your own thoughts would torment you: you would think of Edinburgh or London, and that you could not be there.'

We set out after dinner for *Breacacha*, the family seat of the Laird of Col, accompanied by the young laird, who had now got a horse, and by the younger Mr. M'Sweyn, whose wife had gone thither before us, to prepare every thing for our reception, the laird and his family being absent at Aberdeen. It is called *Breacacha*, or the Spotted Field, because in summer it is enamelled with clover and daisies, as young Col told me. We passed by a place where there is a very large stone, I may call it a *rock*;—' a vast weight for Ajax [3].' The tradition is, that a giant threw such another stone at his mistress, up to the top of a hill, at a small distance; and that she,[a] in return, threw this mass down to him [4]. It was all in sport.

[a] she, 1, 2: she 3.

[1] See *ante*, v. 162. ⟨For a translation of the song see Croker, 1831, ii. 516 n., and 1835, v. 15.⟩

[2] ⟨Allan Macdonald, the 12th Chief of Clanranald, held high command in the Jacobite army at Sherrifmuir, 1715.⟩

† ⟨'We had here the best Goose that I ever eat.' Boswell's *Hebrides*, ed. Pottle and Bennett, 1936, p. 260.⟩

[3] ' When Ajax strives some rock's vast weight to throw,
The line too labours, and the words move slow.'
Pope, *Essay on Criticism*, l. 370.

[4] Johnson's remark on these stones is curious as shewing that he had not even a glimpse of the discoveries to be made by geology. After saying that ' no account can be given ' of the position of one of the stones, he continues :—' There are so many important things, of which human knowledge can give no account, that it may be forgiven us, if we speculate no longer on two stones in Col.' *Western Isl.*, p. 114. See *ante*, ii. 468, for his censure of Brydone's ' antimosaical remark.'

Malo me petit lasciva puella [1].

As we advanced, we came to a large extent of plain ground. I had not seen such a place for a long time. Col and I took a gallop upon it by way of race. It was very refreshing to me, after having been so long taking short steps in hilly countries. It was like stretching a man's legs after being cramped in a short bed. We also passed close by a large extent of sand-hills, near two miles square. Dr. Johnson said, ' he never had the image before. It was horrible, if barrenness and danger could be so.' I heard him, after we were in the house of *Breacacha*, repeating to himself, as he walked about the room,

' And smother'd in the dusty whirlwind, dies [2].'

Probably he had been thinking of the whole of the simile in *Cato*, of which that is the concluding line ; the sandy desert had struck him so strongly. The sand has of late been blown over a good deal of meadow ; and the people of the island say, that their fathers remembered much of the space which is now covered with sand, to have been under tillage [3]. Col's house is situated on a bay called *Breacacha* Bay. We found here a neat new-built gentleman's house, better than any we had been in since we were at Lord Errol's. Dr. Johnson relished it much at first, but soon remarked to me, that ' there was nothing becoming a Chief about it : it was a mere tradesman's box [4].' He seemed quite at home, and no longer found any difficulty in using the Highland address ; for as soon as we arrived, he said, with a spirited familiarity, ' Now, *Col*, if you could get us a dish of tea.'—Dr. Johnson and I had each an excellent bed-chamber.

[1] ' Malo me Galatea petit, lasciva puella.'
' My Phyllis me with pelted apples plies.'
DRYDEN. Virgil, *Eclogues*, iii. 64.

[2] ' The helpless Traveller, with wild Surprize,
Sees the dry Desart all around him rise,
And smother'd in the dusty Whirlwind Dies.'
Cato, act ii. sc. 6.

[3] Johnson seems unwilling to believe this. ' I am not of opinion, that by any surveys or land-marks, its [the sand's] limits have been ever fixed, or its progression ascertained. If one man has confidence enough to say, that it advances, nobody can bring any proof to support him in denying it.' *Western Isl.*, p. 113. He had seen land in like manner laid waste north of Aberdeen ; where ' the owner, when he was required to pay the usual tax, desired rather to resign the ground.' *Ib.* p. 16.

[4] *Box*, in this sense, is not in Johnson's *Dictionary*. ⟨For a description of the house, which still stands, see App. D, p. 552.⟩

We had a dispute which of us had the best curtains. His were rather the best, being of linen; but I insisted that my bed had the best posts, which was undeniable. 'Well, (said he,) if you *have* the best *posts*, we will have you tied to them and whipped.'—I mention this slight circumstance, only to shew how ready he is, even in mere trifles, to get the better of his antagonist, by placing him in a ludicrous view. I have known him sometimes use the same art, when hard pressed, in serious disputation. Goldsmith, I remember, to retaliate for many a severe defeat which he has suffered from him, applied to him a lively saying in one of Cibber's comedies, which puts this part of his character in a strong light.—' There is no arguing with Johnson; for, *if his pistol misses fire, he knocks you down with the but-end of it* [1].'

Wednesday, 6th October.

After a sufficiency of sleep, we assembled at breakfast. We were just as if in barracks †. Every body was master. We went and viewed the old castle of Col, which is not far from the present house, near the shore, and founded on a rock. It has never been a large feudal residence, and has nothing about it that requires a particular description. Like other old inconvenient buildings of the same age, it exemplified Gray's picturesque lines,

' Huge [2] windows that exclude the light,
And passages that lead to nothing.'

It may however be worth mentioning, that on the second story we saw a vault, which was, and still is, the family prison [3]. There was a woman put into it by the laird, for theft, within these ten years; and any offender would be confined there yet; for, from the necessity of the thing, as the island is remote from any power established by law, the laird must exercise his jurisdiction to a certain degree.

We were shewn, in a corner of this vault, a hole, into which Col said greater criminals used to be put. It was now filled up with rubbish of different kinds. He said, it was of a great depth. 'Ay, (said Dr. Johnson, smiling,) all such places, that *are filled up*, were of a great depth.' He is very quick in

[1] See *ante*, ii. 100, and iv. 274.   *A Long Story*, l. 7.
† ⟨See App. D, p. 552.⟩   [3] ⟨See App. D, pp. 552-3.⟩
[2] In the original, ' Rich windows '.

shewing that he does not give credit to careless or exaggerated accounts of things. After seeing the castle, we looked at a small hut near it. It is called *Teigh Franchich*, *i.e.* the Frenchman's House. Col could not tell us the history of it. A poor man with a wife and children now lived in it. We went into it, and Dr. Johnson gave them some charity. There was but one bed for all the family, and the hut was very smoky. When he came out, he said to me, ' *Et hoc secundum sententiam philosophorum est esse beatus*[1].'—*Boswell*. ' The philosophers, when they placed happiness in a cottage, supposed cleanliness and no smoke.' —*Johnson*. ' Sir, they did not think about either.'

We walked a little in the laird's garden, in which endeavours have been used to rear some trees; but, as soon as they got above the surrounding wall, they died. Dr. Johnson recommended sowing the seeds of hardy trees, instead of planting.

Col and I rode out this morning, and viewed a part of the island. In the course of our ride, we saw a turnip-field, which he had hoed with his own hands. He first introduced this kind of husbandry into the Western islands[2]. We also looked at an appearance of lead, which seemed very promising. It has been long known; for I found[3] letters to the late laird, from Sir John Areskine and Sir Alexander Murray, respecting it.

After dinner came Mr. M'Lean, of Corneck, brother to Isle of Muck, who is a cadet of the family of Col. He possesses the two ends of Col, which belong to the Duke of Argyll. Corneck had lately taken a lease of them at a very advanced rent, rather than let the Campbells get a footing in the island, one of whom had offered nearly as much as he. Dr. Johnson well observed, that, ' landlords err much when they calculate merely what their

[1] ' And this according to the philosophers is happiness.' Boswell says of Crabbe's poem *The Village*, that ' its sentiments as to the false notions of rustick happiness and rustick virtue were quite congenial with Johnson's own.' *Ante*, iv. 175.

[2] ' This innovation was considered by Mr. Macsweyn as the idle project of a young head, heated with English fancies; but he has now found that turnips will really grow, and that hungry sheep and cows will really eat them.' Johnson's *Western Isl.*, p. 113. ' The young Laird is heir, perhaps, to 300 square miles of Land, which at 10 shillings an acre, would bring him 96,000£ a year. He is desirous of improving the agriculture of his Country, and in imitation of the Czar travelled for improvement, and worked with his own hands upon a farm in Hertfordshire.' *Letters*, No. 331.

[3] ⟨In Col's cabinet. Boswell's *Hebrides*, ed. Pottle and Bennett, 1936, p. 268.⟩

land *may* yield. The rent must be in a proportionate ratio of what the land may yield, and of the power of the tenant to make it yield. A tenant cannot make by his land, but according to the corn and cattle which he has. Suppose you should give him twice as much land as he has, it does him no good, unless he gets also more stock. It is clear then, that the Highland landlords, who let their substantial tenants leave them, are infatuated ; for the poor small tenants cannot give them good rents, from the very nature of things. They have not the means of raising more from their farms [1].' Corneck, Dr. Johnson said, was the most distinct man that he had met with in these isles ; he did not shut his eyes, or put his fingers in his ears, which he seemed to think was a good deal the mode with most of the people whom we have seen of late.

Thursday, 7th October.

Captain M'Lean joined us this morning at breakfast. There came on a dreadful storm of wind and rain, which continued all day, and rather increased at night. The wind was directly against our getting to Mull. We were in a strange state of abstraction from the world : we could neither hear from our friends, nor write to them. Col had brought Daille *on the Fathers* [2], Lucas *on Happiness* [3], and More's *Dialogues* [4], from the Reverend Mr. M'Lean's, and Burnet's *History of his own Times*, from Captain M'Lean's ; and he had of his own some books of farming, and Gregory's *Geometry* [5]. Dr. Johnson read a good deal of Burnet, and of Gregory, and I observed he made some geometrical notes in the end of his pocket-book [6]. I read a little

---

[1] ' In more fruitful countries, the removal of one only makes room for the succession of another : but in the Hebrides, the loss of an inhabitant leaves a lasting vacuity ; for nobody born in any other parts of the world will choose this country for his residence.' Johnson's *Western Isl.*, p. 87.

[2] ⟨Jean Daillé, 1594–1670, published in 1632 *Traicté de l'employ des saincts Pères pour le Iugement des differends, qui sont auiourd'hui en la Religion*, of which an English version appeared in 1651. This is, no doubt, the work meant.⟩

[3] *Enquiry after Happiness*, by Richard Lucas, D.D., 1685.

[4] *Divine Dialogues*, by Henry More, D.D. See *ante*, ii. 162, note 1.

[5] ⟨Prof. Colin MacLaurin (*ante*, v. 49) published in 1745, under the title *A Treatise of practical Geometry*, his translation, from the Latin, of Prof. David Gregory's mathematical lectures at Edinburgh.⟩

[6] ⟨Boswell originally wrote ' Journal '. Ed. Pottle and Bennett, *op. cit.* p. 270.⟩

of Young's Six Weeks Tour through the Southern Counties †;
and Ovid's Epistles, which I had bought at Inverness, and which
helped to solace many a weary hour.

We were to have gone with Dr. Johnson this morning to
see the mine; but were prevented by the storm. While it
was raging, he said, 'We may be glad we are not *damnati ad
metalla* §.'

Friday, 8th October.

Dr. Johnson appeared to-day very weary of our present confined situation. He said, ' I want to be on the main land, and go on with existence. This is a waste of life.'

I shall here insert, without regard to chronology, some of his conversation at different times.

' There was a man some time ago, who was well received for two years, among the gentlemen of Northamptonshire, by calling himself my brother. At last he grew so impudent as by his influence to get tenants turned out of their farms. Allen the Printer [1], who is of that county, came to me, asking, with much appearance of doubtfulness, if I had a brother; and upon being assured I had none alive, he told me of the imposition, and immediately wrote to the country, and the fellow was dismissed. It pleased me to hear that so much was got by using my name. It is not every name that can carry double; do both for a man's self and his brother (laughing). I should be glad to see the fellow. However, I could have done nothing against him. A man can have no redress for his name being used, or ridiculous stories being told of him in the news-papers, except he can shew that he has suffered damage.—Some years ago a foolish piece ¶ was published, said to be written " *by S. Johnson* ". Some of my friends wanted me to be very angry about this. I said, it would be in vain; for the answer would be, *S. Johnson* may be Simon Johnson, or Simeon Johnson, or Solomon Johnson; and even if the full name, Samuel Johnson, had been used, it might be said; " it is not you; it is a much cleverer fellow."

' Beauclerk and I, and Langton, and Lady Sydney Beauclerk, mother to our friend, were one day driving in a coach by Cuper's Gardens [2], which were then unoccupied. I, in sport, proposed

† ⟨First published in 1768.⟩   ¶ ⟨See App. D, p. 553⟩.
§ ⟨Cf. Plin. *Ep.* II. xi. 8. 'Damnatus in metallum'.⟩   [1] *Ante*, iii. 141.   [2] ' Cuper's Gardens, near the south bank of the Thames, opposite to

that Beauclerk and Langton, and myself should take them; and we amused ourselves with scheming how we should all do our parts. Lady Sydney grew angry, and said, "an old man should not put such things in young people's heads." She had no notion of a joke, sir; had come late into life, and had a mighty unpliable understanding.

'*Carte's Life of the Duke of Ormond* is considered as a book of authority; but it is ill-written. The matter is diffused in too many words; there is no animation, no compression, no vigour. Two good volumes in duodecimo might be made out of the two in folio [1].'

Talking of our confinement here, I observed, that our discontent and impatience could not be considered as very unreasonable; for that we were just in the state of which Seneca complains so grievously, while in exile in Corsica [2]. 'Yes, (said Dr. Johnson,) and he was not farther from home than we are.' The truth is, he was much nearer.

There was a good deal of rain to-day, and the wind was still contrary. Corneck attended me, while I amused myself in

Somerset House. . . . The gardens were illuminated, and the company entertained by a band of music, and fireworks; but this, with other places of the same kind, has been lately discontinued by an act that has reduced the number of these seats of luxury and dissipation.' Dodsley's *London and its Environs*, ed. 1761, ii. 209. The Act was the 25th George II, for 'preventing robberies and regulating places of public entertainment.' *Parl. Hist.* xiv. 1234. ⟨The Gardens were reopened in 1753 and remained open, with varying fortunes, till 1759. See Wroth, *London Pleasure Gardens in 18th c.*, 1896, pp. 247 ff.⟩

[1] ⟨Carte published in 1736 *An History of the Life of James Duke of Ormonde* in two volumes folio; he had published, also in folio, in the preceding year *A Collection of Letters* 'by way of Appendix to that History'.⟩ 'Mr. Johnson,' according to Mr. Langton, 'used to laugh at a passage in Carte's *Life of the Duke of Ormond*, where he gravely observes "that he was always in full dress when he went to court; too many being in the practice of going thither with double lapells."' *Boswelliana*, p. 274. The following is the passage :—' No severity of weather or condition of health served him for a reason of not observing that decorum of dress which he thought a point of respect to persons and places. In winter time people were allowed to come to court with double-breasted coats, a sort of undress. The duke would never take advantage of that indulgence; but let it be never so cold, he always came in his proper habit; and indeed the king himself . . . always did the same, though too many neglected his example to make use of the liberty he was pleased to allow.' Carte's *Life of Ormonde*, 1851, iv. 693. See *ante*, i. 42.

[2] Seneca's two epigrams on Corsica are quoted in Boswell's *Corsica*, first edition, p. 13.

examining a collection of papers belonging to the family of Col. The first laird was a younger son of the Chieftain M'Lean, and got the middle part of Col for his patrimony. Dr. Johnson having given a very particular account [1] of the connection between this family and a branch of the family of Camerons, called M'Lonich, I shall only insert the following document, (which I found in Col's cabinet,) as a proof of its continuance, even to a late period :

> To the Laird of Col.
>
> ' Dear Sir,
> ' THE long-standing tract of firm affectionate friendship 'twixt your worthy predecessors and ours affords us such assurance, as that we may have full relyance on your favour and undoubted friendship, in recommending the bearer, Ewen Cameron, our cousin, son to the deceast Dugall M'Connill of Innermaillie, sometime in Glenpean, to your favour and conduct, who is a man of undoubted honesty and discretion, only that he has the misfortune of being alledged to have

[1] ' Very near the house of Maclean stands the castle of Col, which was the mansion of the Laird, till the house was built. . . . On the wall was, not long ago, a stone with an inscription, importing, that *if any man of the clan of Maclonich shall appear before this castle, though he come at midnight, with a man's head in his hand, he shall there find safety and protection against all but the King.* This is an old Highland treaty made upon a very memorable occasion. Maclean, the son of John Gerves, who recovered Col, and conquered Barra, had obtained, it is said, from James the Second, a grant of the lands of Lochiel, forfeited, I suppose, by some offence against the state. Forfeited estates were not in those days quietly resigned ; Maclean, therefore, went with an armed force to seize his new possessions, and, I know not for what reason, took his wife with him. The Camerons rose in defence of their Chief, and a battle was fought at the head of Loch Ness, near the place where Fort Augustus now stands, in which Lochiel obtained the victory, and Maclean, with his followers, was defeated and destroyed. The lady fell into the hands of the conquerours, and being found pregnant was placed in the custody of Maclonich, one of a tribe or family branched from Cameron, with orders, if she brought a boy, to destroy him, if a girl, to spare her. Maclonich's wife, who was with child likewise, had a girl about the same time at which lady Maclean brought a boy, and Maclonich with more generosity to his captive, than fidelity to his trust, contrived that the children should be changed. Maclean, being thus preserved from death, in time recovered his original patrimony ; and in gratitude to his friend, made his castle a place of refuge to any of the clan that should think himself in danger ; and, as a proof of reciprocal confidence, Maclean took upon himself and his posterity the care of educating the heir of Maclonich.' Johnson's *Western Isl.*, p. 121.

been accessory to the killing of one of M'Martin's family about fourteen years ago, upon which alledgeance the M'Martins are now so sanguine on revenging, that they are fully resolved for the deprivation of his life ; to the preventing of which you are relyed on by us, as the only fit instrument, and a most capable person. Therefore your favour and protection is expected and intreated, during his good behaviour ; and failing of which behaviour, you'll please to [a] use him as a most insignificant person deserves.

'Sir, he had, upon the alledgeance foresaid, been transported, at Lochiel's desire, to France, to gratify the M'Martins, and upon his return home, about five years ago, married : But now he is so much threatened by the M'Martins, that he is not secure enough to stay where he is, being Ardmurchan, which occasions this trouble to you. Wishing prosperity and happiness to attend still yourself, worthy Lady, and good family, we are, in the most affectionate manner,

Dear sir,
Your most obliged, affectionate,
and most humble servants,
DUGALL CAMERON, *of Strone.*
DUGALL CAMERON, *of Barr.*
DUGALL CAMERON, *of Inveriskvouilline.*
DUGALL CAMERON, *of Invinvalie.*'
Strone, 11th March, 1737.'

Ewen Cameron was protected, and his son has now a farm from the Laird of Col, in Mull.

The family of Col was very loyal in the time of the great Montrose [1], from whom I found two letters in his own handwriting. The first is as follows:

For my very loving friend the Laird of Coall.
'Sir,
'I must heartily thank you for all your willingness and good affection to his Majesty's service, and particularly the sending alongs of your son, to who I will heave ane particular respect, hopeing also that you will still continue ane goode instrument for the advanceing ther of the King's service, for which, and all your former loyal carriages,

[a] to *not in Boswell's original copy.*

[1] 'Mr. Croker tells us that the great Marquis of Montrose was beheaded at Edinburgh in 1650. There is not a forward boy at any school in England who does not know that the Marquis was hanged.' Macaulay's *Literary Essays*, 1923, p. 208.

be confident you shall fynd the effects of his Mās favour, as they can be witnessed you by

Your very faithfull freinde,
Montrose.'

Strethearne,
20 Jañ. 1646.

The other is,

For the Laird of Col.

' Sir,
' HAVING occasion to write to your fields, I cannot be forgetful of your willingness and good affection to his Majesty's service. I acknowledge to you, and thank you heartily for it;[a] assuring, that in what lies in my power, you shall find the good. Mean while, I shall expect that you will continue your loyal endeavours, in wishing those slack people that are about you, to appear more obedient than they do, and loyal in their prince's service ; whereby I assure you, you shall find me ever

Your faithful friend,
Montrose [1].'

Petty,
17 April, 1646.

I found some uncouth lines on the death of the present laird's father, intituled ' Nature's Elegy upon the death of Donald Maclean of Col.' They are not worth insertion. I shall only give what is called his Epitaph, which Dr. Johnson said, ' was not so very bad.'

' Nature's minion, Virtue's wonder,
' Art's corrective,[b] here lyes under.'

I asked, what ' Art's corrective ' meant. ' Why, sir, (said he,) that the laird was so exquisite, that he set Art right, when she was wrong.'

I found several letters † to the late Col, from my father's old companion at Paris, Sir Hector M'Lean, one of which was written at the time of settling the colony in Georgia [2]. It dissuades Col from letting people go there, and assures him there will soon be an opportunity of employing them better at home. Hence it appears that emigration from the Highlands, though not in such

---

[a] it; 1 (*Boswell's copy*): it, 2, 3.   [b] corrective, 1, 2: corrective 3.

[1] It is observable that men of the first rank spelt very ill in the last century. In the first of these letters I have preserved the original spelling. Boswell, ed. 1.

† ⟨For a highly interesting letter which Boswell suppressed see *Hebrides*, ed. Pottle and Bennett, 1936, pp. 277–8.⟩

[2] See *ante*, i. 127, note 4.

numbers at a time as of late, has always been practised. Dr. Johnson observed, that, 'the Lairds, instead of improving their country, diminished their people.'

There are several districts of sandy desert in Col. There are forty-eight lochs of fresh water; but many of them are very small, —mere pools. About one half of them, however, have trout and eel. There is a great number of horses in the island, mostly of a small size. Being over-stocked, they sell some in Tir-yi, and on the main land. Their black cattle, which are chiefly rough-haired, are reckoned remarkably good. The climate being very mild in winter, they never put their beasts in any house. The lakes are never frozen so as to bear a man; and snow never lies above a few hours. They have a good many sheep, which they eat mostly themselves, and sell but a few. They have goats in several places. There are no foxes; no serpents, toads, or frogs, nor any venomous creature. They have otters and mice here; but had no rats till lately that an American vessel brought them. There is a rabbit-warren on the north-east of the island, belonging to the Duke of Argyle. Young Col intends to get some hares, of which there are none at present. There are no black-cock, muir-fowl [1], nor partridges; but there are snipe, wild-duck, wild-geese, and swans, in winter; wild-pidgeons, plover, and great numbers [a] of starlings; of which I shot some, and found them pretty good eating. Woodcocks come hither, though there is not a tree upon the island. There are no rivers in Col; but only some brooks, in which there is a great variety of fish. In the whole isle there are but three hills, and none of them considerable, for a Highland country. The people are very industrious. Every man can tan. They get oak, and birch-bark, and lime, from the main land. Some have pits; but they commonly use tubs. I saw brogues [2] very well tanned; and every man can make them. They all make candles of the tallow of their beasts, both moulded and dipped; and they all make oil of the livers of fish. The little fish called Cuddies produce a great deal. They sell some oil out of the island, and they use it much for light in their houses, in little iron lamps, most of which they have from England; but of late their own blacksmith makes them. He

---

[a] numbers 1 : number 2, 3.

[1] Muir-fowl is grouse. *Ante*, v. 44.   [2] See *ante*, v. 162, note 1.

is a good workman; but he has no employment in shoeing horses, for they all go unshod here, except some of a better kind belonging to young Col, which were now in Mull. There are two carpenters in Col; but most of the inhabitants can do something as boat-carpenters. They can all dye. Heath is used for yellow; and for red, a moss which grows on stones. They make broad-cloth, and tartan, and linen, of their own wool and flax, sufficient for their own use; as also stockings. Their bonnets come from the main land. Hard-ware and several small articles are brought annually from Greenock, and sold in the only shop in the island, which is kept near the house, or rather hut, used for publick worship, there being no church in the island.— The inhabitants of Col have increased considerably within these thirty years, as appears from the parish registers. There are but three considerable tacksmen on Col's part of the island [1]: the rest is let to small tenants, some of whom pay so low a rent as four, three, or even two guineas. The highest is seven pounds, paid by a farmer, whose son goes yearly on foot to Aberdeen for education, and in summer returns, and acts as a school-master in Col. Dr. Johnson said, 'There is something noble in a young man's walking two hundred miles and back again, every year, for the sake of learning [2].'

This day a number of people came to Col, with complaints of each other's [a] trespasses. Corneck, to prevent their being troublesome, told them, that the lawyer from Edinburgh was here, and,[b] if they did not agree, he would take them to task. They were alarmed at this; said, they had never been used to go to law, and hoped Col would settle matters himself.—In the evening Corneck left us.

[a] other's 1 (*MS.*): others' 2, 3.   [b] and, 1, 2: and 3.

[1] 'In Col only two houses pay the window tax; for only two have six windows, which, I suppose, are the Laird's and Mr. Macsweyn's.' Johnson's *Western Isl.*, p. 116. 'The window-tax, as it stands at present, (January 1775) ... lays a duty upon every window, which, in England, augments gradually from two-pence, the lowest rate, upon houses with not more than seven windows; to two shillings, the highest rate, upon houses with twenty-five windows and upwards.' Adam Smith, *Wealth of Nations*, v. 2. 2. 1. The tax was first imposed in 1695, as a substitute for hearth money. Macaulay's *England*, ed. 1858, vii. 271. It was abolished in 1851.

[2] ⟨According to Boswell's Orig. Jrnl. Neil Maclean of Crocepole or Crossapoll, 'a most industrious man'. The son was Donald, the eldest of ten children. He gained one bursary at King's College, Aberdeen, 'upon a competition', and Coll procured him another 'for four years as a student of Divinity'. Ed. Pottle and Bennett, 1936, p. 283. See App. D, p. 553.⟩

Saturday, 9th October.

As, in our present confinement, any thing that had even the name of curious was an object of attention, I proposed that Col should show me the great stone, mentioned in a former page [1], as having been thrown by a giant to the top of a mountain. Dr. Johnson, who did not like to be left alone, said he would accompany us as far as riding was practicable. We ascended a part of the hill on horseback, and Col and I scrambled up the rest. A servant held our horses, and Dr. Johnson placed himself on the ground, with his back against a large fragment of rock. The wind being high, he let down the cocks of his hat, and tied it with his handkerchief under his chin. While we were employed in examining the stone, which did not repay our trouble in getting to it, he amused himself with reading *Gataker on Lots and on the Christian Watch* [2], a very learned book, of the last age, which had been found in the garret of Col's house, and which he said was a treasure here. When we descried him from above, he had a most eremitical appearance; and on our return told us, he had been so much engaged by Gataker, that he had never missed us. His avidity for a variety [a] of books, while we were in Col, was frequently expressed; and he often complained that so few were within his reach. Upon which I observed to him, that it was strange he should complain of want of books, when he could at any time make such good ones.

We next proceeded to the lead mine. In our way we came to a strand of some extent, where we were glad to take a gallop, in which my learned friend joined with great alacrity. Dr. Johnson, mounted on a large bay mare without shoes, and followed by a foal, which had some difficulty in keeping up with him, was a singular spectacle.

After examining the mine, we returned through a very uncouth district, full of sand hills; down which, though apparent precipices, our horses carried us with safety, the sand always gently sliding away from their feet. Vestiges of houses were pointed out to us, which Col, and two others who had joined us,

[a] a variety 1 (*and Contents*): variety 2, 3.

[1] *Ante*, v. 290.
[2] *Of the Nature and Use of Lots; a Treatise historicall and theologicall.* By Thomas Gataker. London, 1619.

The Spirituall Watch, or Christ's Generall Watch-word. By Thomas Gataker. London, 1619.

asserted had been overwhelmed with sand blown over them. But, on going close to one of them, Dr. Johnson shewed the absurdity of the notion, by remarking, that ' it was evidently only a house abandoned, the stones of which had been taken away for other purposes ; for the large stones, which form the lower part of the walls, were still standing higher than the sand. If *they* were not blown over, it was clear nothing higher than they could be blown over.' This was quite convincing to me ; but it made not the least impression on Col and the others, who were not to be argued out of a Highland tradition.

We did not sit down to dinner till between six and seven. We lived plentifully here, and had a true welcome. In such a season, good firing was of no small importance. The peats were excellent, and burned cheerfully. Those at Dunvegan, which were damp, Dr. Johnson called ' a sullen fuel.'—Here a Scottish phrase was singularly applied to him. One of the company having remarked that he had gone out on a stormy evening, and brought in a supply of peats from the stack, old Mr. M'Sweyn said, ' that was *main honest* [1] ! '

Blenheim being occasionally mentioned, he told me he had never seen it [2] : he had not gone formerly ; and he would not go now, just as a common spectator, for his money : he would not put it in the power of some man about the Duke of Marlborough to say, ' Johnson was here ; I knew him, but I took no notice of him [3].' He said, he should be very glad to see it, if properly invited, which in all probability would never be the case, as it was not worth his while to seek for it.—I observed, that he might be easily introduced there by a common friend of ours, nearly related to the duke [4]. He answered, with an uncommon attention to delicacy of feeling, ' I doubt whether our friend be on such a footing with the duke as to carry any body there ;

[1] ⟨Boswell's Orig. Jrnl., 14 Oct., tells us that M'Sweyn's son was the relater of this incident, which he himself had witnessed : he observed that Johnson tied his handkerchief round his head. The story was inserted in the second edition at Malone's suggestion.⟩
[2] He visited it with the Thrales on Sept. 22, 1774 (*post*, v. 458), when returning from his tour to Wales, and with Boswell in 1776 (*ante*, ii. 451).
[3] Mr. Croker says, 1848, that 'this, no doubt, alludes to Jacob Bryant,

the secretary or librarian at Blenheim, with whom Johnson had had, perhaps, some coolness now forgotten.' The supposition of the coolness seems needless. With so little to go upon, guessing is very hazardous.
[4] Topham Beauclerk, who had married the Duke's sister, after she had been divorced for adultery with him from her first husband, Viscount Bolingbroke. *Ante*, ii. 246, note 1. ⟨This identification is confirmed by Boswell's Orig. Jrnl., ed. Pottle and Bennett, 1936, p. 289.⟩

and I would not give him the uneasiness of seeing that I knew he was not, or even of being himself reminded of it.'

Sunday, 10th October.

There was this day the most terrible storm of wind and rain that I ever remember [1]. It made such an awful impression on us all, as to produce, for some time, a kind of dismal quietness in the house. The day was passed without much conversation: only, upon my observing that there must be something bad in a man's mind, who does not like to give leases to his tenants, but wishes to keep them in a perpetual wretched dependence on his will, Dr. Johnson said, 'You are right: it is a man's duty to extend comfort and security among as many people as he can. He should not wish to have his tenants mere *Ephemeræ*,—mere beings of an hour [2].'—*Boswell.* 'But, sir, if they have leases, is there not some danger that they may grow insolent? I remember you yourself once told me, an English tenant was so independent, that, if provoked, he would *throw* his rent at his landlord.'—*Johnson.* 'Depend upon it, sir, it is the landlord's own fault, if it is thrown at him. A man may always keep his tenants in dependence enough, though they have leases. He must be a good tenant indeed, who will not fall behind in his rent, if his landlord will let him; and if he does fall behind, his landlord has him at his mercy. Indeed, the poor man is always much at the mercy of the rich; no matter whether landlord or tenant. If the tenant lets his landlord have a little rent beforehand, or has lent him money, then the landlord is in his power. There cannot be a greater man than a tenant who has lent money to his landlord; for he has under subjection the very man to whom he should be subjected.'

Monday, 11th October.

We had some days ago engaged the Campbelltown vessel to carry us to Mull, from the harbour where she lay. The morning was fine, and the wind fair and moderate; so we hoped at length to get away.

[1] See *post*, v. 407.
[2] See *ante*, ii. 340, where Johnson said that 'if he were a gentleman of landed property, he would turn out all his tenants who did not vote for the candidate whom he supported.'

Mrs. M'Sweyn †, who officiated as our landlady here, had never been on the main land. On hearing this, Dr. Johnson said to me, before her, ' That is rather being behind-hand with life. I would at least go and see Glenelg.'—*Boswell*. ' You yourself, sir, have never seen, till now, any thing but your native island.' —*Johnson*. ' But, sir, by seeing London, I have seen as much of life as the world can shew ¹.'—*Boswell*. ' You have not seen Pekin.' —*Johnson*. ' What is Pekin ? Ten thousand Londoners would drive all the people of Pekin : they would drive them like deer.'

We set out about eleven for the harbour ; but, before we reached it, so violent a storm came on, that we were obliged again to take shelter in the house of Captain M'Lean, where we dined, and passed the night.

Tuesday, 12th October.

After breakfast, we made a second attempt to get to the harbour ; but another storm soon convinced us that it would be in vain. Captain M'Lean's house being in some confusion, on account of Mrs. M'Lean being expected to lie-in, we resolved to go to Mr. M'Sweyn's, where we arrived very wet, fatigued, and hungry. In this situation, we were somewhat disconcerted by being told that we should have no dinner till late in the evening ; but should have tea in the mean time. Dr. Johnson opposed this arrangement ; but they persisted, and he took the tea very readily. He said to me afterwards, ' You must consider, sir, a dinner here is a matter of great consequence. It is a thing to be first planned, and then executed. I suppose the mutton was brought some miles off, from some place where they knew there was a sheep killed.'

Talking of the good people with whom we were, he said, ' Life has not got at all forward by a generation in M'Sweyn's family ; for the son is exactly formed upon the father. What the father says, the son says ; and what the father looks, the son looks.'

There being little conversation to-night, I must endeavour to recollect what I may have omitted on former occasions.—When I boasted, at Rasay, of my independency of spirit, and that I

---

† ⟨' She was one of the hardest favoured women that I ever saw, swarthy & marked with the small-pox, & of very ungainly manners.' Boswell's *Hebrides*, ed. Pottle and Bennett, 1936, p. 291.⟩
¹ See *ante*, iii. 378.

could not be bribed, he said, ' Yes, you may be bribed by flattery.'—At the Reverend Mr. M'Lean's, Dr. Johnson asked him, if the people of Col had any superstitions. He said, ' No.' The cutting peats at the increase of the moon was mentioned as one ; but he would not allow it, saying, it was not a superstition, but a whim. Dr. Johnson would not admit the distinction. There were many superstitions, he maintained, not connected with religion ; and this was one of them [1].—On Monday we had a dispute at the Captain's, whether sand-hills could be fixed down by art. Dr. Johnson said, ' How *the devil* can you do it ? ' but instantly corrected himself, ' How can you do it [2] ? ' —I never before heard him use a phrase of that nature.

He has particularities which it is impossible to explain [3]. He never wears a night-cap, as I have already mentioned ; but he puts a handkerchief on his head in the night.—The day that we left Talisker, he bade us ride on. He then turned the head of his horse back towards Talisker, stopped for some time ; then wheeled round to the same direction with ours, and then came briskly after us. He sets open a window in the coldest day or night, and stands before it. It may do with his constitution ; but most people, amongst whom I am one, would say, with the frogs in the fable, ' This may be sport to you ; but it is death to us.'—It is in vain to try to find a meaning in every one of his particularities, which, I suppose, are mere habits, contracted by chance ; of which every man has some that are more or less remarkable. His speaking to himself, or rather repeating, is a common habit with studious men accustomed to deep thinking ; and, in consequence of their being thus rapt, they will even laugh by themselves, if the subject which they are musing on is

---

[1] ' They have opinions, which cannot be ranked with superstition, because they regard only natural effects. They expect better crops of grain, by sowing their seed in the moon's increase. The moon has great influence in vulgar philosophy. In my memory it was a precept annually given in one of the English Almanacks, " to kill hogs when the moon was increasing, and the bacon would prove the better in boiling." '

Johnson's *Western Isl.*, p. 97. Bacon, in his *Natural History* (No. 892) says :—' For the Increase of Moisture, the Opinion Receiued is, that Seeds will grow soonest . . . if they be Set, or Cut, in the Increase of the Moone.'

[2] The question which Johnson asked with such unusual warmth might have been answered, ' by sowing the bent, or couch-grass.' SCOTT, 1831.

[3] See *ante*, i. 484.

a merry one. Dr. Johnson is often uttering pious ejaculations, when he appears to be talking to himself; for sometimes his voice grows stronger, and parts of the Lord's Prayer are heard [1]. I have sat beside him with more than ordinary reverence on such occasions [2].

In our Tour, I observed that he was disgusted whenever he met with coarse manners. He said † to me, ' I know not how it is, but I cannot bear low life [3] : and I find others, who have as good a right as I to be fastidious, bear it better, by having mixed more with different sorts of men. You would think that I have mixed pretty well too.'

He read this day a good deal of my Journal, written in a small book with which he had supplied me, and was pleased, for he said, ' I wish thy books were twice as big [4].' He helped me to fill up blanks which I had left in first writing it, when I was not quite sure of what he had said, and he corrected any mistakes that I had made. ' They call me a scholar, (said he,) and yet how very little literature is there in my conversation.'—*Boswell.* ' That, sir, must be according to your company. You would not give literature to those who cannot taste it. Stay till we meet Lord Elibank.'

We had at last a good dinner, or rather supper, and were very well satisfied with our entertainment.

Wednesday, 13th October.

Col called me up, with intelligence that it was a good day for a passage to Mull; and just as we rose, a sailor from the vessel arrived for us. We got all ready with dispatch. Dr. Johnson was displeased at my bustling, and walking quickly up and down. He said, ' It does not hasten us a bit. It is getting on

---

[1] See *ante*, i. 483.

[2] It is remarkable, that Dr. Johnson should have read this account of some of his own peculiar habits, without saying any thing on the subject, which I hoped he would have done. BOSWELL, ed. 1.

See *ante*, v. 128, note 2, and iv. 183, where Boswell ' observed, he must have been a bold laugher who would have ventured to tell Dr. Johnson of any of his particularities.'

† ⟨At McSweyn's. Boswell's *Hebrides*, ed. Pottle and Bennett, 1936, p. 293.⟩

[3] In this he was very unlike Swift, who, in his youth, when travelling in England, ' generally chose to dine with waggoners, hostlers, and persons of that rank; and he used to lye at night in houses where he found written over the door *Lodgings for a penny.* He delighted in scenes of low life.' Orrery's *Swift*, ed. 1752, p. 22.

[4] ⟨See App. C, p. 425.⟩

horseback in a ship [1]. All boys do it ; and you are longer a boy than others.' He himself has no alertness, or whatever it may be called ; so he may dislike it, as *Oderunt hilarem tristes* [2].

Before we reached the harbour, the wind grew high again. However, the small boat was waiting, and took us on board. We remained for some time in uncertainty what to do : at last it was determined, that, as a good part of the day was over, and it was dangerous to be at sea at night, in such a vessel, and such weather, we should not sail till the morning tide, when the wind would probably be more gentle. We resolved not to go ashore again, but lie here in readiness. Dr. Johnson and I had each a bed in the cabbin. Col sat at the fire in the forecastle, with the captain, and Joseph, and the rest. I eat † some dry oatmeal, of which I found a barrel in the cabbin. I had not done this since I was a boy. Dr. Johnson owned that he too was fond of it when a boy [3] ; a circumstance which I was highly pleased to hear from him, as it gave me an opportunity of observing that, notwithstanding his joke on the article of OATS [4], he was himself a proof that this kind of *food* was not peculiar to the people of Scotland.

Thursday, 14th October.

When Dr. Johnson awaked this morning, he called ' *Lanky !* ' having, I suppose, been thinking of Langton ; but corrected himself instantly, and cried, ' *Bozzy !* ' He has a way of contracting the names of his friends. Goldsmith feels himself so important now, as to be displeased at it. I remember one day, when Tom Davies was telling that Dr. Johnson said, ' We are all in labour for a name to *Goldy's* play,' Goldsmith cried, ' I have often desired him not to call me *Goldy* [5].'

Between six and seven we hauled our anchor, and set sail with a fair breeze ; and, after a pleasant voyage, we got safely and agreeably into the harbour of Tobermorie, before the wind rose, which it always has done, for some days, about noon.

Tobermorie is an excellent harbour. An island lies before

---

[1] ⟨This is xxiv. of the *Facetiæ* of Hierocles, where we read that ' Scholasticus, wishing to cross a river, embarked on the vessel on horseback and when some one asked him the cause of this, replied that he was in haste '. E. B.⟩

[2] ' The grave a gay companion shun.' FRANCIS. Horace, 1 *Epis.*

xviii. 89.

† ⟨The word Boswell first wrote in his Journal was ' licked '.⟩

[3] Boswell in 1776 found that ' oats were much used as the *food of the people* in Dr. Johnson's own town.' *Ante*, ii. 463.

[4] *Ante*, i. 294.

[5] See *ante*, ii. ⟨205 and⟩ 258.

it, and it is surrounded by a hilly theatre [1]. The island is too low, otherwise this would be quite a secure port; but, the island not being a sufficient protection, some storms blow very hard here. Not long ago, fifteen vessels were blown from their moorings. There are sometimes sixty or seventy sail here: to-day there were twelve or fourteen vessels. To see such a fleet was the next thing to seeing a town. The vessels were from different places; Clyde, Campbelltown, Newcastle, &c. One was returning to Lancaster from Hamburgh. After having been shut up so long in Col, the sight of such an assemblage of moving habitations, containing such a variety of people, engaged in different pursuits, gave me much gaiety of spirit. When we had landed, Dr. Johnson said, ' Boswell is now all alive. He is like Antæus; he gets new vigour whenever he touches the ground.'—I went to the top of a hill fronting the harbour, from whence I had a good view of it. We had here a tolerable inn †. Dr. Johnson had owned to me this morning, that he was out of humour. Indeed, he shewed it a good deal in the ship; for when I was expressing my joy on the prospect of our landing in Mull, he said, he had no joy, when he recollected that it would be five days before he should get to the main land. I was afraid he would now take a sudden resolution to give up seeing Icolmkill. A dish of tea, and some good bread and butter, did him service, and his bad humour went off. I told him, that I was diverted to hear all the people whom we had visited in our Tour, say, ' Honest man ! he's pleased with every thing; he's always content ! '—' Little do they know,' said I. He laughed, and said, ' You rogue [2] ! '

[1] ' The richness of the round steep green knolls, clothed with copse, and glancing with cascades, and a pleasant peep at a small fresh-water loch embosomed among them—the view of the bay, surrounded and guarded by the island of Colvay—the gliding of two or three vessels in the more distant Sound—and the row of the gigantic Ardnamurchan mountains closing the scene to the north, almost justify the eulogium of Sacheverell, [post, v. 336] who, in 1688, declared the bay of Tobermory might equal any prospect in Italy.' Lockhart's Scott, iii. 253.

† ⟨It was kept by a Mr. McArthur. Boswell's Hebrides, ed. Pottle and Bennett, 1936, p. 298. In 1814 it was called The Old Portmor Inn.⟩

[2] 'The saying of the old philosopher, who observes, That he who wants least is most like the gods, who want nothing; was a favourite sentence with Dr. Johnson, who on his own part required less attendance, sick or well, than ever I saw any human creature. Conversation was all he required to make him happy.' Piozzi's Anec. p. 275 : Johnson, Misc. i. 329.

Thursday 14 October 1773 — Mull

We sent to hire horses to carry us across the island of Mull to the shore opposite to Inchkenneth, the residence of Sir Allan M'Lean, uncle to young Col, and Chief of the M'Leans, to whose house we intended to go the next day. Our friend Col went to visit his aunt, the wife of Dr. Alexander[a] M'Lean, a physician, who lives about a mile from Tobermorie.

Dr. Johnson and I sat by ourselves at the inn, and talked a good deal.—I told him, that I had found, in Leandro Alberti's Description of Italy, much of what Addison has given us in his *Remarks*[1]. He said, ' The collection of passages from the Classicks has been made by another Italian : it is, however, impossible to detect a man as a plagiary in such a case, because all who set about making such a collection must find the same passages ; but, if you find the same applications in another book, then Addison's learning in his *Remarks* tumbles down. It is a tedious book ; and, if it were not attached to Addison's previous reputation, one would not think much of it. Had he written nothing else, his name would not have lived. Addison does not seem to have gone deep in Italian literature : he shews nothing of it in his subsequent writings. He shews a great deal of French learning.—There is, perhaps, more knowledge circulated in the French language than in any other [2]. There is more original knowledge in English.'—' But the French (said I) have the art of accommodating [3] literature.'—*Johnson*.

[a] read Hector

[1] *Remarks on Several Parts of Italy* (ante, ii. 346, 519). Johnson (*Addison*, 23) says of these *Travels* :—' Of many parts it is not a very severe censure to say that they might have been written at home.' He adds that ' the book, though a while neglected, became in time so much the favourite of the publick, that before it was reprinted it rose to five times its price.' ⟨See App. D, p. 554⟩.

[2] See *ante*, iii. 254, and iv. 237.

[3] Johnson (*Pope*, 295) says of Pope that ' he had before him not only what his own meditation suggested, but what he had found in other writers that might be *accommodated* to his present purpose.' Boswell's use of the word is perhaps derived, as Mr. Croker suggests, from *accommoder*, in the sense of *dressing up* or *cooking meats*. This word occurs in an amusing story that Boswell tells in No. 17 of his *Hypochondriack* (*London Mag.* 1779, p. 55) :—' A friend of mine told me, that he engaged a French cook for Sir Benjamin Keen, when ambassador in Spain, and when he asked the fellow if he had ever dressed any magnificent dinners, the answer was, " Monsieur, j'ai accommodé un dîner qui faisoit trembler toute la France." ' Scott, in *Guy Mannering* (ch. xiii), describes ' Miss Bertram's solicitude to soothe and *accommodate* her parent.' See *ante*, iv. 39, note 1, for ' *accommodated* the ladies.' To

Mull *Thursday 14 October* 1773 311

'Yes, sir; we have no such book as Moreri's Dictionary¹.' *Boswell.* 'Their *Ana*² are good.'—*Johnson.* 'A few of them are good; but we have one book of that kind better than any of them; Selden's *Table-talk* †. As to original literature, the French have a couple of tragick poets who go round the world, *Racine* and *Corneille*, and one comick poet, *Moliere.*'—*Boswell.* 'They have *Fenelon.*'—*Johnson.* 'Why, sir, *Telemachus* is pretty well.' —*Boswell.* 'And *Voltaire*, sir.'—*Johnson.* 'He has not stood his trial yet. And what makes Voltaire chiefly circulate, is collection; such as his *Universal History.*'—*Boswell.* 'What do you say to the Bishop of *Meaux?* '—*Johnson.* ' Sir, nobody reads him 3.'—He would not allow *Massillon* and *Bourdaloue* to go round the world. In general, however, he gave the French much praise for their industry.

He asked me whether he had mentioned, in any of the papers of the *Rambler*, the description in Virgil of the entrance into Hell, with an application to the press; 'for (said he) I do not much remember them.' I told him, 'No.' Upon which he repeated it:

> Vestibulum ante ipsum, primisque in faucibus orci,
> Luctus et ultrices posuere cubilia Curæ;
> Pallentesque habitant Morbi, tristisque Senectus,
> Et metus, et malesuada Fames, et turpis Egestas,
> Terribiles visu formæ; Lethumque, Laborque 4.

---

sum up, we may say with Justice Shallow:—'Accommodated! it comes of *accommodo*; very good; a good phrase.' 2 *Henry IV*, act iii. sc. 2.

¹ 'Louis Moréri, né en Provence en 1643. On ne s'attendait pas que l'auteur du *Pays d'amour*, et le traducteur de *Rodriguez*, entreprît dans sa jeunesse le premier dictionnaire de faits qu'on eût encore vu. Ce grand travail lui coûta la vie . . . Mort en 1680.' Voltaire's *Œuvres*, 1878, xiv. 409. ⟨*Le Grand Dictionaire historique* was first published, in one volume folio, in 1673; the last edition, ' revu, corrigé et augmenté par Drouet' appeared, in ten volumes folio, in 1759.⟩

² Johnson looked upon *Ana* as an English word, for he gives it in his *Dictionary.*

† ⟨*Table-Talk: being the Discourses of John Selden Esq.* Compiled by Richard Milward, Selden's secretary, and published posthumously in 1689.⟩

3 I take leave to enter my strongest protest against this judgement. Bossuet I hold to be one of the first luminaries of religion and literature. If there are who do not read him, it is full time they should begin. BOSWELL, ed. 1.

4 Just in the gate, and in the jaws
of hell,
Revengeful cares, and sullen
sorrows dwell;
And pale diseases, and repining
age;
Want, fear, and famine's unresisted rage;
Here toils and death, and death's
half-brother, sleep,
Forms terrible to view, their
sentry keep.
Dryden, [*Æneid*, vi. 273.] BOSWELL, ed. 2. ⟨See *post*, v. 554.⟩ Voltaire,

'Now, (said he,) almost all these apply exactly to an authour; all these are the concomitants of a printing-house.' I proposed to him to dictate an essay on it, and offered to write it. He said, he would not do it then, but perhaps would write one at some future period.

The Sunday evening that we sat by ourselves at Aberdeen, I asked him several particulars of his life, from his early years, which he readily told me; and I wrote them down before him. This day I proceeded in my inquiries, also writing them in his presence. I have them on detached sheets. I shall collect authentic materials for THE LIFE OF SAMUEL JOHNSON, LL.D.; and, if I survive him, I shall be one who will most faithfully do honour to his memory. I have now a vast treasure of his conversation, at different times, since the year 1762 [1], when I first obtained his acquaintance; and, by assiduous inquiry, I can make up for not knowing him sooner [2].

A Newcastle ship-master †, who happened to be in the house, intruded himself upon us. He was much in liquor, and talked nonsense about his being a man for *Wilkes and Liberty*, and against the ministry. Dr. Johnson was angry, that 'a fellow should come into *our* company, who was fit for *no* company.' He left us soon.

Col returned from his aunt, and told us, she insisted that we should come to her house that night. He introduced to us Mr. Campbell, the Duke of Argyle's factor in Tyr-yi. He was a genteel, agreeable man. He was going to Inveraray, and promised to put letters into the post-office for us [3]. I now found that Dr. Johnson's desire to get on the main land, arose from

in a letter to a young poet named Lefebvre or Lefèvre, who died in 1732 or 1734 (*Œuvres*, 1880, t. xxx, p. 293), says:—'Enfin, après un an de refus et de négociations, votre ouvrage s'imprime; c'est alors qu'il faut ou assoupir les Cerbères de la littérature, ou les faire aboyer en votre faveur.' He therefore carries on the resemblance one step further,—

'Cerberus haec ingens latratu regna trifauci
Personat.' *Æneid*, vi. 417.
[1] It was in 1763 that Boswell made Johnson's acquaintance. *Ante*, i. 391. ⟨Boswell refers to his Journal, the greater part of which has now been published: see *ante*, i, p. xix, n. 3.⟩

[2] It is no small satisfaction to me to reflect, that Dr. Johnson read this, and, after being apprized of my intention, communicated to me, at subsequent periods, many particulars of his life, which probably could not otherwise have been preserved. BOSWELL, ed. 1. See *ante*, i. 26; ii. 166, 217; iii. 196.

† ⟨According to Boswell's Orig. Jrnl. his name was Nisbet.⟩

[3] Though Mull is, as Johnson says, the third island of the Hebrides in extent, there was no post there. Johnson's *Letters*, No. 332.

Mull *Thursday 14 October 1773*

his anxiety to have an opportunity of conveying letters to his friends.

After dinner, we proceeded to Dr. M'Lean's, which was about a mile from our inn †. He was not at home, but we were received by his lady and daughter, who entertained us so well, that Dr. Johnson seemed quite happy. When we had supped, he asked me to give him some paper to write letters. I begged he would write short ones, and not *expatiate*, as we ought to set off early. He was irritated by this, and said, ' What must be done, must be done ; the thing is past a joke.'—' Nay, sir, (said I,) write as much as you please ; but do not blame me, if we are kept six days before we get to the main land. You were very impatient in the morning : but no sooner do you find yourself in good quarters, than you forget that you are to move.' I got him paper enough, and we parted in good humour.

Let me now recollect whatever particulars I have omitted.— In the morning I said to him, before we landed at Tobermorie, ' We shall see Dr. M'Lean, who has written the History of the M'Leans.'—*Johnson*. ' I have no great patience to stay to hear the history of the M'Leans. I would rather hear the History of the Thrales.'—When on Mull, I said, ' Well, sir, this is the fourth of the Hebrides that we have been upon.'—*Johnson*. ' Nay, we cannot boast of the number we have seen. We thought we should see many more. We thought of sailing about easily from island to island ; and so we should, had we come at a better season [1] ; but we, being wise men, thought it would be summer all the year where *we* were. However, sir, we have seen enough to give us a pretty good notion of the system of insular life.'

Let me not forget, that he sometimes amused himself with very slight reading ; from which, however, his conversation shewed that he contrived to extract some benefit. At Captain M'Lean's he read a good deal in *The Charmer*, a collection of songs [2].

---

† ⟨Johnson was mounted. ' Coll and I and the servants walked. A Highlander led Mr. Johnson's horse, and Coll's servant walked holding a candle which burned till we saw the light of a candle at Dr. MacLean's.' Boswell's *Hebrides*, ed. Pottle and Bennett, 1936, p. 301. For Dr. MacLean's house and his History of the MacLeans see App. D, pp. 554–5.⟩

[1] This observation is very just. The time for the Hebrides was too late by a month or six weeks. I have heard those who remembered their tour express surprise they were not drowned. SCOTT, 1831.

[2] ⟨*The Charmer ; a choice Collection of Songs, English and Scots*. Edinburgh, 1749. Sir Gilbert Elliot's ' Amynta ' made its first appearance in it. Second and third editions were published in 1752 and 1765, and a second volume was added in 1751 ; in 1782 an augmented edition of both volumes appeared. The compiler, ' J. G.', has not been identified.⟩

Friday, 15th October.

We this morning found that we could not proceed, there being a violent storm of wind and rain, and the rivers being impassable. When I expressed my discontent † at our confinement, Dr. Johnson said, 'Now that I have had an opportunity of writing to the main land, I am in no such haste.' I was amused with his being so easily satisfied; for the truth was, that the gentleman who was to convey our letters, as I was now informed, was not to set out for Inveraray for some time; so that it was probable we should be there as soon as he: however, I did not undeceive my friend, but suffered him to enjoy his fancy.

Dr. Johnson asked, in the evening, to see Dr. M'Lean's books. He took down Willis *de Anima Brutorum* [1], and pored over it a good deal.

Miss M'Lean produced some Erse poems by John M'Lean, who was a famous bard in Mull, and had died only a few years ago. He could neither read nor write. She read and translated two of them; one, a kind of elegy on Sir John M'Lean's being obliged to fly his country in 1715; another, a dialogue between two Roman Catholick young ladies, sisters, whether it was better to be a nun or to marry. I could not perceive much poetical imagery in the translation. Yet all of our company who understood Erse, seemed charmed with the original. There may, perhaps, be some choice of expression, and some excellence of arrangement, that cannot be shewn in translation.

After we had exhausted the Erse poems, of which Dr. Johnson said nothing, Miss M'Lean gave us several tunes on a spinnet, which, though made so long ago, as in 1667, was still very well toned. She sung along with it. Dr. Johnson seemed pleased with the musick, though he owns he neither likes it, nor has hardly any perception of it. At Mr. M'Pherson's, in Slate, he told us, that 'he knew a drum from a trumpet, and a bagpipe

---

† ⟨Boswell had had a bad night. He writes in his Journal: 'when I was going to bed, Joseph perceived that the sheets were not clean. I looked at them and was shocked at their dirtiness. I threw off only my boots and coat and waistcoat, and put on my greatcoat as a night-gown, and so lay down. The mixture of brandy punch at the inn and rum punch here, joined with a comfortless bed, made me rest very poorly.' He could hardly keep from 'repining indecently'. Ed. Pottle and Bennett, 1936, p. 303.⟩

[1] By Thomas Willis, M.D. It was published in 1672.

from a guittar, which was about the extent of his knowledge of musick.' To-night he said, that, 'if he had learnt musick, he should have been afraid he would have done nothing else but play. It was a method of employing the mind, without the labour of thinking at all, and with some applause from a man's self [1].'

We had the musick of the bagpipe every day, at Armidale, Dunvegan, and Col. Dr. Johnson appeared fond of it, and used often to stand for some time with his ear close to the great drone.

The penurious gentleman of our acquaintance, formerly alluded to [2], afforded us a topick of conversation to-night. Dr. Johnson said, I ought to write down a collection of the instances of his narrowness, as they almost exceeded belief. Col told us, that O'Kane [3], the famous Irish harper, was once at that gentleman's house. He could not find in his heart to give him any money, but gave him a key for a harp, which was finely ornamented with gold and silver, and with a precious stone, and was worth eighty or a hundred guineas. He did not know the value of it; and when he came to know it, he would fain have had it back; but O'Kane took care that he should not.—*Johnson.* 'They exaggerate the value; every body is so desirous that he should be fleeced. I am very willing it should be worth eighty or a hundred guineas; but I do not believe it.'—*Boswell.* 'I do not think O'Kane was obliged to give it back.'—*Johnson.* 'No, sir. If a man with his eyes open, and without any means used to deceive him, gives me a thing, I am not to let him have it again when he grows wiser. I like to see how avarice defeats itself: how, when avoiding to part with money, the miser gives something more valuable.'—Col said, the gentleman's relations were angry at his giving away the harp-key, for it had been long in the family.—*Johnson.* 'Sir, he values a new guinea more than an old friend.'

Col also told us, that the same person having come up with a serjeant and twenty men, working on the high road, he entered into discourse with the serjeant, and then gave him sixpence for the men to drink. The serjeant asked, 'Who is this fellow?'

---

[1] See *ante*, ii. 409 and iii. 242.
[2] *Ante*, v. 277 ⟨and *Letters*, No. 337⟩.
[3] ⟨Eachmarcach O'Kane, 1720–90: see *D.N.B.* Sir Alexander in the letter, 26 Nov. 1785, which nearly caused the duel, explains that O'Kane, 'after having slurred over some tunes' for a week at his house, 'under the inordinate influence of Bacchus, was dismissed with two guineas in his pocket and a key which he valued more than one hundred Guineas, made of common Agate'. *Boswell Papers*, xvi. 239.⟩

Upon being informed, he said, 'If I had known who he was, I should have thrown it in his face.'—*Johnson.* 'There is much want of sense in all this. He had no business to speak with the serjeant. He might have been in haste, and trotted on. He has not learnt to be a miser: I believe we must take him apprentice.'—*Boswell.* 'He would grudge giving half a guinea to be taught.'—*Johnson.* 'Nay, sir, you must teach him *gratis*. You must give him an opportunity to practice your precepts.'

Let me now go back, and glean *Johnsoniana*.—The Saturday before we sailed from Slate, I sat awhile in the afternoon with Dr. Johnson in his room, in a quiet serious frame. I observed, that hardly any man was accurately prepared for dying; but almost every one left something undone, something in confusion; that my father, indeed, told me he knew one man, (Carlisle of Limekilns †,) after whose death all his papers were found in exact order; and nothing was omitted in his will.—*Johnson.* 'Sir, I had an uncle § who died so; but such attention requires great leisure, and great firmness of mind. If one was to think constantly of death, the business of life would stand still. I am no friend to making religion appear too hard. Many good people have done harm, by giving severe notions of it. In the same way, as to learning §§: I never frighten young people with difficulties; on the contrary, I tell them that they may very easily get as much as will do very well. I do not indeed tell them that they will be *Bentleys*.'

The night we rode to Col's house, I said, 'Lord Elibank is probably wondering what is become of us.'—*Johnson.* 'No, no ; he is not thinking of us.'—*Boswell.* 'But recollect the warmth with which he wrote [1]. Are we not to believe a man, when he says that [a] he has a great desire to see another? Don't you believe that I was very impatient for your coming to Scotland?' *Johnson.* 'Yes, sir; I believe you were; and I was impatient to come to you. A young man feels so, but seldom an old man.' I however convinced him that Lord Elibank, who has much of the spirit of a young man, might feel so.—He asked me if our jaunt had answered expectation. I said it had much exceeded it. I expected much difficulty with him, and had not

[a] that *omitted* 3.

† ⟨See App. D, p. 555.⟩ *Gleanings*, iii. 142.⟩
§ ⟨Probably Dr. Joseph Ford. §§ ⟨See *Rambler*, No. 25.⟩
Ante, i. 49, n. 3. See A. L. Reade, [1] *Ante*, v. 181.

found it. 'And (he added) wherever we have come, we have been received like princes in their progress.'

He said, he would not wish not to be disgusted in the Highlands; for that would be to lose the power of distinguishing, and a man might then lie down in the middle of them. He wished only to conceal his disgust.

At Captain M'Lean's, I mentioned Pope's friend, Spence. —*Johnson.* 'He was a weak conceited man [1].'—*Boswell.* 'A good scholar, sir?'—*Johnson.* 'Why, no, sir.'—*Boswell.* 'He was a pretty scholar.'—*Johnson.* 'You have about reached him.'

Last night at the inn, when the factor in Tyr-yi spoke of his having heard that a roof was put on some part of the buildings at Icolmkill, I unluckily said, 'It will be fortunate if we find a cathedral with a roof on it.' I said this from a foolish anxiety to engage Dr. Johnson's curiosity more. He took me short at once. 'What, sir? how can you talk so? If we shall *find* a cathedral roofed! as if we were going to a *terra incognita*; when every thing that is at Icolmkill is so well known. You are like some New-England-men who came to the mouth of the Thames. "Come, (said they,) let us go up and see what sort of inhabitants there are here." They talked, sir, as if they had been to go up the Susquehannah, or any other American river.'

Saturday, 16th October.

This day there was a new moon, and the weather changed for the better. Dr. Johnson said of Miss M'Lean, 'She is the most accomplished lady that I have found in the Highlands. She knows French, musick, and drawing, sews neatly, makes shell-

[1] Mr. Langton thinks this must have been the hasty expression of a splenetick moment, as he has heard Dr. Johnson speak of Mr. Spence's judgement in criticism with so high a degree of respect, as to shew that this was not his settled opinion of him. Let me add that, in the preface to the *Preceptor*, he recommends Spence's *Essay on Pope's Odyssey*, and that his admirable Lives of the English Poets are much enriched by Spence's Anecdotes of Pope. Bos-well, ed. 3, 1786.

For the *Preceptor* see *ante*, i. 192, and Johnson's *Works*, v. 231 ff. Johnson, in his *Life of Pope* (137), speaks of Spence as 'a man whose learning was not very great, and whose mind was not very powerful. His criticism, however, was commonly just; what he thought, he thought rightly; and his remarks were recommended by his coolness and candour.' See *ante*, iv. 9, 63, ⟨482⟩.

work, and can milk cows ; in short, she can do every thing. She talks sensibly, and is the first person whom I have found, that can translate Erse poetry literally [1].'—We set out, mounted on little Mull horses. Mull corresponded exactly with the idea which I had always had of it ; a hilly country, diversified with heath and grass, and many rivulets. Dr. Johnson was not in very good humour. He said, it was a dreary country, much worse than Sky. I differed from him. ' O, sir, (said he,) a most dolorous country [2] !'

We had a very hard journey to-day. I had no bridle for my sheltie, but only a halter ; and Joseph rode without a saddle. At one place, a loch having swelled over the road, we were obliged to plunge through pretty deep water. Dr. Johnson observed, how helpless a man would be, were he travelling here alone, and should meet with any accident ; and said, ' he longed to get to *a country of saddles and bridles* †.' He was more out of humour to-day, than he has been in the course of our Tour, being fretted to find that his little horse could scarcely support his weight ;—and having suffered a loss, which, though small in itself, was of some consequence to him, while travelling the rugged steeps of Mull, where he was at times obliged to walk. The loss that I allude to was that of the large oak-stick, which, as I formerly mentioned, he had brought with him from London [3]. It was of great use to him in our wild peregrination ; for, ever since his last illness in 1766 [4], he has had a weakness in his knees, and has not been able to walk easily. It had too the properties of a measure; for one nail was driven into it at the length of a foot ; another at that of a yard. In return for the services it had done him, he said, this morning, he would make a present of it to some Museum ; but he little thought he was so soon to lose it. As he preferred riding with a switch, it was

---

[1] ' She was the only interpreter of Earse poetry that I could ever find.' Johnson's *Western Isl.*, p. 124. See *ante*, v. 241. ⟨For Miss Maclean see App. D, p. 555.⟩

[2] ' After a journey difficult and tedious, over rocks naked and valleys untracked, through a country of barrenness and solitude, we came, almost in the dark, to [the] seaside, weary and dejected having met with nothing but water falling from the mountains that could raise any image of delight.' *Letters*, No. 332. ' It is natural, in traversing this gloom of desolation, to inquire, whether something may not be done to give nature a more cheerful face.' *Western Isl.*, p. 126. ⟨'Dolorous country ' is perhaps a reminiscence of Milton's 'region dolorous '. *P.L.* ii. 619.⟩

† ⟨See *post*, v. 362 and 375.⟩

[3] *Ante*, v. 19.

[4] See *ante*, i. 521.

intrusted to a fellow to be delivered to our baggage-man, who followed us at some distance; but we never saw it more. I could not persuade him out of a suspicion that it had been stolen. ' No, no, my friend, (said he,) it is not to be expected that any man in Mull, who has got it, will part with it. Consider, sir, the value of such a *piece of timber* here!'

As we travelled this forenoon, we met Dr. M'Lean, who expressed much regret at his having been so unfortunate as to be absent while we were at his house.

We were in hopes to get to Sir Allan Maclean's,[a] at Inchkenneth, to-night; but the eight miles, of which our road was said to consist, were so very long, that we did not reach the opposite coast of Mull till seven at night, though we had set out about eleven in the forenoon; and when we did arrive there, we found the wind strong against us. Col determined that we should pass the night at M'Quarrie's, in the island of Ulva, which lies between Mull and Inchkenneth; and a servant was sent forward to the ferry, to secure the boat for us: but the boat was gone to the Ulva side, and the wind was so high that the people could not hear him call; and the night so dark that they could not see a signal. We should have been in a very bad situation, had there not fortunately been lying in the little sound of Ulva an Irish vessel, the Bonnetta, of Londonderry, Captain M'Lure, master. He himself was at M'Quarrie's; but his men obligingly came with their long-boat, and ferried us over.

M'Quarrie's house [1] was mean; but we were agreeably surprised with the appearance of the master, whom we found to be intelligent, polite, and much a man of the world. Though his clan is not numerous, he is a very ancient Chief, and has a burial place at Icolmkill. He told us, his family had possessed Ulva for nine hundred years; but I was distressed to hear that it was soon to be sold for payment of his debts [2].

Captain M'Lure, whom we found here, was of Scotch extraction, and properly a M'Leod, being descended of some of the M'Leods who went with Sir Normand of Bernera to the battle of Worcester; and, after the defeat of the royalists, fled to Ireland, and, to conceal themselves, took a different name. He told me, there was a great number of them about Londonderry; some of good property. I said, they should now resume their

[a] Maclean's, 1, 2: Maclean's 3.

[1] ⟨See App. D, p. 556.⟩ [2] ⟨It was sold in 1777. *Ante*, iii. 126.⟩

real name. The Laird of M'Leod should go over, and assemble them, and make them all drink the large horn full [1], and from that time they should be M'Leods.—The captain informed us, he had named his ship the Bonnetta, out of gratitude to Providence; for once, when he was sailing to America with a good number of passengers, the ship in which he then sailed was becalmed for five weeks, and during all that time, numbers of the fish Bonnetta swam close to her, and were caught for food; he resolved therefore that the ship he should next get, should be called the Bonnetta.

M'Quarrie told us a strong instance of the second sight. He had gone to Edinburgh, and taken a man-servant along with him. An old woman, who was in the house, said one day, 'M'Quarrie will be at home to-morrow, and will bring two gentlemen with him;' and she said, she saw his servant return in red and green. He did come home next day. He had two gentlemen with him; and his servant had a new red and green livery, which M'Quarrie had bought for him at Edinburgh, upon a sudden thought, not having the least intention when he left home to put his servant in livery; so that the old woman could not have heard any previous mention of it. This, he assured us, was a true story.

M'Quarrie insisted that the *Mercheta Mulierum*, mentioned in our old charters, did really mean the privilege which a lord of a manor, or a baron, had, to have the first night of all his vassals' wives. Dr. Johnson said, the belief of such a custom having existed was also held in England, where there is a tenure called *Borough English*, by which the eldest child does not inherit, from a doubt of his being the son of the tenant [2]. M'Quarrie told us, that still, on the marriage of each of his tenants, a sheep is due

---

[1] See *ante*, v. 212.

[2] Sir William Blackstone says, in his COMMENTARIES, that 'he cannot find that ever this custom prevailed in *England*;' and therefore he is of opinion that it could not have given rise to *Borough-English*. BOSWELL, ed. 2. 'I cannot learn that ever this custom prevailed in England, though it certainly did in Scotland (under the name of *mercheta* or *marcheta*), till abolished by Malcolm III.' *Commentaries*, ed. 1778, ii. 83. Sir H. Maine, in his *Early History of Institutions*, p. 222, writes:—'Other authors, as Blackstone tells us, explained it ["Borough English"] by a supposed right of the Seigneur or lord, now very generally regarded as apocryphal, which raised a presumption of the eldest son's illegitimacy.'

to him ; for which the composition is fixed at five shillings [1]. I suppose, Ulva is the only place where this custom remains.

Talking of the sale of an estate of an ancient family, which was said to have been purchased much under its value by the confidential lawyer of that family, and it being mentioned that the sale would probably be set aside by a suit in equity, Dr. Johnson said, ' I am very willing that this sale should be set aside, but I doubt much whether the suit will be successful ; for the argument for avoiding the sale is founded on vague and indeterminate principles,—as that the price was too low, and that there was a great degree of confidence placed by the seller in the person who became the purchaser. Now, how low should a price be ? or what degree of confidence should there be to make a bargain be set aside ? a bargain, which is a wager of skill between man and man.—If, indeed, any fraud can be proved, that will do.'

When Dr. Johnson and I were by ourselves at night, I observed of our host, ' *aspectum generosum habet ;* '— *et generosum animum*,' he added.—For fear of being overheard in the small Highland houses, I often talked to him in such Latin as I could speak, and with as much of the English accent as I could assume, so as not to be understood, in case our conversation should be too loud for the space.

We had each an elegant bed in the same room ; and here it was that a circumstance occurred, as to which he has been strangely misunderstood. From his description of his chamber, it has erroneously been supposed, that, [a] his bed being too short for him, his feet, during the night, were in the mire ; whereas he has only said, that, [a] when he undressed, he felt his feet in the mire : that is, the clay-floor of the room, on which he stood [b] before he went into bed, was wet, in consequence of the windows being broken, which let in the rain [2].

[a] that, 1, 2: that 3.   [b] stood 1, 2 : stood upon 3

[1] ' Macquarry was used to demand a sheep, for which he now takes a crown, by that inattention to the uncertain proportion between the value and the denomination of money, which has brought much disorder into Europe. A sheep has always the same power of supplying human wants, but a crown will bring at one time more, at another less.' Johnson's *Western Isl.*, p. 129.

[2] ' The house and the furniture are not always nicely suited. We were driven once, by missing a passage, to the hut of a gentleman, where, after a very liberal supper, when I was conducted to my chamber, I found an elegant bed of Indian cot-

Sunday 17 October 1773

Sunday, 17th October.

Being informed that there was nothing worthy of observation in Ulva, we took boat, and proceeded to Inchkenneth, where we were introduced by our friend Col to Sir Allan M'Lean, the Chief of his clan, and to two young ladies, his daughters. Inchkenneth is a pretty little island, a mile long, and about half a mile broad, all good land [1].

As we walked up from the shore, Dr. Johnson's heart was cheered by the sight of a road marked with cart-wheels [2], as on the main land; a thing which we had not seen for a long time. It gave us a pleasure similar to that which a traveller feels, when, whilst wandering on what he fears is a desert island, he perceives the print of human feet.

Military men acquire excellent habits of having all con-

ton, spread with fine sheets. The accommodation was flattering; I undressed myself, and felt my feet in the mire. The bed stood upon the bare earth, which a long course of rain had softened to a puddle.' *Ibid.*, p. 91.

[1] Inchkenneth is a most beautiful little islet of the most verdant green, while all the neighbouring shore of Greban, as well as the large islands of Colinsay and Ulva, are as black as heath and moss can make them. But Ulva has a good anchorage, and Inchkenneth is surrounded by shoals. It is now uninhabited. The ruins of the huts, in which Dr. Johnson was received by Sir Allan M'Lean, were still to be seen, and some tatters of the paper hangings were to be seen on the walls. Sir George Onesiphorus Paul was at Inchkenneth with the same party of which I was a member. [See Lockhart's *Scott*, ed. 1837, ii. 312.] He seemed to me to suspect many of the Highland tales which he heard, but he showed most incredulity on the subject of Johnson's having been entertained in the wretched huts of which we saw the ruins. He took me aside, and conjured me to tell him the truth of the matter. ' This Sir Allan,' said he, ' was he a *regular*

baronet, or was his title such a traditional one as you find in Ireland?' I assured my excellent acquaintance that, ' for my own part, I would have paid more respect to a knight of Kerry, or knight of Glynn; yet Sir Allan M'Lean was a *regular baronet* by patent;' and, having giving him this information, I took the liberty of asking him, in return, whether he would not in conscience prefer the worst cell in the jail at Gloucester (which he had been very active in overlooking while the building was going on) to those exposed hovels where Johnson had been entertained by rank and beauty. He looked round the little islet, and allowed Sir Allan had some advantage in exercising ground; but in other respects he thought the compulsory tenants of Gloucester had greatly the advantage. Such was his opinion of a place, concerning which Johnson has recorded that ' it wanted little which palaces could afford [a].' SCOTT, 1831.

[2] ⟨Boswell mentions later that ' one of the young Ladies had been overturned on the road a day or two before. It seems they rode in a cart, as the only carriage that they could get to take an airing in '. *Hebrides*, 1936, p. 315.⟩

[a] We . . . wanted little that palaces afford. *Western Isl.* 130.

Inchkenneth *Sunday* 17 *October* 1773

veniencies about them. Sir Allan M'Lean, who had been long in the army, and had now a lease of this ᵃ island, had formed a commodious habitation, though it consisted but of a few small buildings, only one story high [1]. He had, in his little apartments, more things than I could enumerate in a page or two.

Among other agreeable circumstances, it was not the least, to find here a parcel of the *Caledonian Mercury*, published since we left Edinburgh; which I read with that pleasure which every man feels who has been for some time secluded from the animated scenes of the busy world.

Dr. Johnson found books here. He bade me buy Bishop Gastrell's *Christian Institutes* [2], which was lying in the room. He said, ' I do not like to read any thing on a Sunday, but what is theological; not that I would scrupulously refuse to look at any thing which a friend should shew me in a news-paper; but in general, I would read only what is theological.—I read just now some of Drummond's Travels [3], before I perceived what books were here. I then took up Derham's Physico-Theology [4].'

Every particular concerning this island having been so well described by Dr. Johnson, it would be superfluous in me to present the publick with the observations that I made upon it, in my Journal.

I was quite easy with Sir Allan almost instantaneously. He knew the great intimacy that had been between my father and his predecessor, Sir Hector, and was himself of a very frank disposition.—After dinner, Sir Allan said he had got Dr. Campbell about an hundred subscribers to his *Britannia Elucidata*,

ᵃ this 1 : the 2, 3.

[1] ' Sir Allan's affairs are in disorder by the fault of his ancestors, and while he forms some scheme for retrieving them, he has retreated hither.' Johnson's *Letters*, No. 332. ⟨See App. D, p. 556.⟩
[2] Published in 1707 by Dr. Francis Gastrell, later Bishop of Chester.
[3] *Travels through different Cities of Germany, Italy, Greece, &c.*, by Alexander Drummond, 1754. ⟨The work was seen through the press by Smollett. Smollett's *Letters*, 1926, pp. 24, 29, 134. Drummond was Consul at Aleppo and brother of George, the famous Lord Provost of Edinburgh (*ante*, v. 43).⟩
[4] *Physico-Theology : or, a Demonstration of the Being and Attributes of God, from His Works of Creation.* By William Derham, D.D., 1713. ⟨The 12th edition was published in 1754, and an edition in two vols. appeared in 1798.⟩ Voltaire, in *Micromégas*, ch. 1, speaks of ' l'illustre vicaire Derham ', but the Kehl editors add in a note :—' Malheureusement, lui et ses imitateurs se trompent souvent dans l'exposition de ces merveilles : ils s'extasient sur la sagesse qui se montre dans l'ordre d'un phénomène, et on découvre que ce phénomène est tout différent de ce qu'ils ont supposé ; alors c'est ce nouvel ordre qui leur paraît un chef-d'œuvre de sagesse.' Voltaire's *Œuvres*, 1879, t. xxi, p. 107, note 2.

(a work since published under the title of *A Political Survey of Great Britain* [1],) of whom he believed twenty were dead, the publication having been so long delayed.—*Johnson*. 'Sir, I imagine the delay of publication is owing to this ;—that, after publication, there will be no more subscribers, and few will send the additional guinea to get their books : in which they will be wrong ; for there will be a great deal of instruction in the work. I think highly of Campbell [2]. In the first place, he has very good parts. In the second place, he has very extensive reading ; not, perhaps, what is properly called learning, but history, politicks, and, in short, that popular knowledge which makes a man very useful. In the third place, he has learned much by what is called the *vox viva*. He talks with a great many people.'

Speaking of this gentleman, at Rasay, he told us, that he one day called on him, and they talked of *Tull's Husbandry* [3]. Dr. Campbell said something. Dr. Johnson began to dispute it. ' Come, (said Dr. Campbell,) we do not want to get the better of one another : we want to encrease each other's ideas.' —Dr. Johnson took it in good. part, and the conversation then went on coolly and instructively.—His candour in relating this anecdote does him much credit, and his conduct on that occasion proves how easily he could be persuaded to talk from a better motive than ' for victory [4].'

Dr. Johnson here shewed so much of the spirit of a Highlander, that he won Sir Allan's heart : indeed, he has shewn it during the whole of our Tour.—One night, in Col, he strutted about the room with a broad-sword and target, and made a formidable appearance ; and, another night, I took the liberty to put a large blue bonnet on his head. His age, his size, and his bushy grey wig, with this covering on it, presented the image of a venerable *Senachi* [5] : and, however unfavourable to

---

[1] ⟨Campbell's ' Proposals ' for *Britannia Elucidata* were issued on 13 Jan. 1755. For the book see *ante*, ii. 447, 531.⟩

[2] See *ante*, i. 417.

[3] *The Horse-hoing Husbandry*, by Jethro Tull, 1733.

[4] ' He owned he sometimes talked for victory.' *Ante*, iv. 111, and v. 17.

[5] ' They said that a great family had a *Bard* and a *Senachi*, who were the poet and historian of the house ; and an old gentleman told me that he remembered one of each. Here was a dawn of intelligence. . . . Another conversation indeed informed me, that the same man was both Bard and Senachi. This variation discouraged me. . . . Soon after I

the Lowland Scots, he seemed much pleased to assume the appearance of an ancient Caledonian. We only regretted that he could not be prevailed with to partake of the social glass. One of his arguments against drinking, appears to me not convincing. He urged, that, 'in proportion as drinking makes a man different from what he is before he has drunk, it is bad ; because it has so far affected his reason.'—But may it not be answered, that a man may be altered by it *for the better* ; that his spirits may be exhilarated, without his reason being affected [1] ? On the general subject of drinking, however, I do not mean positively to take the other side. I am *dubius, non improbus.*

In the evening, Sir Allan informed us that it was the custom of his house to have prayers every Sunday ; and Miss M'Lean read the evening service, in which we all joined. I then read Ogden's second and ninth Sermons on Prayer, which, with their other distinguished excellence, have the merit of being short. Dr. Johnson said, that it was the most agreeable Sunday he had ever passed [2] ; and it made such an impression on his mind, that he afterwards wrote the following Latin verses upon Inchkenneth [3] :

INSULA SANCTI KENNETHI.

Parva quidem regio, sed relligione priorum
Nota, Caledonias panditur inter aquas ;
Voce ubi Cennethus populos domuisse feroces
Dicitur, et vanos dedocuisse deos.

---

was told by a gentleman, who is generally acknowledged the greatest master of Hebridian antiquities, that there had indeed once been both Bards and Senachies ; and that *Senachi* signified *the man of talk*, or of conversation ; but that neither Bard nor Senachi had existed for some centuries.' Johnson's *Western Isl.*, p. 101.

[1] See *ante*, iii. 41, 327.

[2] ⟨Boswell in his Orig. Jrnl. reported that Miss Maclean ' read the evening service with a beautiful decency '. He continued : ' we read the Responses and other parts that Congregations read. When she came to the prayer for the Royal Family, she stopt. I bid her go to the prayer for the Clergy. She did so. Mr. J. pointed out to her some prayers, which she read.' Ed. Pottle and Bennett, p. 317.⟩ ' Towards evening, Sir Allan told us, that Sunday never passed over him like another day. One of the Ladies read, and read very well, the Evening services—And Paradise was open'd in the wild.' Johnson's *Letters*, No. 332. The quotation is from Pope's *Eloisa to Abelard*, l. 134 :—

' You rais'd these hallow'd walls ;
    the desert smil'd,
And Paradise was open'd in the Wild.'

[3] He sent these verses to Boswell in 1775. *Ante*, ii. 293.

Sunday 17 October 1773 — Inchkenneth

Huc ego delatus placido per cœrula cursu
Scire locum volui quid daret ille novi.
Illic Leniades humili regnabat in aula,
Leniades magnis nobilitatus avis :
Una duas habuit casa cum genitore puellas,
Quas Amor undarum fingeret esse deas :
Non tamen inculti gelidis latuere sub antris,
Accola Danubii qualia sævus habet ;
Mollia non deerant vacuæ solatia vitæ,
Sive libros poscant otia, sive lyram.
Luxerat illa dies, legis gens docta supernæ
Spes hominum ac curas cum procul esse jubet,
Ponti inter strepitus sacri non munera cultus
Cessarunt ; pietas hic quoque cura fuit :
Quid quod sacrifici versavit femina libros,
Legitimas faciunt pectora pura preces [1].
Quo vagor ulterius ? quod ubique requiritur hic est ;
Hic secura quies, hic et honestus amor [2].

---

[1] Boswell wrote to Johnson on Feb. 2, 1775, (*ante*, ii. 295) :—' Lord Hailes bids me tell you he doubts whether
" Legitimas faciunt pectora pura preces"
be according to the rubrick : but that is your concern ; for, you know, he is a Presbyterian.'

[2] In Johnson's *Works*, 1787, xi. 393, these lines are given with amendments and additions, mostly made by Johnson, but some, Mr. Croker believes, by Mr. Langton. In the following copy the variations are marked in italics.

INSULA KENNETHI, INTER HEBRIDAS.

Parva quidem regio, sed religione priorum
Clara, Caledonias panditur inter aquas.
Voce ubi Cennethus populos domuisse feroces
Dicitur, et vanos dedocuisse deos.
Huc ego delatus placido per cærula cursu,
Scire *locus* volui quid daret *iste* novi.

Illic Leniades humili regnabat in aula,
Leniades, magnis nobilitatus avis.
Una duas *cepit* casa cum genitore puellas,
Quas Amor undarum *crederet* esse deas.
Nec tamen inculti gelidis latuere sub antris,
Accola Danubii qualia sævus habet.
Mollia non *desunt* vacuæ solatia vitæ,
Sive libros poscant otia, sive lyram.
Fulserat illa dies, legis *qua* docta supernæ
Spes hominum *et* curas *gens* procul esse jubet.
*Ut precibus justas avertat numinis iras,
Et summi accendat pectus amore boni.*
Ponti inter strepitus *non sacri* munera cultus
Cessarunt, pietas hic quoque cura fuit :
*Nil opus est æris sacra de turre sonantis
Admonitu, ipsa suas nunciat hora vices.*

Inchkenneth   *Monday 18 October 1773*   327

Monday, 18th October.

We agreed to pass this day with Sir Allan, and he engaged to have every thing in order for our voyage to-morrow.

Being now soon to be separated from our amiable friend young Col, his merits were all remembered. At Ulva he had appeared in a new character, having given us a good prescription for a cold. On my mentioning him with warmth, Dr. Johnson said, ' Col does every thing for us : we will erect a statue to Col.'—' Yes, said I, and we will have him with his various attributes and characters, like Mercury, or any other of the heathen gods. We will have him as a pilot ; we will have him as a fisherman, as a hunter, as a husbandman, as a physician.'

I this morning took a spade, and dug a little grave in the floor of a ruined chapel [1], near Sir Allan M'Lean's house, in which I buried some human bones I found there. Dr. Johnson praised me for what I had done, though he owned, he could not have done it. He shewed in the chapel at Rasay [2] his horrour at dead men's bones. He shewed it again at Col's house. In the Charter-room there was a remarkably[a] large shin-bone, which was said to have been a bone of *John Garve* [3], one of the lairds. Dr. Johnson would not look at it ; but started away.

At breakfast, I asked, ' What is the reason that we are angry at a trader's having opulence [4] ? '—*Johnson.* ' Why, sir, the

[a] remarkably 1, 2 : remarkable 3.

Quid, quod sacrifici versavit fœmina libros ?
Sint pro legitimis pura labella sacris.
Quo vagor ulterius ? quod ubique requiritur hic est,
Hic secura quies, hic et honestus amor.
Mr. Croker says, 1848, of the third line from the end, that in a copy of these verses in Johnson's own hand which he had seen, ' Johnson had first written
Sunt pro legitimis pectora pura sacris.
He then wrote
Legitimas faciunt pura labella preces.
That line was erased, and the line as it stands in the *Works* is substituted in Mr. Langton's hand, as is also an alteration in the 16th line, *velit* into *jubet*.' *Jubet* however is in the copy as printed by Boswell. Mr. Langton edited some, if not all, of

Johnson's Latin poems. (*Ante*, iv. 384.) ⟨For Sir D. K. Sandford's translations (1833) of the version given by Boswell see L. Maclean's *Account of Iona* (ed. 4, 1841, pp. 133–4.⟩

[1] ⟨Boswell had prayed before the cross on Sunday night. ' I was for going into the chapel ; but a tremor seized me for ghosts, and I hastened back to the house.' *Hebrides*, ed. Pottle and Bennett, p. 317. See Johnson's *Letters*, No. 332. Boswell in his Journal says, under 19 Oct., ' It was this day, and not yesterday, that I buried the bones '. *Op. cit.* p. 324.⟩

[2] *Ante*, v. 169.

[3] ⟨He was the ' first of the Macleans of Coll '. Sir R. Douglas, *Baronage of Scotl.*, 1798, 372.⟩ See Johnson's *Western Isl.*, p. 111.

[4] Lord Chatham in the House of Lords, on Nov. 22, 1770, speaking of ' the honest, industrious tradesman,

reason is, (though I don't undertake to prove that there is a reason,) we see no qualities in trade that should entitle a man to superiority. We are not angry at a soldier's getting riches, because we see that he possesses qualities which we have not. If a man returns from a battle, having lost one hand, and with the other full of gold, we feel that he deserves the gold; but we cannot think that a fellow, by sitting all day at a desk, is entitled to get above us.'—*Boswell*. ' But, sir, may we not suppose a merchant to be a man of an enlarged mind, such as Addison in the *Spectator* † describes Sir Andrew Freeport to have been?'—*Johnson*. ' Why, sir, we may suppose any fictitious character. We may suppose a philosophical day-labourer, who is happy in reflecting that, by his labour, he contributes to the fertility of the earth, and to the support of his fellow-creatures; but we find no such philosophical day-labourer. A merchant may, perhaps, be a man of an enlarged mind; but there is nothing in trade connected with an enlarged mind [1].'

I mentioned that I had heard Dr. Solander say he was a Swedish Laplander [2].—*Johnson*. ' Sir, I don't believe he is a Laplander. The Laplanders are not much above four feet high. He is as tall as you; and he has not the copper colour of a Laplander.'—*Boswell*. ' But what motive could he have to make himself a Laplander?'—*Johnson*. ' Why, sir, he must either mean the word Laplander in a very extensive sense, or may mean a voluntary degradation of himself. " For all my being who holds the middle rank, and has given repeated proofs, that he prefers law and liberty to gold,' had said :— ' I love that class of men. Much less would I be thought to reflect upon the fair merchant, whose liberal commerce is the prime source of national wealth. I esteem his occupation, and respect his character.' *Parl. Hist.* xvi. 1107.

† ⟨Steele describes Sir Andrew as ' a person of indefatigable industry, strong reason, and great experience. His notions of trade are noble and generous and . . . he calls the sea the British Common '. *Spectator*, No. 2.⟩

[1] See *ante*, iii. 382.
[2] ⟨Daniel Charles Solander was born in Pitea, Norrland, Sweden, on 12 Feb. 1735. See *Nordisk Familjebok*, 1917, and *D.N.B.*⟩ Miss Burney wrote of him in 1780 :—' My father has very exactly named him, in calling him a philosophical gossip.' Mme D'Arblay's *Diary*, i. 297. Horace Walpole the same year, just after the Gordon Riots, wrote (*Letters*, xi. 225, 15 June 1780) :—' Who is secure against Jack Straw and a whirlwind? How I abominate Mr. Banks and Dr. Solander, who routed the poor Otaheitians out of the centre of the ocean, and carried our abominable passions amongst them! Not even that poor little speck could escape European restlessness.' See *ante*, ii. 148.

the great man that you see me now, I was originally a Barbarian; " as if Burke should say, " I came over a wild Irishman,[a]"— which he might say in his present state of exaltation.'

Having expressed a desire to have an island like Inchkenneth, Dr. Johnson set himself to think what would be necessary for a man in such a situation. ' Sir, I should build me a fortification, if I came to live here ; for, if you have it not, what should hinder a parcel of ruffians to land in the night, and carry off every thing you have in the house, which, in a remote country, would be more valuable than cows and sheep ? add to all this the danger of having your throat cut.'—*Boswell.* ' I would have a large dog.'—*Johnson.* ' So you may, sir ; but a large dog is of no use but to alarm.'—He, however, I apprehend, thinks too lightly of the power of that animal. I have heard him say, that he is afraid of no dog. ' He would take him up by the hinder legs, which would render him quite helpless,—and then knock his head against a stone, and beat out his bráins.'—Topham Beauclerk told me, that at his house in the country, two large ferocious dogs were fighting. Dr. Johnson looked steadily at them for a little while ; and then, as one would separate two little boys, who are foolishly hurting each other, he ran up to them, and cuffed their heads till he drove them asunder [1]. But few men have his intrepidity, Herculean strength, or presence of mind. Most thieves or robbers would be afraid to encounter a mastiff.

I observed, that, when young Col talked of the lands belonging to his family, he always said, ' *my* lands [2].' For this he had a plausible pretence ; for he told me, there has been a custom in this family, that the laird resigns the estate to the eldest son

[a] Irishman, 1, 2: Irishman. 3.

[1] Boswell tells this story again, *ante*, ii. 299. Mrs. Piozzi's account (*Anec.* p. 114 : *Johnson. Misc.*, i. 225) is evidently so inaccurate that it does not deserve attention ; she herself admits that Beauclerk was truthful. In a marginal note on Wraxall's *Memoirs*, she says :—' Topham Beauclerc (wicked and profligate as he wished to be accounted) was yet a man of very strict veracity. Oh Lord ! how I did hate that horrid Beauclerc !' Hayward's *Piozzi*, ed. 2, ii. 112. Johnson testified to ' the correctness of Beauclerk's memory, and the fidelity of his narrative'. *Ante*, ii. 405.

[2] ' Mr. Maclean of Col, having a very numerous family, has, for some time past, resided at Aberdeen, that he may superintend their education, and leaves the young gentleman, our friend, to govern his dominions, with the full power of a Highland Chief.' Johnson's *Western Isl.*, p. 109.

when he comes of age, reserving to himself only a certain liferent. He said, it was a voluntary custom; but I think I found an instance in the charter-room, that there was such an obligation in a contract of marriage. If the custom was voluntary, it was only curious; but if founded on obligation, it might be dangerous; for I have been told, that in Otaheité, whenever a child is born, (a son, I think,) the father loses his right to the estate and honours, and that this unnatural, or rather absurd custom, occasions the murder of many children.

Young Col told us he could run down a greyhound; 'for, (said he,) the dog runs himself out of breath, by going too quick, and then I get up with him [1].' I accounted for his advantage over the dog, by remarking that Col had the faculty of reason, and knew how to moderate his pace, which the dog had not sense enough to do. Dr. Johnson said, ' He is a noble animal. He is as complete an islander as the mind can figure. He is a farmer, a sailor, a hunter, a fisher : he will run you down a dog : if any man has a *tail* [2], it is Col. He is hospitable; and he has an intrepidity of talk, whether he understands the subject or not. I regret that he is not more intellectual.'

Dr. Johnson observed, that there was nothing of which he would not undertake to persuade a Frenchman in a foreign country. ' I'll carry a Frenchman to St. Paul's Church-yard, and I'll tell him, " by our law you may walk half round the church; but, if you walk round the whole, you will be punished capitally:" and he will believe me at once. Now, no Englishman would readily swallow such a thing : he would go and inquire of somebody else [3].'—The Frenchman's credulity, I observed, must be owing to his being accustomed to implicit submission; whereas every Englishman reasons upon the laws of his country, and instructs his representatives, who compose the legislature.

[1] This is not spoken of hare-coursing, where the game is taken or lost before the dog gets out of wind; but in chasing deer with the great Highland greyhound, Col's exploit is feasible enough. SCOTT, 1831.

[2] See *ante*, v, pp. 45, 111, for Monboddo's notion.

[3] Mme Ricccoboni in 1767 wrote to Garrick of the French :—' Un mensonge grossier les révolte. . . . Si on vouloit leur persuader que les Anglois vivent de grenouilles, meurent de faim, que leurs femmes sont barbouillées, et jurent par toutes les lettres de l'alphabet, ils lèveroient les épaules, et s'écriroient, *quel sot ose écrire ces misères-là ?* mais à Londres, diantre, cela prend!' *Garrick Corres.* ii. 524.

Tuesday 19 October 1773

This day was passed in looking at a small island † adjoining Inchkenneth, which afforded nothing worthy of observation; and in such social and gay entertainments as our little society could furnish.

Tuesday, 19th October.

After breakfast we took leave of the young ladies, and of our excellent companion Col, to whom we had been so much obliged. He had now put us under the care of his Chief; and was to hasten back to Sky. We parted from him with very strong feelings of kindness and gratitude; and we hoped to have had some future opportunity of proving to him the sincerity of what we felt; but in the following year he was unfortunately lost in the Sound between Ulva and Mull [1]; and this imperfect memorial, joined to the high honour of being tenderly and respectfully mentioned by Dr. Johnson, is the only return which the uncertainty of human events has permitted us to make to this deserving young man.

Sir Allan, who obligingly undertook to accompany us to Icolmkill [2], had a strong good boat, with four stout rowers. We coasted along Mull till we reached *Gribon*, where is what is called Mackinnon's cave, compared with which that at Ulinish [3] is inconsiderable. It is in a rock of a great height, close to the sea. Upon the left of its entrance there is a cascade, almost perpendicular from the top to the bottom of the rock. There is a tradition that it was conducted thither artificially, to supply the inhabitants of the cave with water. Dr. Johnson gave no credit to this tradition. As, on the one hand, his faith in the Christian religion is firmly founded upon good grounds; so, on the other, he is incredulous when there is no sufficient reason for belief [4]; being in this respect just the reverse of modern infidels, who, however nice and scrupulous in weighing the evidences of religion, are yet often so ready to believe the most absurd and improbable tales of another nature, that Lord Hailes

† ⟨Samland. 'We found a great many of the small yellow whelks... Mr. J. lay down & gathered, as he is short-sighted.' Boswell's *Hebrides*, p. 321.⟩

[1] Just opposite to M'Quarrie's house the boat was swamped by the intoxication of the sailors, who had partaken too largely of M'Quarrie's wonted hospitality. SCOTT, 1831.

Johnson wrote from Lichfield on June 13, 1775:—'There is great lamentation here for the death of Coll. Lucy is of opinion that he was wonderfully handsome.' *Letters*, No. 406. See *ante*, ii. 287 ⟨and *post*, App. D, p. 557⟩.

[2] Iona. [3] See *ante*, v. 237.
[4] See *ante*, ii. 247; iii. 188 and 229.

well observed, a good essay might be written *Sur la credulité des Incredules.*

The height of this cave I cannot tell with any tolerable exactness : but it seemed to be very lofty, and to be a pretty regular arch. We penetrated, by candlelight, a great way ; by our measurement, no less than four hundred and eighty-five feet. Tradition says, that a piper and twelve men once advanced into this cave, nobody can tell how far ; and never returned. At the distance to which we proceeded the air was quite pure ; for the candle burned freely, without the least appearance of the flame growing globular ; but as we had only one, we thought it dangerous to venture farther, lest, should it have been extinguished, we should have had no means of ascertaining whether we could remain without danger. Dr. Johnson said, this was the greatest natural curiosity he had ever seen.

We saw the island of Staffa, at no very great distance, but could not land upon it, the surge was so high on its rocky coast [1].

Sir Allan, anxious for the honour of Mull, was still talking of its *woods*, and pointing them out to Dr. Johnson, as appearing at a distance on the skirts of that island, as we sailed along.—*Johnson*. ' Sir, I saw at Tobermorie what they called a wood, which I unluckily took for *heath.* If you shew me what I shall take for *furze*, it will be something.'

In the afternoon we went ashore on the coast of Mull, and partook of a cold repast, which we carried with us. We hoped to have procured some rum or brandy for our boatmen and servants, from a publick-house near where we landed ; but unfortunately a funeral a few days before had exhausted all their store [2]. Mr. Campbell however, one of the Duke of Argyle's tacksmen, who lived in the neighbourhood, on receiving a message from Sir Allan, sent us a liberal supply.

[1] Sir James Mackintosh says (*Life*, ii. 252) :—' Dr. Johnson visited Iona without looking at Staffa, which lay in sight, . . . with that indifference to natural objects, either of taste or scientific curiosity, which characterised him.' This is a fair enough sample of much of the criticism under which Johnson's reputation has suffered.

[2] Smollett in *Humphry Clinker* (Letter of Sept. 3) describes a Highland funeral. ' Our entertainer . . . seemed to think it a disparagement to his family, that not above a hundred gallons of whisky had been drank upon such a solemn occasion.'

Tuesday 19 October 1773

We continued to coast along Mull, and passed by Nuns' Island, which, it is said, belonged to the nuns of Icolmkill, and from which, we were told, the stone for the buildings there was taken. As we sailed along by moon-light, in a sea somewhat rough, and often between black and gloomy rocks, Dr. Johnson said, ' If this be not *roving among the Hebrides*, nothing is [1].'—The repetition of words which he had so often previously used [†], made a strong impression on my imagination; and, by a natural course of thinking, led me to consider how our present adventures would appear to me at a future period.

I have often experienced, that scenes through which a man has passed, improve by lying in the memory: they grow mellow. *Acti labores sunt jucundi* [2]. This may be owing to comparing them with present listless ease. Even harsh scenes acquire a softness by length of time [3]; and some are like very loud sounds, which do not please, or at least do not please so much, till you are removed to a certain distance. They may be compared to strong coarse pictures, which will not bear to be viewed near. Even pleasing scenes improve by time, and seem more exquisite in recollection, than when they were present; if they have not faded to dimness in the memory. Perhaps, there is so much evil in every human enjoyment, when present,—so much dross mixed with it, that it requires to be refined by time; and yet I do not see why time should not melt away the good and the evil in equal proportions;—why the shade should decay, and the light remain in preservation.

After a tedious sail, which, by our following various turnings of the coast of Mull, was extended to about forty miles, it gave

[1] ' We then entered the boat again, the night came upon us, the wind rose, the sea swelled, and Boswel desired to be set on dry ground. We however persued our navigation, and passed by several little Islands in the silent solemnity of faint moon-shine, seeing little, and hearing only the wind and the water.' *Letters*, No. 332. ⟨For Boswell's alarm, see *Hebrides*, ed. Pottle and Bennett, 1936, p. 330.⟩
† ⟨For one previous use see *ante*, v. 278.⟩
[2] Cicero, *De Finibus*, ii. 32.
[3] I have lately observed that this thought has been elegantly expressed by Cowley:
' Things which offend when present, and affright,
In memory, well painted, move delight.' BOSWELL, ed. 3.
The lines are found in the *Ode upon His Majesty's Restoration and Return*, stanza 12. They may have been suggested by Virgil's lines—
' Revocate animos, maestumque timorem
Mittite; forsan et haec olim meminisse iuvabit.' *Æneid*, i. 202.

us no small pleasure to perceive a light in the village at Icolmkill, in which almost all the inhabitants of the island live, close to where the ancient buildings ᵃ stood. As we approached the shore, the tower of the cathedral, just discernible in the air, was a picturesque object.

When we had landed upon this ᵇ sacred place, which, as long as I can remember, I had thought on with veneration, Dr. Johnson and I cordially embraced †. We had long talked of visiting Icolmkill ; and, from the lateness of the season, were at times very doubtful whether we should be able to effect our purpose. To have seen it, even alone, would have given me great satisfaction ; but the venerable scene was rendered much more pleasing by the company of my great and pious friend, who was no less affected by it than I was ; and who has described the impressions it should make on the mind, with such strength of thought, and energy of language, that I shall quote his words, as conveying my own sensations much more forcibly than I am capable of doing :

' WE were now treading that illustrious Island, which was once the luminary of the Caledonian regions, whence savage clans and roving barbarians derived the benefits of knowledge, and the blessings of religion. To abstract the mind from all local emotion would be impossible, if it were endeavoured, and would be foolish,ᶜ if it were possible. Whatever withdraws us from the power of our senses, whatever makes the past, the distant, or the future, predominate over the present, advances us in the dignity of thinking beings. Far from me, and from my friends, be such frigid philosophy as may conduct us indifferent and unmoved over any ground which has been dignified by wisdom, bravery,ᵈ or virtue. That man is little to be envied, whose patriotism would not gain force upon the plain of *Marathon*, or whose piety would not grow warmer among the ruins of *Iona* ¹ ! '

ᵃ buildings 1, 2 (*MS.*) : building 3.   ᵇ this 1 : the 2, 3.   ᶜ, ᵈ *comma omitted* 3.

† ⟨' I shook hands with him cordially ' is Boswell's original version. For Johnson's landing see v. 368.⟩

¹ Had our Tour produced nothing else but this sublime passage, the world must have acknowledged that it was not made in vain. The present respectable President of the Royal Society was so much struck on reading it, that he clasped his hands together, and remained for some time in an attitude of silent admiration. BOSWELL, ed. 1. Boswell again quotes this passage (which is found in Johnson's *Western Isl.*, p. 134), ante, iii. 173, note 3. The President was Sir Joseph Banks. Johnson says in *Rasselas*, ch. xi :—

Upon hearing that Sir Allan M'Lean was arrived, the inhabitants, who still consider themselves as the people of M'Lean, to whom the island formerly belonged, though the Duke of Argyle has at present possession of it, ran eagerly to him.

We were accommodated this night in a large barn †, the island affording no lodging that we should have liked so well. Some good hay was strewed at one end of it, to form a bed for us, upon which we lay with our clothes on; and we were furnished with blankets from the village [1]. Each of us had a portmanteau for a pillow. When I awaked in the morning, and looked round me, I could not help smiling at the idea of the chief of the M'Leans, the great English Moralist, and myself, lying thus extended in such a situation.

Wednesday, 20th October.

Early in the morning we surveyed the remains of antiquity at this place, accompanied by an illiterate fellow, as *Cicerone*, who called himself a descendant of a cousin of Saint Columba, the founder of the religious establishment here. As I knew that many persons had already examined them, and as I saw Dr. Johnson inspecting and measuring several of the ruins of which he has since given so full an account, my mind was quiescent; and I resolved to stroll among them at my ease, to take no trouble to investigate minutely, and only receive the general impression of solemn antiquity, and the particular ideas of such objects as should of themselves strike my attention.

We walked from the monastery of Nuns to the great church or cathedral, as they call it, along an old broken causeway.

'That the Supreme Being may be more easily propitiated in one place than in another, is the dream of idle superstition; but that some places may operate upon our own minds in an uncommon manner, is an opinion which hourly experience will justify. He who supposes that his vices may be more successfully combated in Palestine, will, perhaps, find himself mistaken, yet he may go thither without folly: he who thinks they will be more freely pardoned, dishonours at once his reason and religion.'

† ⟨Pennant pitched a tent formed of oars and sails as his 'day residence' during his short stay in the island. *Tour Hebrides 1772*, 1774, p. 245.⟩

[1] 'Sir Allan went to the headman of the Island, whom Fame, but Fame delights in amplifying, represents as worth no less than fifty pounds. He was perhaps proud enough of his guests, but ill prepared for our entertainment; however, he soon produced more provision than men not luxurious require.' Johnson's *Western Isl.*, p. 135.

They told us, that this had been a street; and that there were good houses built on each side. Dr. Johnson doubted if it was any thing more than a paved road for the nuns. The convent of Monks, the great church, Oran's chapel, and four other chapels, are still to be discerned †. But I must own that Icolmkill did not answer my expectations; for they were high, from what I had read of it, and still more from what I had h•ard and thought of it, from my earliest years. Dr. Johnson said, it came up to his expectations, because he had taken his impression from an account of it subjoined to Sacheverel's History of the Isle of Man [1], where it is said, there is not much to be seen here. We were both disappointed, when we were shewn what are called the monuments of the kings of Scotland, Ireland, and Denmark, and of a King of France. There are only some grave-stones flat on the earth, and we could see no inscriptions. How far short was this of marble monuments, like those in Westminster-Abbey, which I had imagined here! The grave-stones of Sir Allan M'Lean's family, and of that of M'Quarrie, had as good an appearance as the royal grave-stones; if they were royal, which we [a] doubted.

My easiness to give credit to what I heard in the course of our Tour was too great. Dr. Johnson's peculiar accuracy of investigation detected much traditional fiction, and many gross mistakes. It is not to be wondered at, that he was provoked by people carelessly telling him, with the utmost readiness and confidence, what he found, on questioning them a little more, was erroneous [2]. Of this there were innumerable instances.

I left him and Sir Allan at breakfast in our barn, and stole back again to the cathedral, to indulge in solitude and devout meditation [3]. While contemplating the venerable ruins, I re-

[a] which we 1 (which Mr. J. *MS.*): we 2, 3.

† ⟨For all these chapels see W. Reeves, *Adamnan's Life of St. Columba*, 1857, pp. 415 ff.⟩
[1] *An Account of the Isle of Man. With a Voyage to I-Columb-kill.* By W. Sacheverell, Esq., late Governour of Man. 1702. ⟨Sacheverell expresses his vexation and disappointment at seeing ' so many noble Monuments ... Buried in their own Ruins ' (p. 142).⟩
[2] ' He that surveys it [the church-yard], attended by an insular antiquary, may be told where the Kings of many nations are buried, and if he loves to sooth his imagination with the thoughts that naturally rise in places where the great and the powerful lie mingled with the dust, let him listen in submissive silence; for if he asks any questions, his delight is at an end.' Johnson's *Western Isl.*, p. 137.
[3] On quitting the island Johnson wrote: ' We now left those illustrious ruins, by which Mr. Boswell was

flected with much satisfaction, that the solemn scenes of piety never lose their sanctity and influence, though the cares and follies of life may prevent us from visiting them, or may even make us fancy that their effects are only ' as yesterday, when it is past [1],' and never again to be perceived. I hoped, that, ever after having been in this holy place, I should maintain an exemplary conduct. One has a strange propensity to fix upon some point of time from whence a better course of life may begin [2].

Being desirous to visit the opposite shore of the island, where Saint Columba is said to have landed, I procured a horse from one M'Ginnis [3], who ran along as my guide. The M'Ginnises are said to be a branch of the clan of M'Lean. Sir Allan had been told that this man had refused to send him some rum, at which the knight was in great indignation. ' You rascal ! (said he,) don't you know that I can hang you, if I please ? '—Not adverting to the Chieftain's power over his clan, I imagined that Sir Allan had known of some capital crime that the fellow had committed, which he could discover, and so get him condemned ; and said, ' How so ? '—' Why, (said Sir Allan,) are they not all my people ? '—Sensible of my inadvertency, and most willing to contribute what I could towards the continuation of feudal authority, ' Very true,' said I.—Sir Allan went on : ' Refuse to send rum to me, you rascal ! Don't you know that, if I order you to go and cut a man's throat, you are to do it ? '—' Yes, an't please your honour ! and my own too, and hang myself too.' —The poor fellow denied that he had refused to send the rum. His making these professions was not merely a pretence in presence of his Chief ; for after he and I were out of Sir Allan's hearing, he told me, ' Had he sent his dog for the rum, I would have given it : I would cut my bones for him.'—It was very remarkable to find such an attachment to a Chief, though he had

much affected, nor would I willingly be thought to have looked upon them without some emotion.' *Ib.* p. 138. ⟨See *Hebrides*, ed. Pottle and Bennett, 1936, p. 335.⟩

[1] *Psalm* xc. 4.
[2] Boswell wrote on Nov. 9, 1767 :—
' I am always for fixing some period for my perfection as far as possible. Let it be when my *Account of Corsica*

is published. I shall then have a character which I must support.' *Letters*, No. 76. Five weeks later he wrote :—' I have . . . been as wild as ever, and for these ten days I have been suffering justly for my conduct.' *Ib.*, No. 84.

[3] Boswell here speaks as an Englishman. He should have written ' *a* M'Ginnis.' See *ante*, v. 135, note 3.

then no connection with the island, and had not been there for fourteen years.—Sir Allan, by way of upbraiding the fellow, said, ' I believe you are a *Campbell.*'

The place which I went to see is about two miles from the village. They call it *Portawherry* †, from the wherry in which Columba came ; though, when they shew the length of his vessel, as marked on the beach by two heaps of stones, they say, ' Here is the length of the *Currach,*' using the Erse word.

Icolmkill is a fertile island. The inhabitants export some cattle and grain ; and,[a] I was told, they import nothing but iron and salt. They are industrious, and make their own woollen and linen cloth ; and they brew a good deal of beer, which we did not find in any of the other islands [1].

We set sail again about mid-day, and in the evening landed on Mull, near the house of the Reverend Mr. Neil M'Leod [2], who having been informed of our coming, by a message from Sir Allan, came out to meet us. We were this night very agreeably entertained at his house. Dr. Johnson observed to me, that he was the cleanest-headed [b] man that he had met with in the Western islands. He seemed to be well acquainted with Dr. Johnson's writings, and courteously said, ' I have been often obliged to you, though I never had the pleasure of seeing you before.'

He told us, he had lived for some time in St. Kilda, under the tuition of the minister or catechist there, and had there first read Horace and Virgil. The scenes which they describe must have been a strong contrast to the dreary waste around him.

[a] and, 1, 2: and 3.   [b] *the reading is no longer in doubt.*

† ⟨The English representative of the Gaelic name ' Port-a-Churaich '.⟩

[1] ' The fruitfulness of Iona is now its whole prosperity. The inhabitants are remarkably gross, and remarkably neglected : I know not if they are visited by any Minister. The Island, which was once the metropolis of learning and piety, has now no school for education, nor temple for worship, only two inhabitants that can speak English, and not one that can write or read.' Johnson's *Western Isl.*, p. 138. Scott, who visited it in 1810, writes :—' There are many monuments of singular curiosity forming a strange contrast to the squalid and dejected poverty of the present inhabitants.' Lockhart's *Scott,* ii. 319. In 1814, on a second visit, he writes :—' Iona, the last time I saw it, seemed to me to contain the most wretched people I had any where seen. But either they have got better since I was here, or my eyes, familiarized with the wretchedness of Zetland and the Harris, are less shocked with that of Iona.' He found a schoolmaster there. *Ib.* iii. 243. ⟨Boswell noted, ' In this Island which once enlightened us all, there is not now one man that can read, & but two that can speak english.' Orig. Jrnl.⟩

[2] ⟨See App. D, pp. 557-8.⟩

Thursday, 21st October.

This morning the subject of politicks was introduced.—*Johnson.* ' Pulteney was as paltry a fellow as could be [1]. He was a Whig, who pretended to be honest ; and you know it is ridiculous for a Whig to pretend to be honest. He cannot hold it out [2].'—He called Mr. Pitt a meteor ; Sir Robert Walpole a fixed star [3].—He said, ' It is wonderful to think that all the force of government was required to prevent Wilkes from being chosen the chief magistrate of London [4], though the liverymen knew he would rob their shops,—knew he would debauch their daughters [5].'

[1] Johnson's Jacobite friend, Dr. King (*ante*, i. 279), says of Pulteney, on his being made Earl of Bath :— ' He deserted the cause of his country : he betrayed his friends and adherents : he ruined his character ; and from a most glorious eminence sunk down to a degree of contempt. The first time Sir Robert (who was now Earl of Orford) met him in the House of Lords, he threw out this reproach : " My Lord Bath, you and I are now two as insignificant men as any in England." In which he spoke the truth of my Lord Bath, but not of himself. For my Lord Orford was consulted by the ministers, to the last day of his life.' King's *Anec.* p. 43.

[2] See *ante*, i. 431, and iii. 326.

[3] ' Sir Robert Walpole detested war. This made the late acute Dr. Johnson . . . say of him, " He was the best minister this country ever had ; as, if *we* would have let him (he speaks of his own violent faction), he would have kept the country in perpetual peace." ' Seward's *Biographiana*, 1799, ii, p. 554. See *ante*, i. 131.

[4] See *ante*, iii, Appendix C, 460–2.

[5] I think it incumbent on me to make some observation on this strong satirical sally on my classical companion, Mr. Wilkes. Reporting it lately from memory, in his presence, I expressed it thus :—' They knew he would rob their shops, *if he durst ;* they knew he would debauch their daughters, *if he could ;* ' which, according to the French phrase, may be said *rencherir* on Dr. Johnson ; but on looking into my Journal, I found it as above, and would by no means make any addition. Mr. Wilkes received both readings with a good humour that I cannot enough admire. Indeed both he and I (as, with respect to myself, the reader has more than once had occasion to observe in the course of this Journal,) are too fond of a *bon mot*, not to relish it, though we should be ourselves the object of it.

Let me add, in justice to the gentleman here mentioned, that, [a] at a subsequent period, he *was* elected chief magistrate of London [in 1774], and discharged the duties of that high office with great honour to himself, and advantage to the city.—Some years before Dr. Johnson died, I was fortunate enough to bring him and Mr. Wilkes together ; the consequence of which was, that they were ever afterwards on easy and not unfriendly terms. The particulars I shall have great pleasure in relating at large in my LIFE OF DR. JOHNSON. BOSWELL, ed. i.

In a copy of Boswell's second *Letter to the People of Scotland* (1785) in the

[a] that, 1: that 2, 3.

Boswell. ' The History of England is so strange, that, if it were not so well vouched as it is, it would hardly be credible.' —*Johnson.* ' Sir, if it were told as shortly, and with as little preparation for introducing the different events, as the History of the Jewish Kings, it would be equally liable to objections of improbability.'—Mr. M'Leod was much pleased with the justice and novelty of the thought.—Dr. Johnson illustrated what he had said, as follows : ' Take, as an instance, Charles the First's concessions to his parliament, which were greater and greater, in proportion as the parliament grew more insolent, and less deserving of trust. Had these concessions been related nakedly, without any detail of the circumstances which gradually [a] led to them, they would not have been believed.'

Sir Allan M'Lean bragged, that Scotland had the advantage of England, by its having more water.—*Johnson.* ' Sir, we would not have your water, to take the vile bogs which produce it. You have too much ! A man who is drowned has more water than either of us ; '—and then he laughed.—(But this was surely robust sophistry : for the people of taste in England, who have seen Scotland, own that its variety of rivers and lakes makes it naturally more beautiful than England, in that respect.) —Pursuing his victory over Sir Allan, he proceeded : ' Your country consists of two things, stone and water. There is, indeed, a little earth above the stone in some places, but a very little ; and the stone is always appearing. It is like a man in rags ; the naked skin is still peeping out.'

He took leave of Mr. M'Leod, saying, ' Sir, I thank you for your entertainment, and your conversation.'

Mr. Campbell, who had been so polite yesterday, came this morning on purpose to breakfast with us, and very obligingly furnished us with horses to proceed on our journey to Mr. M'Lean's of *Lochbuy*, where we were to pass the night. We dined at the house of Dr. Alexander M'Lean, another physician in

[a] gradually 1 : generally 2, 3.

British Museum (1103 g. 86) is entered in Boswell's own hand:
' Comes jucundus in via pro vehiculo est.
To John Wilkes Esq: as pleasant a companion as ever lived. From the

Authour.
     —will my Wilkes retreat,
And see, once seen before, that ancient Seat! &c.'
See *ante,* iii. 64, 183 ; iv. 101, 224, note 2.

Mull, who was so much struck with the uncommon conversation of Dr. Johnson, that he observed to me, ' This man is just a *hogshead* of sense.'

Dr. Johnson said of the *Turkish Spy* [1], which lay in the room, that it told nothing but what every body might have known at that time ; and that what was good in it, did not pay you for the trouble of reading to find it.

After a very tedious ride, through what appeared to me the most gloomy and desolate country I had ever beheld [2], we arrived, between seven and eight o'clock, at *Moy*, the seat of the Laird of *Lochbuy*.—*Buy*, in Erse, signifies yellow, and I at first imagined that the loch or branch of the sea here, was thus denominated, in the same manner as the *Red Sea ;* but I afterwards learned that it derived its name from a hill above it, which,[a] being of a yellowish hue, has the epithet of *Buy*.

We had heard much of Lochbuy's being a great roaring braggadocio, a kind of Sir John Falstaff, both in size and manners ; but we found that they had swelled him up to a fictitious size, and clothed him with imaginary qualities.—Col's idea of him was equally extravagant, though very different : he told us he was quite a Don Quixote ; and said, he would give a great deal to see him and Dr. Johnson together. The truth is, that Lochbuy proved to be only a bluff, comely, noisy old gentleman, proud of his hereditary consequence, and a very hearty and hospitable landlord. Lady Lochbuy was sister to Sir Allan M'Lean, but much older. He said to me, ' They are quite *Antediluvians*.' Being told that Dr. Johnson did not hear well, Lochbuy bawled out to him, ' Are you of the Johnstons of Glencro, or of Ardnamurchan [3] ? '—Dr. Johnson gave him a significant look, but made no answer ; and I told Lochbuy that he was not Johns*ton*, but John*son*, and that he was an Englishman [4].

[a] which, 1, 2: which 3.

[1] See *ante*, iv. 199 ⟨and 517 ff.⟩.
[2] ' Our afternoon journey was through a country of such gloomy desolation, that Mr. Boswell thought no part of the Highlands equally terrifick.' Johnson's *Western Isl.*, p. 139.
[3] Johnson describes Lochbuy as ' a true Highland Laird, rough and haughty, and tenacious of his dignity ; who, hearing my name, inquired whether I was of the Johnstons of Glencroe, or of Ardnamurchan.' *Ib*. ⟨For Lochbuy see App. D, p. 558.⟩
[4] Boswell totally misapprehended Lochbuy's meaning. There are two septs of the powerful clan of M'Donald, who are called Mac-Ian, that is *John's-son ;* and as Highlanders often translate their names when they go to the Lowlands,—as Gregor-son for Mac-Gregor, Farquhar-son for Mac-

Lochbuy some years ago tried to prove himself a weak man, liable to imposition, or, as we term it in Scotland, a *facile* man, in order to set aside a lease which he had granted ; but failed in the attempt. On my mentioning this circumstance to Dr. Johnson, he seemed much surprized that such a suit was admitted by the Scottish law, and observed, that ' In England no man is allowed to *stultify* himself [1].'

Sir Allan, Lochbuy, and I, had the conversation chiefly to ourselves to-night : Dr. Johnson, being extremely weary, went to bed soon after supper.

Friday, 22d October.

†Before Dr. Johnson came to breakfast, Lady Lochbuy said, ' he was a *dungeon* of wit ; ' a very common phrase in Scotland to express a profoundness of intellect, though he afterwards told me, that he had never [a] heard it. She proposed that he should have some cold sheep's-head for breakfast. Sir Allan seemed displeased at his sister's vulgarity, and wondered how such a thought should come into her head. From a mischievous love of sport, I took the lady's part ; and very gravely said, ' I think it is but fair to give him an offer of it. If he does not choose it, he may let it alone.'—' I think so,' said the lady, looking at her brother with an air of victory. Sir Allan, finding the matter desperate, strutted about the room, and took snuff. When Dr. Johnson came in, she called to him, ' Do you choose any cold sheep's-head, sir ? '—' No, MADAM,' said he, with a tone of surprise and anger [2].—' It is here, sir,' said she, supposing he

[a] had never 1 (*MS.*) : never had 2, 3.

Farquhar,—Lochbuy supposed that Dr. Johnson might be one of the Mac-Ians of Ardnamurchan, or of Glencro. Boswell's explanation was nothing to the purpose. The *Johnstons* are a clan distinguished in Scottish *border* history, and as brave as any *Highland* clan that ever wore brogues ; but they lay entirely out of Lochbuy's knowledge—nor was he thinking of *them*. SCOTT, 1831.

[1] This maxim, however, has been controverted. See Blackstone's COMMENTARIES, Vol. II. p. 292 ; and the authorities there quoted. BOSWELL.

' Blackstone says :—From these loose authorities, which Fitzherbert does not scruple to reject as being contrary to reason, the maxim that a man shall not stultify himself hath been handed down as settled law : though later opinions, feeling the inconvenience of the rule, have in many points endeavoured to restrain it.' *Ib.* bk. ii, ch. xix, p. 292.

† ⟨The first draft of this paragraph was written in 1779: see Preface, p. vi.⟩

[2] Begging pardon of the Doctor and his conductor, I have often seen and partaken of cold sheep's head at

had refused it to save the trouble of bringing it in. They thus went on at cross purposes, till he confirmed his refusal in a manner not to be misunderstood ; while I sat quietly by, and enjoyed my success.

†After breakfast, we surveyed the old castle, in the pit or dungeon of which Lochbuy had some years before taken upon him to imprison several persons [1] ; and though he had been fined in a considerable sum by the Court of Justiciary, he was so little affected by it, that, while we were examining the dungeon, he said to me, with a smile, ' Your father knows something of this ; ' (alluding to my father's having sat as one of the judges on his trial.) Sir Allan whispered me, that the laird could not be persuaded, that he had lost his heritable jurisdiction [2].

We then set out for the ferry, by which we were to cross to the main land of Argyleshire. Lochbuy and Sir Allan accompanied us. We were told much of a war-saddle, on which this reputed Don Quixote used to be mounted ; but we did not see it, for the young laird had applied it to a less noble purpose, having taken it to Falkirk fair *with a drove of black cattle.*

We bade adieu to Lochbuy, and to our very kind conductor [3],

as good breakfast-tables as ever they sat at. This protest is something in the manner of the late Culrossie, who fought a duel for the honour of Aberdeen butter. I have passed over all the Doctor's other reproaches upon Scotland, but the sheep's head I will defend *totis viribus.* Dr. Johnson himself must have forgiven my zeal on this occasion ; for if, as he says, *dinner* be the thing of which a man thinks *oftenest during the day, breakfast* must be that of which he thinks *first in the morning.* SCOTT, 1831. I do not know where Johnson says this. Perhaps Scott was thinking of a passage in Mrs. Piozzi's *Anec.,* p. 149 (*John. Misc.* i. 249) where she writes that he said : ' A man seldom thinks with more earnestness of any thing than he does of his dinner.'

† ⟨Boswell wrote up his Journal for the rest of this day on 23 Aug. 1780 : see the Preface, p. vi, to this volume.⟩

[1] A horrible place it was. Johnson describes it (*Western Isl.,* p. 140) as ' a deep subterraneous cavity, walled on the sides, and arched on the top, into which the descent is through a narrow door, by a ladder or a rope.'

[2] See *ante,* v. 177.

[3] Sir Allan Maclean, like many Highland chiefs, was embarrassed in his private affairs, and exposed to unpleasant solicitations from attorneys, called, in Scotland, *writers* (which, indeed, was the chief motive of his retiring to Inchkenneth). Upon one occasion he made a visit to a friend, then residing at Carron lodge, on the banks of the Carron, where the banks of that river are studded with pretty villas : Sir Allan, admiring the landscape, asked his friend, whom that handsome seat belonged to. ' M——, the writer to the signet,' was the reply. ' Umph ! ' said Sir Allan, but not with an accent of assent, ' I mean that other house.' ' Oh ! that belongs to a very honest

Saturday 23 October 1773 — Oban

Sir Allan M'Lean, on the shore of Mull, and then got into the ferry-boat, the bottom of which was strewed with branches of trees or bushes, upon which we sat. We had a good day and a fine passage, and in the evening landed at Oban, where we found a tolerable inn†. After having been so long confined at different times in islands, from which it was always uncertain when we could get away, it was comfortable to be now on the main land, and to know that, if in health, we might get to any place in Scotland or England in a certain number of days.

Here we discovered,[a] from the conjectures which were formed, that the people on the main land were entirely ignorant of our motions; for in a Glasgow news-paper [1] we found a paragraph, which, as it contains a just and well-turned compliment to my illustrious friend, I shall here insert:

'We are well assured that Dr. Johnson is confined by tempestuous weather to the isle [b] of Sky; it being unsafe to venture, in a small boat, upon such a stormy surge as is very common there at this time of the year. Such a philosopher, detained on an almost barren island, resembles a whale left upon the strand. The latter will be welcome to every body, on account of his oil, his bone, &c. and the other will charm his companions, and the rude inhabitants, with his superior knowledge and wisdom, calm resignation, and unbounded benevolence.'

Saturday, 23d October.

After a good night's rest, we breakfasted at our leisure. We talked of Goldsmith's *Traveller*, of which Dr. Johnson spoke highly; and, while I was helping him on with his great coat, he repeated from it the character of the British nation, which he did with such energy, that the tear started into his eye:

'Stern o'er each bosom reason holds her state,
'With daring aims irregularly great,

---

[a] discovered, 1; discovered 2, 3.   [b] island *Glasgow Journal*.

fellow, Jamie——, also a writer to the signet.' 'Umph!' said the Highland chief of M'Lean, with more emphasis than before, 'And yon smaller house?' 'That belongs to a Stirling man; I forget his name, but I am sure he is a writer, too; for——.' Sir Allan, who had recoiled a quarter of a circle backward at every response, now wheeled the circle entire, and turned his back on the landscape, saying, 'My good friend, I must own, you have a pretty situation here; but d—n your neighbourhood.' SCOTT, 1831.

† ⟨See App. D, p. 559.⟩
[1] ⟨*Glasgow Journal*, 14–21 Oct. 1773. Boswell improved the punctuation of the paragraph. He noted in his Journal, 10 April 1784: 'See at Glasgow The Newspaper about Dr. Johnson, Oct. 1773.' *Boswell Papers*, xvi. 51.⟩

–Inveraray *Saturday 23 October 1773*

' Pride in their port, defiance in their eye,
' I see the lords of humankind pass by,
' Intent on high designs, a thoughtful band,
' By forms unfashion'd, fresh from nature's hand ;
' Fierce in their native hardiness of soul,
' True to imagin'd right, above control,
' While ev'n the peasant boasts these rights to scan,
' And learns to venerate himself as man.'

We could get but one bridle here, which, according to the maxim *detur digniori*, was appropriated to Dr. Johnson's sheltie. I and Joseph rode with halters. We crossed in a ferry-boat a pretty wide lake [1], and on the farther side of it, close by the shore, found a hut for our inn. We were much wet. I changed my clothes in part, and was at pains to get myself well dried. Dr. Johnson resolutely kept on all his clothes, wet as they were, letting them steam before the smoky turf fire. I thought him in the wrong ; but his firmness was, perhaps, a species of heroism.

I remember but little of our conversation†. I mentioned Shenstone's saying of Pope, that he had the art of condensing sense more than any body [2]. Dr. Johnson said, ' It is not true, sir. There is more sense in a line of Cowley than in a page (or a sentence, or ten lines,—I am not quite certain of the very phrase) of Pope.' He maintained that Archibald, Duke of Argyle [3], was a narrow man. I wondered at this ; and observed, that his building so great a house at Inveraray was not like a narrow man. ' Sir, (said he,) when a narrow man has resolved to build a house, he builds it like another man. But Archibald, Duke of Argyle, was narrow in his ordinary expences, in his quotidian expences.'

[1] Loch Awe.

† ⟨Boswell wrote his Journal for this day on 23 Aug. 1782 : see the Preface to this volume, p. vi.⟩

[2] ' Pope's talent lay remarkably in what one may naturally enough term the condensation of thoughts. I think no other English poet ever brought so much sense into the same number of lines with equal smoothness, ease, and poetical beauty. Let him who doubts of this peruse his Essay on Man with attention.' Shenstone's *Essays on Men and Manners* ⟨*Works*, 1764, ii. 178⟩. ' He [Gray] approved an observation of Shenstone, that

" Pope had the art of condensing a thought." ' Nicholls' *Reminiscences of Gray*, p. 37 ⟨Gray's *Corresp.*, 1935, iii. 1292⟩. And Swift [in his *Lines on the death of Dr. Swift*], himself a great condenser, says
' In Pope I cannot read a line
But with a sigh I wish it mine ;
When he can in one couplet fix
More sense than I can do in six.'
P. CUNNINGHAM.

[3] He is described by Walpole to Lord Hailes, 10 Feb. 1781, as ' undoubtedly a dark shrewd man.' *Letters*, ed. Toynbee, xi. 393.

The distinction is very just. It is in the ordinary expences of life that a man's liberality or narrowness is to be discovered.—I never heard the word *quotidian* in this sense, and I imagined it to be a word of Dr. Johnson's own fabrication ; but I have since found it in Young's *Night Thoughts*, (Night fifth,)

'Death's a destroyer of quotidian prey.'

and in my friend's Dictionary, supported by the authorities of Charles I. and Dr. Donne.

It rained very hard as we journeyed on after dinner. The roar of torrents from the mountains, as we passed along in the dusk, and the other circumstances attending our ride this evening, have been mentioned with so much animation by Dr. Johnson, that I shall not attempt to say any thing on the subject [1].

We got at night to Inveraray, where we found an excellent inn [†]. Even here, Dr. Johnson would not change his wet clothes.

The prospect of good accommodation cheered us much. We supped well ; and after supper, Dr. Johnson, whom I had not seen taste any fermented liquor during all our travels, called for a gill of whisky. ' Come, (said he,) let me know what it is that makes a Scotchman happy [2] ! ' He drank it all but a drop, which I begged leave to pour into my glass, that I might say we had

---

[1] 'The night came on while we had yet a great part of the way to go, though not so dark, but that we could discern the cataracts which poured down the hills, on one side, and fell into one general channel that ran with great violence on the other. The wind was loud, the rain was heavy, and the whistling of the blast, the fall of the shower, the rush of the cataracts, and the roar of the torrent, made a nobler chorus of the rough musick of nature than it had ever been my chance to hear before.' Johnson's *Western Isl.*, p. 143. He wrote to Mr. Thrale :—' All the rougher powers of Nature, except thunder were in motion, but there was no danger. I should have been sorry to have missed any of the inconveniences, to have had more light, or less rain, for their cooperation crowded the scene, and filled the mind.' *Letters*, No. 333.

[†] ⟨See App. D, p. 559.⟩

[2] 'I never tasted whisky, except once for experiment at the inn in Inverary, when I thought it preferable to any English malt brandy. It was strong, but not pungent, and was free from the empyreumatick taste or smell. What was the process I had no opportunity of inquiring, nor do I wish to improve the art of making poison pleasant.' Johnson's *Western Isl.*, p. 49. Smollett, medical man though he was, looked upon whisky as anything but poison. ' I am told that it is given with great success to infants, as a cordial, in the confluent small-pox.' *Humphry Clinker*, Letter of Sept. 3. ⟨Arnot (*Hist. Edinburgh*, 1779, p. 302) describes whisky as 'a spirituous liquor used by the poorer class of people in Scotland'. Pennant (*Tour Hebrides 1772*, 1774, p. 194) calls it '*liqueur d'enfer*'.⟩

drunk whisky together. I proposed Mrs. Thrale should be our toast. He would not have *her* drunk in whisky, but rather ' some insular lady ; ' so we drank one of the ladies† whom we had lately left.—He owned to-night, that he got as good a room and bed as at an English inn.

I had here the pleasure of finding a letter from home, which relieved me from the anxiety I had suffered, in consequence of not having received any account of my family for many weeks. I also found a letter from Mr. Garrick, which was a regale [1] as agreeable as a pine-apple would be in a desert [2]. He had favoured me with his correspondence for many years ; and when Dr. Johnson and I were at Inverness, I had written to him as follows :

Inverness,
Sunday, 29 August, 1773.

' My dear Sir,

' HERE I am, and Mr. Samuel Johnson actually with me. We were a night at Fores, in coming to which, in the dusk of the evening, we passed over the bleak and blasted heath where Macbeth met the witches [3]. Your old preceptor [4] repeated, with much solemnity, the speech—

" How far is't called to Fores ? What are these,
" So wither'd and so wild in their attire," &c.

This day we visited the ruins of Macbeth's castle at Inverness. I have had great romantick satisfaction in seeing Johnson upon the classical scenes of Shakspeare in Scotland ; which I really looked upon as almost as improbable as that " Birnam wood should come to Dunsinane [5]." Indeed, as I have always been accustomed to view him as a permanent London object, it would not be much more wonderful to me to see St. Paul's church moving along where we now are. As yet we have travelled in post-chaises ; but to-morrow we are to mount on

† ⟨Boswell says in his Original Journal ' I think Miss Macpherson '. See *ante*, v. 265.⟩
[1] *Regale* in this sense is not in Johnson's *Dictionary*. It was, however, a favourite word at this time. Thus, Mrs. Piozzi, in her *Journey through France*, ii. 297, says :—' A large dish of hot chocolate thickened with bread and cream is a common afternoon's regale here.' Miss Burney often uses the word.
[2] ⟨The comparison of Garrick's letter to a pine-apple first occurs in Boswell's reply to Garrick, 11 April 1774: ' It was,' he writes, ' a pine-apple of the finest flavour, which had a high zest indeed among the heath-covered mountains of Scotia.' *Letters*, No. 124, i. 201. The comparison was introduced into the *Tour* in 1785. See Pottle and Bennett's edition, 1936, p. 349.⟩
[3] See *ante*, v. 76 and 115.
[4] See *ante*, i. 97.
[5] ' Though Birnam wood be come to Dunsinane.'
Macbeth, act v. sc. 7.

horseback, and ascend into the mountains by Fort Augustus, and so on to the ferry, where we are to cross to Sky. We shall see that Island fully, and then visit some more of the Hebrides; after which we are to land in Argyleshire, proceed by Glasgow to Auchinleck, repose there a competent time, and then return to Edinburgh, from whence the Rambler will depart for old England again, as soon as he finds it convenient. Hitherto,[a] we have had a very prosperous expedition. I flatter myself, *servetur ad imum, qualis ab incepto processerit* [1]. He is in excellent spirits, and I have a rich journal of his conversation. Look back, *Davy* [2], to Lichfield,—run up through the time that has elapsed since you first knew Mr. Johnson,—and enjoy with me his present extraordinary Tour. I could not resist the impulse of writing to you from this place. The situation of the old castle corresponds exactly to Shakspeare's description. While we were there to-day [3], it happened oddly, that a raven perched upon one of the chimney-tops, and croaked. Then I in my turn repeated—

> "The raven himself is hoarse,
> That croaks the fatal entrance of Duncan,
> Under my battlements."

'I wish you had been with us. Think what enthusiastick happiness I shall have to see Mr. Samuel Johnson walking among the romantick rocks and woods of my ancestors at Auchinleck [4]! Write to me at Edinburgh. You owe me his verses on great George and tuneful Cibber, and the bad verses which led him to make his fine ones on Philips the musician [5]. Keep your promise, and let me have them. I offer my very best compliments to Mrs. Garrick, and ever am

'Your warm admirer and friend,

JAMES BOSWELL.'

'*To David Garrick, Esq;
London.*'

His answer was as follows:

[a] Hitherto, 1, 2: Hitherto 3.

[1] 'From his first entrance to the closing scene
Let him one equal character maintain.'
FRANCIS. Horace, *Ars Poet.* l. 126.

[2] I took the liberty of giving this familiar appellation to my celebrated friend, to bring in a more lively manner to his remembrance the period when he was Dr. Johnson's pupil. BOSWELL, ed. 1.

[3] See *ante*, v. 129.

[4] Boswell is here quoting the Preface to the third edition of his *Corsica*:—'Whatever clouds may overcast my days, I can now walk here among the rocks and woods of my ancestors, with an agreeable consciousness that I have done something worthy.'

[5] See *ante*, i. 148, ii. 25; *post*, v. 404.

Inveraray *Saturday 23 October* 1773

'Hampton, September 14, 1773.

'DEAR SIR,

'YOU stole away from London, and left us all in the lurch ; for we expected you one night at the club, and knew nothing of your departure. Had I payed you what I owed you, for the book you bought for me, I should only have grieved for the loss of your company, and slept with a quiet conscience ; but, wounded as it is, it must remain so till I see you again, though I am sure our good friend Mr. Johnson will discharge the debt for me, if you will let him.—Your account of your journey to *Fores*, the *raven, old castle*, &c. &c. made me half mad. Are you not rather too late in the year for fine weather, which is the life and soul of seeing places ?—I hope your pleasure will continue *qualis ab incepto*, &c.

'Your friend [1] ——————— threatens me much. I only wish that he would put his threats in execution, and, if he prints his play, I will forgive him. I remember he complained to you, that his bookseller called for the money for some copies of his ————, which I subscribed for, and that I desired him to call again.—The truth is, that my wife was not at home, and that for weeks together I have not ten shillings in my pocket [2].—However, had it been otherwise, it was not so great

[1] I have suppressed my friend's name from an apprehension of wounding his sensibility ; but I would not withhold from my readers a passage which shews Mr. Garrick's mode of writing as the Manager of a Theatre, and contains a pleasing trait of his domestick life. His judgment of dramatick pieces, so far as concerns their exhibition on the stage, must be allowed to have considerable weight. But from the effect which a perusal of the tragedy here condemned had upon myself, and from the opinions of some eminent criticks, I venture to pronounce that it has much poetical merit ; and its authour has distinguished himself by several performances which shew that the epithet *poetaster* was, in the present instance, much misapplied. BOSWELL, ed. 3, 1786.

⟨Boswell's friend was Mickle, whose tragedy, *Chateaubriant*, or as it was re-named *The Siege of Marseilles*, he strongly recommended to Garrick. Writing to Mickle, 22 June 1769, he says: 'I now return you Chateaubriant, with a letter of recommendation for Mr. Garrick. I am sure it is in Mr. Garrick's power to make it appear to advantage in Drury-Lane.' On 23 Sept. 1771 he says: 'I wrote to Mr. Garrick in favour of your tragedy, at the very time when you first wished me to do it, this year. That letter was written before your's came to my hands. It was a spontaneous application. Since receiving both your last, I have again written to Mr. Garrick.' Boswell then quotes a paragraph from one of his letters, presumably the last, to Garrick, which reveals the names of 'some eminent criticks' : 'Permit me . . . again to recommend to your patronage, Mr. Mickle's tragedy ; which, I rejoice to hear, has now passed through the hands of both the Wartons.' On 24 Sept. 1772 he tells Mickle that he has 'written again to Mr. Garrick on the subject of your play '. See *Universal Mag.*, 1809, xi. 24, 224 ff., 301 ff. For Mickle's threats and complaints see App. D, p. 559.⟩

[2] ⟨Mickle told Boswell that Becket, Garrick's bookseller, paid his bookseller £6, the first payment of twenty subscriptions. He was convinced that 'the greatest part of Garrick's twenty subscriptions were taken in Becket's shop'. *Universal Mag.*, 1809, xi. 303.⟩

a crime to draw his poetical vengeance upon me.—I despise all that he can do, and am glad that I can so easily get rid of him and his ingratitude.—I am hardened both to abuse and ingratitude.

'You, I am sure, will no more recommend your poetasters to my civility and good offices.

'Shall I recommend to you a play of Eschylus, (the Prometheus,) published and translated by poor old Morell, who is a good scholar [1], and an acquaintance of mine? It will be but half a guinea, and your name shall be put in the list I am making for him. You will be in very good company.

'Now for the Epitaphs!

[*These, together with the verses on George the Second, and Colley Cibber, as his Poet Laureat, of which imperfect copies are gone about, will appear in my Life of Dr. Johnson* [2].]

'I have no more paper, or I should have said more to you. My love [3] and respects to Mr. Johnson.

'Yours ever,
'D. GARRICK.'

'I can't write. I have the gout in my hand.'
'*To James Boswell, Esq. Edinburgh.*'

Sunday, 24th October.

We passed the forenoon calmly and placidly. I prevailed on Dr. Johnson to read aloud Ogden's sixth Sermon on Prayer, which he did with a distinct expression, and pleasing solemnity. He praised my favourite preacher, his elegant language, and

[1] ⟨Dr. Thomas Morell's edition of *Prometheus Vinctus* was published in 1767 and reissued, together with Stanley's Latin version and an English translation by Morell, in 1773 (see App. D, p. 560). Morell's reputation as a scholar rests chiefly on his *Thesaurus Græcæ Poeseos*, 1762, the frontispiece of which is Basire's engraving of Hogarth's portrait of Morell 'in the character of a cynic philosopher'.⟩ Morell once entered the school-room at Winchester College, 'in which some junior boys were writing their exercises, one of whom, struck no less with his air and manner than [with] the questions he put to them, whispered to his schoolfellows, "Is he not a fine old Grecian!" The Doctor, overhearing this, turned hastily round, and exclaimed, "I am indeed an old Grecian, my little man! Did you never see my head before my Thesaurus?"' The Praepostors, learning the dignity of their visitor, in a most respectful manner showed him the College. Wooll's *Life of Dr. Warton*, p. 329. ⟨Morell supplied the libretti for a number of Handel's oratorios, including 'Judas Maccabaeus', 'Joshua', and 'Jephtha'. See *D.N.B.*⟩

[2] *Ante*, i. 148–9.

[3] I doubt whether any other instance can be found of *love* being sent to Johnson.

remarkable acuteness ; and said, he fought infidels with their own weapons.

As a specimen of Ogden's manner, I insert the following passage † from the sermon which Dr. Johnson now read. The preacher, after arguing against that vain philosophy which maintains, in conformity with the hard principle of eternal necessity, or unchangeable predetermination, that the only effect of prayer for others, although we are exhorted to pray for them, is to produce good dispositions in ourselves towards them ; thus expresses himself :

' A plain man may be apt to ask, But if this then, though enjoined in the holy scriptures, is to be my real aim and intention, when I am taught to pray for other persons, why is it that I do not plainly so express it ? Why is not the form of the petition brought nearer to the meaning ? Give them, say I to our heavenly father, what is good. But this, I am to understand, will be as it will be, and is not for me to alter. What is it then that I am doing ? I am desiring to become charitable myself ; and why may I not plainly say so ? Is there shame in it, or impiety ? The wish is laudable : why should I form designs to hide it ?

' Or is it, perhaps, better to be brought about by indirect means, and in this artful manner ? Alas ! who is it that I would impose on ? From whom can it be, in this commerce, that I desire to hide any thing ? When, as my Saviour commands me, I have *entered into my closet, and shut my door*, there are but two parties privy to my devotions, GOD and my own heart ; which of the two am I deceiving ? '

He wished to have more books, and, upon inquiring if there were any in the house, was told that a waiter had some, which were brought to him ; but I recollect none of them, except *Hervey's Meditations* §. He thought slightly of this admired book. He treated it with ridicule, and would not allow even the scene of the dying Husband and Father to be pathetick [1]. I am not an impartial judge ; for *Hervey's Meditations* engaged my affections in my early years.—He read a passage concerning the moon, ludicrously, and shewed how easily he could, in the same style, make reflections on that planet, the very reverse of Hervey's [2], representing her as treacherous to mankind. He did

† ⟨Taken, with some adaptation, from *Sermons on the Efficacy of Prayer and Intercession*, 1770, pp. 65 ff.⟩
§ ⟨By the Rev. James Hervey. The first edition of *Meditations among the Tombs* was published in 1746 ; the second, enlarged to two volumes and entitled *Meditations and Contempla-*tions, in 1748.⟩
[1] The passage begins :—' A Servant or two, from a revering Distance, cast many a wishful Look, and condole their honoured Master in the Language of Sighs.' Hervey's *Meditations*, ed. 1748, i. 40.
[2] *Ib*. ii. 84.

this with much humour ; but I have not preserved the particulars. He then indulged a playful fancy, in making a *Meditation on a Pudding* [1], of which I hastily wrote down, in his presence, the following note ; which, though imperfect, may serve to give my readers some idea of it.

MEDITATION ON A PUDDING.

' LET us seriously reflect of what a pudding is composed. It is composed of flour that once waved in the golden grain, and drank the dews of the morning ; of milk pressed from the swelling udder by the gentle hand of the beauteous milkmaid, whose beauty and innocence might have recommended a worse draught ; who, while she stroked the udder, indulged no ambitious thoughts of wandering in palaces, formed no plans for the destruction of her fellow-creatures : milk, which is drawn from the cow, that useful animal, that eats the grass of the field, and supplies us with that which made the greatest part of the food of mankind in the age which the poets have agreed to call golden. It is made with an egg, that miracle of nature, which the theoretical Burnet [2] has compared to creation. An egg contains water within its beautiful smooth surface ; and an unformed mass, by the incubation of the parent, becomes a regular animal, furnished with bones and sinews, and covered with feathers.—Let us consider ; can there be more wanting to complete the Meditation on a Pudding ? If more is wanting, more may be found. It contains salt, which keeps the sea from putrefaction : salt, which is made the image of intellectual excellence, contributes to the formation of a pudding.'

In a Magazine I found a saying of Dr. Johnson's, something to this purpose ; that the happiest part of a man's life is what he passes lying awake in bed in the morning. I read it to him. He said, ' I may, perhaps, have said this ; for nobody, at times, talks more laxly than I do [3].' I ventured to suggest to him, that this was dangerous from one of his authority.

I spoke of living in the country, and upon what footing one should be with neighbours. I observed that some people were afraid of being on too easy a footing with them, from an apprehension that their time would not be their own. He made the obvious remark, that it depended much on what kind

[1] ⟨See Boswell's *Hebrides*, ed. Pottle and Bennett, 1936, p. 350.⟩ The *Meditation* was perhaps partly suggested by Swift's *Meditation upon a Broom-Stick*, *Prose Works* (ed. Temple Scott), i. 331.

[2] Thomas Burnet of the Charterhouse, in his *Sacred Theory of the Earth*, bk. 1, chs. iv and vi, ed. 1719, pp. 71, 97.

[3] See *ante*, i. 476, and ii. 73.

of neighbours one has, whether it was desirable to be on an easy footing with them, or not. I mentioned a certain baronet †, who told me, he never was happy in the country, till he was not on speaking terms with his neighbours, which he contrived in different ways to bring about. ' Lord ────── † (said he) stuck long ᵃ ; but at last the fellow pounded my pigs, and then I got rid of him.' —*Johnson.* ' Nay, sir, My Lord got rid of Sir John, and shewed how little he valued him, by putting his pigs in the pound.'

I told Dr. Johnson I was in some difficulty how to act at Inveraray. I had reason to think that the Duchess of Argyle disliked me, on account of my zeal in the Douglas cause ¹ ; but the Duke of Argyle had always been pleased to treat me with great civility. They were now at the castle, which is a very short walk from our inn ; and the question was, whether I should go and pay my respects there. Dr. Johnson, to whom I had stated the case, was clear that I ought ; but, in his usual way, he was very shy of discovering a desire to be invited there himself. Though,ᵇ from a conviction of the benefit of subordination ² to society, he has always shewn great respect to persons of high rank, when he happened to be in their company, yet his pride of character has ever made him guard against any appearance of courting the great. Besides, he was impatient to get ᶜ to Glasgow, where he expected letters. At the same time he was, I believe, secretly not unwilling to have attention paid him by so great a Chieftain, and so exalted a nobleman. He insisted that I should not go to the castle this day before dinner, as it would look like seeking an invitation. ' But, (said I,) if the duke invites us to dine with him to-morrow, shall we accept ? '—' Yes, sir ; ' I think he said, ' to be sure.' But, he added, ' He won't ask us ! '—I mentioned, that I was afraid my company might be disagreeable

ᵃ long 1 : along 2, 3.   ᵇ Though, 1, 2 : Though 3.   ᶜ get 1: go 2, 3.

† ⟨Sir John Dalrymple and Lord Adam Gordon : see App. D, p. 560.⟩
¹ Elizabeth Gunning (see *post*, v. 359, n. 2) . . . was mother of Douglas, Duke of Hamilton, the competitor for the Douglas property with the late Lord Douglas : she was, of course, prejudiced against Boswell, who had shown all the bustling importance of his character in the Douglas cause, and it was said, I know not on what authority, that he headed the mob which broke the windows of some of the judges, and of Lord Auchinleck, his father, in particular. SCOTT, 1831. See *ante*, ii. 50 ⟨and *post* App. D, p. 560⟩.
² See *ante*, i. 408, and ii. 329.

to the duchess. He treated this objection with a manly disdain: 'That, sir, he must settle with his wife.'—We dined well. I went to the castle just about the time when I supposed the ladies would be retired from dinner. I sent in my name; and, being shewn in, found the amiable duke sitting at the head of his table with several gentlemen. I was most politely received, and gave his grace some particulars of the curious journey which I had been making with Dr. Johnson. When we rose from table, the duke said to me, 'I hope you and Dr. Johnson will dine with us to-morrow.' I thanked his grace; but told him, my friend was in a great hurry to get back to London. The duke, with a kind complacency, said, 'He will stay one day; and I will take care he shall see this place to advantage.' I said, I should be sure to let him know his grace's invitation.—As I was going away, the duke said, 'Mr. Boswell, won't you have some tea?'—I thought it best to get over the meeting with the duchess this night; so respectfully agreed. I was conducted to the drawing-room by the duke, who announced my name; but the duchess, who was sitting with her daughter, Lady Betty Hamilton [1], and some other ladies †, took not the least notice of me. I should have been mortified at being thus coldly received by a lady of whom I, with the rest of the world, have always entertained a very high admiration, had I not been consoled by the obliging attention of the duke.

When I returned to the inn, I informed Dr. Johnson of the Duke of Argyle's invitation, with which he was much pleased, and readily accepted of it.—We talked of a violent contest which was then carrying on, with a view to the next general election for Ayrshire; where one of the candidates, in order to undermine the old and established interest, had artfully held himself out as a champion for the independency of the county against aristocratick influence, and had persuaded several gentlemen into a resolution to oppose every candidate who was supported by peers [2].—'Foolish fellows! (said Dr. Johnson,) don't they see that they are as much dependent upon the peers one way as the other. The peers have but to *oppose* a candidate,

---

[1] ⟨She was born 26 Jan. 1753 and on 23 June 1774 married the 12th Earl of Derby. She in 1778 had an intrigue with the third Duke of Dorset and was in consequence separated from her husband, who on her death, in 1797, married Elizabeth Farran. See G. E. C., *Complete Peerage*, 1916, iv. 218, and *post*, v. 358, 562–3.⟩
† ⟨See App. D, p. 561.⟩
[2] See *ante*, iv. 248.

to ensure him success. It is said, the only way to make a pig go forward, is to pull him back by the tail. These people must be treated like pigs.'

Monday, 25th October.

My acquaintance, the Reverend Mr. John M'Aulay [1], one of the Ministers of Inveraray, and brother to our good friend at Calder [2], came to us this morning, and accompanied us to the castle, where I presented Dr. Johnson to the Duke of Argyle. We were shewn through the house; and I never shall forget the impression made upon my fancy by some of the ladies' maids tripping about in neat morning dresses. After seeing for a long time little but rusticity, their lively manner, and gay inviting appearance, pleased me so much, that I thought, for the moment, I could have been a knight-errant for them [3].

We then got into a low one-horse chair, ordered for us by the duke, in which we drove about the place. Dr. Johnson was much struck by the grandeur and elegance of this princely seat †. He thought, however, the castle too low, and wished it had been a story higher.—He said, ' What I admire here, is the total defiance of expence.' I had a particular pride in shewing him a great number of fine old trees, to compensate for the nakedness which had made such an impression on him on the eastern coast of Scotland.

When we came in, before dinner, we found the duke and some gentlemen in the hall. Dr. Johnson took much notice of the large collection of arms, which are excellently disposed there. I told what he had said to Sir Alexander M'Donald, of his ancestors not suffering their arms to rust [4]. ' Well, (said the doctor,) but let us be glad we live in times when arms *may* rust. We can sit to-day at his grace's table, without any risk of being attacked, and perhaps sitting down again wounded or maimed.' The duke placed Dr. Johnson next himself at table. I was in fine spirits; and though sensible that I had the misfortune of

---

[1] Lord Macaulay's grandfather. ⟨See App. D, p. 561.⟩
[2] See *ante*, v. 118.
[3] On reflection, at the distance of several years, I wonder that my venerable fellow-traveller should have read this passage without censuring my levity. BOSWELL, ed. 1. ⟨See App. D, p. 561.⟩
† ⟨See App. D, p. 562.⟩ [4] *Ante*, v. 151.

not being in favour with the duchess, I was not in the least disconcerted, and offered her grace some of the dish that was before me. It must be owned that I was in the right to be quite unconcerned, if I could. I was the Duke of Argyle's guest; and I had no reason to suppose that he adopted the prejudices and resentments of the Duchess of Hamilton.

I knew it was the rule of modern high life not to drink to any body; but, that I might have the satisfaction for once to look the duchess in the face, with a glass in my hand, I with a respectful air addressed her,—' My Lady Duchess, I have the honour to drink your grace's good health.'—I repeated the words audibly, and with a steady countenance. This was, perhaps, rather too much; but some allowance must be made for human feelings.

The duchess was very attentive to Dr. Johnson. I know not how a *middle state* [1] came to be mentioned. Her grace wished to hear him on that point. ' Madam, (said he,) your own relation, Mr. Archibald Campbell, can tell you better about it than I can. He was a bishop of the nonjuring communion, and wrote a book upon the subject [2].'—He engaged to get it for her grace. He afterwards gave a full history of Mr. Archibald Campbell, which I am sorry I do not recollect particularly. He said, Mr. Campbell had been bred a violent Whig, but afterwards ' kept *better company*, and became a Tory.' He said this with a smile, in pleasant allusion, as I thought, to the opposition between his own political principles and those of the duke's

---

[1] See *ante*, i. 240. ⟨Boswell himself believed in 'a middle state' after death: see App. D, p. 562.⟩

[2] As this book is now become very scarce, I shall subjoin the title, which is curious:

'The Doctrines of a Middle State between Death and the Resurrection: Of Prayers for the Dead: And the Necessity of Purification; plainly proved from the holy Scriptures, and the Writings of the Fathers of the Primitive Church: And acknowledged by several learned Fathers and great Divines of the Church of England and others since the Reformation. To which is added, an Appendix concerning the Descent of the Soul of Christ into Hell, while his Body lay in the Grave. Together with the Judgment of the Reverend Dr. Hickes concerning this Book, so far as relates to a Middle State, particular Judgment, and Prayers for the Dead as it appeared in the first Edition. And a Manuscript of the Right Reverend Bishop Overall [a] upon the Subject of a Middle State [b], and never before printed. Also, a Preservative against several of the Errors of the Roman Church, in six small Treatises. By the Honourable Archibald Campbell.' Folio, 1721. BOSWELL, ed. 2. ⟨Johnson had a copy in his own collection. See the sale *Catalogue*, lot 219.⟩

[a] Overal, *orig.*

[b] State, &c., *orig.*

clan. He added that Mr. Campbell, after the Revolution, was thrown into gaol on account of his tenets; but, on application by letter to the old Lord Townshend [1], was released : that he always spoke of his Lordship with great gratitude, saying, ' though a *Whig*, he had humanity.'

Dr. Johnson and I passed some time together, in June 1784 [2], at Pembroke college, Oxford, with the Reverend Dr. Adams, the master; and I having expressed a regret that my note relative to Mr. Archibald Campbell was imperfect, he was then so good as to write with his own hand, on the blank page of my Journal, opposite to that which contains what I have now mentioned, the following paragraph; which, however, is not quite so full as the narrative he gave at Inveraray :

' *The Honourable* ARCHIBALD CAMPBELL *was, I believe, the nephew* [3] *of the Marquis of Argyle. He began life by engaging in Monmouth's rebellion, and, to escape the law, lived some time in Surinam. When he returned, he became zealous for episcopacy and monarchy; and at the Revolution adhered not only to the Nonjurors, but to those who refused to communicate with the Church of England, or to be present at any worship where the usurper was mentioned as king. He was, I believe, more than once apprehended in the reign of King William, and once at the accession of George. He was the familiar friend of Hickes* [4] *and Nelson* [5] *; a man of letters, but injudicious; and very curious and inquisitive, but credulous. He lived* [6] *in* 1743, *or* 44, *about* 75 *years old.*'

The subject of luxury having been introduced, Dr. Johnson

---

[1] The release gained for him by Lord Townshend must have been from his last imprisonment after the accession of George I; for, as Mr. Croker points out, Townshend was not Secretary of State till 1714.

[2] See *ante*, iv. 286. ⟨Johnson wrote the paragraph on 15 June 1784.⟩

[3] He was the grandson of the first Marquis, who was beheaded by Charles II in 1661, and nephew of the ninth Earl, who was beheaded by James II in 1685. Burke's *Peerage*. He died on June 15, 1744, according to the *Gent. Mag.* xiv. 339; where he is described as ' the last consecrated Archbishop of St. Andrews.' See *ante*, ii. 216, ⟨App. D to this vol., p. 562, and *D.N.B.*⟩.

[4] George Hickes, 1642–1715. A non-juror, consecrated on 24 Feb. 1694 suffragan bishop of Thetford by three of the deprived non-juror bishops. *D.N.B.* s.v. Hickes. Burnet (*Hist. of his own Time*, ii. 603) describes him as ' an ill-tempered Man, who was now [1712] at the Head of the Jacobite Party, [and who] had in several Books promoted a Notion, that there was a proper Sacrifice made in the Eucharist.' ⟨His great *Thesaurus* was published at Oxford, 1703–5.⟩

[5] See *ante*, ii. 458.

[6] ⟨Johnson wrote, as Dr. Hill conjectured, *He died*. See the facsimile reproduction in Pottle and Bennett's edition of Boswell's *Tour*, 1936.⟩

defended it. 'We have now (said he) a splendid dinner before us; Which of all these dishes is unwholesome [a]?' The duke asserted, that he had observed the grandees of Spain diminished in their size by luxury. Dr. Johnson politely refrained from opposing directly an observation which the duke himself had made; but said, 'Man must be very different from other animals, if he is diminished by good living; for the size of all other animals is increased by it [1].' I made some remark that seemed to imply a belief in *second sight*. The duchess said, 'I fancy you will be a *Methodist*.'—This was the only sentence her grace deigned to utter to me; and I take it for granted, she thought it a good hit on my *credulity* in the Douglas cause.

A gentleman [2] in company, after dinner, was desired by the duke to go to another room, for a specimen of curious marble, which his grace wished to shew us. He brought a wrong piece, upon which the duke sent him back again. He could not refuse; but, to avoid any appearance of servility, he whistled as he walked out of the room, to show his independency. On my mentioning this afterwards to Dr. Johnson, he said, it was a nice trait of character.

Dr. Johnson talked a great deal, and was so entertaining, that Lady Betty Hamilton [3], after dinner, went and placed her chair close to his, leaned upon the back of it, and listened eagerly. It would have made a fine picture to have drawn the Sage and her at this time in their several attitudes. He did not know, all the while, how much he was honoured. I told him afterwards. I never saw him so gentle and complaisant as this day.

We went to tea. The duke and I walked up and down the drawing-room, conversing. The duchess still continued to shew the same marked coldness for me; for which, though I suffered from it, I made every allowance, considering the very warm part that I had taken for Douglas, in the cause in which she thought her son deeply interested. Had not her grace discovered some

[a] unwholesome 1, 2: unwholsome 3.

[1] 'It is generally supposed, that life is longer in places where there are few opportunities of luxury; but I found no instance here of extraordinary longevity. A cottager grows old over his oaten cakes, like a citizen at a turtle feast. He is indeed seldom incommoded by corpulence. Poverty preserves him from sinking under the burden of himself, but he escapes no other injury of time.' Johnson's *Western Isl.*, p. 76.

[2] ⟨Lt.-Col. A. Livingstone, M.P.: see App. D, p. 562.⟩

[3] ⟨See App. D, pp. 562-3.⟩

displeasure towards me, I should have suspected her of insensibility or dissimulation.

Her grace made Dr. Johnson come and sit by her, and asked him why he made his journey so late in the year. ' Why, madam, (said he,) you know Mr. Boswell must attend the Court of Session, and it does not rise till the twelfth of August.'—She said, with some sharpness, 'I *know nothing* of Mr. Boswell.' Poor Lady Lucy Douglas [1], to whom I mentioned this, observed, ' She knew *too much* of Mr. Boswell.' I shall make no remark on her grace's speech. I indeed felt it as rather too severe ; but when I recollected that my punishment was inflicted by so dignified a beauty, I had that kind of consolation which a man would feel who is strangled by a *silken cord*. Dr. Johnson was all attention to her grace. He used afterwards a droll expression, upon her enjoying the three titles of Hamilton, Brandon, and Argyle [2]. Borrowing an image from the Turkish empire, he called her a *Duchess* with *three tails*.

He was much pleased with our visit at the castle of Inveraray. The Duke of Argyle was exceedingly polite to him, and, upon his complaining of the shelties which he had hitherto ridden being too small for him, his grace told him he should be provided with a good horse to carry him next day.

Mr. John M'Aulay passed the evening with us at our inn. When Dr. Johnson spoke of people whose principles were good, but whose practice was faulty, Mr. M'Aulay said, he had no notion of people being in earnest in their good professions, whose practice was not suitable to them [a]. The Doctor grew warm, and said, 'Sir, are you [b] so grossly ignorant of human

[a] to them *added in* 3.   [b] are you 1, 2 (*MS.*): you are 3.

[1] Lady Lucy Graham, daughter of the second Duke of Montrose, and wife of Mr. Douglas, the successful claimant : she died in 1780, whence Boswell calls her '*poor* Lady Lucy.' CROKER, 1831. ⟨She was born on 28 July 1751.⟩

[2] ⟨She married first, 14 Feb. 1752, James, the sixth Duke of Hamilton and Brandon, and secondly, 3 Mar. 1759, Col. John Campbell, who became Duke of Argyll in 1770. She was created Baroness Hamilton of Hameldon, Leicester, in 1770, and died, aged 57, in 1790. She was the mother of the seventh and eighth Dukes of Hamilton and the sixth and seventh Dukes of Argyll. Her elder sister married, 5 Mar. 1752, the sixth Earl of Coventry. They were the daughters of a poor Irish squire, John Gunning, of Castle Coote, Roscommon. G. E. C., *Compl. Peerage*, 1910, i. 210 ; 1926, vi. 270.⟩

nature, as not to know that a man may be very sincere in good principles, without having good practice [1] ? '

Dr. Johnson was unquestionably in the right; and whoever examines himself candidly, will be satisfied of it, though the inconsistency between principles and practice is greater in some men than in others.

I recollect very little of this night's conversation. I am sorry that indolence came upon me towards the conclusion of our journey, so that I did not write down what passed with the same assiduity as during the greatest part of it.

Tuesday, 26th October.

Mr. M'Aulay breakfasted with us, nothing hurt or dismayed by his last night's correction. Being a man of good sense, he had a just admiration of Dr. Johnson.

Either yesterday morning, or this, I communicated to Dr. Johnson, from Mr. M'Aulay's information, the news that Dr. Beattie had got a pension of two hundred pounds a year [2]. He sat up in his bed, clapped his hands, and cried, ' O brave we [3] ! ' —a peculiar exclamation of his when he rejoices [4].

As we sat over our tea, Mr. Home's Tragedy of *Douglas* was mentioned. I put Dr. Johnson in mind, that once, in a coffee-house at Oxford, he called to old Mr. Sheridan, ' How came you, Sir, to give Home a gold medal for writing that foolish play ? ' and defied Mr. Sheridan to shew ten good lines in it. He did not insist they should be together; but that there were not ten good lines in the whole play [5]. He now persisted in this. I endeavoured to defend that pathetic and beautiful tragedy, and repeated the following passage :

[1] See *ante*, iv. 397, v. 210, ⟨and *post*, App. D, p. 563⟩. It was Lord Macaulay's grandfather who was thus reprimanded. Mr. Trevelyan remarks (*Life of Macaulay*, i. 6), ' When we think what well-known ground this [subject] was to Lord Macaulay, it is impossible to suppress a wish that the great talker had been at hand to avenge his grandfather.' The result might well have been, however, that the great talker would have been reduced to silence—one of those brilliant flashes of silence for which Sydney Smith longed, but longed in vain.

[2] See *ante*, ii. 264, note 2.

[3] See *ante*, iv. 8, for his use of ' O brave ! '

[4] Having mentioned, more than once, that my Journal was perused by Dr. Johnson, I think it proper to inform my readers that this is the last paragraph which he read. BOSWELL, ed. 1. He began to read it on August 18 (*ante*, v. 58, note 2). ⟨The manuscript of Boswell's original Journal as preserved concludes with the antepenultimate paragraph of the preceding day's record; but a leaf, at least, is missing.⟩

[5] See *ante*, ii. 320.

'————————————————' Sincerity,
Thou first of virtues ! let no mortal leave
Thy onward path, although the earth should gape,
And from the gulph of hell destruction cry,
To take dissimulation's winding way [1].'

Johnson. 'That will not do, sir. Nothing is good but what is consistent with truth or probability, which this is not. Juvenal, indeed, gives us a noble picture of inflexible virtue :

> '*Esto bonus miles, tutor bonus, arbiter idem*
> *Integer : ambiguæ si quando citabere testis,*
> *Incertæque rei, Phalaris licet imperet, ut sis*
> *Falsus, et admoto dictet perjuria tauro,*
> *Summum crede nefas animam præferre pudori,*
> *Et propter vitam vivendi perdere causas* [2].'

He repeated the lines with great force and dignity ; then

---

[1] Act i. sc. 1. The best-known passage in *Douglas* is the speech beginning ' My name is Norval.' Act ii. The play affords a few quotations more or less known, as :—
'I found myself—
As women wish to be who love their lords.' Act i.
'He seldom errs
Who thinks the worst he can of womankind.' Act iii.
Honour, sole judge and umpire of itself.' Act iv.
⟨Boswell quotes this line at the end of his second *Letter to the People of Scotland*, 1785.⟩
' Unknown I die ; no tongue shall speak of me.—
Some noble spirits, judging by themselves,
May yet conjecture what I might have prov'd,
And think life only wanting to my fame.' Act v.
[2] ' An honest guardian, arbitrator just,
Be thou ; thy station deem a sacred trust.
With thy good sword maintain thy country's cause ;
In every action venerate its laws :
The lie suborn'd if falsely urg'd to swear,
Though torture wait thee, torture firmly bear ;
To forfeit honour, think the highest shame,
And life too dearly bought by loss of fame ;
Nor, to preserve it, with thy virtue give
That for which only man should wish to live.'
[*Satires*, viii. 79.]
For this and the other translations to which no signature is affixed, I am indebted to the friend whose observations are mentioned in the notes, [p. 78] and [p. 399]. BOSWELL, ed. 2. I have little doubt that it was Malone. ' One of the best criticks of our age,' Boswell calls this friend in the other two passages. This was a compliment Boswell was likely to pay to Malone, to whom he dedicated this book. Malone was a versifier. See Prior's *Malone*, p. 463. ⟨Dr. Hill was correct, see *ante*, v. 1, note 5.⟩

added, 'And, after this, comes Johnny Home, with his *earth gaping*, and his *destruction crying* :—Pooh [1] ! '

While we were lamenting the number of ruined religious buildings which we had lately seen, I spoke with peculiar feeling of the miserable neglect of the chapel belonging to the palace of Holyrood-house, in which are deposited the remains of many of the Kings of Scotland, and of many of our nobility. I said, it was a disgrace to the country that it was not repaired : and particularly complained that my friend Douglas, the representative of a great house, and proprietor of a vast estate, should suffer the sacred spot where his mother lies interred, to be unroofed, and exposed to all the inclemencies of the weather. Dr. Johnson, who, I know not how, had formed an opinion on the Hamilton side, in the Douglas cause, slily answered, ' Sir, sir, don't be too severe upon the gentleman ; don't accuse him of want of filial piety ! Lady Jane Douglas was not *his* mother †.'—He roused my zeal so much,[a] that I took the liberty to tell him he knew nothing of the cause ; which I do most seriously believe was the case [2].

We were now ' in a country of bridles and saddles [3],' and set out fully equipped. The Duke of Argyle was obliging enough

[a] much, 1 : much 2, 3.

[1] I am sorry that I was unlucky in my quotation. But notwithstanding the acuteness of Dr. Johnson's criticism, and the power of his ridicule, the Tragedy of Douglas still continues to be generally and deservedly admired. BOSWELL, ed. 3, 1786.

Johnson's scorn was no doubt returned, for Dr. A. Carlyle (*Auto.*, p. 295) says of Home:—'As John all his life had a thorough contempt for such as neglected or disapproved of his poetry, he treated all who approved of his works with a partiality which more than approached to flattery.' Carlyle tells (pp. 301–305) how Home started for London with his tragedy in one pocket of his great coat and his clean shirt and nightcap in the other, escorted on setting out by ' six or seven Merse ministers '. ' Garrick, after reading the play, returned it with an opinion that it was totally unfit for the stage.' It was brought out first in Edinburgh, and in the year 1757 in Covent Garden, where it had great success. ' This tragedy,' wrote Carlyle forty-five years later, ' still maintains its ground, has been more frequently acted, and is more popular, than any tragedy in the English language.' *Ib.* p. 325. Hannah More recorded in 1786 (*Memoirs*, ii. 22), ' I had a memorable quarrel with Lord Monboddo one night lately. . . . He said *Douglas* was a better play than Shakspeare could have written. He was angry and I was pert. . . . Lord Mulgrave sat spiriting me up, but kept out of the scrape himself, and Lord Stormont seemed to enjoy the debate, but was shabby enough not to help me out.'

† ⟨Douglas resented Boswell's publication of this remark : see App. D, p. 563.⟩

[2] See *ante*, ii. 230, note 1.
[3] See *ante*, v. 318, and *post*, v. 375.

to mount Dr. Johnson on a stately steed from his grace's stable. My friend was highly pleased, and Joseph said, ' He now looks like a bishop.'

We dined at the inn † at Tarbat, and at night came to Rosedow, the beautiful seat of Sir James Colquhoun §, on the banks of Lochlomond, where I, and any friends whom I have introduced, have ever been received with kind and elegant hospitality.

Wednesday, 27th October.

When I went into Dr. Johnson's room this morning, I observed to him how wonderfully courteous he had been at Inveraray, and said, ' You were quite a fine gentleman, when with the duchess.' He answered, in good humour, ' Sir, I look upon myself as a very polite man : ' and he was right, in a proper manly sense of the word [1]. As an immediate proof of it, let me observe, that he would not send back the Duke of Argyle's horse without a letter of thanks, which I copied.

' To his Grace the Duke of ARGYLE.
' My Lord,
' THAT kindness which disposed your grace to supply me with the horse, which I have now returned, will make you pleased to hear that he has carried me well.

' By my diligence in the little commission with which I was honoured by the duchess [2], I will endeavour to shew how highly I value the favours which I have received, and how much I desire to be thought,
' My lord,
' Your grace's most obedient,
' and most humble servant,
' SAM. JOHNSON.'
' Rosedow, Oct. 29 *, 1773.'

The duke was so attentive to his respectable [3] guest, that on the same day, he wrote him an answer, which was received at Auchinleck :

' To Dr. JOHNSON, Auchinleck, Ayrshire.
' Sir,
' I am glad to hear your journey from this place was not unpleasant,

†, § ⟨See App. D, pp. 563-4.⟩
[1] See ante, iii. 54.
[2] See ante, v. 356.
* ⟨The printer misread Boswell's cramped 27 as 29. The Duke's reply is probably correctly dated. Pottle and Bennett, Hebrides, 1962, pp. 437-8.⟩
[3] See ante, iii. 241, note 2.

in regard to your horse. I wish I could have supplied you with good weather, which I am afraid you felt the want of.

'The Duchess of Argyle desires her compliments to you, and is much obliged to you for remembering her commission.

'I am, sir,
'Your most obedient humble servant,
'ARGYLE.'

'Inveraray, Oct. 29, 1773.'

I am happy to insert every memorial of the honour done to my great friend. Indeed, I was at all times desirous to preserve the letters which he received from eminent persons, of which, as of all other papers, he was very negligent; and I once proposed to him, that they should be committed to my care, as his *Custos Rotulorum*. I wish he had complied with my request, as by that means many valuable writings might have been preserved, that are now lost [1].

After breakfast, Dr. Johnson and I were furnished with a boat, and sailed about upon Lochlomond, and landed on some of the islands which are interspersed [2]. He was much pleased with the scene, which is so well known by the accounts of various travellers, that it is unnecessary for me to attempt any description of it.

I recollect none of his conversation, except that, when talking of dress, he said, 'Sir, were I to have any thing fine, it should be very fine. Were I to wear a ring, it should not be a bauble, but a stone of great value. Were I to wear a laced or embroidered waistcoat, it should be very rich. I had once a very rich laced waistcoat, which I wore the first night of my tragedy [3].'

[1] As a remarkable instance of his negligence, I remember some years ago to have found lying loose in his study, and without the cover, which contained the address, a letter to him from Lord Thurlow, to whom he had made an application as Chancellor, in behalf of a poor literary friend. It was expressed in such terms of respect for Dr. Johnson, that, in my zeal for his reputation, I remonstrated warmly with him on his strange inattention, and obtained his permission to take a copy of it; by which probably it has been preserved, as the original I have reason to suppose is lost. BOSWELL, ed. 1. See *ante*, iii. 441.

[2] ⟨Writing to Mrs. Thrale, 28 Oct. 1773, Johnson says: 'We took a boat to rove upon the Lake.... We passed up and down, and landed upon one small island on which are the ruins of a Castle, and upon another much larger, which serves Sir James for a park, and is remarkable for a large wood of Eugh trees.' *Letters*, No. 336. See also *Western Isl.*, p. 144.⟩

[3] See *ante*, i. 200, and iv. 179.

Lady Helen Colquhoun † being a very pious woman, the conversation, after dinner, took a religious turn. Her ladyship defended the presbyterian mode of publick worship; upon which Dr. Johnson delivered those excellent arguments for a form of prayer which he has introduced into his ' Journey ' [1]. I am myself fully convinced that a form of prayer for publick worship is in general most decent and edifying. *Solennia verba* have a kind of prescriptive sanctity, and make a deeper impression on the mind than extemporaneous effusions, in which, as we know not what they are to be, we cannot readily acquiesce. Yet I would allow also of a certain portion of extempore address, as occasion may require. This is the practice of the French Protestant churches. And although the office of forming supplications to the throne of Heaven is, in my mind, too great a trust to be indiscriminately committed to the discretion of every minister, I do not mean to deny that sincere devotion may be experienced when joining in prayer with those who use no Liturgy.

We were favoured with Sir James Colquhoun's coach to convey us in the evening to Cameron, the seat of Commissary Smollet [2]. Our satisfaction at finding ourselves again in a comfortable carriage was very great. We had a pleasing conviction of the commodiousness of civilization, and heartily laughed at the ravings of those absurd visionaries who have attempted to persuade us of the superior advantages of a *state of nature* [3].

Mr. Smollet was a man of considerable learning, with abundance of animal spirits; so that he was a very good companion for Dr. Johnson, who said to me, ' We have had more solid talk here than at any place where we have been.'

† ⟨See App. D, p. 563.⟩
[1] In these arguments he says :—' Reason and truth will prevail at last. The most learned of the Scottish Doctors would now gladly admit a form of prayer, if the people would endure it. The zeal or rage of congregations has its different degrees. In some parishes the Lord's Prayer is suffered: in others it is still rejected as a form; and he that should make it part of his supplication would be suspected of heretical pravity.' Johnson's *Western Isl.*, p. 95. See *ante*, v. 121.

[2] ' A very little above [the source of the Leven], on the lake, stands the house of Cameron, belonging to Mr. Smollett, so embosomed in an oak wood that we did not see it till we were within fifty yards of the door.' *Humphry Clinker*, letter of Aug. 28. ⟨James Smollett, the cousin of the novelist, bought the house in 1763; it is still, 1939, in the possession of the family. See App. D, p. 564.⟩

[3] Boswell himself was at times one of ' those absurd visionaries.' *Ante*, ii. 73.

I remember Dr. Johnson gave us this evening an able and eloquent discourse on the *Origin of Evil* [1], and on the consistency of moral evil with the power and goodness of GOD. He shewed us how it arose from our free agency, an extinction of which would be a still greater evil than any we experience. I know not that he said any thing absolutely new, but he said a great deal wonderfully well ; and perceiving us to be delighted and satisfied, he concluded his harangue with an air of benevolent triumph over an objection which has distressed many worthy minds : ' This then is the answer to the question, Ποθεν το Κακον ? '—Mrs. Smollet whispered me, that it was the best sermon she had ever heard. Much do I upbraid myself for having neglected to preserve it.

Thursday, 28th October.

Mr. Smollet pleased Dr. Johnson, by producing a collection of news-papers in the time of the Usurpation, from which it appeared that all sorts of crimes were very frequent during that horrible anarchy. By the side of the high road to Glasgow, at some distance from his house, he had erected a pillar to the memory of his ingenious kinsman, Dr. Smollet ; and he consulted Dr. Johnson as to an inscription for it. Lord Kames, who, though he had a great store of knowledge, with much ingenuity, and uncommon activity of mind, was no profound scholar, had it seems recommended an English inscription [2]. Dr. Johnson treated this with great contempt, saying, ' An English inscription would be a disgrace to Dr. Smollet [3] ; ' and, in answer to what Lord Kames had urged, as to the advantage of its being in English, because it would be generally understood, I observed, that all to whom Dr. Smollet's merit could be an object of respect and imitation, would understand it as well in Latin ; and that surely it was not meant for the Highland drovers, or other such people, who pass and repass that way.

We were then shewn a Latin inscription, proposed for this monument. Dr. Johnson sat down with an ardent and liberal

---

[1] See *ante*, v. 117.
[2] Lord Kames wrote one, which is published in R. Chambers's *Traditions of Edinburgh*, ed. 1825, i. 280. In it he bids the traveller to ' indulge the hope of a Monumental Pillar.'
[3] See *ante*, iii. 85, and v. 154.

earnestness to revise it, and greatly improved it by several additions and variations. I unfortunately did not take a copy of it, as it originally stood ; but I have happily preserved every fragment of what Dr. Johnson wrote :

Quisquis ades, viator [1],
Vel mente felix, vel studiis cultus,
Immorare paululum memoriæ
TOBIÆ SMOLLET, M.D.
Viri iis virtutibus
Quas in homine et cive
Et laudes, et imiteris,
* * * * *
Postquam mira * * *
Se * * * * * * * *
* * * *
Tali tantoque viro, suo patrueli,
* * * * * *
Hanc columnam,
Amoris eheu ! inane monumentum,
In ipsis Leviniæ ripis,
Quas primis infans vagitibus personuit,
Versiculisque jam fere moriturus illustravit [2],
Ponendam curavit [3]
* * * * * * *

[1] This address does not offend against the rule that Johnson lays down in his *Essay on Epitaphs* (*Works*, v. 263), where he says :—' It is . . improper to address the epitaph to the passenger.' The impropriety consists in such an address in a church. He however did break through his rule in his epitaph in Streatham Church on Mr. Thrale, where he says :—'Abi, Viator.' *Ib.* i. 154.

[2] In *Humphry Clinker* (letter of Aug. 28), which was published a few months before Smollett's death, is his *Ode to Leven-Water*.

[3] The epitaph which has been inscribed on the pillar erected on the banks of the Leven, in honour of Dr. Smollet, is as follows. The part which was written by Dr. Johnson, it appears, has been altered ; whether for the better, the reader will judge. The alterations are distinguished by Italicks.

Siste viator !
Si lepores ingeniique venam benignam,
Si morum callidissimum pictorem,
Unquam es miratus,
Immorare paululum memoriæ
TOBIÆ SMOLLET, M.D.
Viri virtutibus *hisce*
Quas in homine et cive
Et laudes et imiteris,
Haud mediocriter ornati :
Qui in literis variis versatus,
Postquam felicitate *sibi propria*
Sese posteris commendaverat,
Morte acerba raptus
Anno ætatis 51,
Eheu ! quam procul a patria !

Thursday 28 October 1773   Dumbarton

We had this morning a singular proof of Dr. Johnson's quick and retentive memory. Hay's translation of Martial was lying in a window. I said, I thought it was pretty well done, and shewed him a particular epigram, I think, of ten, but am certain of eight, lines. He read it, and tossed away the book, saying—' No,.it is *not* pretty well.' As I persisted in my opinion, he said, ' Why, sir, the original is thus,'—(and he repeated it ;) ' and this man's translation is thus,'—and then he repeated that also, exactly, though he had never seen it before, and read it over only once, and that too, without any intention of getting it by heart [1].

Here a post-chaise, which I had ordered from Glasgow, came for us, and we drove on in high spirits. We stopped at Dunbarton, and though the approach to the castle there is very steep, Dr. Johnson ascended it with alacrity, and surveyed all that was to be seen. During the whole of our Tour he shewed uncommon spirit, could not bear to be treated like an old or infirm man, and was very unwilling to accept of any assistance, insomuch that, at our landing on[a] Icolmkill, when Sir Allan M'Lean and I submitted to be carried on men's shoulders from the boat to the shore, as it could not be brought quite close to land, he sprang into the sea, and waded vigorously out.

[a] on 1, 2 : at 3.

Prope Liburni portum in Italia,
　Jacet sepultus.
Tali tantoque viro, patrueli suo,
　Cui in decursu lampada
Se potius tradidisse decuit,
　Hanc Columnam,
Amoris, eheu ! inane monumentum
　In ipsis Leviniæ ripis,
Quas *versiculis sub exitu vitæ
　illustratas*
Primis infans vagitibus personuit,
　Ponendam curavit
JACOBUS SMOLLET de Bonhill.
　Abi et reminiscere,
　Hoc quidem honore,
Non modo defuncti memoriæ,
Verum etiam exemplo, prospectum
　esse ;
Aliis enim, si modo digni sint,
Idem erit virtutis præmium !
　　　　　　BOSWELL, ed. 2.
⟨See App. D, p. 564.⟩
[1] Baretti told Malone in 1789 that having proposed to teach Johnson Italian ' they went over a few stanzas of Ariosto's *Orlando Inamorato*, and Johnson then grew weary. Some years afterwards, Baretti reminded him of his promise to study Italian, and said he would give him another lesson ; but added, I suppose you have forgot what we read before. " Who forgets, sir ? " said Johnson, and immediately repeated three or four stanzas of the poem. Baretti was astonished, and took an opportunity before he went away of privately taking down the book to see if it had been recently opened ; but the leaves were entirely covered with dust.' Prior's *Malone*, pp. 159–60. Johnson had learnt to translate Italian before he knew Baretti. *Ante*, i. 107. For other instances of his memory, see *ante*, i. 39, 48 ; iii. 318, note 1 ; and iv. 103, note 2. ⟨For Hay's *Martial*, see App. D, p. 565.⟩

Friday 29 *October* 1773

On our arrival at the Saracen's Head Inn †, at Glasgow, I was made happy by good accounts from home ; and Dr. Johnson, who had not received a single letter since we left Aberdeen [1], found here a great many, the perusal of which entertained him much. He enjoyed in imagination the comforts which we could now command, and seemed to be in high glee. I remember, he put a leg up on each side of the grate, and said, with a mock solemnity, by way of soliloquy, but loud enough for me to hear it, ' Here am I, an ENGLISH man, sitting by a *coal* fire! '

Friday, 29*th October.*

The professors [2] of the university being informed of our arrival, Dr. Stevenson, Dr. Reid [3], and Mr. Anderson, breakfasted with us. Mr. Anderson accompanied us while Dr. Johnson viewed this beautiful city. He had told me, that one day in London, when Dr. Adam Smith was boasting of it, he turned to him and said, ' Pray, sir, have you ever seen Brentford [4] ? '—This was surely a strong instance of his impatience, and spirit of contradiction. I put him in mind of it to-day, while he expressed his admiration of the elegant buildings, and whispered him, ' Don't you feel some remorse [5] ? '

† ⟨'The paragon of inns, in the eyes of the Scotch, but most wretchedly managed.' *Gent. Mag.* 1771, xli. 545. See *post*, App. D, p. 565.⟩

[1] For sixty-eight days he received no letter—from August 21 (*ante*, v. 84) to October 28. ⟨He received six at Glasgow, *Letters*, No. 337.⟩

[2] Among these professors might have been Hume had not a Mr. Clow been the successful competitor in 1752 as the successor to Adam Smith in the chair of Logic. ' Mr. Clow ... has acquired a curious title to fame, from the greatness of the man to whom he succeeded, and of those over whom he was triumphant.' J. H. Burton's *Hume*, i. 351. ⟨For Stevenson and Anderson see App. D, pp. 565–6⟩.

[3] ⟨For Thomas Reid, 1710–96, Professor of Moral Philosophy, see Dugald Stewart's *Account* of his life and writings first published in 1802 and reprinted, with additional notes, in Sir W. Hamilton's edition of Reid's *Works*, 1846, and *D.N.B.*⟩

[4] See *ante*, iv. 186 ⟨and 513⟩.

[5] Mr. Boswell has chosen to omit, for reasons which will be presently obvious, that Johnson and Adam Smith met at Glasgow ; but I have been assured by Professor John Miller that they did so, and that Smith, leaving the party in which he had met Johnson, happened to come to another company where Miller was. Knowing that Smith had been in Johnson's society, they were anxious to know what had passed, and the more so as Dr. Smith's temper seemed much ruffled. At first Smith would only answer, ' He's a brute—he's a brute ; ' but on closer examination, it appeared that Johnson no sooner saw Smith than he attacked him for some point of his famous letter on the death of Hume (*ante*, v. 30). Smith vindicated the

Friday 29 *October* 1773   Glasgow

We were received in the college by a number of the professors, who shewed all due respect to Dr. Johnson ; and then we paid a visit to the principal, Dr. Leechman [1], at his own house, where Dr. Johnson had the satisfaction of being told that his name had been gratefully celebrated in one of the parochial congregations in the Highlands, as the person to whose influence it was chiefly owing, that the New Testament was allowed to be translated into the Erse language. It seems some political members of the Society in Scotland for propagating Christian Knowledge, had opposed this pious undertaking, as tending to preserve the distinction between the Highlanders and Lowlanders. Dr. Johnson wrote a long letter upon the subject to a friend, which being shewn to them, made them ashamed, and afraid of being publickly exposed ; so they were forced to a compliance. It is now in my possession, and is, perhaps, one of the best productions of his masterly pen [2].

Professors Reid and Anderson, and the two Messieurs Foulis [3], the Elzevirs of Glasgow, dined and drank tea with us at our inn, after which the professors went away ; and I, having a letter to write, left my fellow-traveller with Messieurs Foulis. Though good and ingenious men, they had that unsettled speculative mode of conversation which is offensive to a man regularly taught at an English school and university. I found that, instead of listening to the dictates of the Sage, they had teazed truth of his statement. ' What did Johnson say ? ' was the universal inquiry. ' Why, he said,' replied Smith, with the deepest impression of resentment, ' he said, *you lie !* ' ' And what did you reply ? ' ' I said, you are a son of a ——— ! ' On such terms did these two great moralists meet and part, and such was the classical dialogue between two great teachers of philosophy. SCOTT, 1831.

This story is *certainly* erroneous in the particulars of the *time, place*, and *subject* of the alleged quarrel ; for Hume did not die for [nearly] three years after Johnson's only visit to Glasgow ; nor was Smith then there. Johnson had, previous to 1763 (see *ante*, i. 427, and iii. 331), had an altercation with Adam Smith at Mr. Strahan's table. This . . . may have been the foundation of Professor Miller's strange misrepresentation.

But, even *then*, nothing of this very offensive kind could have passed, as, if it had, Smith could certainly not have afterwards solicited admission to the Club of which Johnson was the leader, to which he was admitted 1st Dec. 1775, and where he and Johnson met frequently on civil terms. I, therefore, disbelieve the whole story. CROKER. ⟨1835-48. See also *ante*, iii. 331 ; Napier's Boswell, v. 370 ff., and Middendorf in *Philol. Q.* xi, 1961, 281 ff.⟩

[1] ' His appearance,' says Dr. A. Carlyle (*Auto.*, p. 68), ' was that of an ascetic, reduced by fasting and prayer.' See *ante*, v. 68, note 4.
[2] See *ante*, ii. 27, 279.
[3] ⟨Neither of the brothers lived to read this passage, Robert dying in 1776 and Andrew in 1775. See David Murray, *R. and A. Foulis*, 1913.⟩

him with questions and doubtful disputations. He came in a flutter to me, and desired I might come back again, for he could not bear these men. ' O ho ! sir, (said I,) you are flying to me for refuge ! ' He never, in any situation, was at a loss for a ready repartee. He answered, with a quick vivacity, ' It is of two evils choosing the least.' I was delighted with this flash bursting from the cloud which hung upon his mind, closed my letter directly, and joined the company.

We supped at professor Anderson's. The general impression upon my memory is, that we had not much conversation at Glasgow, where the professors, like their brethren at Aberdeen [1], did not venture to expose themselves much to the battery of cannon which they knew might play upon them [2]. Dr. Johnson, who was fully conscious of his own superior powers, afterwards praised Principal Robertson for his caution in this respect [3]. He said to me, ' Robertson, sir, was in the right. Robertson is a man of eminence, and the head of a college at Edinburgh. He had a character to maintain, and did well not to risk its being lessened.'

Saturday, 30th October.

We set out towards Ayrshire. I sent Joseph on to *Loudoun*, with a message, that, if the earl was at home, Dr. Johnson and I would have the honour to dine with him. Joseph met us on the road, and reported that the earl '*jumped for joy*,' and said, ' I shall be very happy to see them.'—We were received with a most pleasing courtesy by his lordship, and by the countess his mother, who, in her ninety-fifth year, had all her faculties quite unimpaired [4]. This was a very cheering sight to Dr. Johnson, who had an extraordinary desire for long life. Her ladyship was sensible and well-informed, and had seen a great deal

[1] See *ante*, v. 92.
[2] Johnson wrote to Mrs. Thrale :—
' I was not much pleased with any of the Professors.' *Letters*, No. 337. Mme D'Arblay says :—' Whenever Dr. Johnson did not make the charm of conversation, he only marred it by his presence ; from the general fear he incited, that if he spoke not, he might listen ; and that if he listened— he might reprove.' *Memoirs of Dr. Burney*, ii. 187. See *ante*, ii. 63.
[3] Boswell has not let us see this caution. When Robertson first came in, ' there began,' we are told, ' some animated dialogue ' (*ante*, v. 32). The next day we read that ' he fluently harangued to Dr. Johnson ' (*ante*, v. 43).
[4] See *ante*, iii. 366 ⟨and *post*, App. D, p. 566⟩.

of the world. Her lord had held several high offices, and she was sister to the great Earl of Stair [1].

I cannot here refrain from paying a just tribute to the character of John Earl of Loudoun, who did more service to the county of Ayr in general, as well as to individuals in it, than any man we have ever had. It is painful to think that he met with much ingratitude from persons both in high and low rank : but such was his temper, such his knowledge of ' base mankind [2],' that, as if he had expected no other return, his mind was never soured, and he retained his good-humour and benevolence to the last. The tenderness of his heart was proved in 1745-6, when he had an important command in the Highlands, and behaved with a generous humanity to the unfortunate. I cannot figure a more honest politician ; for, though his interest in our county was great, and generally successful, he not only did not deceive by fallacious promises, but was anxious that people should not deceive themselves by too sanguine expectations. His kind and dutiful attention to his mother was unremitted. At his house was true hospitality ; a plain but a plentiful table ; and every guest, being left at perfect freedom, felt himself quite easy and happy. While I live, I shall honour the memory of this amiable man [3].

At night, we advanced a few miles farther, to the house of Mr. Campbell of Treesbank [4], who was married to one of my wife's sisters, and were entertained very agreeably by a worthy couple.

Sunday, 31st October.
We reposed here in tranquillity. Dr. Johnson was pleased to find a numerous and excellent collection of books, which had

[1] ⟨John Dalrymple, 2nd earl, 1673-1747. He had a most distinguished career as soldier and diplomat, becoming in turn Ambassador at Paris, Field-Marshal and Commander-in-Chief. See J. Murray Graham, *Annals and Corresp.* 1875, and *D.N.B.*⟩

[2] The unwilling gratitude of base mankind. POPE. [*Imitations of Horace*, 2 *Epis.* i. 14.] BOSWELL, ed. 1.

[3] ⟨John Campbell, 4th Earl of Loudoun, 1705-1782. Writing on 16 Nov. 1774 Boswell says : ' This was the first time that Lord Loudoun was in my house. I liked to be well with one of the Nobles of the County of Ayr. But I must own that I was somewhat cooled towards the Peers when, upon talking to Lord Loudoun of the Sherrifship of our county yesterday, he told me that he was not at liberty to speak on the subject, . . . I also perceived that his Lordship had not that dignity of spirit which I should have wished ; but was ready to join with Sir Adam Fergusson if he saw it for his interest.' *Boswell Papers*, x. 54. See also App. D, p. 566.⟩

[4] ⟨See App. D, p. 566.⟩

–Dundonald Castle *Monday 1 Nov.* 1773

mostly belonged to the Reverend Mr. John Campbell †, brother of our host. I was desirous to have procured for my fellow-traveller, to-day, the company of Sir John Cuninghame, of Caprington, whose castle was but two miles from us. He was a very distinguished scholar, was long abroad, and during part of the time lived much with the learned Cuninghame [1], the opponent of Bentley as a critick upon Horace. He wrote Latin with great elegance, and, what is very remarkable, read Homer and Ariosto through,[a] every year. I wrote to him,[b] to request he would come to us ; but unfortunately he was prevented by indisposition.

Monday, 1st November.

Though Dr. Johnson was lazy, and averse to move, I insisted that he should go with me, and pay a visit to the Countess of Eglintoune, mother of the late and present earl. I assured him, he would find himself amply recompensed for the trouble ; and he yielded to my solicitations, though with some unwillingness. We were well mounted, and had not many miles to ride. He talked of the attention that is necessary in order to distribute our charity judiciously. ' If thoughtlessly done, we may neglect the most deserving objects ; and, as every man has but a certain proportion to give, if it is lavished upon those who first present themselves, there may be nothing left for such as have a better claim. A man should first relieve those who are nearly connected with him, by whatever tie ; and then, if he has any thing to spare, may extend his bounty to a wider circle [2].'

As we passed very near the castle of Dundonald, which was one of the many residencies of the kings of Scotland, and in which Robert the Second lived and died, Dr. Johnson wished to survey it particularly. It stands on a beautiful rising ground, which is seen at a great distance on several quarters, and from whence there is an extensive prospect of the rich district of Cuninghame, the western sea, the isle of Arran, and a part of the northern coast of Ireland. It has long been unroofed ; and, though of considerable size, we could not, by any power of imagination, figure it as having been a suitable habitation for

[a] through, 1, 2 : through 3.   [b] him, 1, 2 : him 3.

† ⟨See App. D, p. 567.⟩
[1] ⟨For the two Cuninghams see App. D, p. 567.⟩
[2] He had paid but little attention to his own rule. See *ante*, ii. 119.

Monday 1 Nov. 1773 ⟨Old Auchans⟩

majesty[1]. Dr. Johnson, to irritate my *old Scottish*[2] enthusiasm, was very jocular on the homely accommodation of 'King *Bob*,' and roared and laughed till the ruins echoed.

Lady Eglintoune, though she was now in her eighty-fifth year, and had lived in the retirement of the country for almost half a century, was still a very agreeable woman. She was of the noble house of Kennedy, and had all the elevation which the consciousness of such birth inspires. Her figure was majestick, her manners high-bred, her reading extensive, and her conversation elegant. She had been the admiration of the gay circles of life, and the patroness of poets[3]. Dr. Johnson was delighted with his reception here. Her principles in church and state were congenial with his. She knew all his merit, and had heard much of him from her son, Earl Alexander[4], who loved to cultivate the acquaintance of men of talents, in every department.

All who knew his lordship, will allow that his understanding and accomplishments were of no ordinary rate. From the gay habits which he had early acquired, he spent too much of his time with men, and in pursuits,[a] far beneath such a mind as his. He afterwards became sensible of it, and turned his thoughts to objects of importance; but was cut off in the prime of his life. I cannot speak, but with emotions of the most affectionate regret, of one, in whose company many of my early days were passed, and to whose kindness I was much indebted.

Often must I have occasion to upbraid myself, that,[b] soon after our return to the main land, I allowed indolence to prevail over me so much, as to shrink from the labour of continuing my Journal with the same minuteness as before; sheltering myself in the thought, that we had done with the *Hebrides*; and not considering, that Dr. Johnson's *Memorabilia* were likely to be

[a] pursuits, 1, 2: pursuits 3.   [b] that, 1: that 2, 3.

[1] ⟨' This castle was a favourite habitation of Robert II and Robert III, the former of whom died here in 1390. It is therefore naturally on a much more extensive scale than most of the keeps of the fourteenth century.' Macgibbon and Ross, *Castellated and Domestic Architecture* i. 167.⟩

[2] See *ante*, v. 40.

[3] Johnson described her as 'a Lady who for many years, gave the laws of Elegance to Scotland.' *Letters*, No. 337. Allan Ramsay dedicated to her his *Gentle Shepherd*, and W. Hamilton, of Bangour, wrote to her verses on the presentation of Ramsay's poem. Hamilton's *Poems*, 1748, p. 40. ⟨See also App. D, p. 567.⟩

[4] See *ante*, ii. 66, iii. 188, ⟨and *post*, v, App. D, p. 568.⟩

more valuable when we were restored to a more polished society. Much has thus been irrecoverably lost.

In the course of our conversation this day, it came out, that Lady Eglintoune was married the year before Dr. Johnson was born; upon which she graciously said to him, that she might have been his mother,[a] and that she now adopted him; and when we were going away, she embraced him, saying, ' My dear son, farewell [1] ! '—My friend was much pleased with this day's entertainment, and owned that I had done well to force him out.

Tuesday, 2d November.

We were now in a country not only ' *of saddles and bridles* [2],' but of post-chaises; and having ordered one from Kilmarnock, we got to Auchinleck [3] before dinner.

My father was not quite a year and a half older than Dr. Johnson; but his conscientious discharge of his laborious duty as a judge in Scotland, where the law proceedings are almost all in writing,—a severe complaint which ended in his death,—and the loss of my mother, a woman of almost unexampled piety and goodness,—had before this time in some degree affected his spirits [4], and rendered him less disposed to exert his faculties: for he had originally a very strong mind, and cheerful temper. He assured me, he never had felt one moment of what is called low spirits, or uneasiness [b] without a real cause. He had a great many good stories, which he told uncommonly well, and he was remarkable for ' humour, *incolumi gravitate* [5],' as Lord Monboddo used to characterise it. His age, his office, and his character, had long given him an acknowledged claim to great attention, in whatever

[a] mother, 1, 2: mother; 3.   [b] uneasiness 1, 2 : uneasiness, 3.

[1] ' She called Boswel the boy, yes Madam, said I, we will send him to school. He is already, said she, in a good school, and expressed her hope of his improvement. At last night came, and I was sorry to leave her.' Johnson's *Letters*, No. 337. See *ante*, iii. 366 ⟨and *post*, v. 401⟩.
[2] See *ante*, v. 318, 362.
[3] ⟨Mickle in 1768 thought of introducing Boswell into a poem on Liberty and Slavery; Boswell wrote, 22 June 1769 : ' I could wish you to represent me among the rocks and woods of my ancestors. Auchinleck is a most unpoetical name. But it may be mentioned at the foot of a page.' *Universal Mag.*, 1809, xi. p. 25.⟩
[4] He had, however, married again. *Ante*, ii. 140, note 1.
[5]   ' Asper
Incolumi gravitate jocum tentavit.'
' Though rude his mirth, yet laboured to maintain
The solemn grandeur of the tragic scene.'
FRANCIS. Horace, *Ars Poet.* l. 221.

company he was; and he could ill brook any diminution of it. He was as sanguine a Whig and Presbyterian, as Dr. Johnson was a Tory and church of England man: and as he had not much leisure to be informed of Dr. Johnson's great merits by reading his works, he had a partial and unfavourable notion of him, founded on his supposed political tenets; which were so discordant to his own, that, instead of speaking of him with that respect to which he was entitled, he used to call him 'a *Jacobite fellow.*' Knowing all this, I should not have ventured to bring them together, had not my father, out of kindness to me, desired me to invite Dr. Johnson to his house.

I was very anxious that all should be well; and begged of my friend to avoid three topicks, as to which they differed very widely; Whiggism, Presbyterianism, and—Sir John Pringle [1]. He said courteously, 'I shall certainly not talk on subjects which I am told are disagreeable to a gentleman under whose roof I am; especially, I shall not do so to *your father*.'

Our first day went off very smoothly. It rained, and we could not get out; but my father shewed Dr. Johnson his library, which, in curious editions of the Greek and Roman classicks, is, I suppose, not excelled by any private collection in Great Britain. My father had studied at Leyden, and been very intimate with the Gronovii, and other learned men there. He was a sound scholar, and, in particular, had collated manuscripts and different editions of Anacreon, and others of the Greek Lyrick poets, with great care; so that my friend and he had much matter for conversation, without touching on the fatal topicks of difference.

Dr. Johnson found here Baxter's *Anacreon* [2], which he told me he had long enquired for in vain, and began to suspect there was no such book. Baxter was the keen antagonist of Barnes [3]. His life is in the *Biographia Britannica* [4]. My father has written

---

[1] See *ante*, iii. 65, and v. 97.
[2] See *ante*, iv. 163, 241, ⟨265, 525⟩.
[3] Johnson (*Addison*, 27) says of Addison's dedication of the opera of *Rosamond* to the Duchess of Marlborough, that 'it was an instance of servile absurdity, to be exceeded only by Joshua Barnes's dedication of a Greek *Anacreon* to the Duke.'

For Barnes see *ante*, iii. 284, and iv. 19.
[4] ⟨The life, which is in the first edition, 1747, i. 565–6, is not superseded by that in the *D.N.B.*⟩ William Baxter, the editor of *Anacreon*, was the nephew of Richard Baxter, the nonconformist divine.

many notes on this book, and Dr. Johnson and I talked of having it reprinted.

Wednesday, 3d November.

It rained all day, and gave Dr. Johnson an impression of that incommodiousness of climate in the west, of which he has taken notice in his 'Journey [1]'; but, being well accommodated, and furnished with variety of books, he was not dissatisfied.

Some gentlemen of the neighbourhood came to visit my father; but there was little conversation. One of them asked Dr. Johnson how he liked the Highlands. The question seemed to irritate him, for he answered, ' How, sir, can you ask me what obliges me to speak unfavourably of a country where I have been hospitably entertained ? Who *can* like the Highlands [2] ?—I like the inhabitants very well [3].'—The gentleman asked no more questions.

Let me now make up for present [a] neglect, by again gleaning from the past. At Lord Monboddo's, after the conversation upon the decrease of learning in England, his Lordship mentioned *Hermes* by Mr. Harris of Salisbury [4], as the work of a living authour, for whom he had a great respect. Dr. Johnson said nothing at the time; but when we were in our post-chaise, told me, he thought Harris 'a coxcomb.' This he said of

[a] present 1 : the present 2, 3.

[1] He says of Auchinleck (*Western Isl.*, p. 146) that ' like all the Western side of Scotland, [it is] incommoded by very frequent rain.' ' In all September we had according to Boswels register, only one day and a half of fair weather, and in October perhaps not more.' Johnson's *Letters*, No. 336.

[2] 'By-the-bye,' wrote Sir Walter Scott, ' I am far from being of the number of those angry Scotsmen who imputed to Johnson's national prejudices all or a great part of the report he has given of our country in [his *Journey to the Western Islands*]. I remember the Highlands ten or twelve years later, and no one can conceive of how much that could have been easily remedied travellers had to complain.' *Croker Corres.* ii. 34.

[3] ' Of these Islands it must be confessed, that they have not many allurements, but to the mere lover of naked nature. The inhabitants are thin, provisions are scarce, and desolation and penury give little pleasure.' Johnson's *Western Isl.*, p. 142. In an earlier passage (p. 127), in describing a rough ride in Mull, he says :—' We were now long enough acquainted with hills and heath to have lost the emotion that they once raised, whether pleasing or painful, and had our mind employed only on our own fatigue.' ⟨For another version of Johnson's answer see App. D, p. 568.⟩

[4] See *ante*, ii. 225.

him, not as a man, but as an authour [1] ; and I give his opinions of men and books, faithfully, whether they agree with my own, or not. I do admit, that there always appeared to me something of affectation in Mr. Harris's manner of writing ; something of a habit of clothing plain thoughts in analytick and categorical formality. But all his writings are imbued with learning ; and all breathe that philanthropy and amiable disposition, which distinguished him as a man [2].

At another time, during our Tour, he drew the character of a rapacious Highland Chief [3] with the strength of Theophrastus or La Bruyere ; concluding with these words : ' Sir, he has no more the soul of a Chief, than an attorney who has twenty houses in a street, and considers how much he can make by them.'

He this day, when we were by ourselves, observed, how common it was for people to talk from books ; to retail the sentiments of others, and not their own ; in short, to converse without any originality of thinking. He was pleased to say, ' You and I do not talk from books [4].'

---

[1] In like manner Wesley said, 3 Feb. 1770, of Rousseau :—' Sure a more consummate coxcomb never saw the sun. . . . He is a cynic all over. So indeed is his brother-infidel, Voltaire ; and well nigh as great a coxcomb.' Wesley's *Journal*, v. 352.

[2] This gentleman, though devoted to the study of grammar and dialecticks, was not so absorbed in it as to be without a sense of pleasantry, or to be offended at his favourite topicks being treated lightly. I one day met him in the street, as I was hastening to the House of Lords, and told him, I was sorry I could not stop, being rather too late to attend an appeal of the Duke of Hamilton against Douglas. ' I thought (said he) their contest had been over long ago.' I answered, ' The contest concerning Douglas's filiation was over long ago ; but the contest now is, who shall have the estate.' Then, assuming the air of ' an antient sage philosopher,' I proceeded thus : ' Were I to *predicate* concerning him, I should say, the contest formerly was, What *is* he ? The contest now is, What *has* he ? '—' Right, (replied Mr. Harris, smiling,) you have done with *quality*, and have got into *quantity*.' BOSWELL, ed. 1.

[3] ⟨Sir A. Macdonald, as Dr. Hill conjectured.⟩ *Ante*, v. 148.

[4] Boswell wrote on March 18, 1775 : —' Mr. Johnson once, when enumerating our Club, observed of some of us, that they talked from books, Langton in particular. " Garrick," he said, " would talk from books, if he talked seriously." " *I*," said he, " do not talk from books. You do not talk from books."—This was a compliment to my originality. But I am afraid I have not read books enough to be able to talk from them.' Boswell's *Letters*, No. 136, i. 214. See *ante*, ii. 360, where Johnson said to Boswell :—' I don't believe you have

Thursday, 4th November.

I was glad to have at length a very fine day, on which I could shew Dr. Johnson the *Place* of my family, which he has honoured with so much attention in his ' Journey '. He is, however, mistaken in thinking that the Celtick name, *Auchinleck*, has no relation to the natural appearance of it. I believe every Celtick name of a place will be found very descriptive. *Auchinleck* does not signify a *stony field*, as he has said, but a *field of flag-stones* [a] ; and this place has a number of rocks, which abound in strata of that kind. The ' sullen dignity of the old castle,' as he has forcibly expressed it, delighted him exceedingly [1]. On one side of the rock on which its ruins stand, runs the river *Lugar*, which is here of considerable breadth, and is bordered by other high rocks, shaded with wood. On the other side runs a brook, skirted in the same manner, but on a smaller scale. I cannot figure a more romantick scene.

I felt myself elated here, and expatiated to my illustrious Mentor on the antiquity and honourable alliances of my family, and on the merits of its founder, Thomas Boswell, who was highly favoured by his sovereign, James IV. of Scotland, and fell with him at the battle of Flodden-field [2]; and,[b] in the glow of what, I am sensible, will, in a commercial age, be considered as genealogical enthusiasm, did not omit to mention,[c] what I was sure my friend would not think lightly of, my relation [3] to the Royal Personage, whose liberality, on his accession to the throne, had given him comfort and independence [4]. I have, in

[a] *flag-stones* 1, 2 : *flag stones* 3.   [b] and, 1, 2 : and 3.   [c] mention, 1, 2 : mention 3.

borrowed from Waller. I wish you would enable yourself to borrow more ; ' and i. 105, where he described ' a man of a great deal of knowledge of the world, fresh from life, not strained through books.'

[1] ' Lord Auchinleck has built a house of hewn stone, very stately, and durable, and has advanced the value of his lands with great tenderness to his tenants. I was, however, less delighted with the elegance of the modern mansion, than with the sullen dignity of the old castle.' Johnson's *Western Isl.*, p. 146. ' The house is scarcely yet finished, but very magni-ficent and very convenient.' Johnson's *Letters*, No. 337. See *ante*, i. 462.

[2] See *ante*, ii. 413, and v. 91.

[3] The relation, it should seem, was remote even for . Scotland. Their common ancestor was Robert Bruce, some sixteen generations back. Boswell's mother's grandmother was a Bruce of the Earl of Kincardine's family, and so also was his father's mother. Rogers's *Boswelliana*, pp. 4, 5.

[4] He refers to Johnson's pension, which was given nearly two years after George III's accession. *Ante*, i. 372.

a former page [1], acknowledged my pride of ancient blood, in which I was encouraged by Dr. Johnson : my readers therefore will not be surprised at my having indulged it on this occasion.

Not far from the old castle is a spot of consecrated earth, on which may be traced the foundations of an ancient chapel, dedicated to St. Vincent, and where,[a] in old times, was the 'place [b] of graves' for the family. It grieves me to think that the remains of sanctity here, which were considerable, were dragged away, and employed in building a part of the house of Auchinleck, of the middle age † ; which was the family residence, till my father erected that 'elegant modern mansion,' of which Dr. Johnson speaks so handsomely. Perhaps this chapel may one day be restored.

Dr. Johnson was pleased, when I shewed him some venerable old trees, under the shade of which my ancestors had walked. He exhorted me to plant assiduously [2], as my father had done to a great extent.

As I wandered with my revered [c] friend in the groves of Auchinleck, I told him, that, if I survived him, it was my intention to erect a monument to him here, among scenes which, in my mind, were all classical ; for in my youth I had appropriated to them many of the descriptions of the Roman poets. He could not bear to have death presented to him in any shape ; for his constitutional melancholy made the king of terrours more frightful. He turned off the subject, saying, ' Sir, I hope to see your grand-children ! '

This forenoon he observed some cattle without horns, of which he has taken notice in his ' Journey [3] ', and seems undecided whether they be of a particular race. His doubts appear to have had no foundation ; for my respectable neighbour, Mr. Fairlie [4], who, with

[a] where, 1 : where 2, 3.　　[b] was the ' place 1, 2 : ' was the place 3.
[c] revered 1, 2 : reverend 3.

[1] *Ante*, v. 51.
[2] He repeated this advice in 1777. *Ante*, iii. 207.
[3] ' Of their black cattle, some are without horns, called by the Scots *humble* cows, as we call a bee an *humble* bee, that wants a sting. Whether this difference be specifick, or accidental, though we inquired with great diligence, we could not be informed.' Johnson's *Western Isl.*, p. 74. Johnson, in his *Dictionary*, gives the derivation of humble-bee, from *hum* and *bee*. The word *Humble-cow* is found in *Guy Mannering*, ch. ix.

† ⟨For the old castle, the Renaissance mansion, and the site of the ancient chapel, see Boswell's *Hebrides*, 1962, pp. 485–6.⟩

[4] ⟨Alexander Fairlie of Fairlie : see App. D, pp. 568–9.⟩

all his attention to agriculture, finds time both for the classicks and his friends, assures me they are a distinct species, and that, when any of their calves have horns, a mixture of breed can be traced. In confirmation of his opinion, he pointed out to me the following passage in Tacitus,—' *Ne armentis quidem suus honor, aut gloria frontis* [1] ; ' (De mor. Germ. § 5.) which he wondered had escaped Dr. Johnson.

On the front of the house of Auchinleck is this inscription :

———— Quod petis, hic est ;
Est Ulubris ; animus si te non deficit æquus [2].

It is characteristick of the founder ; but the *animus æquus* is, alas ! not inheritable, nor the subject of devise. He always talked to me as if it were in a man's own power to attain it ; but Dr. Johnson told me that he owned to him, when they were alone, his persuasion that it was in a great measure constitutional, or the effect of causes which do not depend on ourselves, and that Horace boasts too much, when he says, *æquum mi animum ipse parabo* [3].

Friday, 5th November.

The Reverend Mr. Dun, our parish minister, who had dined with us yesterday, with some other company, insisted that Dr. Johnson and I should dine with him to-day. This gave me an opportunity to shew my friend the road to the church, made by my father at a great expence, for above three miles, on his own estate, through a range of well enclosed farms, with a row of trees on each side of it. He called it the *Via sacra*, and was very fond of it. [4] Dr. Johnson, though he held notions far distant from those of the presbyterian clergy, yet could associate on good terms with them. He indeed occasionally attacked them. One of them discovered a narrowness of information

---

[1] ' Even the cattle have not their usual beauty or noble head.' Church and Brodribb's *Tacitus*.
[2] ' The peace you seek is here—where is it not ? If your own mind be equal to its lot.' Horace, 1 *Epistles*, xi. 29. CROKER.
[3] Horace, 1 *Epistles*, xviii. 112.
[4] This and the next paragraph are not in the first edition. The paragraph that follows has been altered so as to hide the fact that the minister spoken of was Mr. Dun. Originally it stood :—' Mr. Dun, though a man of sincere good principles, as a presbyterian divine, discovered ' &c. First edition, p. 478. ⟨For Mr. Dun see App. D, p. 569.⟩

concerning the dignitaries of the church of England, among whom may be found men of the greatest learning, virtue, and piety, and of a truly apostolick character. He talked before Dr. Johnson, of fat bishops and drowsy deans ; and, in short, seemed to believe the illiberal and profane scoffings of professed satyrists, or vulgar railers. Dr. Johnson was so highly offended, that he said to him, ' Sir, you know no more of our church than a Hottentot [1].' I was sorry that he brought this upon himself.

Saturday, 6th November.

I cannot be certain, whether it was on this day, or a former, that Dr. Johnson and my father came in collision. If I recollect right, the contest began while my father was shewing him his collection of medals ; and Oliver Cromwell's coin unfortunately introduced Charles the First, and Toryism. They became exceedingly warm, and violent, and I was very much distressed by being present at such an altercation between two men, both of whom I reverenced ; yet I durst not interfere. It would certainly be very unbecoming in me to exhibit my honoured father, and my respected friend, as intellectual gladiators, for the entertainment of the publick ; and therefore I suppress what would, I dare say, make an interesting scene in this dramatick sketch,— this account of the transit of Johnson over the Caledonian Hemisphere [2].

[1] ⟨See Boswell's *Hebrides*, 1962, pp. 440, 442.⟩

[2] Old Lord Auchinleck was an able lawyer, a good scholar, after the manner of Scotland, and highly valued his own advantages as a man of good estate and ancient family, and, moreover, he was a strict presbyterian and Whig of the old Scottish cast. This did not prevent his being a terribly proud aristocrat ; and great was the contempt he entertained and expressed for his son James, for the nature of his friendships and the character of the personages of whom he was *engoué* one after another. ' There's nae hope for Jamie, mon,' he said to a friend. ' Jamie is gaen clean gyte.—What do you think, mon ? He's done wi' Paoli—he's off wi' the land-louping scoundrel of a Corsican ; and whose tail do you think he has pinned himself to now, mon ? ' Here the old judge summoned up a sneer of most sovereign contempt. ' A *dominie*, mon—an auld dominie : he keeped a schūle, and cau'd it an acaadamy.' Probably if this had been reported to Johnson, he would have felt it more galling, for he never much liked to think of that period of his life [*ante*, i. 97, note 2] ; it would have aggravated his dislike of Lord Auchinleck's Whiggery and presbyterianism. These the old lord carried to such an unusual height, that once, when a countryman came-in to state some justice business, and being required to make his oath, declined to do so before his lordship, because he was not a *covenanted*

Yet I think I may, without impropriety, mention one circumstance, as an instance of my father's address. Dr. Johnson challenged him, as he did us all at Talisker [1], to point out any theological works of merit written by Presbyterian ministers in Scotland. My father, whose studies did not lie much in that way, owned to me afterwards, that he was somewhat at a loss how to answer, but that luckily he recollected having read in catalogues the title of *Durham on the Galatians;* upon which he boldly said, ' Pray, sir, have you read Mr. Durham's excellent commentary on the Galatians ? '—' No, sir,' said Dr. Johnson. By this lucky thought my father kept him at bay, and for some time enjoyed his triumph [2]; but his antagonist soon made a retort, which I forbear to mention.

magistrate. ' Is that a' your objection, mon ? ' said the judge ; ' come your ways in here, and we'll baith of us tak the solemn league and covenant together.' The oath was accordingly agreed and sworn to by both, and I dare say it was the last time it ever received such homage. It may be surmised how far Lord Auchinleck, such as he is here described, was likely to suit a high Tory and episcopalian like Johnson. As they approached Auchinleck, Boswell conjured Johnson by all the ties of regard, and in requital of the services he had rendered him upon his tour, that he would spare two subjects in tenderness to his father's prejudices ; the first related to Sir John Pringle, president of the royal society, about whom there was then some dispute current : the second concerned the general question of Whig and Tory. Sir John Pringle, as Boswell says, escaped, but the controversy between Tory and Covenanter raged with great fury, and ended in Johnson's pressing upon the old judge the question, what good Cromwell, of whom he had said something derogatory, had ever done to his country ; when, after being much tortured, Lord Auchinleck at last spoke out, ' God, Doctor ! he gart kings ken that they had a *lith* in their neck '— he taught kings they had a *joint* in their necks. Jamie then set to mediating between his father and the philosopher, and availing himself of the judge's sense of hospitality, which was punctilious, reduced the debate to more order. SCOTT, 1831. ⟨See also App. D, pp. 569–70.⟩ Paoli had visited Auchinleck. Boswell wrote to Garrick on Sept. 18, 1771 :—' I have just been enjoying the very great happiness of a visit from my illustrious friend Pascal Paoli. He was two nights at Auchinleck, and you may figure the joy of my worthy father and me at seeing the Corsican Hero in our romantick groves.' *Letters*, No. 110, i. 184. Johnson was not blind to Cromwell's greatness, for he says (*Waller*, 71), that ' he wanted nothing to raise him to heroick excellence but virtue.' Lord Auchinleck's famous saying had been anticipated by Quin, who, according to Davies (*Life of Garrick*, 1808, ii. ch. xxxviii. 112), had said that ' on a thirtieth of January every King in Europe would rise with a crick in his neck.'

[1] See *ante*, v. 252.

[2] ⟨James Durham, 1622–1658, wrote many theological works, but none on the *Galatians*. The book that Lord Auchinleck saw was probably, as Croker suggested in 1831, *A Commentary on the Book of Revelation*, of which there were editions in 1658 (Amsterdam) and 1680 ; it was

Sunday 7, Monday 8 Nov. 1773   Auchinleck

In the course of their altercation, Whiggism and Presbyterianism, Toryism and Episcopacy, were terribly buffeted. My worthy hereditary friend, Sir John Pringle, never having been mentioned, happily escaped without a bruise.

My father's opinion of Dr. Johnson may be conjectured from the name he afterwards gave him, which was URSA MAJOR [1]. But it is not true, as has been reported, that it was in consequence of my saying that he was a *constellation* [2] of genius and literature. It was a sly abrupt expression to one of his brethren on the bench of the Court of Session, in which Dr. Johnson was then standing ; but it was not said in his hearing.

Sunday, 7th November.

My father and I went to publick worship in our parish-church †, in which I regretted that Dr. Johnson would not join us ; for, though we have there no form of prayer, nor magnificent solemnity, yet, as GOD is worshipped in spirit and in truth, and the same doctrines preached as in the church of England, my friend would certainly have shewn more liberality, had he attended. I doubt not, however, but he employed his time in private to very good purpose. His uniform and fervent piety was manifested on many occasions during our Tour, which I have not mentioned.—His reason for not joining in Presbyterian worship has been recorded in a former page [3].

Monday, 8th November.

Notwithstanding the altercation that had passed, my father,

---

considered worth a new edition in 1788. See *D.N.B.* and J. Darling's *Cycl. Bibl.*, 1854, i. 991.⟩

[1] Gray, it should seem, had given the name earlier. His friend Bonstetten says that about the year 1769 he was walking with him, when Gray 'exclaimed, with some bitterness, "Look, look, Bonstetten !—the great bear !—There goes *Ursa Major !*" This was Johnson : Gray could not abide him.' Sir Egerton Brydges, *Autobiog.*, 1834, ii. 111. For the epithet *bear* applied to Johnson see *ante*, ii. 66, 269, note 1, and iv. 113, note 2. Boswell wrote on June 19,

1775 :—' My father harps on my going over Scotland with a *brute* (think how shockingly erroneous), and wandering (or some such phrase) to London.' *Letters*, No. 147.

[2] It is remarkable that Johnson in his *Life of Blackmore* [paragraph 26] calls the imaginary Mr. Johnson of the *Lay Monastery* 'a constellation of excellence.' CROKER, 1848.

† ⟨It was replaced by a new church which was opened in 1843 and destroyed by fire on 3 March 1938. *Scotsman*, 4 Mar. 1938.⟩

[3] Page [121]. BOSWELL. See also *ante*, iii. 336.

who had the dignified courtesy of an old Baron, was very civil to Dr. Johnson, and politely attended him to the post-chaise, which was to convey us to Edinburgh [1].

Thus they parted.—They are now in another, and a higher, state of existence : and as they were both worthy christian men, I trust they have met in happiness. But I must observe, in justice to my friend's political principles, and my own, that they have met in a place where there is no room for *Whiggism* [2].

We came at night to a good inn † at Hamilton.—I recollect no more.

Tuesday, 9th November.

I wished to have shewn Dr. Johnson the Duke of Hamilton's house, commonly called the *Palace* of Hamilton, which is close by the town §. It is an object which, having been pointed out to me as a splendid edifice, from my earliest years, in travelling between Auchinleck and Edinburgh, has still great grandeur in my imagination. My friend consented to stop, and view the outside of it, but could not be persuaded to go into it.

We arrived this night at Edinburgh, after an absence of eighty-three days. For five weeks together, of the tempestuous season, there had been no account received of us. I cannot express how happy I was on finding myself again at home.

Wednesday, 10th November.

Old Mr. Drummond, the bookseller [3], came to breakfast. Dr. Johnson and he had not met for ten years. There was respect on his side, and kindness on Dr. Johnson's. Soon afterwards Lord Elibank came in, and was much pleased at seeing Dr. Johnson in Scotland. His lordship said, ' hardly any thing seemed to him more improbable.' Dr. Johnson had a very high opinion of him. Speaking of him to me, he characterized

---

[1] ' The late Sir Alexander Boswell,' wrote Scott, ' was a proud man, and, like his grandfather, thought that his father lowered himself by his deferential suit and service to Johnson. I have observed he disliked any allusion to the book or to Johnson himself, and I have heard that Johnson's fine picture by Sir Joshua was sent up-stairs out of the sitting apartments at Auchinleck.' *Croker Corres.* ii. 32. This portrait, which was given by Sir Joshua to Boswell, ⟨came into the possession of his second son, James, and was sold after his death in 1825 : it is now, 1935, in The National Portrait Gallery. See the frontispiece to vol. i and *ante*, iv. 448.⟩

[2] ' I have always said, the first Whig was the Devil.' *Ante*, iii. 326.

†, § ⟨See App. D, p. 570.⟩

[3] See *ante*, ii. 26. ⟨His death is recorded in the *Scots Mag.* 1774, xxxvi. 679 : ' 21 Dec. At Edinburgh, in the 66th year of his age, William Drummond, Esq ; of Callander, bookseller in Edinburgh '.⟩

him thus: 'Lord Elibank has read a great deal. It is true, I can find in books all that he has read; but he has a great deal of what is in books, proved by the test of real life.'—Indeed, there have been few men whose conversation discovered more knowledge enlivened by fancy. He published several small pieces of distinguished merit; and has left some in manuscript, in particular an account of the expedition against Carthagena, in which he served as an officer in the army. His writings deserve to be collected. He was the early patron of Dr. Robertson, the historian, and Mr. Home, the tragick poet; who, when they were ministers of country parishes, lived near his seat. He told me, ' I saw these lads had talents, and they were much with me.'—I hope they will pay a grateful tribute to his memory [1].

The morning was chiefly taken up by Dr. Johnson's giving him an account of our Tour.—The subject of difference in political principles was introduced.—*Johnson.* ' It is much increased by opposition. There was a violent Whig, with whom I used to contend with great eagerness. After his death I felt my Toryism much abated.'—I suppose he meant Mr. Walmsley,[a] of Lichfield, whose character he has drawn so well in his Life of Edmund Smith [2].

Mr. Nairne [3] came in, and he and I accompanied Dr. Johnson

[a] Walmsley, 1, 2: Walmsley 3.

[1] Dr. A. Carlyle (*Auto.*, p. 266) has paid this tribute. ' Lord Elibank,' he writes, ' had a mind that embraced the greatest variety of topics, and produced the most original remarks. ... He had been a lieutenant-colonel in the army, and was at the siege of Carthagena, of which he left an elegant ... account (which I'm afraid is lost). He was a Jacobite, and a member of the famous Cocoa-tree Club, and resigned his commission on some disgust.' Dr. Robertson and John Home were his neighbours in the country, ' who made him change or soften down many of his original opinions, and prepared him for becoming a most agreeable member of the Literary Society of Edinburgh.' Smollett in *Humphry Clinker* (Bramble's letter of July 18), describes him as a ' nobleman whom I have long revered for his humanity and universal intelligence, over and above the entertainment arising from the originality of his character.' Boswell, in No. 19 of his *Hypochondriack*, thus mentions the Cocoa-tree Club :—' But even at court, though I see much external *obeisance*, I do not find congenial sentiments to warm my heart; and except when I have the conversation of a very few select friends, I am never so well, as when I sit down to a dish of coffee in the Cocoa-Tree, sacred of old to loyalty, look round me to men of ancient families, and please myself with the consolatory thought 'that there is perhaps more good in the nation than I know.' ⟨For Lord Elibank and his writings see App. D, pp. 570 ff.⟩

[2] Johnson's *Lives of the Poets*, ed. Hill, ii. 20. See *ante*, i. 81.

[3] See *ante*, v. 53.

to Edinburgh castle, which he owned was 'a great place.' But I must mention, as a striking instance of that spirit of contradiction to which he had a strong propensity, when Lord Elibank was some days after talking of it with the natural elation of a Scotchman, or of any man who is proud of a stately fortress in his own country, Dr. Johnson affected to despise it, observing, that ' it ᵃ would make a good *prison* in ENGLAND.'

Lest it should be supposed that I have suppressed one of his sallies against my country, it may not be improper here to correct a mistaken account that has been circulated, as to his conversation this day. It has been said, that being desired to attend to the noble prospect from the Castle-hill, he replied, ' Sir, the noblest prospect that a Scotchman ever sees, is the high road that leads him to London.'—This lively sarcasm was thrown out at a tavern [1] in London, in my presence, many years before.

We had with us to-day at dinner, at my house, the Lady Dowager Colvill, and Lady Anne Erskine, sisters of the Earl of Kelly [2]; the Honourable Archibald Erskine, who has now succeeded to that title ; Lord Elibank ; the Reverend Dr. Blair ; Mr. Tytler, the acute vindicator of Mary Queen of Scots [3], and some other friends [4].

Fingal being talked of, Dr. Johnson, who used to boast that he had, from the first, resisted both Ossian [5] and the Giants of Patagonia [6], averred his positive disbelief of its authenticity.

ᵃ observing, that 'it 1, 2 : observing that, ' it 3.

[1] The Mitre tavern. *Ante*, i. 425.
[2] Of this Earl of Kelly Boswell records the following pun :—' At a dinner at Mr. Crosbie's, when the company were very merry, the Rev. Dr. Webster told them he was sorry to go away so early, but was obliged to catch the tide, to cross the Frith of Forth to Fife. " Better stay a little," said Thomas Earl of Kelly, " till you be half seas over." ' Rogers's *Boswelliana*, p. 325. ⟨He died 9 Oct. 1781 and was succeeded by his brother Archibald, who died 8 May 1797. Sir James Balfour Paul's *Scots Peerage*, 1908, v. 89–90. For his sisters see *post*, App. D, p. 572.⟩
[3] See *ante*, i. 354.
[4] In the first edition, 'and his son the advocate '. Under this son, A. F. Tytler, afterwards a Lord of Session by the title of Lord Woodhouselee, Scott studied history at Edinburgh College. Lockhart's *Scott*, ed. 1837, i. 43, 205.
[5] See *ante*, i. 396, and ii. 296.
[6] ' If we know little of the ancient Highlanders, let us not fill the vacuity with Ossian. If we have not searched the Magellanick regions, let us however forbear to people them with Patagons.' Johnson's *Western Isl*., p. 108. Walpole wrote on May 22, 1766 (*Letters*, vii. 2) :— ' Oh, but we have discovered a race of giants ! Captain Byron has found a nation of Brobdignags on the coast of Patagonia ; the inhabitants on foot

Lord Elibank said, ' I am sure it is not M'Pherson's. Mr. Johnson, I keep company a great deal with you ; it is known I do. I may borrow from you better things than I can say myself, and give them as my own ; but, if I should, every body will know whose they are.'—The Doctor was not softened by this compliment. He denied merit to *Fingal,* supposing it to be the production of a man who has had the advantages that the present age affords ; and said, ' nothing is more easy than to write enough in that style, [a] if once you begin [1].'—[2] One gentleman in company [3] expressing his opinion ' that *Fingal* was certainly genuine, for that he had heard a great part of it repeated in the original,' Dr. Johnson indignantly asked him whether he understood the original ; to which an answer being given in the negative, ' Why then, (said Dr. Johnson,) we see to what *this* testimony comes :—thus it is.'

I mention [b] this as a remarkable proof how liable the mind of man is to credulity, when not guarded by such strict examination as that which Dr. Johnson habitually practised. [4] The talents and integrity of the gentleman who made the remark, are unquestionable ; yet, had not Dr. Johnson made him advert to the consideration, that he who does not understand a language, cannot know that something which is recited to him is in that language, he might have believed, and reported to this hour,

[a] style, 1, 2 : style 3.   [b] mention 1, 2 : mentioned 3

taller than he and his men on horseback. I don't indeed know how he and his sailors came to be riding in the South Seas.' ⟨See Hawkesworth's *Voy.* 1773, i. 28–32, T. Falkner's *Patagonia,* 1774, p. 26, Pennant's *Literary Life,* 1793, pp. 47 ff., and the *D.N.B.* s.v. Byron, John.⟩

[1] I desire not to be understood as agreeing *entirely* with the opinions of Dr. Johnson, which I relate without any remark. The many imitations, however, of *Fingal,* that have been published, confirm this observation in a considerable degree. BOSWELL, ed. 1.

Johnson said to Sir Joshua of Ossian :—' Sir, a man might write such stuff for ever, if he would *abandon* his mind to it.' *Ante,* iv. 183.

[2] In the first edition (p. 485) this paragraph ran thus :—' Young Mr. Tytler stepped briskly forward, and said, " *Fingal* is certainly genuine ; for I have heard a great part of it repeated in the original."—Dr. Johnson indignantly asked him, " Sir, do you understand the original ? "—*Tytler.* " No, Sir."—*Johnson.* " Why, then, we see to what this testimony comes :—Thus it is."—He afterwards said to me, " Did you observe the wonderful confidence with which young Tytler advanced, with his front ready *brased* ? " ' ⟨See App. D, p. 572.⟩

[3] For *in company* we should perhaps read *in the company.*

[4] In the first edition, ' This gentleman's talents and integrity are,' &c.

that he had 'heard a great part of *Fingal* repeated in the original.'

For the satisfaction of those on the north of the Tweed, who may think Dr. Johnson's account of Caledonian credulity and inaccuracy too strong [1], it is but fair to add, that he admitted the same kind of ready belief might be found in his own country. ' He would undertake, (he said) to write an epick poem on the story of *Robin Hood* [2], and half England, to whom the names and places he should mention in it are familiar, would believe and declare they had heard it from their earliest years.'

One of his objections to the authenticity of *Fingal*, during the conversation at Ulinish [3], is omitted in my Journal, but I perfectly recollect it.—' Why is not the original deposited in some publick library, instead of exhibiting attestations of its existence [4]? Suppose there were a question in a court of justice, whether a man be dead or alive : You aver he is alive, and you bring fifty witnesses to swear it : I answer, " Why do you not produce the man ? " '—This is an argument founded on one of the first principles of the *law of evidence*, which *Gilbert* [5] would have held to be irrefragable.

I do not think it incumbent on me to give any precise decided opinion upon this question, as to which I believe more than some, and less than others [6]. The subject appears to have now become very uninteresting to the publick. That *Fingal* is not from beginning to end a translation from the Gallick, but that *some* passages have been supplied by the editor to connect the whole, I have heard admitted by very warm advocates for its authenticity. If this be the case, why are not these distinctly ascertained ? Antiquaries, and admirers of the work, may complain, that they are in a situation similar to that of the unhappy gentleman whose wife informed him, on her death-bed, that one

---

[1] ' A Scotchman must be a very sturdy moralist, who does not love *Scotland* better than truth : he will always love it better than inquiry ; and if falsehood flatters his vanity, will not be very diligent to detect it.' Johnson's *Western Isl.*, p. 108. See ante, ii. 311 ⟨and *post* App. D, p. 572⟩.

[2] See *ante*, v. 164.
[3] See *ante*, v. 242.
[4] See *ante*, iv. 253.
[5] ⟨Sir Geoffrey Gilbert's *Law of Evidence*, first published, posthumously (like all his works), in 1761, was the standard authority on the subject for the rest of the century.⟩
[6] See *ante* ii. 302.

of their reputed children was not his; and, when he eagerly begged her to declare which of them it was, she answered, ' *That you shall never know;* ' and expired, leaving him in irremediable doubt as to them all.

I beg leave now to say something upon *second sight*, of which I have related two instances [1], as they impressed my mind at the time. I own, I returned from the Hebrides with a considerable degree of faith in the many stories of that kind which I heard with a too easy acquiescence, without any close examination of the evidence: but, since that time, my belief in those stories has been much weakened [2], by reflecting on the careless inaccuracy of narrative in common matters, from which we may certainly conclude that there may be the same in what is more extraordinary.—It is but just, however, to add, that the belief in second sight is not peculiar to the Highlands and Isles [3].

Some years after our Tour, a cause [4] was tried in the Court of Session, where the principal fact to be ascertained was, whether a ship-master, who used to frequent the Western Highlands and Isles, was drowned in one particular year, or in the year after. A great number of witnesses from those parts were examined on each side, and swore directly contrary to each other, upon this simple question. One of them, a very respectable Chieftain [5], who told me a story of second sight, which I have not mentioned, but which I too implicitly believed, had in this case, previous to his[a] publick examination, not only said, but attested under his hand, that he had seen the ship-master in the year subsequent to that in which the court was finally satisfied he was drowned. When interrogated with the strictness of judicial inquiry, and under the awe of an oath, he recollected himself better, and retracted what he had formerly asserted, apologising for his inaccuracy, by telling the judges, ' A man will *say* what he will not *swear*.'—By many he was much censured, and it was maintained that every gentleman would be as attentive to truth

[a] his 1 : this 2, 3.

[1] Three instances, *ante*, v. 160, 320.
[2] See *ante*, ii. 318.
[3] An instance is given in Sacheverell's *Account of the Isle of Man*, ed. 1702, p. 14. ⟨Lord Monboddo was a believer. *Boswell Papers*, x. 91.⟩

[4] In the margin of the copy of Boswell's *Journal* in the National Library of Scotland it is stated that this cause was *Wilson versus Maclean*. ⟨See App. D, pp. 572–3.⟩
[5] ⟨Sir Allan Maclean: see App. D, p. 556.⟩

Edinburgh   *Wednesday* 10 *November* 1773   391
without the sanction of an oath, as with it. Dr. Johnson, though he himself was distinguished at all times by a scrupulous adherence to truth, controverted this proposition ; and, as a proof that this was not, though it ought to be, the case, urged the very different decisions of elections under Mr. Grenville's Act [1], from those formerly made. ' Gentlemen will not pronounce upon oath, what they would have said, and voted in the house, without that sanction.'

However difficult it may be for men who believe in preternatural communications, in modern times, to satisfy those who are of a different opinion, they may easily refute the doctrine of their opponents, who impute a belief in *second sight* to *superstition*. To entertain a visionary notion that one sees a distant or future event, may be called *superstition ;* but the correspondence of the fact or event with such an impression on the fancy, though certainly very wonderful, *if proved*, has no more connection with superstition, than magnetism or electricity.

After dinner, various topicks were discussed ; but I recollect only one particular. Dr. Johnson compared the different talents of Garrick and Foote [2], as companions, and gave Garrick greatly the preference for elegance, though he allowed Foote extraordinary powers of entertainment. He said, ' Garrick is restrained by some principle ; but Foote has the advantage of an unlimited range. Garrick has some delicacy of feeling ; it is possible to put him out ; you may get the better of him ; but Foote is the most incompressible fellow that I ever knew : when you have driven him into a corner, and think you are sure of him, he runs through between your legs, or jumps over your head, and makes his escape.'

Dr. Erskine [3] and Mr. Robert Walker [3], two very respectable ministers of Edinburgh, supped with us, as did the Reverend Dr. Webster [4].—The conversation turned on the Moravian missions, and on the Methodists. Dr. Johnson observed in general, that missionaries were too sanguine in their accounts of their success among savages, and that much of what they tell is not to be believed. He owned that the Methodists had done good ;

[1] See *ante*, iv. 74, note 3.
[2] See *ante*, iii. 69, 183.
[3] ⟨For Drs. John Erskine and

Robert Walker see App. D, p. 573.⟩
[4] See *ante*, v. 50 ⟨and *post*, App. D, pp. 472–3⟩.

Thursday 11 *November* 1773   *Edinburgh*
had spread religious impressions among the vulgar part of mankind [1] : but, he said, they had great bitterness against other Christians, and that he never could get a Methodist to explain in what he excelled others ; that it always ended in the indispensible necessity of hearing one of their preachers [2].

Thursday, 11th November.

Principal Robertson came to us as we sat at breakfast : he advanced to Dr. Johnson, repeating a line of Virgil, which I forget. I suppose, either

   Post [a] *varios casus, per tot discrimina rerum* [3],—

or

   —*multum ille et terris jactatus, et alto* [4].

Every body had accosted us with some studied compliment on our return. Dr. Johnson said, ' I am really ashamed of the congratulations which we receive. We are addressed as if we had made a voyage to Nova Zembla, and suffered five persecutions in Japan [5].' And he afterwards remarked, that, ' to see a man come up with a formal air, and a Latin line, when we had had [b] no fatigue and no danger, was provoking [6].'—I told him, he was not sensible of the danger, having lain under cover in the

[a] *Per* Virgil.
[b] had had 1 : had 2, 3.

[1] See *ante*, i. 458.

[2] 'We now observe, that the methodists, where they scatter their opinions, represent themselves, as preaching the gospel to unconverted nations ; and enthusiasts of all kinds have been inclined to disguise their particular tenets with pompous appellations, and to imagine themselves the great instruments of salvation.' Johnson's *Life of Cheynel, Works*, vi. 417.

[3] Through various hazards and events we move.
Dryden,[*Æneid*,I. 204]. BOSWELL,ed.2.

[4] Long labours both by sea and land he bore.
Dryden, [*Æneid*, I. 3]. BOSWELL, ed. 2.

[5] The Jesuits, headed by Francis Xavier, made their appearance in Japan in 1549. The first persecution was in 1587 ; it was followed by others in 1590, 1597, 1637, 1638.

Encycl. Brit. 8th edit. xii. 697.

[6] 'They congratulate our return as if we had been with Phipps or Banks ; I am ashamed of their salutations.' Johnson's *Letters*, No. 338. Phipps had gone this year to the Arctic Ocean (*ante*, v. 236), and Banks had accompanied Captain Cook in 1768–1771. Johnson says however (*Western Isl.*, p. 79), that ' to the southern inhabitants of Scotland, the state of the mountains and the islands is equally unknown with that of Borneo or Sumatra.' See *ante*, v. 283, note 1, where Scott says that ' the whole expedition was highly perilous.' Smollett, in *Humphry Clinker* (Melford's letter of July 18), says of Scotland in general :— ' The people at the other end of the island know as little of Scotland as of Japan.'

boat during the storm [1] : he was like the chicken, that hides its head under its wing, and then thinks itself safe.

Lord Elibank came to us, as did Sir William Forbes. The rash attempt in 1745 being mentioned, I observed, that it would make a fine piece of History. Dr. Johnson said it would [2]. Lord Elibank doubted whether any man of this age could give it impartially.—*Johnson.* ' A man, by talking with those of different sides, who were actors in it, and putting down all that he hears, may in time collect the materials of a good narrative. You are to consider, all history was at first oral. I suppose Voltaire was fifty years [3] in collecting his *Louis XIV.* which he did in the way that I am proposing.'—*Robertson.* ' He did so. He lived much with all the great people who were concerned in that reign, and heard them talk of every thing ; and then either took Mr. Boswell's way, of writing down what he heard, or, which is as good, preserved it in his memory ; for he has a wonderful memory.'—With the leave, however, of this elegant historian, no man's memory can preserve facts or sayings with such fidelity as may be done by writing them down when they are recent.—Dr. Robertson said, ' it was now full time to make such a collection as Dr. Johnson suggested ; for many of the people who were then in arms, were dropping off ; and both Whigs and Jacobites were now come to talk with moderation.' —Lord Elibank said to him, ' Mr. Robertson, the first thing that gave me a high opinion of you, was your saying in the Select Society [4], while parties ran high, soon after the year 1745, that you did not think worse of a man's moral character for his having been in rebellion. This was venturing to utter a liberal sentiment, while both sides had a detestation of each other.'

Dr. Johnson observed, that being in rebellion from a notion

[1] In sailing from Skye to Col. *Ante*, v. 280.
[2] Johnson, four years later, suggested to Boswell that he should write this history. *Ante*, iii. 162, 414.
[3] ⟨' Voltaire pensait, dès 1732, à donner l'histoire du Siècle de Louis XIV.' *Œuvres*, ed. 1878, t. xiv, p. ix. It was published in 1751. He was born in 1694.⟩
[4] A society for debate in Edinburgh, consisting of the most eminent men. BOSWELL, ed. 1. ⟨The Select Society was founded by

Allan Ramsay, the painter. The first meeting was held on 22 May 1754 and the last on 8 Feb. 1763 (when it had ceased to be ' select '). Among the original members were Hume, Adam Smith, Robertson, Wedderburn, Alex. Carlyle, Lord Kames, and Lord Auchinleck (*Minutes* in Nat. Libr. Scot., MS. 23. 1. 1). See Hume's *Letters*, ed. Greig, i. 219, Dugald Stewart's *Life of Robertson*, 1801, pp. 10 and 137 ff., and Alex. Carlyle's *Autobiog.*, 1860, pp. 297 ff. and 390.⟩

of another's right, was not connected with depravity ; and that we had this proof of it, that all mankind applauded the pardoning of rebels ; which they would not do in the case of robbers and murderers. He said, with a smile, that ' he wondered that the phrase of *unnatural* rebellion should be so much used, for that all rebellion was natural to man.'

As I kept no Journal of any thing that passed after this morning, I shall, from memory, group together this and the other days, till that on which Dr. Johnson departed for London. They were in all nine days ; on which he dined at Lady Colvill's, Lord Hailes's, Sir Adolphus Oughton's, Sir Alexander Dick's, Principal Robertson's, Mr. M'Laurin's [1], and thrice at Lord Elibank's seat in the country, where we also passed two nights [2]. He supped at the Honourable Alexander Gordon's [3], now one of our judges, by the title of Lord Rockville ; at Mr. Nairne's †, now also one of our judges, by the title of Lord Dunsinan ; at Dr. Blair's, and Mr. Tytler's ; and at my house thrice, one evening with a numerous company, chiefly gentlemen of the law ; another with Mr. Menzies of Culdares §, and Lord Monboddo, who disengaged himself on purpose to meet him ; and the evening on which we returned from Lord Elibank's, he supped with my wife and me by ourselves [4].

He breakfasted at Dr. Webster's, at old Mr. Drummond's, and at Dr. Blacklock's ; and spent one forenoon at my uncle Dr. Boswell's [5], who shewed him his curious museum ; and, as he was an elegant scholar, and a physician bred in the school of Boerhaave [6], Dr. Johnson was pleased with his company.

---

[1] See *ante*, i. 469.
[2] ⟨Lord Elibank's country seat was at Ballencrieff, near Haddington. The mansion was burnt down in 1868. See J. Martine, *Reminisc. Fourteen Parishes*, 1890, p. 12, and C. E. Green, *East Lothian*, 1907, pp. 101 ff.⟩
[3] ⟨The sentence ' by . . . Rockville ' was added in the third edition. Gordon was raised to the bench in 1784, when he took his title from his estate in Haddingtonshire. See Brunton and Haig, 1832, p. 537. See also *ante*, i. 469.⟩
† ⟨The sentence ' now . . . Dunsinan ' was added in the third edition. Nairne was promoted in 1786. See Brunton and Haig, p. 538.⟩

§ ⟨See App. D, pp. 573-4.⟩
[4] For the alarm he gave to Mrs. Boswell before this supper, see *ante*, i. 469.
[5] On Dr. Boswell's death, in 1780, Boswell wrote of him :—' He was a very good scholar, knew a great many things, had an elegant taste, and was very affectionate. But he had no conduct. His money was all gone ; and, do you know, he was not confined to one woman ? He had a strange kind of religion. But, I flatter myself, he will be e'er long, if he is not allready, in Heaven.' *Letters*, No. 200, ii. 309. ⟨See also *post*, App. D, p. 574.⟩
[6] Johnson had written the *Life* of

Edinburgh *Thursday* 11—*Saturday* 20 *Nov.* 1773   395

On the mornings when he breakfasted at my house, he had, from ten o'clock till one or two, a constant levee of various persons, of very different characters and descriptions. I could not attend him, being obliged to be in the Court of Session; but my wife was so good as to devote the greater part of the morning to the endless task of pouring out tea for my friend and his visitors.

Such was the disposition of his time at Edinburgh. He said one evening to me, in a fit of languor, ' Sir, we have been harrassed by invitations.' I acquiesced. ' Ay, sir, he replied; but how much worse would it have been, if we had been neglected 1 ? '

From what has been recorded in this Journal, it may well be supposed that a variety of admirable conversation has been lost, by my neglect to preserve it.—I shall endeavour to recollect some of it, as well as I can.

At Lady Colvill's, to whom I am proud to introduce any stranger of eminence, that he may see what dignity and grace is to be found in Scotland, an officer observed, that he had heard Lord Mansfield was not a great English lawyer.—*Johnson*. ' Why, sir, supposing Lord Mansfield not to have the splendid talents which he possesses, he must be a great English lawyer, from having been so long at the bar, and having passed through so many of the great offices of the law. Sir, you may as well maintain that a carrier, who has driven a packhorse between Edinburgh and Berwick for thirty years, does not know the road, as that Lord Mansfield does not know the law of England 2.'

At Mr. Nairne's, he drew the character of Richardson, the author of *Clarissa*, with a strong yet delicate pencil. I lament much that I have not preserved it : I only remember that he expressed a high opinion of his talents and virtues ; but observed, that ' his perpetual study was to ward off petty inconveniencies, and procure petty pleasures ; that his love of continual superiority was such, that he took care to be always surrounded by

---

' the great Boerhaave,' as he called him. *Works*, vi. 292.

1 ' We now returned to Edinburgh, where I passed some days with men of learning, whose names want no advancement from my commemoration, or with women of elegance, which perhaps disclaims a pedant's praise.' Johnson's *Western Isl.*, p. 147.

2 See *ante*, iv. 178.

Thursday 11—Saturday 20 Nov. 1773 Edinburgh women [1], who listened to him implicitly, and did not venture to controvert his opinions; and that his desire of distinction was so great, that he used to give large vails to the Speaker Onslow's servants, that they might treat him with respect.'

On the same evening, he would not allow that the private life of a judge, in England, was required to be so strictly decorous as I supposed. 'Why then, sir, (said I,) according to your account, an English judge may just live like a gentleman.' —*Johnson*. 'Yes, sir [2],—if he *can*.'

At Mr. Tytler's, I happened to tell that one evening, a great many years ago, when Dr. Hugh Blair and I were sitting together in the pit of Drury-lane play-house, in a wild freak of youthful extravagance, I entertained the audience *prodigiously* [3], by imitating the lowing of a cow. A little while after I had told this story, I differed from Dr. Johnson, I suppose too confidently, upon some point, which I now forget. He did not spare me. 'Nay, sir, (said he,) if you cannot talk better as a man, I'd have you bellow like a cow [4].'

---

[1] 'My acquaintance,' wrote Richardson (*Corres.* iv. 317), 'lies chiefly among the ladies; I care not who knows it.' Mrs. Piozzi, in a marginal note on her own copy of the *Piozzi Letters*, says:—' Dr. Johnson said, that if Mr. Richardson had lived till *I* came out, my praises would have added two or three years to his life: "For," says Dr. Johnson, "that fellow died merely for want of change among his flatterers: he perished for want of *more*, like a man obliged to breathe the same air till it is exhausted."' Hayward's *Piozzi*, ed. 1, i. 311. In her *Journey*, i. 265, she says:—' Richardson had seen little, and Johnson has often told me that he had read little.' See *ante*, iv. 28.

[2] He may live like a gentleman, but he must not ' call himself *Farmer*, and go about with a little round hat.' *Ante*, v. 111.

[3] Boswell italicizes this word, I think, because Johnson objected to the misuse of it. '"Sir," said Mr. Edwards, "I remember you would not let us say *prodigious* at College."' *Ante*, iii. 303.

[4] As I have been scrupulously exact in relating anecdotes concerning other persons, I shall not withhold any part of this story, however ludicrous.—I was so successful in this boyish frolick, that the universal cry of the galleries was, ' Encore the cow! Encore the cow!' In the pride of my heart, I attempted imitations of some other animals, but with very inferior effect. My reverend friend, anxious for my *fame*, with an air of the utmost gravity and earnestness, addressed me thus: ' My dear sir, I would *confine* myself to the cow!' BOSWELL, ed. 1.

Blair's advice was expressed more emphatically, and with a peculiar burr—' *Stick to the cow*, mon!' SCOTT, 1831. Boswell's record, which moreover is far more humorous, is much more trustworthy than Scott's tradition.

Edinburgh *Thursday* 11—*Saturday* 20 *Nov.* 1773   397

At Dr. Webster's, he said, that he believed hardly any man died without affectation. This remark appears to me to be well founded, and will account for many of the celebrated death-bed sayings which are recorded [1].

On one of the evenings at my house, when he told that Lord Lovat boasted to an English nobleman, that though he had not his wealth, he had two thousand men whom he could at any time call into the field, the Honourable Alexander Gordon observed, that those two thousand men brought him to the block. —' True, sir, (said Dr. Johnson :) but you may just as well argue, concerning a man who has fallen over a precipice to which he has walked too near,—" His two legs brought him to that." Is [a] he not the better for having two legs ? '

At Dr. Blair's I left him, in order to attend a consultation, during which he and his amiable host were by themselves. I returned to supper, at which were Principal Robertson, Mr. Nairne, and some other gentlemen. Dr. Robertson and Dr. Blair, I remember, talked well upon subordination [2] and government ; and, as my friend and I were walking home, he said to me, ' Sir, these two doctors are good men, and wise men [3].'

[a] that." Is 1, 2 : that," is 3.

[1] Mme de Sévigné in describing a death wrote :—' Cela ... nous fit voir qu'on joue long-temps la comédie, et qu'à la mort on dit la vérité.' Letter of June 24, 1672. Addison says :—' The end of a Man's Life is often compared to the winding up of a well-written Play, where the principal Persons still act in Character, whatever the Fate is which they undergo. ... That innocent Mirth, which had been so conspicuous in Sir Thomas More's Life, did not forsake him to the last. ... His Death was of a piece with his Life. There was nothing in it new, forced, or affected.' *The Spectator*, No. 349. Young also thought, or at least, wrote differently.
A death-bed 's a detector of the heart.
Here tir'd dissimulation drops her masque.'
Night Thoughts, ii. 639.
'L'expression de l'évêque d'Autun [Talleyrand] était si heureuse que je n'ai pu l'oublier : "Il ⟨Mirabeau⟩ a dramatisé sa mort"', says Dumont in his *Souvenirs sur Mirabeau*, 1832, p. 309. See *ante*, iii. 154.

[2] See *ante*, i. 408, 447 ; ii. 219, 329.

[3] Dr. A. Carlyle (*Auto.*, p. 291) says of Blair's conversation that ' it was so infantine that many people thought it impossible, at first sight, that he could be a man of sense or genius. He was as eager about a new paper to his wife's drawing-room, or his own new wig, as about a new tragedy or a new epic poem.' He adds, that he was ' capable of the most profound conversation, when circumstances led to it. [He] had not the least desire to shine, but was delighted beyond measure to show other people in their best guise to his friends. " Did not I show you the lion well to-day ? " used he to say after the exhibition of a remarkable

398 *Thursday* 11—*Saturday* 20 *Nov.* 1773 Edinburgh
—I begged of Dr. Blair to recollect what he could of the long conversation that passed between Dr. Johnson and him alone, this evening, and he obligingly wrote to me as follows :

March 3, 1785.
' *Dear Sir*,

' — AS so many years have intervened, since I chanced to have that conversation with Dr. Johnson in my house, to which you refer, I have forgotten most of what then passed, but remember that I was both instructed and entertained by it. Among other subjects, the discourse happening to turn on modern Latin poets, the Dr. expressed a very favourable opinion of Buchanan, and instantly repeated, from beginning to end, an ode of his, intituled *Calendæ Maiæ*, (the eleventh in his *Miscellaneorum Liber*,) beginning with these words, ' *Salvete sacris deliciis sacræ*,' with which I had formerly been unacquainted ; but upon perusing it, the praise which he bestowed upon it, as one of the happiest of Buchanan's poetical compositions, appeared to me very just. He also repeated to me a Latin ode he had composed in one of the Western Islands, from which he had lately returned. We had much discourse concerning his excursion to those islands, with which he expressed himself as having been highly pleased ; talked in a favourable manner of the hospitality of the inhabitants ; and particularly spoke much of his happiness in having you for his companion ; and said, that the longer he knew you, he loved and esteemed you the more. This conversation passed in the interval between tea and supper, when we were by ourselves. You, and the rest of the company who were with us at supper, have often taken notice that he was uncommonly bland and gay that evening, and gave much pleasure to all who were present. —This is all that I can recollect distinctly of that long conversation.

' Yours sincerely,
' HUGH BLAIR.'

At Lord Hailes's [1], we spent a most agreeable day ; but again I must lament that I was so indolent as to let almost all that passed evaporate into oblivion. Dr. Johnson observed there, that ' it is wonderful how ignorant many officers of the army are, considering how much leisure they have for study, and the stranger.' He had no wit, and for humour hardly a relish. Robertson's reputation for wisdom may have been easily won. Dr. A. Carlyle says (*ib.*, p. 287) :—' Robertson's translations and paraphrases on other people's thoughts were so beautiful and so harmless that I never saw anybody lay claim to their own.' He may have flattered Johnson by dexterously echoing his sentiments.

[1] ⟨Either at Lord Hailes's town house in New Street or at New Hailes, Musselburgh : the last-named mansion is still, 1964, in the possession of the Dalrymple family.⟩

acquisition of knowledge [1].' I hope he was mistaken; for he maintained that many of them were ignorant of things belonging immediately to their own profession; ' for instance, many cannot tell how far a musket will carry a bullet;' in proof of which, I suppose, he mentioned some particular person, for Lord Hailes, from whom I solicited what he could recollect of that day, writes to me as follows :

' As to Dr. Johnson's observation about the ignorance of officers, in the length that a musket will carry, my brother, Colonel Dalrymple, was present, and he thought that the doctor was either mistaken, by putting the question wrong, or that he had conversed on the subject with some person out of service.

' Was it upon that occasion that he expressed no curiosity to see the room at Dumfermline, where Charles I. was born ? " I know that he was born, (said he ;) no matter where."—Did he envy us the birth-place of the king ? '

Near the end of his ' Journey ', Dr. Johnson has given liberal praise to Mr. Braidwood's academy for the deaf and dumb [2]. When he visited it, a circumstance occurred which was truly characteristical of our great Lexicographer. ' Pray, (said he,) can they pronounce any *long* words ? '—Mr. Braidwood informed him they could. Upon which Dr. Johnson wrote one of his *sesquipedalia verba* [3], which was pronounced by the scholars, and he was satisfied.—My readers may perhaps wish to know what the word was ; but I cannot gratify their curiosity. Mr. Braidwood told me, it remained long in his school, but had been lost before I made my inquiry [4].

[1] In the *Marmor Norfolciense* (*ante*, i. 141) Johnson says :—' I know that the knowledge of the alphabet is so disreputable among these gentlemen [of the army], that those who have, by ill fortune, formerly been taught it, have partly forgot it by disuse, and partly concealed it from the world, to avoid the railleries and insults to which their education might make them liable.' Johnson's *Works*, vi. 111. See *ante*, iii. 265.

[2] ' One of the young Ladies had her slate before her, on which I wrote a question consisting of three figures, to be multiplied by two figures. She looked upon it, and quivering her fingers in a manner which I thought very pretty, but of which I know not whether it was art or play, multiplied the sum regularly in two lines, observing the decimal place ; but did not add the two lines together, probably disdaining so easy an operation.' Johnson's *Western Isl.*, p. 148. ⟨For the academy see *post*, App. D, p. 574.⟩

[3] Horace, *Ars Poet.* l. 97.

[4] One of the best criticks of our age ' does not wish to prevent the admirers of the incorrect and nerveless style which generally prevailed for a century before Dr. Johnson's energetick writings were known,

400 *Thursday* 11—*Saturday* 20 *Nov.* 1773 Edinburgh

Dr. Johnson one day visited the Court of Session [1]. He thought the mode of pleading there too vehement, and too much addressed to the passions of the judges. 'This (said he) is not the Areopagus.'

At old Mr. Drummond's, Sir John Dalrymple quaintly said, the two noblest animals in the world were, a Scotch Highlander and an English Sailor [2]. 'Why, sir, (said Dr. Johnson,) I shall say nothing as to the Scotch Highlander; but as to the English Sailor, I cannot agree with you.'—Sir John said, he was generous in giving away his money.'—*Johnson*. 'Sir, he throws away his money, without thought, and without merit. I do not call a tree generous, that sheds its fruit at every breeze.'—Sir John having affected to complain of the attacks made upon his *Memoirs* [3], Dr. Johnson said, 'Nay, sir, do not complain. It is advantageous to an authour, that his book should be attacked as well as praised. Fame is a shuttlecock. If it be struck only at one end of the room, it will soon fall to the ground. To keep it up, it must be struck at both ends [4].'—Often have I reflected on

---

from enjoying the laugh that this story may produce, in which he is very ready to join them.' He, however, requests me to observe, that 'my friend very properly chose a *long* word on this occasion, not, it is believed, from any predilection for polysyllables, (though he certainly had a due respect for them,) but in order to put Mr. Braidwood's skill to the strictest test, and to try the efficacy of his instruction by the most difficult exertion of the organs of his pupils.' BOSWELL, ed. 1. ⟨'One of the best criticks of our age' is Malone, as Dr. Hill suggested. See *ante*, v. 1, note 5.⟩

[1] It was here that Lord Auchinleck called him *Ursa Major*. *Ante*, v. 384.

[2] See *ante*, iii. 266, and v. 20, where 'Mr. Crosbie said, that the English are better animals than the Scots.'

[3] ⟨*Memoirs of Great Britain and Ireland*, 2 vols., 1771–3.⟩ Johnson himself had laughed at them (*ante*, ii. 210) and accused them of foppery (*ante*, ii. 237).

[4] Johnson said, 'I never think I have hit hard, unless it rebounds' (*ante*, ii. 335), and, 'I would rather be attacked than unnoticed' (*ante*, iii. 375 : see also note *ad loc.*). When he was told of a caricature 'of the nine muses flogging him round Parnassus,' he said, 'Sir, I am very glad to hear this. I hope the day will never arrive when I shall neither be the object of calumny or ridicule, for then I shall be neglected and forgotten.' Croker's *Boswell*, 1831, v. 413. ⟨This particular caricature was published 29 July 1783. Mrs. M. D. George, *Catal. Polit. & Personal Satires*, 1935, v, No. 6328.⟩ See *ante*, ii. 61, and v. 174, 273. 'There was much laughter when M. de Lesseps mentioned that on his first visit to England the publisher who brought out the report of his meeting charged, as the first item of his bill, "£50 for attacking the book in order to make it succeed." "Since then," observed M. de Lesseps, "I have been attacked gratuitously, and have got on without paying."' *The Times*, Feb. 19, 1884.

Edinburgh *Thursday* 11—*Saturday* 20 *Nov.* 1773　401
this since; and, instead of being angry at many of those who have written against me, have smiled to think that they were unintentionally subservient to my fame, by using a battledoor to make me *virum volitare per ora* [1].

At Sir Alexander Dick's, from that absence of mind to which every man is at times subject, I told, in a blundering manner, Lady Eglintoune's complimentary adoption of Dr. Johnson as her son †; for I unfortunately stated that her ladyship adopted him as her son, in consequence of her having been married the year *after* he was born. Dr. Johnson instantly corrected me. 'Sir, don't you perceive that you are defaming the countess? For, supposing me to be her son, and that she was not married till the year after my birth, I must have been her *natural* son.' A young lady of quality §, who was present, very handsomely said, 'Might not the son have justified the fault?'—My friend was much flattered by this compliment, which he never forgot. When in more than ordinary spirits, and talking of his journey in Scotland, he has called to me, 'Boswell, what was it that the young lady of quality said of me at Sir Alexander Dick's?' Nobody will doubt that I was happy in repeating it.

My illustrious friend, being now desirous to be again in the great theatre of life and animated exertion, took a place in the coach, which was to set out for London on Monday the 22d of November [2]. Sir John Dalrymple pressed him to come on the Saturday before, to his house * at Cranston, which being twelve miles from Edinburgh, upon the middle road to Newcastle, (Dr. Johnson had come to Edinburgh by Berwick, and along the naked coast [3],) it would make his journey easier, as the coach

[1] 'To wing my flight to fame.' DRYDEN. Virgil, *Georgics*, iii. 9.
† ⟨See *ante*, v. 375 and iii. 366.⟩
§ ⟨Lady Anne Lindsay: see App. D, pp. 575–6.⟩
[2] On Nov. 12 he wrote to Mrs. Thrale from Edinburgh:—' We came hither on the ninth of this month. I long to come under your care, but for some days cannot decently get away.' *Letters*, No. 338.
* ⟨Stated in H. H. Dalrymple's *Acc. Oxenfoord Castle*, 1901, to be 'now demolished' (p. 34 n.).⟩
[3] He would have been astonished had he known that a few miles from Edinburgh he had passed through two villages of serfs. The coal-hewers and salt-makers of Tranent and Preston-Pans were still sold with the soil. 'In Scotland domestic slavery is unknown, except so far as regards the coal-hewers and salt-makers, whose condition, it must be confessed, bears some resemblance to slavery; because all who have once acted in either of these capacities, are compellable to serve, and fixed to their respective places of employment during life.' F. Hargrave's *Argument in the case of James Sommersett*, 1772, p. 70. ⟨Brit. Mus. 884 k. 26.⟩

would take him up at a more seasonable hour than that at which it sets out. Sir John, I perceived, was ambitious of having such a guest; but, as I was well assured, that at this very time he had joined with some of his prejudiced countrymen in railing at Dr. Johnson [1], and had said, 'he [a] wondered how any gentleman of Scotland could keep company with him,' I thought he did not deserve the honour : yet, as it might be a convenience to Dr. Johnson, I contrived that he should accept the invitation, and engaged to conduct him. I resolved that, on our way to Sir John's, we should make a little circuit by Roslin Castle, and Hawthornden, and wished to set out soon after breakfast ; but young Mr. Tytler came to shew Dr. Johnson some essays which he had written ; and my great friend, who was exceedingly obliging when thus consulted [2], was detained so long that it was, I believe, one o'clock before we got into our post-chaise. I found that we should be too late for dinner at Sir John Dalrymple's, to which we were engaged : but I would by no means lose the pleasure of seeing my friend at Hawthornden,—of seeing *Sam Johnson* at the very spot where *Ben Jonson* [b] visited the learned and poetical Drummond [3].

We surveyed Roslin Castle, the romantick scene around it, and the beautiful Gothick chapel [4], and dined and drank tea at the inn ; after which we proceeded to Hawthornden, and viewed the caves ; and I all the while had *Rare Ben* [5] in my mind, and was

[a] 'he 1, 2: he 3.   [b] *Johnson* 3.

[1] The year following in the House of Commons he railed at the London booksellers, 'who, he positively asserted, entirely governed the newspapers.' 'For his part,' he added, 'he had ordered that no English newspaper should come within his doors for three months.' *Parl. Hist.* xvii. 1090.

[2] See *ante*, iii. 373.

[3] ⟨Ben Jonson walked from London to Edinburgh in 1618 and spent two or three weeks at Hawthornden, about Christmas. Drummond's record of his talk is given in the so-called *Conversations with William Drummond*. See Herford and Simpson, *Ben Jonson*, 1925, i. 77 ff., 132 ff.⟩

[4] Perhaps the same woman showed the chapel who was there 29 years later, when Scott visited it. '[William] Erskine expressed a hope that they might, as habitual visitors, escape hearing the usual endless story of the silly old woman that showed the ruins ' ; but Scott answered, ' There is a pleasure in the song which none but the songstress knows, and by telling her we know it all already, we should make the poor devil unhappy.' Lockhart's *Scott*, 1837, i. 362.

[5] *O rare Ben Jonson* is on Jonson's tomb in Westminster Abbey. ⟨For the history of the inscription see Herford and Simpson, *Ben Jonson*, 1925, i. 180, 183.⟩

pleased to think that this place was now visited by another celebrated wit of England.

By this time '' the waning night was growing old,' and we were yet several miles from Sir John Dalrymple's. Dr. Johnson did not seem much troubled at our having treated the baronet with so little attention to politeness; but when I talked of the grievous disappointment it must have been to him that we did not come to the *feast* that he had prepared for us, (for he told us he had killed a seven-year-old sheep on purpose,) my friend got into a merry mood, and jocularly said, '. I dare say, sir, he has been very sadly distressed : Nay, we do not know but the consequence may have been fatal. Let me try to describe his situation in his own historical style.[a] I have as good a right to make him think and talk, as he has to tell us how people thought and talked a hundred years ago, of which he has no evidence. All history, so far as it is not supported by contemporary evidence, is romance [1].
——Stay now.——Let us consider ! '——He then (heartily laughing all the while) proceeded in his imitation, I am sure to the following effect, though now, at the distance of almost twelve years, I cannot pretend to recollect all the precise words :

' Dinner being ready, he wondered that his guests were not yet come.
' His wonder was soon succeeded by impatience. He walked about the
' room in anxious agitation ; sometimes he looked at his watch, some-
' times he looked out at the window with an eager gaze of expectation,
' and revolved in his mind the various accidents of human life. His
' family beheld him with mute concern. " Surely (said he, with a sigh,)
' they will not fail me."—The mind of man can bear a certain pressure ;
' but there is a point when it can bear no more. A rope was in his view,
' and he died a Roman death [2].'

[a] style. 1, 2: style, 3.

[1] See *ante*, ii. 365.
[2] ' Essex was at that time confined to the same chamber of the Tower from which his father Lord Capel had been led to death, and in which his wife's grandfather had inflicted a voluntary death upon himself. When he saw his friend carried to what he reckoned certain fate, their common enemies enjoying the spectacle, and reflected that it was he who had forced Lord Howard upon the confidence of Russel, he retired, and, by a *Roman death*, put an end to his misery.' Dalrymple's Memoirs of Great Britain and Ireland. Vol. I, p. 36. BOSWELL, ed. 1.

In the original after ' his wife's grandfather ' is added ' Lord Northumberland.' It was his wife's great-grandfather, the ninth Earl of Northumberland. ⟨He was found dead in his bed in the Tower from a pistol-shot, supposed to have been self-inflicted, 21 June 1585. G. E. C., *Compl. Peerage*, 1895, vi. 90. Dalrymple lived till 1810 and therefore must have read this anecdote.⟩

It was very late before we reached the seat of Sir John Dalrymple, who, certainly with some reason,[a] was not in very good humour. Our conversation was not brilliant. We supped, and went to bed in ancient rooms, which would have better suited the climate of Italy in summer, than that of Scotland in the month of November.

I recollect no conversation of the next day, worth preserving, except one saying of Dr. Johnson, which will be a valuable text for many decent old dowagers, and other good company, in various circles,[b] to descant upon.—He said, ' I am sorry I have not learnt to play at cards. It is very useful in life : it generates kindness, and consolidates society [1].'—He certainly could not mean deep play.

My friend and I thought we should be more comfortable at the inn † at Blackshiels [c], two miles farther on. We therefore went thither in the evening, and he was very entertaining ; but I have preserved nothing but the pleasing remembrance, and his verses on George the Second and Cibber [2], and his epitaph on Parnell [3], which he was then so good as to dictate to me. We breakfasted together next morning, and then the coach came, and took him up. He had, as one of his companions in it, as far as Newcastle, the worthy and ingenious Dr. Hope [4], botanical professor at Edinburgh. Both Dr. Johnson and he used to speak of their good fortune in thus accidentally meeting ; for they had much instructive conversation, which is always a most valuable enjoyment, and, when found where it is not expected, is peculiarly relished.

I have now completed my account of our Tour to the Hebrides. I have brought Dr. Johnson down to Scotland, and seen him into the coach which in a few hours carried him back into England.

[a] reason 1, 2, 3.   [b] circles, 1, 2: circles 3.   [c] Blackshields 3.

[1] Dr. A. Carlyle (*Auto.*, p. 293) says of Robertson and Blair :—' Having been bred at a time when the common people thought to play with cards or dice was a sin, and everybody thought it an indecorum in clergymen, they could neither of them play at golf or bowls, and far less at cards or backgammon, and on that account were very unhappy when from home in friends' houses in the country in rainy weather. As I had set the first example of playing at cards at home with unlocked doors, and so relieved the clergy from ridicule on that side, they both learned to play at whist after they were sixty.' See *ante*, iii. 23.

† ⟨See App. D, p. 576.⟩
[2] See *ante*, i. 149, and v. 350.
[3] See *ante*, iv. 54.
[4] ⟨Dr. John Hope, 1725–86; see *D.N.B.*⟩

He said to me often, that the time he spent in this Tour was the pleasantest part of his life [1], and asked me if I would lose the recollection of it for five hundred pounds. I answered I would not; and he applauded my setting such a value on an accession of new images in my mind [2].

Had it not been for me, I am persuaded Dr. Johnson never would have undertaken such a journey; and I must be allowed to assume some merit from having been the cause that our language has been enriched with such a book as that which he published on his return; a book which I never read but with the utmost admiration, as I had such opportunities of knowing from what very meagre materials it was composed.

But my praise may be supposed partial; and therefore I shall insert two testimonies, not liable to that objection, both written by gentlemen of Scotland, to whose opinions I am confident the highest respect will be paid, Lord Hailes [3], and Mr. Dempster [4].

---

[1] He wrote to Boswell on Nov. 16, 1776 (*ante*, iii. 93) :—' The expedition to the Hebrides was the most pleasant journey that I ever made.' In his *Diary* he recorded on Jan. 9, 1774 :—' In the Autumn I took a journey to the Hebrides, but my mind was not free from perturbation.' *Pr. and Med.* ¶ 106. ⟨Dr. Hill was enabled to print the following letter (*Letters*, No. 342), by the courtesy of Mr. M. M. Holloway. He reproduced it in facsimile in *Footsteps of Johnson*, 1890. It is now, 1964, in the Hyde collection, Somerville, New Jersey.⟩
' DEAR SIR
' When I was at Edinburgh I had a letter from you, telling me that in answer to some enquiry you were informed that I was in the Sky. I was then I suppose in the western Islands of Scotland; I set out on the northern expedition August 6. and came back to Fleet-Street, November 26. I have seen a new region.
' I have been upon seven of the Islands, and probably should have visited many more, had we not begun our Journey so late in the year, that the stormy weather came upon us, and the storms have I believe for about five months hardly any intermission.
' Your Letter told me that you were better. When you write do not forget to confirm that account. I had very little ill health while I was on the journey, and bore rain and wind tolerably well. I had a cold and deafness only for a few days, and those days I passed at a good house. I have traversed the east coast of Scotland from south to north from Edinburgh to Inverness, and the west coast from north to south, from the Highland[s] to Glasgow, and am come back as I went,
' Sir
' Your affectionate humble servant
' SAM. JOHNSON.'
' Jan. 15. 1774.
' To the Reverend Dr. Taylor
' in Ashbourn
' Derbyshire. '

[2] Johnson speaking of this tour on April 10, 1783, said :—' I got an acquisition of more ideas by it than by any thing that I remember.' *Ante*, iv. 199.

[3] See *ante*, v. 48. ⟨Boswell put into Johnson's hands a copy of *Western Islands* annotated by Lord Hailes and Sir Alexander Dick. Boswell's *Letters*, No. 168, i. 256.⟩

[4] See *ante*, i. 408, 443, note 2, ⟨549,⟩ and ii. 303.

⟨*Monday* 6 *February* 1775⟩

'*To James Boswell, Esq.*

' Sir,

' I have received much pleasure and much instruction, from perusing " The Journey " to the Hebrides.

' I admire the elegance and variety of description, and the lively picture of men and manners. I always approve of the moral, often of the political, reflections. I love the benevolence of the authour.

' They who search for faults, may possibly find them in this, as well as in every other work of literature.

' For example, the friends of the old family say that *the æra of planting* is placed too late, at the Union of the two kingdoms [1]. I am known to be no friend of the old family; yet I would place the æra of planting at the Restoration; after the murder of Charles I. had been expiated in the anarchy which succeeded it.

' Before the Restoration, few trees were planted, unless by the monastick drones: their successors, (and worthy patriots they were,) the barons, first cut down the trees, and then sold the estates. The gentleman [a] at St. Andrews, who said that there were but two trees in Fife [2], ought to have added, that the elms of Balmerino [3] were sold within these twenty years, to make pumps for the fire-engines.

' In J. Major *de Gestis Scotorum*, L. i. C. 2. last edition, there is a singular passage:

' " Davidi Cranstoneo conterraneo, dum de prima theologiæ licentia foret, duo ei consocii et familiares, et mei cum eo in artibus auditores, scilicet Jacobus Almain Senonensis, et Petrus Bruxcellensis, Prædicatoris [b] ordinis, in Sorbonæ curia die Sorbonico commilitonibus [c] suis publice objecerunt, *quod pane avenaceo plebeii* [d] *Scoti*, sicut a quodam religioso intellexerant, *vescebantur, ut virum, quem cholericum noverant, honestis salibus tentarent, qui hoc inficiari tanquam patriæ dedecus nisus est.*"

' Pray introduce our countryman, Mr. Licentiate David Cranston, to the acquaintance of Mr. Johnson.

' The syllogism seems to have been this:

' They who feed on oatmeal are barbarians;
But the Scots feed on oatmeal:
Ergo—

[a] gentleman 1, 2: gentlemen 3.
[b] Prædicatorii *orig.*
[c] coram commilitonibus *orig.*
[d] plebei *orig.*

[1] ' It may be doubted whether before the Union any man [Lowlander *in the second impression*] between Edinburgh and England had ever set a tree.' Johnson's *Western Isl.*, p. 9.
[2] See *ante*, v. 69.
[3] Lord Balmerino's estate was forfeited to the Crown on his conviction for high treason in 1746 (*ante*, i. 180).

⟨*Thursday* 16 *February* 1775⟩

The licentiate denied the *minor*.

'I am, sir,
'Your most obedient servant,
'DAV. DALRYMPLE.'

Newhailes, 6th Feb. 1775.

'To JAMES BOSWELL, *Esq. Edinburgh*.

Dunnichen, 16th February, 1775.

'My dear Boswell,
'I cannot omit a moment to return you my best thanks for the entertainment you have furnished me, my family, and guests, by the perusal of Dr. Johnson's " Journey to the Western Islands ; "—and now for my sentiments of it.—I was well entertained. His descriptions are accurate and vivid. He carried me on the Tour along with him. I am pleased with the justice he has done to your humour and vivacity. " The noise of the wind being all its own," is a *bon-mot*, that it would have been a pity to have omitted, and a robbery not to have ascribed to its author [1].

'There is nothing in the book, from beginning to end, that a Scotchman need to take amiss [2]. What he says of the country is true, and his observations on the people are what must naturally occur to a sensible, observing, and reflecting inhabitant of a *convenient* Metropolis, where a man on thirty pounds a year may be better accommodated with all the little wants of life, than *Col* or *Sir Allan*. He reasons candidly about the *second sight ;* but I wish he had enquired more, before he ventured to say he even doubted of the possibility of such an unusual and useless deviation from all the known laws of nature [3]. The notion of the second sight I consider as a remnant of superstitious ignorance and credulity, which a philosopher will set down as such, till the contrary is clearly proved, and then it will be classed among the other certain, though unaccountable, parts of our nature, like dreams [4], and—I do not know what.

'In regard to the language, it has the merit of being all his own.

[1] 'I know not that I ever heard the wind so loud in any other place ; and Mr. Boswell observed, that its noise was all its own, for there were no trees to increase it.' Johnson's *Western Isl.*, p. 113. See *ante*, v. 304.
[2] See *ante*, ii. 300.
[3] 'Strong reasons for incredulity will readily occur. This faculty of seeing things out of sight is local, and commonly useless. It is a breach of the common order of things, without any visible reason or perceptible benefit.' Johnson's *Western Isl.*, p. 99.
[4] 'To the confidence of these objections it may be replied, . . that the *Second Sight* is only wonderful because it is rare, for, considered in itself, it involves no more difficulty than dreams.' *Ib.*

⟨*Thursday* 16 *February* 1775⟩

Many words of foreign extraction are used, where, I believe, common ones would do as well, especially on familiar occasions. Yet I believe he could not express himself so forcibly in any other stile. I am charmed with his researches concerning the Erse language, and the antiquity of their manuscripts. I am quite convinced; and I shall rank *Ossian*, and his *Fingals* and *Oscars*, amongst the Nursery Tales, not the true history of our country, in all time to come.

'Upon the whole, the book cannot displease, for it has no pretensions. The author neither says he is a Geographer, nor [a] an Antiquarian, nor very learned in the History of Scotland, nor a Naturalist, nor a Fossilist [1]. The manners of the people, and the face of the country, are all he attempts to describe, or seems to have thought of. Much were it to be wished, that they who have travelled into more remote, and of course more curious, regions, had all possessed his good sense. Of the state of learning, his observations on Glasgow university [2] shew he has formed a very sound judgement. He understands our climate too, and he has accurately observed the changes, however slow and imperceptible to us, which Scotland has undergone, in consequence of the blessings of liberty and internal peace. I could have drawn my pen through the story of the old woman at St. Andrews, being the only silly thing in the book [3]. He has taken the opportunity of ingrafting into the work several good observations, which I dare say he had made upon men and things, before he set foot on Scotch ground, by which it is considerably enriched [4]. A long journey, like a tall May-pole, though not very beautiful itself, yet is pretty enough, when ornamented with flowers and garlands: it furnishes a sort of cloak-pins for hanging the furniture of your mind upon; and whoever sets out upon a journey, without furnishing his mind previously with much study and useful knowledge, erects a May-pole in December, and puts up very useless cloak-pins [5].

'I hope the book will induce many of his countrymen to make the same jaunt, and help to intermix the more liberal part of them still more with us, and perhaps abate somewhat of that virulent antipathy which many of them entertain against the Scotch; who certainly would never have

[a] nor 1: not 2, 3.

[1] The fossilist of last century is the geologist of this. Neither term is in Johnson's *Dictionary*, but Johnson in his *Journey* (p. 44) speaks of 'Mr. Janes the fossilist.'

[2] *Ib*. p. 145.

[3] *Ib*. p. 8. I do not see anything silly in the story. It is however better told in a letter to Mrs. Thrale. *Letters*, No. 321.

[4] Mr. Orme, one of the ablest historians of this age, is of the same opinion. He said to me, 'There are in that book thoughts, which, by long revolution in the great mind of Johnson, have been formed and polished —like pebbles rolled in the ocean!' BOSWELL, ed. 1. See *ante*, ii. 300, and iii. 284.

[5] See *ante*, iii. 301.

⟨*Thursday* 16 *February* 1775⟩ 409

formed those *combinations* [1] which he takes notice of, more than their ancestors, had they not been necessary for their mutual safety, at least for their success, in a country where they are treated as foreigners. They would find us not deficient, at least in point of hospitality, and they would be ashamed ever after to abuse us in the mass.

' So much for the Tour.—I have now, for the first time in my life, passed a winter in the country ; and never did three months roll on with more swiftness and satisfaction. I used not only to wonder at, but pity, those whose lot condemned them to winter any where but in either of the capitals. But every place has its charms to a cheerful mind. I am busy planting and taking measures for opening the summer campaign in farming ; and I find I have an excellent resource, when revolutions in politicks perhaps, and revolutions of the sun for certain, will make it decent for me to retreat behind the ranks of the more forward in life.

' I am glad to hear the last was a very busy week with you. I see you as counsel in some causes which must have opened a charming field for your humorous [a] vein. As it is more uncommon, so I verily believe it is more useful than the more serious exercise of reason ; and, to a man who is to appear in publick, more eclat is to be gained, sometimes more money too, by a *bon-mot*, than a learned speech. It is the fund of natural humour which Lord North possesses, that makes him so much a favourite [b] of the house, and so able, because so amiable, a leader of a party [2].

' I have now finished *my* Tour of *Seven Pages*. In what remains, I beg leave to offer my compliments, and those of *ma tres chere femme*, to you and Mrs. Boswell. Pray unbend the busy brow, and frolick a little in a letter to,
　　　　　　　　　　' My dear Boswell,
　　　　　　　　　　　　' Your affectionate friend,
　　　　　　　　　　　　　　　　' GEORGE DEMPSTER [3].'

I shall also present the publick with a correspondence with the Laird of Rasay, concerning a passage in the *Journey to the*

[a] humourous 3.　　　　　　[b] a favourite 1, 2 : the favourite 3.

[1] Johnson (*Western Isl.*, p. 146) mentions ' a national combination so invidious, that their friends cannot defend it.' See *ante*, ii. 307, 311.
[2] See *ante*, v. 269, note 1. ⟨See also Wraxall's *Mem.*, 1884, i. 364.⟩
[3] Every reader will, I am sure, join with me in warm admiration of the truly patriotick writer of this letter. I know not which most to applaud,—

that good sense and liberality of mind, which could see and admit the defects of his native country, to which no man is a more zealous friend ;— or that candour, which induced him to give just praise to the minister whom he honestly and strenuously opposed. BOSWELL, ed. 1. ⟨For Dempster see App. D, p. 576.⟩

⟨*Monday* 10 *April* 1775⟩
Western Islands, which shews Dr. Johnson in a very amiable light.

To JAMES BOSWELL, *Esq.*

'*Dear Sir*, Rasay, April 10th, 1775.

' I take this occasion of returning you my most hearty thanks for the civilities shown to my daughter by you and Mrs. Boswell. Yet, though she has informed me that I am under this obligation, I should very probably have deferred troubling you with making my acknowledgments at present, if I had not seen Doctor [a] Johnson's " Journey to the Western Isles," in which he has been pleased to make a very friendly mention of my family, for which I am surely obliged to him, as being more than an equivalent for the reception you and he met with. Yet there is one paragraph I should have been glad he had omitted, which I am sure was owing to misinformation ; that is, that I had acknowledged M'Leod to be my chief, though my ancestors disputed the pre-eminence for a long tract of time.

' I never had occasion to enter seriously on this argument with the present laird or his grandfather, nor could I have any temptation to such a renunciation from either of them. I acknowledge, the benefit of being chief of a clan is in our days of very little significancy, and to trace out the progress of this honour to the founder of a family, of any standing, would perhaps be a matter of some difficulty.

' The true state of the present case is this : the M'Leod family consists of two different branches ; the M'Leods of Lewis, of which I am descended, and the M'Leods of Harris. And though the former have lost a very extensive estate by forfeiture in king James the sixth's time, there are still several respectable families of it existing, who would justly blame me for such an unmeaning cession, when they all acknowledge me head of that family ; which though in fact it be but an ideal point of honour, is not hitherto so far disregarded in our country, but it would determine some of my friends to look on me as a much smaller man than either they or myself judge me at present to be. I will, therefore, ask it as a favour of you to acquaint the Doctor with the difficulty he has brought me to. In travelling among rival clans, such a silly tale as this might easily be whispered into the ear of a passing stranger ; but as it has no foundation in fact, I hope the Doctor will be so good as to take his own way in undeceiving the publick, I principally mean my friends and connections, who will be first angry at me, and next sorry to find such an instance of my littleness recorded in a book which has a very fair chance of being much read. I expect you will let me know what he will write you in return, and we here beg to

[a] Doctor 1, 2 : Dr. 3.

⟨*Monday* 8 *May* 1775⟩

make offer to you and Mrs. Boswell of our most respectful compliments. I am,
'Dear sir,
'Your most obedient humble servant,
'JOHN M'LEOD.'
TO THE LAIRD OF RASAY.

London, May 8, 1775.
'*Dear Sir*,
'THE day before yesterday I had the honour to receive your letter, and I immediately communicated it to Dr. Johnson. He said he loved your spirit, and was exceedingly sorry that he had been the cause of the smallest uneasiness to you. There is not a more candid man in the world than he is, when properly addressed, as you will see from his letter to you, which I now enclose. He has allowed me to take a copy of it, and he says you may read it to your clan, or publish it if you please. Be assured, sir, that I shall take care of what he has entrusted to me, which is to have an acknowledgement of his errour inserted in the Edinburgh newspapers. You will, I dare say, be fully satisfied with Dr. Johnson's behaviour. He is desirous to know that you are; and therefore when you have read his acknowledgement in the papers, I beg you may write to me; and if you choose it, I am persuaded a letter from you to the Doctor also will be taken kind. I shall be at Edinburgh the week after next.

'Any civilities which my wife and I had it [a] in our power to shew to your daughter, Miss M'Leod [1], were due to her own merit, and were well repaid by her agreeable company. But I am sure I should be a very unworthy man if I did not wish to shew a grateful sense of the hospitable and genteel manner in which you were pleased to treat me. Be assured, my dear sir, that I shall never forget your goodness, and the happy hours which I spent in Rasay.

'You and Dr. M'Leod were both so obliging as to promise me an account in writing, of all the particulars which each of you remember, concerning the transactions of 1745–6. Pray do not forget this, and be as minute and full as you can; put down every thing; I have a great curiosity to know as much as I can, authentically.

'I beg that you may present my best respects to Lady Rasay, my compliments to your young family, and to Dr. M'Leod; and my hearty good wishes to Malcolm, with whom I hope again to shake hands cordially. I have the honour to be,
'Dear sir,
'Your obliged and faithful humble servant,
'JAMES BOSWELL.'

[a] had it 1, 2 : had 3.   [1] ⟨See App. D, p. 577.⟩

⟨*Saturday* 6 *May* 1775⟩

ADVERTISEMENT, written by Dr. Johnson, and inserted by his desire in the Edinburgh newspapers :—Referred to in the foregoing letter [1].

' *THE authour of the* Journey to the Western Islands, *having related that the M'Leods of Rasay acknowledge the chieftainship or superiority of the M'Leods of Sky, finds that he has been misinformed or mistaken. He means in a future edition to correct his errour* [2], *and wishes to be told of more, if more have been discovered.*'

Dr. Johnson's letter was as follows :

TO THE LAIRD OF RASAY.

Dear Sir,
' MR. Boswell has this day shewn me a letter, in which you complain of a passage in " the Journey to the Hebrides." My meaning is mistaken. I did not intend to say that you had personally made any cession of the rights of your house, or any acknowledgement of the superiority of M'Leod of Dunvegan. I only designed to express what I thought generally admitted,—that the house of Rasay allowed the superiority of the house of Dunvegan. Even this I now find to be erroneous, and will therefore omit or retract it in the next edition.

' Though what I had said had been true, if it had been disagreeable to you, I should have wished it unsaid ; for it is not my business to adjust precedence. As it is mistaken, I find myself disposed to correct it [a], both by my respect for you, and my reverence for truth.

' As I know not when the book will be reprinted, I have desired Mr.

[a] correct it 1, 2 : correct 3.

[1] The original MS. is now in my possession. BOSWELL, ed. 1.

[2] The passage that gave offence was as follows :—' Mr. Macleod is the proprietor of the islands of Raasay, Rona, and Fladda, and possesses an extensive district in Sky. The estate has not, during four hundred years, gained or lost a single acre. He acknowledges Macleod of Dunvegan as his chief, though his ancestors have formerly disputed the pre-eminence.' First edition, p. 132. ⟨Ed. 1924, p. 53.⟩ The second edition was not published till the year after Johnson's death. In it the passage remains unchanged. To it the following note was prefixed : ' Strand, Oct. 26, 1785. Since this Work was printed off, the Publisher having been informed that the Author, some years ago, had promised the Laird of Rasay, to correct, in a future edition, a passage concerning him, . . . thinks it a justice due to that Gentleman to insert here the Advertisement relative to this matter, which was published, by Dr. Johnson's desire, in the Edinburgh Newspapers in the year 1775, and which has been lately reprinted in Mr. Boswell's *Tour to the Hebrides.*' (It is not unlikely that the publication of Boswell's *Tour* occasioned a fresh demand for Johnson's *Journey*.) In later editions all the words after ' a single acre ' are silently struck out. Johnson's *Works*, ix. 55. See *ante*, ii. 382.

Boswell to anticipate the correction in the Edinburgh papers. This is all that can be done.

' I hope I may now venture to desire that my compliments may be made, and my gratitude expressed, to Lady Rasay, Mr. Malcolm M'Leod, Mr. Donald M'Queen, and all the gentlemen and all the ladies whom I saw in the island of Rasay ; a place which I remember with too much pleasure and too much kindness, not to be sorry that my ignorance, or hasty persuasion, should, for a single moment, have violated its tranquillity.

' I beg you all to forgive an undesigned and involuntary injury, and to consider me as,
                    ' Sir, your most obliged,
                        ' And most humble servant,
                                ' SAM. JOHNSON [1].'
London, May 6, 1775.

It would be improper for me to boast of my own labours ; but I cannot refrain from publishing such praise as I received from such a man as Sir William Forbes, of Pitsligo, after the perusal of the original manuscript of my Journal [2].

To JAMES BOSWELL, *Esq.*

Edinburgh, March 7, 1777.
' *My dear Sir*,
' I ought to have thanked you sooner, for your very obliging letter, and for the singular confidence you are pleased to place in me, when you trust me with such a curious and valuable deposite as the papers you have sent me [3]. Be assured,[a] I have a due sense of this favour, and shall

[a] assured, 1, 2: assured 3.

[1] Rasay was highly gratified, and afterwards visited and dined with Dr. Johnson, at his house in London. BOSWELL, ed. 1.

Johnson wrote to Mrs. Thrale, May 12, 1775:—' I have offended, and, what is stranger, have justly offended the Nation of Rasay. If they could come hither, they would be as fierce as the Americans. Rasay has written to Boswel an account of the injury done him, by representing his House as subordinate to that of Dunvegan. Boswel has his letter and, I believe, copied my answer. I have appeased him, if a degraded Chief can possibly be appeased, but it will be thirteen days, days of resentment and discontent, before my recantation can reach him. Many a dirk will imagination, during that interval fix in my heart. I really question if at this time my life would not be in danger, if distance did not secure it. Boswel will find his way to Streatham before he goes, and will detail this great affair.' *Letters*, No. 390.

[2] In like manner he communicated to Sir William Forbes part of his journal from which he made the *Life of Johnson*. *Ante*, iii. 208.

[3] In justice both to Sir William Forbes and myself, it is proper to mention, that the papers which were submitted to his perusal contained only an account of our Tour from the time that Dr. Johnson and I set

faithfully and carefully return them to you. You may rely that I shall neither copy any part, nor permit the papers to be seen.

'They contain a curious picture of society, and form a journal on the most instructive plan that can possibly be thought of; for I am not sure that an ordinary observer would become so well acquainted either with Dr. Johnson, or with the manners of the Hebrides, by a personal intercourse, as by a perusal of your Journal.

'I am very truly,
'Dear Sir,
'Your most obedient,
'And affectionate humble servant,
'WILLIAM FORBES.'

When I consider how many of the persons mentioned in this Tour are now gone to 'that undiscovered country, from whose bourne no traveller returns [1],' I feel an impression at once awful and tender.—*Requiescant in pace!*

It may be objected by some persons, as it has been by one of my friends, that he who has the power of thus exhibiting an exact transcript of conversations is not a desirable member of society. I repeat the answer which I made to that friend :—'Few, very few, need be afraid that their sayings will be recorded. Can it be imagined that I would take the trouble to gather what grows on every hedge, because I have collected such fruits as the *Nonpareil* and the BON CHRETIEN [2]?

On the other hand, how useful is such a faculty, if well exercised! To it we owe all those interesting apothegms and *memorabilia* of the ancients, which Plutarch, Xenophon, and Valerius Maximus, have transmitted to us. To it we owe all those instructive and entertaining collections which the French have made under the title of *Ana*, affixed to some celebrated name. To it we owe the *Table-Talk* of Selden [3], the *Conversation* between Ben Jonson and Drummond of Hawthornden [4], Spence's

out from Edinburgh (p. [58]), and consequently did not contain the elogium on Sir William Forbes, (p. [24]), which he never saw till this book appeared in print; nor did he even know, when he wrote the above letter, that this Journal was to be published. BOSWELL. ⟨This note was added in the second edition. See App. D, p. 577.⟩

[1] *Hamlet*, act iii. sc. 1.
[2] Both *Nonpareil* and *Bon Chretien* are in Johnson's *Dictionary* (1755); *Nonpareil* is defined as *a kind of apple*, and *Bon Chretien* as *a species of pear*. ⟨See Boswell's *Letters*, ii. 438.⟩
[3] See *ante*, v. 311.
[4] ⟨See *ante*, v. 402, note 3.⟩

Anecdotes of Pope[1], and other valuable remains in our own language. How delighted should we have been, if thus introduced into the company of Shakspeare and of Dryden[2], of whom we know scarcely any thing but their admirable writings! What pleasure would it have given us, to have known their petty habits, their characteristick manners, their modes of composition, and their genuine opinion of preceding writers and of their contemporaries! All these are now irrecoverably lost. —Considering how many of the strongest and most brilliant effusions of exalted intellect must have perished, how much is it to be regretted that all men of distinguished wisdom and wit have not been attended by friends, of taste enough to relish, and abilities enough to register, their conversation!

> *Vixere fortes ante Agamemnona*
> *Multi, sed omnes illacrymabiles*
> *Urgentur, ignotique longa*
> *Nocte, carent quia vate sacro*[3].

They whose inferiour exertions are recorded, as serving to explain or illustrate the sayings of such men, may be proud of being thus associated, and of their names being transmitted to posterity, by being appended to an illustrious character.

Before I conclude, I think it proper to say, that I have suppressed[4] every thing which I thought could *really* hurt any one

[1] See *ante*, iv. 9, ⟨63, and 482⟩.

[2] 'Dryden's contemporaries, however they reverenced his genius, left his life unwritten; and nothing therefore can be known beyond what casual mention and uncertain tradition have supplied.' Johnson's *Life of Dryden*, 1. See *ante*, iii. 71.

[3] 'Before great Agamemnon reign'd
  Reign'd kings as great as he, and brave,
  Whose huge ambition's now contain'd
  In the small compass of a grave;
  In endless night they sleep, unwept, unknown,
  No bard had they to make all time their own.'
  FRANCIS. Horace, *Odes*, iv. 9. 25.

[4] Having found, on a revision of the first edition of this work, that, notwithstanding my best care, a few observations had escaped me, which arose from the instant impression, the publication of which might perhaps be considered as passing the bounds of a strict decorum, I immediately ordered that they should be omitted in the subsequent editions. I was pleased to find that they did not amount in the whole to a page. If any of the same kind are yet left, it is owing to inadvertence alone, no man being more unwilling to give pain to others than I am.

A contemptible scribbler, of whom I have learned no more than that, after having disgraced and deserted the clerical character, he picks up in London a scanty livelihood by now living. Vanity and self-conceit indeed may sometimes suffer. With respect to what *is* related, I considered it my duty to 'extenuate nothing, nor set down aught in malice [1];' and with those lighter strokes of Dr. Johnson's satire, proceeding from a warmth and quickness of imagination, not from any malevolence of heart, and which, on account of their excellence, could not be omitted, I trust that they who are the subject of them have good sense and good temper enough not to be displeased.

I have only to add, that I shall ever reflect with great pleasure on a Tour, which has been the means of preserving so much of the enlightened and instructive conversation of one whose virtues will, I hope, ever be an object of imitation, and whose powers of mind were so extraordinary, that ages may revolve before such a man shall again appear.

scurrilous lampoons under a feigned name, has impudently and falsely asserted that the passages omitted were *defamatory*, and that the omission was not voluntary, but compulsory. The last insinuation I took the trouble publickly to disprove; yet, like one of Pope's dunces, he persevered in 'the lie o'erthrown.' [*Prologue to the Satires*, l. 350.] As to the charge of defamation, there is an obvious and certain mode of refuting it. Any person who thinks it worth while to compare one edition with the other, will find that the passages omitted were not in the least degree of that nature, but exactly such as I have represented them in the former part of this note, the hasty effusion of momentary feelings, which the delicacy of politeness should have suppressed. BOSWELL.

In the second edition this note ended at the first paragraph, the latter part being added in the third. For the 'few observations omitted' see *ante*, v. pp. 148, 381, 388. The 'contemptible scribbler' was, I believe, John Wolcot, better known by his assumed name of Peter Pindar. He had been a clergyman. In his *Epistle to Boswell* (*Works*, 1794, i. 320), he says in reference to the passages about Sir A. Macdonald (afterwards Lord Macdonald):— 'A letter of severe remonstrance was sent to Mr. B., who, in consequence, omitted, in the second edition of his *Journal*, what is so generally pleasing to the public, viz., the scandalous passages relative to this nobleman.' It was in a letter to the *Gent. Mag.* 1786, i. 285, that Boswell 'publickly disproved the insinuation' made 'in a late scurrilous publication' that these passages 'were omitted . . . in consequence of a letter from his lordship.' 'Nor was any application,' he continues, 'made to me by the nobleman alluded to, at any time, to make any alteration in my *Journal*.' ⟨For this letter and its consequences see App. D, p. 578.⟩

[1]   'Nothing extenuate,
   Nor set down aught in malice.'
            Othello, act v. sc. 2.

APPENDIX

No. I.

In justice to the ingenious DR. BLACKLOCK, *I publish the following letter from him, relative to a passage in p.* [47] [1].

To JAMES BOSWELL, ESQ.

'DEAR SIR,

HAVING lately had the pleasure of reading your account of the journey which you took with Dr. Samuel Johnson to the Western Isles, I take the liberty of transmitting my ideas of the conversation which happened between the doctor and myself concerning Lexicography and Poetry, which, as it is a little different from the delineation exhibited in the former edition of your Journal, cannot, I hope, be unacceptable; particularly since I have been informed that a second edition of that work is now in contemplation, if not in execution : and I am still more strongly tempted to encourage that hope, from considering that, if every one concerned in the conversations related, were to send you what they can recollect of these colloquial entertainments, many curious and interesting particulars might be recovered, which the most assiduous attention could not observe, nor the most tenacious memory retain. A little reflection, sir, will convince you, that there is not an axiom in Euclid more intuitive nor more evident than the doctor's assertion that poetry was of much easier execution than lexicography. Any mind therefore endowed with common sense, must have been extremely absent from itself, if it discovered the least astonishment from hearing that a poem might be written with much more facility than the same quantity of a dictionary.

The real cause of my surprise was,[a] what appeared to me much more paradoxical, that he could write a sheet of dictionary *with as much pleasure* as a sheet of poetry. He acknowledged, indeed, that the latter was much easier than the former. For in the one case, books and a desk were requisite; in the other, you might compose when lying in bed, or walking in the fields, &c. He did not, however, descend to explain, nor to this moment can I comprehend, how the labours of a

[a] was, 2: was 3.

[1] ⟨This Appendix was added in the second edition, which reads after 'him', 'which did not come to my hands till this edition was nearly printed off'. Blacklock's letter was forwarded to Boswell by Forbes, 6 Dec. 1785. *Fettercairn Catal.*, Nos. 355, 1116, 1331.⟩

mere Philologist, in the most refined sense of that term, could give equal pleasure with the exercise of a mind replete with elevated conceptions and pathetic ideas, while taste, fancy, and intellect were deeply enamoured of nature, and in full exertion. You may likewise, perhaps, remember, that when I complained of the ground which Scepticism in religion and morals was continually gaining, it did not appear to be on my own account, as my private opinions upon these important subjects had long been inflexibly determined. What I then deplored, and still deplore, was the unhappy influence which that gloomy hesitation had, not only upon particular characters, but even upon life in general; as being equally the bane of action in our present state, and of such consolations as we might derive from the hopes of a future.

I have the pleasure of remaining with sincere esteem and respect,
Dear Sir,
Your most obedient humble servant,
THOMAS BLACKLOCK.

Edinburgh, Nov. 12, 1785.

I am very happy to find that Dr. Blacklock's apparent uneasiness on the subject of Scepticism was not on his own account, (as I supposed,) but from a benevolent concern for the happiness of mankind. With respect, however, to the question concerning poetry, and composing a dictionary, I am confident that my state of Dr. Johnson's position is accurate. One may misconceive the motive by which a person is induced to discuss a particular topick (as in the case of Dr. Blacklock's speaking of Scepticism); but an assertion, like that made by Dr. Johnson, cannot be easily mistaken. And indeed it seems not very probable, that he who so pathetically laments the *drudgery*[1] to which the unhappy lexicographer is doomed, and is known to have written his splendid imitation of Juvenal with astonishing rapidity[2], should have had 'as much pleasure in writing a sheet of a dictionary as a sheet of poetry[3].' Nor can I concur with

---

[1] See *ante*, i. 189, note 2, 296, 297; and Johnson's *Preface to Dictionary*.

[2] Of his two imitations Boswell means *The Vanity of Human Wishes*, of which one hundred lines were written in a day. *Ante*, i. 192, and ii. 15.

[3] Johnson, it should seem, did not allow that there was any pleasure in writing poetry. 'It has been said, there is pleasure in writing, particularly in writing verses. I allow you may have pleasure from writing, after it is over, if you have written well; but you don't go willingly to it again.' *Ante*, iv. 219. What Johnson always sought was to occupy the mind sufficiently. So long

Appendix. No. II

the ingenious writer of the foregoing letter, in thinking it an axiom as evident as any in Euclid, that 'poetry is of easier execution than lexicography.' I have no doubt that Bailey [1], and the 'mighty blunderbluss of law [2],' Jacob, wrote ten pages of their respective Dictionaries with more ease than they could have written five pages of poetry.

If this book should again be reprinted, I shall with the utmost readiness correct any errours I may have committed, in stating conversations, provided it can be clearly shewn to me that I have been inaccurate. But I am slow to believe, (as I have elsewhere observed, [3]) that any man's memory, at the distance of several years, can preserve facts or sayings with such fidelity as may be done by writing them down when they are recent: and I beg it may be remembered, that it is not upon *memory*, but upon what was *written at the time*, that the authenticity of my Journal rests.

No. II.

VERSES written by Sir Alexander (now Lord) Macdonald; addressed and presented to Dr. Johnson, at Armidale in the Isle of Sky [4].

> *Viator, o qui nostra per æquora*
> *Visurus agros Skiaticos venis,*
>   *En te salutantes tributim*
>   *Undique conglomerantur oris* [a]
>
> *Donaldiani,—quotquot in insulis*
> *Compescit arctis limitibus mare ;*
>   *Alitque jamdudum, ac alendos*
>   *Piscibus indigenas fovebit.*

[a] oris 2 : oris. 3.

---

as that was done, that labour would, I believe, seem to him the pleasanter which required the less thought.

[1] Nathan Bailey first published his *English Dictionary* in 1721.

[2] 'W⟨oolsto⟩n, the scourge of Scripture, mark with awe ! And mighty J⟨aco⟩b, Blunderbus of Law !' *The Dunciad*, first ed., bk. iii. l. 156. Giles Jacob first published his *Law Dictionary* in 1729.

[3] *Ante*, v. 393.

[4] ⟨This appendix first appeared in

the second edition, with this introduction :—

'The following verses, written by Sir Alexander (now Lord) Macdonald, and addressed and presented to Dr. Johnson, at Armidale, in the Isle of Sky, should have appeared in the proper place, if the authour of this Journal had been possessed of them; but this edition was almost printed off, when he was accidentally furnished with a copy by a friend.' Carruthers printed in his edition of the *Tour* (p. 113 note), from a copy given to

Appendix. No. II

Ciere fluctus siste, Procelliger,
Nec tu laborans perge, precor, ratis,
Ne conjugem plangat marita,
  Ne doleat soboles parentem.

Nec te vicissim pœniteat virum
Luxisse ;—vestro scimus ut æstuant
In corde luctantes dolores,
  Cum feriant inopina corpus.

Quidni ! peremptum clade tuentibus
Plus semper illo qui moritur pati
Datur, doloris dum profundos
  Pervia mens aperit recessus.

Valete luctus ;—hinc lacrymabiles
Arcete visus :—ibimus, ibimus
Superbienti qua theatro
  Fingaliæ memorantur aulæ.

Illustris hospes ! mox spatiabere
Qua mens ruinæ ducta meatibus
Gaudebit explorare cœtus,
  Buccina qua cecinit triumphos ;

Audin ? resurgens spirat anhelitu
Dux usitato, suscitat efficax
Poeta manes, ingruitque
  Vi solitâ redivivus horror.

Ahæna quassans tela gravi manu
Sic ibat atrox Ossiani pater :
Quiescat urnâ, stet fidelis
  'Phersonius vigil ad favillam.

him by Sir David Brewster, the following letter of Sir Alexander Macdonald to James Macpherson :
'London, 5th June, 1774.
' Sir,—The annexed congratulatory Ode was written and presented by me to Mr. Samuel Johnson the day of his arriving at my house. I had assembled some of my friends to welcome him when he landed. From my windows he viewed the ocean ; he trembled for the distress of the small boats which were fishing, and likely to be overwhelmed in the gulf—a sight unusual to him, a station frequently experienced by them. I wish my time and my abilities had been such as to have permitted and enabled me to have conducted and placed you on the right hand of Fingal when we trod the hallowed mansions of the hero. A sketch drawn by me is unworthy of your acceptance, whose genius is above my capacity, and unnecessary, as your pencil has already made our every sense of feeling to catch the fire and glow with the warmth of perfection ! I am, with the greatest pride in ranking myself amid your admirers, dear Sir, your most humble servant,
  Alex. Macdonald.
James Macpherson, Esq., London.'
These verses were brought to Boswell's knowledge by their author on 26 Nov. 1785. See App. D, p. 579.〉

Preparing for the Press, in one Volume Quarto,

THE LIFE OF SAMUEL JOHNSON, LL.D.

By *JAMES BOSWELL*, Esq.

MR. Boswell has been collecting materials for this work for more than twenty years, during which he was honoured with the intimate friendship of Dr. Johnson ; to whose memory he is ambitious to erect a literary monument, worthy of so great an authour, and so excellent a man. Dr. Johnson was well informed of his design, and obligingly communicated to him several curious particulars. With these will be interwoven the most authentick accounts that can be obtained from those who knew him best ; many sketches of his conversation on a multiplicity of subjects, with various persons, some of them the most eminent of the age ; a great number of letters from him at different periods, and several original pieces dictated by him to Mr. Boswell, distinguished by that peculiar energy, which marked every emanation of his mind.

Mr. Boswell takes this [1] opportunity of gratefully acknowledging the many valuable communications which he has received to enable him to render his Life of Dr. Johnson more complete. His thanks are particularly due to the Rev. Dr. Adams, the Rev. Dr. Taylor, Sir Joshua Reynolds, Mr. Langton, Dr. Brocklesby, the Rev. Thomas Warton, Mr. Hector of Birmingham, Mrs. Porter, and Miss Seward.

He has already obtained a large collection of Dr. Johnson's letters to his friends, and shall be much obliged for such others as yet remain in private hands ; which he is the more desirous of collecting, as all the letters of that great man, which he has yet seen, are written with peculiar precision and elegance ; and he is confident that the publication of the whole of Dr. Johnson's epistolary correspondence will do him the highest honour.

[1] ⟨This and the next paragraph appear first in the second edition.⟩

APPENDIX A

(Page 80.)

As no one reads Warburton now—I bought the five volumes of his *Divine Legation* in excellent condition, bound in calf, for ten pence—one or two extracts from his writing may be of interest. His Dedication of that work to the Free-Thinkers is as vigorous as it is abusive. It has such passages as the following :—' Low and mean as your buffoonery is, it is yet to the level of the people : ' vol. 1, part 1, 1755, p. xi. ' I have now done with your buffoonery: which, like chewed bullets, is against the law of arms ; and come next to your scurrilities, those stink-pots of your offensive war.' *Ib.* p. xxii. On page xl he returns again to their ' *cold* buffoonery.' In the Appendix to vol. v, 1765, p. 414, he thus wittily replies to Lowth, who had maintained that ' idolatry was punished under the DOMINION of Melchisedec ' (p. 409) :—
' Melchisedec's story is a short one ; he is just brought into the scene to *bless* Abraham in his return from conquest. This promises but ill. Had this *King and Priest of Salem* been brought in *cursing*, it had had a better appearance : for, I think, punishment for opinions, which generally ends in a *Fagot*, always begins with a *curse*. But we may be misled perhaps by a wrong translation. The Hebrew word to *bless*, signifies likewise to *curse*, and, under the management of an intolerant Priest, good things easily run into their contraries. What follows, is his taking *Tythes* from Abraham. Nor will this serve our purpose, unless we interpret these *Tythes* into *Fines for non-conformity* ; and then, by the *blessing*, we can easily understand *absolution*. We have seen much stranger things done with the *Hebrew Verity*. If this be not allowed, I do not see how we can elicite fire and fagot from this adventure ; for I think there is no inseparable connexion between *Tythes* and *Persecution*, but in the ideas of a Quaker.—And so much for *king Melchisedec*. But the learned *Professor*, who has been hardily brought up in the keen Atmosphere of WHOLESOME SEVERITIES, and early taught to distinguish between *de facto* and *de jure*, thought it needless to enquire into *Facts*, when he was secure of the *Right*.'

424 *Appendix B*

This 'keen atmosphere of wholesome severities' reappears by the way in Mason's continuation of Gray's ode *On the Pleasure arising from Vicissitude* :—

> 'That breathes the keen yet wholesome air
> Of rugged Penury.'

And later in the first book of Wordsworth's *Excursion* (ed. 1857, vi. 29) :—

> 'The keen, the wholesome, air of poverty.'

Johnson said of Warburton : ' His abilities gave him an haughty confidence, which he disdained to conceal or mollify ; and his impatience of opposition disposed him to treat his adversaries with such contemptuous superiority as made his readers commonly his enemies, and excited against the advocate the wishes of some who favoured the cause. He seems to have adopted the Roman Emperor's determination, *oderint dum metuant ;* he used no allurements of gentle language, but wished to compel rather than persuade.' Johnson's *Life of Pope*, 184. (The quotation is from Suetonius, *Caligula*, xxx.) See *ante*, ii. 36, and iv. 46.

APPENDIX B

(*Page* 158.)

Johnson's Ode written in Skye was thus translated by Lord Houghton :—

> 'Where constant mist enshrouds the rocks,
> Shattered in earth's primeval shocks,
> And niggard Nature ever mocks
>   The labourer's toil,
> I roam through clans of savage men,
> Untamed by arts, untaught by pen ;
> Or cower within some squalid den
>   O'er reeking soil.
>
> Through paths that halt from stone to stone,
> Amid the din of tongues unknown,
> One image haunts my soul alone,
>   Thine, gentle Thrale !
> Soothes she, I ask, her spouse's care ?
> Does mother-love its charge prepare ?
> Stores she her mind with knowledge rare,
>   Or lively tale ?

Appendix C

Forget me not ! thy faith I claim,
Holding a faith that cannot die,
That fills with thy benignant name
These shores of Sky.'
Hayward's *Piozzi*, 1861, first edition, i. 29.

⟨Miss Cornelia Knight, 1737–1837, also translated the ode, and her version was printed by Carruthers in his edition of Boswell's *Tour to the Hebrides* (1852, pp. 120–1). Mr. R. B. Adam, who owned the holograph manuscript of the Latin ode, reproduced it in facsimile in the catalogue of his collection. *The R. B. Adam Library*, 1929, i, between pp. 115 and 116. It is now, 1964, in the Hyde collection. See also Johnson's *Letters*, No. 333.⟩

APPENDIX C

(*Page* 307.)

Johnson's use of the word *big*, where he says ' I wish thy books were twice as big,' enables me to explain a passage in *The Life of Johnson* (*ante*, iii. 348) which had long puzzled me. Boswell there represents him as saying :—' A man who loses at play, or who runs out his fortune at court, makes his estate less, in hopes of making it bigger.' Boswell adds in a parenthesis :—' I am sure of this word, which was often used by him.' He had been criticized by a writer in the *Gent. Mag.* 1785, lv. pt. ii, p. 968, who, quoting from the text the words ' a *big* book,' says :—' Mr. Boswell has made his friend (as in a few other passages) guilty of a *Scotticism*. An Englishman reads and writes a *large* book, and wears a *great* (not a *big* or *bag*) coat.' When Boswell came to publish *The Life of Johnson*, he took the opportunity to justify himself, though he did not care to refer directly to his anonymous critic. This explanation I discovered too late to insert in the text.

⟨Johnson says, *ante*, i. 471 : ' Don't, Sir, accustom yourself to use big words for little matters.' Cf. *ante*, v. 175, where Boswell draws attention to his use of *large* by italics ; he originally wrote ' great '. Beattie records *big* as a Scotticism in ' *Big-coat*, Great coat '. Beattie's *Scotisms*, 1787, p. 13.⟩

A JOURNEY
INTO
NORTH WALES,
IN
THE YEAR 1774[1].

JULY 5, TUESDAY.

11. a.m. We left Streatham.
Price of 4 horses 2s. a mile.

[1] ⟨Boswell did not know of this diary. He dismisses Johnson's tour in Wales in a paragraph and says : ' it . . . did not give occasion to such a discursive exercise of his mind as our tour to the Hebrides. I do not find that he kept any journal or notes of what he saw there ' (*ante*, ii. 285). The earliest known mention of the diary occurs in a letter, 7 Jan. 1813, of the Rev. Henry White to Dr. Robert Myddelton of Gwaynynog. White writes : ' I mentioned to you when you favoured me with your Company t'other day my anxious desire to inform Mrs. Piozzi of the manuscript of Dr. Samuel Johnson which you saw. Should this Lady be now in your neighbourhood will you do me the great kindness to ask her whether she remembers the Journal of the Year 1774 wch. contains the Doctor's remarks on his tour through N. W. . . . I have not the least doubt of my making what is called a good thing of its publication—but God forbid that I should . . . for the *lucre* of gain commit the High Character of Johnson's pen by the publication of what He might have intended to keep from the Public Eye.' Myddelton on 12 Jan. informed Mrs. Piozzi that he had seen the MS. and wrote : 'Should you be disposed to patronise Mr. White, and encourage the publication . . . Mr. White will be happy in dedicating it to you.' (These letters, which were brought to my notice by Mr. J. L. Clifford, are in the John Rylands Library, Manchester. Henry Gostling White was born in 1769, admitted pensioner at Pembroke College, Cambridge, in 1788, migrated to Clare in 1789, of which he was a Fellow 1792–95 ; he was curate of Barking in 1794.) Mrs. Piozzi met the two gentlemen in the following April and saw the MS. Writing to Queeney, 15 May 1813, she says : ' Did I mention to dear Lady Keith a literary curiosity that was shewn me in Town ? The Journal Doctor Johnson kept of our Tour in Wales ? . . . If the proprietor resolves to print it, he must exchange Peace for Pelf, and so I had the honour to tell him.' (*Bowood MSS*.) White, according to Mrs. Piozzi, ' repeatedly observed he would print it, only it was not sufficiently bulky for publication '. Hayward's *Piozzi*, ii. 177. He never proceeded beyond a resolution and disposed of the MS., which is next heard of in the hands of Richard Duppa (see *D.N.B.*). In a letter to Mrs. Piozzi, which is undated but was probably written in

1. p.m. 1.40 Barnet.†
At night to Dunstable.
On the road I read Tully's Epistles.

6 [JULY].

To Lichfield 83 miles.
To the Swan[1].

7 [JULY].

To Mrs. Porters[2], to the Cathedral. To Mrs. Astons. To Mr. Greens.
Mr. Greens Museum was much admired, and Mr. Newton's China.

8 [JULY].

To Mr. Newton's §. To Mrs. Cobb.
Dr. Darwin's[3].
I went again to Mrs. Aston's. She was sorry to part.

June or July 1816, Duppa says: 'A fragment in the handwriting of Dr. Johnson has lately been put into my hands and I am preparing it for the press'; in this and a second letter, dated 6 Aug. 1816, he puts questions to her about it 'which she alone can answer'. The R. B. Adam Library, iii. 89, 90. The edition was published in October: on the 14th Mrs. Piozzi wrote: 'Johnson's Diary is selling rapidly, though the contents are bien maigre, I must confess. Mr. Duppa has sent me the book, and I perceive has politely suppressed some sarcastic expressions about my family, the Cottons, whom we visited at Combermere (post, v. 434), and at Lleweney.' Hayward's Piozzi, ed. 1, ii. 178–9. Duppa suppressed other passages and his edition is very inaccurate. The diary has here been re-edited from the MS., which is now in the British Museum (Add. MS. 12,070).

Mrs. Thrale also kept a diary during the tour which was edited by A. M. Broadley in his Dr. Johnson and Mrs. Thrale (1910). The original manuscript is now, 1964, owned by Mr. and Mrs. Donald F. Hyde.⟩

† ⟨The travellers stopped at The Mitre and went on to St. Albans, where they were given 'a good cold dinner' by Mr. and Mrs. Ralph Smith, Mr. Thrale's relatives. Broadley, Dr. Johnson and Mrs. Thrale, 1910, p. 158.⟩

[1] ⟨They arrived just before midnight and Johnson said 'how much pleasanter it was travelling by night than by day'. Broadley, op. cit., p. 160.⟩ 'When I went with him [Johnson] to Litchfield, and came down stairs to breakfast at the inn, my dress did not please him, and he made me alter it entirely before he would stir a step with us about the town, saying most satirical things concerning the appearance I made in a riding-habit.' Piozzi's Anec. p. 288: Johns. Misc. i. 339. ⟨The dress that displeased Johnson was, according to Mrs. Thrale's diary, 'a morning nightgown and close cap.' Broadley, op. cit., p. 160.⟩

[2] For Miss Porter, Miss Aston, Mr. Green, Mrs. Cobb, and Mr. Peter Garrick, see ante, ii. 462–473.

§ ⟨Andrew Newton, wine-merchant, and brother of Thomas Newton, bishop of Bristol. See A. L. Reade, Reades of Blackwood Hill, p. 200, n. 1.⟩

[3] Dr. Erasmus Darwin, the physio-

9 [JULY].

Breakfast at Mr Garricks.
Visited Miss Vise [1]. Miss Seward †.
Went to Dr Taylors [2].
I read a little on the road in Tully's Epistles and Martial.

10 [JULY].

Morning at Church. Company at Dinner.

11 [JULY].

At Ilam[3]. At Okeover.
I was less pleased with Ilam than when I saw it first; but my friends were much delighted.

12 [JULY].

At Chatsworth [4]. The water willow, the Cascade, shot out from many spouts. The fountains. The water tree [5]. The smooth floors in the highest rooms. Atlas 15 hands inch and half [6]. Surly's Humours [7]. River running through the park. The porticos on the sides, support two galleries for the first floor.

My friends were not struck with the house. It fell below my ideas of the furniture. The Staircase is in the corner of the house. The Hall in the corner the grandest room, though only a room of passage. On the ground floor only the Chappel, and

---

logist and poet, grandfather of Charles Darwin. ⟨See the *D.N.B.* and Hesketh Pearson, *Dr. Darwin*, 1930. Dr. Darwin's house was in the Cathedral Close. Mrs. Thrale was greatly impressed by his roses. Broadley, *Dr. Johnson and Mrs. Thrale*, p. 162, and Piozzi, *Journey*, i. 278.⟩

[1] ⟨Mary Vyse, 1745–1827, daughter of the Ven. W. Vyse, archdeacon of Salop (*ante*, iii. 124 : she married, 1796, Spencer Madan, bishop of Peterborough. See F. Madan, *The Madan Family*, 1933, p. 136.⟩

† ⟨Mrs. Piozzi noted, ' Dr. Johnson would not suffer me to speak to Miss Seward.' CROKER, 1835.⟩

[2] ⟨At Ashbourne : see *ante*, ii. 473 and 542.⟩

[3] See *ante*, iii. 187 ⟨and Broadley, *Dr. Johnson and Mrs. Thrale*, p. 165⟩.

[4] Johnson wrote on Nov. 27, 1772,

' I was yesterday at Chatsworth. . . . They complimented me with playing the fountains, and opening the cascade. But I am of my friend's opinion, that when one has seen the Ocean, cascades are but little things.' *Letters*, No. 288. ⟨Mrs. Thrale records her opinion : ' Dr. Taylor took us to Chatsworth, where I was pleased with scarcely anything.' Broadley, *op. cit.*, p. 166.⟩

[5] ' A water-work with a concealed spring, which, upon touching, spouted out streams from every bough of a willow tree.' *Piozzi MS*. CROKER, 1835.

[6] A race-horse, which was very handsome and very gentle, and attracted so much of Dr. Johnson's attention, that he said ; ' of all the Duke's possessions, I like Atlas best.' DUPPA. ⟨See App. D, p. 579.⟩

[7] ⟨Surley was another of the Duke's race-horses.⟩

430 **Tuesday 12—Saturday 16 July 1774** Dovedale
breakfast room, and a small library. The rest servants rooms and offices.

A bad inn †.

13 [JULY].

At Matlock.

14 [JULY].

At Dinner, at Oakover §, too deaf to hear or much converse. Mrs. Gell.

The chapel at Oakover. The wood of the pews grossly painted. I could not read the epitaph. Would learn the old hands.

15 [JULY].

Mart 8, 44. lino pro limo [1].

At Ashbourne. Mrs. Diot and her daughters came in the morning. Mr. Diot dined with us. We visited Mr. Flint.

Τὸ πρῶτον Μῶρος, τὸ δὲ δεύτερον εἷλεν Ἐρασμός,
Τὸ τρίτον ἐκ Μουσῶν στέμμα Μίκυλλος ἔχει[2].

16 [JULY].

At Dovedale, with Mr. Langley[3] and Mr. Flint. It is a place that deserves a visit, but did not answer my expectation. The river is small, the rocks are grand. Reynard's hall is a cave very high in the rock, [it][a] goes backward several yards, perhaps eight. To the left is a small opening through which I crept, and found another cavern perhaps four yards square, at the back was a breach yet smaller, which I could not easily have entered, and, wanting light did not inspect. I was in a cave yet higher called Reynard's kitchen. There is a rock called the Church, in which I saw no resemblance, that could justify the name. Dovedale is about two miles long. We walked towards the head of the Dove which is said to rise about five miles above two caves called the dog holes[4], at the end of Dovedale.

[a] *MS. torn.*

† ⟨At Edensor. Broadley, *op. cit.*, p. 166. See App. D, p. 580.⟩

§ ⟨For Oakover, or Okeover, and its squire, Mrs. Gell, the Dyotts, and Mr. Flint, see App. D, pp. 580-1.⟩

[1] The verse in *Martial* is :—
'Defluat, et lento splendescat turbida limo.'
In the common editions it has the number 45, and not 44. DUPPA. ⟨See App. D, p. 581.⟩

[2] 'From the Muses, Sir Thomas More bore away the first crown, Erasmus the second, and Micyllus has the third.' In the MS. Johnson has introduced ᾖρεν by the side of εἷλεν. DUPPA. ⟨The use by Johnson of these alternatives supports the opinion that the epigram is original. For Micyllus (Jacob Moltzer or Molsheym) 1503-1558, see *Allgemeine Deutsche Biographie*, xxi. 704 ff.⟩

[3] See *ante*, ii. 324, note 1, iii. 138 ⟨and 494-6⟩.   [4] ⟨*read* Dove-holes.⟩

In one place where the Rocks approached I propose to build an arch from rock to rock over the stream, with a summerhouse upon it. The water murmured pleasantly among the stones.

I thought that the heat and exercise mended my hearing. I bore the fatigue of the walk, which was very laborious without inconvenience.

There were with us Gilpin[1] and Parker[2]. Having heard of this place before, I had formed some confused idea, to which it did not answer. Brown[3] says he was disappointed. I certainly expected a larger river where I found only a clear quick brook. I believe I had imaged a valley enclosed by rocks, and terminated by a broad expanse of water.

He that has seen Dovedale has no need to visit the Highlands.

In the afternoon we visited old Mrs. Dale †.

17 [JULY].

Sunday. Morning at Church.
Afternoon at Mr. Dyot's.
$K\alpha\theta$.

18 [JULY].

Dined at Mr. Gell's[4].

19 JULY.

We went to Kedleston[5] to see Lord Scarsdales new house, which is very costly but illcontrived. The hall is very stately, lighted by three sky lights; it has two rows of marble pillars dug as I hear from Langley in a quarry of Northamptonshire. The pillars are very large and massy and take up ⟨too⟩[a] much room. They were better away. Behind the hall is a circular salon, useless and therefore illcontrived. The corridors that join the wings to the body, are mere passages, through segments of circles. The state bedchamber was very richly furnished. The dining

[a] two MS.

---

[1] Mr. Gilpin was an undergraduate at Oxford. DUPPA. ⟨See App. D, p. 582.⟩
[2] John Parker, of Brownsholme, in Lancashire [Browsholme, in Yorkshire], Esq. DUPPA. ⟨See App. D, p. 582.⟩
[3] Mrs. Piozzi ' rather thought ' that this was Capability Brown. CROKER,

1835.   † ⟨See App. D, p. 581.⟩
[4] ⟨Philip Gell, of Hopton Hall. He was Sheriff of Derbyshire, 1755, and died 5 Aug. 1795, aged 72. See Johnson's Letters, No. 418.⟩
[5] See ante, iii. 160 ⟨and 499, Broadley, op. cit. p. 173, and post, App. D, pp. 582–3.⟩

parlour was more splendid with gilt plate than any that I have seen. There were many pictures. The grandeur was all below; the bedchambers were small, low, dark and fitter for a prison than a house of splendour. The Kitchen has an opening into the gallery, by which its heat and its fumes are dispersed over the house. There seemed in the whole more cost than judgement.

We went then to the Silkmil⟨l⟩ at Derby[1], where I remarked a particular manner of propagating motion from a horizontal to a vertical wheel. We were desired to leave the men only two shillings. Mr. Thrales bill at the inn for dinner was 0–18–10.

At night I went to Mr. Langley, Mrs. Wood, Captain Astle †, &c.

20 [July].

We left Ashbourn, and went to Buxton, thenc[e] to Pool's hole which is narrow at first, but then rises into a high arch, but is so obstructed with crags that it is difficult to walk in it. There are two ways to the end which is, they say six hundred and fifty yards from the mouth. They take passengers up the higher way and bring them back the lower. The higher way was so difficult and dangerous, that having tried it I desisted. I found no level part.

At night we came to Macclesfield a very large town in Cheshire, little known. It has a silk mill. It has a handsome church, which however is but a chapel, for the town belongs to some parish of another name [2] as Stourbridge lately did to Old Swinford. Macclesfield has a town hall and is, I suppose, a corporate town.

21 [July].

We came to Congleton, where there is likewise a silk mill. Then to Middlewich a mean old town, without any manufacture, but I think a corporation. Thence we proceeded to Namptwich, an old town, from the Inn, I saw scarcely any but black timber houses. I tasted the brine water, which contains much more salt than the sea-water. By slow evaporation they make large

---

[1] See *ante*, iii. 164 ⟨and 501⟩.

† ⟨For Captain Astle, who in or about 1778 resigned his commission and took holy orders, see *ante*, iv. 311

and 536–7. Mrs. Wood was almost certainly his sister. *Ib.* 537.⟩

[2] The parish of Prestbury. DUPPA.

crystals of salt, by quick boiling small granulations. It seemed to have no other preparation.

At evening we came to Combermere[1], so called from a wide lake.

22 [JULY].

We went upon the Mere. I pulled a bulrush of about ten feet.

23 [JULY].

We visited Lord Kilmurrey's house[2]. It is large and convenient, with many rooms, none of which are magnificently spacious. The furniture was not splendid. The bed curtains were guarded[3]. Lord K. showd the place with too much exultation. He has no park, and little water[4].

24 [JULY].

We went to a Chapel built by Sir Linch Cotton for his Tenants. It is consecrated and therefore, I suppose, endowed. It is neat and plain. The communion plate is handsome. It has iron pales and gates of great elegance, brought from Llewenny. " For Robert has laid all open[5]."

25 [JULY].

We saw Ha⟨w⟩keston⟨e⟩, the seat of Sir Rowland Hill[6], and were conducted by Miss Hill over a large tract of rocks and woods, a region abounding with striking scenes and terrifick grandeur. We were always on the brink of a precipice, or at the foot of a lofty rock, but the steeps were seldom naked; in many places Oaks of uncommon magnitude shot up from the crannies of stone, and where there were not tall trees, there were underwoods and

[1] At this time the seat of Sir Lynch Salusbury Cotton, now, of Lord Combermere, his grandson, from which place he takes his title. DUPPA. ⟨See App. D, p. 583.⟩

[2] Shavington Hall, in Shropshire. DUPPA.

[3] ' To guard. To adorn with lists, laces, or ornamental borders. Obsolete.' Johnson's *Dictionary*.

[4] Johnson wrote to Mrs. Thrale on Nov. 13, 1783 :—' You seem to mention Lord Kilmurrey as a stranger. We were at his house in Cheshire [Shropshire]. . . . Do not you remember how he rejoiced in having *no* park; He could not disoblige his neighbours by sending them *no* venison.' *Letters*, No. 900. ⟨For Mrs. Thrale's description of Lord Kilmorey, see App. D, pp. 584–5.⟩

[5] This remark has reference to family conversation. Robert was the eldest son of Sir L. S. Cotton, and lived at Lleweney. DUPPA. ⟨See App. D, p. 583.⟩

[6] ⟨See App. D, p. 585.⟩

bushes. Round the rocks is a narrow path, cut upon the stone which is very frequently hewn into steps, but art has proceeded no further than ⟨to⟩ª make the succession of wonders safely accessible. The whole circuit is somewhat laborious, it is terminated by a grotto cut in the rock to a great extent with many windings and supported by pillars, not hewn into regularity, but such as imitate the sports of nature, by asperi⟨ties⟩ and protuberances.

The place is without any dampness, and would afford a habitation not uncomfortable. There were from space to space seats in the rock. Though it wants water it excells Dovedale, by the extent of its prospects, the awfulness of its shades, the horrors of its precipices, the verdure of its hollows and the loftiness of its rocks. The Ideas which it forces upon the mind, are the sublime, the dreadful, and the vast. Above, is inaccessible altitude, below, is horrible profundity. But it excells the Garden of Ilam only in extent.

Ilam has grandeur tempered with softness. The walker congratulates his own arrival at the place, and is grieved to think that he must ever leave it. As he looks up to the rocks his thoughts are elevated; as he turns his eyes on the vallies, he is composed and soothed.

He that mounts the precipices at Hawkeston, wonders how he came hither, and doubts how he shall return. His walk is an adventure and his departure an escape[b]. He has not the tranquillity, but the horrour of solitude, a kind of turbulent pleasure between fright and admiration.

Ilam is the fit[c] abode of pastoral virtue, and might properly diffuse its shades over nymphs and swains. Hawkeston can have[d] no fitter inhabitants than Giants of mighty bone, and bold emprise[1], men of lawless courage and heroic violence. Hawkestone should be described by Milton and Ilam by Parnel.

Miss Hill showed the whole succession of wonders with great civility. The House was magnificent compared with the rank of the owner.

26 [JULY].

We left Cumbermere, where we have been treated with great civility. Sir L. is gross, the Lady weak and ignorant. The

---

[a] the MS. for proper erased.   [b] an escape *interlinear and in different ink.*   [c] substituted for proper erased.   [d] substituted for proper erased.

[1] *Paradise Lost*, book xi. v. 642. DUPPA.

House is spacious but not magnificent, built at different times with different materials, part is of timber, part of stone or brick, plaistered and painted to look like timber. It is the best house that I ever saw of that kind.

The Meer or lake is large with a small island, on which there is a summer house shaded with great trees. Some were hollow and have seats in their trunks.

In the afternoon we came to West Chester (my Father went to the fair when I had the small pox). We walked round the walls which are compleat, and contain one Mile, three quarters, and one hundred and one yards⟨:⟩ within them are many gardens. They are very high, and two may walk very commodiously side by side. On the inside is a rail; there are towers from space to space not very frequent, and I think, not all compleat [1].

27 [JULY].

We staid at Chester and saw the Cathedral, which is not of the first rank. The Castle, in one of the rooms the Assizes are held, and the refectory of the old abbey of which part is a Grammar School. The Master seemed glad to see me. The cloister is very solemn, over it a⟨re⟩ chambers, in which the singing men live.

In one part of the street was a subterranean arch very strongly built, in another what they called, I believe rightly, a Roman hypocaust.

Chester has many curiosities.

28 [JULY].

We entered Wales, dined at Mold, and came to Llewenny [2].

29 [JULY].

We were at Llewenny.

---

[1] ⟨See App. D, p. 585.⟩

[2] ⟨Mrs. Thrale wrote on 29 July 1774: 'Yesterday evening we came into Llewenny, which struck me extremely as an old family seat of no small dignity. Superfluous space seems to be one source of satisfaction in a house, and here is a hall and a gallery which never seem intended for use, but merely stateliness of appearance.' Broadley, *op. cit.*, p. 182. At this time it was the residence of her cousin Robert Salusbury Cotton, eldest son of Sir Lynch Salusbury

Saturday 30—*Sunday* 31 *July* 1774

30 [JULY].

We went to Bachycraig where we found an old house built 1567 in an uncommon and incommodious form. My Mistress[1] chattered about tiring, but I prevailed on her to go to the top. The floors have been stolen; the windows are stopped. The house was less than I seemed to expect.

The River Clwyd is a brook with a bridge of one arch about one third of a mile.

The woods[2] have many trees generally young, but some which seem to decay. They have been lopped. The house never had a garden. The addition of another story would make an useful house, but it cannot be great; some buildings which Clough the founder intended for ware houses would make store-chambers and servants rooms[3]. The ground seems to be good. I wish it well.

31 [JULY].

We went to Church at St. Asaph. The Cathedral though

Cotton (*ante*, v. 433). He sold it, some time after his father's death in 1775, to the Hon. Thomas Fitzmaurice, brother of the Earl of Shelburne, who in May 1780 invited Johnson to pass the summer there. Johnson's *Letters*, No. 664. Mr. Fitzmaurice erected a linen bleachery in the grounds. R. Twining, *Sel. from Papers of Twining Family*, 1887, pp. 115-16. The mansion was pulled down in 1817. Hayward's *Piozzi*, ii. 206. See *ante*, ii. 282, note 3, and Pennant, *Tour in Wales*, 1784, ii. 27.⟩

[1] Johnson's name for Mrs. Thrale. *Ante*, i. 494.

[2] Johnson wrote to Mrs. Thrale on Sept. 13, 1777:—' Boswell wants to see Wales, but except the woods of Bachycraigh what is there in Wales? What that can fill the hunger of ignorance, or quench the thirst of curiosity?' *Letters*, No. 545. *Ante*, iii. 134, note 1.

[3] Pennant gives a description of this house, in a tour he made into North Wales in 1780:—' Not far from Tremerchion, lies, half buried in woods, the singular house of Bachegraig. It consists of a mansion, and three sides, inclosing a square court. The first consists of a vast hall, and parlour: the rest of it rises into six wonderful stories, including the cupola; and forms from the second floor the figure of a pyramid: the rooms small, and inconvenient. The bricks are admirable, and appear to have been made in Holland; and the model of the house was probably brought from Flanders, where this species of building was not unfrequent. Sir Richard Clough, an eminent merchant, in the reign of queen Elizabeth, seems to have a better title to the honor [of building it]. The initials of his name are in iron on the front, with the date 1567; and on the gateway that of 1569.' *Tour in Wales*, 1784, ii. 22. ⟨See App. D, p. 586.⟩

St. Asaph–Denbigh *Sun.* 31 *July*—*Mon.* 1 *August* 1774
not large has something of dignity and Grandeur. The cross isle is very short. It has scarcely any monuments. The Quire has, I think thirty two stalls, of antique workmanship. On the backs were Canonicus, Prebend, Cancellarius, Thesaurarius, Præcentor. The constitution I do not know but it has all the usual titles and dignities. The service was sung only in the Psalms and hymns.

The Bishop was very civil [1]. We went to his palace, which is but mean. They have a library, and design a room. Here lived Lloyd [2] and Dodwel [3].

AUGUST 1.

We visited Denbigh and the remains of its Castle. The town consists of one main street, and some that cross it which I have not seen. The chief street ascends with a quick rise for a great length. The houses are built some with rough stone, some with brick, and a few are of timber.

The Castle, with its whole enclosure has been a prodigious pile, it is now so ruined that the form of the inhabited part cannot easily be traced. There are as in all old buildings said to be extensive vaults which the ruins of the upper works cover and conceal but into which boys sometimes find a way. To clear all passages and trace the whole of what remains would require much labour and expence.

We saw a church, which was once the chapel of the castle, but is used by the town, it is dedicated to St. Hilary and has an income of about

At a small distance is the ruin of ⟨a⟩ Church said to ⟨have⟩ been

---

[1] ⟨Dr. Jonathan Shipley. Mrs. Thrale remarks: 'His Lordship invited us all to his Palace, which, as he said, would be a good creditable Parsonage House in any of the less remote Counties. His Wife ... pressed us to stay dinner, and was as civil as she knew how.' Broadley, *op. cit.*, p. 184.⟩ See *ante*, iv. 246.

[2] William Lloyd, successively bishop of St. Asaph, Lichfield and Coventry, and Worcester. He was one of the seven bishops who were sent to the Tower in 1688. His character is drawn by Burnet, *History of His Own Time*, 1724, i. 190. See *ante*, ii. 256, note 3.

[3] ⟨Henry Dodwell, the non-juror, 1641–1711, did not reside in St. Asaph, but spent a considerable time there with his friend Bishop Lloyd. Francis Brokesby's *Life of Dodwell*, 1715, p. 39. He resigned his Fellowship of Trinity College, Dublin, as he was unwilling to take Holy Orders, and was deprived of the Camden Professorship of Ancient History at Oxford for refusing to take the Oath of Allegiance. He returned to the Church in 1710. *Ib.* pp. 23, 221, and the *D.N.B.* See also Burnet, *o.c.s.* ii. 604, Hearne in Leland's *Itin.*, 1744, v. 127, and Macaulay's *Hist. Eng.*, ch. xii, 1874, iv. 226.⟩

Mon. 1—Tues. 2 Aug. 1774 Denbigh–Tremeirchion begun by the great Earl of Leicester [1], and left unfinished at his death. One side and I think the East end are yet standing. There was a stone in the wall over the doorway, which it was said, would fall and crush the best scholar in the diocese. One Price would not pass under it [2]. They have taken it down.

We then saw the Chapel of ⟨Lleweney⟩, founded by one of the Salusburies. It is very complete, the monumental stones lye in the ground. A chimney has been added to it, but it is otherwise not much injured, and might be easily repaired.

We then went to the parish church of Denbigh which being near a mile from the town is only used when the Parish Officers are chosen.

In the chapel on Sundays the service is read thrice, the second time only in English, the first and third in Welsh.

The Bishop came to survey the Castle and visited likewise St Hilary's chapel which is that which the town uses.

N⟨ote⟩. In the lawn of Lleweney is a spring of fine water which rises above the surface into a stone basin, from which it runs to waste in a continual stream through a pipe. There are very large trees.

The Hay barn built with brick pillars from space to space, and covered with a roof. A mere [3] elegant and lofty Hovel.

The rivers here are mere torrents which are suddenly swelled by the rain to great breadth and great violence but have very little constant stream. Such are the Clwyd and the Elwas †. There are yet no mountains. The ground is beautifully embellished with woods, and diversified by inequalities.

AUGUST 2.

We rode to a summerhouse of Mr. C⟨otton⟩, which has a very extensive prospect. It is meanly built and unskilfully disposed.

We then went to Dimerchion [4] Ch⟨urch⟩ where the old Clerk acknowledged his mistress. It is the parish Church of Bachycraig, a mean fabrick. Mr. Salusbury [5] was buried in it. Bachicraig has fourteen seats in it.

[1] ⟨In 1579. According to Pennant Leicester borrowed, and never repaid, the money raised for its completion. *Tour in Wales*, 1784, ii. 35–6.⟩
[2] See *ante*, iii. 357, and v. 42.
[3] ⟨Duppa read *more*.⟩ † ⟨Elwy.⟩
[4] ⟨Tremeirchion. Mrs. Thrale states that the church was in ' a dismal condition '. Broadley, *op. cit.*, p. 186. See also Pennant, *Tour in Wales*, 1784, ii. 22. Mrs. Thrale lies buried in the church in the same vault with her second husband. A memorial tablet was erected to her in 1909. Broadley, pp. 75 and 154.⟩
[5] ⟨Mrs. Thrale's father, John Salus-

Llanerch   *Tuesday 2 August* 1774

As we rode by I looked at the house again. We saw Llannerch †, a house not mean, with a small park very well watered. There was an avenue of oaks, which in a foolish compliance with the present mode, has been cut down [1]. A few are yet standing. The owner's name is Davies †. The way lay through pleasant lanes, and overlooked a region beautifully diversified with trees and grass [2].

bury, 1707–62 ; see J. L. Clifford, H. L. Piozzi, 1941, pp. 5 ff.⟩

† ⟨Llanerch was, according to Pennant, formerly called Lleweni Vechan. It was the chief seat of his kinsman, John Davies († 1785), the great-grandson of the Welsh antiquary, Robert Davies (1684–1728). Pennant, *Tour in Wales*, 1784, ii. 21. Mrs. Thrale wrote : 'We went to Llanerch, the seat of Mr. Davies, with elegant grounds and a very pleasing piece of water about it. I took the more interest in its appearance as I had often heard my Mother say that was the house in Wales where she had spent the happiest hours.' Broadley, *op. cit.*, p. 187.⟩

[1] Cowper wrote a few years later in the first book of *The Task*, lines 252 ff., in his description of the grounds at Weston Underwood :—

'Not distant far, a length of colonnade
Invites us. Monument of ancient taste,
Now scorn'd, but worthy of a better fate.
Our fathers knew the value of a screen
From sultry suns ; and, in their shaded walks
And long protracted bow'rs, enjoy'd at noon
The gloom and coolness of declining day.'

[2] Such a passage as this shews that Johnson was not so insensible to nature as is often asserted. Mrs. Piozzi (*Anec.* p. 99 : John. Misc. i. 215) says :—' Mr. Thrale loved prospects, and was mortified that his friend could not enjoy the sight of those different dispositions of wood and water, hill and valley, that travelling through England and France affords a man. But when he wished to point them out to his companion : "Never heed such nonsense," would be the reply : "a blade of grass is always a blade of grass, whether in one country or another : let us if we *do* talk, talk about something ; men and women are my subjects of enquiry ; let us see how these differ from those we have left behind."' She adds (p. 265, John. Misc. i. 323) :—' Walking in a wood when it rained, was, I think, the only rural image he pleased his fancy with ; " for (says he) after one has gathered the apples in an orchard, one wishes them well baked, and removed to a London eating-house for enjoyment."' See *ante*, v. pp. 132, note 1, 141, note 2, 333, note 1, and 346, note 1, for Johnson's descriptions of scenery. Passages in his letters shew that he had some enjoyment of country life. Thus he writes :—' I hope Mrs. Porter when she came to her favourite place, found her house dry, and her woods growing, and the breeze whistling, and the birds singing, and her own heart dancing.' *Letters*, No. 74. ' I hope ... to see standing corn in some part of the earth this summer, but I shall hardly smell hay, or suck clover flowers.' *Ib.* No. 674. ' What I shall do next I know not ; all my schemes of rural pleasure have been some way or other disappointed.' *Ib.* No. 966.

Tuesday 2—Wednesday 3 August 1774 Holywell

The old Clerk had great appearance of joy at the sight of his Mistress, and foolishly said, that he was now willing to die.

NOTES AND OMISSIONS.

In the parish Church of Denbigh is a bas relief of Lluyd the antiquary who was before Camden. He is kneeling at his prayers [1].

I saw no convenient boat upon Cumbermere.

At Dymerchion Church there is English service only once a Month. This is about twenty miles from the English Border. The old Clerk had only [a] a crown given him by my mistress [2].

The Hall at Llewenny is 40 feet long and 28 broad. The Gallery 120 feet long (all paced); the Library 42 feet long, and 28 broad. The dining parlour 30 feet long 26 broad.

At Dymerchion Church, the Texts on the walls are in Welsh.

Ll⟨ewenny⟩ is partly sashed and partly has casements.

AUGUST 3.

We went in the coach to Holywel. Talk with Mistress about flattery [3].

[a] only *and* given ... mistress *added in different ink.*

In this very trip to Wales, after describing the high bank of a river ' shaded by gradual rows of trees,' he writes :—' The gloom, the stream, and the silence, generate thoughtfulness.' *Post*, v. 453.

[1] Humphry Llwyd was a native of Denbigh, and practised there as a physician, and also represented the town in Parliament. He died 1568, aged 41. DUPPA. ⟨See App. D, p. 592.⟩

[2] ' If Mr. Duppa,' wrote Mrs. Piozzi, ' does not send me [a copy of Johnson's *Diary*], he is as shabby as it seems our Doctor thought me, when I gave but a crown to the old clerk. The poor clerk had probably never seen a crown in his possession before. Things were very distant A.D. 1774, from what they are 1816.' Hayward's *Piozzi*, ed. 1, ii. 178.

[3] Mrs. Piozzi has the following note on this:—' He said that I flattered the people to whose houses we went : I was saucy, and said I was obliged to be civil for *two*—meaning himself and me. He replied, nobody would thank me for compliments they did not understand. At Gwaynynog ... *he* was flattered, and was happy of course.' CROKER, 1835. Sept. 21, 1778. Mrs. Thrale. ' I remember, Sir, when we were travelling in Wales, how you called me to account for my civility to the people; "Madam," you said, " let me have no more of this idle commendation of nothing. Why is it, that whatever you see, and whoever you see, you are to be so indiscriminately lavish of praise ? " " Why I'll tell you, Sir," said I, " when I am with you, and Mr. Thrale, and Queeny, I am obliged to be civil for four! " ' Mme. D'Arblay's *Diary*, i. 111. See also Johnson's *Letters*, No. 405, Piozzi, *Anecd.* p. 184 (John. Misc. i. 273), and *ante*, iii. 293.

Holywell **Wednesday 3 August 1774**

Holywel is a Market town neither very small nor mean. The spring called Winifred's Well† is very clear, and so copious that it yields one hundred tuns of water in a minute. It is all at once a very great stream which within perhaps thirty yards of its eruption turns a mill and in a course of two miles eighteen mills more. In descent it ⟨is⟩ very quick. It then falls into the sea. The Well is covered by a lofty circular arch supported by pillars, and over this arch is an old Chapel, now a school. The Chancel is separated by a wall. The Bath is completely and indecently open. A Woman bathed while we all looked on.

In the Church, which makes a good appearance, and is surrounded by galleries to receive a numerous congregation, we were present while a child was christened in Welsh.

We went down by the stream to see a prospect in which I had no part. We then saw a brass work where the lapis Calaminaris [1] is gath⟨e⟩red, broken, washed from the earth and the lead, though how the lead was separated I did not see, then calcined, afterwards ground fine, and then mixed by fire with the copper.

We saw several strong fires with melting pots, but the construction of the fireplaces I did not learn.

At a copper work, which receives its pigs of copper, I think, from Warrington, we saw a plate of copper put hot between steel rollers, and spread thin. I know not whether ⟨the⟩ upper roller was set to a certain distance, as I suppose, or acted only by its weight.

At an iron work I saw round bars formed by a notched hammer and anvil. Then I saw a bar of about half an inch or more square, cut with sheers worked by water and then beaten hot into a thinner bar; the hammers, all worked as they were by water, acting upon small bodies moved very quick, as quick as by the hand.

† ⟨For St. Winifred's Well, one of the Seven Wonders of Wales, and the arch and chapel over it, see *Inventory of Ancient Monuments, County of Flint*, 1912, p. 44, and Pennant's *History of Whiteford and Holywell*, 1796, pp. 219 ff.⟩

[1] Johnson, in his *Dictionary*, defines *calamine* or *lapis calaminaris* as *a kind of fossile bituminous earth, which, being mixed with copper, changes it into brass*. ⟨'Calamine is worked in a rich mine of galena at Holywell.' Ure's *Dict. Arts*, iii. 1187. See the Oxford Dictionary.⟩

I then saw wire drawn, and gave a shilling. I have enlarged my notions [1]. Though not being able to see the movements, and having not time to peep closely, I know less than I might. I was less weary, and had better breath as I walked further.

I had καθ the day before, and had some of the effects this morning.

Aug⟨ust⟩ 4.

Ruthlan Castle is still a very noble ruin. All the walls still remain so that a compleat platform, and elevations not very imperfect may be taken. It incloses a square of about thirty yards. The middle space was always open. The wall is I believe about thirty feet high very thick, flanked with six round towers each about eighteen feet, or less, in diameter. Only one tower had a chimney, so that here was [2] commodity of living. It was only a place of strength. The Garrison had perhaps tents in the area.

Stapiltons house is pretty [3]⟨;⟩ there are pleasing shades about it, with a constant spring that supplies a cold bath.

We then went to see a cascade, I trudged unwillingly, and was not sorry to find it dry †. The water was however turned on, and produced a very striking cataract. They are paid an hundred pounds a year, for permission to divert the stream to the mines. The River for such it may be termed [4] rises from a single spring, which like that of Winifred is covered with a building.

We called then at another house belonging to Mr. Lloyd [5] which made a handsome appearance. This country seems full of very splendid houses.

Mrs. T⟨hrale⟩ lost her purse. She expressed so much uneasiness that I concluded the sum to be very great, but when I heard

---

[1] See *ante*, iii. 164.

[2] 'No' or 'little' is here probably omitted. CROKER, 1848.

[3] The name of this house is Bodryddan; formerly the residence of the Stapyltons, the parents of ⟨four⟩ co-heiresses, of whom Mrs. Cotton, afterwards Lady Salusbury Cotton, was one. DUPPA. ⟨Mrs. Thrale described it as 'an agreeable place hastening to decay for want of a male heir.' Broadley, *op. cit.*, p. 189.⟩

† ⟨Mrs. Piozzi noted: 'He teased Mrs. Cotton about her dry cascade till she was ready to cry.' CROKER, 1848. See also App. D, p. 587.⟩

[4] 'Dr. Johnson . . . asked of one of our sharp currents in North Wales —Has this BROOK e'er a name?—and received for answer—Why, dear Sir, this is the RIVER Ustrad.—Let us, said he, turning to his friend, jump over it directly, and shew them how an *Englishman* should treat a *Welch* RIVER.' Piozzi's *Synon.* i. 82.

[5] ⟨See App. D, p. 587.⟩

of only seven guineas, I was glad to find she had so much sensibility of money.

I could not drink this day either coffee or tea after dinner. I know not when I missed before.

AUG⟨UST⟩ 5.

Last night my sleep was remarkably quiet. little flatus. I know not whether by fatigue in walking, or by forbearance of tea [1]. I gave the Ipecacuanha [2]—Vin. Emet. had failed, so had tartar Emet. The Ipec. did but little.

I dined at Mr. Middleton's of Gwaynynog †. The house was a Gentlemans house below the second rate, perhaps below the third⟨,⟩ built of stone roughly cut. The rooms were low, and the passage above stairs gloomy, but the furniture was good. The table was well supplied, except that the fruit was bad. It was truly the dinner of a country Gentleman. Two tables were filled with company not inelegant. After dinner the talk was of preserving the Welsh language. I offered them a scheme. Poor Evan Evans § was mentioned as incorrigibly addicted to strong drink. Worthington [3] was commended. Middleton is the only man who in Wales has talked to me of literature. I wish he were truly zealous. I recommended the republication of David ap Rhees's Welsh Grammar *.

Two sheets of Hebrides came to me for correction to day, F. G.[4]

AUGUST 6.

$Ka\theta\langle a\rho\sigma\iota s\rangle$ $\delta\rho\langle a\sigma\tau\iota\kappa\dot{\eta}\rangle$. I corrected the two sheets. My sleep last night was disturbed.

Washing at Chester, and here — 5s. 1d.

I did not read. Atterbury's version [5] a heap of barbarity. The $\kappa a\theta$ did not much, but I hope, enough.

I saw to day more of the outhouses at Lleuwenny. It is in the whole a very spacious house.

[1] See *ante*, i. 313, note 4.
[2] On Aug. 16 he wrote to Mr. Levett :—' I have made nothing of the Ipecacuanha.' *Ante*, ii. 282. Croker suggests that *up* is omitted after ' I gave'.
† ⟨For John Myddelton of Gwaynynog, see App. D, pp. 587–8.⟩
§ ⟨See App. D, p. 589.⟩

[3] See *post*, v. 453.
* ⟨See App. D, p. 589.⟩
[4] F. G. are the printer's signatures, by which it appears that at this time four sheets (B, C, D, E), or 64 pages had already been printed. See *ante*, ii. 278.
[5] ⟨See Johnson, *Diaries, Prayers, and Annals*, 1958, pp. 191–2.⟩

August 7.

I was at Church at Botfarry. There was a service used for a sick woman, not canonically, but such as I have heard, I think, formerly at Lichfield, taken out of the visitation. Καθ μετριῶς. The Church is mean but has a square tower for the bells, rather too stately for the Church †.

Observations.

Bit and bridle Ps. 32. Southwel.
Dixit injustus. Ps. 36 has no relation to the English [1].
"Preserve us Lord" has the name of Robert Wisedome, 1618. Barkers Bible [2].
Battologiam ab iteratione recte distinguit Erasmus. Mod. Orandi Deum p. 56–144 [3].
Southwells thought of his own death [4].
Baudius on Erasmus [5]. Infinitum debet. q.

---

† ⟨Mrs. Thrale records :—' When the Parson saw us, he gave out that service should be performed in English. We had neither singing nor preaching. . . . Texts, some Welch, some English, were strewed about the Church, which was really below a stable for convenience or beauty.' Broadley, *op. cit.*, p. 190.⟩

[1] The Prayer Book (Coverdale) version of Psalm 36 begins,—' My heart sheweth me the wickedness of the ungodly,' which has no relation to 'Dixit injustus.'

[2] This alludes to 'A prayer by R. W., (evidently Robert Wisedom) which Sir Henry Ellis, of the British Museum, has found among the Hymns which follow the old version of the singing Psalms, at the end of Barker's Bible of 1639. It begins,
'Preserve us, Lord, by thy deare word,
From Turk and Pope, defend us Lord,
Which both would thrust out of his throne
Our Lord Jesus Christ, thy deare son.' Croker, 1835.

[3] ' Proinde quum dominus Matth. 6 docet discipulos suos, ne in orando multiloqui sint, nihil aliud docet, quam ne credant deum inani uerborum strepitu flecti rem eandem subinde flagitantium. Nam Græcis est βαττολογήσατε. Βαττολογεῖν autem illis dicitur, qui uoces easdem frequenter iterant sine causa, uel loquacitatis, uel naturæ, uel consuetudinis uitio. Alioqui iuxta precepta rhetorum nonnunquam laudis est iterare uerba, quemadmodum et Christus in cruce clamauit. Deus meus, deus meus : non erat illa βαττολογία, sed ardens ac uehemens affectus orantis.' Erasmus's *Opera*, ed. 1540, v. 927.

[4] ⟨Croker suggested, 1835, that the reference is to Southwell's stanzas ' Upon the Image of Death,' in his *Mæoniæ*, 1595, p. 24 :—
' Before my face the picture hangs,
That daily should put me in mind,
Of those cold names and bitter pangs,
That shortly I am like to find :
But yet alas full little I
Do thinke here on that I must die.'
For Southwell, 1561–95, see Pierre Janelle, *Robert Southwell the Writer*, 1935.⟩

[5] ⟨The reference is to Dominic Baudius's *Epistolae*, cent. ii, epist. xxvii, which contains the criticism of Erasmus quoted by Johnson in his *Life of Milton* (165), and concludes: 'Multum tamen imo infinitum ei debet posteritas.'⟩

Lleweny *Monday 8—Saturday 13 August 1774* 445

⟨AUGUST⟩ 8.

The Bishop and much company dined at Llewenny. Talk of Greek—and of the Army [1]. The D⟨uke⟩ of M⟨arlborough⟩s officers useless. Read Phocyllides [2], distinguished the paragraphs.

⟨AUGUST⟩ 9.

Looked in Leland, an unpleasant book of mere hints. Lichfield School 10 l. and 5 l from the hospital [3].

⟨AUGUST⟩ 10.

At Lloyds of Macemunnon †, a good house, and very large walled garden. I read Windus's Account of his journey to Mequinez, and of Stuarts Embassy [4]. I had read in the Morning Wasse's Greek trochaics to Bentley. They appeared inelegant and made with difficulty. The Latin Elegy contains only common places harshly expressed so far as I have read, for it is long. They seem to be the verses of a Scholar, who has no practice of writing. The Greek I did not always fully understand. I am in doubt about ⟨the⟩ 6th and last paragraphs. Perhaps they are not printed right; for εὔτοκον perhaps εὔστοχον. q.

The following days I read here and there. The Bibl. Literaria, was so little supplied with papers that could interest curiosity, tha⟨t⟩ it could not hope for long continuance [5]. Wasse the chief contributor was an unpolished Scholar, who with much literature, had no art or elegance of diction, at least in English.

---

[1] Bishop Shipley had been an Army Chaplain. *Ante*, iii. 251.
[2] The title of the poem is Ποίημα νουθετικόν. DUPPA. ⟨See *post*, v. 461, n. 2.⟩
[3] This entry refers to the following passage in Leland's *Itinerary*, published by Thomas Hearne, ed. 1744, iv. 112. ' B. *Smith* in K. *H.* 7. dayes, and last Bishop of *Lincolne*, beganne a new Foundation at this Place settinge up a Mr. there with 2. Preistes, and 10. poore Men in an Hospitall. He sett there alsoe a Schoole-Mr. to teach Grammer that hath 10. *l.* by the yeare, and an Under- Schoole-Mr. that hath 5. *l.* by the Yeare. King *H.* 7. was a great Benefactour to this new Foundation, and gave to it an ould Hospitall called Denhall in Wirhall in Cheshire.'
† ⟨See Broadley, *op. cit.*, pp. 191, 207.⟩
[4] *A Journey to Mequinez, the Residence of the present Emperor of Fez and Morocco, on the Occasion of Commodore Stewart's Embassy thither, for the Redemption of the British Captives, in the Year* 1721. DUPPA.
[5] The *Bibliotheca Literaria* was published in London, 1722–4, in 4to numbers, but only extended to ten numbers. DUPPA. ⟨Wasse's Greek and Latin lines to Bentley occur in No. 6, pp. 9–14: see Monk, *Life of Bentley*, 1830, p. 467, and *Johnson Club Papers*, 1899, i. 36.⟩

Sunday 14—Thursday 18 August 1774 Conway
August 14.
At Botfarry I heard the second Lesson read, and the sermon preached in Welsh. The text was pronounced both in Welsh and English. The sound of the Welsh in a continued discourse is not unpleasant.

Βρῶσις ὀλίγη [1]. Καθ⟨αρσις⟩ α⟨νευ⟩ φ⟨αρμακων⟩

The Letter of Chrysostom † against transubstantiation. Erasmus to the Nuns*, full of mystick notions, and allegories.

Aug⟨ust⟩ 15.
Καθ. Imbecillitas genuum non sine aliquantulo doloris inter ambulandum, quem a prandio magis sensi [2].

Aug⟨ust⟩ 18.
We left Llewenni, and went forwards on our Journey. We came to Abergeler [3] a mean town in which little but Welsh is spoken, and Divine Service is seldom performed in English. Our way then lay by the sea side, at the foot of a Mountain called Penman ross [4]. Here the way was so steep that we walked on the lower edge of the hill to meet the Coach that went upon a road higher on the hill. Our walk was not long nor unpleasant, the longer I walk the less I feel its inconvenience. As I grow warm my breath mends and I think my limbs grow pliable.

We then came to Conway Ferry, and passed in small boats, with some passengers from the Stage coach, Among whom were an Irish Gentlewoman with two maids and three little children of which the youngest was only a few months old. The tide did not serve the large ferry boat, and therefore our Coach could not very soon follow us. We were therefore to stay at the Inn. It is now the day of the race at Conway and the town was so full of company, that no money could purchase lodging. We were not very readily supplied with cold dinner. We would have stayed at Conway, if we could have found entertainment, for we were

---

[1] By this expression it would seem, that on this day Johnson ate sparingly. Duppa.

† ⟨The apocryphal Letter to Caesarius. See *Dict. of Christian Biography*, 1877, i. 378 and *Catholic Encycl.* viii. 456. It is in *Bibliotheca Literaria*, No. 5.⟩

* ⟨Published as *Epistola consolatoria* (Leiden, 1528). See *Opus Epist.*, ed. Allen, 1928, vii. 283.⟩

[2] 'A weakness of the knees, not without some pain in walking, which I feel increased after I have dined.' Duppa.

[3] ⟨Abergele.⟩   [4] ⟨Penmaen Rhôs.⟩

afraid of passing Penmanmawr over which lay our way to Bangor but by bright daylight, and the delay of our coach made our departure necessarily late. There was however no stay on any other terms than of sitting up all night.

The poor Irish Lady was still more distressed. Her children wanted rest. She would have been content with one bed, but for a time none could be had. Mrs. T⟨hrale⟩ gave her what help she could. At last two gentlemen were persuaded to yield up their room with two beds, for which she gave half a guinea.

Our coach was at last brought and we set out with some anxiety but we came to Penmanmawr by day light, and found a way lately made, very easy and very safe [1]. It was cut smooth and inclosed between parallel walls. The outer of which secures the ⟨traveller ?⟩ from the precipice which is deep and dreadful. This wall is here and there broken by mischievous wantonness [2]. The inner wall preserves the road from the loose stones which the shatter⟨ed⟩ steeps above it would pour down. That side of the mountain seems to have a surface of loose stones which every accident may crumble. The old road was higher and must have been very formidable. The sea beats at the bottom of the way. At Evening the Moon shone eminently bright, and our thoughts of danger being now past, the rest of our journey was very pleasant. At an hour somewhat late we came to Bangor, where we found a very mean Inn, and had some difficulty to obtain lodging. I lay in a room where the other bed had two men [3]. I had a flatulent night.

August 19.

We obtained a boat to convey us to Anglesea, and saw Lord Bulkley's house [4] and Beaumaris Castle. I was accosted by Mr Lloyd [5] the Schoolmaster of Beaumaris who had seen me at University College and he with Mr. Roberts [6] the Register of Bangor whose boat we borrowed, accompanied us. Lord Bulkeley's house is very mean, but his garden is spacious and shady, with

---

[1] Penmaen Mawr is a huge rock, rising nearly 1550 feet perpendicular above the sea. Along a shelf of this precipice, is formed an excellent road, well guarded . . . by a strong wall, supported in many parts by arches turned underneath it. Before this wall was built, travellers sometimes fell down the precipices. Duppa. ⟨The road was built in 1772.⟩

[2] See *post*, v. 452.

[3-6] ⟨See App. D, pp. 590-1.⟩

large trees and smaller interspersed. The walks are strait and cross each other with no variety of plan but they have a pleasing coolness and solemn gloom, and extend to a great length.

The Castle is a mighty pile ⟨:⟩ the outward wall has fifteen round towers, besides square towers at the angles. There is then a void space between the wall and the castle, which has an area enclosed with a wall which again has towers larger than those of the outer wall ; the towers of the inner castle are I think eight. There is likewise a chapel entire, bui⟨l⟩t upon an arch as I suppose, and beautifully arch⟨ed⟩ with a stone roof which is yet [a] unbroken. The entrance into the Chapel is about eight or nine feet high, and was I suppose, higher when there was no rubbish in the area.

This castle corresponds with all the representations of romancing narratives. Here is not wanting the private passage, the dark cavity, the deep dungeon or the lofty tower. We did not discover the well. This is ⟨the⟩ most complete view that I have yet had of an old castle [1]. It had a moat.

The towers.

We returned to Bangor.

AUGUST 20.

We went by water from Bangor to Caernarvon, where we met Poali and Sir Thomas Wynne †. Meeting by chance with one Troughton [2], an intelligent and loquacious wanderer, Mr. T⟨hrale⟩ invited him to din⟨n⟩er. He attended us to the Castle, an Edifice of stupendous magnitude and strength. It has in it all that we observed at Beaumaris, of [b] much greater dimensions ; many of the smaller rooms floored with stone are entire ; of the larger rooms, the beams and planks are all lost ; this is ⟨the⟩ state of all buildings left to time. We mounted the Eagle tower by 169 steps each of ten inches. We did not find the well, nor did I trace the moat, but moats there were I believe to all castles on the plain, which not only hindred access, but prevented mines. We saw but a very small part of this mighty ruin. And in all these

[a] yet yet MS.   [b] ? read and is of

[1] See *ante*, ii. 285. ⟨For a full description of Beaumaris Castle see the Royal Commission's *Inventory of Ancient Monuments in Wales, Anglesey*, 1937, pp. 8 ff.⟩
† ⟨See App. D, p. 591.⟩
[2] ⟨See App. D, pp. 591–2.⟩

Carnarvon–Bodvil Sat. 20—Mon. 22 Aug. 1774   449
old buildings, the subterraneous works are concealed by the rubbish. To survey this place would take much time.· I did not think there had been such buildings. It surpassed my Ideas.

⟨AUGUST⟩ 21.

We were at Church, the service in the town is always English, at the Parish Church at a small distance always Welsh. The town has by degrees, I suppose, been brought nearer to the sea side. We received an invitation to Dr Worthington †. We then went to din⟨n⟩er at Sir T. Wynne's. The Dinner mean, Sir T. civil. His Lady nothing [1]. Poali civil.

We supped with Colonel Wynne's Lady [2] who lives in one of the towers of the Castle.

I have not been very well.

AUGUST 22.

We went to visit Bodville, the place where Mrs. T⟨hrale⟩ was born, and the churches called Tydweilliog and Llangynnidle which she holds by impropriation. We had an invitation to the House of Mr Griffith [3] of Brinoddle, where we found a small neat new built house, with square rooms. The walls are of unhewn stone and therefore thick, for the stones not fitting with exactness are not strong without great thickness. He had planted a great

† ⟨See *post*, v. 453.⟩
[1] ⟨Sir Thomas Wynn's wife was Lady Catharine Perceval, daughter of the second Earl of Egmont. Mrs. Thrale describes her as 'an empty woman of quality, insolent, ignorant, and ill bred, without either beauty or fortune to atone for her faults,' and relates : ' She set a vile dinner before us, and on such linen as shocked one ; no plate, no china to be seen, nothing but what was as despicable as herself. Mr. Johnson compared her at our return to sour small beer ; she could not have been a good thing, he said, and even that poor thing was spoilt.' Broadley, *op. cit.* p. 200. Mrs. Piozzi introduces Johnson's ' denunciation ', anonymously and in a different form, in her *Anecdotes* (p. 171 : John. Misc. i. 264).⟩
[2] ⟨Lt. Col. Glynn Wynn, M.P. for

Carnarvon Borough, 1768–90, Sir Thomas Wynn's brother, married Bridget, daughter of E. P. Pugh, of Penrhyn. Burke's *Peerage and Baronetage*, 1833, ii. 221.⟩
[3] ⟨Hugh Griffith, 1724–95, Sheriff of Carnarvonshire, 1777–8, married Mary, daughter and heiress of William Wynn of Llanfairisgaer. Brynodol, which was the party's head-quarters for three days, is described by Mrs. Thrale as ' an excellent house, of the tight warm kind, like those near London. . . . The look from the windows, however, soon reminds you of the immence distance of this from any English habitation.' A. M. Broadley, *Dr. Johnson and Mrs. Thrale*, 1910, pp. 200 ff. It is to-day a farm-house and in the possession of the same family. See also Pennant, *Tour in Wales*, 1784, ii. 202.⟩

Mon. 22—Wed. 24 Aug. 1774 Clynnog–Bodvil
deal of young wood in walks. Fruit trees do not thrive, but having grown a few years reach some barren stratum and wither.

We found Mr Griffiths not at home, but the provisions were good. Mr. Griffith came home the next day. He married a Lady who has a house and estate at ⟨Llanfairisgaer⟩, over against Anglesea, and near Caernarvon, where she is more disposed, as it seems, to reside than at Brinodl.

I read Lluyds account of Mona which he proves to be Anglesea†.

In our way to Br⟨ynodol⟩, we saw at Llanerk§ a Church built crosswise very spacious and magnificent for this country; we could not see the Parson and could get no intelligence about it.

⟨AUGUST⟩ 24.

We went to see Bodvil. Mrs. T⟨hrale⟩ remembered the rooms, and wandred over them, with recollection of her childhood. This species of pleasure is always melancholy. The walk was cut down, and the pond was dry. Nothing was better [1].

We surveyed the churches, which are mean and neglected to a degree scarcely imaginable. They have no pavement, and the earth is full of holes, the seats are rude benches. The altars have no rails; one of them has a breach in the roof. On the desk I think of each lay a Folio Welsh Bible of the black letter, which the Curate cannot easily read [2]. Mr. T⟨hrale⟩ proposes to beautify the Churches, and, if he prospers, will probably restore the tithes.

† ⟨See App. D, p. 592.⟩
§ ⟨Clynnog: see App. D, pp. 592–3.⟩
[1] Cf. Johnson's description of his own disappointment on his return to Lichfield in 1762. *Ante*, i. 370.
[2] 'It was impossible not to laugh at the patience he shewed, when a Welch parson of mean abilities, though a good heart, struck with reverence at the sight of Dr. Johnson, whom he had heard of as the greatest man living, could not find any words to answer his inquiries concerning a motto round somebody's arms which adorned a tomb-stone in Ruabon church-yard. If I remember right the words were,
Heb Dw, Heb Dym,
Dw o' diggon.

And though of no very difficult construction, the gentleman seemed wholly confounded, and unable to explain them; till Mr. Johnson having picked out the meaning by little and little, said to the man, "*Heb* is a preposition, I believe Sir, is it not?" My countryman recovering some spirits upon the sudden question, cried out, "So I humbly presume, Sir," very comically.' Piozzi's *Anec.* p. 238 : John. Misc. i. 308. The Welsh words, which are the Myddelton motto, mean, 'Without God, without all. God is all-sufficient.' *Piozzi MS.* Croker, 1835. ⟨There is to-day, 1939, no tombstone in Ruabon churchyard or church with this motto.⟩

Pwllheli–Snowdon Wed. 24—Fri. 26 Aug. 1774

The two parishes are Llangynnidle and Tydweilliog [1]. The Methodists are here very prevalent. A better church will impress the people with more reverence of publick Worship.

Mrs. Thrale visited a house where she had been used to drink milk, which was left with an estate of 200 l a year, by one Lloyd † to a married woman who lived with him.

We went to Pwlhely a mean old town at the extremity of the country. Here we bought something to remember the place *.

⟨AUGUST⟩ 25.

We returned to Carnarvon where we eat with Mrs Wynne §.

⟨AUGUST⟩ 26.

We visited with Mrs. Wynne Llyn Badarn and Llyn Beris, two lakes joined by a narrow strait. They are formed by the waters which fall from Snowden and the opposite Mountains. On the side of Snowden are the remains of a large fort, to which we climbed with great labour. I was breathless and harrassed. The lakes have no great breadth so that the boat is always near one bank or the other [2].

[1] In 1809 the whole income for Llangwinodyl, including surplice fees, amounted to forty-six pounds two shillings and twopence, and for Tydweilliog, forty-three pounds nineteen shillings and tenpence ; so that it does not appear that Mr. Thrale carried into effect his good intention. DUPPA.

† ⟨See App. D, pp. 593–4.⟩

* ⟨Mrs. Thrale tells us that Johnson 'could find nothing to purchase but a Primmer.' Broadley, op. cit. p. 203.⟩

§ ⟨See ante, v. 449, n. 2.⟩

[2] ⟨Duppa printed as the next line the following cryptic sentence : ' Queeny's goats, one hundred and forty-nine, I think,' which is one of a number of miscellaneous notes written by Johnson on a blank page of his diary (see post, v. 461). Duppa added the following explanation, which was, no doubt, supplied by Mrs. Piozzi:—'Mr. Thrale was near-sighted, and could not see the goats browsing on Snowdon, and he promised his daughter, who was a child of ten years old, a penny for every goat she would shew him, and Dr. Johnson kept the account ; so that it appears her father was in debt to her one hundred and forty-nine pence. Queeny was the epithet, which had its origin in the nursery, by which Miss Thrale was always distinguished by Johnson.' Her name was Hester Maria. The name ' Queeney ' was used by Johnson and Mrs. Thrale as early as July 1771 (Letters, No. 260, and The Queeney Letters, 1934, p. 5, note 3) and soon became established : in 1772 Johnson wrote ' I think Mrs. Queeney might write again ' (Letters, No. 286). Mrs. Thrale uses it throughout her Welsh diary, rarely varying it with ' Niggey ' or ' Nig '. See also ante, iii. 422, n. 4.⟩

⟨August⟩ 27.

We returned to Bangor where Mr. T⟨hrale⟩ was lodged at Mr. Roberts's the Register.

⟨August⟩ 28.

We went to worship at the Cathedral. The Quire is mean, the service was not well read.

⟨August⟩ 29.

We came to Mr Middelton's of Gyuannog. To the first place as my Mistress observed, where we have been welcome.

N⟨ote⟩. On the day when we visited Bodvil, we turned to the house of Mr. Griffiths of Kefnamwllch, a Gentleman of large fortune remarkable for having made great and sudden improvements in his seat and Estate. He has inclosed a large Garden with a brick wall. He is considered as a Man of great accomplishments. He was educated in literature at the University and served some time in the army, then quitted his commission, and retired to his Lands. He is accounted a good Man and endeavours to bring the people to church.

In our way from Bangor to Conway, we passed again the new road upon the edge of Penmanmaur, which would be very tremendous but that the wall shuts out the idea of danger. In the wall are several breaches made as Mr. T⟨hrale⟩ very reasonably conjectures, by fragments of rocks which roll down the mountain, broken perhaps by frost, or worn through by rain.

We then viewed Conway.

To spare the horses at Penman Ross, between Conway and St. Asaph we sent the coach over the road cross the Mountain, with Mrs Th⟨rale⟩ who had been tired with a walk some time before, and I with Mr Th⟨rale⟩ and Miss, walked along the edge where the path is very narrow, and much encumbred by little loose stones which had fallen [*MS.* falled] down as we thought upon the way since we passed it before.

At Conway we took a short survey of the Castle, which afforded us nothing new. It is larger than that of Beumarris, and less than that of Caernarvon. It is built upon a rock so high and steep that it is even now very difficult of access. We found a round pit which was called the well, it is now almost filled and therefore dry. We found the well in no other castle. There are some re-

Gwaynynog–Llanrhaiadr *Mon. 29 Aug.—Th. 8 Sept.* 1774   453
mains of leaden pipes at Caernarvon, which, I suppose only conveyed water from one part of the building to another. Had the Garrison had no other supply, the Welsh who must know where the pipes were laid could easily have cut them.

Aug⟨ust⟩ 29.

We came to the house of Mr. Middelton (on Monday) where we staid to Sept. 6, and were very kindly entertained.

How we spent our time I am not very able to tell [1]. We saw the wood which is diversified and romantick.

Sept⟨ember⟩ 4, Sunday.

We dined with Mr Middelton † the Clergyman at Denbigh, where I saw the Harvestmen ᵃ very decently dressed ᵃ after the afternoon service standing to be hired. On other days they stand at about four in the morning. They are hired from day to day.

Sept⟨ember⟩ 6, Tuesday.

We lay at Wrexham, a busy, extensive and well-built town. It has a very large and magnificent Church. ᵃIt has a famous fair.ᵃ

Sept⟨ember⟩ 7.

We came to Chirk Castle §.

Sep⟨tember⟩ 8, Thursday.

We came to the House of Dr Worthington [2] at Llanrhaiadur. Our entertainment was poor though his house was not bad. The Situation is very pleasant by the side of a small river, of which the bank rises high on the other side shaded by gradual rows of trees. The gloom, the stream, and the silence generate thoughtfulness.

ᵃ⁻ᵃ *added later.*

[1] See *ante*, iv. 421 ⟨and 554⟩, for the inscription on an urn erected by Mr. Myddelton 'on the banks of a rivulet where Johnson delighted to stand and repeat verses.' On Sept. 18, 1777, Johnson wrote to Mrs. Thrale:—' Mr. Myddleton's erection of an urn looks like an intention to bury me alive; I would as willingly see my friend, however benevolent and hospitable quietly inurned. Let him think for the present of some more acceptable memorial.' *Letters*, No. 548.

† ⟨The Rev. Robert Myddelton, the rector of Denbigh, 1772–97. He was the brother of John Myddelton of Gwaynynog, *post*, v, pp. 587–8.⟩

§ ⟨See App. D, p. 594.⟩

[2] ⟨The Rev. W. Worthington, D.D., was Vicar of Llanrhaiadr from 1745 till his death on 6 Oct. 1778. He was a Prebendary of St. Asaph and York. Writing on 24 Oct. 1778 Johnson said :—' I have known Worthington long . . . I believe he was a very good Man.' *Letters*, No. 585. See next page for his house and the *D.N.B.* for his numerous writings.⟩

Th. 8—Sat. 10 *Sept.* 1774 Llanrhaiadr–Shrewsbury

The town is old and very mean, but has, I think, a market. In this house the Welsh translation of the old testament was made †.

The Welsh Singing Psalms were written by Archdeacon Price §. They are not considered as elegant, but as very literal and accurate.

We came to Llanrhaiadur through Oswestry, a town not very little nor very mean. The Church which I saw only at a distance seems to be an edifice much too grand for the present state of the place.

Sept⟨ember⟩ 9.

We visited the Waterfal which is very high, and in rainy weather very copious. There is a reservoir made to supply it. In its fall it has perforated a rock. There is a room built for entertainment. There was some difficulty in climbing to a near view. Lord Littelton [1] came near it, and turned back.

When we came back we took some cold meat, and notwithstanding the D⟨octo⟩r's importunities went that day to Shrewsbury.

Sept⟨ember⟩ 10.

I sent for Gwin [2], and he showed us the town. The walls are broken, and narrower than those of Chester. The town is large

† ⟨The Bible was first translated into Welsh by the Rev. William Morgan, 1545–1604, who was Vicar of Llanrhaiadr from 1578 to 1588: the translation was published in 1588. Morgan became successively Bishop of Llandaff and St. Asaph. See the *D.N.B.* and Owen Evans, *op. cit. infra*, pp. 123–8.

Mrs. Thrale wrote:—' We slept at Dr. Worthington's, where the warmth of our welcome made some amends for the wretchedness of our accommodation.' Broadley, *op. cit.* p. 208. The present (1937) Vicar, the Rev. Canon Silas Evans, informs me that the vicarage, save for some alterations and improvements, is the same to-day as it was in Johnson's time.⟩

§ ⟨The metrical version of the Psalms by Edmund Prys, 1544–1623, archdeacon of Merioneth, was first published as an appendix, with a separate title-page and pagination, to the new edition of the Welsh Book of Common Prayer, 1621; it has since been included in over a hundred editions of the Welsh Prayer Book, Bible, or Metrical Psalms. The hymn-books of every denomination in Wales to-day contain many of Prys's psalms. The Venerable A. Owen Evans in a life of Prys writes: ' His version is a pleasing and correct translation and something more; it is a commentary and an exposition.' See *Trans. Soc. Cymmrodorion,* 1924, pp. 112 ff., and *D.N.B.*⟩

[1] Thomas, the second Lord Lyttelton. Duppa.

[2] Mr. Gwynn the architect was a native of Shrewsbury, and was at this time completing a bridge across the Severn, called the English Bridge: besides this bridge, he built one at A⟨t⟩cham, over the Severn, near to Shrewsbury; and the bridges at Worcester and Oxford. Duppa. ⟨For John Gwynn see *ante*, ii. 438, Johnson's *Letters*, Nos. 533 and 570, and *D.N.B.*⟩

and has many Gentlemens houses, but the streets are narrow. I saw Taylors library †. We walked in the Quarry, a very pleasant walk by the river [1]. Our inn was not bad.

Sept⟨ember⟩ 11. Sunday.

We were at St. Chads, a very large and luminous Church. We were on the Castle hill.

⟨September⟩ 12.

We called on Dr. Adams [2], and travelled towards Worcester through Wenlock, a very mean place though a borough. At noon we came to Bridgenorth, and walked about the town, of which one part stands on a high rock and part very low by the river. There is an old tower § which being crooked leans so much that it is frightful to pass by it.

In the afternoon we went through Kinver a town in Staffordshire, neat and closely built. I believe it has only one street.

The Road was so steep and miry, that we were forced to stop at Hartlebury, where we had a very neat inn, though it made a very poor appearance.

Sept⟨ember⟩ 13.

We came to Lord Sandys at Ombersley where we were treated with great civility [3]. The house is large. The Hall is a very noble room.

[1] An ancestor of mine, a nurserygardener, Thomas Wright by name, after whom my grandfather, Thomas Wright Hill, was called, planted this walk. The tradition preserved in my family is that on his wedding-day he took six men with him and planted these trees. When blamed for keeping the wedding-dinner waiting, he answered, that if what he had been doing turned out well, it would be of far more value than a wedding-dinner.

[2] ⟨Dr. Adams was Perpetual Curate of St. Chad's, Shrewsbury. He lived in an early 17th-c. brick-built house, known as Rowley's mansion, in Hill's Lane : the house still (1937) stands, almost entirely devoid of the original interior and no longer used as a residence. See H. E. Forrest, *Old Houses of Shrewsbury*, 1912, pp. 51–4. Mrs. Thrale's account of the visit is not pleasing : she writes :—' We breakfasted with Dr. Adams, . . .

whose welcome, and whose breakfast, and whose conversation were so cold that I was most impatient of delay.' Broadley, *op. cit.* p. 209. Dr. Adams was appointed Master of Pembroke College, Oxford, next year. See Macleane's *Pembroke College*, p. 393, and *ante*, ii. 441.⟩

†, § ⟨See App. D, pp. 594–5.⟩

[3] ⟨Edwin, Lord Sandys, 1726–97, was an old friend of the Thrales. He had been M.P. for Droitwich, 1747–54, Bossiney, 1754–62, and Westminster, 1762–70. He married the widow of W. Payne King. See G. E. C. *Compl. Peerage*, 1896, vii. 54. Mrs. Thrale says that the travellers were entertained ' with a liberality of friendship which cannot be surpassed. The Lady's attention to her friends makes more than amends for her ignorance and deformity.' Broadley, *op. cit.* p. 210.⟩ ' I have heard Dr.

⟨SEPTEMBER⟩ 15.

We went to Worcester a very splendid city. The Cathedral is very noble with many remarkable monuments. The Library is in the Chapter house, on the table lay the Nuremburg Chronicle, I think, of the first Edition †. We went to the China Warehouse. The Cathedral has a cloister. The long isle is in my opinion neither so wide [a] nor so high as that of Lichfield.

⟨SEPTEMBER⟩ 16.

We went to Hagley, where we were disappointed of the respect and kindness that we expected [1].

⟨SEPTEMBER⟩ 17.

We saw the house and park which equalled my expectation. The house is one square mass. The offices are below. The rooms of elegance on the first floor with two stories of bed Chambers very well disposed above it. The Bedchambers have low windows which abates the dignity of the house.

The park has an artificial ruin [2], and wants water. There is however one temporary cascade. From the farthest hill there is a very wide prospect.

[a] wide *substituted for* long *erased*.

Johnson protest that he never had quite as much as he wished of wall-fruit except once in his life, and that was when we were all together at Ombersley.' Piozzi's *Anec.* p. 103 : John. Misc. i. 217.

† ⟨Schedel's *Liber cronicarum*, 1493, is still in the Cathedral library.⟩

[1] This visit was not to Lord Lyttelton, but to his uncle [William Henry Lyttelton, afterwards, by successive creations, Baron Westcote (1776) and Baron Lyttelton (1794)], the father of the present Lord Lyttelton, who lived at a house called Little Hagley. Duppa. ⟨Mrs. Thrale writes :—' We dressed and dined at Hagley, where the day passed in the common formalities till the evening came and the ladies pressed me to play at cards, notwithstanding all my excuses, with an ill-bred but irresistible importunity. . . . Mr. Johnson sate to read awhile and then walked about, when Mr. Lyttelton advertised if he did not use his candle to put it out.' Broadley, *op. cit.* p. 210. Mrs. Thrale was forced to play cards again on the next evening : ' Cards again and cruel vexation to me, but to-night I scarce troubled myself to hold them. The ladies had made themselves so disagreeable to me that I thought they deserved no unpleasant compliance from me, and they shall have none.' *Ibid.* See next page, note 1, for a different version of the rudeness to Johnson. Mr. Lyttelton, who was Mr. Thrale's friend, had invited Johnson to visit him in 1771. Johnson's *Letters*, No. 257.⟩

[2] Walpole, writing of Hagley in Sept. 1753 (*Letters*, iii. 186), says :— ' There is extreme taste in the park : the seats are not the best, but there is not one absurdity. There is a ruined castle, built by Miller, that would get him his freedom even of Strawberry : it has the true rust of the Barons' Wars. Then there is a scene of a small lake, with cascades falling down such a Parnassus ! . . . and there is such a fairy dale, with more cascades gushing out of rocks ! '

⟨SEPTEMBER⟩ 18.

I went to Church. The Church is externally very mean, and is therefore diligently hidden by a plantation. There are in it several modern monuments of the Littletons.

The⟨re⟩ dined with us, Lord Dudley, and Sir   Littelton †
of Staffordshire and His Lady, they were all persons of agreeable conversation.

I found time to reflect on my Birthday, and offered a prayer which I hope, was heard.

SEPT⟨EMBER⟩ 19.

We made haste away from a place where all were offended [1]. In the way we visited the Leasires [2]. It was rain, yet we visited all the waterfalls; there are in one place fourteen falls in a short line. It is the next place to Ilam Garden [3]. Poor Shenstone never tasted his pension. It is not very well proved that any pension was obtained for him. I am afraid that he died of misery [4].

† ⟨Sir Edward Littleton, c. 1725–1812.⟩

[1] ' Mrs. Lyttelton, *ci-devant* Caroline Bristow, forced me to play at whist against my liking, and her husband took away Johnson's candle that he wanted to read by at the other end of the room. Those, I trust, were the offences.' *Piozzi MS.* CROKER. ⟨See *ante*, v. 456, n. 1.⟩

[2] Johnson thus writes of Shenstone and the Leasowes (*Life of Shenstone*, 10–12): ' He began . . . to point his prospects, to diversify his surface, to entangle his walks, and to wind his waters, which he did with such judgement and such fancy as made his little domain the envy of the great and the admiration of the skilful: a place to be visited by travellers, and copied by designers. . . . For a while the inhabitants of Hagley affected to tell their acquaintance of the little fellow that was trying to make himself admired; but when by degrees the Leasowes forced themselves into notice, they took care to defeat the curiosity which they could not suppress by conducting their visitants perversely to inconvenient points of view, and introducing them at the wrong end of a walk to detect a deception; injuries of which Shenstone would heavily complain. Where there is emulation there will be vanity; and where there is vanity there will be folly. The pleasure of Shenstone was all in his eye: he valued what he valued merely for its looks: nothing raised his indignation more than to ask if there were any fishes in his water.' ⟨For a very full account of the Leasowes, see T. Martyn's *The English Connoisseur*, 1766, i. 151 ff.⟩ See *ante*, v. 345.

[3] See *ante*, iii. 187, and v. 429.

[4] ' He spent his estate in adorning it, and his death was probably hastened by his anxieties. He was a lamp that spent its oil in blazing. It is said that if he had lived a little longer he would have been assisted by a pension: such bounty could not have been ever more properly bestowed.' Johnson's *Life of Shenstone*, 14. His friend, Mr. Graves, the author of *The Spiritual Quixote*, in a note on this passage says that, if he was sometimes

Mon. 19—Th. 22 Sept. 1774 Birmingham–Woodstock

We came to Birmingham and I sent for Hector [1], whom I found well.

⟨SEPTEMBER⟩ 20.

We breakfasted with Hector and visited the Manufacture of Papier machè. The paper which the⟨y⟩ use is smooth whited brown; the varnish is polished with [a] rotten stone. Hector gave me a tea [a] board. We then went to Boltons [2], who with great civility led us through his shops. I could not ⟨d⟩istinctly see his enginery.

Twelve dozen of Buttons for three ⟨s⟩hillings [3]. Spoons struck at once.

⟨SEPTEMBER⟩ 21.

Hector came to us again. We came easily to Woodstock †.

⟨SEPTEMBER⟩ 22.

We saw Blenheim and Woodstock park [4]. The park contains 2500 Acres about four square miles. It has red deer.

Mr. Bryant [5] shewed me the Library with great civility.

[a–a] *one line of MS. at foot of leaf almost cut away.*

distressed for money, yet he was able to leave legacies and two small annuities. *Recoll. Shenstone,* p. 72.

[1] ⟨Edmund Hector, Johnson's school friend, who had been established in Birmingham as a surgeon since about 1731, and at whose house Johnson often stayed. He was born in 1708 and died in 1794. See A. L. Reade, *Gleanings,* iii. 124–5, v. 93 ; *ante,* ii. 459, iv. 135, 270, and 375. Hector's sister, Mrs. Carless, made breakfast for the visitors next morning, and in the evening Johnson said how much he had been in love with her. See *ante,* ii. 537.⟩

[2] ⟨For Boulton and his works see *ante,* ii. 459, 536, and H. W. Dickinson, *Matthew Boulton* (1937).⟩

[3] ⟨Mrs. Thrale notes :—' He [Boulton] showed us his Buttons at 3s. the six dozen, and his watch chains at two pence each.' Broadley, *op. cit.* p. 214.⟩

† ⟨Mrs. Thrale records :—' At the last stage of the journey Mr. Seward (*ante,* iii. 123) came up to the coach-side and so went with us to Woodstock, where we sent for our friend Mr. King and consulted how to see Blenheim in the morning. Horses were accordingly provided and we rode about the Park.' Broadley, *op. cit.* p. 215.⟩

[4] Johnson and Boswell drove through the Park in 1776. *Ante,* ii. 451. ⟨For Johnson's desire to see Blenheim, ' if properly invited', see *ante,* v. 303.⟩

[5] ' My friend, the late Lord Grosvenor, had a house at Salt-Hill, where I usually spent a part of the summer, and thus became a neighbour of that great and good man, Jacob Bryant. Here the conversation turned one morning on a Greek criticism by Dr. Johnson in some volume lying on the table, which I ventured (*for I was then young*) to deem incorrect, and pointed it out to him. I could not help thinking that he was somewhat of my opinion ; but he was cautious and reserved. " But, Sir," said I, willing to overcome his scruples, " Dr. Johnson himself . . . admitted that he was not a good Greek scholar." " Sir," he replied, with a serious and impressive air, " it is not easy for us to say what such a man as Johnson would call a good Greek scholar." I hope that I profited by that lesson —certainly I never forgot it.' Gifford's

Oxford   Thursday 22—Saturday 24 Sept. 1774   459
Durandi Rationale. 1459 [1]. Lascaris Grammar of the first
edition, well printed, but much less than latter Editions [2]. The
first Batrachomyomachia [3].
The Duke † sent Mr. Thrale Partridges and fruit. At night
we came to Oxford.

⟨SEPTEMBER⟩ 23.

We visited Mr. Colson [4]. The Ladies wandred about the
University.

⟨SEPTEMBER⟩ 24.

$Ka\theta$. We dine with Mr. Colson.

Works of Ford, vol. i. p. lxii. ' So notorious is Mr. Bryant's great fondness for studying and proving the truths of the creation according to Moses, that he told me himself, and with much quaint humour, a pleasantry of one of his friends in giving a character of him :—" Bryant," said he, "is a very good scholar, and knows all things whatever up to Noah, but not a single thing in the world beyond the Deluge!"' Mme D'Arblay's *Diary*, iii. 229. ⟨As Secretary to the Duke of Marlborough Bryant resided at Blenheim for many years.⟩

[1] ⟨*Rationale Divinorum Officiorum*, the chief work of Gulielmus Durandus, bishop of Mende, *c*. 1230–1296 : it was first printed by Fust and Schoeffer at Mainz in 1459.⟩ See *ante*, ii. 397, n. 2.

[2] ⟨See p. 461, n. 4.⟩

[3] ⟨Formerly attributed to Homer. The first edition was printed by Laonicus Cretensis at Venice in 1486. See *Catal. of Books printed in the XVth c. in the British Museum*, v. 408, and Legrand, *Bibl. hellénique*, i. 6.⟩

† ⟨George, the 4th duke, 1738–1817. Mrs. Thrale writes : ' I hear the Duke and Duchess were very attentive and polite, and said they would have asked us to dinner but that they were engaged abroad.' The Duke's son, the Marquis of Blandford, asked to see Mrs. Thrale, but as he had the ' Hooping Cough', she ' declined the honour.' Broadley, *op. cit*. p. 215.⟩

[4] Under the date 24 Sept. Mrs. Thrale writes :—' We dined in the Hall at University College, where I sat in the seat of honour as Locum Tenens forsooth ; and saw the ceremonies of the Grace Cup and Butler's Book. Mr. Coulson entertained us with liberality and with kindness. . . . We drank tea in the Common Room, had a World of talk and passed the evening [of the 24th], with cheerfulness and comfort. I like Mr. Coulson much and pressed him to come to Streatham with a very honest importunity.' Broadley, *op. cit*. p. 216. Mr. Coulson was a senior Fellow of University College, in habit and appearance something like Johnson himself. . . . Lord Stowell informed me that he was very eccentric. He would on a fine day hang out of the college windows his various pieces of apparel to air, which used to be universally answered by the young men hanging out from all the other windows, quilts, carpets, rags, and every kind of trash, and this was called an *illumination*. His notions of the eminence and importance of his academic situation were so peculiar, that, when he afterwards accepted a college living, he expressed to Lord Stowell his doubts whether, after living so long in the great *world*, he might not grow weary of the comparative retirement of a country parish. CROKER, 1835–48. ⟨John Coulson, son of Edward Coulson of Lee Hall, Northumberland, matriculated from New College, Oxford, 17 Dec. 1739, aged 20 ; he took his first degree in 1743, migrated to University College, and proceeded M.A. in 1746. Foster, *Alumni Oxon*. i. 304. He was Rector of Checkendon, Oxon., from 18 Oct. 1779 till his death on 4 Nov. 1788. *Gent. Mag*., 1788, lviii. ii. 1032.⟩ See *ante*, ii. 382, note.

460 **Sunday 25—Friday 30 Sept.** 1774 Oxford–London
Van Sittaert[1] told me his distemper.
[a]Afterwards we were at Burke's, where we heard of the dissolution of the parliament. We went home [2].[a]

[a-a] *added later.*

[1] Dr. Robert Vansittart, who was Regius Professor of Civil Law at this time. ⟨Mrs. Thrale says, under date 25th Sept., that the visitors dined with Vansittart; she adds : ' His politeness and desire to oblige would be still more valuable than they are did one not easily observe that all is a mere effort to get rid of himself, not to oblige his friends. This unhappy man has had by accident his spirits much disordered and seeks that refuge from coxcomry and assiduity which has been denied him by literature, and that liveliness of disposition which seems natural to him.' Broadley, *op. cit.* p. 216. See *ante*, i. 348, 546, and *D.N.B.*⟩

[2] ⟨The party left Oxford on the 27th for Benson, staying the night at the inn there ; on the next day they visited some of Mrs. Thrale's farm property near Crowmarsh and reached Beaconsfield late at night, where they stayed with Burke, at Gregories, till the 30th, when they left for London and Streatham. Broadley, *op. cit.* p. 217. Mrs. Thrale wrote on the 30th in what she calls ' The Children's Book', now, 1964, owned by Brigadier Hugh Mainwaring : ' I returned safe home from my long Tour ; bro[t]. Queeney safe back, called on my Girls at Kensington, whom I found quite well . . ., and got in good time to Streatham where Harry met & rejoyced over us very kindly.' Mrs. Thrale returned, however, not to the peace of Streatham, but to the turmoil of an election at Southwark. The news of the dissolution of Parliament on 30 Sept. caused great excitement at Gregories. Mrs. Thrale writes, under date 29 Sept. : ' Last night we were received with open arms by our friends at Beaconsfield ; each seemed to contend who should be kindest, but to-day Mr. Burke himself was obliged to go out somewhere about Election matters. There was an old Mr. Lowndes dined with us and got very drunk talking Politics with Will Burke and my Master after dinner. Lord Verney and Edmund came home at night very much flustered with liquor, and I thought how I had spent three months from home among dunces of all ranks and sorts, but had never seen a man drunk till I came among the Wits.' Under the date 30 Sept., she writes : ' When I rose Mr. Thrale informed me that the Parliament was suddenly dissolved and that all the World was to bustle, that we were to go to Southwark, not to Streatham, and canvass away.' Broadley, *op. cit.*, pp. 217–19. Johnson returned to London and wrote ' with energetick vivacity ' his political pamphlet, *The Patriot* (*ante*, ii. 286) ; he also wrote Mr. Thrale's election address, the following draft of which, in Johnson's handwriting, was discovered by Mr. J. L. Clifford at Bach-y-Graig in 1936:
' To the worthy Electors of the Borough of Southwark.
' Gentlemen,
'.A new Parliament being called, I propose to solicit the honour of continuing to represent you, and request your votes and interest, with the respect due to the collective voice of a Borough so numerous and opulent, and that hope of your Favour which may be modestly indulged by a man not conscious either of negligence in his attendance or unfaithfulness in his trust, who if he shall be again dignified by your choice, will have no other purpose than that of promoting the true and permanent interest of our country.
' I am
' Gentlemen
' with great respect.'
Nathaniel Polhill and Henry Thrale were returned on 18 Oct. *Parl. Return Members of Parl.* ii. 156. See *ante*, iii. 440, for another specimen of Johnson's election addresses. For Johnson's parting words to Burke at Beaconsfield, see *ante*, ii. 285, n. 3.⟩

NOTES[1]

Indidem from the same place.
Θαλίαις for Δολίαις in Phocylides [2].
To note down my Father's stock, expences, and profit.
Queeny's Goats 149 I think [3].
Potato set whole at the latter end of May produced Sept. 5, 7lb 7 oz in a hundred potatoes great and small.
First Printed Book in Greek, Lascaris's Grammar 4to Mediolani 1476 per Dionysium Palavisinum qu⟨aere⟩. Bowyer [4].

[1] ⟨These notes are written in the blank column opposite part of the entry for 18 August with which they have no clear connexion. It is hardly possible to say exactly when they were written, but Dr. Robin Flower is of the opinion that the handwriting belongs to the period of the diary itself.⟩

[2] ⟨The reference is to the didactic poem, Ποίημα νουθετικόν or γνῶμαι, long thought to be by the gnomic poet Phocylides of Miletus, but shown by Bernays in 1856 to be the work of an Alexandrian Jew or Christian. The emendation noted by Johnson was actually made by R. F. P. Brunck (1729–1803): it occurs in the following precept (verses 81, 82):

Καλὸν ξεινίζειν ταχέως λιταῖσι τραπέζαις
ἢ πλείσταις θαλίαισι βραδυνούσαις παρὰ καιρόν.

Brunck's text was first printed, so far as I have been able to discover, in his 'Ηθικὴ ποίησις sive Gnomici Poetae Graeci (1784). In making the emendation he says (p. 317): 'Absurde vulgo legitur ἢ πλείσταις δολίαισι. Vere θαλίαι, opiparae, lautae epulae opponuntur λιταῖσι τραπέζαις, quae etiamsi sint tenuissimae tamen subdolae esse possunt.' Most modern editors accept the emendation, but Rubenauer does not approve and suggests θοίναισι (Poetae elegiaci et iambographi, 1915, p. 92). See Bernays, Über das Phokylideische Gedicht, 1856; Nicole in Album Gratulatorium in honorem H. V. Herwerden, 1902, pp. 163 ff.; Jewish Encycl. 1915, x. 255–6; and Diehl, Anthologia lyrica Graeca, 1936, t. i, pars 2, pp. 96 ff.⟩

[3] ⟨See ante, v. 451, n. 2.⟩

[4] ⟨W. Bowyer, the learned printer, has the same record in his Origin of Printing (p. 102), which was published in June 1774 and therefore available to Johnson. Gent. Mag. xliv. 277. No earlier book printed in Greek type than Lascaris's Grammar has been found. See E. Legrand, Bibl. hellénique, 1885, i. 1, and Introd. pp. cxxxi ff. Johnson saw the book at Blenheim on 22 Sept. Ante, v. 459.⟩

APPENDIX D

THIS General Appendix consists of notes to this volume for which room could not be found on the pages to which they relate. The numbers of these pages are, for convenience of reference, given in the headline.

Page 14, lines 1 ff. Boswell had his first interview with Voltaire on 24 Dec. 1764 at Ferney. Of this he wrote a full account. He records: ' I told him that Mr. Johnson and I intended to make a tour thro' the Hebrides, the Northern Isles of Scotland. He smiled, and cried, " *Eh bien ; mais Je resterai ici. Vous me laisserez rester ici ?* " " *Sans doute.*" " *Eh bien, donc, Allez. Je n'ai point d'objections* ".' *Boswell Papers*, iv. 130.

Page 18, last line. By an Act of the 7th of George I for encouraging the consumption of raw silk and mohair, buttons and button-holes made of cloth, serge, and other stuffs were prohibited. In 1738 a petition was presented to Parliament stating that in evasion of this Act 'great quantities of stuffs made of horse-hair, or mixed therewith, have been . . . used only for making and binding of buttons and button-holes to the great detriment and impoverishing of many thousands . . . and prejudice of the woollen manufactures of the kingdom '. An Act was brought in to prohibit the use of horse-hair, and was only thrown out on the third reading. *Parl. Hist.* x. 787.—HILL.

Page 21, line 1. The Court of Session ' sits two terms in the year, from the 12th of November to the 12th of March, and from the 12th of June to the 12th of August, with an interruption of about three weeks during the Christmas holidays '. H. Arnot, *Hist. Edinburgh*, 1779, p. 469. The time of the Summer Session was found to be inconvenient and was altered in 1790, by 30 Geo. III, cap. 17, to begin on 12 May and end on 11 July. *Scots Mag.* lii, p. 255.

Page 21, line 4. Boswell's journal for Saturday 14 August 1773 reads: ' Was in anxiety all the evening lest Mr. Johnson should come while our country company sat. So there is ALLWAYS some uneasiness. Got a card from him about half an hour after 11 that he was at Boyd's. This relieved me. I took a chairman to light me thither. I thought all the way of the Rambler, etc.' *Boswell Papers*, vi. 175. When they met Johnson said : ' " Shall I see your Lady ? " BOSWELL " Yes". JOHNSON " Then I'll put on a clean shirt ". I said, " 'Tis needless. Either don't see her tonight, or don't put on a clean shirt ". JOHNSON " Sir, I'll do both".' *Ibid.* Boswell adds at the end of the entry ' We sat till near two in the morning. I was fatigued a little'. *Ibid.* 176.

Pages 22–5   *Appendix D*   463

Page 22, line 10 and note 2. Boswell on Whitsunday, 1773, removed from Hume's ' house ', which he sub-let to Lady Wallace, to the larger ground-floor apartment on the same stair, and it was in this apartment that he received Johnson. E. C. Mossner in *Mod. Lang. Notes*, 1948, pp. 516–19. Boswell lived there till 1786.

Page 24, lines 3 ff. *Vicennial prescription.* The trial was that of Callum Macgregor *alias* John Grant. He was indicted before the circuit-court, held at Aberdeen in the spring of 1773, for the murder of John Stuart on 25 Dec. 1747. ' He, in bar of the prosecution, pleaded prescription; and as this was an important, and hitherto undecided point, the advocate-depute deserted the diet, and the prisoner was recommitted upon a new warrant, in order that the question might be argued before the whole court at Edinburgh.' J. Maclaurin's *Arguments & Decisions*, 1774, pp. 595 ff. This was done in May 1773 and on 9 Aug. the Court pronounced the interlocutor : ' In respect it does not appear that any sentence of fugitation passed against the pannel, sustain the defence, and dismiss the indictment.' *Ibid.* 607. The case is fully reported by Maclaurin, who questioned the justice of the Court's decision. Lord Auchinleck thought the question ' new and extremely nice '. The case was cited as a precedent in 1934 (Sugden *v.* H.M. Advocate, fully reported in *Scots Law Times Reports*, 1934, pp. 465 ff.), when the Court, by a majority, dismissed the appeal and held that the vicennial prescription of crime did not form part of the law of Scotland, and that the above-cited case was not a decision to the contrary.

Page 25, note 2. Boswell's great-grandmother was Veronica, one of the sixteen children of Cornelis van Aerssen, heer van Sommelsdijk (1600–62), and his wife Lucia van Waltha (d. 1674): she was born in 1633 and married Alexander Bruce, second Earl of Kincardine (*c.* 1629–80). Her brother Cornelis (1637–88) was Governor of Surinam, where he was murdered. The son of this Cornelis, François (1669–1740), was appointed Governor of Surinam, but declined the office: he was the admiral of the Dutch fleet that co-operated with Sir Charles Wager in 1729, when the conclusion of peace between England and Spain seemed uncertain ; he married, 1712, Maria van Aerssen van Wernhout, and had four daughters and two sons : his younger son was Boswell's correspondent. His full style was François Cornelis (baron) van Aerssen, heer van de Plaat, Sommelsdijk, Ooltgensplaat met den Bommel en Craayestein ; he was born 5 Aug. 1725, entered the army and became a general-major and colonel in 1766 ; he was ennobled 14 Jan. 1772, and held various offices, the most important of which was that of 'Houtvester en Jagermeestergeneraal van Holland ', or head of the department which controlled the forests and waste lands, which was a greatly desired post and was usually held by a member of the nobility (see

Tegenwoordige staat der Vereenigde Nederlanden, 1742, iv, pp. 206 ff.). He married Everdina Petronella, Countess of Hogendorp, and died at The Hague, 26 Dec. 1793. He was the last of his line, as his only son, François Jean (1764-84), predeceased him. See *Adelsarchief: Jaarboek voor den Nederlandschen Adel*, ed. D. G. van Epen, 1902, iii. 166-77; *Nieuw Nederlandsch Biografisch Woordenboek*, 1914, iii. 8-13; G. E. C., *Complete Peerage*, 1929, vii. 271; and *Boswell Papers*, ii. 168 ff.

Boswell visited the van Sommelsdijks at Christmas, 1763. In some notes made for his 'Hague Jaunt' he wrote:

'You are to wait on Mynheer de Somelsdyke of whom you have heard so much from your Infancy, and who may be of infinite use to you. Your father considers this as a matter of great moment.' *Boswell Papers*, ii. 190.

Boswell agreed, 6 June 1764, with van Sommelsdijk 'to have a correspondence', but very few letters have survived. *Boswell Papers*, ii. 137, 176-8; vii. 116; viii. 214-15.

Page 30, line 3. Boswell's journal tells us what he suppressed as too violent. Boswell asked 'Why attack his [i.e. Hume's] heart?' Johnson's reply was: 'Why, Sir, because his head has corrupted it. Or perhaps it has perverted his head. I know not indeed whether he has first been a blockhead and that has made him a rogue, or first been a rogue and that has made him a blockhead.' *Boswell Papers*, vi. 178.

Page 30, lines 14 ff. and note 3. Adam Smith's letter to William Strahan was written for publication as an addendum to Hume's brief autobiography, *The Life of David Hume written by Himself* (Strahan and Cadell, 1777); both pieces are prefixed to editions of Hume's *History of England*, published from 1778 to 1864. The letter is reprinted by Dr. Birkbeck Hill in his *Letters of David Hume to William Strahan*, 1888, pp. xxxiv ff., and by Dr. J. Y. T. Greig in his edition of Hume's *Letters*, 1932 (ii. 450-2).

Page 32, line 25. Evidence of the time when the morning and afternoon services were held in the Edinburgh churches is scanty. Boswell's younger brother, John, records in his diary (which was courteously placed at my disposal by the late Dr. Alexander Boswell), under date 31 Dec. 1769, 'Brackfasted about ten, after brackfast went to the New Church, after sermon took a turn to the Castle Hill, dined betwixt one and two, after dinner went back to the New Church'. On the next Sunday he dined at the same time, went to the same church, and 'came home betwixt three and four'; the services were held at the same time in the summer; on 10 June 1770 he records: 'Brackfasted about ten, after brackfast went to the New Church, . . . came out betwixt twelve and one, . . . dined betwixt one and two. . . . After dinner went back to the New Church.'

Farington, who visited Scotland in 1788, noted on Sunday 6 July:

Pages 32-4   *Appendix D*

'This morning went to St. Giles Church. . . . The service began at half-past ten.' (*The Scotsman*, 7 Feb. 1935, p. 10.) Unfortunately he did not go to church in the afternoon.

At the Tron Kirk the services were in 1790 held later : ' The Council appointed the Bells for the Church to be continued to be rung as at present, viz : at a quarter before eleven in the forenoons and at two o'clock afternoons of the Sundays ' (Dugald Butler, *The Tron Kirk*, 1906, p. 262) : presumably the services would be held at 11.0 and 2.15. The Rev. J. Campbell, D.D., Minister of the Tolbooth Church, to whom I am indebted, thinks that services in the other churches would be held at the same time, as otherwise the bells of some would have disturbed others. He also tells me that the hour of afternoon service, as long as afternoon services continued, down to thirty years ago, was 2.15 or 2.30.

Cockburn, who was born in 1779, says that in his youth ' the prevailing dinner hour was about three o'clock. Two o'clock was quite common, if there was no company. Hence it was no great deviation from their usual custom for a family to dine on Sundays *between sermons* —that is between one and two.' *Memorials*, 1910, p. 30.

Page 32, note 3 (last line of note in the first column of page 33). For *turpissima bestia* see the line of Ennius cited by Cicero (*De natura deorum*, i. 35, 97), ' Simia quam similis, turpissima bestia, nobis ! '

Page 32, note 3 (lines 27 ff. of the second column of page 33). Malone, who was the virtual editor of the second edition of the *Tour*, made the long and important addition, beginning ' I find, since the former edition ', in defence of Burke's reputation for wit, entirely on his own initiative : he told Boswell, in a letter dated 19 Oct. 1785, that he had ' tacked a rider ' to his note. *Fettercairn Catalogue*, No. 556. Boswell, in a letter to Burke dated 20 Dec. 1785, accompanying a presentation copy of the book, gave Malone full credit. *Ibid.*, No. 1065. Burke, in reply, 4 Jan. 1786, thanked Boswell and Malone, but made it clear that he was willing to accept Johnson's judgement. *Ibid.* No. 161.

For the friendship of Boswell and Burke see Mr. Dixon Wecter in *Modern Philology*, Aug. 1938, pp. 47 ff. They met first on 6 May 1772 and not on 30 April 1773, as Boswell inadvertently stated in the *Life* (*ante*, ii. 240).

Page 34, lines 4-9. Johnson's remark on Burke, as originally reported by Boswell, 15 Aug. 1773, was very different from the printed version. It ran :

' Burke, Sir, is such a man, that if you met him for the first time in a street where there was a shower of cannon bullets & you & he ran up a stair to take shelter he'd talk to you in such a manner that when you came down you'd say this is an extraordinary man.'

Appendix D

See *Boswell Papers*, 1929, vi. 172 and plate facing p. 178, and Dr. Chapman's edition of *Hebrides*, 1924, p. 463.

Page 35, note 3. John Wesley published his pamphlet, *A Calm Address to our American Colonies*, in 1775, probably in September. (The reply by ' Germanicus ' is dated 19 Oct. 1775.) Toplady, under the pseudonym of ' An Hanoverian ', issued his virulent attack, *An Old Fox tarr'd and feathered*, in the following October. He showed, by printing extracts from the two pamphlets in parallel columns, that Wesley had borrowed freely from Johnson's *Taxation no Tyranny*. Wesley made no mention whatever of Johnson's pamphlet in his first edition, but in ' a new edition, corrected and enlarged ', he gave as the opening paragraph of the Preface :

' I was of a different judgment on this head, till I read a tract intitled, " Taxation no Tyranny ". But as soon as I received more light myself, I judged it my duty to impart it to others. I therefore extracted the chief arguments from that treatise, and added an application to those whom it most concerns. I was well aware of the treatment this would bring upon myself : but let it be, so I may in any degree serve my King and Country.'

The Johnsonian passages, which number over thirty, are not distinguished in the text. Toplady's pamphlet is included in his *Works* (1794, v. 449–67). See also R. Polwhele's *Traditions*, 1826, ii. 556–7.

Page 37, line 1. Thomas Cooke, 1703–56, first published his translation of Hesiod in 1728. One volume only, containing the Amphitruo, of his edition and translation of Plautus appeared ; this is dated 1746 and has an impressive list of subscribers, including Garrick, Handel, Chesterfield, and well over a hundred peers. For a mild criticism of Pope, in his *Battle of the Poets*, he was put in *The Dunciad* (ii. 138) : he replied with great bitterness in a second edition. See his *Original Poems*, &c., 1742, pp. 177 ff., and the *D.N.B.*

Page 40, line 4 from foot. James Kerr was appointed Joint Keeper of the Public Records 20 Oct. 1746; he demitted office in 1773. If, as seems probable, he is identical with James Kerr, Writer, who was admitted Burgess and Guild Brother of Edinburgh, 12 Dec. 1753, in right of his wife Margaret, daughter of Thomas Buchanan, Writer, he was alive in 1780, but died before 12 Sept. 1781. I have to thank the former Keeper of the Records, Mr. W. Angus, for this information.

Page 40, line 2 from foot. Alexander Brown was appointed Keeper of the Library and Clerk to the Faculty of Advocates on 14 Jan. 1766 in succession to William Wallace, advocate. He had assisted in the Library before he was appointed Keeper. At a meeting of the Faculty on 5 Jan. 1762 it was agreed that there should be an assistant in addition to Walter Goodall (1706?–1766: see *D.N.B.*); on 11 Jan. 1763 the Treasurer was ordered to pay Mr. Alexander Brown £20 sterling ' on account of his extraordinary trouble during the late Survey of the Library'; similar entries occur every year till he was appointed Keeper. He held office till 1801. At a Faculty meeting held on 20 Jan. 1794 a motion was adopted ' that it be remitted to the Curators of the Library for this and the four preceding Years to consider of the propriety of appointing an assistant to Mr. Brown on account of his bad state of health '. On 8 July following Alexander Manners was appointed assistant and successor to Brown in both offices. Manners was in office as Principal Librarian on 20 June 1801, when Brown was spoken of as ' the late '. These facts are obtained from the MS. Minutes of the Faculty of Advocates, who have courteously permitted me to print them. Alexander Brown was the compiler of the second volume of the Library Catalogue, published in 1776. Hugo Arnot records that his ' accuracy and obliging dispositions render his management of this library extremely acceptable to the proprietors '. *Hist. Edinburgh*, 1779, p. 296.

Page 41, line 7. The ' signed assurance ' is what is generally known as the Accession Oath. This is taken ' at the first meeting of the Privy Council, and, when subscribed by the sovereign and the members of Council present, is transmitted to the Lord President of the Court of Session, registered in the Books of Sederunt, and thereafter deposited in the Register House '. M. Livingstone, *Guide to the Public Records of Scotland*, 1905, p. 2. William and Mary were the first to take the oath.

Page 42, line 15. A few years before Johnson's visit to Edinburgh it was proposed ' to rebuild the fabric of the University according to a regular plan, and in a decent manner ', on the ground where it then stood. Robertson, as Principal of the University, issued a *Memorial Relating to the University of Edinburgh*, 1768, a pamphlet not included in his *Works*, in which he described the buildings as they then existed. He says (p. 4) :

' A public Hall, a Divinity School, and some other buildings were erected by the year 1617. But these buildings, poor in themselves, seem not to have been carried on according to any regular plan, such as takes place in other Academical Structures which have been erected on more opulent foundations ; and hence the whole fabric has a mean, irregular, and contemptible appearance. Some of the houses which were found upon the area when it was purchased were converted, as they stood, into a part of the University buildings ; and many of the schools or teaching-rooms are, at this day, crowded into what was formerly the Marquis of Hamilton's house.'

The Principal, after enlarging on the high degree of reputation to which the University had attained, and mentioning the number of students as ' betwixt six and seven hundred ', continues (p. 6) :

' The buildings of the University must, on the first inspection, appear to every one to be extremely unsuitable, both to the rank which this University has for several years held, and to the present advancing and improved state of this country. They are so far inferior to all other structures of the same kind in our own, or in other countries, that they cannot fail to prejudice every stranger against Scotland, its education, and its manners. A stranger, when conducted to view the University of Edinburgh, might, on seeing such courts and buildings, naturally enough imagine them to be alms-houses for the reception of the poor ; but would never imagine that he was entering within the precincts of a noted and flourishing seat of learning. An area, which, if entire, would have formed one spacious quadrangle, is broken into three paltry divisions, and encompassed partly with walls which threaten destruction to the passenger, and partly with a range of low houses, several of which are now become ruinous, and not habitable. With the exception of one large upper gallery, which has lately been repaired, and made the public library, and of an anatomical theatre, there is no room or building belonging to the University that has any degree of academical decency. The teaching rooms of the Professors are, in general, mean, straitened, and inconvenient ; more enlarged accommodation is wanted ; and some Professors, whose hours of teaching follow immediately on one another, are obliged to occupy the same room.'

He concludes (p. 8) :

'In Edinburgh . . . the great improvements which have been lately made, and are still going forwards, large buildings arising suddenly on all hands, a magnificent bridge, and new streets and squares begun, carry all the marks of a country growing in arts and in industry. The University-fabric alone remains in such a neglected state, as to be generally accounted a dishonour to the city of Edinburgh, and to this part of the kingdom.'

The old buildings were pulled down in 1789, and Robert Adam was called upon to plan new ones ; these were completed in 1816 by W. H. Playfair, one of whose principal objects was ' to maintain as much as possible the spirit of that style of architecture which has been adopted in the buildings already executed [by R. Adam] '. See Playfair's *Report*, 1816, p. 4.

Page 42, line 19. The University Library took its rise from the bequest, in 1580, by Clement Little of his books ' to the Town of Edinburgh '. The Town Council, which had ordered that ' a house or library ' should be provided, four years later handed over the books to the custody of the Principal of the College, which had been recently, in 1582, founded. Subsequently the Council thought that the College had not provided sufficient accommodation for the Library and in 1616 allotted to it the room over the public Academical Hall. In 1642 it was removed to an adjacent building, but in 1753 the Upper Hall was renovated and restored to its original function. This was the Library that Johnson saw ; it remained in use till 1825, long after the rest of the old college buildings had been replaced by those that now stand. See A. Dalzel, *Hist. of the University of Edinburgh*, 1862, i. 269 ff., and Sir A. Grant, *Story of the University of Edinburgh*, 1884, ii. 168 ff.

Page 42, line 19. James Robertson, 1714–95, was Librarian of Edinburgh University from 1763 to 1785. He, with the help of an assistant, Mr. Duke Gordon, and three or four students, compiled the first catalogue of the Library. The assistant was paid £15 per annum, with board, and the students five shillings a week ; they for the most part dined with the Librarian during the carrying out of the work. The Librarian himself received no salary for the first two years, but in 1768 was given ' a gratification of seventy guineas '. See Andrew Dalzel, *Hist. of the University of Edinburgh*, 1862, ii. 438–9, 456, and Sir Alexander Grant, *Story of the University of Edinburgh*, 1884, ii. 174. Robertson was appointed conjunct Professor of Hebrew and Oriental Languages in 1751 and was, according to Sir Alexander Grant (*op. cit. supra*, ii. 289), the first really qualified professor to hold the chair. See also A. Bower, *Hist. of the University of Edinburgh*, 1817, ii. 360 ff. ; Hew Scott, *Fasti Eccl. Scot.*, 1928, vii. 386 ; and the *D.N.B.* s.v. Robertson, James.

This manuscript catalogue was in four folio volumes : it remained in use till *c.* 1820. Duke Gordon, according to Dalzel (*o.c.s.* i. 269), had been private tutor to Boswell's father, a statement which is certainly erroneous. He matriculated at Edinburgh in March 1753 in the class of Robert Hunter, Professor of Greek, and in March 1755 he was in the class of John Stevenson, Professor of Rational Philosophy. On 12 April 1800 he was granted the Honorary Degree of M.A. He died on 20 December following, bequeathing a large number of books to the Library in which he had worked for thirty-five years. *Senatus Minutes.* There is a full account of him in A. Bower's *Hist. of the University of Edinburgh*, 1830, iii. 134 ff.

Page 42, last line. ' Friar Bacon's Study ' at Oxford was the medieval tower and gatehouse on South or Folly Bridge ; it did not acquire this name till the seventeenth century, and in the sixteenth was sometimes called Bachelor's Tower. Anthony Wood, in his collections for the history of the city, writes :

' Before I goe any farther, I must take notice of the tower with a gate and common passage underneath, called Fryar Bacon his Study, which standeth on this bridge neare to the end next the city. A name though meerly traditionall and not in any record to be found ; yet neverthelesse their might be some matter of truth in it, being soe delivered from one generation to another.' *City of Oxford*, ed. A. Clark, Oxf. Hist. Soc., 1889, i. 425.

Wood had been told by ' eminent persons of this University ' that Roger Bacon ' did sometimes use in the night season to ascend this place invironed with waters and there to take the altitude and distance of starrs ', but he believed ' all this was at Little Gate ' in the neighbouring Grey Friars, where there was in his youth a decrepit building known as 'Roger Bacon's and Thomas Bongei's study '. *Ibid.* and ii. 411.

Thomas Hearne, in 1724, was more credulous (*Remarks & Collections*, Oxf. Hist. Soc., 1907, viii. 271); neither he nor Wood mentions the tradition that the 'study' would fall on some learned man. The Oxford City Council on 22 Jan. 1779 appointed a committee ' to view Friar Bacon's Study and treat with the Trustees of the Hinksey Turnpikes for the sale of the City's interest in the same ' (*City Council Book*), and it was pulled down later in the year. The *St. James's Chronicle* has, in the issue for 8–10 April 1779, some ' Lines occasioned by the intended Demolition of Friar Bacon's Study in Oxford'. See H. E. Salter, *Oxford City Properties*, Oxf. Hist. Soc., 1926, p. 102, and, for two good views, the *Book of Words* of the Oxford Historical Pageant, 1907.

· It is stated that Robert Henderson, 1685–1747, Librarian of the University of Edinburgh, was afraid the ruinous Edinburgh wall would fall on him. Andrew Dalzel, *Hist. University of Edinburgh*, 1862, i. 272.

Page 43, line 6. The Royal Infirmary, the successor of the original infirmary or hospital built in 1729, was erected on a site, lying to the south of Robinson's Close and to the east of the College Garden on Kirk o' Field, in the present Infirmary Street. The foundation stone was laid on 2 Aug. 1738, one wing was opened in 1741, and the building was completed in 1748 : the architect was William Adam, father of the more famous brothers, Robert and John. The Infirmary, with successive extensions in 1829, 1833, and 1853, lasted till 1879, when the present hospital, known at first as the New Royal Infirmary, between Lauriston Place and the West Meadows, was completed. The old building was demolished in 1884 and no part of it now remains.

George Drummond (1687–1766), who had been deeply concerned in the building of the original Infirmary, was chiefly instrumental in the establishment of its successor, as the bust of him by Nollekens, 1772, testifies. This was erected in the entrance hall of the Royal Infirmary and now stands in the main entrance of the New Royal Infirmary. Principal Robertson composed for it the following inscription : ' George Drummond, To whom this Country is indebted for all the Benefits which it derives from The Royal Infirmary.' See William Maitland, *Hist. of Edinburgh*, 1753, pp. 450 ff. ; James Grant, *Old and New Edinburgh*, 1882, ii. 297 ff. ; and, especially, Dr. A. Logan Turner, *The Story of a Great Hospital, the Royal Infirmary of Edinburgh* (Oliver & Boyd), 1937. · For a description of the building as it appeared in Johnson's time see the anonymous *History and Statutes of the Royal Infirmary*, 1778.

Page 49, line 19 and note 4. Viscount Perceval, afterwards the first Earl of Egmont, writes in his diary under date 13 March 1732 :

' Colonel Schutz . . . told me that he had been with Mrs. Vane, that he avoided it as long as he could, till the Prince [Frederick] took notice of his not going. . . .

Page 49 'This fat, and ill-shaped dwarf has nothing good to recommend her that I know of; neither sense nor wit, and is, besides (if report be true), the leavings of others.' *MSS. of the Earl of Egmont, Diary* (Hist. MSS. Comm., 1920), i. 235.

The Hon. Anne Vane was the eldest daughter of Gilbert, second Baron Barnard, 1678–1753. She was the mother, by Frederick Prince of Wales, of a son, Fitz-Frederick, who was born 24 June 1732 and who predeceased her. She died, unmarried, at Bath 27 March 1736. *Gent. Mag.* 1736, vi. 168, and G. E. C., *Complete Peerage*, 1910, i. 425 note.

Page 49, line 3 from foot. John Maclaurin, 1734–96, was one of Boswell's closest friends. He and his father are complimented in Boswell's second *Letter to the People of Scotland*, 1785, p. 43 : 'Mr. John Maclaurin (*filius Colini fama super æthera noti*, and a son of no common talents)'. John Ramsay of Ochtertyre gives a full account of him :

' A more singular young man, or one less prepossessing in his appearance to a stranger, could hardly be seen. The affected gravity of his dress and demeanour formed a strange contrast to the brilliant sallies of wit, with which he never failed to enliven his discourse, in season and out of season. . . . As he had a most lively imagination, and a levity which spurned all rules, he could not preserve the mask of gravity for any length of time among people of his own years. Though regarded as a pleasant good-natured fellow, the exuberance of his fancy, which was ever too strong to be controlled by discretion, made him perpetually deal in poetical squibs or burlesque pieces on some of his companions. . . . Notwithstanding his vivacity, he was a good scholar and a hard student. . . . Next to the law, he paid most attention to polite literature, particularly to light poetry and works of wit and humour, which coincided with his own genius.' *Scotland & Scotsmen in the 18th century*, 1888, i. 441 ff.

Among his writings are *The Philosopher's Opera*, 1757, and *Apology for the Writers against the Tragedy of Douglas*, 1759, two somewhat ill-natured attacks on Home and his friends, *The Keekeiad*, 1760, an obscene skit on Mr. John Jolly, ' a very eminent Citizen of Edinburgh ', and *Essays in Verse*, three parts, 1769–72. A manuscript note by David Rae in a copy of the first part in the National Library of Scotland reads :

' These Essays were presented to me by the ingenious Author John MacLaurin, Esq[r] Advocate.—They were not only wrote, but printed by him at a portable press—And he told me the printing cost him much more labour and pains than the writing ! D. R.'

In a copy of the third part, presented to Sir James Foulis and now in the Bodleian, Maclaurin wrote :

' These Essays tho printed are not published or sold and therefore it is requested that this copy be not lent or lost.'

This part contains (p. 39) the verses ' On Johnson's Dictionary ' mentioned *ante*, v. 273. His more serious works include *Observations on some Points of Law, with a System of the Judicial Law of Moses,*

Appendix D

1759 ; *Considerations on the Nature and Origin of Literary Property*, 1767 ; and the important compilation *Arguments and Decisions in Remarkable Cases, Before the High Court of Justiciary, and other Supreme Courts, in Scotland*, 1774. In the Preface to this bulky quarto of over 800 pages he says (p. vi) :

'I chearfully submitted to be the transcriber of judgements frequently unjust, the abridger of arguments often absurd, and the *sad historian* of dooms and executions.'

He was raised to the Bench in 1788, when he took the title of Lord Dreghorn. He died 24 Dec. 1796. *Scots Mag.* lviii, p. 865. An edition of his *Works* was published by his son in two volumes in 1798. There are numerous references to him in Boswell's Journals, see the *Index to the Private Papers of James Boswell* (1937), s.v. *Dreghorn*. See also *ante*, ii. 363 ; iii. 86 ; and the *D.N.B.*

Page 50, note 2. Professor Colin Maclaurin was buried in Greyfriars' Churchyard, near the south-west corner of New Greyfriars' Church, and close to the wall. The grave is covered by an altar tomb, consisting of a rectangular slab raised on four ornamental pillars one and a half feet above the ground. On the slab is engraved ' C. M. Nat. MDCXCVIII Ob. MDCCXLVI '. On the church wall, immediately above the grave, is a mural monument having as a base a square tablet with a Latin inscription, now undecipherable. A third monument to his memory is situated on the church wall, high above the monument just described. On this is the inscription, still legible, printed by Boswell. John Maclaurin's inscription and his own translation, which was intended to be inscribed on the tomb, are given in his *Works*, 1798, i. 23 ; where the fourth line is expanded to ' Hunc lapidem posuit filius '. The grave and monuments are situated in what is known as the Poets' Corner : memorials to Allan Ramsay and Hugh Blair are near by.

Page 50, line 9. The wife of Alexander Murray, Lord Henderland (see *ante*, iii. 8 and 469), was Katharine, the daughter of Sir Alexander Lindsay of Evelick and Amelia Murray, Lord Mansfield's sister. G. E. C., *Complete Baronetage*, iv. 250.

Page 50, line 16. Dr. Alexander Webster, 1707–84, minister of the Tolbooth Church, 1737–84, was a great friend both of Boswell and his father, whose first wife's sister, Mary Erskine, daughter of Col. John Erskine of Alva, he had married in 1737. He combined great business ability and powers of organization with a conviviality which sometimes, in the opinion of his contemporaries, passed the bounds of clerical decorum. John Ramsay of Ochtertyre has a long and, on the whole, favourable account of him : he concludes by saying :

' Dr. Webster was a sort of clerical Aristippus, for he knew how to live *cum tristibus severe, cum remissis jucunde, cum senibus graviter, cum juventute comiter,*

Page 50   *Appendix D*   473

without letting himself down, or forgetting his duty to God or man.' *Scotland & Scotsmen in the 18th century*, 1888, i. 261.

Dr. Alexander Carlyle, a hostile witness, whose account is perhaps too harsh, says:

'He could pass at once from the most unbounded jollity to the most fervent devotion; yet I believe that his hypocrisy was no more than habit grounded merely on temper, and that his aptness to pray was as easy and natural to him as to drink a convivial glass.' *Rem.*, 1860, p. 240.

There is in Boswell's Journal abundant evidence of his conviviality. He records under date 27 Oct. 1762:

'I dined at Mr Webster's and was very hearty. He is a man of great talents—little literature but great Application to Business. He is vivacious and loves Society and is very jolly and merry over a Bottle.' *Boswell Papers*, i. 120.

On 24 Sept. 1774 Boswell and Webster travelled from Edinburgh to Valleyfield together:

'I found that Dr. Webster and I by ourselves could not make good company. I suppose he is never lively but when he has a considerable circle.' *Ibid.* x. 5.

On 8 Nov. following Boswell supped with the Synod of Lothian and Tweeddale:

'Dr. Webster took the lead. I was disgusted with their coarse merriment, which frequently seemed to me to be profane, as it turned on absurd passages in sermons. Webster kept so many sitting till towards two in the morning.' *Ibid.* x. 51.

On 29 Dec. 1774 he says:

'Webster is so social it is not easy to resist the inclination of taking a good glass with him.' *Ibid.* x. 74.

Webster died on 25 Jan. 1784. Boswell notes:

'Grange, who went up to inquire how Dr. Webster was, informed me about ten o'clock that *it was all over*. Both he and I were struck with the removal of so eminent a Man, and regretted that we had not been more with him of late.' *Ibid.* xvi. 26.

The last important entry occurs under date 29 Jan. 1784:

'The Weather had all this time been very severe. This day was uncommonly so. Yet a most numerous company attended the funeral of Dr. Webster. I was affected with a dreary impression of Mortality, but not with tenderness. For Webster was a Man more to be admired for his talents and address than to touch the heart with affection.' *Ibid.* xvi. 26–7.

Boswell, who was writing on 3 Feb. 1784, appears to have got the date of the funeral wrong. The record of interment is: ' 1784 Jany. 28. The Revd. Dr. Webster, buried 1 D[ouble] p[ace] E[ast] Frances Kinloch's Tomb.' W. P. Anderson, *Silences that Speak*, 1931, p. 372.

474   *Appendix D*   Page 50

Webster appointed Boswell one of the trustees of his will. *Boswell Papers*, xvi. 27. Boswell collected anecdotes for a life of him; they have not, up to the present (1937), been discovered. *Ibid.* xiv. 127; xvi. 37.

The clergy of the Established Church of Scotland and the Professors of the Scottish Universities are deeply indebted to him, as he was the author of the pension scheme, established by Act of Parliament 17 George II, cap. 11, and now known as the Scottish Widows' Fund. He was also responsible for the first population return of Scotland. This was obtained in 1755. Webster ' prevailed with the Society for Propagating Christian Knowledge to require every Minister within the Bounds of those Presbyteries where they had erected Schools to make up and transmit a List of his Parishioners, distinguishing them into Protestants and Papists '. One of the manuscript copies of this return, which was entitled *An Account of the Ecclesiastical Benefices, the Patrons of the several Parishes, and the Number of People in Scotland*, is in the National Library of Scotland. The total population was 1,265,380. Adam Smith had the use of this return, and said of its compiler, ' of all the men I have ever known, [he was] the most skilful in Political Arithmetic ' (Letter to George Chalmers, 10 Nov. 1785, in the National Library of Scotland). These works are Webster's memorial. See also *ante*, ii. 274, *A Letter from the Rev. Dr. Webster ... to the Rev. Dr. Price ... relative to the Establishment for a Provision to the Widows and Children of the Ministers and Professors in Scotland*, Edinburgh, 1771; R. Chambers, *Tradit. Edinb.* 1869, p. 30; Hew Scott, *Fasti Eccl. Scot.*, 1915, i. 119; and the *D.N.B.*

Page 50, lines 6 ff. from foot. Hinton of London brought an action for damages and reparation against Donaldson and others for reprinting and publishing Stackhouse's *History of the Bible*, a work which he claimed to be his property by virtue of a supposed common law right derived from the original publisher. The cause was heard in the Court of Session 20–4 July 1773, and the Court held, by eleven to one, that no such right existed in authors and publishers at common law. The judges delivered their opinions on 27 July: these were published by Boswell: *The Decision of the Court of Session upon the Question of Literary Property in the Cause John Hinton ... against Alexander Donaldson, ... John Wood, ... and James Meurose ...* Edinburgh, 1774. The judge whose argument Boswell quoted to Johnson was Lord Gardenston. He is reported to have said:

' But property, when applied to ideas, or literary and intellectual compositions, is perfectly new and surprising. In a law-tract upon this species of property, the division of its subjects would be perfectly curious; by far the most comprehensive denomination of it would be, a property in nonsense. It must also be branched out into the property of bawdy, blasphemy, and treason.' (p. 25.)

Pages 52-3   Appendix D   475

Johnson's own views on copyright and literary property are given in his letter to William Strahan, 7 March 1774 : he held ' That after the Authours death his work should continue an exclusive property capable of bequest and inheritance, and of conveyance by gift or sale for thirty years.' *Letters*, No. 349. See *ante*, i. 439.

Page 52, line 2. The following are the chief references by Boswell to his military ambitions :

23 Sept. 1762. ' Mr. Murray [of Broughton] and I had a long conversation about my scheme of the Guards.' *Boswell Papers*, i. 74.

26 Oct. 1762. ' I was in raptures to think of being an officer of the Guards, and I doubted not to make a good figure there, and be distinguished as a good Officer and a Gentleman of wit and spirit.' *Ibid.* 119.

11 May 1767, on receipt of a letter from Marischal Keith. ' For a moment old ideas revived and you felt warm ambition, love of grandeur, Germany, etc., etc., Spanish Colonel, etc., etc., but checked yourself and was again Mr. James Boswell of Auchinleck, Advocate.' *Ibid.* vii. 129.

1 July 1769. ' I walked out early and met the 6 Regt. of foot and marched with my Cousin, Capt. Maxwell of Dalswinton, a Captain in it, from about half a mile west from town, through the City, and till the Regt. was fairly out at the Water get. I have always had a great fondness for the army, at least for the shew and parade of it, though I am fixed to the law. I am like a Man who has married one woman while he is in love with another. Perhaps, indeed, if I had enjoyed my military Mistress, I should have been heartily tired of her.' *Ibid.* viii. 39.

17 Oct. 1773. At Inchkenneth his ' old soldierly inclinations revived ' on sleeping in a camp-bed which had seen service in America. *Hebrides*, ed. Pottle and Bennett, p. 318.

14 Oct. 1775. When the Royal Highland Regiment marched into the Castle at Edinburgh Boswell 'was quite military and highland '. He showed his enthusiasm by drinking beer with three of the guardsmen, one of whom had been tried for murder, for two hours ' in the little room in which Queen Mary was delivered of King James VI '. *Boswell Papers*, x. 239-41.

22 Aug. 1793. ' At breakfast I read in the Newspaper that there had been an Action in Flanders, in which Colonel Bosville was killed. This agitated me much. . . . I was in a kind of distraction of mind from time to time. My *military ardour* was quite extinguished.' *Ibid.* xviii. 202-3.

Page 53, line 8 and note 1. Sir Walter Scott told Croker that Joseph Ritter undertook the management of the large inn at Paisley called the Abercorn Arms, but did not succeed in that concern (Croker's *Boswell*, 1831, ii. 288 note).

Page 53, last line and note 3. Mr. William Nairne, according to Boswell, was ' a heaven-born judge '. *Letter to the People of Scotland*, 1785, p. 43. In the confidential report on the county voters drawn up in 1788 he is briefly described : ' Mr. William Nairne of Coull. Lord Dunsinnane in the Court of Session. Got his gown from this Ministry. Independant estate. A batchelor. His nephew, Sir William Nairne, his heir.' Sir C. Elphinstone Adam, *View Pol. State Scotland*, 1887,

Appendix D

p. 151. See also Brunton and Haig, and the *D.N.B.* He died 23 March 1811. *Scots Mag.* lxxiii. 320. Scott confessed to Croker that he wrote the note on Lord Dunsinnan lest ' I should be thought to have gone out of my way to insult his memory ', and added ' he was positively the dullest man I ever knew '. F. A. Pottle in *Yale University Library Gazette*, 1928, ii, No. 3, p. 43.

Page 55, lines 18-19. Brantôme's designation of Inch Keith occurs in his *Discours sur les duels* (livre ii, ch. ii). Describing a duel between ' le sieur de d'Ussac ' and ' le capitaine Hautefort ' he writes :

' Ils esmeurent dispute ensemble et querelle, pour l'amour d'une grand'dame. . . . Ils s'assignarent et s'appellarent tous deux à l'Isle aux Chevaux, qui est devant le Petit Lict [*i.e.* Leith]. Ceux qui ont veu le lieu comme moy sçavent où c'est, où s'y estant faicts passer.' *Œuvres*, 1891, t. viii. 126.

Brantôme accompanied Mary Queen of Scots on her return to Scotland in 1561. *Ibid.* 1890, x. 123 ff.

Page 56, line 15. The ferry-boats from Leith crossed to Pettycur, near Kinghorn, and it was probably here that the travellers landed. The inn at which they dined was, according to Boswell's original Journal, kept by one Monro : Johnson commended the dinner. It was in the parish of Kinghorn, upon the farm of Balbarton, that Boswell's eldest son, Sir Alexander, was fatally shot in his duel with James Stuart of Dunearn, 26 March 1822 : he was carried to Balmuto House, the home of the Boswells of Balmuto, where he died. See *Statistical Acct. of Scotland*, 1794, xii. 229 ff. ; Sir R. Sibbald, *Fife & Kinross*, 1803, pp. 311-13 ; Alan Reid, *Kinghorn*, 1906 ; and *Trial of James Stuart*, 1822, pp. 2, 23, 50-1.

Page 57, line 8 and note 2. Boswell noted in his journal, 1 June 1785, ' Sat some time at Nichols's, trying to find a quotation of Dr. Johnson's in Butler's " Remains ", but could not.' *Boswell Papers*, xvi. 97.

Page 57, line 10. The site of Glass's inn is not now known. If, as is probable, the inn was identical with, or the immediate ancestor of, the ' Black Bull ', it stood at or near the corner of South Street and Heukster's Wynd, now called South Castle Street, where that inn is shown, by Wood's *Plan of St. Andrews*, 1820, to have been situated. Andrew Glass in 1786 sold his vintner's business, together with several other properties, one of which was on this site, but the sale missive does not clearly indicate which property was used as the inn. When the ' Black Bull ' was to be let in 1840 it was stated in the advertisement that ' There is no good Inn at St. Andrews except the Black Bull and the whole of the Trade would be concentrated in this Inn under proper Management '. Lord Cockburn stayed at the ' Black Bull ' in 1844. *Circuit Journeys*, 1889, p. 230. There has been no inn on or near this site in living memory.

Pages 57-8   *Appendix D*   477

The distance from this corner of South Street to St. Leonard's College would be about 250 yards ; the travellers made a much longer ' procession ' from their inn at Tobermory to Dr. Maclean's house at Erray (see *ante*, v. 313, note †).

I am greatly indebted to Mr. John J. Smith and Mr. J. C. Cantley, the Town Clerk of St. Andrews, for their assistance in this investigation.

Page 57, lines 12 ff. King James I made a progress through Scotland 13 May to 4 August 1617. Numerous speeches in Latin and English were delivered, poems read or presented, and disputations held, at the various places at which he was publicly received. The speeches and poems are preserved in the collection entitled : Τὰ τῶν Μουσῶν Εἰσόδια : *The Muses Welcome to the high and mighty Prince Iames. . . . At his Majesties happie Returne to his olde and natiue Kingdome of Scotland, after 14 yeeres absence, in Anno 1617. Digested according to the order of his Majesties Progresse, by I. A.* Edinburgh, 1618. There are two editions, which differ mainly in the title-page and preliminary matter, one with Thomas Finlason's imprint on the title-page, the other without printer's name, but with title-page and preliminaries printed by Andro Hart. See J. F. Kellas Johnstone and A. W. Robertson, *Bibliographia Aberdonensis*, 1929, i. 178-9. The digester was John Adamson, who became later Principal of Edinburgh University (see *D.N.B.*). Among the contributors of Latin poems are Robert Boyd (1578-1627), David Hume (?1560-?1630), and David Wedderburn (1580-1646). The chief contributors of English poems are Alexander Craig (?1567-1627), Sir William Mure (1594-1657), and Drummond of Hawthornden, who presented his famous panegyric, *Forth Feasting*, on 15 May (pp. 27-37). Not all the speeches to which His Majesty was compelled to listen were included, e.g. that delivered in Hebrew by Andrew Ker, ' a boy of nyne yeeres age ' (p. 116). See also *Register of the Privy Council of Scotland*, xi, 1894, pp. xlii ff., 418-19, &c.

Page 58, line 10. The University of St. Andrews was originally composed of three colleges, St. Salvator's, St. Leonard's, and St. Mary's: the two first mentioned were in 1747 incorporated into one, called the United College. The Act of Parliament (20 Geo. II, cap. 32) by which this union was established states that ' the Masters and Professors in both the said Colleges, taking into their consideration, that the Meanness of the present Salaries will discourage Men of Learning and Abilities from accepting of vacant Professorships, and that in the present ruinous state and Condition of one of the Fabricks, the same cannot be repaired or supported without an Expence far exceeding what the publick Funds of the said College can afford ', came to an agreement to unite them. The buildings, area, and garden of St. Leonard's College were valued at £400. Professor Watson bought the property in 1772, when ' it was

Appendix D Pages 58–61

arranged that £200 should be paid in cash, and that in place of the remaining £200 there should be an annual feu duty of £10 '. The walls and area of St. Leonard's Church were reserved as College property. J. Herkless and R. K. Hannay, *The College of St. Leonard*, 1905, pp. 27–8.

Wesley, who visited Scotland in May 1776, records in his *Journal* on the 27th (ed. Curnock, vi. 110):

'What is left of St. Leonard's College is only a heap of ruins. Two colleges remain. One of them has a tolerable square, but all the windows are broke, like those of a brothel. We were informed that the students do this before they leave the college.'

St. Leonards Girls' School now stands on the site of the College.

Page 58, line 14. Boswell's original Journal for this day began:

'Slept till near ten . . . waked well. Prayed fervtly, read new test. Found Mr. Johns. up. He shewed me his notes of yesterday's jaunt. Wonderfully minute, and exact except as to not seeing trees and hedges.' *Hebrides*, ed. Pottle and Bennett, 1936, p. 38, note 12.

Page 60, lines 4 ff. There is corroboration of Johnson's statement that smoking had, in the latter half of the eighteenth century, become unfashionable; Richard Graves notes in his *Senilities* (1801, p. 291):

'On a publick day, 1743, on my scrupling to take a pipe, his Grace [the Duke of Devonshire] observed, " They were good times, when the Clergy smoked tobacco ".'

Smoking in Common Rooms at Oxford was said to be dying out in 1773. Wood's *City of Oxford*, ed. A. Clark (1889), i. 632.

Speaking of the youth of George IV, H. D. Best says:

'Our smoking-rooms were turned into powdering closets, our summerhouses into conservatories. A coat tainted with the fumes of tobacco was a title of exclusion from good company. " Nobody smokes now ", said they.' *Literary Memorials*, 1829, p. 279.

He lived to see the restoration of tobacco during the Napoleonic wars:

'Military glory and smoking became the fashion of the day; and the tobaccopipe is re-established in all its former honours.' *Ibid.* p. 280.

Boswell, writing on 21 Sept. 1769 of his attendance at a club in London, says ' Some of us smoak a pipe '. *Boswell Papers*, viii. 122. See *ante*, v. 142, and *ante*, i. 317, where the following quotation from Burke might have been given:

'Tobacco is the delight of Dutchmen, as it diffuses a torpor and pleasing stupefaction.' *Sublime and Beautiful* (ed. 2, 1759), Introd., p. 13.

Page 61, line 23. George Martine's account of St. Andrews, entitled *Reliquiæ divi Andreæ*, was written in 1683, revised by the author in 1699, and published, from the original manuscript, now in the Library

Pages 61-3   *Appendix D*   479

of the University of Edinburgh, in 1797: the section dealing with St. Rule, *The History and Antiquities of St. Rule's Chapel in the Monastery of St. Andrew's*, was printed in 1787 and included in Nichols' *Bibl. Topogr. Britannica* (vol. v, 1790). Three manuscript copies were traced by the 1797 editor.; one in the Library of the University of St. Andrews, another in the Harleian Collection, and a third in the possession of Prof. John Adamson of St. Andrews (this is now in the Library of the University of Edinburgh). For Martine see *D.N.B.*

Page 61, line 24. The late Dr. C. H. Bennett pointed out to me that William Douglass published a ' small account of St. Andrews ' in London in 1728 under the title *Some Historical Remarks on the City of St. Andrews in North Britain*. This anonymous pamphlet is inscribed to the Lord Chancellor by ' William Douglass '. The Provost of the city at that time was William Douglas, eldest son of Sir Robert Douglas of Glenbervie, and I suggest that he was the author. (The present Town Clerk, Mr. N. C. Mackenzie, to whom I am indebted, reports that he consistently signed the Minute Books ' Will. Douglas ', but that the Clerk used the form ' Douglass ' on the minute of his election.) He was born in 1689, admitted Advocate in 1712; he engaged in the 1715 Rebellion, was attainted, but pardoned in 1720; he was elected Provost, 1724 to 1736, and 1738 to 1746, when he succeeded his father in the baronetcy. He was Inspector of Customs on Tobacco in Scotland. He died 23 July 1764. *See* Sir Francis J. Grant, *Faculty of Advocates in Scotland*, 1944, p. 58. The picture Douglas gives of the city is a sad one. He notes that the ' great Square Spire [of St. Rule] is still very intire ' and advocates that the ancient Chapel be restored and adopted as the Chapel and Chapter-house of the Knights of the Thistle (p. 13).

Page 61, line 1 from foot and note 4. Knox was buried in the churchyard of St. Giles, now Parliament Square; a tablet, bearing the initials ' I. K.' and the date ' 1572 ', marks what is presumably the exact spot; the equestrian statue of Charles II is near by.

Page 63, note 2. *The University of St. Andrews in 1778.* In the preface to *Poems by George Monck Berkeley* (1797), it is recorded (p. cccxlviii) that when ' Mr. Berkeley entered at the university of St. Andrews, [in 1781], one of the college officers called upon him to deposit a crown to pay for the windows he might break. Mr. Berkeley said, that as he should reside in his Father's house, it was little likely he should break any windows, having never, that he remembered, broke one in his whole life. He was assured that he *would* do it at St. Andrews. . . . On the rising of the session, several of the students said, " Now for the windows. Come, it is time to set off; let us sally forth." Mr. Berkeley, being called upon, enquired what was to be done ? They . . . replied

Appendix D   Page 64

"Why, to break every window in college."—"For what reason?" —"Oh! no reason; but that it has always been done from time immemorial".' The Editor goes on to say that Mr. Berkeley prevailed on them to give up the practice. How poor some of the students were is shown by the following anecdote, told by the College Porter, who had to collect the crowns. 'I am just come', he said, 'from a poor student indeed. I went for the window *croon*; he cried, begged, and prayed not to pay it, saying, "he brought but a croon to keep him all the session, and he had spent six-pence of it; so I have got only four and six-pence".' His father, a labourer, who owned three cows, had sold one 'to dress his son for the University, and put the lamented croon in his pocket, to purchase coals. All the lower students study by fire light. He brought with him a large tub of oatmeal, and a pot of salted butter, on which he was to subsist from the 20th of October until the 20th of May.' Berkeley raised 'a very noble [subscription]' for the poor fellow.

In another passage (p. cxcviii) it is recorded that Berkeley 'used to boast to his Father, "Well, Sir, *idle* as *you* may think me, . . . I never have once bowed at . . . any Professor's lectures".' An explanation being requested of the word *bowing*, it was thus given : 'Why, if any poor fellow has been a little idle, and is not prepared to speak when called upon by the Professor, he gets up and makes a respectful bow, and sits down again.' Berkeley was a grandson of Bishop Berkeley.—HILL.

Page 64, line 2. The 'library-room' that Principal Murison showed Johnson was not the Library of St. Mary's College, but the upper room of the University Library. This Library was founded in 1612 by James I and was originally housed in a two-story building completed in 1643 ; the lower hall, the Parliament Hall, so named because the Scottish Parliament sat there in 1645–6, was then and for over a hundred years after used for University meetings and functions. The growth of the Library after the passing of the Copyright Act in 1709, when it became entitled to a copy of every work entered at Stationers' Hall, rendered extension necessary, and in 1765–7 the original library room was greatly enlarged ' by increasing the height of the walls and carrying a gallery along the north side and the east and west ends '. The Parliament Hall is now a part of the Library, which has been successively extended in 1829, 1889–90, and 1907–8. The copyright privilege was commuted for an annual grant of £630 in 1836. See J. Maitland Anderson in *Votiva Tabella*, 1911, pp. 93 ff., and the same writer's *Handbook to the City and University of St. Andrews*, 1911, pp. 92 ff.

Page 64, lines 3–5. The professors who entertained Johnson and Boswell were : (1) Dr. James Murison, Principal of St. Mary's College, 1747–79. He was an Aberdeen graduate, minister at Edzell, 1729–43,

Page 64 *Appendix D*

and Kinnell, 1743–7, Moderator of the General Assembly, 1767. Hew Scott, *Fasti Eccl. Scot.*, 1928, vii. 391, 421, 470, and J. M. Anderson, *Matriculation Roll of St. Andrews*, 1905, p. lxxxi. John Ramsay of Ochtertyre says of him :

'His learning . . . was barely sufficient for the discharge of his duty. The lads, therefore, sometimes made themselves merry with his slips in Latinity. But though he did not superabound in classical lore, he had an ample share of mother-wit and discretion, which made him be respected, if not admired.' *Scotland and Scotsmen in the 18th century*, 1888, i. 269.

(2) Andrew Shaw, Professor of Divinity and Biblical Criticism, 1739–79 ; minister of St. Madoes, Perthshire, 1729–39. Hew Scott, *o.c.s.* vii. 429. ' Though not a deep philosopher or original thinker, [he] was a painstaking man, exceedingly well informed, and well-disposed to do good.' Ramsay, *o.c.s.* i. 269.

(3) John Cook, Professor of Moral Philosophy, 1769–73, Professor of Ethics and Pneumatics, 1773–1815. J. M. Anderson, *o.c.s.* pp. lxxvi, lxxviii. He was the father and grandfather of two St. Andrews professors, John Cook, Professor of Biblical Criticism, 1808–24, and John Cook, Professor of Ecclesiastical History, 1860–8. Hew Scott, *o.c.s.* vii. 429, 433.

(4) Dr. George Hill, 1750–1819. Professor of Greek, 1772–88, Professor of Biblical Criticism, 1788–91, Principal of St. Mary's College, 1791–1819. He was Moderator of the General Assembly in 1789, and succeeded Robertson as the leader of the Moderate party in the Church. Lord Cockburn somewhat grudgingly admits that he had talent : he says that ' his influence depended on a single power—that of public speaking '. *Memorials*, 1856, p. 231. See also *D.N.B.*, George Cook's *Life of George Hill*, 1820, and Hew Scott, *o.c.s.* vii. 422.

(5) George Hadow, son of James Hadow (*c.* 1670–1747), Principal of St. Mary's College, was Professor of Hebrew and Oriental Languages, 1748–80. Hew Scott, *o.c.s.* vii. 426.

(6) Robert Watson, *c.* 1730–81, the son of an apothecary and brewer of St. Andrews, was Professor of Logic, Rhetoric, and Metaphysics at the United College from 1756 to 1778, and Principal from 1778 to 1781. He must have been preparing his *History of the Reign of Philip II* (*ante*, iii. 104) at the time of Johnson's visit. See Hew Scott, *o.c.s.* vii. 414, and the *D.N.B.*

(7) James Flint was Professor of Medicine from 1770 to 1810. J. M. Anderson, *o.c.s.* p. lxxx.

(8) William Brown was Professor of Divinity and Ecclesiastical History, 1757–91. He had previously been minister of the Scottish church at Utrecht (see *ante*, ii. 9, note 2). His son, Dr. William Laurence Brown, 1755–1830, was Principal of Marischal College, Aberdeen.

J. M. Anderson, *o.c.s.* p. lxxxii, Hew Scott, *o.c.s.* vii. 432, and the *D.N.B.* (*s.v.* Brown, W. L.).

Page 65, lines 3 ff. There is in *The Gentleman and Lady's Weekly Magazine*, an Edinburgh periodical, of 22 April 1774, a story, reprinted from the *Aberdeen Journal*, that Johnson reproved the Principal of St. Andrews for saying grace in the vernacular and ' said a long blessing in Latin ' himself. ' R. S.', in a letter dated from St. Andrews 1 May 1774, gives, in the number for 11 May (pp. 73–5), what he describes as ' a short account of the affair as it really happened '. It is as follows :

> The Principal, having said grace, turned about, while the company were yet standing, to Dr Johnson, and observed to him, that he was told, they never asked a blessing in their mother tongue, in any of the English universities ; but that, instead of an English grace, they always used these words, on any public occasion, *Benedictus benedicat*. The Doctor assured him, that it was not so ; that indeed, they always asked a blessing in *Latin* in the English universities; but he never had heard these two words used in any of them. ' For my part,' says he, ' I remember perfectly the words which were used, in the university of Oxford, by one of the heads of the college, of which I was a member, and for your satisfaction, I shall repeat them.' Upon this the Doctor repeated a pretty long Latin grace.

I owe the reference to this rare periodical, a copy of which is in the Signet Library, Edinburgh, to Professor D. Nichol Smith.

Page 66, lines 1 ff. The nonjuring clergyman was, there can be little doubt, the Reverend David Lindsay, the Episcopal minister at St. Andrews from 1742, or perhaps earlier, to 1791, when he died. He was a younger son of Lindsay of Glenquiech in Angus. See T. T. Oliphant, *Hist. Notes relating to the Episcopal Congregation at St. Andrews*, 1896, p. 18. Bp. David Low, who is generally regarded as a good authority, told Lord Lindsay that Johnson, on meeting him, inquired who he was, and, on being told ' Only a poor episcopal minister ', replied ' Sir, I honour him '. Lord Lindsay, *Lives of the Lindsays*, 1840, i. 75–6, note. Boswell's silence makes the story doubtful.

Page 66, line 5 from foot. According to Mrs. Thrale, Johnson did more than advise Chambers on composition. In the list of Johnson's works, ' a Catalogue of such writings as I *know* to be his ', she included ' Law Lectures for Chambers '. *Thraliana*, ed. K. C. Balderston, 1942, i. 204. Johnson himself says that he ' learnt some law ' from Chambers (*ante*, iii. 22). But the ease with which he dictated to Boswell numerous legal arguments (*ante*, ii. 183–5, 196–200, 242–6, 372–4 ; iii. 59–62, 202–3 ; iv. 74 and 129–31) shows that the writing of such lectures would not have been beyond his powers. Since the above was written Prof. E. L. McAdam has shown that Johnson helped Chambers in the actual composition of his Vinerian Lectures : see *R.E.S.* xv. 385 ff., xvi. 159 ff., and *Dr. Johnson and the English Law* (1951).

Johnson knew Chambers certainly as early as 1754 when he was an

Page 67   *Appendix D*   483

exhibitioner of Lincoln College (*ante*, i. 274), and stayed with him at Oxford in 1768, 1769, and 1770 when he was Principal of New Inn Hall (ii. 67 ; iii. 453 ; and *Letters*, Nos. 216–18, 227·1): Chambers was Vinerian Professor of Law at Oxford from 1762 till 1777.

Page 67, note 1. The Hervey for whom, according to Mrs. Thrale, Johnson wrote sermons, was the Hon. Henry Hervey, fourth (not ' third ' as Boswell states *ante*, i. 106, note 1) son of John Hervey, first Earl of Bristol (1663–1751). He was born in 1701 and, after an unsuccessful career at Oxford, entered the army in which he rose to the rank of captain in the 1st Dragoon Guards. He left the army in 1742, and in the following year was ordained and presented to the family living of Shotley, Suffolk. He married, in 1730, Catherine Aston, the elder sister of Johnson's friends, Mrs. Gastrell, Mrs. Walmsley, and ' Molly ' Aston (*ante*, i. 83, note 4) : his wife, on the death of her brother in 1744, inherited the Aston estates and Mr. Hervey took her name (*ante*, i. 106, note 1). He died in 1748. The Rev. William Cole, who did not know him, wrote, 16 June 1757, that ' he was greatly followed as an admired Preacher in London ' (Add. MSS. 5829, fol. 137, in the British Museum). He was, in 1745, chosen to preach the Festival sermon of the Corporation of the Sons of the Clergy in St. Paul's Cathedral and the sermon was, in accordance with custom, published. This is the only sermon published by him : copies are in the British Museum, Cambridge University Library, and Lambeth Palace Library. (It was edited by Prof. J. L. Clifford for the Augustan Reprint Society, No. 50, at Los Angeles in 1955.) The title runs :

A | Sermon | Preached at the | Cathedral Church of St. Paul, | Before the Sons of the Clergy, | on Thursday the Second of May, 1745, | Being the Day of their | Annual Feast, | By the Honourable and Reverend | Henry Hervey Aston, A.M. | Rector of Shottely in the County of Suffolk. | London : | Printed for J. Brindley, Bookseller to His Royal | Highness the Prince of Wales, at the Feathers in | New-Bond-Street ; and sold by M. Cooper, in Pater- | Noster-Row. |

The sermon, which is on the text Heb. xiii. 16, opens :

    ' The great Duty of charity and Beneficence, however it may be sometimes forgotten or neglected, is so generally admitted, and so zealously professed, that it may seem superfluous to recommend, and difficult to enforce it : Superfluous, because those that omit it, seem rather inclined to conceal their conduct, and shew, by their Desire of Secrecy, their Consciousness of Guilt, and difficult, because what is universally known, must be, of itself, easily discoverable ; and it is vain to labour for Forms of Argument, to evince that of which Sensation or Intuition will inform us.'

This eminently Johnsonian style is generally maintained. Two other short passages may be given from different parts of the sermon.

    ' It is, indeed, not easy to prevail upon Avarice to remit its Anxieties ; upcr Gaiety to be attentive, or upon Luxury to reason ; but, surely, when Doctrines, thus important, are to be delivered, a short Pause of Action might be obtained from the most laborious of all the Slaves of Wealth or Greatness, and a Suspence of Sensuality might be granted by Those, who have resigned themselves to Jollity and Pleasure ' (p. 18).

' It should, likewise, be remember'd, that he best shews his Regard for Truth, who most contributes to its Propagation, and that he will propagate it with most success, who recommends it by Benevolence ' (p. 23).

I have no hesitation in ascribing this sermon to Johnson. It is not, as I once thought, the sermon which Dr. Douglas (*ante*, i. 407) had in mind when he told Boswell that Johnson ' gave an excellent sermon to a clergyman, who preached and published it in his own name, on some public occasion ' (*ante*, iii. 507) ; that sermon was preached on the fifth of November. Boswell's *Letters*, ii. 455.

Johnson probably first met Hervey Aston at Lichfield when his regiment was quartered there about the year 1730 : he was on intimate terms with him when he went to live in London in 1737. See *ante*, i. 106, 194 ; and iii. 195.

The life and character of Hervey Aston have been fully described by the Rev. Sydenham H. A. Hervey in his *Suffolk Green Books*, 1906, xiv, pp. xlix ff., and 1912, xvi, pt. ii, pp. 329 ff., and Mr. A. L. Reade's *Gleanings*, 1928, v. 245 ff. See also *The Times*, 25 Nov. 1938, pp. 15, 16.

I have great pleasure in recording my obligations in this investigation to the Marquis of Bristol, who courteously sent to me such manuscripts of Hervey Aston as are in his possession (these include the earliest known copies of four of Johnson's poems : see Nichol Smith and McAdam, *The Poems of Johnson*, pp. 119 ff.) ; Miss Irene V. Churchill, of the Lambeth Palace Library; Mr. E. Baillie Reynolds, Registrar of the Corporation of the Sons of the Clergy; and Mr. A. S. Whyte, of the War Office Library.

A sermon which Johnson may have composed was described in *The Times* of 29 Sept. 1933 by Dr. R. W. Chapman. The manuscript was given by Hugo Meynell (*ante*, i. 82) to the Rev. Richard Gifford (*ante*, v. 118), who found it at Bradley Park, near Ashbourne, Derbyshire. It is a fair copy, with corrections in two hands, one of which is certainly Johnson's. Gifford believed the sermon to be by Johnson and endeavoured to persuade Cadell to publish it. He does not give the name of the clergyman for whom, in his opinion, Johnson wrote the sermon. The place where it was found points to the Rev. John Kennedy, as Dr. Chapman suggests : he was Rector of Bradley from 1732 to 1782, and Johnson had not only contributed to his *Astronomical Chronology*, but had ' looked at it before it was printed ' (*ante*, i. 366 and 547).

Page 68, lines 6 ff. James Craig, who was born in 1740, was the son of William Craig and Mary Thomson, the youngest sister of the poet. He was a pupil of Sir Robert Taylor, 1714-88, the London architect and founder of the Taylor Institution at Oxford. In 1763 he submitted a plan for the new bridge over the recently drained North Loch, Edin-

Page 68   *Appendix D*   485

burgh, which was not accepted, but in 1766 his design for the New Town was awarded the first prize, approved by the Council, and put into execution in 1767. The plan was submitted by the Council to George III and the Queen, who showed great interest in the names proposed for the new streets : Sir John Pringle (*ante*, iii. 65, and v. 376) assured the Lord Provost in December, 1767,

'that the appellations of George Street, Queen's Street, and Hanover Street were not overlooked and that His Majesty when he objected to the name of St. Giles Street, and was graciously pleased to desire that it should be called Prince's Street, had more in view the addressing himself to the Magistrates of the City than to the Draughtsman.' W. Cowan, *Maps of Edinburgh*, ed. C. B. Boog Watson, 1932, p. 45.

Pringle was responsible for the naming of Frederick Street ; he says : ' It was the Bishop of Osnaburgh I meant and not the late Prince of Wales.' *Ibid.* p. 46. Frederick Augustus, the second son of George III, was born in 1763, and in 1764 was elected Bishop of Osnaburgh : he is now better known to Londoners as the Duke of York whose column is visible in Carlton House Terrace. Craig published his plan 1 Jan. 1768 under the title *Plan of the New Streets and Squares intended for the City of Edinburgh*, with a dedication to the King and an apt quotation from his uncle's *Liberty* (v. 701–6).

The building of the New Town was rapid. Pennant, who saw it in 1769, reports :

' On the north side of the City lies the new town, which is planned with great judgement, and will prove a magnificent addition to Edinburgh.' *Tour in Scotland*, 1771, p. 54.

Arnot, writing ten years later, says :

' The buildings along Prince's street have run to a considerable length. St. Andrews square, and the streets connected with it, are almost compleat. Indeed, the natural advantages of the situation, joined to the regulation of the whole being built conform to a regular and beautiful plan, give the extended royalty a superiority over any city in Great Britain.' *Hist. Edinburgh*, 1779, p. 318.

In our own days Craig's work has been highly praised :

' Craig was a man of exceptional foresight. His street planning—more especially his project for the North and South Bridges area [which the authorities did not adopt]—was in advance of anything of the time. . . . The New Town of Edinburgh . . . will always be one of the fine things that this country has produced.' T. H. Hughes, ' James Craig ', in *Quarterly of The Incorporation of Architects of Scotland*, No. 9, 1924, p. 76.

Craig died, a comparatively young man, on 23 June 1795, having done for Edinburgh what the two Woods, father and son, did more nobly for Bath. See also *ante*, iii. 360, *D.N.B.*, and L. Morel, *James Thomson*, 1895, p. 10, n. 1.

Page 68, line 13. The ' worthy gentleman ' who forgot his own name cannot be definitely identified. Boswell gave his name in his original Journal, but the reading is uncertain ; the editors, Prof. Pottle and Dr. Bennett, suggest ' Ro. Irv ', perhaps Robert Irvine or Irving, W.S., who is described by Boswell, 6 Oct. 1762, ' Mr. Irvine is a Writer in Edinburgh and a very good plain man and more genteel than usual '. *Boswell Papers*, i. 86. He lived at Bonshaw near Annan. *Ibid.* 88.

Page 69, lines 7 ff. Colonel John Nairne was the second son of the Hon. John Nairne, *c.* 1691–1770, who was twice attainted for the part he took in the 1715 and 1745 risings. He was in the 1st Foot Regiment, married Brabazon, daughter of Richard Wheeler of Lyrath, co. Kilkenny, and died at St. Andrews 7 Nov. 1782. The barony, which he had never assumed, was restored to his son William in 1824, and is now held by the Marquis of Lansdowne. See Sir James Balfour Paul, *Scots Peerage*, 1909, vi. 397–9, and G. E. C., *Complete Peerage*, 1936, ix. 448.

Colonel Nairne lived in the house known as ' Queen Mary's House ', No. 4 South Street, from 1769–79, which has since 1927 been the Library of St. Leonard's Girls' School. The grotto remains, but the solitary tree, known as ' Dr. Johnson's tree ', was, according to Sir Auckland Colvin (*John Russell Colvin*, 1895, p. 19), uprooted *c.* 1817 ' in the sight of John Colvin and his younger brother, Binny '. This house, which dates from the first quarter of the sixteenth century, was owned in 1779 by Mary Lillias Sharp, the widow of James Lumisden and a descendant of Archbishop Sharp. See also Birkbeck Hill, *Footsteps*, p. 102 ; J. Maitland Anderson, *City and University of St. Andrews*, 1911, p. 24; and Macgibbon and Ross, *Castellated and Domestic Architecture of Scotland*, 1889, iii. 563–6.

Page 70, line 5 from foot. The minister of Leuchars at the time of Johnson's visit was the Reverend James Walker. He was licensed 28 Oct. 1731, presented to the living 15 Aug. 1732, and ordained 9 Jan. 1733. He died 27 Dec. 1773. See Hew Scott, *Fasti Eccles. Scoticanæ*, 1925, v. 222. The church of Leuchars is remarkable for its Norman apse, one of the few left in Scotland ; this and the choir alone remain of the original church. Macgibbon and Ross, *Eccl. Archit. of Scotl.*, 1896, i. 309–314.

Page 72, lines 14 ff. Lord Monboddo, who was the only member of the Court to support the pursuer or claimant John Hinton against Donaldson (see *ante*, v. 50 and 474), argued :

' I allow every man who purchases a book to *appropriate* the ideas of it to himself as much as he can, and the words too, if his memory be good enough. I think I could go further without hurting my argument, and admit that he may carry those ideas in his mind, and those words in his memory, to a printing press, and get them thrown off. Such a man I would call a *plagiary*, but not the *pirate* of a book.' Boswell, *Decision of the Court of Session upon the Question of Literary Property*, 1774, pp. 9–10.

Pages 72-3   *Appendix D*   487

Page 72, lines 8 and 7 from foot. Sir John Hawkins's history was announced in the *Public Advertiser* for 17 July 1773 :

'In the Press, And in great Forwardness, A General History of the Science and Practice of Music. . . . In four Volumes in Quarto. By Sir John Hawkins, Knt.

☞ The Third Volume is now in the Press.'

The work was published, in five volumes, in 1776.

Dr. Burney's published Proposals for his history are dated 20 April 1773. They will be found in the second edition, 1773, of his *Present State of Music in France and Italy*. In the first edition, 1771, of this work Burney had printed the following ' Advertisement ' :

'A General Plan of the Author's intended *History of Music*, with Proposals for Printing it by Subscription, will be submitted to the public as soon as the work is sufficiently advanced to enable him to fix a time with any degree of certainty for its appearance.'

Burney's history had in fact been well advertised by this work and the companion volume, *The Present State of Music in Germany, &c.*, 1773, which stated on their title-pages that they were journals ' undertaken to collect Materials for a General History of Music '. The first volume was published in 1776, the second in 1782, and the third and fourth in 1789. Johnson wrote the Dedication to the Queen (vol. i) for Burney (see *ante*, iv. 546) and translated the lines from the Medea of Euripides in vol. ii, p. 340 (see Courtney, p. 154).

' Both books ', writes an authority, ' are of the highest value, and form the foundation of nearly every English work on musical history which has appeared since.' (Barclay Squire in the *D.N.B.* s.v. Burney, Charles.) Hawkins's *History* was republished in 1853 and 1875, but Burney's had to wait for a completely new edition till 1935, when it was edited with critical and historical notes by Mr. Frank Mercer. Burney's copy of his rival's *History* in the British Museum (press-mark C 45, f. 4-8) contains a number of corrections and strictures, and his unpublished attack on it, in heroic couplets, entitled ' The Trial of Midas the Second ', is in the John Rylands Library, Manchester (see Mr. W. Wright Roberts in *The Bulletin of the John Rylands Library*, 1933, xvii, pp. 322 ff.).

Page 73, line 15. The Reverend Charles Nisbet, the established minister of St. John's, Montrose, was born 21 Jan. 1736, took his M.A. at Edinburgh 1754, was licensed 24 Sept. 1760, and presented to the living 25 Nov. 1763. The College of New Jersey conferred the degree of D.D. upon him in 1783. He defended the cause of the American Colonists from the pulpit, got into trouble with the magistrates, and in 1785 went to America, where he was appointed first President of·Dickinson College, Carlisle, Pennsylvania. This office he resigned, owing to illness and depression, within a few months, and determined to return to Scotland, but was prevented by a prejudice against sailing in a vessel commanded by an Irish captain. Whereupon he was induced to reconsider his resignation and was formally re-elected. In his *Address to Dickinson College . . . on his re-election* (Edinburgh, 1786) he endeavoured to persuade his students of his goodwill to his adopted country, and to Dickinson College, by expatiating upon his abandonment of ' an honourable and independent station, and renouncing the society of many valuable and long tried friends, [by] crossing the vast Atlantic, and exposing [his] life to the perils of a new climate' (p. 2). He did not hide his light under a bushel :

' After a pretty long life spent in the pursuit of learning, and undergoing so many dangers and troubles for promoting its increase in this country, I flatter myself that I have a name to lose ; and you would do me a sensible and grievous injury, if it should be lost by your negligence ' (pp. 3–4).

He remained President till his death in 1804 in spite of the fact that he was ' anti-republican, had no faith in American institutions, [and] did not believe in their stability '. See the *Dictionary of American Biography*, 1934, xiii. 526 (from which the last-quoted sentence is taken) ; Hew Scott, *Fasti Eccl. Scot.*, 1925, v. 411 ; David Mitchell, *History of Montrose*, 1866, pp. 36–7 ; and the *D.N.B.*

Page 73, line 16. The Reverend Joseph Spooner went to St. Peter's, the Episcopal or English chapel, on probation in Sept. 1756 for three months and was thereafter appointed incumbent. He held office till his death in 1779 : his stipend was originally £60, raised later to £70, a year.

The Episcopal chapel was founded in 1722 and burned down in 1857. David Mitchell, *History of Montrose*, 1866, p. 107. According to Pennant it was ' very neat ' and had ' a painted altar-piece, and a small organ '. *Tour in Scotland, 1772*, pt. ii, 1776, p. 143. The congregation remained an independent unit till 1920, when it was absorbed by that of St. Mary's Episcopal church, now known as the Church of St. Mary and St. Peter.

I owe this information to the late Canon H. M. Ranken, formerly Rector of Montrose, and to the present Rector, the Reverend W. R. Torvany.

Page 73, lines 20–1. Pennant notes of the Montrose buildings : ' The houses are of stone, and, like those in Flanders, often with their gable ends towards the streets '. *Tour in Scotland, 1772*, pt. ii, 1776, p. 142. Not many of the houses so built remain to-day, but the inhabitants of Montrose are still known as ' Gable-endies '.

Page 73, line 21. 'Mr Gleg ', the merchant, was almost certainly Mr. Adam Glegg, Provost of Montrose, 1781–2, 1785–6, 1789–90, and 1793–4.

Pages 75-6   Appendix D   489
Page 75, lines 9 ff. and note 4. Lord Gardenstone is described in the confidential report on the Scottish freeholders made in the interest of the Whig party in 1788 :

'A very independant fortune, £3000 or £4000 a year. A great personal interest all over the north of Scotland. An old Batchelor. A virtuoso. Does not value money. An able man. Connected at present with Mr. Dundas and his friends.' See Sir C. Elphinstone Adam, *View Polit. State Scotl.*, 1887, p. 5.

His writings include, in addition to *A Letter to the People of Laurencekirk*, three volumes of *Travelling Memorandums, made in a Tour upon the Continent of Europe in the years 1786, 1787, and 1788*, published respectively in 1791, 1792, and 1795 (at the end of the first volume are some ' Memorandums concerning the village of Lawrencekirk ' which had previously been printed, without their author's permission, by John Knox in his *Tour through the Highlands*, 1787) ; a *Plan of a Scheme for an Academy of Useful Arts at Laurencekirk, c.* 1789, of which there is a copy in the National Library of Scotland ; and at least a part of the anonymous *Miscellanies in Prose and Verse*, 1791. In the second edition of the first volume of *Travelling Memorandums*, 1792, a second edition of this work is announced : ' Miscellanies in Prose and Verse ; Including Remarks on English Plays, Operas, Farces, And on a Variety of other Modern Publications. By the Honourable Lord Gardenstone ' ; but in the second volume brackets are placed before ' Including ' and after ' Gardenstone ', and it is only the part of the book thus indicated that can with certainty be ascribed to him : these ' Remarks ' were reprinted as Gardenstone's in *The Bee*, ed. by James Anderson, volumes ii–v, 1791 ; in volumes iii–v of which the *Travelling Memorandums* were also printed.

The following uncomplimentary description of Boswell occurs at the end of the ' Remarks ' (1791, p. 240) :

' Boswell has no character at all. He is all foolery and affectation. He has gone to England for the same reason that Hamlet went there.'

Page 75, last line. The minister of Laurencekirk whom Boswell reproved for inhospitality to strangers was the Reverend David Forbes, the son of a blacksmith and a graduate of King's College, Aberdeen. He was presented to the living in July 1759, and ordained 27 Aug. 1760. He died 24 March 1795. See Hew Scott, *Fasti Eccl. Scot.*, 1925, v. 477. He contributed an account of the parish to Sir John Sinclair's *Statistical Account of Scotland*, 1793, v. 175–81. A more recent historian of the town records that :

' Mr. Forbes had the reputation of being a man not over-active in his habits, and of performing his duties in a very perfunctory manner.' W. R. Fraser, *Hist. of Laurencekirk*, 1880, p. 236.

Page 76, lines 10 ff. The inn at which Johnson and Boswell stopped at Laurencekirk was the Boar's Head, now (1936) called the Gardenstone Arms. The library, a square building with a pyramidal roof, joins it on the north side ; it consists of a single room which is now innocent of books. John Ramsay of Ochtertyre, like Johnson, thought well of the design ; he says :

> 'The public... was much indebted to his lordship for an excellent inn, and for the pains he took to amuse travellers.... Many a one has been agreeably amused on a bad day or long night with the library, which is well chosen for desultory reading.' *Scotland and Scotsmen in the 18th century*, 1888, i. 377.

Among those books that survived till the end of the nineteenth century were an edition of Aristophanes, with Latin notes, Newton's *Principia*, Watts's *Logic*, Jethro Tull's *Horse-hoeing Husbandry*, Dryden's *Virgil*, Le Sage's *Gil Blas*, and Clarke's *Sermons*. See W. R. Fraser's *Hist. of Laurencekirk*, 1880, p. 335 ; G. Birkbeck Hill's *Footsteps*, 1890, p. 110; and Mr. W. Fraser Mitchell in *Univ. of Edinburgh Jrnl.*, 1934, pp. 234 ff. Francis Douglas spoke in high praise of the inn and the landlord. *East Coast of Scotl.* 1782, p. 264.

Page 77, line 8. The great-great-grandmother of Lord Monboddo was Elisabeth, daughter of Sir Robert Douglas of Glenbervie, second son of William, ninth Earl of Angus. She married Capt. Robert Irvine, who bought Monboddo in 1633 and rebuilt the house in 1635. Their daughter, Elisabeth, married James Burnett of Lagavin, who acquired the estate *c.* 1671. Monboddo House has been greatly enlarged and altered since Johnson's time, but the dining-room in which he was entertained remains almost unchanged. The arms over the door of the house are those of Irvine of Monboddo impaled with Douglas of Glenbervie ; above the shield is a helmet surmounted by a ' C ' and below are the initials ' R I ' and ' E D ' with the date ' 1635 '. See Sir Robert Douglas, *Baronage of Scotland*, 1798, i. 19 ; *The Family of Burnett of Leys*, ed. from the manuscripts of Dr. G. Burnett by Col. J. Allardyce (New Spalding Club, 1901), pp. 143 ff., and G. Birkbeck Hill, *Footsteps*, pp. 113 ff. I am indebted to Mr. Fraser Mitchell for his friendly assistance.

Page 80, lines 8 ff. from foot. Pope published his edition of Shakespeare in 1723-5 : it was openly attacked by Theobald in his *Shakespeare restored*, 1726, and anonymously by Warburton in three letters in the *Daily Journal*, 22 March, 8 and 22 April 1729. T. R. Lounsbury, *First Editors of Shakespeare*, 1906, pp. 352-62, and A. W. Evans, *Warburton*, 1932, pp. 73 ff. (Warburton also attacked Pope's character and described *The Dunciad* as ' a most outrageous libel, the disgrace of the good sense, politeness and humanity of Great Britain '. Lounsbury, *op. cit.* p. 358.) Warburton first met Theobald on 1 Jan. 1727 and during 1729-30 corresponded with him very freely on Shakespearian

Page 84   *Appendix D*   491
problems (for the correspondence see Nichols, *Illustr.* ii. 204–654, and R. F. Jones, *Lewis Theobald*, 1919, 258–344). Theobald published his edition of Shakespeare in 1733–4 and in the Preface, which he submitted to Warburton, made the following acknowledgement of his debt to him :

' My most ingenious and ever-respected Friend, the Reverend Mr. Warburton . . . not only read over the whole Author for me, with the exactest Care ; but enter'd into a long and laborious Epistolary Correspondence ; to which I owe no small Part of my best Criticisms upon my Author.' Theobald's edition of Shakspeare, ed. 1733, vol. i, p. lxvi.

He also added Warburton's name to passages amended or explained by him. After the edition was published Warburton wrote to Theobald, 20 June 1734 :

' I have been so exact in my inquisitorial search after faults, that I dare undertake to defend every note throughout the whole bulky work, save these *thirteen* I have objected to.' Nichols, *Illustr.* ii. 645.

Warburton continued to send Theobald notes for a future edition, but the two friends subsequently, in 1736, became so completely estranged that Warburton demanded the return of his letters and Theobald omitted all reference to Warburton in the Preface to his second edition of Shakespeare published in 1740. See R. F. Jones, *Lewis Theobald*, 1919, 203 ff. and 343–4, D. Nichol Smith, *Eighteenth-century Essays on Shakespeare*, p. xlvi, and A. W. Evans, *op. cit.* p. 147.

Warburton's defence of Pope against the attacks of Crousaz originally appeared, as a series of five letters, in *The History of the Works of the Learned*, Dec. 1738–May 1739. In 1740 he revised these letters, added a sixth, and published the whole in a pamphlet entitled *A Vindication of Mr Pope's Essay on Man, from the Misrepresentations of Mr de Crousaz* ; this was followed, in the same year, by *A Seventh Letter*, and in 1742 by an enlarged edition, *A Critical and Philosophical Commentary on Mr Pope's Essay on Man*. Warburton's original defence brought him a grateful letter from Pope, 2 Feb. 1739, whom he visited in the following year. In 1741 Allen and Pope invited him to Prior Park and in Sept. 1745 he married Gertrude Tucker, Allen's favourite niece. It was through Allen's influence that he was made, in Sept. 1757, Dean of Bristol and two years later Bishop of Gloucester. See the *D.N.B. s.v.* Warburton.

Page 84, lines 6 ff. from foot. The English chapel at Aberdeen was Old St. Paul's Episcopal Church ; it was erected on the west side of the Gallowgate in 1721–2 by a number of ' respectable ' families of the episcopal persuasion who became English independents, ' formed themselves into a congregation, and appointed a clergyman, ordained by an English bishop, to administer the ordinances of religion according to the forms of the Church of England '. W. Kennedy, *Annals of Aberdeen*,

Appendix D Page 84
1818, ii. 182. Kennedy describes the church as 'a handsome and commodious place of worship, capable of containing a thousand hearers' (p. 183). A view of it will be found in Alexander Gammie's *The Churches of Aberdeen*, 1909, p. 307. It was replaced by the present church in 1866 and the only relic of it that now remains is the Duke of Gordon's coat of arms affixed to the west wall.

When the church was established two clergymen were appointed to serve it: at the time of Johnson's visit these were the Rev. James Riddoch (see *post*, v. 494) and Professor Thomas Gordon, who was 'minister of the second charge'. Gordon, who belonged to a family closely connected with the University since the sixteenth century, was a Professor of it for nearly 60 years : he was born in 1714, Humanist 1739–65, Professor of Philosophy 1765–96, Professor of Greek 1796, and died in 1797. He apparently took his duties lightly, for the Principal complained, 26 Jan. 1760, that ' he has scarcely ever had the face of a publick class '. P. J. Anderson, *Officers and Graduates of University and King's College*, 1893, pp. 48–9. If two independent witnesses are to be believed he could not have obtained the ear of his congregation at St. Paul's. Wesley, who visited Aberdeen in 1772 and attended the English church, writes, 3 May 1772, of him :

' So miserable a reader I have never heard before. Listening with all attention, I understood but one single word, " Balak ", in the First Lesson, and one more, " begat ", was all I could possibly distinguish in the Second.' *Journal*, ed. Curnock, v. 457.

Boswell, in his original Journal of the Tour, says :

' Gordon, who officiated, had the most unhappy defects of speech. His tongue was too big. He made such efforts to articulate, 'twas like convulsions. There was no understanding him. 'Twas just the same as speaking in an unknown tongue. It was wrong to put him in orders.' *Hebrides*, ed. Pottle and Bennett, 1936, p. 59.

John Ramsay of Ochtertyre, who met him towards the end of the century, applies to him Swift's saying of Arbuthnot that he could ' do everything but walk '. *Scotland & Scotsmen*, 1888, i. 296. The historian of Aberdeen, William Kennedy, owed many of the particulars in his account of the University to his industry and research. *Annals of Aberdeen*, 1818, ii. 384.

Mr. Tait, whose Christian name was Andrew, had in 1773 been organist for many years : he married Ann Ochterloney in 1759 and died in 1778. His successor, the well-known John Ross (1763–1837 : see the *D.N.B.*), married his daughter. See *Scottish Notes and Queries*, 3 Ser. xiii, 1935, pp. 79–80.

The ' admirable organ ' was built in 1721 and lasted till 1818. Kennedy, *o.c.s.* ii, p. 183. Edward Burt says that it was the only church

Pages 85–6 *Appendix D* 493

organ in Scotland known to him. *Letters from a Gentleman in the North of Scotland*, 1754, i. 258.

Page 85, line 11. Professor Thomas Gordon had in 1753, when he was the Humanist, been responsible for the abolition of the teaching of elementary Latin in King's College. At the same time the Senate had decided that ' the ancient practice of the same Regent carrying the Students through the whole course should be continued '. *Report relating to University and King's College, Aberdeen*, 1830, in *Report . . . into the State of the Universities of Scotland*, 1831, p. 309. The authorities of Marischal College took the opposite view, which was that of Dr. Gerard. They decided that, after spending a year on the classics, ' the Students should be made acquainted with the elements of History, natural and civil ; with Geography and Chronology, and with the elements of Mathematics ; that they should then proceed to Natural Philosophy, and terminate the course by studying Moral Philosophy '. *Report relating to Marischal College, Aberdeen*, 1830, *ibid.* p. 345. See also Dr. Alexander Gerard's *Plan of Education in the Marischal College*, 1755.

Pages 85, line 12, and 86, line 1. The English student at Aberdeen was Waller's great-great-grandson, not great-grandson, as the following entry in the records of the University shows :

' Mr. Edmundus Waller, Anglus de Beaconsfield, inclyti poetae E. W. abnepos.'

He took the degree of M.A. 28 March 1776. P. J. Anderson, *Officers and Graduates of Univ. and King's College, Aberdeen*, 1893, p. 252. He was born in 1757 and died in 1810. Burke's *Landed Gentry*, 1886, p. 1911. His father, ' the present Mr. Waller ', and grandfather, both named Edmund, sat in Parliament for Buckinghamshire boroughs ; both were elected for Chipping, or High, Wycombe on 27 June 1747. *Return of Members of Parl.* ii, pp. 50, 61, 72, 85, 98, and 109.

Page 86, lines 10 ff. Sir Alexander Gordon, of Lesmoir or Lismore, 7th baronet, born *c.* 1720, was the third son of Alexander Gordon, Collector of Customs, Aberdeen. He was the heir of his cousin, Sir William Gordon, who died in 1750 : he ' succeeded to a reduced estate ' and ' found himself under the necessity of executing a trust disposition of his whole estate for behoof of his creditors. . . . The landed estate, what remained of Newton Garie, was purchased by the Duke of Gordon in 1765 '; J. M. Bulloch, *House of Gordon*, 1907, ii. 260. He was appointed assistant and successor to Dr. John Gregory as Professor of Medicine, King's College, Aberdeen, in 1764, and full professor in 1766 : he demitted office on 19 March 1782 and died six days later. P. J. Anderson, *Officers and Graduates of University and King's College, Aberdeen*, 1893, p. 38. Boswell, in his original Journal, describes him as a ' worthy, harmless man '. His house no longer exists : it was

Appendix D

situated opposite King's College and stood on ground now (1937) occupied by professorial houses; part of the grotto remains.

Page 87, lines 6 ff. The Rev. James Riddoch was ' minister of the first charge ' at St. Paul's Episcopal Church, Aberdeen, from 20 June 1757 to the time of his death at the end of 1778. He had previously been minister of the Episcopal congregation at Glasgow. According to Sir William Forbes his ' manner in the pulpit was extremely energetic '. *Life of Beattie*, 1806, ii. 45. He published *Six Occasional Sermons* in 1762, and his widow, with the aid of Beattie and Dr. George Campbell (*post*, v. 495), published in 1782 a larger collection, *Sermons on Several Subjects and Occasions*, in two volumes, to which a third was added in 1799; these ran into five editions. The present Rector, the Rev. Charles S. Caldwell, to whom I am indebted, says that Mr. Riddoch's stipend during the whole of his incumbency was £60 a year.

Boswell first met his ' cousin ', Miss Dallas, in 1761, when on the Northern Circuit with his father, and described her as ' a charming creature indeed : excessively pretty, a most engaging manner. Great good sense, surprising propriety of language and facility of Expression. . . . Upon my soul, a delightfull Girl . . . . Was in raptures to myself w^t her.' *Hebrides*, ed. Pottle and Bennett, 1936, p. 61, note. In his original Journal of the Tour he describes her as an ' old flame ' and notes :

' I was in a kind of uneasiness from thinking that I should see a great change upon her at the distance of twelve years. But I declare I thought she looked better in every respect, except that some of her fore-teeth were spoiled. . . . My mind was sensibly affected at seeing her. I believe there was sincere joy on both sides.' *Ibid.* p. 61.

Mrs. Riddoch's niece was Miss Stuart (or Stewart) Dallas, the daughter and only child of William Dallas and his wife Stewart, daughter of Sir Alexander Mackenzie of Coul. See James Dallas, *Hist. of Family of Dallas*, 1921, pp. 190 and 574.

Page 88, line 8. Massillon's ' discourses on the Psalms ' were *Sentimens d'une âme touchée de Dieu, tirés des Pseaumes de David, ou Paraphrase morale de plusieurs pseaumes en forme de prière*, first published, in two volumes, in 1747.

Page 89, line 11. Baxter's commendation occurs in *The Grotian Religion Discovered* (1658, p. 4) :

' I must in Gratitude Profess, that I have learnt more from Grotius, then from almost any Writer in those subjects, that ever I read : (I speak not of Practical Divinity, which my soul doth live upon, and is the happiest part of my learning :) Especially his Books *de satisfactione Christi, de veritate Religionis Christi*.'

Grotius's treatise, *Defensio Fidei Catholicae de Satisfactione Christi, adversus Faustum Socinum*, was first published at Leyden in 1617.

Page 90, line 2. Principal George Campbell was born in 1719, took his M.A. in 1738 and his D.D. in 1764 : he was appointed Principal of Marischal College, Aberdeen, chiefly by the influence of his relative Archibald, 3rd Duke of Argyll, 14 Aug. 1759, and held the office till 18 Jan. 1796 : he was also Professor of Divinity, Marischal College, and Minister of Greyfriars, Aberdeen, 1771–95. He died 6 April 1796. His chief works are a reply to Hume, *A Dissertation on Miracles*, 1762, a translation from the Greek of the Gospels, 1789 (ed. 7 in 1834), and *Lectures on Ecclesiastical History*, ed. with a life by G. S. Keith in 1800. See Hew Scott, *Fasti Eccl. Scot.* 1926, vi. 3, 8, 80 ; 1928, vii. 359 ; Wesley, *Journal*, ed. Curnock, iv. 451 ; John Ramsay of Ochtertyre, *Scotland and Scotsmen in 18th century*, 1888, i. 482–3 ; and the *D.N.B.* For a portrait of him see P. J. Anderson, *Fasti Acad. Mariscall. Aberd.* 1898, ii. 29.

Page 90, line 3. John Ross was Professor of Hebrew, King's College, Aberdeen, from 1767 to 1790. P. J. Anderson, *Officers and Graduates of University and King's College, Aberdeen*, 1893, p. 74. He died, according to the *Aberdeen Journal*, on 9 July 1814. His death was prematurely announced in the magazines in 1777 :

' 21 Jan. John Ross, LL.D. professor of languages in the King's College, Old Aberdeen. His death was occasioned by swallowing a spider in a glass of wine. Upon dissecting his stomach, it was found to be ulcered [*Gent. Mag.* ulcerated] and extended beyond an ordinary size.' *Scots Mag.* Jan. 1777, xxxix. 55 ; and *Gent. Mag.* Jan. 1777, xlvii. 48.

There was no other professor of the name at King's College at the time, and the notice was no doubt malicious. There is in *The Scots Magazine* for the following April the somewhat belated correction : ' It is with pleasure we learn, that the report of the death of Prof. Ross . . . is false ' (p. 223). The Professor of Hebrew was, so Dr. Douglas Simpson informs me, expected to teach Oriental languages.

Page 92, line 2. Dr. James Dunbar was Professor of Philosophy from 1765 to 1794. He was the author of *Essays on the History of Mankind in rude and cultivated Ages*, 1780, second edition 1781, in which he pays a tribute to ' the texture of Johnson's brain ' (p. 89). He died in 1798. P. J. Anderson, *Officers and Graduates of Univ. and King's Coll.*, 1893, p. 63 ; and W. Kennedy, *Ann. Aberdeen*, 1818, ii. 383. See *antè*, iii. 436.

Page 92, line 3. John Leslie was appointed Professor of Greek at King's College on 29 April 1754. He died 24 May 1790, in his 69th year. See P. J. Anderson, *Officers and Graduates of Univ. and King's Coll.*, Aberdeen, 1893, p. 63 ; and *Scots Mag.*, June 1790, lii. 310.

Page 93, lines 17, 18. Boswell talked of ' the difference of genius ' because Dr. Gerard was about to publish his *Essay on Genius*, which had been in preparation since 1758 : it was published in 1774.

Appendix D Pages 94–8

Alexander Gerard, 1728–95, was Deputy Professor of Moral Philosophy at Marischal College in 1750, full Professor 1752 to 1760, Professor of Divinity, 1760–71, Professor of Divinity, King's College, 1771–95. See P. J. Anderson, *Fasti Acad. Mariscall. Aberd.* 1898, ii. 45; John Ramsay of Ochtertyre, *Scotl. and Scotsmen in the 18th century*, 1888, i. 482–5; and the *D.N.B.* His *Plan of Education for the Marischal College*, drawn up by order of the Faculty in 1753 and published, anonymously, in 1755, produced a revolutionary change in the curriculum of the college. See note to p. 85, line 11, above.

Page 94, note. Locke's complimentary verses were first appended to the second edition of Sydenham's *Methodus curandi Febres*, 1668: there are a few variants, chiefly of spelling and punctuation, from Boswell's text. Locke's first published compositions were two poems, one in Latin and the other in English, in *Musarum Oxoniensium 'Ελαιοφορία*, 1654, a collection of verses complimentary to Cromwell on the conclusion of peace with Holland; the editor was the eminent Puritan divine, Dr. John Owen, Dean of Christ Church and Vice-Chancellor of the University; Locke's verses are reprinted in H. R. Fox Bourne's *Life of Locke* (1876, i. 50 ff.).

Page 95, line 12. Roderick Macleod, 1727–1815, the son of Donald Macleod, the third, of Talisker, was appointed Professor of Philosophy at King's College in 1749 and Principal in 1800. Hew Scott, *Fasti Eccl. Scot.*, 1928, vii. 367.

Page 96, line 14. There was only one inn at Ellon in the eighteenth century, The New Inn. See *Statistical Acc. of Scotland*, 1792, iii. 102, and *The Book of Buchan*, ed. J. F. Tocher, 1910, pp. 191, 342. The present inn, so named, on the old Aberdeen road, is no doubt its successor: it was clearly a post-house.

Page 98, line 4. Mr. Irvine of Drum was Alexander, 18th Laird of Drum, 1754–1844. ' Independant estate. In the Army. Married a daughter of Forbes of Shivas, niece of Gardenstone's, who directs him. A family', says the confidential report made in 1788. Sir C. Elphinstone Adam, *View Polit. State Scotland*, 1887, p. 13. See also D. Wimberley, *Short Acc. of the Family of Irvine of Drum*, 1893, pp. 52 ff.; and J. F. Leslie, *The Irvines of Drum*, 1909, pp. 142 ff.

Page 98, line 9 and note 1. Tom Cumming died at Tottenham 29 May 1774. *Gent. Mag.* xliv. 287. Boswell appears to have met him only once, at Dilly's on 30 March 1768. *Boswell Papers*, vii. 184. He had from Sheridan, 7 April 1775, a very inaccurate account of an incident in his career:

' He [Sheridan] said he saw Cumming the Quaker fairly thresh Johnson one night with a forcible natural eloquence when fully provoked by him; and that Johnson cried mercy. Now Mr. Johnson told me that he had been rather severe upon Cumming; that Cumming was drunk and attacked him with rudeness; and that he did not answer him because he was in such a situation; and that he walked home with him.' *Boswell Papers*, x. 195.

For Cumming see *ante*, iv. 212, 513–14; below; and the *D.N.B.*

Page 99. The Hon. Charles Boyd was the third son of William, 4th Earl of Kilmarnock. He was born in Feb. 1728. He fought under the Prince's standard at Culloden. The name of his first wife, the French lady, is not known : he married secondly Anne Lockhart, sister of his brother's first wife (see below, p. 498). He died at Edinburgh 3 Aug. 1782. See Sir James Balfour Paul, *Scots Peerage*, 1908, v. 179; and *Scots Mag.* 1782, xliv, p. 447.

Page 101, lines 15 ff. Mr. Boyd was in error. Tom Cumming's pamphlet preceded Leechman's sermon and started a famous controversy. It was published anonymously in 1742 under the title *A Rational Inquiry concerning Prayer, wherein is shewn, the Insufficiency of Human Reason, to prove That Mankind ought to Invoke or thank Their Creator*. No place of publication is given, but according to *The Remarks of The Committee of the Presbytery of Glasgow upon Mr Leechman's Sermon on Prayer*, 1744, which also ascribes it to Cumming, it was published at Glasgow (pp. 34–5). Cumming states :

'That Mankind ought Not to Invoke, nor Thank their Creator. That they ought not to Invoke, that is, To pray for, wish or desire any Thing from him, more or less, then they are already endow'd with ; or, by natural Causes, in due Time may, or will have in actual Possession ' (p. 18).

His argument is that :

'The very Meaning of a Prayer to God implies, That he has withheld Something necessary for, or permitted Something to be done, in the general Oeconomy of the World, destructive or injurious to our Happiness. . . . To Thank God for, or to acknowledge Favours from him implies, That it was in his Option, whether to have given or withheld Good from us ; *i.e.* in other words, God might have, or may, chuse whether to be Good or Wicked, Just or Unjust; which is no less, if I may be allow'd the Expression, then a Devilizing of the Deity ' (p. 19).

The only copy of this pamphlet known to me is in the Library of New College, Edinburgh. Leechman's reply, *The Nature, Reasonableness, and Advantages of Prayer*, was published at Glasgow in 1743. The Presbytery of Glasgow found this reply unsatisfactory, accused Leechman of heresy, and refused to enrol him a member of their court on his election to the Professorship of Divinity of Glasgow University. The Synod of Glasgow and Ayr did not confirm the accusation and the General Assembly adopted the judgement of the Synod. See Wodrow's Life of Leechman in Leechman's *Sermons*, 1789, vol. i, pp. 22 ff. ; and W. Law Mathieson, *Scotland and the Union*, 1905, pp. 255–6. For Cumming, see *ante*, iv. 212 and 513–14, and above (note to p. 98, line 9).

498 *Appendix D* Pages 102-5

Page 102, line 18. Slains Castle was built in the seventeenth century to replace the old castle, the remains of which are still to be seen a few miles to the south, blown up by James VI in 1594. It was added to early in the eighteenth century and almost entirely rebuilt in 1836-7 ; it is now, 1938, a ruin. See J. B. Pratt, *Buchan*, ed. 4, 1901, pp. 50 ff. There is an engraving of the castle, as Johnson saw it, in C. Cordiner's *Remarkable Ruins and Romantic Prospects*, 1788, vol. i.

The collection of books was purchased in 1918 by the Libraries Committee of Glasgow and is now housed in the Mitchell Library : it consists of approximately 2,600 volumes and contains a few manuscripts, chiefly household accounts and memoranda. (Information courteously supplied by Mr. R. Bain, the Librarian of Glasgow.) The library was described by the late J. F. Kellas Johnstone in a paper read before the Bibliographical Society of Edinburgh, 8 March 1917, and subsequently revised and reprinted in the *Aberdeen University Library Bulletin*, April 1917.

Page 103, line 1. Alexander Falconer, 1682-1745, advocate, second son of Sir David Falconer, Lord President, married Mary, *suo jure* Countess of Erroll, eldest sister of Charles, 13th Earl. She died in 1758, when she was succeeded by her great-nephew, James Boyd (later Hay), 15th Earl, Johnson's host. G. E. C., *Complete Peerage*, 1926, v. 99-100.

Page 103, line 3. Captain John Gordon was the second son of Sir James Gordon of Park, second baronet. His half-brother, Sir William, took part in the '45 in the Jacobite interest and was attainted : Captain John Gordon claimed the forfeited estate and retained it till his death in Sept. 1781. See G. E. C., *Complete Baronetage*, iv. 345. For his military career see J. M. Bulloch, *The House of Gordon*, 1912, iii. 199.

Page 103, lines 6 ff. James Boyd, second son of the 4th Earl of Kilmarnock, to whose estates (but not peerage) he succeeded, was born in 1726 and became Earl of Erroll on the death of his great-aunt Mary in 1758. He married first Rebecca, daughter of Alexander Lockhart, Lord Covington (see *ante*, iii. 513), and secondly, in 1762, Isabella, elder daughter of William Carr of Etall, Northumberland. He died 3 July 1778. He and his second wife had, in 1773, ten children ; two more were born subsequently. Their eldest son, George, whose birth in May 1767 was celebrated by Beattie, committed suicide in 1798. Lady Erroll was born in 1742 and died 3 Nov. 1808. See J. P. Wood's edition of Sir Robert Douglas's *Peerage of Scotland*, i. 554 ; Sir James Balfour Paul, *Scots Peerage*, 1906, iii. 581; and G. E. C., *Complete Peerage*, 1926, v. 100.

Page 105, lines 16 ff. Beattie's *Ode on Lord Hay's Birthday* was apparently first printed for private distribution. (There is no copy in

Page 105   Appendix D   499
the Slains Castle Collection in the Mitchell Library, *ante*, v. 102, 498.)
Gray saw it at the end of December 1767. Writing to Beattie on the 24th of the month he says :

' I have read with much pleasure an Ode of yours (in wch you have done me the honour to adopt a measure, that I have used) on Ld Hay's birth-day. Tho' I do not love *panegyrick*, I can not but applaud this, for there is nothing mean in it.' *Correspondence of Gray*, ed. Toynbee and Whibley, 1935, iii. 983.

The ode was first published in *The Edinburgh Magazine and Review*, Nov. 1773, i. 81, where it is printed along with *The Hermit*. There is the following note :

' This beautiful Poem [i.e. *The Hermit*] was some time ago published in a news-paper from an imperfect copy. The ingenious author has done us the honour to permit us to print it from his own hand-writing. We have also to acknowledge our obligation to him for the elegant verses which follow it. They now appear for the first time.' (I owe this reference to Dr. L. W. Sharp, of the University Library, Edinburgh.)

Gray approved of the poem and objected to only two words (*o.c.s.* 984), but Lord Hailes was offended by Beattie's historical inaccuracy :

' No poetical merit ', he writes, ' can ever in my eyes justify a poem that alludes to the Hays at Luncarty—it is the fable of fables.' Margaret Forbes, *Beattie and his Friends*, 1904, p. 149.

Beattie included the ode in the 1776 edition of his poems, and did not reject it from the later editions, as he did so many of his pieces.

Page 105, line 28. *Dolus latet in universalibus*. Dryden has it in English ' For fallacies in universals live ' (*Hind and Panther*, ii. 651). The legal maxim *dolus versatur in generalibus*, or *dolosus versatur in universalibus*, dates from the end of the sixteenth century : see *Englefield's Case* (1590) Moore K. B. 321 ; *Doddington's Case* (1594) 2 Rep. 34 (a) ; *Twyne's Case* (1601) 3 Rep. 81 (a) ; *Stone* v. *Grubham* (1615) 2 Bulstr. 226 ; *Warren* v. *Smith* (The Magdalen College Case) (1616) 1 Rolle 157 ; and H. Broom's *Selection of Legal Maxims*, 1911, p. 240. (I owe the references to Mr. W. Hussey Griffith.)

Page 105, line 2 from foot. The ' old lawyer, who had much experience in making wills ' was, according to Mrs. Piozzi, Charles Scrase. In a copy of the second edition of *Hebrides* she wrote, on this passage, ' Scrase told me and I told Johnson '. Scrase lent Mr. Thrale money and frequently advised him on legal matters; writing to Queeney, 1 Aug. 1784, Mrs. Thrale says : ' Mr. Scrase *is* a Friend to every thing belonging to your Father ; I am glad you love him, but 'tis impossible not.' *The Queeney Letters*, ed. Ld. Lansdowne, 1934, p. 173. See also *ibid.*, pp. 177, 193, 199, 204. Johnson, in whose letters to Mrs. Thrale he is frequently mentioned, wished he had ' his knowledge of Business, and of law ' and described him as ' a friend upon all occasions,

500   *Appendix D*   Page 107

whether assistance was wanted for the purse or the understanding '. *Letters*, Nos. 591 (14 Nov. 1778) and 636 (21 Oct. 1779). He lived at Brighton, where he died 13 Jan. 1792 ' at his house on the Steine, aged 83 ' ; the obituary notice adds that 'he was for many years partner with the late Mr. Robson of Lincoln['s Inn].' *Gent. Mag.* Jan. 1792, lxii, pt. i. 92. There is in the John Rylands Library a letter from Scrase to Thrale, dated 30 July 1775, in which he speaks of Robson as aiding in drawing up Mrs. Thrale's marriage settlement, under which Johnson and Cator were made trustees of all the Welsh property (J.R.L., Eng. MS. 600, 26). See also Hayward's *Piozzi*, ed. 1, 1861, ii. 244 (where Mrs. Piozzi, with great exaggeration, says that he was 86 in 1765); Fanny Burney's *Diary*, 1842, ii. 19; and *Thraliana*, ed. Balderston, ii. 864.

Page 107, lines 3 ff. The great manufacturer of whom this story is told was, there can be no doubt, Jean de Jullienne, 1686-1766 ; he was not, however, ' at the Gobelins '. He acquired the dye-works and cloth manufactory of his uncles, Jean Glucq († 1715) and François Jullienne († 1733), and made a fortune : both works were situated near the Gobelins and the house in which he lived was styled ' la grande Maison des Gobelins '. He was ennobled in 1736 and in the ' lettres de noblesse ' was described as ' entrepreneur des manufactures royales des draps fins et teintures en hautes couleurs façon d'Angleterre et de Hollande '. In his youth he attended the Académie Royale de Peinture et Sculpture, where he met Watteau, whose friend and patron he became, and whose drawings he published in 1736. See J. Hérold and A. Vuaflart, *Jean de Jullienne et les graveurs de Watteau*, t. i, Notices et documents biographiques, Paris, 1929, and Thieme-Becker, *Künstler-Lexikon*, xix, 1926, p. 312. Mr. Boyd's story does not seem to be in keeping with what is known of Jean de Jullienne's life.

Page 107, last line and note 1. The hospitable Mr. Fraser was Alexander Fraser, the son of Lord Strichen, a judge in the Court of Session, a Lord of Justiciary, and General of the Mint, who died on 15 Feb. 1775 at the age of 76. Brunton and Haig, *Senators of the College of Justice*, 1832, pp. 502-3. His mother was Ann, daughter of Archibald, 1st Duke of Argyll, and widow of James, 2nd Earl of Bute. He received the estate of Strichen from his father by disposition in 1759. He died 17 Dec. 1794. See John Anderson, *Hist. Acct. of the Family of Fraser*, 1825, p. 186 ; Sir James Balfour Paul, *Scots Peerage*, 1908, v. 545 ; and Johnson's *Letters*, No. 323. Johnson in his *Western Isl.* (1924, p. 18) says :

' We dined this day at the house of Mr. Frazer of Streichton, who shewed us in his grounds some stones yet standing of a druidical circle, and what I began to think more worthy of notice, some forest trees of full growth.'

He was said to be politically ' very independant ' and to have ' much

Pages 108-10   *Appendix D*   501
to say with those of his own name '. Sir C. Elphinstone Adam, *View of the Political State of Scotland*, 1887, pp. 9 and 180.

Page 108, line 4 from foot. Johnson could not refrain from a gibe at Langton. Boswell records in his original Journal under this date, 25 Aug. 1773 :

'He said that we'd persuade Langton to lodge in the garret, as best for him, and if he should take a fancy of making his Will, we'd get him to leave his estate to the College.' *Hebrides*, ed. Pottle and Bennett, 1936, p. 79.

For Langton's ' bad management ', poor table, &c., see *ante*, iii. 48 ; for the making of his will, see *ante*, ii. 261-2.

Page 108, line 3 from foot. Dr. Christopher Nugent died on 12 November (not October as stated in the *D.N.B.*) 1775, at his house in Suffolk Street. *Gent. Mag.*, Nov. 1775, p. 551. Mr. Dixon Wecter has printed Johnson's letter of condolence to his daughter, Burke's wife, in *The Times Literary Suppl.*, 2 July 1938, p. 449 : *Letters*, No. 437 1.

Page 109, last line and note 6. The inn at Banff in which the travellers stayed was probably either The Black Bull or The Ship, the chief hostelries in the town at the time. The former was pulled down in 1879, the latter, which was described by a fastidious traveller in 1771 as ' good ', is at present, 1938, in a good state of preservation : it is in an old part of the town and next door to the house once occupied by Thomas Edward, the noted Banff naturalist. See W. Cramond, *Annals of Banff*, 1891, i. 223, and *Gent. Mag.* 1771, p. 544.

Page 110, lines 11 ff. William Robertson, 1740-1803, gained a bursary at King's College, Aberdeen University, where he distinguished himself by his proficiency in Greek. He became, on the recommendation of Prof. Leslie (*ante*, v. 92, 495), clerk to Lord Monboddo, who wanted a young Greek scholar ' properly qualified to aid him in his literary pursuits '. He remained with Monboddo till 1766, when he was appointed Chamberlain to James, Earl of Findlater, who died in 1770. In 1777 he was appointed, as a colleague to his brother Alexander, Joint Deputy Keeper of the Records of Scotland, a post which he held till his death. See the Memoir prefixed to the ninth edition of his *History of Greece*, 1829, pp. xi-xviii.

The translation of La Condamine's *Histoire d'une jeune fille sauvage* (1755), was the first of his literary works. It was published at Edinburgh in 1768 under the title *An Account of a Savage Girl, Caught Wild in the Woods of Champagne. With a Preface, Containing several Particulars omitted in the Original Account*. Monboddo acknowledged the authorship of the Preface and stated that the translation was made by his clerk. *Antient Metaphysics*, 1795, iv. 33-4 (Monboddo met the ' Savage Girl ' in Paris in March 1765. *Ibid.*, App., pp. 403 ff.). Robertson's translation is rare : it was issued, without Monboddo's Preface, as a chap-book *c.* 1822. The present Keeper of the Records, Mr. W. Angus, tells me that his *Proceedings Relative to the Peerage of Scotland*, 1794, is still occasionally consulted in connexion with the election of Representative Peers, that his Index of Missing Charters, 1798, was in use till 1912, when it was superseded by the more scholarly version prepared by Dr. Maitland Thomson, and that his posthumous *Records of the Parliament of Scotland*, 1804, was so unsatisfactory that it had to be withdrawn.

It is stated in the *D.N.B.* that Robertson was responsible for the haddocks at Johnson's breakfast: this is highly improbable, as the travellers breakfasted at the inn and not at Cullen House, as is implied. Another story, told in the Memoir (p. xv), that Johnson disdained to look at some very fine trees to which Robertson had drawn his attention ' when they were going over the grounds at Cullen House ', and said ' Sir, I can see nothing less than a mountain in Scotland ', appears to be derived from Boswell's narrative, which refutes it.

Page 114, line 4. The chief residence of the Bishop of Moray was Spynie Castle, about two miles north of Elgin, but there was a smaller sixteenth-century residence or manse, still called ' the Bishop's House ', near the cathedral : it was situated in what was the north-west corner of the enclosing wall of the cathedral grounds ; a wing of it still remains. See Shaw, *Hist. of Province of Moray*, 1775, p. 285; Macgibbon and Ross, *Castellated & Domestic Archit.*, 1887, ii. 58–60 ; 1892, v. 91 ; and Muirhead, *Scotland* (Blue Guides), 1927, p. 312.

Page 114, note 1. Johnson's original censure in his *Journey to the Western Islands* was directed against the Dean and Chapter of Lichfield Cathedral ; it ran thus, after ' neighbours ' (p. 48) :

' There is now, as I have heard, a body of men, not less decent or virtuous than the Scotish council, longing to melt the lead of an English cathedral. What they shall melt, it were just that they should swallow.'

This was suppressed, and the more general stricture substituted, by Johnson out of gratitude to Dean Addenbroke, who had been kind to him in his youth. *Letters*, No. 364. Gough's transcript of the passage, in his copy of the book, now in the Bodleian, was discovered by Dr. Birkbeck Hill, who commented on it in his edition of the *Life* (vi, p. xxxiii) ; the cancelled leaf (D 8) is now in the Hyde Collection and is otherwise recorded. No copy of the book with the leaf uncancelled has so far been discovered. See Courtney, p. 123, and Dr. R. W. Chapman's edition, 1924, pp. 452–3.

Page 114, note 2. The cathedral of Elgin was, after its destruction in 1390, gradually rebuilt by successive bishops. The central tower fell in 1506, but was re-erected by 1538. During the episcopate of Patrick Hepburn, a notorious profligate and ' the greatest dilapidator of the church's possessions ', the lead was stripped from the roof by order of the Privy Council, of which he was a member, on the ground

Pages 114-15   *Appendix D*   503

that it was being stolen by private persons. The actual order, dated 14 Feb. 1567/68, is in the following terms :

'[The Lords] understanding that the leid upoun the Cathedrall Kirkis of Abirdene and Elgin is for ane greit part be diverse personis thiftuouslie stowin and takin away, . . . theirefoir . . . ordanit . . . that the leidis of the saidis kirkis salbe takin doun with diligence and sauld and disponit upoun, for interteneing and sustentatioun of the saidis men of weir and utheris neidfull chargeis of the commoun weill.' *Register Privy Council Scotl.* 1877, i. 609.

Two burgesses of Edinburgh were empowered to carry out the work, and a number of Sheriffs, Sheriffs-depute, Provosts, and others, including the bishops of the cathedrals concerned, were commanded to assist them. The roof rafters fell in 1637, and three years later the Rev. Gilbert Ross, minister of Elgin, and other Covenanters, without authority, but probably influenced by the 'Act anent the demolishing of idolatrous monuments' (*Acts of the General Assembly*, 1843, i. 44), broke down the screen between the nave and the choir ; the great tower fell in 1711 ; the north transept and nave arcades quickly followed. No attempt was made in the eighteenth century to restore a building which for size and ornament was unrivalled in Scotland. Early in the nineteenth century John Shanks, a shoemaker, established himself as the preserver of the cathedral ; he cleared away effectively, but not very carefully, masses of rubbish ' with his solitary spade and mattock ', and was rewarded by being appointed the official custodian. He died in 1841, and Lord Cockburn, after much delay, succeeded in getting the authorities to erect a tablet to his memory within the cathedral precincts. See Billings, *Baronial and Eccl. Antiq. Scotl.*, vol. ii; Lord Cockburn, *Circuit Journeys*, 1888, pp. 42-3, 264 ; Macgibbon and Ross, *Eccl. Archit. Scotl.* ii. 122 ff. ; and H. B. Mackintosh, *Elgin, Past and Present*, 1914, pp. 60 ff. The ruined cathedral has long been cared for by H.M. Office of Works.

Page 114, note 3. The Duke of Gordon in 1773 was Alexander, the fourth duke, 1743-1827. His father, the third duke, Cosmo George, was named after Cosmo de Medicis the third, Grand Duke of Tuscany, who was the second Duke of Gordon's close friend. Burke's *Peerage*, 1829, p. 320. The first and second dukes were Catholics. For the fourth duke's son, Lord George Gordon, the leader of the ' No Popery ' riots, see *ante*, iii. 428, 430, and iv. 87. He became a Jew in 1786.

Page 115, lines 14 ff. Johnson says of the inn at Elgin, The Red Lion, where he stayed : ' This was the first time, and except one, the last, that I found any reason to complain of a Scotish table.' *Western Isl.*, 1924, p. 20. Boswell's original Journal supplies more details :

' Baillie Leslie, at whose house we put up, gave us good fish, but beef collops and mutton chops which absolutely could not be eat.' *Hebrides*, ed. Pottle and Bennett, 1936, p. 83.

Appendix D   Pages 115–16

Dr. Birkbeck Hill prints in his *Footsteps* (1890, p. 130) what he describes as ' a satisfactory explanation ' of the badness of the food. It consists of a story, stated to occur in a manuscript ' as early ' as 1837, that Johnson was mistaken by a waiter for a poor commercial traveller (or, according to Mr. H. B. Mackintosh, merchant), a regular customer of the inn, and given such a dinner as this man ' was wont to receive '. As this man ' cared little about eating . . . and was in the habit of ordering only a very slender dinner, that he might spend the more on the pleasures of the bottle ', Johnson suffered by the mistake, ' for ', the story continues, ' he did not ask for that which was to follow '. This is an explanation, not so much of the poor quality of the food, as of its exiguous quantity, of which no complaint was made, and of which, as Boswell's record shows, no complaint was justified. The story completely ignores the presence of Boswell : it is, *pace* Dr. Hill, and the distinguished historian of Elgin (Mr. H. B. Mackintosh, *Elgin*, 1914, p. 11), out of respect for whom it is mentioned here, unworthy of credence. It is some consolation to know that if Johnson had visited Elgin a year or two earlier he would have fared better, for a nice observer of Scottish inns commends this one : ' Elgin . . . Red Lion, Leslie ; good. The only landlord in Scotland who wears ruffles.' *Gent. Mag.* 1771, xli. 544. The building is now (1938) a shop, Nos. 44 and 46 High Street. See H. B. Mackintosh, *Elgin*, 1914, pp. 9–10, where a picture of it is given.

Mr. A. G. Cockburn, the Town Clerk of Elgin, tells me from the records of the Burgh, that from about 1770 to 1777 there was a Bailie Robert Leslie, who was almost certainly the landlord of the Red Lion Inn.

Page 115, lines 17 ff. and note 3. Hannah More says that Johnson told her in 1774 that ' when he and Boswell stopt a night at the spot (as they imagined) where the Weird Sisters appeared to Macbeth, the idea so worked upon their enthusiasm, that it quite deprived them of rest : however, they learnt, the next morning, to their mortification, that they had been deceived, and were in quite another part of the country '. *Memoirs*, 1834, i. 50. Carruthers, in his edition of Boswell's *Hebrides*, 1852, p. 81, has the following note :

' The " blasted heath " lies to the west of Forres, about half-way between that town and Nairn. A round knoll planted with fir-trees, and known by the name of " Macbeth's Hillock ", has from time immemorial been pointed out as the place where the Thane met the weird sisters.'

' Macbeth's Hill ' is marked on the O.S. six-inch maps, 1868–70 and revision of 1904 ; it is Hardmuir Wood, on the Elgin–Nairn road, just inside the Elgin border : the hill is about 160 feet high.

Page 116, line 3 from foot. *Leonidas, a Poem* was published, in quarto, by R. Dodsley on 2 April 1737 and cost 10*s*. 6*d*. bound ; a

Page 118   *Appendix D*   505

second edition appeared in 1738, a fourth in 1739, and a fifth in 1770, all in duodecimo : the fifth edition, published by Cadell, was thoroughly revised and enlarged from nine books to twelve. ' Few poems ', says Dr. Warton, who knew Glover well, ' on their first appearance, have been received with greater applause than *Leonidas*. . . . Nothing else was read or talked of at Leicester House; and by all the members that were in opposition to Sir R. Walpole.' Swift's *Works*, 1824, xix. 73. See also Fielding's *Works*, 1882, v. 230 ; Swift's *Corresp.* 1914, vi. 17 ; Horace Walpole, *Letters*, ed. Toynbee, i. 76 ; Henry Pemberton, *Obs. on Poetry*, 1738 ; R. Straus, *Robert Dodsley*, 1910, pp. 41 ff. and 318 ; and the *D.N.B.* s.v. Glover.

Page 118, lines 4 ff. The Rev. Kenneth Macaulay, or McAulay, was the third son of the Rev. Aulay Macaulay, *c.* 1673–1758, minister of Harris ; he was born in 1723, educated at King's College, Aberdeen, where he took his M.A. in 1742 ; ordained as assistant and successor to his father in 1750, and sent on a special mission to St. Kilda in 1758 ; appointed minister of Ardnamurchan, Argyleshire, in 1761, and translated to the living of Cawdor in 1772, which he held till his death on 2 March 1779. Hew Scott, *Fasti Eccl. Scot.* 1926, vi. 439. He was buried in Cawdor churchyard, opposite the west door of the church, and his tombstone, in addition to the usual biographical facts, tells us that he was ' notus in fratres animi paterni ' [Horace, *Odes*, ii. 2. 6]. He married, in 1758, Penelope, daughter of Alexander Macleod, third son of Norman Macleod IV, of Drynoch, and Penelope, daughter of Mackinnon of Mackinnon, seventeenth chief. She died in 1799. A. Mackenzie, *Hist. of Macleods*, 1889, p. 217. Their second son, Aulay, ' the smart young lad about eleven years old ' (*ante*, v. 122), was born 25 May 1762 ; he became a Lieutenant in the Marines, 27 Feb. 1779, was placed on half-pay 7 June 1780, and died, without further service, in 1842. Boswell notes in his original Journal that ' he had a governor in the house to teach him ' and that his father did not take Johnson's offer to get him a servitorship so warmly as he should have done and as his mother did. *Hebrides*, ed. Pottle and Bennett, 1936, p. 89.

Kenneth Macaulay published *The History of St. Kilda* in 1764. Boswell wrote in his original Journal, 27 Aug. 1773 :

' From his conversation Mr. Johnson was persuaded that he had not written the book which goes under his name. I myself always suspected so. Mr. Johnson said there was a combination in it of which Macaulay was not capable, and said to me privately, " Crassus homo est ".' *Hebrides*, ed. Pottle and Bennett, 1936, p. 86.

Boswell had not, however, read it at that time : in his Journal for 26 Nov. 1775 he wrote :

' I . . . came home and began for the first time MacAulay's *History of St. Kilda*. I read about one half of it.' *Boswell Papers*, xi. 20.

On the next day he wrote more fully :

'Having no business immediately pressing, I finished *St. Kilda*. . . . Dr. Johnson and I had discovered from McAulay's conversation, and from what we were told in Sky, that he had not written the Book to which his name is prefixed, but only collected some materials for it. Dr. McPherson, Minister of Slate, is supposed to have arranged them and put them in language, with illustrations and reflections. The Book indeed is not like the genuine narrative of a Traveller himself and is too much loaded with dissertation and allusion. It is deficient in many respects. There is not near so minute an account of the peculiar state of life in St. Kilda as might have been given. I am sure I could give a much better.' *Ibid.* xi. 20, 21.

Johnson clearly held Macaulay in contempt. He told Coll that he was ' as obstinate as a mule and as ignorant as a bull ', and when the Scottish clergy were discussed at Talisker, 23 Sept. 1773, he named him as an outstanding example of their ignorance : ' There is Macaulay— the most ignorant booby and the grossest bastard.' *Hebrides*, ed. Pottle and Bennett, 1936, p. 215.

William Macpherson, 1812–93, the eminent legal author and son of Professor Hugh Macpherson, 1767–1854, when he was a young man informed Croker that Dr. John Macpherson, to whom he was distantly related, was ' certainly the author ' of *The History of St. Kilda*. Croker's *Boswell*, 1835, iv, p. 122, n. 2. Kenneth Macaulay's own family and friends, according to Robert Carruthers, ' always strenuously denied ' this ascription. Carruthers stated that Kenneth's nephew, the Rev. Aulay Macaulay (1758–1819), the Vicar of Rothley, intended to republish the book, with notes, ' showing the work to have been altogether his uncle's composition '. *Boswell's Hebrides*, 1852, p. 286 note. The edition was not published and the materials for it have not been found. The Rev. Thomas Fraser, minister of Cawdor, told Dr. Birkbeck Hill that in the Kirk Session Records of Cawdor is a minute by Kenneth Macaulay ' most beautifully expressed '. *Footsteps of Dr. Johnson*, 1890, p. 136.

It appears from letters in the National Library of Scotland that Macaulay submitted his manuscript to Dr. Macpherson for revision. Writing to the Rev. John Macaulay (*post*, v. 561), Kenneth's elder brother, Dr. Macpherson says, 27 July 1759 :

' Kenneth was here till about three daies ago. We read his History of St. Kilda tête à tête. The Subject is truly curious—but to say the truth, handled in a careless way. If that Essay is to be published some one ought surely to retouch it—and what hinders the Dean to assist a young Adventurer in the Republic of Letters. For my share, if the truth be in me, there is nothing more irksome to me, & to say a great deal more, nothing can be more prejudicial to my health than the scribbling business. . . . But after all, as my friends are not a little interested in this thing, & as Mr. Smollet takes the matter so much to heart, I will undertake to do what I can. . . . The subject may possibly lead me into the large field of our Scottish Antiquities, and perhaps tempt me to make some little

Page 119   *Appendix D*   507

Remarks in the Critical & Etymological way &c. &c. How far my Imagination may carry me, I am not just now able to determine or foresee. . . . Ask your Friend [Mr. Smollett], whether he will give me leave to ramble a little, or whether he chuses to confine me to the Text of my Author.'

He thought that his task would take him six or seven weeks, but it was apparently not completed in 1762. Writing on 5 April of that year to Kenneth Macaulay he says of his own work, the *Critical Dissertations* :
' I correspond now with my friend Sir James Macdonald & Ossian principally. My sheets I send up in franks to the former from time to time and they are to be printed at London. Some people of the highest character there for literary merit are impatient to have them in print and I am not. I have drawn out a new & much fuller edition of the first volume. . . . As to St. Kilda I know not yet whether it shall make a part of the 2d volume as I may perhaps have materials enough without it. If I use any freedoms with it, nothing shall be done without your advice & consent & depend on it, no injury shall be done to your character.'

In his letter of 27 July 1759, Dr. Macpherson assured the Rev. John Macaulay that his brother ' is to answer for all my Lucubrations, or in other words, to publish all under his own name, if the Paper shall ever make any sort of appearance in the world ', but now he apparently contemplated attaching *St. Kilda* to his own *Critical Dissertations*. This procedure, coupled with the long delay, probably alarmed Kenneth Macaulay and his friends and caused them to urge separate publication. However that may be, Macaulay's History appeared during Dr. Macpherson's lifetime, while his own *Dissertations* did not. There can be little doubt that Dr. Macpherson did revise and enlarge *The History of St. Kilda*, as I have endeavoured to show elsewhere (*R.E.S.*, xvi, 1940, pp. 44 ff.), but his contribution, although extensive, was not so interesting or so valuable as that made by the Rev. Kenneth Macaulay.

Boswell in his original Journal says, at the end of his record for 27 Aug. 1773, ' Macaulay had a remarkably good manse. Mr. Grant and I slept in the same room. Mr. Johnson had a room to himself. The house was very decently furnished.' Pottle and Bennett, *o.c.s.* p. 89. Mr. Grant (*post*, v. 509) stated that the manse was built about 1730. *Statist. Acct.* 1792, iv. 353. It lasted a hundred years, its successor, the present manse, being built, so the Rev. William Metcalfe informs me, in 1829–30.

Page 119, line 5 and note 1. The communion tokens were circular, oval, oblong, or square pieces of metal, usually lead, stamped with the name of the parish and often the date of original issue, sometimes, among the ' Seceders ', with the initials of the minister. At the present time tokens are in pretty general use in the Islands and country parishes of the Highlands : in the towns and farther south cards, on which the name and address of the communicant can be written, are used.

At Cawdor, so the present minister, the Reverend William Metcalfe, informs me, the Session in 1730 procured 204 new tokens at a cost of 8s. 4d. The oldest tokens of Boswell's own parish are of the eighteenth century and undated ; they bear the name ' Afleck ' ; the dated tokens of 1817 are lettered ' Auchinleck '. Helen J. Steven, *Auchinleck*, p. 40. For a full account of the tokens see the Rev. Thomas Burns, *Old Scottish Communion Plate*, 1892, pp. 435–68. There is a large collection of the older tokens in the General Assembly Library, Tolbooth Church, Edinburgh.

Page 119, lines 19 ff. Cawdor Castle is not so old as Boswell thought, or as it looks ; the licence to build the castle was granted in 1454 and the tower or keep dates from the late fifteenth century, but the surrounding structures are seventeenth-century work. See Cosmo Innes, *Thanes of Cawdor*, 1859, pp. 20, 48, 68, 295–9, and Macgibbon and Ross, *Castellated and Domestic Architecture of Scotland*, 1887, ii. 314. Lachlan Shaw, who was minister of Cawdor 1719–34, in his *History of the Province of Moray* (1882, ii. 269) writes : ' It [the castle] is built upon a rock of freestone, washed by a brook to the west, and on the other sides having a dry ditch, with a draw-bridge.' This ditch or fosse, which both Boswell and Johnson (*Western Isl.* 1924, p. 22) took for a moat, was, as the Earl of Cawdor told Dr. Birkbeck Hill, ' the excavation made in quarrying the stone for the castle '. *Footsteps*, 1890, p. 140. Boswell's original description of the hawthorn tree, round which according to legend the castle was built, is more accurate than his revised version : it is ' There is a hawthorn tree in one of the rooms, still undecayed, that is to say, the stock still remains.' *Hebrides*, ed. Pottle and Bennett, 1936, p. 86. The stock is still (1937) to be seen in the ground floor of the old donjon. Lord Cockburn, who saw the castle in 1844, was severe *more suo* : ' The edifice, though pretended to be still maintained as a place of residence, is all in the most humiliating condition of paltry disrepair.' *Circuit Journeys*, 1888, p. 216. That is not so to-day.

Page 119, line 21 and note 4. The sentence, ' I was sorry that my friend, this " prosperous gentleman," was not there ', was added by Boswell in 1785. It is certain, therefore, that Boswell by ' this ' means ' the present ' laird, as Dr. Chapman conjectured (see *Hebrides*, 1924, p. 468). The laird in 1773 was John Campbell of Cawdor and Castlemartin, Pembrokeshire, on which latter estate he resided ; he died on 6 Sept. 1777 and was succeeded by his grandson, Boswell's friend, also named John. He was M.P. for Nairn, 1777–80, and Cardigan, 1780–96, and was created Baron Cawdor of Castlemartin 21 June 1796 ; he died 1 June 1821, aged 66. G. E. C., *Compl. Peerage*, 1913, ii. 122 ; and *Parl. Return Members of Parl.* 1878, pt. ii. 161, 172 and 197. Boswell records meeting him on 29 July 1782. *Boswell Papers*, xv. 107.

Pages 120-4   *Appendix D*   509

Page 120, line 11. The Rev. Alexander Grant was the son of the Rev. George Grant (1700-72), minister of Kirkmichael, Abernethy; he was born in 1743, graduated at King's College, Aberdeen, in 1759, ordained as missionary at Fort William in 1765, translated to Daviot and Dunlichity in 1771, and to Cawdor in 1780. He died at Cawdor 28 June 1828 and was buried in the churchyard. He married Grace, daughter of Col. Alexander Fraser; their fourth son, James (1790-1853), minister of Nairn, was the father of Col. James Augustus Grant (1827-92), the great African traveller. He wrote the account of the parish of Cawdor in the old *Statistical Account of Scotland* (1792, vol. iv, pp. 349 ff.) and was one of the thirteen gentlemen to whom Pennant returned particular thanks for their assistance to him (*Tour in Scotland, 1769*, ed. 3, 1774, Advt., p. viii). See Hew Scott, *Fasti Eccl. Scot.* 1926, vi. 367, 439, 444.

Page 122, line 4 from foot. Valentine White was a native of Pembrokeshire and a man of some importance at Cawdor. The laird lived chiefly at Stackpole Court, Pembrokeshire, and left the management of the Cawdor estate to White, who carried out great improvements in cultivation on it. He is mentioned in the Sessions minutes as ' factor to the laird of Calder ' as early as 1758. Extracts from the correspondence between him and the laird are printed in George Bain's *History of Nairnshire* (1893, pp. 369 ff.). His tombstone in Cawdor churchyard states that he died on 20 April 1784, at the age of 67, and ' after tuenty-three years faithful discharge of his trust and receving many marks of the favour of his Constituents '.

Page 123, line 17. Fort George, on the point of Ardersier at the head of the Firth of Inverness, was built after the Rebellion of 1745 on the site of a fishing village, Blacktown, the inhabitants of which were removed to Campbelltown, about a mile distant: it was constructed to accommodate over 3,000 officers and men. See R. Wright, *Life of Wolfe*, 1864, p. 178; and G. Bain, *History of Nairnshire*, 1893, p. 378.

Page 123, line 19. John Brewse was Second Engineer in Newfoundland in 1745, where he still was in 1748; ten years later, 1758, he was at the siege of Louisburg with the rank of Captain-Lieutenant; he was promoted Major on 23 July 1772, Lieutenant-Colonel on 29 Aug. 1777, and Colonel on 20 Nov. 1782. He succeeded Col. Patrick Mackellar as Chief Engineer in Minorca in 1778 and held the post during the siege of the island. See Whitworth Porter, *History of the Corps of Royal Engineers*, 1889, i. 158, 166, 184, 209; *Army List*, 1775, p. 176, 1778, p. 206, 1779, p. 238, 1784, p. 7, and 1785, p. 158. His name does not appear in the Army Lists for 1786 and following years.

Page 124, line 5. Shakespeare wrote his name on each of the three sheets of his will (25 March 1616): these signatures are (1) William

Shakspere, (2) Willm̄ Shakspere, (3) William Shakspeare. See Sir E. K. Chambers, *William Shakespeare*, 1930, i. 504 ff. In the *Biographia Britannica* (1763, vi. 3637), where the will was first printed, the third signature, the only one printed, is given as ' Shakespeare ' ; this is followed by Steevens in his first edition of the plays (1773) ; in his second edition, 1778, he reproduces the three signatures in facsimile (vol. i, opposite p. 200) and rejects the reading ' Shakespeare ' for ' Shakspeare ' (*Ib.* p. 199 note). The only other authentic signatures are ' Shaksp ' and ' Shakspē '. Chambers, *o.c.s.*

Page 125, line 2 from foot. Lieut.-Colonel John Pennington was the eldest son of Sir Joseph Pennington, fourth baronet, of Muncaster ; he was born in 1737; he entered the army as an ensign in the 3rd Foot Guards, 17 Dec. 1756, and was promoted Lieutenant and Captain 15 Jan. 1762 ; he exchanged into the 2nd Foot Regiment (*not* 2nd Foot Guards as stated in the *D.N.B.*) with the rank of Major, 21 March 1765, and was appointed Lieut.-Colonel of the 37th Foot Regiment on 15 Feb. 1773 ; he retired from the army on 30 Nov. 1775. (*Army List*, 1773, p. 56, and 1775, p. 91, and information kindly supplied by Mr. A. S. White, Deputy Librarian of the War Office.) Lieut.-Colonel Pennington was M.P. for Milborne Port, Somerset, 1781–96, Colchester 1796–1802, and Westmorland County 1806–13. He was created Baron Muncaster, in the peerage of Ireland, on 21 Oct. 1783. He died on 8 Oct. 1813. See G. E. C., *Compl. Peerage*, 1936, ix. 408 ; *Parl. Return of Members of Parl.*, pt. ii, 1879, pp. 167, 180, 193, 203, 222, 236, 250, 265 ; and the *D.N.B.*

Page 128, line 1 and note †. ' The Horns ' (in the nineteenth century the name was changed to the Commercial Hotel) stood in a court on the south side of Bridge Street. It was originally the town house of the Forbes of Culloden family, and was used as the head-quarters of the Duke of Cumberland's staff in 1746. According to Provost A. Ross it was standing in 1916, but has since been demolished. See C. Fraser-Mackintosh, *Invernessiana*, 1875 (where it is depicted), and A. Ross in *Trans. Inverness Scientific Soc.* viii. 296–7.

Page 128, lines 22 ff. At the time of Johnson's visit to Inverness there were two Episcopalian congregations, served respectively by ' qualified ' and ' unqualified ' ministers, Jurors and Nonjurors. Johnson attended the place of worship of the first-named ; this was an upper room in the house of a former minister, the Rev. John Stewart, in Baron Taylor's Lane. J. B. Craven, *Hist. Episcopal Church in the Diocese of Moray*, 1889, pp. 243, 245–6, 250–1. The house is now, 1961, a shop. Johnson also calls it ' an English chapel '. He thought it was a separate building: ' There is likewise an English chapel, but meanly built, where on Sunday we saw a very decent congregation.' *Journey to the Western Islands*, 1924, p. 24.

Mr. Tait, or Tate, was a chaplain to the garrison at Fort George—a fact which confirms Dr. Hill's conjecture that he knew in advance that

Johnson and Boswell would be in his congregation. The Reverend Allan Cameron, in a note dated 12 Sept. 1770, says : ' Mr. Tate, from the Fort, preaches every Sunday afternoon at Inverness for a Guinea, and no less.' *Journals of the Episcopal Visitations of the Right Rev. Robert Forbes*, ed. J. B. Craven, 1886, p. 326.

Page 129, line 5 and note 2. Boswell and Johnson and others, including the careful Pennant (*Tour in Scotland 1769*, 1774, p. 160), confused Macbeth's Castle, which stood on the eastern extremity, 'The Crown', of the hill overlooking the town, with the Castle of Inverness built on the western extremity, Castle Hill. Macbeth's Castle was razed to the ground by Malcolm Canmore ; the Castle of Inverness was blown up in 1746. See *Statist. Acct.* 1793, ix. 633 ; and John Anderson in *Archaeologia Scotica*, 1831, iii. 234 ff. A view of the ruins that Johnson saw will be found in the last-cited volume facing p. 231. See also Burt's *Letters from the North of Scotland*, 1754, i. 41 ff.

Page 131, line 10. Carruthers prints, in his edition of *Hebrides* (1852, p. 96), the following anecdote of Johnson's sportive behaviour at the inn :

' Mr. Grant used to relate that on this occasion Johnson was in high spirits. In the course of conversation he mentioned that Mr. Banks (afterwards Sir Joseph) had, in his travels in New South Wales, discovered an extraordinary animal called the kangaroo. The appearance, conformation, and habits of this quadruped were of the most singular kind ; and in order to render his description more vivid and graphic, Johnson rose from his chair and volunteered an imitation of the animal. The company stared ; and Mr. Grant said nothing could be more ludicrous than the appearance of a tall, heavy, grave-looking man, like Dr. Johnson, standing up to mimic the shape and motions of a kangaroo. He stood erect, put out his hands like feelers, and, gathering up the tails of his huge brown coat so as to resemble the pouch of the animal, made two or three vigorous bounds across the room!'

For Mr. Grant, who died in 1828, see *ante*, v. 509.

Page 134, line 12. The mean kirk was old Boleskine church, 17¾ miles from Inverness ; its site is marked on Taylor and Skinner's *Survey and Maps of North Britain* (1776, plate 60) as 'Boleskine Kirk Ruins'. According to the *New Statistical Account, Inverness-shire* (1842, xiv. 61), a new church was built in 1777, but it, together with the manse, is marked on the above map as 3¼ miles farther on, 2 miles beyond Foyers, off the high road.

The Rev. Thomas Sinton, writing in 1912, says :

' Soon after leaving Foyers [*i.e.* in Fort Augustus direction], my friend and I were entering the old Parish Churchyard of Boleskine. . . . Over a hundred years ago MacShimi [*i.e.* Chief of Fraser] had excambed the glebe at Boleskine for land on Drumtemple where a new manse and church were erected. . . . The grey mildewed walls within the churchyard . . . are often mistaken for the ruins of what James Boswell writes of as " the meanest parish church I ever saw ".' *Trans. Gaelic Soc. of Inverness*, xxviii. 155 ff.

Appendix D

Page 134

The site of the General's Hut is given on the above-quoted map as close to, but beyond, the old church ruins, nearer to Foyers.

Page 134, line 15. Alexander Trapaud was Deputy Governor and resident governor of Fort Augustus certainly from 1754 till his death, at the age of 84, on 2 Dec. 1796. He had been aide-de-camp to General Ponsonby at Fontenoy and to General Huske at Culloden, where he was wounded. See the *Army List*, 1758, p. 149; Carruthers's edition of Boswell's *Hebrides*, 1852, p. 100; and Dom Odo Blundell's *Kilcumein and Fort-Augustus* (1914), pp. 35, 50 ff. Mrs. Trapaud died at Fort Augustus on 24 May 1774. *Scots Mag.* xxxvi. 279.

General Cyrus Trapaud, who, when an ensign in the Buffs, saved George II from serious injury by stopping his bolting horse at Dettingen, had a distinguished military career : he was Colonel of the 70th Foot from 1760 to 1778 and of the 52nd Foot from 1778 to 1800 ; he was promoted Major-General on 10 July 1762, Lieut.-General on 25 May 1772, and General on 19 Feb. 1783. At his death in 1800 he was the senior general officer below the rank of a Field-Marshal. See Col. H. W. Pearse, *Hist. of the East Surrey Regt.* 1916, i. 27,.243 ; W. S. Moorsom, *Hist. Record of the 52nd Regt.* 1860, p. 22 ; and the *Army List*, 1800, p. 2.

Page 134, line 2 from foot. Captain Timothy Newmarsh received his commission as Lieutenant in the 7th Foot (Royal Fusiliers) on 30 Dec. 1755, and as Captain on 18 July 1766 ; he obtained his majority, in the 60th Regt., on 10 Aug. 1780. He served with his regiment in Gibraltar and Minorca in 1756 and in America from the beginning of the Rebellion ; he was wounded at the Cowpens, when in command of the regiment. He retired from the Army in 1783 and died on 16 May 1802. See W. Wheater, *Hist. Record of the Royal Fusiliers*, 1875 ; and the *Army List*, 1783, p. 134. On a muster-roll dated 24 Feb. 1773 in the P.R.O. (W.O. 12/2474) he signs his name 'Tim. Newmarch'. His wife, who was the only child of General Alexander Trapaud, died on 22 Feb. 1791. *Scots Mag.* liii. 102.

Pages 134–5. Fort Augustus was built by General Wade to replace the old barrack which was too far from Loch Ness ; it was begun in 1727, but not completed till 1742 ; the rebels captured it in 1746 and burnt it on the birthday of the Duke of Cumberland, after whom Wade had named it : it was restored in the following year. Mrs. Grant of Laggan, whose father was barrack-master there, writing on 15 June 1773, describes the fort and the Governor's garden :

'The Fort stands on the brink of the western extremity of Loch Ness, and the Oich and Tarffe discharge their pure streams into it on each side. Near the lake, the Governor has created a most picturesque shrubbery and garden in the dry ditch that surrounds the fort, and hid the masked battery with laurels. That

Page 135   *Appendix D*   513

beautiful spot the glacis is almost an island. . . . The Fort, too, appears the prettiest little thing you can imagine. You would suppose some old veteran had built himself a house with a ditch and drawbridge to remind him of his past exploits.' *Letters from the Mountains*, 1845, i. 93-4.

According to the *New Statistical Account* the Fort was abandoned early in the nineteenth century:

'The garrison is now become unnecessary and useless: The Government some years ago ordered the ramparts to be dismantled, and the ordnance to be sent to Fort George' (*Inverness-shire*, 1842, p. 57: the article was originally written in 1831 and revised in 1835).

The buildings and the land were sold by the Government in 1857 to Thomas Alexander Fraser, twelfth Lord Lovat, whose son, Simon, Lord Lovat, in 1876 presented them to the English Congregation of the Order of St. Benedict, which immediately transformed the fort into a monastery and college. The Right Rev. Sir David Oswald Hunter Blair, O.S.B., who was Lord Abbot from 1913 to 1917, informs me that 'the whole of the four-sided building of the fort remains, except the south block, which was demolished to make way for the new church; the governor's house, married soldiers' quarters, and barracks, are intact, and two of the four bastions. The roofs were raised a story and the windows " gothicized ".'

See E. Burt, *Letters from a Gentleman in the North of Scotland*, ed. R. Jamieson, 1818, ii, App., pp. 282, 314-15; James Ray, *Hist. of the Rebellion*, 1749, p. 352; Pennant, *Tour in Scotland 1769*, 1772, p. 171; Dom Odo Blundell, *Kilcumein and Fort-Augustus*, 1914; and J. B. Salmond, *Wade in Scotland*, 1934, pp. 46-8.

Page 135, lines 9 and 10. The military records of (1) Lewis Ourry and (2) Isaac Augustus D'Aripé are as follows: (1) 2nd Lieut., Churchill's Marines, 22 June 1747; Fort Adjutant, Jersey, 20 Mar. 1750; Lieut., 60th Regiment, 14 Jan. 1756; Captain-Lieut., do., 29 Aug. 1759; Captain, do., 12 Dec. 1760; Captain, 15th Regiment, 15 July 1772. Retired 1 Dec. 1775. (He became Fort Major of Kinsale, Co. Cork, 1777, and Commissary for Prisoners of War, 1778. He died at Kinsale in April 1779. Information supplied by Prof. D. Cornu of Seattle.) (2) Ensign, 15th Regiment, 22 Jan. 1755; Lieut., do., 25 Sept. 1757; Captain-Lieut., do., 22 Sept. 1764; Capt., do., 22 June 1770. Retired 9 Oct. 1775. D'Aripé served in the Rochefort Expedition under Sir John Mordaunt in 1757, at the sieges of Louisburg and Quebec, at the battle of Ste Foy, 1760, and at the capture of Martinique and Havana, 1762. He was appointed Town Adjutant, Quebec, 23 Sept. 1759. I am indebted to Mr. A. S. White, of the War Office, for these details.

Mrs. Grant of Laggan's friend, Miss Ourry, later Mrs. Furzer, was Captain Ourry's daughter. Mrs. Grant's father was barrack-master at Fort Augustus from 1773 to 1794. *Mem. and Corr. of Mrs. Grant of Laggan*, 1844, i. 11, 13, 19; *Letters from the Mountains*, ed. J. P. Grant, 1845, i. 112, and *Misc. Gen. & Herald.*, 3rd ser., v, p. 13.

Page 136, lines 1 ff. and note 1. Carruthers has the following note on the landlord of the inn at Anoch in his edition of Boswell's *Hebrides* (1852, p. 102):

'Macqueen was a gentleman of the old Highland stamp, who considered himself a public benefactor by condescending to keep a change-house. He was married to a laird's daughter, and could both read Latin and write Celtic poetry. He was famous in the glen for his ready wit and his talent at telling a story or rehearsing a legend.... Macqueen did not carry out his intention of going to America. He lived at Anoch fifteen years after his entertainment of the *olla Sassenach*, or jolly Englishman, as he used to call Johnson. He then removed to Dalcataig, another farm in the neighbourhood, and survived till past ninety. His pretty daughter... became Mrs. Mackintosh, wife of a watchmaker in Morayshire, and died without issue.'

Anoch, Aonach, or, as it was named in some eighteenth-century maps, Unach, was about nine miles from Fort Augustus. Johnson said that it consisted of 'three huts, one of which is distinguished by a chimney'; the hut with the chimney was the inn. *Western Isl.*, 1924, p. 31. 'Unach Inn' is marked on the map of Inverness-shire in the *New Statistical Acct.* (xiv. 1842). Carruthers, ten years later, reported that part of the old walls marked its site. See also A. Sinclair, *Reminiscences of the Grants of Glenmoriston*, 1887, p. 5; and W. Mackay, *Urquhart and Glenmoriston*, new ed. 1914, p. 457.

The laird of Glenmoriston at the time of Johnson's visit was Patrick Grant, eighth laird. He died in 1786, aged 86. See William Fraser, *The Chiefs of Grant*, 1883, i. 523; A. Sinclair, *o.c.s.*, pp. 28 ff.; and *Burke's Landed Gentry*, 1937, p. 953.

Page 137 foot. Miss Cornelia Knight records the following highly interesting anecdote:

'He [Johnson] was very curious to see the manner of living and the discipline on board a ship of war, and when my father was appointed to the command of the *Ramilies*, of seventy-four guns, and to sail with the command of a squadron for Gibraltar, at the time when a war with Spain was expected, Johnson went to Portsmouth, and passed a week on board with my father. He inquired into everything, made himself very agreeable to the officers, and was much pleased with his visit. When he was conveyed on shore, the young officer whom my father had sent to accompany him, asked if he had any further commands. "Sir," said Johnson, " have the goodness to thank the commodore and all the officers for their kindness to me, and tell Mr. ——, the first lieutenant, that I beg he will leave off the practice of swearing." The young man, willing, if possible, to justify, or at least excuse, his superior, replied that, unfortunately, there was no making the sailors do their duty without using strong language, and that his Majesty's service required it. "Then, pray, sir," answered Johnson, " tell Mr. —— that I beseech him not to use one oath more than is absolutely required for the service of his Majesty."' *Autobiography*, 1861, i. 15–16.

Miss Knight's father, Captain Joseph Knight, R.N., took up command of H.M.S. *Ramillies* on 30 Oct. 1770, when she was at the Nore. She sailed for the Downs on 1 Nov. and a fortnight later proceeded to

Page 137   *Appendix D*   515

Spithead, where she came to moorings on 18 Nov. Her position, as given by log, was ' The town of Ryde S.W. b S. South Sea Castle E. b N. and Gilkicker N. b W. 1 mile '. She remained moored in this position the whole time she lay at Spithead. She weighed anchor on Christmas Day.

The First Lieutenant of the *Ramillies* was Thomas Tonken : he obtained his promotion to Commander 25 Dec. 1778, and became Captain 15 May 1780. He died in 1791.

The late Sir Oswyn Murray, the Secretary of the Admiralty, kindly favoured me with his expert opinion :

' If Johnson really passed a week on board of the *Ramillies* at this time of the year and when she was lying so far from the shore, it was plucky of him : but not of course more plucky than much of his trip to the Islands. From the point of view of Service routine, I do not think there is any reason to say that the story is improbable. Ships lying off a Home Port in such circumstances were generally infested with bum-boatmen, women, &c. whenever weather conditions permitted, and the Commanding Officer might quite easily have had a guest staying with him, and unless the guest had a liking for the long pull to and from the shore in wintry weather, he would find it necessary to spend most or all of his time in the ship.'

The only other evidence, known to me, of the visit comes from Mrs. Piozzi, who in her *Anecdotes*, written in 1786, says: 'The roughness of the language used on board a man of war, where he passed a week on a visit to Capt. Knight, disgusted him terribly ' : see *ante*, i. 378, n. 1.

Evidence of Johnson's movements during the period, 18 Nov. to 25 Dec. 1770, when he could have paid this visit, is scanty. He wrote to Langton from London on 24 Oct., to Percy on 27 Nov., and to Frank Barber on 7 Dec., presumably from London on both occasions. I have no record of any other letters or of Johnson's movements for the remainder of the year.

Miss Knight, 1757-1837, may have heard the story related by her father, who rose to the rank of Rear-Admiral and died in September 1775, or by her mother, who survived till 1799. Her journal, which was written in 1816, is regarded as accurate.

Croker, who did not know Miss Knight's circumstantial account, suggested that Johnson and Reynolds may have visited Capt. Knight at Plymouth in the summer of 1762, when he was in command of H.M.S. *Belle Isle* (*ante*, i. 378, n. 1). The *Belle Isle*, with Capt. Knight in command, was at Plymouth from 16 Aug. 1761 to 3 March 1762, when she sailed for Barbados ; she was at Cuba in August and September, when Johnson and Reynolds were at Plymouth, and did not return to England till June 1763.

I am greatly indebted to Mr. D. Bonner Smith, the Admiralty Librarian, for invaluable help with this note.

Appendix D

Page 140, last line. The battle of Glenshiel was fought on 10 June 1719, the Old Pretender's birthday, between a combined force of Spaniards and Highlanders, led by the Marquis of Tullibardine and the Earl Marischal, and the British troops commanded by General Wightman : the Jacobite force took up a strong position some five miles above Invershiel, where the road crosses the river Shiel, and was attacked by the Hanoverian troops coming from Inverness : it was all over in about three hours. The Spaniards surrendered in a body the next day, and, in the words of the future Field-Marshal Keith, who was present, ' every body else took the road he liked best'. See C. Sanford Terry in *Scottish Hist. Rev.* 1905, ii. 412 ff., and *Fragment of Memoir of Field-Marshal Keith*, 1843, p. 52. For a full account of this projected invasion, which was organized by Cardinal Alberoni and the Duke of Ormonde, see W. K. Dickson, *The Jacobite Attempt of 1719* (Scottish Hist. Soc. 1895).

Page 142, last line and note 2. Boswell, in his Journal, says, 22 Sept. 1778 :

' I shall not fill my Journal with this Mutiny, as I am to write a particular account of it. . . . I was wonderfully animated by this extraordinary scene, and came home and wrote some account of it in a great hurry for the *Publick Advertiser*.' *Boswell Papers*, xiii. 159-60.

Two days later he noted :

' I wrote a little yesterday and more today about the Mutiny for the *Publick Advertiser*, and sent it off tonight.' *Ibid.* 161.

The account, entitled ' Mutiny in Scotland ', fills a column and a third in the *Public Advertiser* for 29 Sept. and two-thirds of a column in the number for 1 Oct. The final paragraph, dated 25 Sept., states :

' Thus has a very alarming Affair been happily settled, owing to the Patience and good Temper of our present Military Commanders ; and it is hoped that the Soldiers of this 78th Regiment will for the future live in that Harmony which is the Beauty of Subordination. The poor Fellows were the wildest Highlanders, many of them MacCraws, of whom Dr. Johnson gives so picturesque and curious an Account in his Highland Travels.'

Page 145, line 25. The barracks at Bernera were built in 1719-22 and consisted of two houses containing twenty-four apartments and accommodating two hundred soldiers. Pennant, who was there in 1772, describes the barracks as 'handsome and capacious' ; they were then occupied by a corporal and six soldiers. *Tour in Scotland and Voyage to the Hebrides 1772*, 1774, pp. 336-7 ; T. M. Murchison in *Scots Mag.*, Nov. 1934, pp. 97 ff. John Knox in 1786 described their condition as ruinous. He was entertained by ' the commanding officer, and his whole garrison. The former was an old corporal, and the latter was the old corporal's wife : the entertainment, snuff and whiskey.' *Tour through*

Pages 145-9   *Appendix D*   517
the Highlands in 1786, 1787, p. 103. The officers' quarters were still habitable in 1795. *Statist. Acct. of Scotland*, xvi. 271. The walls of the barracks are well preserved to-day.

Page 145, line 28. The site of the inn at Glenelg, where 'the negative catalogue of the provisions was very copious' (Johnson's *Western Isl.*, 1924, p. 43), is not now known. According to Boswell's original Journal, the landlord, 'one Munro from Fort Augustus', paid £8 a year 'for the shell of the house alone, and has not a bit of land in lease'.

Page 146, line 2. John Murchison was factor to the laird of Macleod at Glenelg from 1764 to 1778. He leased Beolary from Macleod. His tombstone in Glenelg churchyard states that he died on the 20th July 1811, aged 80. C. Fraser-Mackintosh, *Antiquarian Notes*, 1897, p. 239, and information kindly supplied by the Rev. T. M. Murchison, formerly minister of Glenelg.

Page 148, lines 1 ff. The most ancient seat of the chief of the Macdonalds was not Duntulm but Dun Scaich on the southern shore of Loch Eishort. See Macgibbon and Ross, *Castellated and Domestic Architecture*, iv. 307 ff. ; and *Royal Commission on Ancient and Hist. Monum. (Scotland)*, 9th Rep. *Outer Hebrides, Skye*, &c., 1928, pp. 167-8, 186 ff.

Page 148, line 4. Mugstot, or Monkstadt, was built by Sir Alexander Macdonald's father about 1740. It became a tacksman's dwelling towards the end of the eighteenth century, when Sir Alexander built a new mansion-house at Armadale, the immediate ancestor of the present Armadale Castle. Mr. James Macintyre, who in his *Castles of Skye* (Inverness, 1938) gives a history of these and other Macdonald strongholds and homes, describes the present condition of the house : ' a large part of the house is now a roofless ruin, but half of the main block is still inhabited. The old crow-stepped gable at the west end—the stones of which may have come from Duntulm—is still intact, and in it and the well-proportioned old Scots windows and gateway pillars much of the former picturesqueness and old-world charm of Monkstadt are still preserved ' (p. 51).

Page 149, line 17. Boswell's original Journal reads : ' We had at dinner a little Aberdeenshire man, one Jeans, a naturalist, with his son, a dwarf with crooked legs. Jeans said', &c. Johnson, in a letter to Mrs. Thrale, says : ' At Macdonald's I was claimed by a Naturalist, who wanders about the Islands to pick up curiosities.' *Letters*, No. 326. Richard Gough naturally knew of him :

' John Jeans, of Aberdeen, a great adept in the mineral kingdom, remarkable for his travelling over this country [Scotland] annually on foot, composed very sensible " General directions for discovering metals, minerals, gems, &c." describing by the colour of the earth and springs in Scotland where these may probably be found. Were this essay enlarged and printed, these inquiries might tend to the public good.' *British Topography*, 1780, ii. 634.

More details of Jeans and his son are given by P. J. Anderson, formerly University Librarian, Aberdeen, in an extract from Prof. W. Knight's Collections regarding Marischal College :

' Jeans ... was the inventor of the screw stair. He afterwards built the beautiful little bridge over the Denburn in the line of the Windmillbrae. But there was then no employment for such a person as he in Aberdeen. Being of an ingenious and active turn, he became an enthusiast for mineralogy, and travelled over the greater part of the Mainland and the Highlands, collecting till he became eminent as a dealer, repairing annually to London, and being the,first finder of numerous Scottish substances. He lived to old age, dying about 1804, aged about eighty. ... From his portrait he seems to have been a spare man of genteel and keen aspect. A son succeeded him in the business of collecting and polishing, a coarse and contemptible character, who was drowned on a dark night by falling into the basin near the New Pier, 1809.' *Notes & Queries*, 10 Ser. ii. 1904, 155.

The son, Alexander, was drowned in May 1809. *Aberdeen Journal*, 3 May 1809. See also *ante*, v. 163 ; and Johnson's *Western Islands*, 1924, p. 471.

Page 149, line 3 from foot. Donald Macdonald was, according to Boswell's original Journal, a son of ' Rorie Macdonald in Sandaig, a near relation of Sir Alexander's ' ; the precise relationship was that of third cousin. His commission as a lieutenant in Colonel Montgomery's regiment was dated 1 Feb. 1757. This regiment was raised in 1757 and originally called the First Highland Battalion ; in the following year it became the 62nd Regiment, and in 1759 or 1760 the 77th Regiment. *Army List*, 1757, p. 98, 1758, p. 128, 1759, p. 130, 1760, p. 133. The regiment was disbanded in 1764.

Page 150, line 14. Sir James Foulis, fifth baronet of Colinton, 1714–91, was, according to Scott, ' one of the few Lowlanders whom Highlanders allowed to be well skilled in the Gaelic'. Croker's *Boswell*, 1831, ii. 382 note. He contributed six articles to the first volume of the *Transactions of the Society of Antiquaries of Scotland* (1792). He was made an honorary member of the Society on its formation, 14 Nov. 1780. *Ibid*., p. xxv. Ritson thought poorly of him and his writings. In his *Bibliographia Scotica*, which at long last has been found and published by Mr. B. H. Bronson, Ritson says of Sir James :

' Though this worthy gentleman could write (which he, certainly, did with equal facility whether he understood the subject or not), there is little appearance of his haveing been able to read or, at least, of his makeing any use of that capacity ; his facts being explodeëd errours and his Conjectures absurd whims. ... The society of " antiquarys " of Scotland could have derive'd no credit from the reveries of sir James Foulis of Colinton, who could not possiblely have been worse employ'd than in writeing upon history or antiquitys.' *Publ. Mod. Lang. Amer.* 1937, lii. 131–2.

Page 156, lines 8, 9. Boswell, in his original Journal, reports that he first met Donald Macleod at Sir Alexander Macdonald's at Armadale on 2 Sept., when he describes him as ' late of Canna, a very genteel

Page 157 Appendix D 519

man'. He advised the travellers to visit Raasay and was one of 'the two other gentlemen' (*ante*, v. 168) who accompanied Boswell and Malcolm Macleod on their long walk in the island. Boswell writes at Dunvegan, under date 15 Sept. :

'Mr. Donald MacLeod, late tenant in Canna but now dispossessed of it, was still with us. He was an obliging serviceable man. His father was one of MacLeod's ministers; and the late Laird educated him, and in particular had him several years at school near London. He was at present in that kind of wandering state that many a Highland younger brother is. I was sometimes angry at his appearing unanimated, speaking a few words slowly and with a weak voice, and then sitting with his mouth open. He was tall and a good sportsman. He gained me at last by saying of Mr. Johnson, " Well, it is really a happiness to be in this man's company." '

On 15 Sept. he went to Loch Bracadale to cash a bill of £30 for Boswell and got 'mortally drunk' at Portree. When he rejoined the travellers at Corrichatachin on the 27th (*ante*, v. 260), he had only £22, having given the rest to a poor family of emigrants in payment of a debt. He accompanied Johnson and Boswell to Ostaig (*ante*, v. 272), where he made Boswell sit up a little longer than was agreeable to him over an extra bowl of punch, and Armadale, and repaid the £8 by ' a good bill' on 3 Oct. *Hebrides*, ed. Pottle and Bennett, 1936, pp. 114, 116, 137, 158, 172, 198, 225, 236, 239, 245.

Page 157, lines 2 ff. Pennant records under date 17 July 1772, 'Mr. Mackinnon, junior, . . . presses us to accept the entertainment of his father's house of Coire-chattachan', and two days later, 19 July, 'Leave Coire-chattachan, after experiencing every civility from the family; and from Mr. Nicholson, the minister'. *Tour to Scotland and Voyage to Hebrides, 1772, 1774*, pp. 285 and 287.

Page 157, line 8 and note 2. Boswell, in his original Journal, gives a more vivid and detailed account of his entertainment at Corrichatachin: he writes under date 6 Sept. :

' We came on a mile to Coirechatachan, a farm-house of Sir Alexander possessed by Mr. Mackinnon, a jolly big man who received us with a kindly welcome. The house was of two storeys. We were carried into a low parlour, with a carpet on the floor, which we had not seen at Armadale. We had tea in good order, a *trea*, silver tea-pot, silver sugar-dish and tongs, silver tea-spoons enough. . . . Mr. Johnson was quite well here. Mrs. Mackinnon was a decent well-behaved old gentlewoman in a black silk gown. At night we had of company Coirechatachan and his wife ; Mrs. Mackinnon, daughter to his wife and widow of his son; Mr. Macpherson, minister of Sleat, and his wife, daughter of Coirechatachan ; a niece of Coirechatachan's, Miss Mackinnon ; Miss Macpherson, sister to the minister ; and Dr. Macdonald, a physician ; as also young Mr. Mackinnon, son to Coirechatachan. We had for supper a large dish of minced beef collops, a large dish of fricassee of fowl, I believe a dish called fried chicken or something like it, a dish of ham or tongue, some excellent haddocks, some herrings, a large bowl of rich milk, frothed, as good a bread-pudding as I ever tasted, full of raisins and lemon or orange peel, and sillabubs made with port wine and in sillabub glasses. There was a good table-cloth with napkins ; china, silver spoons, porter if we chose it, and a large bowl of very good punch. It was really an agreeable meeting.' *Hebrides*, ed. Pottle and Bennett, 1936, pp. 119–20.

Lachlan Mackinnon 3rd. of Corry entered on a wadset of Corry in July 1750, granted by John Mackinnon of Mishnish, who was then Chief of the Clan. He was Factor to the Mackinnon estate. He was a Jacobite and had been 'out' in the '45 as a Captain in Prince Charles's army. He married three times : his third wife, Johnson's hostess, was Mrs. Anne, widow of Ranald MacAlister, and a daughter of Alexander Macdonald of Kingsburgh (*post*, v. 545). He died in 1789. His eldest son, Charles, by his first wife, Janet Mackinnon of Ceann Uachdarach, Strath, married Flora MacAlister, daughter of the above : he died in 1771 or 1772. Lachlan Mackinnon had two other sons, Lachlan (Major, H.E.I.C.S., died unmarried) and John (died at Corry, 1806, unmarried), one of whom was the 'young Mr. M'Kinnon' mentioned by Boswell. I am indebted to the Reverend Donald MacKinnon of Portree for many of these particulars.

Page 158, last line. There is no known print of Macdonald of Clanranald, who was killed at Sherriffmuir, with such an inscription as Boswell describes, but there is one of Ranald Macdonald of Belfinlay. The inscription is :

'Ranaldus Macdonald de Bellfinlay in Benbecula in proelio Cullodino (Aetatis suae 18) multo vulnere saucius, nudatus, sub dio circiter horas 22 restabat; sed tandem humanitate (tunc temporis admodum singulari) cujusdam Iacobi Hamilton, Vicarij de legione Cholmondlyaca salvus evasit dum vulneratos Commilitones (referens tremisco) consultò mactatos, miserrime jugulatos undique videbat ; adeò ut contaminata esset terra caedibus. Monstrum ! Horrendum ! Ingens !'

There can be no doubt that it was this print which Boswell saw. Copies are now very rare ; the only one known to me is in the Scottish National Portrait Gallery, Edinburgh : it is a line engraving and bears in engraved letters ' W. Robertson Pinxit et fecit '. The original painting from which the print was engraved, and the engraving itself, were commissioned by Bp. Robert Forbes. Writing to Dr. John Burton, 19 June 1749, he says :

' Just now a limner is busy about an original picture at my desire upon which he is to draw the following description . . . [Here follows the inscription]. The limner assures me he is determined to work off a plate of it with the same inscription not to cost above a shilling sterling per copy. As it is an historical and undeniable proof of a certain barbarous and shocking scene, so I doubt not but it may circulate far and near. Pray, Dear Sir, be at pains to count noses and see what demand may be for such a commodity in your corner. You may have as many copies as you please and you are sure there can be [no] counterfeit when the plate is to [be] done instantly from the original picture.' *The Lyon in Mourning*, ed. H. Paton, 1895, ii. 326–7.

Page 160   *Appendix D*   521

The engraving was reproduced by James Caulfield (*Portraits, &c., of Remarkable Persons*, 1820, iv, facing page 50), who stated erroneously that Ranald Macdonald was executed in London on 22 Aug. 1746. He actually died at Kinloch Moidart on 27 Sept. 1749, after returning from Edinburgh and Inverness, where he had received treatment for his wounds. *The Lyon in Mourning*, ii. 303 n., 360, and 365. See also *ibid.* ii. 3, 229, 247, 257, and 340–1. The Macdonalds of Belfinlay and the Mackinnons of Corrichatachin were related by marriage. I am indebted to the late Allan R. Macdonald of Belfinlay and Mr. Kenneth Sanderson, W.S., for their aid in writing this note.

Page 160, line 23. Lachlan Mackinnon's house, Corrichatachin, was of two stories and of fair size (it was described to me in 1936 by an old native as having been 'the bonniest house in the islands', no doubt with some exaggeration), but it is to-day so completely ruined that it is hardly possible to say with certainty how many rooms it contained. Thirteen persons were staying in it at the time of Johnson's visit and it is reasonably certain from Boswell's account of the sleeping-arrangements on the nights of 6 and 7 Sept. that they were accommodated in five rooms, including the dining parlour. The three travellers, Johnson, Boswell, and Joseph, alone had beds to themselves. Boswell writes under date 6 Sept. :

'Mr. Johnson got a good bedroom to himself. When I went upstairs Mrs. Mackinnon received me in an opposite bedroom with three beds in it, and with an air of hearty cordiality said, " Come away and see if you can sleep among a heap of folks ". . . . I had a good clean bed with red and white check curtains to myself. In a bed with blue worsted stuff curtains lay Donald MacLeod and Dr. Macdonald ; in a red one of the same kind, the minister and young Mackinnon.' *Hebrides*, ed. Pottle and Bennett, 1936, p. 121.

He records an addition to the company on the 7th, Mr. Macdonald of Breakish, and notes (*op. cit.*, p. 124) :

'Tonight Breakish was laid with Canna [=Donald MacLeod]. What became of Dr. Macdonald, whose place was thus filled up, is more than I could guess. . . . Joseph had a good bed with clean sheets made for him in the parlour.'

John Ramsay of Ochtertyre, writing of the Scottish country gentry of the same period, says :

'With few exceptions, their houses were small, fitter for the reception of day than of night visitors. . . . Even when strangers stayed all night, they were very easily accommodated, nothing being more common than to lay two gentlemen or two ladies that were not acquainted in the same bed.' *Scotland and Scotsmen in the 18th c.*, 1888, ii. 65. See also *ibid.* 93.

Scott, writing to Joanna Baillie in 1811, says :

'I cannot relinquish my border principle of accommodating all the cousins and *dunawastles* who will rather sleep on chairs and on the floor and in the hayloft than be absent when folks are gathered together.' *Letters*, 1932, ii. 527.

Appendix D

Page 161

Page 161, line 21 and note 2. Boswell, in his original Journal under date 17 Oct., notes:

Mr. Johnson marked in his journal that in the islands they call a gentleman's boat his *carriage*. He did this because Mr. Donald Macqueen, in his card to me, called Raasay's boat so; but upon inquiry I found that it was not a common mode of speech, and set Mr. Johnson right. It was just a *conceit* of Mr. Macqueen's and Mr. Johnson took it to be a general phrase.' *Hebrides*, ed. Pottle and Bennett, 1936, p. 315.

Raasay himself, according to Johnson, styled the boat, which was six-oared, ' his coach and six '; ' and ', adds Johnson, ' in the boat, thus dignified with a pompous name, there is no seat, but an occasional bundle of straw '. *Letters*, No. 329 (ed. Chapman, i. 367). It is amusing to find Boswell cited as the authority for the correctness of the use of ' carriage ', as synonymous with ' boat ', in the islands by W. Daniell, who writes: ' The term has been employed in that sense by Mr. Boswell, and is therefore sanctioned, not only by local usage, but by respectable authority.' *Voy. round Great Britain*, 1820, iv. 42.

Page 161, line 27. The Rev. Donald Macqueen was born *c.* 1716, licensed on 4 June 1737, and ordained on 9 May 1740, when he was appointed minister of Kilmuir-in-Trotternish, Skye. He died 1 Feb. 1785. Hew Scott, *Fasti Eccl. Scot.* 1928, vii. 171. He contributed a ' Dissertation on the Government of the People in the Western Isles ' to Pennant's *Tour in Scotland, 1772, Pt. ii* (1776, pp. 419-38) and assisted Dr. John Stuart of Luss in translating the Pentateuch from ' the original language ' into Gaelic. (Mr. Fred. T. Macleod, of Edinburgh, possesses contemporary copies of Macqueen's letters and observations on this version which show that Stuart adopted a number of the translations suggested.) The version, which, so Prof. John Fraser informs me, bears evidence of very extensive use of the A.V., was published in 1783. See also D. MacKinnon, *Gaelic Bible and Psalter*, 1930, p. 60. Macqueen's belief in Ossian was unshakable (see *ante*, v. 241 ff.). Boswell gives his real opinion of him in this connexion in his original Journal:

' Mr. Macqueen is the most obstinate man I ever found. He has not firmness of mind sufficient to break. He is like a supple willow. No sooner is he pressed down than he rises again, just where he was. He always harped on this: "Macpherson's translations are far inferior to Ossian's originals." . . . It was really disagreeable to see how Macqueen shuffled about the matter.' *Hebrides*, ed. Pottle and Bennett, 1936, p. 205.

Dr. John Erskine described him as ' a clergyman who combined with the better qualities of the heart, such politeness as if he had been bred at court, and such learning as if Oxford or Cambridge had been his constant residence '. *Sketches of Church History*, 1797, ii, p. vii. Carruthers, in his edition of Boswell's *Hebrides* (1852, p. 127 note),

Pages 161-5   *Appendix D*   523

confuses him with the Rev. Donald Macqueen (1700-70), minister of North Uist, who believed in the second sight.

Page 161, line 4 from foot. Malcolm Macleod was cousin to Macleod of Raasay. He and the brothers Murdoch and John Macleod of Raasay conducted the Prince from Skye to Raasay on 1 July and back again on the next day, when the party spent the night in a cow-byre near Scorrybreck, near Portree ; the following evening and night Malcolm alone conducted the Prince to the house of his brother-in-law, John Mackinnon, at Elgol in Strath ; Malcolm then left the Prince in the charge of the old Chief of Mackinnon, who took him to Mallaig on the mainland. Malcolm was captured soon afterwards. See *ante*, v. 190 ff. ; H. Paton, *The Lyon in Mourning*, i. 130 ff. ; and W. B. Blaikie, *Itinerary of Prince Charles Edward Stuart*, pp. 54-5.

Malcolm Macleod of Raasay is one of the persons excepted by name out of the King's General Pardon for participation in the Rebellion. *Gent. Mag.* June 1747, xvii. 296. He is sometimes distinguished as 'of Brae '. He married Catherine Macqueen of Rigg, Skye, John Macleod of Raasay's wife's sister (see below). Bp. Forbes, *Journals*, p. 236.

Boswell, writing, 11 Oct. 1775, to inform John Macleod of Raasay of the birth of a son and heir (Alexander), reminded him of his great walk in the island (*ante*, v. 168) and Macleod in reply says :

' Malcolm desires to acquaint you that the young Gentleman must hurry to this Country ; for, notwithstanding of old age, he is determin'd to have as stout a walk with him as he had with his father, and dance a highland reel with him in the top of Duuncan, and then sett him upon the seat wherein he took Breakfast, which is and will be called Boswell's Chair.' *Boswell Papers*, x. 268.

Page 162, line 23. '*Owr the muir amang the heather.*' This tune appears in *A Collection of Scots Reels or Country Dances* (London, 'Printed and sold by Robt. Bremner'), published about 1760 and known as 'Bremner's collection'. It is set in James Johnson's *Scots Musical Museum* (1792, No. 328) to Jean Glover's song (first line 'Comin thro' the craigs o' Kyle'), which was taken down from her mouth by Burns. See also F. Miller's *Poets of Dumfries-shire*, 1910, pp. 169-71. Andrew Fairservice first whistled and then sang it, ' with much glee and little melody ', on his secession from Osbaldistone Hall (*Rob Roy*, ch. xviii). See also Scott's *Lady of the Lake*, note 31, and *D.N.B.* s.v. Glover, Jean.

Page 165, lines 9 and 10. The Laird of Raasay at the time of Johnson's visit was John Macleod, 9th Chief of Raasay. When his father Malcolm, 8th of Raasay, joined Prince Charles in 1745 he conveyed his estates to him (*ante*, v. 174). He was an ardent Jacobite and, with his cousin Malcolm Macleod (see above) and his brother Murdoch (see below), conducted the Prince from Skye to Raasay and back again on July 1 and 2, 1746 (*ante*, v. 190 ff. ; W. B. Blaikie, *Itinerary*, 1897, p. 54 ;

The Lyon in Mourning, 1895, i. 130, 302). He married Jane Macqueen of Rigg, Skye, and had by her thirteen children, of whom the eldest son was James, who succeeded him as Laird. Alex. Mackenzie, *Hist. Macleods*, 1889, pp. 375 ff. He died in 1786. Burke's *Commoners*, 1838, iv. 592. For his eldest daughter, Flora, see *ante*, iii. 118, and v. 178 ; she died 2 Sept. 1780 (Sir R. Douglas's *Baronage of Scotland*, ed. J. P. Wood, 1813, ii. 154). For his visit to Johnson in 1782, see *ante*, iv. 155, and v. 413, n. 1. For Johnson's erroneous statement that he had acknowledged Macleod of Dunvegan as his chief, and the consequent correspondence, see *ante*, ii. 303, 380, 382, 411, and v. 409 ff.

Dr. Murdoch Macleod was the second son of Malcolm, 8th of Raasay. He married Anna, daughter of Alexander Macdonald of Boisdale, and lived at Eyre, Skye (*ante*, v. 183). See also *ibid*. 190, 194–5. His younger brother, whom Johnson met at Eyre, was Norman, who was a retired officer of the Scots Brigade in Holland. Alex. Mackenzie, *Hist. Macleods*, 1889, p. 373.

Page 165, line 11. Col. John Macleod, 4th of Talisker, elder brother of Prof. Roderick Macleod (*ante*, v. 496). He was in command of one of the companies of the Skye militia during the '45 : he captured Capt. Malcolm Macleod (*ante*, v. 523) on 14 July 1746, and he was in a measure responsible for the arrest of Flora Macdonald. After the Rebellion he joined the Scots Brigade in Holland, General-Major Dundas's Regiment, of the 1st Battalion of which he eventually became Colonel. He, together with all the other officers of the battalion, refused to take the oath to the States General in 1782. In 1772 he came to Scotland to help his young chief, Macleod of Macleod, to manage his estates. He married, firstly, Mary, daughter of Hector Maclean of Coll, and, secondly, Christian, daughter of John Mackay of Inverness. He died 14 July 1798, aged 80. See Alex. Mackenzie, *Hist. Macleods*, 1889, pp. 234 ff. ; James Ferguson, *Scots Brigade*, 1899, ii. 501 ff. and 521–2 ; *Scots Mag.* 1798, lx. 576. Pennant (*Tour Scotl. and Voy. to Hebrides*, 1774, p. 289) and John Knox (*Tour Highlands*, 1787, p. 140) testify to his hospitality and politeness. For Johnson's visit to him at Talisker see *ante*, v. 250 ff. : see also *ibid*. 215, 221, 234.

Page 165, line 15. The ' several other persons ' are named in Boswell's original Journal : they were 'Mr. Macqueen, a young divine, son to the Reverend Mr. Donald Macqueen ; Mr. James MacLeod, a boy about — years of age, the future Laird of Raasay ; and Mr. Macqueen, a . . . young man, his tutor '. *Hebrides*, ed. Pottle and Bennett, 1936, p. 132. The young divine was the Reverend John Macqueen, son of Donald (*ante*, v. 522) : he was born in 1750 and was minister of Applecross from 1777 till his death in 1831. Hew Scott, *Fasti*, 1928, vii. 145. James Macleod, 10th Chief of Raasay, died in Oct. 1823.

Pages 166–71   *Appendix D*   525

Burke's *Commoners*, 1838, iv. 592; Alex. Mackenzie, *Hist. Macleods*, 1889, pp. 389–90.

Page 166, line 11 and note 2. Alexander Macleod of Muiravonside, Stirling, was sent, 24 Sept. 1745, to Skye to summon the three chiefs, Sir Alexander Macdonald, Macleod of Macleod, and Mackinnon of Mackinnon to the Prince's standard. Home's *Hist. Rebellion*, App. No. xxviii; A. Mackenzie, *Hist. Macleods*, pp. 132 ff. He was aide-de-camp to Lord George Murray at Culloden and accompanied the Prince off the field. *The Lyon in Mourning*, i. 190. He did not receive a pardon till 1778. W. B. Blaikie, *Origins of the Forty-five*, 1916, p. 227 n. He died at Muiravonside 30 Dec. 1784. *Scots Mag.* xlvi. 664. For his obstreperous mirth see *ante*, v. 178.

Page 168, lines 4 ff. The identity of the over-studious Highland gentleman is disclosed by Boswell's original Journal:

'The Laird of Mackinnon was a young man of small size, delicate constitution, feebleness of voice and nearness of sight, but I was told had great knowledge, and hurt himself by too much study, particularly of infidel metaphysicians.' *Hebrides*, ed. Pottle and Bennett, 1936, p. 136.

Charles Mackinnon of Mackinnon, 18th chief, was the elder surviving son of John, who joined Prince Charles at Edinburgh in 1745 and conducted him from Skye to the mainland, 4–10 July 1746 (*ante*, v. 197–8). He was born in 1753 and married, in July 1774, Alexandra Macleod, sister-german of Norman Macleod, Johnson's host (*post*, v. 526 ff.). The marriage was not happy, and he was separated from his wife in 1790. He sold, in 1778, the estate of Mishnish, comprehending his whole lands in Mull, for £7,000, and, in 1789, the estate of Strathaird, comprehending his whole lands in Skye, for £8,400. He died, by his own hand, at Dalkeith in 1796. His son, John, inherited nothing but the chieftainship: on his death, unmarried, in 1808, the main line of Mackinnon of Mackinnon became extinct. This sad story could not have been told without the courteous aid of Mr. W. Angus and Mr. C. T. McInnes, of the Register House, Edinburgh, and the Reverend Donald MacKinnon, of Portree.

Page 171, lines 17–20. The poem 'Albin and the daughter of Mey: An old tale, translated from the Irish' was printed in the *Scots Mag.* xviii. 1756, p. 15. The author was Jerome Stone, a schoolmaster of Dunkeld, who was born in 1727 and died 11 June 1756. The original, according to Stone's copy, his translation and a literal translation, are given in the Highland Society's *Report on the Poems of Ossian*, 1805, App. No. vii, pp. 99–117. There is very little resemblance between *Albin* and Malcolm Macleod's story. For Stone see *Scots Mag.* xviii. 314; John Ramsay of Ochtertyre, *Scotl. and Scotsmen in the 18th c.*, i. 547 n.; Nigel MacNeill, *Lit. Highlanders*, 1892, pp. 208 ff.; and the *D.N.B.*

Appendix D Pages 172-6

Page 172, lines 12 ff. Johnson, writing to Mrs. Thrale, 24 Sept. 1773, says :

' We were received at Raarsa on the sea-side, and after clambering with some difficulty over the rocks, . . . we were introduced into the house, which one of the company called the court of Raarsa, with politeness which not the Court of Versailles could have thought defective. The house is not large though we were told in our passage that it had eleven fire rooms, nor magnificently furnished, but our utensils were commonly silver. We went up into a dining room about as large as your blue room. . . . At twelve it was bed time. I had a chamber to myself, which in eleven rooms to forty people was more than my share. How the company and the family were distributed is not easy to tell. Macleod the chieftain, and Boswell, and I, had all single chambers on the first floor. There remained eight rooms for at least seven and thirty lodgers. I suppose they put up temporary beds in the dining room, where they [? packed] all the young Ladies. There was a room above stairs with six beds in which they put ten Men.' *Letters*, No. 327.

This house was built by Johnson's host and largely rebuilt by James, his eldest son and heir (*ante*, v. 524) ; it was sold, with the rest of the island, in 1846 to George Rainy, who further enlarged it, as also did E. H. Wood, who bought the estate in 1876 and spent large sums on it. The island has been since 1922 the property of the Department of Agriculture for Scotland, and Raasay House is now, 1937, an hotel. A good view, by W. Daniell, of the house, taken in 1813, showing the original central portion, will be found in his *Voyage round Gt. Britain*, 1820, iv, facing page 42. The room in which Johnson slept is still shown.

Brochel Castle, described by M. Martin in 1703 as ' an Artificial Fort, three Stories high, . . . called Castle Vreokle ' (*Western Islands*, p. 164), is on the east coast of Raasay. It is fully described in the *Ninth Report of the Royal Commission on Ancient and Historical Monuments and Constructions of Scotland*, 1928, pp. 178 ff. : in this it is stated (p. 180) that ' in the inner of the lower rooms on the western wall is a garderobe with an external chute ', which I take to be the ' certain accommodation ' mentioned by Boswell. For Boswell's strictures on the lack of this in Raasay's new house and Johnson's comment see Pottle and Bennett, *Boswell's Hebrides*, 1936, p. 147.

Page 174, line 2. ' Gaul ' is the Lowland Scots form of English ' Gale ', sweet gale, bog myrtle, *Myrica gale* (see *O.E.D.* s.v. GALE *sb.*[1]). J. Lightfoot enters in his *Flora Scotica*, 1777, ii, p. 613 :

' Gale, Goule, Sweet Willow, or Dutch Myrtle, *Anglis*. Roid, *Gaulis*. Gaul, *Scotis*. In bogs and moorish grounds in the Highlands and Hebrides very frequent and plentiful.'

Gaelic speakers in Raasay to-day call the plant ' roid ' and do not know the Lowland Scots word.

Page 176, lines 18 ff. and note 2. Johnson's host, the Laird of Macleod, was Norman Macleod of Macleod, 20th chief. He was born

Page 176   *Appendix D*   527

4 March 1754 and was the son of John, who predeceased his father, Norman, 19th chief. He attended classes at the Universities of Edinburgh, 1766-9, and St. Andrews (the United College), 1769-70, and matriculated from University College, Oxford, 27 Nov. 1770 ; at Oxford, where he ceased to reside on 26 April 1771, his tutor was Johnson's friend, the Reverend George Strahan (*ante*, iv. 415). See J. M. Anderson, *Matriculation Roll St. Andrews*, 1905, p. 19 ; and Foster, *Alumni Oxon*. iii. 898. The record of attendances in Edinburgh has been kindly supplied by Dr. L. W. Sharp. His grandfather, shortly before his death in 1772, handed over the management of the family estates, which were greatly embarrassed, to him and his nearest male relative, Colonel Macleod of Talisker (*ante*, v. 524). He describes in his Memoirs the state of his affairs and the efforts he and Colonel Macleod made to improve it :

'The duty imposed on us was difficult : the estate was loaded with debt, incumbered with a numerous issue from himself and my father, and charged with some jointures. His tenants had lost, in that severe winter, above a third of their cattle, which constituted their substance ; their spirits were soured by their losses, and the late augmentations of rent ; and their ideas of America were inflamed by the strongest representations, and the example of their neighbouring clans. . . . I was young, and had the warmth of the liberal passions natural to that age ; I called the people of the different districts of our estate together ; I laid before them the situation of our family. . . . I combated their passion for America by a real account of the dangers and hardships they might encounter there ; I besought them to love their young chieftain, and to renew with him the ancient manners ; I promised to live among them ; I threw myself upon them. . . . I desired every district to point out some of their oldest and most respected men, to settle with me every claim. . . . My worthy relation ably seconded me, and our labour was not in vain. We gave considerable abatements in the rents ; few emigrated ; and the clan conceived the most lively attachment to me.' Croker's *Boswell*, 1831, ii. 558 ff. See also Johnson's *Letters*, No. 329 (ed. Chapman, i. 365).

He, however, found ' confinement in a remote corner of the world ' intolerable, and in 1775 started on a military career of some distinction by raising an independent company of the 71st Regt. (Fraser's Highlanders), in which his commission as Captain is dated 7 Dec. 1775 : he was promoted to Major, 2nd Batt. 73rd Regt. (MacLeod's Highlanders), 25 Sept. 1778. He raised or assisted in raising the Second Battalion of the 42nd Highlanders (The Black Watch), of which he became Lieut.-Colonel 21 March 1780, and with which he saw much service in India. The dates of his subsequent commissions, as given in the Army Lists, are as follows : Colonel (local rank in East Indies) 12 June 1782 ; Colonel, 18 Nov. 1790 ; Major-General, 3 Oct. 1794 ; Lieut.-General, 1 Jan. 1801. He retained his appointment as Lieut.-Colonel of the 2nd Battalion 42nd Regt., which in 1786 was formed into a separate regiment, the 73rd, till his death. Some details of his service in India are

528   *Appendix D*   Pages 182-3

to be found in Sir John Philippart's *East India Military Calendar*, 1824, ii. 128, 132, 172 ff., 489, and A. G. Wauchope, *Short Hist. of the Black Watch*, 1908, pp. 22 ff.

Macleod married firstly Mary Mackenzie of Suddie in 1775, and after her death, in 1784, Sarah Stackhouse. He was M.P. for Inverness-shire from 1790 till his death in August 1801. Burke's *Landed Gentry*, 1921, p. 1183 ; A. Mackenzie, *Hist. of Macleods*, 1889, pp. 166 ff. ; and *Parl. Return of Members of Parl.* 1878, pt. ii. 198.

He called on Boswell in Edinburgh on 29 Sept. 1774, and they were very social. ' But ', says Boswell, ' MacLeod did not appear so well to me as when I saw him in the Hebrides. He threw out some modern ideas, as if feudal principles could not now be kept up, which made me angry with him.' *Boswell Papers*, x. 9. ' Modern ideas ' combined with prolonged absence on military service did not help him to clear his estates. He was 'the representative of a great family in Scotland' (*ante*, ii. 428), whose death Johnson and Boswell thought desirable and to the interests of the family, because of his extravagance. *Boswell Papers*, iv. 135. Croker says (*op. cit.* ii. 409) that

' So far from extinguishing the debt on his estates, he increased it ; for though he had sold a great tract of land in Harris, he left at his death, the original debt of £50,000 increased to £70,000.'

Page 182, line 12. George Buchanan's complaint occurs in his *Iambon liber*, i. 7-10:

' Vix me in Britannis montibus natum & solo
Inerudito & sæculo
Raræ audiebant, raræ adibant fontium
Deæ sacrorum præsides.'

Poemata, ed. 1609, p. 119

I owe the reference to the late Professor Edward Bensly.

Page 183, line 15. The horses that the travellers remounted were Sir Alexander Macdonald's.

' He had ', says Boswell, ' most inhospitably desired to have them sent back to him when we got to the shore opposite to Raasay. . . . He even gave me a note in my almanac how to try for horses. But since he had not proper reflection, I resolved to supply his place, upon hearing that we should hardly be able to find other horses. Mr. Johnson said, " Don't let us part with *them* till we get others." I said any sensible Justice of Peace would press them for us.' *Hebrides*, ed. Pottle and Bennett, 1936, p. 154.

He accordingly sent them on to Portree. His action was resented by Sir Alexander, who complained that ' the jaded animals ' were ' lame to the ground . . . and consequently for a long time unfit for the Journey which they were originally intended to perform '. *Boswell Papers*, xvi. 236.

Page 183, lines 17, 18. Carruthers points out that ' the Highland computation was not so wide of the mark ' : Dr. Murdoch Macleod's

Pages 184-5   *Appendix D*   529

house at Eyre was barely eight miles from Portree. The only parts of the original house, now (1937) a land-holder's home, that remain are the front wall and the two gables. See Boswell's *Hebrides*, 1962, p. 471.

Page 184, lines 2 ff. Johnson's host at Kingsburgh was Allan Macdonald, eldest son of Alexander Macdonald (*post*, v. 545), factor to Sir Alexander Macdonald of Sleat, 7th baronet (1711-46). He was a lieutenant in one of the Hanoverian Independent Companies commanded by Lord Loudoun in 1745. He married Flora Macdonald on 6 Nov. 1750. On his father's retirement in 1763 he succeeded him as factor but was unbusinesslike and lost the office in two or three years: he was allowed to retain the tack of Kingsburgh. His father continued to live with him till his death on 10 Feb. 1772. See below for his later career. He was born in 1726.

Kingsburgh House has long since disappeared: nothing remained of it in 1852, according to Carruthers. Pennant was also hospitably entertained there, in 1772, and, like Johnson, was 'lodged in the same bed that formerly received the unfortunate Charles Stuart'. *Tour in Scotland & Voy. to Hebrides 1772*, 1774, p. 299. For an interesting gift that was made to him see *post*, v. 532.

Page 185, line 9. The following letter, now in the National Library of Scotland, from Flora Macdonald to John Mackenzie of Delvine, W.S., shows the extent to which Kingsburgh's affairs were embarrassed and that he was preparing to emigrate in 1772:

' Dr Sir

This goes by my Son Johnie wha thank God tho I am missfortunat in othere respects is happy in his haveing so good a freind as you are to take him under his protection, he seemed when here to be a good natured bidable Boy, without any kind of Vice; make of him what you please and may the Blessing of the almighty attend you alangs with him which is all the return I am able to make for your many and repeated freindships shown to me and this family; of which there will soon be no rememberanc in this poor miserable Island, the best of its inhabitance are making ready to follow theire freinds to america, while they have any thing to bring them; and amang the rest we are to go, especially as we cannot promise ourselves but poverty and oppression, haveing last Spring and this time two years lost almost our whole Stock of Cattle and horseis; we lost within thire three years, three hundred and twenty seven heads, so that we have hardly what will pay our Creditors which we are to let them have and begin the world again, anewe, in a othere Corner of it. Allen was to write you but he is not well with a pain in his Side this ten days past. Sir I beg of you if you see any thing amiss in thè Boys conduct to let me know of it as some Children will stand in awe of ther parents more then any body Else.

I am with my respects to you and mrs mckenzie,
    Sir with esteem
    Your most obedient
    humble Servant
    Flora mcdonald

Kings: agust the 12
 1772.'

Appendix D

The Macdonalds left Campbelltown in August 1774 for North Carolina, where they first settled at Cross Creek, then at Mount Pleasant or Cameron's Hill, north-west of Cross Creek, but in 1775 went farther west to Anson County, in the neighbourhood of Rockingham, where they purchased a plantation, identified in 1956 as on Cheek's Creek. Kingsburgh, however, very soon joined the force raised by Governor Martin of North Carolina, in which he had the rank of Lieutenant-Colonel. This force was defeated by the American militia at Widow Moore's Creek Bridge, 27 Feb. 1776, when Kingsburgh and his son Alexander were captured. After being imprisoned in four different places, one of which was Halifax, North Carolina, father and son were liberated on parole, 9 July 1776, and exchanged in Nov. 1777. Kingsburgh joined his regiment, the Royal Highland Emigrant Regiment, in which he held the substantive rank of Captain, at Halifax, Nova Scotia, in 1778, remained with it till it was reduced in 1783, and in the following year he returned to Scotland on half-pay. Meanwhile the estate on Cheek's Creek was confiscated and Flora, who had taken an active part in the Loyalist cause, had a hard time ; acting on the advice of her husband, whom she visited in Halifax, Nova Scotia, she returned to Scotland. She spent the winter of 1779-80 in London and returned to Skye in July 1780. She appears to have stayed at first with her daughter Anne at Dunvegan, then at Kirkibost, North Uist, and at Milton, her brother's home. When her husband returned in 1784 they appear to have lived, not at the old home at Kingsburgh, but at first in South Uist, certainly till 1787, and after this date in Skye. Flora died on 4 March 1790 ; her physician, Dr. John Maclean of Cuidrach, writing to his son, (Sir) Lauchlan Maclean, 24 March 1790, says :

'Nothing new has occurred since I wrote you except the death of the famous Mrs Flora Macdonald, sometime of Kingsburgh. She suffered much distress for a long time in my neighbourhood at Peinduin.'

She was buried at Kilmuir with her husband's kindred. Her husband died on 20 Sept. 1792. See Alex. Macgregor, *Life of Flora Macdonald*, 1882, which is, however, inaccurate, and J. P. MacLean, *Flora Macdonald in America*, 1909. I am particularly indebted to the Rev. Donald MacKinnon, who has in his *Guide to Skye* (1937) and his edition of Allan R. Macdonald's *Truth about Flora Macdonald* (1938) corrected many of Alex. Macgregor's errors, and to Mr. R. E. Wicker of Pinehurst, North Carolina.

Flora's youngest son, John, mentioned in the above letter, attained distinction as both a soldier and an author (see the *D.N.B.*). He married, secondly, Frances Maria, eldest daughter of Johnson's friend, Sir Robert Chambers (*ante*, iv. 68). He placed a marble slab over his mother's grave at Kilmuir, which was carried away piecemeal by visitors. He died in 1831 and was buried in Exeter Cathedral. The

Page 185   *Appendix D*   531

so-called Autobiography of Flora Macdonald, edited by his daughter, Mrs. F. F. Wylde, and published in 1870, is quite untrustworthy.

Page 185, last line and note 4. The choice of the name to be given to Prince Charles Edward in his narrative was a matter of the gravest concern to Boswell. He felt that the King alone could satisfy him, and to the King he appealed by letter. He wrote to him from Paoli's house in Portman Square, where he was staying, on 6 June 1785 :

'I have several authentick curious Anecdotes concerning that person who in 1745-6 attempted to recover the throne upon which his Ancestors sat. I wish to communicate them as they occur in the course of my publication. But I am at a loss how to design him. I have repeatedly taken the oath of Abjuration, and the oath of Allegiance to Your Majesty, whom may GOD long preserve. And I am clear that the right of the House of Stewart is extinguished. Yet I cannot help feeling that it would be an insult to an unfortunate Man who must think very differently, and who is still alive, should I call him *Pretender*. May I not be permitted to call him *Prince Charles* ? Will your Majesty condescend to signify to me your Royal pleasure as to this ? If I am not permitted to avoid what would hurt my tenderness for what even *has been* Blood Royal, I shall leave out those Anecdotes. If I am permitted, I shall thus apologise for the designation : " I do not call him *the Prince*, because I am satisfied that the right which his Family had is extinguished. I do not call him *Pretender*, because I feel it as ungenerous to the representative of a great but unfortunate House who is still alive. And I am confident that the only Person who is entitled to take it amiss will liberally excuse my tenderness for what *has been* Blood Royal ".' *Boswell Papers*, xvi. 277-8.

He received no reply, and went to the Court levee on 15 June, when the King gave him an opportunity to renew his request. Of the ' very remarkable conversation ' between them Boswell has left a full report entitled ' G.R. Wednesday, 15 June 1785 '. The King inquired about the progress of his work, ' How do you go on ? ', and Boswell replied by reminding him of his letter, which he hoped the King had received. He continued :

' " I am come to receive your Majesty's commands." The King then said " I never before was questioned as to this designation.". . . I replied, " I dare say not, Sir. But I intreat to know your Majesty's pleasure." His Majesty PROVED me once more. He said, " What do you think ? How do you feel yourself ? ". . . I made a profound bow and respectfully answered, " That, Sir, I have already stated in writing to your Majesty." The trial was now over. The King found I was a Man. He stept a little forward, and inclining towards me with a benignant smile equal to that of any of Correggio's Angels, he said, " I think and feel as you do." My heart glowed with emotion. . . . " Sir, (said I,) I did suppose that your Majesty's liberality of mind would make your Majesty give the Answer you have done. Then, Sir, I may do as I have proposed ? " KING. " But what designation do you mean to give ? " BOSWELL. " Why, Sir, ' Prince Charles ' I think is the common expression." His Majesty appearing to hesitate or demur, I proceeded, " Or shall it be ' the Grandson of King James the Second ' ? " KING. " Yes." BOSWELL. " Then I have your Majesty's permission to call him so ? " KING. " You have. To tell you the truth . . . .

I do not think it a matter of consequence to my Family how they are called ; for after the abdication, the change of religion, and other circumstances, I think there can be no question as to the right." BOSWELL. " Certainly not, Sir. I am quite clear as to that. My difficulty is merely from sentiment. ' Pretender ' may be a PARLIAMENTARY expression, but it is not a GENTLEMANLY expression ; and, Sir, allow me to inform you that I am his cousin in the seventh degree." ' *Boswell Papers*, xvi. 99 ff.

Page 187, line 20 and note 3. The Macdonalds had owned a copy of the fourth edition of the anonymous pamphlet, ascribed by the British Museum authorities to Bp. Robert Forbes, entitled *A plain, authentic and faithful Narrative of the several Passages of the Young Chevalier from the Battle of Culloden to his Embarkation for France*, 1765 (the first edition was published in 1750), but Flora could not show it to Johnson because her husband had given it to Pennant, who wrote in it, ' Given to me in the isle of Skie July 23d. 1772, by Mr McDonald of Kingsburgh who married Miss Flora Macdonald, Heroine of the Piece '. W. H. Robinson's 67th Catalogue (1938), item 63.

Page 187 foot ff. Boswell compiled his account of Prince Charles's adventures in the Hebrides from information given to him at different times by five persons who had, in varying degrees of importance, been personally concerned : these persons were Flora Macdonald, Mrs. Mackinnon of Corrichatachin ('old Kingsburgh's daughter '), the Laird of Raasay (John Macleod, ' Young Rasay '), Malcolm Macleod, and John Mackenzie, the servant or boatman who wanted to shoot the suspected spy ; Boswell also met Dr. Murdoch Macleod, who played an important part in conveying the Prince to Raasay. The ' paper of information ' which the Laird of Raasay sent to Boswell on 12 July 1775 (*Fettercairn Catalogue*, No. 554) was used by him. (It contained the Prince's severe reflections on Lord George Murray which Boswell, with the concurrence of Lord George's son, heavily censored. See Boswell's *Hebrides*, ed. Pottle and Bennett, 1962, pp. 422-3.) Boswell's narrative, which has been neglected by most historians, is generally accurate ; the error (p. 195) of making the Prince land in Strath, instead of near Portree, on the return passage from Raasay, was not made in his original manuscript, which reads : ' Mr. Malcolm told us that he went with the Prince from Raasay in a boat, landed near Portree, and from thence they walked all night over the mountains till they came into Strath, and the Laird of Mackinnon received him.' *Hebrides*, ed. Pottle and Bennett, 1936, p. 129.

A detailed day-to-day record of the Prince's movements after Culloden (16 April 1746) to his leaving Skye (4 July) and final escape to France (20 Sept.) will be found in W. B. Blaikie's *Itinerary* (Scot. Hist. Soc. 1897). The following is a brief account of Flora Macdonald's assistance to him and of their movements about the islands together.

It should be stated at the outset that the plan of bringing Flora to

Page 187 *Appendix D* 533

the Prince's aid was conceived by her step-father, Hugh Macdonald of Armadale, who was in command of the Government militia in South Uist and whose duty it was to capture him. The evidence for Hugh Macdonald's duplicity is supplied by Neil MacEachain, or, as he sometimes called himself, Neil Macdonald (1719-88), a South Uist schoolmaster and tutor in Clanranald's family, who was chosen to guide the Prince through South Uist and was actually with him, or in close touch with him, from 10 May, when he landed at Benbecula, till 1 July, when he left Skye for Raasay—he subsequently rejoined the Prince on the mainland and escaped with him to France. Neil, in his Narrative which, in the words of its editor, ' carries conviction in every line ', states categorically :

' I forgot to tell that when Captain Scott landed in South-Wist, Hugh MacDonald, who lay in Benbicula then with his party, sent one of the country gentlemen in whom he could repose a great deal of trust, to tell the prince privately that, as it seemed now impossible for him to conceal himself any longer in the country, if he would venter to be advised by him, though an enemy in appearance yet a sure friend in his heart, he would fall upon a scheme to convoy him to the Isle of Skay, where he was sure to be protected by Lady Margaret MacDonald. The scheme was this : to send his stepdaughter, Miss Florence MacDonald, to Sleet, to live with her mother 'till the enemy was out of Wist. The prince at the same time was ordered to dress in woman's close, that he might pass for her servant-maid, and Neil was appointed to take care of both. The scheme pleased the prince mightely, and he seemed very impatient to see it put in execution.'

This statement fully confirms Bishop Forbes's suspicion of Hugh Macdonald's loyalty to the Government : see *The Lyon in Mourning*, i. 176. For Neil MacEachain and his narrative see W. B. Blaikie, *Itinerary*, 1897, pp. 98 ff., and *Origins of the 'Forty-five*, 1916, pp. lxxi ff. and 238 ff. : he appears in Boswell's narrative (v. 189) as ' a servant ' and ' a man-servant ', the quality he assumed when accompanying Flora Macdonald. The Prince, accompanied by Capt. Felix O'Neil and Neil MacEachain, met Flora Macdonald on 20 June 1746, at Alisary, a shieling on Milton, South Uist, her brother's farm, informed her of her step-father's proposal, and asked her assistance. She immediately left for Nunton, Clanranald's home in Benbecula, but was detained by the guard at a ford, where she was found the next day, 22 June, by Neil MacEachain ; both were released by order of Hugh Macdonald, who gave Flora a passport for herself, MacEachain, and ' Betty Burke '. MacEachain returned to the Prince and Flora went to Nunton, where she stayed till 27 June, when she, Lady Clanranald, Capt. O'Neil, MacEachain, and others, went to the Prince and passed the night in a shieling on the south side of Loch Uskevagh. On the next day, the 28th, the Prince, dressed as Betty Burke, Flora, MacEachain, and six boatmen sailed for Skye ; they were at sea all night and, after being driven off by the militia at the point of Waternish, landed at Kilbride, Trotternish, near Monkstadt (or Mugstot), Sir Alexander Macdonald's house. Flora and MacEachain then walked to Monkstadt to inform Lady Macdonald of the Prince's arrival. Lady Margaret sent her factor, Alexander Macdonald, to conduct the Prince to Kingsburgh ; Flora and MacEachain followed and reached Kingsburgh before them, late at night. The next day, 30 June, Flora, who was mounted, and Mac-Eachain left Kingsburgh, by the main road ; the Prince, guided by a herd boy, walked ' thro all by ways ', in the evening ; they met at the inn at Portree, from which Flora went to her mother's house at Armadale, Sleat, and the Prince, in charge of the three Macleods, to Raasay. See W. B. Blaikie's *Itinerary*, 1897, pp. 52-4 ; and *Origins of the 'Forty-five*, 1916, pp. 250 ff. ; *The Lyon in Mourning*, 1895, i. 117-22, 299 ff., ii. 20 ff. ; Archibald Macdonald, *Memorials of the 'Forty-five*, p. 43 ; and Allan R. Macdonald's *The Truth about Flora Macdonald*, ed. Donald Mackinnon, 1938, pp. 9 ff. For Flora Macdonald's own narrative see *The Times*, 29 Nov. 1938.

Page 188, line 5 from foot. The officer whom Flora Macdonald hoodwinked was Lieutenant Alexander Macleod, son of Donald Macleod of Balmeanach, Bracadale, Skye. He received a commission as Lieutenant in the 78th Regiment (Fraser's Highlanders) when that regiment was raised in 1757, and served with it at Quebec, where he was wounded, in 1760 ; he rose to the rank of Captain. He died at Balmeanach on 7 April 1772. *Scots Mag.* xxxiv. 222, and information kindly supplied by the Rev. Donald MacKinnon.

Flora Macdonald gave two, somewhat different, accounts of the incident. She told Bp. Forbes that when at Monkstadt

' she could not help observing Lady Margaret going often out and in as one in great anxiety, while she in the meantime endeavoured all she could to keep up a close chit chat with Lieutenant MacLeod, who put many questions to her, which she answered as she thought fit '. *Lyon in Mourning*, ii. 17 note.

In the account she gave to Dr. Burton she is reported as saying :

' Kingsburgh took some wine, etc., to refresh the Prince with, . . . leaving Miss MacDonald with Lady Margaret at Mougstot, where the commanding officer of the parties in search of the Prince was, and who asked Miss whence she came, whither she was going, what news ?, etc. all which Miss answered as she thought most proper, and so as to prevent any discovery of what she had been engaged in.' *Ibid.* i. 300.

Capt. Donald Roy Macdonald, who had served in Glengarry's regiment, was wounded at Culloden and had escaped to Skye, told Bp. Forbes that Lady Margaret Macdonald sent for him, 29 June 1746, and that on his arrival at Monkstadt Lady Margaret told him of the Prince's presence in the immediate neighbourhood,

' mentioning a circumstance that distressed her much, because it made the case more perplexed, and made her altogether at a loss how to behave in the matter, which was that Lieutenant MacLeod was at that very instant in the dining room with Miss Flora MacDonald . . . and, which still rendered the case worse and worse, that the Lieutenant had three or four of his men about the house with him, the rest of the command being only at a small distance from the house, as he was employed to guard that part of the coast of Sky '. *Ibid.* ii. 13.

Capt. Donald Roy, as he was usually called, met Lieut. Macleod, whom he identified as the ' son of Donald Macleod of Balmeanagh ', again on his return to Monkstadt after seeing the Prince off to Raasay, 1 July, and spent the night with him and his command ' in order to pump them with wariness and at a distance if they knew any thing at all about the Prince '. They knew nothing. *Ibid.* ii. 27. Malcolm Macleod (*ante*, v. 161 and 523) is the only authority who tells us the Lieutenant's Christian name. He met him on 8 July near Kingsburgh :

' What did we see going by in great haste but six of the M'Leods under Sandy M'Leod of Balmainach command, who did command a partty of the M'Leods of Harries near Mogstote.' *Ibid.* iii. 123.

See also W. B. Blaikie, *Origins of the 'Forty-five*, p. 263. The Rev. A. Macgregor (*Flora Macdonald*, 1882, p. 87) and J. P. MacLean (*Flora Macdonald in America*, 1909, p. 15) are in error in stating that the officer was Capt. John Macleod of Balmeanach.

Page 200, line 3 from foot. Malcolm Macleod (see *ante*, v. 161 and 523) was captured at Raasay on July 15 or 16 by his friend (Colonel) John Macleod of Talisker (*ante*, v. 165 and 524). For his own accounts of his capture and subsequent ill treatment on board ship, see H. Paton, *The Lyon in Mourning*, i. 144 ff. and iii. 123 ff.

Page 204, line 17. The Accession speech was drafted by Lord Hardwicke and sent by him to the Prime Minister, the Duke of Newcastle, who submitted it to the King. Lord Bute returned it to Newcastle, with a separate paper bearing in the King's own handwriting the following passage, which he (the King) commanded to be inserted :

' Born & Educated in this Country I glory in the Name of Britain, & the peculiar Happiness of my Life, will ever consist, in promoting the Welfare of a people, whose Loyalty & warm affection to me, I consider ; as the greatest & most permanent Security of my Throne '.

In the Journals of the House of Lords and House of Commons ' Briton ' is substituted for ' Britain ' and the royal punctuation corrected. The original document is in the British Museum.

The Duke of Newcastle, in a letter of explanation to Lord Hardwicke, expressed his disapproval at the King's independence :

' I make no observation, but that this method of proceeding can't last. We must now, (I suppose) submit. . . . There must be some notice taken of these *Royal Words*, both in the *motion* and the *address*. I suppose you will think *Britain* [*sic*] *remarkable*. It denotes the author to all the world.'

Lord Hardwicke responded, and inserted the following exclamation into the draft of the Lords' Address :

'What a Lustre does it cast upon the Name of *Briton*, when you, Sir, are pleased to esteem it amongst Your Glories ! '

The House of Commons acknowledged ' with the liveliest Sentiments of Duty, Gratitude, and Exultation of Mind, those most affecting and animating Words '. The King, in 1804, told the Hon. George Rose that these words were ' his own and suggested to him by no one '. There is no evidence that the King wrote ' Englishman ' and that Lord Bute substituted ' Briton ' (or ' Britain ') for it. See *Journals of the House of Lords*, xxx. 9, 12 ; *Journals of the House of Commons*, xxviii. 938 ; J. Adolphus, *Hist. Eng.* 1802, i. 16 ff. (the accuracy of which was commended by the King) ; G. Harris, *Life of Lord Hardwicke*, 1847, iii. 231 ff. ; G. Rose, *Diaries & Corresp.* 1860, ii. 189 ; and Lord Mahon, *Hist. Engl.* 1844, iv. 318.

Page 206, line 27. Among the numerous anecdotes printed by Croker in the fifth volume of his first edition, 1831, there is one (p. 412) which ultimately derives from the Rev. John Henry Williams, Vicar of Wellesbourne, near Warwick, who ' when a young man performed a stagecoach journey with Johnson ' :

' The coach halted, as usual, for dinner, which seemed to be a deeply interesting business to Johnson, who vehemently attacked a dish of stewed carp, using his fingers only in feeding himself.'

Mr. Williams matriculated from Johnson's own college on 27 July 1763, aged 16. He became Vicar of Winchcomb, Gloucester, in 1774 and was Vicar of Wellesbourne from 1779 (or 1778) till his death in 1829 (or 1830). See Foster, *Alumni Oxon.* 1888, iv. 1567.

Page 208, line 15. The minister of the parish, Duirinish, was the Rev. William Bethune or Beaton, the son of the Rev. Kenneth Bethune, minister of Kilmuir, Skye. He was born in 1738 and ordained to the parish in 1767, of which he was minister till 1811 ; he died 13 May 1814. He wrote the account of the parish in the *Statistical Account of Scotland*, 1792, iv. 130 ff. See Hew Scott, *Fasti Eccl. Scot.* 1928, vii. 169. Under date 19 Sept. 1773 (*ante*, v. 227) Boswell spells his name ' Beaton ', which is in fact the older and more prevalent form in Skye. The Rev. Donald MacKinnon says that ' during recent years the form " Bethune " has become common in Skye, and in some families the parents retain the original, while the sons and daughters adopt the imported form '. *The Clerical Sons of Skye*, 1930, p. 16. There is no difference in the pronunciation (Beeton).

Page 208, line 16. Magnus Macleod of Claggan was the second son of Donald Macleod, 3rd of Talisker. He was born between 1719 and 1726, married Margaret Isabella Macdonald of Skirinish, and succeeded his elder brother, Colonel John Macleod (*ante*, v. 165 and 524) in the estate of Talisker. The statement that he took a commission in Colonel Campbell's Highland Regiment and rose to the rank of Lieutenant-Colonel appears to be erroneous. See A. Mackenzie, *Hist. Macleods*, 1889, p. 238.

The other 'substantial' gentleman was John Macleod, tacksman of Bay and Gillen, Waternish. From a list of the Macleod factors in the Dunvegan Charter Chest it appears that he was the Macleod factor from 1741 to 1748 and again from 1754 to 1758. He signed the remarkable document, dated 16 Sept. 1777, by which all the Macleod tacksmen voluntarily agreed to increased rentals in favour of their young chief, Johnson's host (*ante*, v. 176 and 526 ff.). He died in 1790 or 1791. C. Fraser-Mackintosh (*Antiq. Notes*, Ser. ii, 1897, p. 291) wrongly identifies him with Capt. Alexander Macleod, husband of Flora Macdonald's eldest daughter, Anne.

Page 212, lines 7 ff. Carruthers, writing in 1852, says :

'The ceremony of quaffing claret from Rorie More's horn at the inauguration of each successive Chief of Macleod is still continued ; but an artificial bottom is inserted on these occasions in order to reduce the libation to a moderate draught.' Boswell's *Hebrides*, p. 166 note.

The present Chief, Flora, informs me that it was used as a loving-cup when Norman Magnus, 26th Chief, celebrated his coming of age.

The horn is alluded to by Burns in *The Whistle*, and it induced Johnson to lay a wager : 'Mr Johnson laid me half a crown I should not show him so large a horn in the Lothians.' Boswell's *Hebrides*, ed. Pottle and Bennett, 1936, p. 195.

Page 213, lines 1 ff. Sir David Dalrymple, Lord Hailes, published his Catalogue anonymously at Edinburgh in 1767 : *A Catalogue of the Lords of Session, from the Institution of the College of Justice, in the Year 1532, with Historical Notes*. After quoting Mackenzie's character of Gilmour (see *ante*, v. 213, n. 1) he adds (p. 20) : 'It is hard to say what Sir George Mackenzie means by the antithesis of *gloria* and *palma*.'

This work was reprinted in 1794, with some Additional Notes; one of which is an account of Dalrymple, beginning 'This great ornament of his country' ; a long list of his writings is added (pp. 36–41).

Page 213, lines 3 ff. Boswell refers to 'A sketch of the constitution of the Church of Scotland' which he contributed to the *London Magazine* in April and May 1772 (vol. xli, pp. 181 ff., 237 ff.). He wrote (p. 184) : 'It may be said of the court and popular parties, *penes hanc gloria, penes illam palma est* : The latter appears to the greatest advantage : but the former gains any prize that is to be had.' He, characteristically, introduces his friends :

'The popular party . . . has many lay-elders zealous and active in its interest.'

Appendix D

We may mention, in particular, two gentlemen of the law, Messieurs Crosbie and Mac Laurin, Advocates. Both are masters of the subject; and both speak in a manner that would do them honour in any assembly.'

After praising Crosbie, he quotes himself, so I believe, on Maclaurin's wit and humour:

'It was observed, by a lively friend of his, distinguished for the originality of his comparisons, "Mac Laurin has as much wit and humour as ever he had; but, fearing to overseason the dish, he has clapped the lid upon the castor, and instead of throwing out those qualities copiously as formerly, he sprinkles them with more address".'

For Andrew Crosbie and John Maclaurin see *ante*, ii. 376, n. 1, and v. 49.

Page 214, lines 5 ff. The paragraph which Johnson found to be incorrectly printed in Sir George Mackenzie's *Works* (1716, 1. i, p. 65) occurs in *The Religious Stoic*, ch. xiii ('Of the Immortality of the Soul'): in the first edition, printed at Edinburgh in 1663, it reads (p. 116):

'Aristotle like the devil (who because he knows not what to answer, answers ever in engines) tells us, that *anima* is ἐντελέχεια, a terme fitted to exercise the empty brains of curious Pedants, and apter to beget, then explicat difficulties.'

'Even' was an error of the 1716 edition. There was another error in that edition which the textual critics did not notice, 'fix'd' for 'fitted': this was taken over from one or other of the editions printed at Edinburgh in 1665 and 1685 (reissued at London in 1693).

Page 216, foot. The nature of the 'degrading images' of which Johnson made Boswell the object and his reactions are shown by Boswell's original Journal:

'Mr Macqueen asked him if he would admit me [to his seraglio]. "Yes", said he, "if he were properly prepared; and he'd make a very good eunuch. He'd be a fine gay animal. He'd do his part well." "I take it", said I, "better than you would do your part." Though he treats his friends with uncommon freedom, he does not like a return. He seemed to me to be a little angry. He got off from my joke by saying, "I have not told you what was to be my part" —and then at once he returned to my office as eunuch and expatiated upon it with such fluency that it really hurt me. He made me quite contemptible for the moment. Luckily the company did not take it so clearly as I did. Perhaps, too, I imagined him to be more serious in this extraordinary raillery than he really was. But I am of firmer metal than Langton and can stand a rub better.' *Hebrides*, ed. Pottle and Bennett, 1936, pp. 176-7.

Page 217, lines 4 ff. Mr. Bennet Langton, the lineal descendant of Johnson's friend, informs me that the following account of the original Langton Hall and its successors is substantially correct:

'The oldest known Langton Hall was in the field to the S.E. of the Church, the site being marked by extensive mounds and remains of a moat. To this

Page 227   *Appendix D*   539

succeeded an Elizabethan mansion to the N.E. of the Church and near the present School-house, which was the one visited by Dr. Johnson. It is sometimes supposed to have been the original of " Locksley Hall ", which is hardly likely as it was pulled down (about 1817) in consequence of an outbreak of typhoid fever before Alfred Tennyson was in his teens. In place of it the grandfather of the present proprietor built an Italian villa on the hill side, which, showing signs of subsidence, had to be pulled down in a few years (about 1845). A farmhouse served for a Hall for a time, and then the present mansion was built by B. R. Langton, Esq., in 1866.' G. G. Walker, *Historical Notes of the Parish of Partney*, 1898, p. 128, note.

Mr. Bennet Langton thinks that the Elizabethan mansion was pulled down in 1820, not 1817.

Page 227 foot and note 4. Lady Grange (Rachel, daughter of Chiesley of Dalry) was the first wife of the Hon. James Erskine of Grange, Lord Justice Clerk, 1679-1754 (see the *D.N.B.* s.v. Erskine, James). In the narrative of her abduction, dated from St. Kilda, 20 Jan. 1738, which is apparently what Scott calls her Journal, Lady Grange says that she was carried off from her lodgings in Edinburgh on the night of 22 Jan. 1732 by ' some servants of Lovats and his couson Roderick Macleod ', adding, erroneously, that Roderick ' is a writter to the Signet ' (Laing MS. II. 201 in the University Library, Edinburgh). Lovat was the notorious Simon, Lord Lovat (*ante*, i. 181, n. 1); the identity of Roderick Macleod is uncertain, but he may have been the brother of John Macleod of Muiravonside, who is regarded by some authorities as one of the abductors (see A. Mackenzie, *Hist. Macleods*, 1889, p. 125, and W. Chambers in *Chambers's Jrnl.* 1874, p. 451). Lady Grange was taken first to Macleod of Muiravonside's house, near Linlithgow, then to Polmaise, near Stirling, where she was kept a close prisoner for, according to her own account, ' neir seven moneth ' ; on 15 August 1732 she was removed from Polmaise and carried through the Highlands to Sir Alexander Macdonald's island of Heisker, off the west coast of North Uist, which she reached on 30 September, and where she remained till 14 June 1734, when she was taken to St. Kilda, which belonged to Macleod of Macleod, by John Macleod, steward of the island, and his brother Norman ; she was removed from St. Kilda in 1741 and taken first to Assynt, Sutherlandshire, and then to Skye, where she died on 10 May 1745. See *Edinburgh Mag. and Literary Misc.* 1817, i, pp. 333 ff. (the article was probably written by Sir George Stewart Mackenzie), and Laing in *Proc. Soc. Antiq. Scotl.* 1876, xi. 593 ff. The place of her death and burial has been variously and erroneously given as Harris (by Boswell), St. Kilda, Dunvegan (by the *D.N.B.*), Idrigill in Skye (by Sir James Balfour Paul's *Scots Peerage*, which gives the date as June 1749), and ' the mainland ' : she undoubtedly died and was buried at Trumpan in the

Waternish district of Skye and Macleod country. The Rev. Donald Mackinnon writes in his *Guide to Skye*, 1937, p. 68 :

'To the north of the ruined Church in Trumpan Graveyard may be seen a rough slab, which marks the grave of Lady Grange, who was buried here after two mock funerals had taken place, one in Edinburgh after she had been abducted, and the other in Kilmuir Graveyard, Dunvegan, fifteen years after her abduction, in the presence of a great crowd of people. The real funeral took place at Trumpan, near the cottar's house in which she died in 1745. The slab was erected some years ago by Lord Mar, a descendant of Lady Grange.'

The name of the cottar was Rory Macneill and his bill to Norman Macleod of Macleod for ' ane particular Acct off expenses in Lady Grange's interment ' and ' her board for nine months ' is still preserved at Dunvegan Castle : it amounted to £53 5s. 5d. Scots and it was ' fitted and cleared ' 16 Aug. 1745.

Canon R. C. Macleod left among his papers a full account of Lady Grange, which his daughter, Mrs. Osbaldeston-Mitford, has courteously allowed me to consult. Canon Macleod found evidence that Lord Grange in 1714 and later was in touch with Jacobite agents and attached to the Jacobite cause.

The ' confidential friend ' to whom Lady Grange found means to write was her lawyer, Thomas Hope of Rankeillour, who went in search of her. In a remarkably frank letter to Lord Grange, dated 23 Feb. 1741, he described the abduction as ' cruel and barbarous ', but agreed that ' the lady should have been placed somewhere that she could have given no disturbance ' to him and his family. *Spalding Club Misc.* iii, 1846, pp. 65 ff.

I do not find that Lady Grange was called the ' Corpach ', as Scott states : she herself writes that ' Sr Alexr [Macdonald] any time he wrote about me the name he gave me was the Cargo ' (Laing MS. II. 201 in the University Library, Edinburgh), and one Rory McSweyn threatened to expose Macleod of Macleod for the part he had played in the detention of ' the Cargo '. W. C. Mackenzie, *Simon Fraser, Lord Lovat*, 1908, p. 297, note. Scott's word is otherwise unknown.

Page 235, lines 13 ff. The common practice to-day is to have the grave previously dug, with a long turf, i.e. a piece of turf big enough to cover the whole grave, ready as well. In wet weather the digging is sometimes delayed till the arrival of the coffin. Mr. Fred. T. Macleod, describing a funeral which took place in 1901, writes :

' For the space of an hour and a half we had to remain in the open, exposed to the severity of the storm, while the grave was being dug. Near relations and friends of the deceased, clad in their best, descended into the hollow, and took their turn at the digging.' *The Maccrimons of Skye*, 1933, p. 20.

Dr. A. Edgar records that in Bute it was customary in the seventeenth

Pages 235-44   *Appendix D*   541

century to bring coffins to the churchyard before the graves were dug. *Old Church Life in Scotland*, ser. ii, 1886, p. 251.

Page 235, foot. The Sheriff-Substitute of Skye was Alexander Macleod, second son of Roderick Macleod 1st of Ulinish. His nephew, Donald Macleod, states in his bombastic autobiography, *Memoirs of the Life and Gallant Exploits of Sergeant Donald Macleod*, published in 1791, that he was at that time in his 100th year (p. 190). He was the progenitor of the Macleods of Dalvey, Moray. A. Mackenzie, *Hist. Macleods*, 1889, pp. 275 ff. John Knox, who travelled through the Highlands in 1786, met him :

'At Brackadale, I was introduced to Mr. Macleod of Ulinish, who, from his great probity, and the respect in which he is held, has, in some cases, the duty of a sheriff imposed upon him by the inhabitants, to whom he is a father.' *Tour Highlands*, 1787, p. 139.

Knox adds that Mrs. Macleod ' had not forgot the quantity of tea, which she filled out to [Dr. Johnson], amounting to twenty-two dishes '.

Alexander Macleod's daughter, Margaret, married Norman Macleod 4th, of Greshornish. For his son Roderick, whom Johnson also met, see *ante*, v. 242.

The 'very good farm-house' has been greatly enlarged ; it is now, 1937, known as Ulinish Lodge : over the original front door is the inscription ' 17 A.M. ♡ M.M. 56 ', which gives us the date of the building of the house and, possibly, of the marriage of Alexander and Margaret Macleod.

Page 238, line 2. Hamilton Boyle, sixth Earl of Corke and Orrery, was born in 1730; he matriculated from Christ Church, Oxford, 14 June 1748, and took the degree of B.C.L. 15 May 1755 and was created D.C.L. 6 July 1763 : he was High Steward of the University in 1762. He represented Charleville in the Irish Parliament in 1759-60, and Warwick in the Parliament of the United Kingdom in 1761-2. He succeeded his father 23 Nov. 1762 and died, unmarried, 17 Jan. 1764. Foster's *Alumni Oxon*. 1888, i. 147 ; G. E. C., *Compl. Peerage*, 1913, iii. 423 ; *Parl. Return of Members of Parliament*, 1878, pt. ii. 132 and 657. Both he and his father contributed to *The World* : his own papers are Nos. 60 and 170, his father's 47, 68, and 161. Kippis and Towers, *Biographia Britannica*, 1780, ii. 524. His contributions to *The Adventurer* have not been identified.

Page 244, lines 8 ff. and note 2. Johnson's *ipsissima verba* are given by Boswell in his original Journal :

' When I asked him, going from Forres to Nairn, why he did not mention him in the Preface to Shakespeare, he said, " I would not disgrace my page with a player. Garrick has been liberally paid for mouthing Shakespeare." ' *Hebrides*, ed. Pottle and Bennett, 1936, p. 207.

Appendix D   Pages 245–50

'One of the ablest commentators on Shakspeare', who related the Johnsonian anecdote to Boswell, was Steevens (see *post*, vi. 470–1). It agrees with Malone's opinion which is recorded in a note to his copy of George Steevens's *Verses addressed to Mr. Garrick on the report of his intending to leave the Stage* (Malone 142 in the Bodleian). Malone writes:

'It is remarkable that the celebrated actor to whom these lines are addressed, in the course of a long life never rectified or illustrated a single passage of Shakspeare.'

Page 245, note 2. Mrs. Piozzi, who was in Italy when the *Tour* was published, was informed by Sir Lucas Pepys, and others, of the passage in it relating to her opinion of Mrs. Montagu's *Essay on Shakespear*. They urged her to deny the truth of the statement or to 'soften down the . . . Harsh Criticism on a Sister Author '. She did what she could, and Pepys, and Cadell, her publisher, were satisfied ; they then wrote the Postscript, as Pepys informed Mrs. Piozzi in a letter dated 3 March 1786:

'Mr. Cadell . . . was much pleased that I had had the Foresight to have written to you on the Subject, as it had made some Noise.—We agreed that a Postscript should be added to your Anecdotes—& by making use entirely of your Own Words in your letter to me, a Postscript is drawn up, which I think you will approve of, & which is sufficiently justified by their being your own Words though in a letter to me.'

See Mr. J. L. Clifford's article 'The printing of Mrs. Piozzi's Anecdotes of Dr. Johnson ' in the *Bulletin of the John Rylands Library*, 1936, xx, pp. 157 ff. The secret was well kept : there is no evidence that either Boswell or Malone ever suspected that Mrs. Piozzi owed so much to her friends ; it would, perhaps, have been better for her reputation if they had not interfered.

Boswell's claim that the paragraph was literally accurate is substantiated by his original Journal, which reads : ' I mentioned Mrs Montagu's high praises of Garrick. JOHNSON. " It is fit she should say so much, and I should say nothing." He said Reynolds was fond of her book, and he wondered at it; for neither he nor Mrs. Thrale nor Beauclerk could get through it.' *Hebrides*, ed. Pottle and Bennett, 1936, p. 208. Boswell apparently struck out Mrs. Thrale's name in the manuscript, but restored it in the proofs as they were passing through the press. See *Hebrides*, ed. Pottle and Bennett, 1962, p. 426.

Page 250, line 1. According to Boswell's original Journal Garrick's ironical exclamation was not ' *Very* jocose, to be sure ', but ' Mighty pleasant, sir ; mighty pleasant, sir '. *Hebrides*, ed. Pottle and Bennett, 1936, p. 212.

Page 250, lines 11 ff. The Macleods of Fernilea were descended from Alexander Macleod, brother of Sir Roderick Macleod, Rorie More

Page 250   *Appendix D*   543

(*ante*, v. 207, 212, &c.). Johnson's host was Alexander Macleod. He held a lease of Fernilea from 1754, which was renewed by Norman Macleod of Macleod in 1769, before its expiry in 1773, to endure from then for 42 years. In an abstract of that lease, now preserved in the General Register House, Edinburgh, it is stated that Alexander built the mansion house on the farm of Fernilea. Boswell, in his original Journal, describes him as ' a worthy, sensible, kind man ' and his house as ' very comfortable ', adding that the ' parlour was paved with flagstones, not in squares, but just in the shapes which they naturally had in the quarry '. *Hebrides*, ed. Pottle and Bennett, 1936, pp. 212–13.

Alexander Macleod married Margaret, daughter of Donald Macleod of Bernera : they had no children. *Ibid.* and a manuscript note by the Lord Lyon in the Register House copy of A. Mackenzie's *Hist. of Macleods* (1889, p. 252).

I have much pleasure in recording my obligations to Mr. C. T. McInnes of the General Register House, Edinburgh.

Page 250, line 2 from foot. Donald Maclean, called the young Laird of Coll, was the eldest son of Hugh Maclean, 13th of Coll, and his wife Janet (or Jeannette), eldest daughter of Donald Macleod of Talisker. Sir R. Douglas, *Baronage of Scotland*, 1798, i. 373 ; and J. C. Sinclair, *Account of the Clan Maclean*, 1838, p. 312. He conducted Johnson and Boswell from Talisker to Coll and Mull (including Ulva and Inchkenneth.) Boswell gives, in his original Journal, under date 5 Oct., when in Coll, a character-sketch of him which he for the most part suppressed in his *Tour* :

' It was very agreeable, as we went along, to see all the people come from their work and shake hands with the young laird. Mr. Johnson wished that he had more conversation than that of a mere farmer ; and indeed he seemed to be just a young country lad who had been a while in England. He had worked there with his own hands, while he lived at farmers' houses in Hertfordshire, in order to learn to improve his paternal acres or rather *miles*. Mr. Johnson said that was like the Czar of Muscovy. By this, however, his manners were not those of a chieftain in point of dignity. But if he had not reverence from his people, he had their affection. I could find no traces of learning about him ; though he had been educated under the care of his uncle, the professor at Aberdeen. But he had a constant good humour, and readiness of conversation upon common things. Then he had a clear sharp voice, and was not afraid to talk to Mr. Johnson ; informed him as to many particulars, and stuck to his point when Mr. Johnson opposed what he said, until very handsomely driven off. With all this he had as much civility as could be wished, and very great attention to have everything right about Mr. Johnson.' *Hebrides*, ed. Pottle and Bennett, 1936, p. 258.

Boswell was impressed by his lack of dignity :

' I said [9 Oct.] young Coll's want of dignity made him seem rather a favourite servant of the laird's than the young laird himself. He was quite companionable

Appendix D

with all the people. But I observed they all kept themselves uncovered when they spoke with him. Perhaps he is right to be thus easy. He is of a very diminutive figure, and better adapted for being liked than reverenced.' *Ibid.* p. 287.

Coll was drowned 25 Sept. 1774. See *ante*, ii. 287-8 ; v. 331 ; *post*, v. 557, and Johnson's *Letters*, No. 406.

Hugh Maclean died some time before Oct. 1786, when Coll's brother Alexander was served heir (*Service of Heirs*, 20 Nov. 1786). For the family seat, Breacacha, see *ante*, v. 291, and *post*, 552.

Page 256, line 19. The Scots Brigade in the Dutch service was originally formed in the reign of Queen Elizabeth of independent companies and had a continuous history from 1588, when it consisted of at least one regiment, till 1782, when there were three regiments, except for a period of about ten years from the Revolution till the Peace of Ryswick, when the brigade was in the direct service of Great Britain under William III. In 1782 the States General resolved that the brigade should be placed on the same footing, in every respect, as the national troops of Holland; this involved the renunciation by the officers of their allegiance to Great Britain ; the majority refused to take the oath required of them and returned to Scotland ; they were placed on half-pay in the British Army. See James Ferguson, *Papers illustrating the History of the Scots Brigade in the Service of the United Netherlands* (Scot. Hist. Soc.), 1899-1901.

Page 257, line 9. The old inn at Sconser on Loch Sligachan, which must not be confused with the Sligachan Inn near the head of the loch, was formerly a place of some importance ; the mail coaches stopped there and the Raasay ferry-boat sailed from a landing-stage near by. Sconser Lodge, built in 1885, which occupies its site, has recently (1938) become a private hotel.

Page 257, line 14. Mr. Macqueen does not appear to have written an account of Skye. For his contribution to Pennant's *Tour to Scotland, Pt. ii* (1776), see *ante*, v. 161 note.

Page 259, line 16. John Campbell was, at the time, Major-General and Colonel of the 21st Foot, and Commander of the troops and garrisons in the west of Scotland ; he became Lieutenant-General in 1747 and General in 1765. He succeeded his cousin Archibald, third Duke, in the Dukedom of Argyll in 1761. He died in 1770. See G. E. C., *Complete Peerage*, 1910, i. 209.

Page 259, note 1. ' Peter Pindar ' (John Wolcot) satirized Boswell in two of his pieces, *A poetical and congratulatory Epistle to James Boswell, Esq. on his Journal of a Tour to the Hebrides with the celebrated Dr. Johnson* (1786, 10th ed. 1789) and *Bozzy and Piozzi, or, The British Biographers* (1786, 9th ed. 1788) : he naturally seized upon Boswell's drunkenness at Corrichatachin in both poems. Wolcot also lampooned

Pages 260–4   *Appendix D*   545

Boswell in *Pindariana* (1794). *Works*, 1796, iv, p. 433. See *ante*, v. 415, where Boswell describes him as 'a contemptible scribbler'.

Page 260, line 20. Alexander Macdonald of Kingsburgh, 'old Kingsburgh', as he is often called in the *Tour* to distinguish him from his son Allan, Flora Macdonald's husband, was factor to Sir Alexander Macdonald of Sleat. He took the Prince from Sir Alexander's house at Monkstadt to his own, Kingsburgh, on 29 June 1746, and gave him shelter for the night. He was arrested a few days later, taken to Edinburgh Castle, and not released till the general amnesty in July 1747. He does not appear to have been in serious danger of his life. He died 10 Feb. 1772. See *ante*, v. 160, 188–9, 257–8; *The Lyon in Mourning*, 1895, i. 126 and 300–1; and *Culloden Papers*, 1815, pp. 291–3.

Page 261, foot. The Highland lady who had the temerity to sit on Johnson's knee and kiss him was the young wife of Dr. Alexander Macdonald of Gillen. She was Margaret, one of the fourteen children of Ranald Macalister and his wife Anne Macdonald, who married secondly Lachlan Mackinnon of Corry (*ante*, v. 156–7). This identification was made in 1852 by Carruthers, who was presumably informed by the lady's son, Macdonald of Innis-drynich, Argyllshire. Miss Margaret Williamson, a great-great-grand-niece of Macdonald of Kingsburgh, adds a circumstance which was unknown to Boswell: she writes:

'Mrs. Mackinnon's daughter, Margaret Macalister, then a young bride of sixteen, having just married Dr. Macdonald of Gillen, took a bet with some sprightly young ladies that she would sit on Dr. Johnson's knee in the drawing-room and kiss him. These young ladies dared her to do it, saying he was too ugly for any woman to kiss.' *Notes & Queries*, ser. x, vol. x, 1908, p. 147.

In Boswell's original Journal her name is given as 'Dr. Macdonald's wife, " Mrs. Dr. Roy " (i.e. red Doctor)'. *Hebrides*, ed. Pottle and Bennett, 1936, p. 226.

Page 263, lines 3 ff. Arthur Young relates the same anecdote, with variants, and reveals the name of the proud Irish gentleman:

'Another great family in Connaught is Macdermot, who calls himself prince of Coolavin; he lives at Coolavin in Sligo, and, though he has not above 100*l* a year, will not admit his children to sit down in his presence.... Lord Kingsborough, Mr. Ponsonby, Mr. O'Hara, Mr. Sandford, etc. came to see him, and his address was curious : " *O'Hara ! you are welcome ; Sandford, I am glad to see your mother's son ;* (his mother was an O'Brien) *as to the rest of ye, come in as ye can* ".' *Tour in Ireland*, 1780, pp. 185–6.

Page 264, line 7 from foot. There were occasions when Boswell was unable to save Johnson from the importunity of his hospitable hosts; one was on 13 October, on board ship in Coll harbour, when the skipper, Capt. Hugh Macdonald, according to Boswell's report, ' pressed him much to eat mutton or butter or cheese—in short, pressed him to

Appendix D

all that was on board ' and ' made Mr. Johnson grow surly '. Johnson, it appears, had some qualms of conscience. He said to Boswell :

' I know not whether a man should blame himself for not making a proper return to awkward civility. Here now is this man who thinks he is doing the best he can to me, and I can hardly use him well.' *Hebrides*, ed. Pottle and Bennett, 1936, p. 296.

For Johnson's rebuke to Mrs. Keith for her officious attention and his anger at Lady Lochbuy's ill-breeding in pressing him to partake of cold sheep's head, see *ante*, v. 130 and 342.

Page 265. Dr. John Macpherson was born on 1 Nov. 1713, educated at King's College, Aberdeen (M.A. 1728, D.D. 1761), and ordained in 1734, when he was appointed minister of Barra ; he was transferred to Sleat, Skye, in 1742. He married Janet, daughter of Donald Macleod of Bernera, and died at Ostaig, 5 April 1765. Hew Scott, *Fasti Eccl. Scot.* 1928, vii. 175. His ' original Latin ode ' to the memory of his friend the Rev. Norman Macleod, minister of Duirinish, who was drowned crossing the Minch, was published in *Scots Mag.* 1739, i. 273 ; and his paraphrase of the Song of Moses in the same periodical, 1747, ix. 590. His *Critical Dissertations on the origin, antiquities, &c., of the Ancient Caledonians* appeared in 1768 ; the work was edited by Macpherson's elder son Martin, who probably received assistance with the Preface (see below), in which it is stated :

' His son, to whose care he left it [his work], with a diffidence which ought to be natural to a very young man, chose rather to give his father's dissertations to the world as they stood, than to attempt any amendments, which perhaps might injure the memory of a parent he tenderly loved ' (p. xx).

The Dedication, to Charles Greville, was written by Macpherson's younger son John, who was born in 1744 or 1745; in it he says : ' I am on the eve of setting out for a very distant quarter of the world ' ; he sailed for India in March 1767 and in less than twenty years became Governor General (see the *D.N.B.*). Pennant thought well of the work and made use of it (*Tour in Scotland and Voyage to Hebrides, 1772, 1774*, p. 200), but Ritson, who was better qualified, did not ; he, in his *Bibliographia Scotica* (see *ante*, v. 518), writes :

' Dr. Macpherson . . . though, unquestionabley, a man of abilitys, is confine'd in his researches and erroneous in his ideas ; sacrificeing history and truth to imagination and hypothesis. These dissertations, therefor, are to be peruse'd with diffidence and distrust, by the historical student and wil be rejected, with indignation and contempt, by the enlighten'd antiquary.' *Publ. Mod. Lang. Soc. of America*, 1937, lii, p. 134.

Ritson states that James Macpherson wrote the Preface.

For Dr. Macpherson's contribution to the Rev. Kenneth Macaulay's *History of St. Kilda* see *ante*, v. 506-7.

Martin Macpherson, the elder son, was born in 1743, and was educated at King's College, Aberdeen (M.A. 1764, D.D. 1803); he was ordained in 1765 and succeeded his father at Sleat. He married Mary, daughter of Lachlan Mackinnon (*ante*, v. 519), and died in 1812. He wrote the account of the parish of Sleat in the *Statistical Acct. of Scotland* (1795, xvi. 534–40). He made a bad impression on Boswell when they first met at Corrichatachin, 7 Sept., but Boswell thought better of him when he met him again at his own manse, where ' there was more convenience ' for the guests.

'I altered my opinion of Mr. Macpherson. . . . I viewed him now with a most favourable eye, because I saw real goodness of character in him. He was a young man with his own hair cut short and round, with a pleasing countenance and a most unaffected kindness.' *Hebrides*, ed. Pottle and Bennett, 1936, p. 232. See also *ibid.* p. 122.

Miss Macpherson, whose Christian name was Isabel, married John Macpherson of Uvia, Badenoch, in 1778. Miss Anne MacVicar (later Mrs. Grant of Laggan), writing from Fort Augustus, 5 June 1778, says :

' We have had a visit from the new married couple, who are, doubtless, oddly matched. . . . She is the person whom Johnson mentions in his Tour, whom he met at Rasay, and again at her brother's house, in the Isle of Skye. She looks much up to that surly sage, and receives letters and presents of books from him.' *Letters from the Mountains*, 1845, i. 149.

Johnson mentions her in connexion with this second visit to Corrichatachin :

' Here we staid two days. . . . The house was filled with company, among whom Mr. Macpherson and his sister distinguished themselves by their politeness and accomplishments.' *Western Isl.*, 1924, p. 69.

They had met at Corrichatachin on his first visit, 6–8 Sept., and she was one of the party that accompanied him from Ostaig to Armadale, 1 Oct. Boswell's *Hebrides*, ed. Pottle and Bennett, 1936, pp. 120 and 239. Boswell reports in his original Journal that :

' Mr Johnson had always been merry with Miss Macpherson ; asked her to go to London, and said many little jocular complimentary things to her which afforded us amusement.' *Ibid.* p. 240.

Miss Macpherson was very probably the ' insular lady ' who was considered by Johnson and Boswell as a more appropriate ' toast ' than Mrs. Thrale (*ante*, v. 347). Boswell does not mention meeting her at Raasay, and no letters of Johnson to her are known (but the copy of *Rasselas* would not have been sent to her without one).

Dr. Macpherson's manse is no more. The Reverend Donald MacKinnon informs me that it stood on the left-hand side of the Tarscavaig road, a few yards beyond where it breaks off the main road at Ostaig : there is to-day (1937) nothing to indicate the site but a few trees and the remains of what was once the garden.

Page 268, line 5. Johnson's censure of Garrick was too severe for Boswell to print. Mr. Macpherson having said, in error, that Garrick had written ' a very pretty epitaph ' for Shenstone, Johnson replied, ' Then if he could get up, he should pull it down. He was above having an epitaph upon him by Garrick.' And when Boswell defended Garrick, Johnson retorted, ' The next subject you talk to him of, 'tis two to one he is wrong.' Boswell's *Hebrides*, ed. Pottle and Bennett, 1936, pp. 232–3.

Page 270, lines 7 ff. and note 4. Young, on the marriage of his stepdaughter, Caroline Lee, in 1748, invited Miss Mary Hallows to his house and she probably became his housekeeper from that time onwards till his death in 1765. *Gent. Mag.* Feb. 1782, lii, pp. 70 ff., and W. Thomas, *Edward Young*, 1901, pp. 174, 180. Miss Hallows, who was born c. 1710, was the daughter of Young's friend, the Rev. Daniel Hallows, Rector of All Saints, Hertford, and Gilston, Herts., who died 6 Oct. 1741, aged 71. Nichols, *Lit. Anecd.* ix. 510, and Venn, *Alumni Cantab.* pt. i, vol. 11. 291. The Rev. John Jones, Young's curate at Welwyn, who claimed to have great knowledge of his private affairs, hints broadly at Miss Hallows's undue influence. Writing to Dr. Birch, 25 July 1762, he says :

' There is much mystery in almost all his temporal affairs. . . . Whoever lives in this neighbourhood to see his exit, will probably see and hear of some very strange things. Time will shew :—I am afraid, not greatly to his credit. There is thought to be an irremoveable obstruction to his happiness within his walls, as well as another without them ; but the former is the more powerful and like to continue so.' Nichols, *Lit. Anecd.* ii. 620.

Again, on 4 Sept. 1762, he writes :

' The Gentleman [= Young] himself is allowed by all to be far more harmless and easy in his family, than some one else who hath too much the lead in it.' *Ibid.* 622.

Boswell, in 1772, heard talk of Young's improper relations with Miss Hallows and disbelieved it ; Johnson's disbelief confirmed his own. Percy told him that there was ' no more foundation for such a suspicion than between Mr. Johnson and Mrs. Williams '. *Hebrides*, ed. Pottle and Bennett, 1936, p. 235. See also *Boswell Papers*, ix. 11–12.

Young's only son Frederick was baptized 20 June 1732. He matriculated from Balliol College 12 Nov. 1751, after which nothing is known of his academic career. In the *Biographia Britannica*, 1766, vi, pt. ii, Suppl. 259, it was stated, during his lifetime, that ' he misbehaved himself so much as to be forbidden the college ' and that ' this misconduct had so highly displeased his father that the old gentleman would never suffer him to come into his sight afterwards '. Croft, who was his intimate friend, denies that he was rusticated, and Dr. Thomas, whose research was exhaustive, has found no evidence to support the *Biographia*'s statement. Johnson, *Life of Young*, 96, and W. Thomas, *Edward Young*, 1901, p. 183. Whatever the cause of the quarrel, the estrangement between father and son was complete. When the father was dying Miss Hallows sent for the son. Mr. Jones, writing 13 April 1765, shortly after Young's death, says:

> 'The father, on his death-bed, . . . was applied to in the tenderest manner, by one of his physicians, and by another person, to admit the son into his presence, to make submission, intreat forgiveness, and obtain his blessing. As to an interview with his son, he intimated that he chose to decline it, as his spirits were then low, and his nerves weak. With regard to the next particular he said, *I heartily forgive him.*' Nichols, *Lit. Anecd.* ii. 634.

Young, by his will dated 25 April 1760, made his son his residuary legatee and left to Miss Hallows ' all the wrought work for chairs, &c. in my mahogany chest and eight hundred pounds ', to which he added by a codicil, dated 21 June 1760, another two hundred pounds. His ' dying request ' to Miss Hallows, dated 17 Sept. 1764, was that she ' would see all writings whatever whether in papers or books (except my book of accounts) burnt and destroyed as soon as I am dead '. Thomas, *op. cit.* pp. 621–3. Miss Hallows died before May 1790 ' at her lodgings in Hertford, aged upwards of 80 '. *Gent. Mag.* May 1790, lx. i, p. 476. Frederick Young married six months after his father's death and lived on at Welwyn till 1787, when he apparently removed to London ; the date of his death is not known. Thomas, *op. cit.* pp. 211–12.

John Kidgell, the author of *The Card*, was for a short time Young's curate at Welwyn. W. Thomas, *op. cit.* p. 192. He finds a place in the *D.N.B.* and is shown to have been dissolute and dishonest.

Page 273, lines 10 ff. and note 2. James Barclay's pamphlet in defence of Johnson is very rare. The title-page runs :

An | Examination | of | Mr. Kenrick's Review | of | Mr. Johnson's | Edition of Shakespeare. | London : | Printed for W. Johnston in Ludgate-Street, and | Sold by S. Bladon in Pater-noster Row. | M DCC LXVI. | [Price One Shilling and Six-Pence.]

The book is an octavo (A⁶, B–F, G⁶, pp. xii+92) : the last page, which is unnumbered, consists of a list of Errata.

As a specimen of Barclay's style I quote his reply to Kenrick's criticism of Johnson's note on *Love's Labour's Lost*, IV. iii. 166 :

> ' Mr. Johnson owns himself at a loss for the meaning of *Knot* ; and his opponent, through his sleep, tells him, " The Poet meant a *bird* called a *Knot*, alias *Avis Canuti.*" Mr. Kenrick ! awake, Mr. Kenrick. Rub your eyes and look about you. You should never sit down to criticise when you are sleepy, man ; you see what comes of it—Incoherent raving—When you are broad awake, I shall ask you, Why of all the species of birds must a *water-fowl*, and of these the *Knot*, be picked out for the King to be changed into ? Indeed, Sir,

you must shake off this drowsiness: I have perceived it to be creeping upon you this long time, but here we catch you *napping* indeed! Downright sleepy talk; I wish it may not grow into a lethargy before you doze through the eight volumes of Mr. Johnson's Shakespeare. But now you are pretty well awake, let me ask you, how you came to dream of the *Knot* ? Belike you sat down to write with a belly full of them : I cannot account any other way for such an expected meaning for the word—Let us however endeavour to come at the real signification, fresh and fasting ' (p. 57).

The copy described was once owned by J. O. Halliwell-Phillipps and is now in the Birmingham Public Library, to the Librarian of which, Mr. H. M. Cashmore, I am greatly obliged.

Page 274, lines 7 ff. Boswell, in his original Journal, wrote : ' He [Johnson] said the *Critical* reviewers, on occasion of he and Goldsmith doing something together (i.e., publishing each a book at the same time, Mr. Johnson the *Idler*), let them know that they might review each other.' The passage in parentheses was not in the first draft, but was added when Boswell was revising the manuscript for publication. The editors suggest that it was omitted from the *Tour* ' either because Boswell was not sure that he was quoting Johnson exactly, or else because he had neglected to ascertain what it was that Goldsmith published '. Boswell's *Hebrides*, ed. Pottle and Bennett, 1936, p. 239. *The Idler* originally appeared in *The Universal Chronicle* from 15 April 1758 to 5 April 1760, and was published in a collected edition in October 1761. Messrs. Pottle and Bennett tacitly suggest that Goldsmith's publication was *The Citizen of the World*, which ran through *The Public Ledger* from 24 Jan. 1760 to 14 Aug. 1761.

Page 276, line 5 and note 2. Sir John Philipps, 6th Bt., of Picton Castle, Pembrokeshire, was a member of, and a considerable benefactor to, Johnson's college ; he matriculated 4 Aug. 1720, aged 19, and was created D.C.L. 12 April 1749. He was M.P. for Carmarthen 1741-7, Petersfield 1754-61, and Pembrokeshire 1761-4. He was appointed a Commissioner for Trade and Plantations in 1744. He died 23 June 1764. Lady Philipps (*née* Shepherd), whom he had married 22 Sept. 1725, survived till 28 Sept. 1788. Foster, *Alumni Oxon.* 1888, iii. 1108 ; *Parl. Return of Members of Parl.* 1878, pt. ii. 95, 116, 134 ; D. Macleane, *Pembroke College*, 1897, pp. 301, 323, and G. E. C., *Compl. Baronetage*, i. 177. Sir Erasmus Philipps, whose diary was published in *N. & Q.* (2nd Ser., x, 1860, pp. 365-6, 443-5), was his elder brother.

Johnson's letter to Chambers of 8 April 1758 was franked ' J. Philipps ', and in Dec. 1760, when Sir John was dangerously ill at Oxford, he described him as ' the chief friend of Miss Williams '. *Letters*, Nos. 113·1, and 136·1. According to Whitefield, to whom he made an allowance of £30 a year whilst at the University, Sir John was 'a great encourager of the Oxford Methodists '. Macleane, *o.c.s.* p. 358.

Pages 278–84   *Appendix D*   551

Page 278, lines 10 ff. from foot. The St. Kilda ' cough ' or ' boat cold ' has been the subject of some inquiry. Dr. E. D. Clarke, who visited the island in 1797, attributed it to ' the alteration in manners and in diet, the intemperance and riot, which take place upon the arrival of the tacksman '. *Life and Remains of E. D. Clarke*, 1824, p. 276. Carruthers thought this was the best solution of the problem. Boswell's *Hebrides*, 1852, p. 221, note. It was not, however, accepted by the local minister, who, in 1841, accounted for it to James Wilson ' as arising from exposure ', which accords, more or less, with Johnson's explanation. See J. Wilson, *Voy. round Coasts of Scotland*, 1842, ii. 20. Mr. Douglas M. Gane points out that the same susceptibility to colds, following the arrival of strangers, ' is found among other small island communities similarly cut off, notably Tristan da Cunha and Pitcairn '.

Mrs. Rogers (Rose Annie Hughes), in her account of Tristan da Cunha, reports :

'After the departure of H.M.S. Dublin [in 1923] there was quite an epidemic of very bad colds all through the island, and many of the people were very unwell for some days, but it did not amount to influenza. It is, however, very curious that this is always the case when a ship from outside stays at the island.' *The Lonely Isle*, 1926, p. 131.

Mr. Gane, who cites this, adds :

' Seeing how few people land when a ship does call, it is matter for conjecture whether the infection is not found on the ship itself and the islanders are affected through visiting it.' *The Times*, 10 Sept. 1930.

Professor Sir Humphry Rolleston has courteously given me his opinion on the problem. He reports :

' From their comparative isolation the inhabitants of St. Kilda and similar islands are not constantly exposed to small doses of the micro-organisms which set up colds (and so unconsciously immunized or vaccinated against them); hence they are a virgin soil and go down wholesale when a ship arrives, which is very likely to contain either passengers with an active cold or " carriers " of germs, who do not know that they are capable of conveying the disease. A minor analogy of the St. Kilda cold is that which attacks some people on their return from a winter sports' holiday in pure air to London.'

Page 284, lines 8 ff. from foot. Boswell, in his original Journal, describes Capt. Lauchlan Maclean's house, which was probably near the present Achamore, a little over a mile from the hotel which stands on the site of the ' little miserable publick-house ' of 1773. He says :

' The house here was built of stone without mortar, and had no plaster or finishing at all. It was as cold as a stable.' *Hebrides*, ed. Pottle and Bennett, 1936, p. 255.

He was a little disconcerted at night as ' there were but three rooms or divisions in the house '. *Ibid.* p. 254.

Appendix D

Page 289, lines 8 ff. and note 2. Malone wrote in his copy of Gay's *Beggar's Opera*, now in the Bodleian (Malone 128), the following marginal note on the line:

> 'The author evidently had here the following passage in his thoughts: "Lastly, the Pulp [of Cucumber] in Broth is greatly refreshing, and may be mingl'd in most Sallets, without the least damage, contrary to the common Opinion; it not being long, since Cucumber, however dress'd, was thought fit to be thrown away, being accounted little better than Poyson."'

The quotation is from Evelyn's *Acetaria*, 1699, p. 22.

Page 291, lines 18 ff. Coll's house, on Breacacha Bay, was built by Hector Maclean, 11th laird of Coll, who died on 6 Nov. 1754 in the 65th year of his age. *Scots Mag.* 1754, p. 548. Boswell says, in his original Journal:

> 'We found here [at Breacacha] a neat gentleman's house with four rooms on a floor, three storeys and garrets. The dining-room and the other three rooms on that floor were well wainscoted with good fir, and were very snug in dry weather.... There are two neat wings or pavilions to the house.' *Hebrides*, ed. Pottle and Bennett, 1936, p. 264.

The house is to-day (1938) the residence of the present laird of Coll, Brigadier-General E. M. P. Stewart.

Page 292, line 16. Dr. R. W. Chapman, in his edition of *Hebrides* (1924, p. 475), remarked, on Boswell's sentence 'Every body was master', 'I sometimes think that Boswell wrote *muster'd*, but the text may be sound.' It is. Boswell meant that 'everybody was his own master'. That he regarded a barracks as a place of orderly ease is seen from the following passage in his Journal for 9 March 1777:

> 'It was a picture of desolation to find both Master and Mistress gone [from Treesbank]; yet I know not how, there was a sort of feeling of ease, as in barracks.' *Boswell Papers*, xii. 142.

Page 292, lines 17 ff. Boswell's original description of the old castle of Breacacha, which he surveyed 'very minutely', is much fuller than his published account: see *Hebrides*, ed. Pottle and Bennett, 1936, pp. 265–7. The following passage testifies to the thoroughness of Johnson's survey:

> 'Mr. Johnson examined all this remaining specimen of ancient life with wonderful eagerness. It was very inconveniently arranged. There was one narrow passage which he tried to get through, but found it would not do. He persisted however; opened his waistcoat and pressed through. There was in the thickness of the walls on the southwest what Coll called a closet. It was a narrow passage or stripe to the southwest corner, and then it run at a right angle to the north for a little way. Mr. Johnson had first looked at it from the entry into it. I went in and reported that it was a circular closet. I was mistaken, to be sure, in every sense; for the line which it formed had nothing of the circle. Coll agreed with me. This incited Mr. Johnson's curiosity to

Pages 295–301   *Appendix D*   553

keener pitch, as he was almost positive we were wrong, from the cursory view he had taken. "How the plague is it circular?" said he; and back he went, and proceeded into it, and confuted us.' *Ibid.* pp. 266–7.

Macgibbon and Ross, in their description of the castle (*Castellated and Domestic Architecture of Scotland*, 1887, iii. 117–20), say that ' the place is so encumbered with rubbish that it is difficult to determine the original levels '. The present laird is endeavouring to clear away the rubbish.

John Ramsay of Ochtertyre says that the ' pits ' or ' thieves' holes ', which were usually, but not always, beneath the ground, were all over Scotland ' accounted legal prison for thieves and other meaner criminals till the Jurisdiction Act passed ' in 1747. *Scotland & Scotsmen in the 18th century*, 1888, ii. 93. He stigmatizes them as ' a reproach to humanity '. For examples of these ' pits ' see W. Mackay Mackenzie in G. Scott-Moncrieff, *The Stones of Scotland*, 1938, pp. 67–8.

Page 295, lines 10 ff. from foot. Croker suggested (1831, ii. 523) that the ' foolish piece ' was *Hurlothrumbo*, published by Samuel Johnson, 1691–1773, in 1729. The full title of this work, of which there were two editions in the same year, is *Hurlothrumbo : or, the Super-Natural, as it is acted at the New-Theatre, in the Hay-Market. Written by Mr. Samuel Johnson, from Cheshire.* It is described by the *D.N.B.* as ' a farrago of nonsense, hardly relieved by one or two good burlesque touches and by approaches to wit, probably due to Byrom '. Both editions have two dedications, one to Lady Delves, the other to Lord Walpole of Walpole, Sir Robert Walpole's son. Mr. W. T. Lynn (*N. & Q.* 6 Ser. xi. 290), thought the piece in question was *A compleat Introduction to the Art of Writing Letters . . . to which is prefixed, A Grammar of the English Language. By S. Johnson.* This work, which is not markedly foolish, is an anthology of real and fictitious letters, preceded by a very compendious grammar, and a few brief remarks on letter-writing, trite, but not foolish. It was published in 1758.

Page 301, lines 18 ff. and note 2. Neil Maclean of Crocepole or Crussapoll, who, according to Boswell, acted ' like a judge among his neighbours ', was born *c.* 1724 : he married Julia Stewart. His son Donald was born 12 May 1752, graduated at King's College, Aberdeen, licensed 18 Dec. 1779 and ordained missionary at Salen and Kilfinichen, presented to the living of the Small Isles (Eigg and Canna) 3 Oct. 1787 ; he died in 1810. His only known work is the account of his parish in Sinclair's *Statistical Account*, 1796, xvii. 272 ff. See Hew Scott, *Fasti Eccl. Scot.* vii. 177 ; A. Maclean Sinclair, *The Clan Gillean*, 1899, pp. 389–90. Johnson told Boswell that he would have talked to him if he had known his merit, and promised to send him a copy of his abridged dictionary. Carruthers said that the promise was kept, that the volume was addressed to him in the author's handwriting, and that it was in 1852 ' carefully preserved '. *Hebrides*, ed. Pottle and Bennett, 1936, p. 283, and ed. Carruthers, 1852, p. 239 note. A copy of Johnson's abridged dictionary, dated 1756, inscribed ' To Mr. Maclean Teacher of Languages in the Island of Coll from the Authour ' is in the Rothschild Collection. *Catal.* No. 1240.

Page 310, lines 8 ff. Leandro Alberti (1479-1553) first published his *Descrittione di tutta Italia* at Bologna in 1550 ; it was frequently reprinted and re-edited, and was translated into Latin in 1567. The great Italian savant Muratori thought so highly of it that he suggested a new and revised edition to Pope Benedict XIV. An Italian authority states that Alberti made great use of Flavio Biondo's *Italia Illustrata* (1474), which he sometimes copied almost literally. *Enciclopedia Italiana*, 1929, ii. 180-1. Boswell on 7 April 1775 repeated to Beauclerk, as his own opinion, Johnson's statement that Addison had borrowed from Alberti, when Beauclerk replied that he was also said to have borrowed from G. C. Cappaccio (*c.* 1560-1631), a prolific writer, whose chief work was a history of Naples in Latin (1607). See *ante*, ii. 346.

Page 311, foot and note 4. Professor Edward Bensly suggests that when Johnson associated these lines of Virgil with the miseries of an author's life, he was very likely influenced by Burton, who in his *Anatomy* (1. 2. iii. 15) quotes from the same passage in the same connexion. Johnson quotes the passage in *Adventurer*, No. 41.

Page 313, lines 3 ff. Dr. Maclean's house was at Erray, about a mile from Tobermory. Boswell describes it as ' a strange confused house built by Mackinnon the proprietor about sixty years ago '. *Hebrides*, ed. Pottle and Bennett, 1936, p. 301. The house, which is of two rather low stories, still (1936) stands ; one half of it is used as a cottage, the other as a cow-byre. See C. J. Hindle in *N. & Q.*, 1931, clxi. 133.

Page 313, lines 18 ff. Dr. Hector Maclean's *History of the Macleans* is almost certainly the work entitled 'A brief genealogical account of the Family of Maclean from its first settling in the Island of Mull and parts adjacent ', of which there are two versions, both of which have been printed : (1) that compiled at the instance of Walter Macfarlane (†1767), the antiquarian, whose *Genealogical Collections concerning families in Scotland . . . 1750-1* were edited by James Toshach Clark in two volumes in 1900 ; this version (vol. i, pp. 118-43) was written after 1750, as it notices the death in that year of Sir James Hector Maclean, 17th chief, of Duart; (2) that known as the Ardgour MS. : this, the much fuller version of the two, must have been completed after 1762, as it mentions Sir Allan Maclean's majority in Col. Fitzroy's regiment, 119th Foot (see below) ; it was privately printed at Edinburgh, at the expense of Alexander Maclean of Ardgour, in 1872 ; one of the

Pages 314–18   *Appendix D*   555

twenty-five copies is in the National Library of Scotland. Mr. Hector McKechnie, Advocate, of Edinburgh, to whom I am greatly indebted, possesses a manuscript copy, on paper watermarked 1817, of this version.

Dr. Hector Maclean mentions his own descent in this work, as Carruthers pointed out:

' Lauchlan MacLean of Gruline was married 1st. to Janet Eldest Daughter to John McLeod of Calick [? Cantulick] Tutor of McLean and Isobell McKenzie Sister to the late Sir Kenneth McKenzie of Scatwell and had Issue Hector married to Kathrine only Daughter to Donald MacLean of Coll.' *Breif Genealogical Acct. of the Family of McLean*, 1872, p. 100.

According to Boswell, Dr. Maclean had been ' above thirty years at Glasgow': *Hebrides*, ed. Pottle and Bennett, 1936, p. 301. Carruthers (p. 248, note) states that he died about 1785.

Page 314, lines 15 ff. The Mull bard, John Maclean (Iain Mac Ailein) was born c. 1670 and died c. 1760. His poems were taken down by Dr. Hector Maclean (see above) and included in the collection left by him to his daughter and given by her to the better-known Gaelic poet of Tiree, also named John Maclean (1787–1848): they are printed in *The Glenbard Collection of Gaelic Poetry*, edited by A. Maclean Sinclair (Charlottetown, Prince Edward Island, 1888). See also *Clarsach na Coille*, ed. A. Maclean Sinclair, 1881, Pref., p. v, and J. P. Macleàn, *Hist. of the Clan MacLean*, 1889, p. 382.

Page 316, line 15. Lord Auchinleck's methodical friend was probably John Carlyle of Lymekilns, Dumfries-shire, a writer or solicitor of Edinburgh. He was served heir male of provision to his uncle, Adam Carlyle of Lymekilns, on 12 Sept. 1684. On 3 Sept. 1706 he was admitted a Burgess of Glasgow, gratis, and in 1736 recorded his arms in the Court of the Lord Lyon. He died in the winter of 1741 (*Scots Mag.* Dec., iii. 571) and his will is entered in the Commissariot Register of Edinburgh under date 30 July 1742. I owe this information to the courtesy of the late James R. Anderson, Librarian of Baillie's Institution, Glasgow.

Page 318, line 3 and note 1. Carruthers, in a note to his edition (1852, p. 252), gives the history of Miss Mary Maclean:

' She conceived a warm attachment for a Mr. Duncan Mackenzie, of Aros, whom her friends conceived to be much inferior to her in rank and acquirements. In deference to her father's feelings, Miss Maclean continued single for many years; but after his death she was united to Mr. Mackenzie, June 6th. 1786. They resided at Tobermory, in reduced circumstances, until about 1800, when Mr. Mackenzie died, without issue, and his widow became a pensioner on the bounty of Coll. She died in 1826, and was buried at Kilmore, about seven miles from Tobermory, but no stone marks her grave. A melancholy sequel to the bright morning of her life depicted by Johnson and Boswell.'

The spinet on which she played to Johnson was ignorantly destroyed about the beginning of the 20th century. C. J. Hindle in *N. & Q.*, 22 Aug. 1931, vol. clxi, p. 133.

Page 319, lines 26 ff. Lauchlan MacQuarrie, 16th chief, son of John MacQuarrie (†1735), was born *c.* 1715 ; he married, firstly, Alice, daughter of Donald Maclean of Torloisk, and, secondly, Anne MacQuarrie. Sir Robert Douglas, *Baronage of Scotland*, 1798, p. 509. He sold his estate in 1777. Carruthers says that ' he had been profusely hospitable, and there was little or no reversion after his debts were paid. He was sixty-two years of age. Yet with unsubdued energy the old chief entered the army, served with distinction for many years, and returning to his native country, died at Glenforsa, a valley in Mull, on the 14th of January, 1818.' Boswell's *Hebrides*, 1852, p. 255, note. He is presumably the Lachlan M'Quarie whose commission as lieutenant in the 74th Regiment of Foot is dated 23 Dec. 1777 : this regiment served in America and Lt. M'Quarie was placed on half-pay in 1783, when it was disbanded. *Army List* for 1779 (p. 140) and 1785 (p. 341).

The old house, which consisted of five rooms and some attics, still (1936) stands : it has been converted into two labourer's cottages.

Page 323, lines 1 ff. Boswell, in his original Journal, wrote :

' I was agreeably disappointed in Sir Allan. I had heard of him only as an officer in Lord Eglinton's Highland regiment, and as a great companion of the Earl's, so I apprehended that I should find a riotous bottle companion and be pressed to drink ; in place of which, the Knight was as sober after dinner as I could wish, and let me do as I pleased. And what surprised me still more agreeably, though he swore, as Dr. Campbell does, he was a man of religion like Dr. Campbell.' *Hebrides*, ed. Pottle and Bennett, 1936, p. 316.

Sir Allan Maclean, 18th chief of Duart and 6th baronet of Brolas, was born *c.* 1710. He joined the Scots Brigade (see *ante*, v. 544), 2nd Battalion of Lord Drumlanrig's Regiment, in which he had the rank of captain ; he later entered the British Army, obtaining first, 16 July 1757, a captaincy in the 62nd Regiment (Montgomery's Highlanders), with which he served in North America, and subsequently, 25 June 1762, a majority in the 119th Foot, in which he finally attained the rank of Lieutenant-Colonel, 25 May 1772. He succeeded his cousin, Sir Hector Maclean, 5th baronet, who died unmarried in Oct. 1750. He married Una, daughter of Hector Maclean of Coll, who died in 1760 ; he died 10 Dec. 1783 and was buried at Inchkenneth. See Sir Robert Douglas, *Baronage of Scotland*, 1780, pp. 368–9 ; J. C. Sinclair, *Account of the Clan MacLean*, 1838, p. 207 ; A. Maclean Sinclair, *The Clan Gillean*, 1899, p. 468 ; *Army List* for 1758, 1770, 1774, and 1782 ; and *New Statist. Acct.* 1845, vii. Argyle, 301. See also *ante*, v. 390, where his identity is concealed under the description ' a very respectable Chieftain '.

Pages 331-8   *Appendix D*   557

The remains of Sir Allan's cottage were to be seen in 1845 (*New Statist. Acct.* vii. Argyle, 301), but there is no trace of it to-day (1936). Johnson, in his letter to Mrs. Thrale, described it somewhat curiously as ' a thatched hut with no chambers '. Perhaps he meant 'upper chambers'. *Letters*, No. 332.

Page 331, line 13 and note 1. Coll was drowned on 25 Sept. 1774. The following account of the accident is taken from the *Scots Mag.* Sept. 1774, xxxvi, p. 503 :

'Archibald Murdoch, Esq: younger, of Gartincaber, Mr. Maclean of Coll, Mr. Fisher from England, and Mr. Malcolm Macdonald, drover in Mull, with five attendants, unfortunately drowned in crossing a ferry in the isle of Mull. Mr. Murdoch had gone to Mull on a visit to Mr. Maclean of Lochbuy; and having dined in a friend's house, the melancholy accident happened on their return. The barge overset within a gunshot of the lands of Ulva and Mull. Mr. Maclean of Lochbuy, and three young men in the barge, having got hold of the mast, continued dashing in the waves for three quarters of an hour, and were saved by the ferry-boat of Ulva, which reached them just as they were ready to sink.'

Page 338, lines 15 ff. The account of the Reverend Neil Macleod in Boswell's original Journal gives many interesting details, including a neat remark by Johnson, which were omitted in the printed version :

' We pulled away along Loch Scridain till we landed near to Mr. Neil MacLeod's, to whose house we walked. . . . He came to meet us. His first appearance was taking. He had a black wig and a smart air, like an English parson ; and he had his hat covered with wax-cloth, which showed an attention to convenience. With him was a Lieutenant Hugh Maclean. His house was a good farm-house of one storey, dry and well furnished. His wife a very well-behaved woman. She was the daughter of the former minister; so, as Mr. Johnson said, she knew how to live in the minister's house. We had tea first, and then an excellent supper. Mr. MacLeod talked sensibly and distinctly. . . . Our evening went on well. Sir Allan, Mr. Johnson, and I had each a good clean bed in the room where we supped. There were some good books here, and good pens and ink, which was no small rarity.' *Hebrides*, ed. Pottle and Bennett, 1936, p. 339.

Neil Macleod was born in 1729 and educated at Aberdeen, where he took his M.A. in 1747 ; before being licensed in 1753 he was for a short time schoolmaster at Bracadale, Skye ; he was appointed missionary at Moidart in 1754 and given the living of Kilfinichen and Kilvicheoan, Mull, in 1756 ; he held the living till his death, 28 April 1780. He married in 1756 Margaret, daughter of the Reverend Archibald Maclean, his immediate predecessor : she died in 1789. Hew Scott, *Fasti Eccl. Scot.* 1923, iv. 113.

The place of his birth is unknown, but it is improbable that it was St. Kilda, as is implied by Dr. S. B. Wylie, the biographer of his son. *Mem. Alex. Macleod*, New York, 1855, p. 12. He was a brother of Donald Macleod, the armourer, of Swordale, Dunvegan, who went

558   *Appendix D*   Pages 341-3
to Skye from Ross-shire. The Rev. Donald Mackinnon suggests that they belonged to the Macleods of Assynt. The statement made by Alex. Mackenzie (*Hist. Macleods*, 1889, p. 435) that he was 'Macleod's Chaplain to the Forces during the Rising of 1745' is certainly incorrect.

The house in which he entertained Johnson and Boswell was at Ardchrishnish, a small farm on the southern shore of Loch Scridain, in the district of Brolas: no trace of the house remains to-day; its traditional site is, so I am informed by Dr. Hector MacLean of Broadford, a former minister, in front of the present farm-house.

The collection of books that Mr. Macleod had there was not numerous nor, indeed, entirely satisfactory: the Rev. Donald Mackinnon, in whose *Clerical Sons of Skye* (1930, pp. 65-6) the catalogue may be consulted, describes it as 'sadly lacking in the literature which one would associate with a minister warmly attached to the full contents of the Evangel'; it consisted of fifty-two separate works and contained, like the Rev. John Macpherson's (*ante*, v. 265), Latin, Greek, and French books; there were also one or two Gaelic books and the Old Testament in Irish: for light reading Mr. Macleod had *Joseph Andrews, Roderick Random, Don Quixote*, the *Gentleman's Recreation*, Congreve, Pope, and, in French, *Guzman d'Alfarache* and *Gil Blas*. Horace and Virgil are not represented, so that the catalogue is perhaps incomplete.

Pages 341-3. John Maclean was the 17th laird of Lochbuy: he was served heir male special to Hector Maclean of Lochbuy in Feb. 1751, when he was described as John Maclean, son of Allan Maclean of Garmony, and in the following November he was served heir-general to his cousin Lachlan Maclean of Lochbuy, when he was described as John Maclean of Lochbuy. He married Isabel, daughter of Donald Maclean, of Brolas, sister of Sir Allan Maclean (*ante*, v. 556). See Sir Robert Douglas, *Baronage of Scotland*, 1798, p. 371; and A. Maclean Sinclair, *The Clan Gillean*, 1899, p. 267.

He built the house which Johnson visited. It still (1936) stands, but is used as stables; on it there is a tablet with the following inscription:

'After leaving Moie Castle the Lochbuie Family resided in this House from 1752 to 1790 and it was in this House that Dr. Johnson and Mr. Boswell were entertained in 1773 by John Maclaine XVII Laird of Lochbuie.'

The modern, more commodious house is adjacent to it, and the old castle, which dates from the fourteenth century and is still (1936) in an excellent state of preservation. See Macgibbon and Ross, *Castellated and Domestic Architecture of Scotland*, 1889, iii. 127-8. Boswell reports in his original Journal that when they were surveying the old castle, Lochbuy 'roared out, what excellent cellars he had in the vaults! Mr. Johnson was offended at being disturbed in his antiquarian re-

Pages 344–9   *Appendix D*   559

searches, or rather meditations, and said, " I don't care about cellars ".'
Hebrides, ed. Pottle and Bennett, 1936, p. 345.

Page 344, line 5. The ' tolerable inn ' at Oban stood at the corner of the present Argyll Square and High Street. There is to-day (1936) a commemorative inscription on a shop named The Argyll House :

'On this Site stood the "Tolerable Inn" where Dr. Samuel Johnson and his friend and biographer James Boswell spent the night on their return from the "Tour to the Hebrides" on Friday 22nd October 1773.'

The original inn was, according to Boswell, ' a slated house of two storeys '. The travellers ' were well enough entertained ', though they ' had nothing like what is to be found in good inns upon a frequented road '. *Hebrides*, ed. Pottle and Bennett, 1936, p. 346. Oban at the time was a very small village.

Page 346, line 15. The ' excellent inn ' at Inveraray was the present (1938) Argyll Arms Hotel ; a large bedroom in it is always spoken of as Dr. Johnson's room, and a portrait of him hangs over the mantelpiece. The inn is described by Dorothy Wordsworth, who visited Inveraray with her brother and Coleridge in 1803 :

' The range [of buildings] bordering on the water consisted of little else than the inn, being a large house, with very large stables, the county gaol, the opening into the main street into the town, and an arched gateway, the entrance into the Duke of Argyle's private domain.' *Recoll. of a Tour in Scotland*, 1874, p. 126.

She added that the inn ' was over-rich in waiters and large rooms to be exactly to our taste, though quite in harmony with the neighbourhood '. *Ibid.* p. 127.

Page 349, lines 15 ff. and note 1. Garrick's rejection of *Chateaubriant* made Mickle exceedingly angry. In an undated reply to Boswell's letter of 12 June 1773 he says, evidently alluding to Johnson (but see *ante*, v, p. xv, *n.* 1) :

' I have heard a name at which Garrick would tremble—talk with ineffable contempt of his *Jeu du Theatre*—and the pieces he brings on the stage. When I told the name now mentioned, that I would attack Garrick's taste, through the sides of this damned trash he has brought on the stage : there, said he, is A BROAD MARK, and you will hurt him.' *Universal Mag.* xi, 1809, p. 303.

He had already printed the note in the *Lusiad* attacking Garrick (*ante*, ii. 495, and *Universal Mag.* xi, 1809, p. 303), but he intended severer strictures, as is evident from his letter to Hoole, 15 Nov. 1773 :

' I have planned a new Dunciad, of which he [Garrick] is the hero. As soon as I finish the Lusiad, I will set about it. If you think proper, you may mention this in any company.' *Poet. Works*, 1806, p. xlvi.

This threat was never carried out.

In the above-quoted letter to Boswell, which is neither very lucidly nor elegantly expressed, he complained that Garrick had spoken of him disrespectfully, and had not treated him ' genteely ' ; he also affirmed

560   *Appendix D*   Pages 350–3

that Garrick's subscription for twenty copies of the *Lusiad* was not genuine. *Universal Mag.* xi, 1809, pp. 302–3.

Page 350, lines 6 ff. and note 1. The new edition of Aeschylus for which Garrick solicited Boswell's subscription was published by Longman in 1773: '*Προμηθεὺς Δεσμώτης*. Cum Stanleiana versione, scholiis α, β (et γ ineditis) amplissimisque variorum notis; quibus suas adjecit, necnon scholia de metro, ac Anglicanam interpretationem T. Morell.' The old sheets of the Greek text and the Latin version were used. The English translation, which has a separate title-page and pagination, was dedicated to Garrick in the following flattering terms: 'To David Garrick, Esq; indisputably the First Actor in this (perhaps in any) Age, the Translation of this the First play extant is inscribed, By his most obedient and humble servant, T. Morell.' The date of this dedication is 1 May 1773. Boswell, replying to Garrick's letter on 11 April 1774, says: 'By all means let me be upon your list of subscribers to Mr. Morrell's *Prometheus*.' *Letters*, 1924, i. 201. I have not found a copy containing a list of subscribers. The book was announced as 'in the press' on the verso of the leaf immediately preceding the title-page of the 1767 edition of the Greek text: the price was then 7s. 6d. Perhaps special copies of the English translation were issued, at an enhanced price, to subscribers.

Page 353, lines 2 ff. The unsociable baronet and his neighbour were, according to Boswell's original Journal, Sir John Dalrymple and Lord Adam Gordon. Sir John's estate was at Cranston, Midlothian (*ante*, v. 401). Lord Adam Hope, the youngest son of Alexander, second Duke of Gordon, inherited from his mother the Prestonhall estate in the same parish (see John Small, *Castles and Mansions of the Lothians*, 1883, vol. ii).

Page 353, line 11 and note 1. The news of the result, in his favour, of Archibald Douglas's appeal to the House of Lords (27 Feb. 1769) against the decision of the Court of Session (July 1767), in favour of the Duke of Hamilton, caused considerable excitement in Edinburgh. 'The inhabitants ... testified their satisfaction by splendid illuminations, and other demonstrations of joy.... The populace, however, became unruly, broke windows, etc.', and soldiers were brought into the city ' to prevent further mischief '. *Scots Mag.* 1769, xxxi. 109. The judges who had been for Hamilton had their windows broken, ' and seven asses, in *honour* of them were led round the town '. James Harris, Lord Malmesbury, *Letters*, 1870, i. 175. According to John Ramsay of Ochtertyre Boswell ' headed the mob which broke the judges' windows, and insulted them in the most licentious manner ', *Scotland and Scotsmen in the 18th c.*, 1888, i. 173. He adds:

'At an entertainment to a very miscellaneous company of the friends of

Douglas, Boswell made no scruple of recounting his feats on the night of the mob. On which Mr. Stewart Moncrieff, starting to his feet, said, "Upon my soul, Boswell, you are mad." " Sir," answered he, " swear by your sixty thousand pounds, by your ice-house, by your peach and grape houses, but do not swear by what you value so little as your soul.'

Page 354, line 20. The identity of the 'other ladies' who were present at Inveraray Castle when the Duchess of Argyll completely ignored Boswell is disclosed by his Journal. He recorded :

'The Duchess took not the least notice of me. I did not mind this, as the Duke was exceedingly civil. Lady Betty Hamilton made tea, and I had some. Miss Sempill, with whom I was pretty well acquainted, hardly acknowledged me, I suppose for fear of offending the Duchess. Miss Campbell of Carrick talked a little with me.' *Hebrides*, ed. Pottle and Bennett, 1936, p. 352.

Miss Sempill was one of the three unmarried daughters of Hew, 11th Lord Sempill, probably Jean, the eldest of these. She died in 1800. Sir James Balfour Paul, *Scots Peerage*, 1900, vii. 563. Boswell mentions meeting or dining with a Miss Semple or Sempill on several occasions, but he never gives her Christian name. *Boswell Papers*, xi. 51, xiii. 268, xiv. 38, 42, 45, 52, 53, 143, xv. 136, xvi. 37, 38.

Boswell also mentions dining with Miss Campbell of Carrick, but not so frequently. *Ibid.* ix. 130, xii. 14, 194, xiii. 193.

Page 355, lines 5 ff. The Rev. John Macaulay, the founder of a famous family, was the son of the Rev. Aulay Macaulay, 1673–1758, minister of Harris ; he was born in 1720, educated at King's College, Aberdeen, where he took his M.A. in 1739 ; he was ordained to South Uist in 1745, translated to Lismore and Alpin in 1755 and to Inveraray in 1765, presented by George III to Cardross in 1772, and admitted in 1774 ; he died 31 March 1789. He married, secondly, Margaret Campbell, by whom he had twelve children : Zachary, the father of Lord Macaulay, was his fourth son. Hew Scott, *Fasti*, iii. 336 ; iv. 12. W. B. Blaikie suggests that he was the 'devil of a minister', who did the fugitive Prince and his followers 'a' the mischief that lay in his power'. *Itinerary of Prince Charles*, 1897, p. 48, n. 3 ; *Lyon in Mourning*, i. 204. See also Blaikie, *Origins of the '45*, 1916, p. 232, and *The Highlander*, 1881–2, p. 202. For his ' rusticity ' see below, p. 563.

Page 355, lines 9 ff. and note 3. Boswell wrote the passage that he thought deserving of Johnson's censure on 24 Aug. 1782 : it then read :

' We were shown through the house ; and I never shall forget the enchanting impression made upon my fancy by some of the ladies' maids tripping about in neat morning dresses. After seeing nothing for a long time but rusticity, their elegance delighted me ; and I could have been a knight-errant for them. Such is my amorous constitution.' *Hebrides*, ed. Pottle and Bennett, 1936, p. 353.

Johnson almost certainly read this at Oxford in June 1784, when he wrote the account of Archibald Campbell (*ante*, v. 357).

Page 355, lines 17 ff. Inveraray Castle was modern, having been built by the third Duke of Argyll during 1744-61. The present Duke tells me that the room in which Johnson dined is now a billiard room, but is otherwise unaltered. See Faujas de Saint-Fond, *Voyage en Angleterre*, 1797, i. 283 ff., for full descriptions of the seat and the life there. The trees are said to have numbered above a million. John Knox, *Tour through Scotland*, 1787, pp. 43 ff. Dorothy Wordsworth thought the beeches were the tallest she had ever seen. *Recoll. of a Tour in Scotland in 1803*, 1874, p. 127.

Page 356, line 16. The following passage, which I owe to the courtesy of Prof. F. A. Pottle, from a codicil, dated 30 May 1785, to Boswell's will gives his own views on the ' middle state ' :

' Finally I request the prayers of all my pious friends for my departed soul considering how reasonable it is to suppose that it may be detained some time in a middle state.'

Page 357, line 14. The 'Hon.' Archibald Campbell was the eldest son, by his first wife, of Lord Neil Campbell, the second son of the first Marquis of Argyll. He was consecrated a bishop by three nonjuring bishops in 1711 and elected bishop of Aberdeen in 1721. See *D.N.B*.

Page 358, lines 13 ff. The identity of the gentleman who whistled ' to show his independency ' is disclosed by Boswell's original Journal :

'A Colonel Livingstone was there, the Member for the County of Argyll. He talked a bit vaguely; and the result was that Mr. Johnson afterwards remarked of him, "A mighty misty man, the Colonel ".' *Hebrides*, ed. Pottle and Bennett, 1936, p. 355.

Adam Livingstone, or Levingston, as he is called in the Army List, was promoted Captain on 30 Apr. 1751 and Major on 8 May 1758, in the Royal North British Fusiliers, or 21st Foot ; he became Lieut.-Colonel in the Army on 8 Jan. 1762. He was elected Member of Parliament for Argyllshire at a by-election 20 Feb. 1772 ; he was re-elected 8 Nov. 1774, and held the seat till 1780, when he retired in favour of Lord Frederick Campbell. *Parl. Return of Members of Parliament*, 1878, pt. ii, pp. 147, 159, 173.

Page 358, lines 21-2. Lady Betty Hamilton, only daughter of the 6th Duke of Hamilton and his wife, Elizabeth Gunning (later the Duchess of Argyll), married in 1774 Sir Edward Smith-Stanley, who became the 12th Earl of Derby on the death of his grandfather : in 1778 she had an intrigue with the 3rd Duke of Dorset and was in consequence separated from her husband. Mrs. Piozzi, referring to this intrigue and its results, noted, in 1820, in the margin of the second edition of *Hebrides*, that Lady Betty

' disgraced herself afterwards so that no Man would *let* her lean on his Chair—She lay unburied a long Time, because no one would be at y[e] Expence of putting her Underground.'

The Queen and others refused to receive Lady Derby after her lapse, but the Duchess of Brunswick, the King's sister, and other members of the nobility were more friendly. See Duke of Argyll, *Intimate Society Letters of the 18th c.*, 1910, i. 250, 252, 267. She died in Gloucester Street, Marylebone, on 14 March 1797, and was buried on 2 April at Bromley, Kent. G. E. C., *Compl. Peerage*, iv. 219.

Pages 359 foot and 360 top. Mr. Macaulay was unfortunate on this occasion. He had already been severely rebuked by Johnson for incivility : ' Mr. Macaulay, Mr. Macaulay ! Don't you know it is very rude to cry eh ! eh ! when one is talking ? ' Boswell's comment was : ' Poor Macaulay had nothing to say for himself. But the truth is, it was a sin of ignorance, or mere rusticity.' *Hebrides*, ed. Pottle and Bennett, 1936, p. 357.

Page 362, lines 14–16. Boswell wrote in his Journal, 22 March 1787 :

' Douglas having (weakly as I thought) taken offence at my mentioning a lively saying of Dr. Johnson's against his filiation in my *Tour to the Hebrides*, and as I thought it unpleasant and unbecoming that he and I should be on bad terms, I had written to him a handsome letter on Sunday, to which he on Monday had returned a cold note. I read both to Malone, who advised me to have nothing more to say to him. I was conscious that he had never shewn me any generous gratitude, and thought nothing could be made of him.' *Boswell Papers*, xvii. 17.

Boswell, in his 'handsome letter' of apology, 18 March 1787, admitted great uneasiness and hoped that his inadvertence would not dissolve all connexion between them. *Fettercairn Catalogue*, No. 1099. Douglas, in his ' cold note ', 19 March, accepted the apology, but begged ' that in no future publication of Mr. Bosewell's, his name, or his family may be so inadvertantly mentioned '. *Ibid.*, No. 304.

Page 363, line 4. The inn at Tarbet at which the travellers dined is represented to-day (1938) by the greatly enlarged Tarbet Hotel : some of the original stables remain. Dorothy Wordsworth wrote in 1803 that it was ' a well-sized white house, the best in the village '. *Recoll. of a Tour in Scotland*, 1874, p. 78.

Page 363, line 5. Sir James Colquhoun, 25th chief of Colquhoun, was the son of Sir James Grant (Colquhoun) and Anne Colquhoun ; he was born in 1714 and succeeded to Luss and the other Colquhoun estates in 1738, when he assumed the name of Colquhoun. He served with his regiment, the Black Watch, in Flanders and was present at the battle of Dettingen. He was created a baronet of Great Britain a few months before his death in 1786. He was a Hanoverian Whig. He married, in 1740, Helen, eldest daughter of William, Lord Strathnaver, eldest son of John, 15th Earl of Sutherland : she was born in 1717 and died in 1791. Her husband named Helensburgh after her. See Sir W. Fraser, *Chiefs of Colquhoun*, 1869, i. 332 ff. ; G. E. C., *Compl. Baronetage*,

1906, v. 249-50 ; and Sir James Balfour Paul, *Scots Peerage*, viii. 355-7.

Rossdhu, the family mansion, was built by Sir James *c.* 1770 ; it still stands, greatly enlarged. See T. Garnett, *Observations on a Tour through the Highlands*, 1800, i. 34-5, and Joseph Irving, *Book of Dumbartonshire*, 1879, ii. 257.

Page 365, lines 20 ff. James Smollett, son of George Smollett of Inglestone, was a Commissary of Edinburgh and Sheriff Depute of Dumbartonshire. He succeeded to the family estate of Bonhill in 1738 and removed to Cameron in 1763. He married Jean, daughter of Sir John Clerk of Pennicuik. He died 12 Nov. 1775. Boswell at once applied to his friends, Lord Mountstuart and Col. James Stuart, for their interest in securing the office of Commissary for him, and was disappointed at his failure to get it. *Boswell Papers*, xi. 6, 18.

Page 366, lines 19 ff., and page 367. The monument to Smollett is situated at the west end of the town of Renton. It was erected in 1773, not 1774, as is sometimes stated : the Edinburgh periodical, *The Weekly Magazine*, reports under date 9 Sept. 1773 (xxi. 351) :

' James Smollett of Bonhill, Esq: has erected an elegant monument, sacred to the memory of the late Dr Tobias Smollett, a gentleman well known in the literary world ; and an inscription is preparing for the same. This monument is erected near Loch Lomond, about two miles from Cameron, on the banks of the beautiful water of Leven, the place where the doctor was born.'

Views of the monument are given in T. Garnett's *Observations on a Tour through the Highlands* (1800), R. Anderson's edition of Smollett's *Misc. Works*, vol. i (1817), and Joseph Irving's *Book of Dumbartonshire*, vol. ii (1879)—in the last-named book as it appeared about 1777.

It appears from a memorandum at Cameron House that several inscriptions were submitted to Mr. Smollett. That chosen was composed by Prof. George Stuart, of Edinburgh University ; Lord Kames was not satisfied with the first four lines, and these were replaced by the opening lines of the inscription written by John Ramsay of Ochtertyre. Lord Kames himself, in submitting an English inscription, which he describes as ' no more but giff-gaff ', said, 11 Oct. 1773, ' the inscription ought to be in English, that all may read ; and it ought to be simple and clear, that all may understand '. R. Chambers, *Trad. Edinb.*, 1825, i. 279 ; Joseph Irving, *Book of Dumbartonshire*, 1879, ii. 200 ff. ; and John Ramsay of Ochtertyre, *Scotland and Scotsmen in 18th c.*, 1888, i. 311.

Major-General Telfer-Smollett, to whom I am greatly obliged, informs me that he has among his papers one which is described as ' The original inscription copied in a clerk's hand, with the corrections as made by Dr. Johnson apparently in his autograph '. Coleridge de-

Pages 368-9 *Appendix D* 565

scribed the latinity of the inscription as 'miserably bad'. Dorothy Wordsworth, *Recollections of a Tour in Scotl.*, 1874, p. 63.

Page 368, lines 2 ff. William Hay's Martial (*Select Epigrams of Martial, Translated and Imitated*) was published by the Dodsleys in 1755. According to the publishers' Advertisement they were 'at the expence of two different impressions . . ., to accommodate the reader. One is in Octavo; with the English only. . . . The other is in Duodecimo; with the original in the opposite page'. Hay introduced Dodsley into two of his 'translations'.

Page 369, line 1. The Saracen's Head Inn stood on the north side of the Gallowgate on the site of the pre-Reformation churchyard of St. Mungo. The original inn was built in 1755, as the following notice in *The Glasgow Courant* of 27 October 1755 shows:

'Robert Tennent, who formerly kept the White Hart Inn, without the Gallowgate Port, is removed to the Saracen's Head, where the Port formerly stood. He takes this opportunity to acquaint all Ladies and Gentlemen that, at the desire of the Magistrates of Glasgow, he has built a convenient and handsome new Inn, agreeable to a Plan given him, containing thirty-six Fire-Rooms, now fit to receive Lodgers. The Bed-Chambers are all separate, none of them entering through another, and so contrived that there is no need of going out of doors to get to them. The Beds are all very good, clean, and free from Bugs.'

in John McUre's *Glasghu Facies*, ed. J. F. S. Gordon, 1872, i. 550.

Tennent died in 1757, a bankrupt. His widow carried on till her death in 1768. The inn was then sold to James Graham, who died, a bankrupt, in 1771. *Glasgow Jrnl.* 3 Oct. 1771 and John McUre's *Glasghu Facies*, ed. J. F. S. Gordon, 1872, ii. 834. Mrs. Graham succeeded and she was the landlady when Johnson stayed there. *Glasgow Jrnl.* 4. Nov. 1773. The original inn was replaced by a new one early in the nineteenth century—it was a 'new building' in 1803 when the Wordsworths stayed in it (Dorothy Wordsworth's *Recollections of a Tour in Scotland*, 1874, p. 52)—which was demolished some time between 1905 and 1908.

I am greatly indebted to Dr. W. R. Cunningham († 25 Oct. 1953), of the University Library, Glasgow, and to Mr. R. H. Small of Glasgow, for aid in writing this note.

Page 369, line 12. Dr. Alexander Stevenson (M.D. 1749) was Professor of the Practice of Medicine at Glasgow, 1766-89: he died 29 May 1791. W. Innes Addison, *Roll of Graduates of the Univ. of Glasgow*, 1898, p. 578.

Page 369, line 12. John Anderson was born at Rosneath, Dumbartonshire, where his father was minister, in 1726. He matriculated at Glasgow in 1741 and took his M.A. in 1745; he was elected Professor of Oriental Languages in 1755 and transferred to the Chair of Natural Philosophy in 1757. He died 13 Jan. 1796, leaving practically 'the whole of his property of every sort for the good of mankind and the improvement of science in an institution to be denominated "Anderson's University".' The Andersonian or, as it has been variously called, Anderson's Institution (1797–1828), Anderson's University (1828–77), Anderson's College (1877–87), was incorporated in 1797, and in 1887 amalgamated with kindred institutions, when it was denominated the Glasgow and West of Scotland Technical College : it is now affiliated to the University of Glasgow. See Hew Scott, *Fasti Eccl. Scot.* vii. 406 ; W. Innes Addison, *Matriculation Albums of the Univ. of Glasgow*, 1913, p. 26 ; A. Humboldt Sexton, *The First Technical College*, 1894 ; and the *D.N.B.*

Anderson, who was a strong anti-Jacobite and a supporter of the French Revolution, was a difficult colleague. In 1775 he brought an action against Prof. Traill and other professors of the University alleging particularly that the accounts of the University were improperly kept. See *Process of Declarator concerning the Management of the Revenues of Glasgow College*, 1778 : the action failed.

Page 371, line 5 from foot. The Dowager Countess of Loudoun was Margaret, third daughter of John Dalrymple, 1st Earl of Stair : she was born in August 1684, married Hugh Campbell, 3rd Earl of Loudoun, 6 April 1700, and died 3 April 1779. Sir James Balfour Paul, *Scots Peerage*, 1911, viii. 151. Johnson, in the long letter to Mrs. Thrale, 3 Nov. 1773, which he calls his ' narrative ', gives a picture of this vigorous lady, whose age he over-estimated.

'We dined [30th Oct.] with the Earl of Loudon, and saw his Mother the Countess, who at ninety three has all her faculties, helps at table, and exerts all the powers of conversation she ever had. Though not tall, she stoops very much. She had lately a daughter, Lady Betty, whom at seventy, she used to send after supper early to bed, for girls must not use late hours, while she sat up to entertain the company.' *Letters*, No. 337.

Page 372, lines 4 ff. and note 3. Lord Loudoun was not a successful soldier. His attempt to capture Prince Charles at Moy Castle in Feb. 1746 was foiled by a simple ruse, and the force under his command was completely dispersed by the Duke of Perth at Dornoch in the following month. He was appointed Governor of Virginia and C.-in-C. in America in 1756, but was recalled next year. According to Lord Shelburne, he was ' a mere pen and ink man ', and so dilatory that an American said of him that he was ' like Saint George upon the signposts, always on horseback but never advancing '. See A. C. Ewald, *Prince Charles Stuart*, 1883, pp. 214 ff. ; Lord E. Fitzmaurice, *Life of Shelburne*, 1912, i. 63 ; W. B. Blaikie, *Origins of the '45*, p. 108 ; and the *D.N.B.*

Page 372, lines 5 ff. from foot. James Campbell of Treesbank married firstly, in 1764, Helen McCredie, and secondly, in 1768, Mary, daughter of David Montgomerie of Lainshaw, Mrs. Boswell's sister. He died 23 Oct. 1776 and his wife died 4 March 1777. There are many references to him and his wife in Boswell's Journal : see F. A. Pottle, *Index*

Pages 373-4 *Appendix D* 567

to the *Private Papers of James Boswell* (1937). See also G. Robertson, *Genealogical Acct. of Principal Families in Ayrshire*, 1824, ii. 242 ; and J. Paterson, *History of County of Ayr*, 1852, ii. 412.

Page 373, line 1. John Campbell, brother of the above, was licensed in 1738 and ordained to Riccarton in 1739 : he died 3 April 1761. Hew Scott, *Fasti Eccl. Scot.* iii. 64. Boswell records in his Journal, 10 March 1777 :

'We had a very creditable interment of worthy Mrs. Campbell. . . . It was striking that in digging her grave the sculls of the first Mrs. Campbell (Nelly Macredie) and of my good friend, The Reverend Mr. John Campbell, were thrown out.' *Boswell Papers*, xii. 142.

Page 373, lines 3 ff. Sir John Cuninghame, or Cunningham, of Caprington, third baronet, married, 1749, Lady Elizabeth Montgomerie, eldest daughter of Alexander, ninth Earl of Eglintoune. He died 30 Nov. 1777. *Burke's Peerage and Baronetage*, 1934, p. 687. For Caprington Castle, which has been greatly altered since Boswell's time, see Macgibbon and Ross, *Castellated and Domestic Architecture of Scotland*, 1892, v. 243-6.

Alexander Cuninghame, or Cunningham, the critic and editor of Horace, was born *c.* 1655 and died at The Hague in Dec. 1730. His criticism of Bentley (*Animadversiones in Richardi Bentleii Notas et Emendationes ad Q. Horatium Flaccum*) was a companion volume to his edition of the text of Horace ; both were first published at The Hague in 1721. Monk describes the *Animadversiones*, which is dedicated to Bentley, as ' one continued objurgation, delivered in dry and bitter terms, unvaried by the least humour or playfulness ; it is the effusion of a person who feels an advantage in the contest, and thinks that his own superior industry and research have given him a right to scold and insult his adversary without forbearance '. *Life of Bentley*, 1830, p. 462. Monk thought highly of Cuninghame's edition of Horace. *Ibid.* p. 464. He was erroneously identified with Alexander Cunningham, 1654-1737, the historian, by Dr. W. Thomson, who, in 1787, translated and published the latter's *History of Great Britain.* See Thomson's letter to Parr, 24 Oct. 1787 (Parr's *Works*, 1828, vii. 565) ; *Scots Magazine*, Oct. 1804, pp. 731-4, and the *D.N.B.* under Cunningham, Alexander (1654-1737).

Page 374, lines 4 ff. Lady Eglintoune was Susanna, daughter of Sir Archibald Kennedy, first baronet, of Culzean. She married, as his third wife, Alexander, ninth Earl of Eglintoune, in June 1709. She died 18 March 1780, aged 92, ' having preserved the stately mien and beautiful complexion to the last '. She was an ardent Jacobite. In her old age she became eccentric and amused herself by taming rats. R. Chambers, *Traditions of Edinburgh*, 1869, pp. 210 ff. See also Johnson's *Letters*, No. 337.

Her jointure house was Auchans Castle, Old Auchans, four miles from Troon. See Macgibbon and Ross, *Castellated and Domestic Architecture of Scotland*, 1887, ii. 174–9.

Alexander, her son, the tenth Earl of Eglintoune, was born 10 Feb. 1723. He was Governor of Dumbarton Castle, 1759–61, Lord of the Bedchamber, 1760–7, and a Representative Peer of Scotland, 1761–9. G. E. C., *Compl. Peerage*, 1926, v. 24. He was shot by Mungo Campbell on 24 Oct. 1769: see *ante*, iii. 188. Lord Holland had a very poor opinion of him: writing of his appointment as Lord of the Bedchamber, he says: ' Everybody was asham'd and vex'd to see so worthless and silly a wretch so placed.' *Memoir* in *Life and Letters of Lady Sarah Lennox*, ed. Countess of Ilchester and Lord Stavordale, 1901, i, p. 17. Boswell had very good reason to speak well of him. John Ramsay of Ochtertyre reports:

' Having eloped from Edinburgh, Alexander, Earl of Eglinton, discovered him [Boswell] by chance in London in very bad company. He took the young man to his own house, and thinking it the best way of redeeming him from wrong connections, gave him a Pisgah view of the gay world.' *Scotland and Scotsmen in the 18th c.*, 1889, i. 171.

Boswell actually ' eloped ' from Glasgow, not Edinburgh, in March 1760. *Hebrides*, ed. Pottle and Bennett, 1936, p. 48, note 2.

There are many references to him in Boswell's journal: see F. A. Pottle, *Index to the Private Papers of James Boswell* (1937). See also *ante*, ii. 66 and Boswell's *Hebrides*, 1962, pp. 438–9.

Page 377, lines 10 ff. and note 3. There is in the *Scots Magazine* (Nov. 1773, vol. xxxv. 613) a brief record of Johnson's tour. It concludes:

'In his travels through Scotland, proper attention was paid him by the great and the learned. It is said, that being asked how he liked his entertainment in the highlands, he answered, " The sauce to every thing was the benevolence of the inhabitants, which cannot be enough praised. I love the people better than the country." '

Page 380, last line. Alexander Fairlie of Fairlie succeeded his father in 1744. ' He was a gentleman of much ability and public spirit, taking an active part in the affairs of the county. He took a prominent lead in promoting agricultural improvement.' James Paterson, *Hist. of the Counties of Ayr and Wigton*, 1863, vol. i. 478. He instructed Boswell in farming, and in 1791 lent him £1,500 for the purchase of Knockroon. *Boswell Papers*, xv. 130–1, xvi. 69, and xviii. 107, and *Fettercairn Catalogue*, 1936, No. 333. In the confidential report drawn up in the Whig interest in 1788 is the following account of him:

' Batchelor, very rich; entire manager for the Earl of Eglinton, whose estate he has restored. Uncle to Sir W. Cuninghame of Robertland and to M'Adam of Craigengillan's wife. Will go with Lord Eglinton, and support at next election Sir Adam [Fergusson].' Sir C. Elphinstone Adam, *View of the political state of Scotland*, 1887, p. 31.

Pages 381-2   *Appendix D*   569

He died, unmarried, at an advanced age, in 1803. J. Paterson, *o.c.s.* 478. The family has long been extinct. J. Paterson, *Hist. of the County of Ayr*, 1852, ii. 302.

Fairlie House, the family mansion, which stood on the south bank of the Irvine water, about three miles from Kilmarnock, was the scene of the ballad of *Hardyknute* (*ante*, ii. 91) : it is now (1937) a ruin. See J. Paterson, *Hist. of the Counties of Ayr and Wigton*, 1863, i. 479.

Page 381, lines 20 ff. The Reverend John Dun was educated at the University of Edinburgh ; he was licensed on 11 Sept. 1750 and ordained to Auchinleck on 9 Nov. 1752. Hew Scott, *Fasti Eccl. Scot.* 1920, iii. 4. Boswell, who received his early religious training from him, did not think very highly of him, but their relations were generally cordial.

Dun published his *Sermons* in two volumes at Kilmarnock in 1790 ; in which are contained some poetical effusions, including ' The Deil's answer to his verra Friend, R. Burns ', and some letters. He makes (vol. ii. 64) a curious apology for having mentioned in an Advertisement a gift by the Earl and Countess of Dumfries for distribution among the poor of Auchinleck :

' I was impelled to it by feeling a greater weight of their humanity, and of the generosity of the family, than I was at liberty to particularize. I could instance more five pounds than one of theirs, which have been distributed in charity to the poor of this parish ; and even five pounds was a most refreshing thing to the poor at that season.'

His manuscript was not revised by Boswell or any other person (vol. ii, Errata slip). He also wrote the account of the parish of Auchinleck in Sinclair's *Statistical Account*, xi. 430-4, the inadequacy of which is explained by his death before publication. He died on 16 Oct. 1792, aged 68. For numerous references to him in Boswell's journal see Prof. F. A. Pottle's *Index* (1937) ; see also *Fettercairn Catalogue*, Nos. 308-10, 1102, and Boswell's *Letters*, 1924, pp. 240, 374, 387, 491.

Page 382, note 2. John Ramsay of Ochtertyre, who knew Lord Auchinleck intimately and venerated his memory, left a long account of him ; in this he wrote :

' It was assuredly one of the cruellest mortifications [Lord Auchinleck] could have met with in the evening of life, to see his son entirely under the influence of a Tory and High Churchman. . . . No wonder, then, that his lordship should consider the Doctor as the person who had misled his son. . . . Two such antipodes could hardly meet without quarrelling.' *Scotland and Scotsmen in the 18th c.*, 1888, i. 175.

Of the quarrel itself Ramsay had no special knowledge. He says :

' Considering Boswell's preposterous passion for recording private conversation, he deserves credit for withholding from the public the angry dialogue that passed between his father and the Doctor. Yet amidst all his professions of filial reverence, it is plain he thinks his father had the worst of the argument.' *Ibid.* p. 176.

Boswell made no record of the altercation at the time and wrote his short account of it in 1785, when he was preparing his Journal for publication. Professor Pottle says that the account Scott gave to Croker ' should be read as historical fiction, not as a record of fact ', *Hebrides*, ed. Pottle and Bennett, 1936, p. 375 note. See *post*, v., Addenda.

John Ramsay reports that in the year after the altercation took place Lord Auchinleck told him ' at Stirling, with more warmth than common, that the great Dr. Johnson of whom he had heard wonders, was just a *dominie*, and the worst-bred dominie he had ever seen '. *Scotland and Scotsmen in the 18th c.*, 1888, i. 176 note.

Page 385, line 9. The ' good inn ' at Hamilton was almost certainly the present ' Hamilton Arms ', sometimes known as the ' Old Head Inn ' : it is situated close by the site of the Palace on what was until 1830 the main street of the town. It was described in 1771 by David Henry, an observer who was not easily pleased, as ' tolerable ' :

' Hamilton Arms, Burns ; tolerable.—The landlord, from pure insipidity, will laugh at you if you come in wet through ; yet he can tell a good deal about the Duke's family.' *Gent. Mag.* 1771, xli. 545.

Dorothy Wordsworth, in 1803, said ' it was a townish place, with a great larder set out ; the house throughout dirty '. *Recollections of a Tour in Scotland*, 1874, p. 45.

Page 385, lines 12 ff. Pennant describes Hamilton Palace as ' a large disagreeable pile, with two deep wings at right angles with the centre : the gallery is of great extent, furnished (as well as some other rooms) with most excellent paintings '. *Tour in Scotl. and Voy. to Hebrides*, 1774, p. 122. A full description of the paintings follows. Dorothy Wordsworth, who with her brother and Coleridge was refused admission to the Palace in 1803, describes it as ' a large building, without grandeur, a heavy lumpish mass '. *Recollections of a Tour in Scotland*, 1874, p. 45.

Mr. W. Crawford, the Town Clerk of Hamilton, informs me that the Palace was sold to a contractor for demolition in or soon after October 1921, but that some of the buildings have not yet (1938) been removed. The Town Council of Hamilton purchased, in 1924, the Hamilton Low Parks, in which the Palace and Mausoleum were situated, from the Hamilton Trustees for £20,250. For an account of the town and Palace, see *Hamilton Past and Present* (1932).

Page 386, lines 1 ff. and note 1. Patrick Murray, fifth Baron Elibank, was born in 1703. He was educated at Edinburgh University and admitted, 22 June 1723, a member of the Faculty of Advocates. He succeeded his father in 1736. He was gazetted a Major in Ponsonby's

Page 386   *Appendix D*   571

Foot (26th Regiment of Foot or Cameronians) on 11 Aug. 1737, and promoted Lieut.-Colonel in Wynard's Marines, one of the new battalions recruited for service in Spain, in 1739 : he was invalided home next year, when he resigned his commission. He married, in 1735, a rich heiress, Maria Margaretta, the daughter of Cornelius de Jonge, Lord of Elmeet in Holland, and widow of William North, Lord North and Baron Grey of Rolleston : she died in 1763. (For Johnson's Latin translation of Lord Elibank's English epitaph to his wife, see *ante*, iv. 10 and 477.) Lord Elibank's account of the expedition against Carthagena is preserved, in the first of two volumes of dispatches about the expedition, in the Public Record Office : this consists of 41 foolscap pages. Other writings, copies of which he promised to give to Johnson (*ante*, ii. 275), are chiefly anonymous pamphlets ; the following is a list of those I have been able to discover : *An Inquiry into the original of the Public Debt*. By a Person of Distinction, 1753. *Essays : Of the Public Debt ; On Paper Money ; On Frugality*. [Anon.], 1755. *Thoughts on Money, Circulation, and Paper Currency*. [Anon.], 1758. *Queries relating to the proposed Plan for altering the Entails in Scotland*. [Anon.], 1765. *Considerations on the Present State of the Peerage of Scotland*. By a Peer of Scotland, 1770. *A Letter to Sir David Dalrymple on his Remarks on the History of Scotland*. [Anon.], 1775. *Eight Sets of Queries upon the Subject of Wool and of the Woollen Manufacture*. By a Peer of the Realm, 1775.

He died 3 Aug. 1778 and, having no legitimate children, was succeeded by his younger brother, George. The eldest of his six natural children, William Young (so named at the wish of Lady Elibank), rose to high office in the service of the East India Co. See Col. Arthur C. Murray, *The Five Sons of 'Bare Betty'*, 1936, pp. 35 ff., and, for Lord Elibank's letters to his son, pp. 159 ff., John Ramsay of Ochtertyre, *Scotland and Scotsmen in the 18th c.*, 1889, i. 318 ff., and G. E. C., *Complete Peerage*, 1926, v. 47.

Lord Elibank's knowledge greatly impressed Johnson : ' I never am ', he told Boswell on 1 April 1772, ' with Lord Elibank but I learn something.' *Boswell Papers*, ix. 53. That this knowledge was worldly is shown by his later pronouncements :

' Lord Elibank's great excellence was not his having read a great many books ... ; but it was his having improved his knowledge by being much in the World.' 16 April 1775. *Ibid*. x. 219.
' Lord Elibank has acquired much knowledge by comparison of books with life.' 13 May 1776. *Ibid*. xi. 281.

Of his conversation, however, he did not think so highly : ' Sir, there is nothing *conclusive* in his talk.' *Ante*, iii. 57. In Johnson's diary discovered at Malahide Castle in 1936, and now, 1964, in the Hyde collection, is the entry, under date 28 Jan. 1765, 'L. Ellibank. Lady Shelburne'. This is the earliest reference known to me of Johnson's acquaintance with Lord Elibank.

Page 387, lines 17-18. The Lady Dowager Colville was Elisabeth Erskine, daughter of Alexander, fifth Earl of Kellie, and his second wife, the daughter of Dr. Alexander Pitcairne. She married firstly Walter Macfarlane, the antiquary, who died in 1767 (see *D:N.B.*), and secondly Alexander, seventh Baron Colville of Culross, who died 21 May 1770. She died 2 Nov. 1794 in her 60th year. See Sir James Balfour Paul, *Scots Peerage*, 1908, v. 89. She was one of the many ladies for whom Boswell had a passion. *Boswell Papers*, i. 133 and xii. 88.

Her younger sister, Anne, was born 18 Feb. 1735 and died unmarried on 18 March 1802. See Sir James Balfour Paul, *op. cit.*

These ladies were Boswell's lifelong friends and there are many references to them in his Journal. See Prof. F. A. Pottle's *Index* (1937). The Hon. Andrew Erskine (*ante*, i. 383 note 3, 408 and iii. 150) was their brother.

Page 388, lines 9 ff. and note 2. The publication of this anecdote in its original form caused much trouble. 'Young Mr. Tytler' thought that Boswell's intention was malicious: he was deeply offended and made a discourteous request for a correction of the passage in accordance with the terms of the copy he himself suggested. Boswell, who appears to have been under the impression that Tytler had no objection to the insertion of the anecdote, agreed to the revised form, but, in his turn, was offended by Tytler's rude letter, for which he demanded an apology: this was, somewhat reluctantly, given. See *Fettercairn Catalogue*, 1936, Nos. 792-4, 985-6, 1288-9, 1300-1, 1453. Boswell asked Dr. Barnard to see that the passage was corrected in the Dublin edition, and was even prepared to pay for its cancellation. *Ibid.*, No. 1150.

See also *Boswell Papers*, xvi. 137, 140, 241.

For A. F. Tytler, later Lord Woodhouselee, see the *D.N.B.*

Page 389, line 5 and note 1. Boswell records in his Journal, under date 21 March 1775, Johnson's strongly-worded opinion that Scotsmen generally preferred Scotland to truth :

'I mentioned David Hume's Observation that he would not believe the authenticity of *Fingal*, though fifty barearsed highlanders should swear it. "No", said Mr. Johnson, "nor though fifty lowlanders should ; for you know that all Scotsmen to a man—nay, not all, but *Droves* of 'em—would come and attest any thing which they think for the honour of Scotland."' *Boswell Papers*, x. 134.

Page 390, lines 16 ff. The cause, *John Wilson and others*, contra *Archibald Maclean*, was tried in 1777. According to the *Pursuer's Memorial* (Advocates' Library : Session Papers, Campbell's Collection,

Pages 391-4   *Appendix D*   573

vol. 33, No. 22), Sir Allan Maclean was examined on 14 June 1777, when

' the defender produced a letter from the deponent, dated 6th of February 1775. . . . And it being observed by the Court, that said letter contained a variety of other particulars beside those now deponed to by the deponent, depones, That in writing said letter, which he did at the defender's desire, he did not imagine that it was to be produced, or made use of as evidence in this cause ; nor did he, the deponent, expect that himself was to be adduced as a witness therein; and that there are several particulars in said letter, to the truth of which the deponent would not depone ' (p. 157).

See also *Memorial for Archibald M'Lean in Laggan, Ulva*, ... against *John Wilson*, 1777. (Signet Library: Old Session Papers, vol. 595, No. 12.) I owe these references to Mr. W. Beattie and Dr. C. A. Malcolm. See also *Boswell Papers*, xiii. 79-82.

Page 391, line 7 from foot. Dr. John Erskine, 1721-1803, was the colleague of Dr. William Robertson at the Old Greyfriars and opposed to him in Church policy and doctrine. ' He was a man of great influence in his day, well known for his literary and theological works, as well as for his piety and practical benevolence.' James Nasmyth, *Autobiog.*, 1885, p. 21. Boswell, who ' engaged ' him to baptize his son Alexander, apostrophized him as ' that primitive Saint '. *Boswell Papers*, x. 237 and 246. Scott describes him and his style of preaching in *Guy Mannering*, ch. xxxvii. See the *D.N.B.*

Dr. Robert Walker was born in 1716, educated at the University of Edinburgh, licensed 6 April 1737, and ordained to Straiton 14 Sept. 1738: he was appointed minister of the second charge, South Leith, 20 Nov. 1746, and translated to the High Church (or New Church), Edinburgh, 10 Oct. 1754, where he had Dr. Hugh Blair as his colleague. He was Moderator of the General Assembly in 1771. He died 6 April 1783 and was buried in Greyfriars Churchyard. Hew Scott, *Fasti Eccl. Scot.* 1915, i. 60, and W. Pitcairn Anderson, *Silences that Speak*, 1931, p. 484. Mr. Walker was Calvinistic in his views, and ' an enemy to many public amusements ', particularly the theatre. Like Boswell he considered Foote's *Minor* ' profane ', and he attacked it from the pulpit. His sermons, of which a collected edition, in four volumes, appeared in 1784-96, with a ' character ' of the author by Blair, were popular. See J. Kay's *Original Portraits*, 1877, i. 347-9. Boswell records in his Journal that his father, his step-mother, and he himself, at different times (1777, 1780, and 1784), read his sermons. *Boswell Papers*, xii. 155, xiv. 27, xvi. 61. He is frequently confused with a contemporary of the same names who was minister of the Canongate.

Page 394, line 20. ' Mr. Menzies of Culdares ' was either James Menzies or, more probably, his son Archibald, both of whom were living in 1773 and both would be styled ' of Culdares ', the father being the life renter, the son the fear. James Menzies died in 1776. Archibald was one of the Scottish Commissioners of Customs from 4 May 1770 till his death 23 Oct. 1777. Boswell got ' sadly intoxicated ' at his house on 28 June 1777, and records dining with his widow on 25 March 1794. See *Gent. Mag.* Oct. 1777, xlvii. 508, and *Boswell Papers*, xii. 204 and xviii. 270. Mr. R. H. Lindsay, to whom I am greatly obliged, informs me from documents in the General Register House, Edinburgh, that Archibald Menzies married, 17 Oct. 1776, Frances, only daughter of John Rutherford of North Carolina, and that she became the wife of Alexander Shaw, store-keeper, of Plymouth, 15 Oct. 1790.

Page 394, line 3 from foot. Boswell's uncle, Dr. John Boswell, was born in 1707. He graduated M.D. at Leyden in 1736 and was made a Fellow of the Royal College of Physicians, Edinburgh, in August 1748 ; he was Treasurer from December 1748 to December 1756 and again from August 1758 to December 1763 ; he was elected President in December 1770. See Sir W. Hale-White in *Proc. R. Soc. Med.*, Jan. 1930, p. 283. He became a Sandemanian or Glassite and thereby lost his practice (see *ante*, ii. 466, where he is not actually named, and *Boswell Papers*, xi. 192–3), but was excommunicated for immorality (*Boswell Papers*, xii. 173)—he is the licentious sectary described by Boswell in March 1776 under the disguise of ' an acquaintance of mine ' (see *ante*, ii. 472–3, and cf. *Boswell Papers*, xi. 193). He was living near the Meadows when Johnson visited him, in a house which Boswell afterwards rented (*ante*, iii. 116, and *Boswell Papers*, xii. 135). The position of this house is given in Williamson's *Edinburgh Directory* for 1773–4 (1889, p. 6) as ' back of the meadow '; the house is now No. 15a Meadow Place. See W. Forbes Gray in *The Scotsman*, 18 Nov. 1940.

Boswell and he were on the best of terms and there are many references to him in Boswell's Journal : see Prof. F. A. Pottle's *Index* (1937). See also *ante*, i. 437, v. 48, and, for Dr. Boswell's description of Johnson, iii. 7. Dr. Boswell died 15 May 1780 (*Boswell Papers*, xiv. 79).

Page 399, lines 18 ff. and note 2. Thomas Braidwood, 1715–1806, opened his 'Academy for the deaf and dumb ' in 1760, when he had a single pupil ; in 1783 he had as many as twenty pupils, most of whom came from England. The house was situate on St. Leonard's Hill, under Arthur's Seat, and is now (1937) divided into tenements and numbered Nos. 93 and 95 Dumbiedykes Road. For accounts of the school see Johnson's *Western Islands*, 1924, pp. 147 ff. ; Monboddo's *Origin of Language*, 1773, i. 179 ff., Pennant's *Tour in Scotland, Pt. II*, 1776, pp. 256 ff. ; Arnot's *Hist. of Edinb.*, 1779, p. 425 ; and Francis Green's ' *Vox Oculis Subjecta* ', 1783, pp. 135 ff. Mr. W. Forbes Gray, who kindly pointed the house out to me, tells me that he was in error in

Page 401   *Appendix D*   575

identifying it with Peffermill House in his book *An Edinburgh Miscellany* (1925, p. 228). Braidwood in 1783 removed to Hackney. See the *D.N.B.*

Page 401, lines 5 ff. Sir Alexander Dick (*ante*, v. 48) lived at Prestonfield, near Duddingston, at the foot of Arthur's Seat ; the mansion, which was built by Sir James Dick, Provost of Edinburgh, in 1687, from the designs of Sir William Bruce, is still in the possession of the Dick-Cunyngham family.

The ' young lady of quality ' whose compliment so delighted Johnson was, as Malone pointed out, Lady Anne Lindsay. She was the eldest child of James, fifth Earl of Balcarres, and his wife, the daughter of Sir Alexander Dick's sister Anne. She was born in 1750 and, in 1793, ' stood the world's smile ', as she herself expressed it, by marrying Andrew Barnard, son of Johnson's friend Dr. Barnard (*ante*, i. 479, iii. 84, iv. 115, &c.) and her junior by twelve years. (See Dorothea Fairbridge, *Lady Anne Barnard in the Cape of Good Hope*, 1924, and the *D.N.B.* s.v. Barnard, Anne.) She was staying with her great-uncle at the time of Johnson's visit and sent an account of it to her sister, Lady Margaret Fordyce, which she amplified when she wrote her ' Memoirs ' in 1815 onwards. Her version of the conversation in which she took so prominent a part differs considerably from Boswell's. She writes :

' He [Johnson] told us that the old Countess of Eglinton always called him " Son ", as he was born the year after she was married.—" No ", said Boswell, " the year before Sir "—" Had that been the case " said Johnson, " she would have had little to boast of "—" Would not the *son* have excused the *sin* " said I, " Doctor ? " The dose took. He became excessively agreeable & entertaining.'

She adds in a parenthesis :

' I saw Boswell steal to the window to put down the *jeu de mot* in his commonplace book.—Little did I expect however to see it in print afterwards, tho' without my name accompanying it; he states it however in his tour thro' Scotland, as a compliment which gratified Johnson so much, that he often reminded him of it, to put him in good humour.'

It was not Boswell's practice to make notes in public, although he occasionally did so (see *Boswell Papers*, vi. 19 ff.) : the latter part of the statement is clearly inaccurate.

Lady Anne concludes her account by saying :

'Amongst the variety of our conversation, which I forget in its quantity, I remember only what Dr. J. said of the great Burke, the orator and statesman— " Is he " said my Uncle, " so distinguished a speaker, Doctor, as I have heard, in point of expression and imagination ? " The Doctor see-sawed with his person as he generally does when preparing a reply—" Burke " said he, " is unequal—he is a lion, who lashes himself into a fury with his own tail, Sir ". And now having said so much of this great Ursus Major, I will quote the words of Mr. Newberry—" See here he is "—I stole his likeness as he spoke and have finished it since—he seems to have a thousand enemies (the poor Bear) but in spite of something very uncouth about him, such as I have described, I see a goodness of heart and simplicity of mind, that might be engaging in him if he did not offend the nerves and senses in twenty ways.'

Lady Anne had evidently read and imperfectly remembered Boswell's description of his introduction to Johnson by Davies (*ante*, i. 391).

The manuscript of Lady Anne's ' Memoirs '. is in the possession of the Earl of Crawford and Balcarres, and I have great pleasure in thanking him for his courtesy in allowing me to print the above extracts from it.

Sir Alexander Dick's daughter Mary told her grandson, Sir Colin Scott-Moncrieff, that on this visit Johnson took her on his knee and said, ' Child, can ye read yet ? ' Mary Albright Hollings, *Life of Sir Colin C. Scott-Moncrieff*, 1917, p. 23. Cf. *ante*, ii. 238, note 5, for another instance of Johnson's fatherly interest in a child's reading.

Page 404, line 15. The inn at Blackshiels was about 16 miles from Edinburgh on the road to Newcastle by Coldstream. It was described as ' good ' by a contributor to the *Gent. Mag.* in 1771 (xli. 543) and by Pennant, *Tour in Scotland, Pt. II*, 1776, p. 260. It is no longer an inn, but is used as farm buildings.

Boswell in 1774 thus describes the state of his mind after parting with Johnson at this inn :

> After Mr Samuel Johnson left me, which was on Monday the 22 of November, when we parted at Blackshiels, I was long in a state of languor. My mind had been kept upon it's utmost stretch in his company. I had exhausted all my powers to entertain him. While he was with me, his noble exuberance of genius excited my spirits to a high degree, so that I did not feel at the time how much I was weakened. I was like a man who drinks hard and is kept in high glee by what is wasting his constitution, but perceives it's enfeebling effects as soon as he lives without it. I was not, however, in a state of despondency. I waited patiently till my force should be restored.' *Boswell Papers*, ix. 117.

Page 409, line 3 from foot and note 3. George Dempster, 1732–1818, known as ' Honest George ', was M.P. in the Whig interest for Forfar Burghs almost continuously from 1761 to 1790 ; he was not a keen party man and used his position, in Parliament and out, to promote or support measures for the improvement of Scottish industries. He was mainly responsible for the Act for erecting lighthouses on the Scottish coasts, 1786, and was, in the same year, one of the four founders of the Fishery Society, the chief aim of which was the establishment of fishing villages in the islands and on the west coast. He founded the village of Letham on his own estate, Dunnichen, near Forfar. A series of letters, covering a long period, to his most intimate friend, Sir Adam Fergusson (*ante*, ii. 169), has been published by Mr. James Fergusson (*Letters of George Dempster to Sir Adam Fergusson, 1756–1813*, 1934) : it is significant that Boswell is never mentioned in them. See *ante*, i. 408 ff., 440 ff. ; ii. 303, 305 ; iii. 301 ; the *D.N.B.* ; and Prof. Pottle's

Pages 411-13   *Appendix D*   577

Index to the Boswell Papers, for numerous references to him. He was a member of the 'jury' which sat on and applauded Boswell's *Tour* at Malone's house 22 Sept. 1785 (*ante*, v. 1 note 5 *ad finem*).

Page 411, line 25. Miss Flora Macleod of Raasay dined with Boswell and his wife three times during her visit to Edinburgh in 1775, on 28 January, 28 February, and 7 March. *Boswell Papers*, x. 89, 107, 111. On the first-mentioned date Boswell wrote:

'Lady Colville and Lady Anne Erskine, Miss MacLeod of Raasay, and Mrs. Vernon, with whom she lodged, . . . dined with us. . . . My wife and I had called for Miss McLeod, but missed her. I was pleased at seeing her again, and she appeared as well at Edinburgh as in Raasay.'

Miss Macleod married Colonel James Mure Campbell, later fifth Earl of Loudoun, on 30 April 1777, and died 2 September 1780; see *ante*, iii. 118 and v. 178.

Page 413, note 3. Boswell lent the original manuscript of his Journal, or rather that part of it which he had written during the tour, to Sir William Forbes, twice: the first occasion was in 1775. He wrote in his diary on 1 January of that year:

'I drank tea by special appointment with worthy Sir William Forbes, to let him read my *Hebrides Journal* to prepare him for Mr. Johnson's Book. He was much entertained, and I left him my three volumes, after reading him a great deal.' *Boswell Papers*, x. 75.

Sir William returned the volumes within a few days and was impatient for the rest of the Journal. *Fettercairn Catalogue*, No. 351. Boswell, on 6 January, sent him nine more sheets, probably all that he had, and told him that as he did not complete the manuscript at the time he must finish the account from memory. *Ibid.* No. 1320. Boswell lent his Journal to Forbes for the second time on 24 February 1777—both he and Forbes seem to have forgotten the previous loan—and particularly requested that he would neither copy nor communicate any part of it. *Ibid.* No. 1321. On 27 March Forbes called on Boswell and praised it highly—'we had no travels like it', was his verdict. *Boswell Papers*, xii. 160.

Lord Macdonald, in his letter to Boswell dated 26 November 1785 (see below), slyly alludes to the letter from Forbes that Boswell published as 'a Letter from a respectable person annexed to your publication who gives his sanction and approbation to the work in which he must have discovered his own just panegyric'. *Boswell Papers*, xvi. 237. Forbes at about the same time, 6 December, wrote to Boswell expressing his fear that the publication of this reciprocity of praise might cause criticism, and stating his own innocence. Whereupon Boswell, influenced perhaps by Macdonald's letter, added the note to the second edition and informed Forbes, 20 December, that he had made it quite

Appendix D — Page 415

clear that he was 'not consulted as to the publication' of the *Tour*. *Fettercairn Catalogue*, Nos. 355 and 1331.

Page 415, last line and note 4. The story of the quarrel between Boswell and Lord Macdonald over the *Tour* is fully and admirably told by Prof. F. A. Pottle in *Boswell Papers*, xvi. 221 ff., where the complete dossier of the numerous letters and notes is printed. Macdonald, who was very angry at the reflections made on him, sent Boswell an unsigned letter, dated 26 November 1785, of great length and extreme offensiveness. The following is a specimen of his invective and his style:

> 'Your violation of the acknowledged Laws of Hospitality by the wanton affront put upon me in it [the *Tour*] . . . is without a parallel in the annals of civilized nations, and could only have proceeded from a mind tainted with prejudices of the most dark and malignant kind, unsusceptible of the least spark of generosity and refinement, and accustomed to arrogate to itself a licence to treat mankind in general with indignity and insolence.' *Boswell Papers*, xvi. 233.

He asked for no apology, indeed he contended that no apology could ever 'wipe away' Boswell's 'aspersions'. 'It is not', he wrote, 'my intention to comment upon your mass of fabricated Apothegms . . ., [but] I think it is time to justify myself . . . from the obloquy with which it [the *Tour*] abounds.' He then proceeds to defend his views on emigration and to refute charges of parsimony. His intention was, according to his brother-in-law, William Bosville (*ante*, iii. 541), to frighten Boswell into an admission of inaccuracy and then to publish the correspondence. Boswell responded by informing Bosville, in an ostensible letter, of his suppression of the 'three exceptionable passages', and expressed regret for having printed them in the first edition. Macdonald remained silent, and Boswell, fearing the worst, wrote to him directly, giving him permission to publish the letter to Bosville, of which he enclosed a copy, on the express condition that he made no use of his own. Macdonald was obstinate and at first refused to comply, but after much negotiation and the threat of a challenge by Boswell, matters were accommodated. Macdonald agreed to expunge all the injurious passages in his original letter and produced what he ingeniously described as a 'second edition', stated to be 'the only surviving record which Lord Md. means at any time to use either publicly or privately in answer to Mr. Boswell's remarks upon him in his first Edition'. So far as is known he made no public use of this revised letter, but news of the affair was 'noised abroad' as early as 8 December. It was, therefore, as Prof. Pottle points out, 'not unnaturally concluded that Macdonald had forced Boswell to make the changes' in the second edition of the *Tour*, which appeared two weeks later. Boswell's statement to the contrary is amply vindicated.

Pages 419, 429   *Appendix D*   579

Page 419, lines 18 ff. and note 4. Lord Macdonald, formerly Sir Alexander Macdonald, reminded Boswell of his own verses: he was clearly piqued by his failure to mention them in the first edition. In the long letter of 26 November 1785, which nearly caused a duel between Boswell and himself (see above), he wrote

'I composed some congratulatory Alcaic verses in the room where you were minuting your Journal before dinner on the first day of your arrival, and presented them to yourself to read before you quitted your place. I asked you if you thought that Dr. Johnson would be pleased with such an oblation; you answered in the affirmative, and rose hastily to put them into his hand. When he had perused them he said I must have been bred at Eton, for they bore the Stamp of that Seminary. As they evinced my belief in the Originality of Fingal's poems, and contained a Compliment due to Mr. Macpherson, they have not been deemed worthy of any notice in your Memorabilia.' *Boswell Papers*. xvi. 234-5.

Boswell briefly noted in his original Journal on 3 September, the day after their arrival at Armadale, 'Sir Alexander composed today some Latin verses with which he presented Mr. Johnson.' He was, perhaps, too angry to read them. The friend who provided him with a copy was almost certainly William Bosville (*ante*, iii. 541), Lord Macdonald's brother-in-law. It was through him that Lord Macdonald gave Boswell permission to print the verses. *Fettercairn Catalogue*, No. 71.

Page 429, line 15 and note 6. Atlas, 'by Babraham (1752) out of a mare by Ld. Halifax's Justice' (*General Stud Book*, i. 416), was a famous horse: he won the King's Plate at York, Lincoln, and Newmarket on four occasions in 1758 and 1759, and other important races in the latter year; in 1760 he was beaten by Careless in 'a great subscription' race at York in a four-mile heat. See R. Heber's *Historical List of Horse-Matches* for the years in question, vols. viii. 49, 58, 71, ix. 4, 12, 71, and x. 49. In 1761 he, with the help of his jockey, beat his old rival, Careless. There is an account of the race in J. F. Sutton's *Date-book of remarkable and memorable Events connected with Nottingham*, 1852, p. 54.

'A race was run on the Nottingham course, which excited immense interest, a greater amount of money depending upon its issue, than upon any race ever run in the Midland counties. The horses were, John Borlase Warren Esq.'s Careless, and the Duke of Devonshire's famous horse Atlas: they were the best horses of the day, and had beaten all they had contended with. Careless was the Nottingham favourite, and on him the local sportsmen risked every shilling they could raise. The animals had once before met at York, on the 30th of August, 1760, when Atlas was beaten. It was then determined by the owners to try at Nottingham which of the two was really the best horse in England. Alas! for the "knowing ones" of Nottingham, Careless was second in the contest, the superior skill of his opponent's jockey having ensured the laurels for what was probably the worst horse.'

Thomas Holcroft (1745-1809), whose earliest occupation was that of a stable-boy, saw this race and described it in his *Memoirs*, posthumously published in 1816 : he thought it took place in 1756 or 1757 (*Memoirs*, i. 70 ff.).

There is an engraved portrait of Atlas by J. Miller after Shaw, dated 17 Jan. 1764.

Page 430, line 3. Mr. Francis Thompson, the Duke of Devonshire's librarian, has courteously supplied me with the following note :

' There have been at different times three inns at Edensor. (1) The ancient village inn at the south end of the former High Street. Owing to its proximity to the new Park Gates erected *c*. 1765, when the land west of the river was imparked, this inn was demolished and replaced by a parsonage (W. Bray, *Sketch of a Tour into Derbyshire*, &c., ed. 2, 1783, p. 168). When Bray first visited Chatsworth in or shortly before 1777 he found the inn "at the parkgate" (*ibid*. 1778, p. 98). (2) A house in the upper (still surviving) part of Edensor, on the west side of the green. This, being marked as " the Inn " in an estate-plan dated 1773, may be presumed to have taken the place of no. 1. (3) The fine red-brick building, just outside the present public entrance to the Park, which continued to serve as an inn till 1910. This does not appear in the 1773 plan but is described in unmistakable terms by Bray (*loc. cit*. 1783). It must therefore have been built between 1778 and 1783. There can thus be little doubt that no. 2 was the inn at which Johnson stayed. His opinion of it was shared by Arthur Young, who had stayed there a few years earlier and in his *Farmer's Tour through the East of England* (1771) printed a caustic footnote warning the traveller against it : " he will find here nothing but dirt and impertinence " (i. 213, n.).'

Page 430, lines 7 ff. Okeover Hall, where Johnson dined with a numerous company on 14 July 1774 (see also A. M. Broadley, *Dr. Johnson and Mrs. Thrale*, 1910, p. 168), was the mansion of the ancient family of Okeover : it stands on the Staffordshire side of the Dove, two and a half miles from Ashbourne ; it is still the family seat. There is a description of it in Stebbing Shaw's *The Topographer* (1790, ii. 314) :

' The house is not the ancient mansion, of which a view is given in Plot (p. 227), but stands exactly in the same situation. . . . This is quite modern, consisting of a middle and two wings, in form of an half H, built of red brick, edged and ornamented with white stone-work.'

Johnson's host was Edward Walhouse Okeover, who in 1763 had inherited the estate of his grand-uncle, Leake Okeover, and taken his name ; he died in 1793, aged 41.

The ' chapel ' at Okeover is in fact, and always has been, the parish church : its close proximity to the Hall and its small size may be responsible for the erroneous designation, which persists among the natives of the district to this day : the living is a donative in the gift of the Okeover family. The church was thoroughly ' restored ' by Sir Gilbert Scott in 1859.

The epitaph which Johnson could not read was almost certainly that

Page 430   *Appendix D*   581

originally inscribed to the memory of William, Lord Zouch, who died in 1447, but altered to commemorate Humphrey Okeover, who died in 1538. The anonymous author of *The History and Topography of Ashbourn*, 1839, reported that the inscription was partly effaced (p. 200). See also the *Portfolio of the Brass Rubbing Society*, 1898, Pt. 9.

Page 430, line 8. Mrs. Gell was, there can be little doubt, the wife of Philip Gell (*ante*, v. 431, note 4): they were married on 11 May 1774. She was Dorothy, daughter and co-heir of William Milnes of Aldercar Park, Derbyshire; she was born on 4 Feb. 1758 and died on 29 April 1808. Sir William Gell, 1777–1836, the archaeologist and traveller, was her second son. For the Gell pedigree see Ince and Sleigh in *The Reliquary*, 1870–71, xi, pl. 31.

Page 430, line 12 and note 1. Johnson wrote on fol. 35 verso of the manuscript of this tour: ' There seem to be few books less depraved by transcription than Martial.'

Martial was apparently not among the books that Johnson owned when an undergraduate, but Miss Carter told her father, in 1738, that he was ' very fond ' of this poet. See A. L. Reade, *Gleanings*, v. 30, and M. Pennington, *Memoirs of Mrs. Carter*, 1808, i. 39.

Page 430, lines 13 and 14. The Dyotts were a wealthy Staffordshire family, which had its principal seat at Freeford Hall, near Lichfield. The members of it whom Johnson met were the reigning squire, Richard Dyott (1723–87), his wife, Catherine Herrick (1724–1810), and their daughters, of whom they had four: Catherine (*c.* 1752–1830), Mary, Hannah (or Anne), and Lucy. The eldest of these daughters married, 2 May 1775, Robert Dale of Ashbourne (1749–1835). The ' old Mrs. Dale ' mentioned by Johnson under date 16 July (*ante*, v. 431) was either this Robert Dale's mother (*c.* 1694–1783) or his grandmother (†1777). See S. Glover, *Hist. and Gazetteer of the County of Derby*, 1829, ii. 47; Erdeswicke, *Survey of Staffordshire*, 1844, pp. 310–11; Burke's *Landed Gentry*, 1921, p. 542; Johnson's *Letters*, Nos. 414 and 418; A. M. Broadley, *Dr. Johnson and Mrs. Thrale*, 1910, pp. 169, 171; and General Wm. Dyott's *Diary*, ed. R. W. Jeffery, 1907, i. 21. General Dyott was Richard Dyott's second son: see *D.N.B.*

Page 430, line 14. Thomas Flint was Dr. Taylor's confidential clerk and factotum. He married on 2 Sept. 1766, as his second wife, Mary, the widow of Thomas Collier; she was the only daughter of John Dunn, innkeeper, of Wolseley Bridge, Staffs., and was claimed by Johnson as his ' cousin '; she was born in 1733 and died in the spring of 1776, leaving two daughters, Mary and Sophia, by her first husband, and a son and daughter by Flint. Flint appears to have wrongfully deprived, for a considerable time at any rate, his step-daughters of their share of their mother's estate. They appealed to Johnson to help them to get their wrongs righted and he did what he could. Flint married a third time in 1783 and died in June 1787, aged 63. Mr. A. L. Reade has, with his customary thoroughness, assembled all the known facts about Flint and Johnson's assistance to his step-daughters, the Miss Colliers: see *Gleanings*, 1939, ix. 25 ff., 75, and 228.

Page 431, line 7. Mrs. Thrale, in her diary of the tour, described 'Mr. Gilpin and his friend Parker' as 'young men travelling about England for pleasure and improvement'. A. M. Broadley, *Dr. Johnson and Mrs. Thrale*, 1910, p. 170. Many years later, in 1816, she gave Duppa further information about them; that about Parker, although imperfect, enables us to establish his identity; that about Gilpin appears to be inaccurate. What I take to be her original note to Duppa on Gilpin was printed by Croker; it is:

'Mr. Gilpin was an accomplished youth, at this time an undergraduate at Oxford. His father was an old silversmith near Lincoln's Inn Fields.' Croker's *Boswell*, 1835, v, p. 196.

The 'old silversmith' was almost certainly Thomas Gilpin, goldsmith, whose business address was, from 1731 to 1773, Lincoln's Inn Back Gate, Serle Street, next door to Will's Coffee-house. Sir A. Heal, *London Goldsmiths*, 1935, p. 160, and *Daily Post*, 21 Dec. 1731. There is no evidence that any son of his went to Oxford. The only Oxford undergraduate of the name at the time was William Gilpin (1757–1848), who matriculated from Queen's College 13 July 1773; his father was the Reverend William Gilpin (1724–1804), Master of Cheam School and author of the various 'Picturesque Tours'; no member of his family was a silversmith or goldsmith. At Cambridge the only Gilpins at the time were Jeremiah, admitted at St. John's in 1770, son of Robert and born at Broughton-in-Furness; and Richard, admitted a Fellow-Commoner of Clare in the same year; he was born in London, and, according to the University records, ' probably a son of Thomas Gilpin of Hockliffe, Beds.' The present adverse circumstances prevent further research and the 'accomplished' Mr. Gilpin must remain unidentified.

John Parker, of Browsholme Hall, West Riding, Yorks., was born *c.* 1755; he went to Eton and was admitted Fellow-Commoner of Christ's College, Cambridge, 2 October 1771, where he resided till Michaelmas 1774. He was Bowbearer of the Forest of Bowland and M.P. for Clitheroe from 11 Sept. 1780 till 20 April 1782. He married Beatrix, daughter of Thomas Lister of Gisburn Park, Yorks., in 1778, and died 25 May 1797. See T. D. Whitaker, *Whalley*, 1872, i. 340; *Parl. Return of Members of Parl.* 1878, Pt. ii, p. 165; and Burke's *Landed Gentry*, 1937, p. 1748. Thomas Lister Parker, 1779–1858, the antiquary, was his eldest son (see the *D.N.B.*).

Page 431, lines 23 ff. Kedleston House was built by Nathaniel Curzon,

Page 433   *Appendix D*

first Baron Scarsdale, in 1761–5 and later ; Robert Adam was the chief architect. For a general description of the mansion see Swarbrick, *Robert Adam and his brothers*, 1916, pp. 84 ff. The Reverend William Langley's statement that the marble pillars were ' dug . . . in a quarry of Northamptonshire ' is incorrect ; they are of veined alabaster from the quarries of Red-hill, Nottinghamshire, which belonged to Lord Scarsdale. Lysons, *Magna Brit.* v, *Derbyshire*, 1817, p. 194.

Page 433, lines 3 ff. and notes 1 and 5. Sir Lynch Salusbury Cotton, 4th baronet, was Mrs. Thrale's uncle. He was born *c.* 1705, was Member of Parliament for Denbigh during four parliaments, 1749–74, and died 14 Aug. 1775. He married Elizabeth Abigail, daughter of Rowland Cotton of Bellaport, Shropshire, and Etwall, Derbyshire ; she died on 4 Jan. 1777.

Mrs. Thrale, writing on 26 July 1774, says :

' On this day we took our leave of Combermere where we had been very kindly treated. I left them, too, liking them better than ever I liked them, though Sir Lynch's rusticity and his Wife's emptiness afforded nothing but a possibility of change from disgust to insipidity.' A. M. Broadley, *Dr. Johnson and Mrs. Thrale*, 1910, p. 180.

After her uncle's death she wrote :

' Sir Lynch Cotton my Uncle was an odd Man as I have seen ; impudent yet bashful, full of rusticity which offended, but had humour to divert one, he would say Things nobody else thought on, and would be merry about his own Fortune, his own Children, and his own Vices, with a sort of steady Insensibility, that looked like archness.' *Thraliana*, ed. Miss K. C. Balderston, i. 103.

Sir Lynch's eldest son and successor, Sir Robert Salusbury Cotton, entertained Johnson and the Thrales at Llewenny (see *ante*, v. 435, note 2) from 28 July to 18 August and took them to numerous places in the neighbourhood. He was born *c.* 1739, married, in 1767, Frances, youngest daughter and coheir of J. R. Stapleton of Bodrhyddan, Flint., was one of the Members of Parliament for Cheshire from 1780 to 1796, and died on 24 August 1809. See G. E. C., *Complete Baronetage*, iv. 84 ; G. Ormerod's *Cheshire*, ed. Helsby, 1882, iii. 415 ; and *Parl. Report of Members of Parl.*, 1878, Pt. ii, pp. 149, 162, 175, and 188. Mrs. Thrale describes him and his wife in her diary of the tour :

' Mr. Cotton seems to live very hospitably, rather in my own opinion splendidly, but his neighbours who should know best seem to think differently of him. I believe he is a man who obstinately resists imposition, and declares it his intention to clear the estate by frugality and diligence. . . . The lady is a most amiable being, charitable, compassionate, modest, and gentle to a degree, almost unequalled by any woman whose want of fortune, person, or understanding did not set her apparently below her husband. She is, however, proportionately equal to him in both knowledge and riches, but so pliant, so tender, so attentive to his health, his children, and expenses, that I sincerely think of all the people I ever yet knew—he is the *happiest* in a Wife.' A. M. Broadley, *Dr. Johnson and Mrs. Thrale*, 1910, p. 191.

Johnson barely mentions Sir Robert and he had a poor opinion of his wife :

' Mr. Johnson does not value Mrs. Cotton as much as she deserves. I mentioned her sweetness of disposition. True, says he, but it is in her nature, and one thanks her no more for being sweet than a honeycomb.' *Ibid.* pp. 192–3. See also *Thraliana*, ed. Miss K. C. Balderston, i. 169.

Combermere, in Cheshire, 3½ miles north-east of Whitchurch, came into the possession of the Cottons at the Dissolution of the Monasteries ; it was sold by the present Viscount Combermere in 1918 to Sir Kenneth Crossley ; the last member of the family to live there was the third Viscount Combermere, who died in 1898. The mansion house, Combermere Abbey, was built on the site of a twelfth-century Cistercian monastery. The lake, said to be the largest natural lake in a private park in England, is long rather than wide. See G. Ormerod's *Cheshire*, ed. Helsby, 1882, iii. 402 ff.

The chapel which Sir Lynch had built for his tenants was at Burleydam, about a mile and a half from Combermere Abbey ; it is now, 1940, the church of St. Mary the Virgin and St. Michael and the parish church of Burleydam Dodcott-cum-Wilkesley. It was consecrated in 1769 and endowed with £1,000—its present annual income from the Combermere endowment is £22. The present vicar, the Rev. A. Lowndes Moir, courteously informs me that, while the existing chalice and paten are not particularly striking, the ewer is remarkable ; all the communion vessels are engraved with the Cotton arms. The pales and gates, which were brought from Llewenny, were replaced in 1878 by plain iron railings with gates to match, but some handsome wrought-iron gate-posts remain. See Broadley, *op. cit.*, p. 178, Ormerod, *op. cit.* iii. 401, and S. Bagshaw, *History, Gazetteer and Directory of Chester*, 1850, pp. 356–60.

Page 433, lines 8 ff. and note 4. John Needham, 10th Viscount Kilmorey, was the third son of Robert, the 7th viscount. He was born in January 1711, commanded a company of Grenadiers in the 2nd Foot Guards from 1737 to 1748, succeeded to the peerage on the death of his brother Thomas, the 9th viscount, in 1768, and died in 1791. See G. E. C., *Complete Peerage*, 1929, vii. 262. He made an extremely unfavourable impression on Mrs. Thrale, who, in her diary of the tour, described him as :

' A man who, joining the bluster of an Officer to the haughtiness of a Nobleman newly come to his estate—an estate which had held his Soul in suspense perhaps for twenty years—endeavours to swell the gay Jack Needham into the magnificent Lord Kilmorey, and is to me extremely offensive.' A. M. Broadley, *Dr. Johnson and Mrs. Thrale*, 1910, p. 177.

She continues :

'His severity is mere clownishness, his civilities carry an air of condescension no way pleasing, and his general behaviour is so turgid that if one is not shocked at it, one must be diverted. So absurdly triumphant too, comparing his house to Keddlestone, his estate with Lord Scarsdale's, and his pool with Sir Lynch Cotton's Lake. All that he said and did, even his politeness, excited and promoted disgust.' *Ibid.* pp. 177–8.

The Shavington estate (in the parish of Adderley, Salop), which had been in the Needham family since the fifteenth century, was sold in 1884. G. E. C., *op. cit. supra*, p. 265.

Page 433, lines 20 ff. Sir Rowland Hill was the son of John Hill, of Wem, and nephew of Richard Hill (1655–1727), the diplomatist (see *D.N.B.*), whose estate he inherited. He was baptized on 28 Sept. 1705, created a baronet on 20 Jan. 1726/7, sheriff of Shropshire, 1731–2, and Member of Parliament for Lichfield, 1734–41 ; he died on 7 Aug. 1783. See G.E.C., *Complete Baronetage*, 1906, v. 65, and *Parl. Return of Members of Parl.* 1878, pt. ii, p. 78. Sir Rowland's first wife, Jane, daughter of Sir Brian Broughton, died in December 1773. 'Miss Hill' was presumably their daughter. Mrs. Thrale thought her deserving of more than ordinary notice. She writes :

'Her conversation is elegant, her dress uncommonly vulgar, her manner lofty if not ostentatious, and her whole appearance below that of a common housemaid. She is, however, by far the most conversible Female I have seen since I left home, her character, I hear, is respectable, and her address is as polite as can be wished.' A. M. Broadley, *Dr. Johnson and Mrs. Thrale*, 1910, p. 181.

Hawkstone Park, near Hodnet, Shropshire, remained the seat of the Hill family till 1906.

Page 435, line 14. Croker printed the following extract from a letter of Mrs. Piozzi to Duppa :

'Of those *ill-fated* walls Dr. Johnson might have learned the extent from any one. He has since put me fairly out of countenance by saying, "I have known *my mistress* fifteen years, and never saw her fairly out of humour but on Chester wall " ; it was because he would keep Miss Thrale beyond her hour of going to bed to walk on the wall, where, from the want of light, I apprehended some accident to her—perhaps to him.' Croker's *Boswell*, 1848, p. 417, note 7.

According to Mrs. Piozzi Johnson was also out of humour at Chester, for it was here that he rebuked her for what she describes as 'a foolborn jest':

'Oh, madam, you had rather crack a Joke, I know, than stop to learn any thing I can teach; so take the road you were born to run.' *British Synonymy*, 1794, i. 324.

Page 435, line 19. The headmaster of the King's School, Chester, at the time of Johnson's visit was the Reverend Robert Vanbrugh. He was born in 1728 and educated at Sedbergh, Eton, and Cambridge. He was admitted sizar at St. John's College in 1748, graduated B.A. in 1753, and commenced M.A. in 1770. After holding curacies at Aldingham, Lancs., and Dent, Yorks., where he was also a master of the local school, he was, in 1768, appointed to the King's School. On his appointment, 8 Jan. 1768, it was ordered that ' as an encouragement he be paid the further sum of Forty-two Pounds (over and above his salary) at the rate of 10 guineas on each of the next 4 quarter days ' (Act Book of Institutions to Livings, &c., in the Diocese of Chester). He resigned his headmastership in 1783. Mr. Vanbrugh was the Rector of Buckland, Glos., from 1776 to 1784: he was appointed a Minor Canon of Chester in 1780. His death is recorded in the March number of the *Gent. Mag.* 1784 (vol. liv, pt. i, p. 235) as having occurred ' lately, at Hartford, near Huntingdon '. See Venn, *Alumni Cantabrigienses*, pt. i, vol. iv, p. 293; but I owe many of the details to the courtesy of Mr. T. Cann Hughes, of Lancaster.

The present headmaster, Mr. C. W. Baty, tells me that the refectory of the abbey remained in use as the King's School from 1541 to 1876: it is still used by the school on special occasions.

Page 436, and note 3. Mrs. Thrale gives a description of Bach-y-Graig in her diary of the tour: she writes under date 30 July:

'I went to see my possessions, which I found are worse than I had expected. The house less spacious and the woods less thick. In the house, however, are three excellent rooms, over which there seems little else but pigeon-holes in a manner peeping out of the roof, and at the top of all a ridiculous Lanthorn with a ladder to get up to it. . . . The walls of the house and the roof of it have, I think, solidity enough to last some centuries, and such is the situation that the place might really be made delightful if one pleased. . . . I really think if the top was taken off and a story of decent rooms built in their stead, the house might yet be convenient and fit for a family.' A. M. Broadley, *Dr. Johnson and Mrs. Thrale*, 1910, pp. 183-4.

The house, of which there is a drawing in Broadley's book, was pulled down early in the nineteenth century; the present farm-house, which bears its name, was built out of the stone of the stables and coach-house. (The sixteenth-century weather-vane is now, 1939, at Brynbella, the house which Mrs. Piozzi built in the neighbourhood.) Major E. P. Salusbury, the grandson of Sir John Salusbury, Mrs. Piozzi's adopted nephew and heir, lived for some years in the house with his tenants; he died in 1908 and ten years later his daughter, Mrs. R. V. Colman, sold the property.

Mrs. Thrale tried hard to save the woods from destruction when her husband was in financial difficulties. Her efforts were seconded by Johnson. Writing in 1810 she says:

' Dr. Johnson tho' he scorned my Country . . . and wanted *me* to scorn it . . . so far was pliant even to my Prejudices as to help me to request Mr. Thrale not

Pages 438-43   *Appendix D*   587

to cut down old Bachygraig wood. . . . After Mr. Thrale had endured a little Solicitation for my Timber [he] coldly replied " Ladies have a charter for teizing . . . but be pleased to have a care, and not set your old Bull Dog upon me— for I will bear nothing of that sort . . . except from a Lady ".' (*Piozziana*, vol. i, folio 76, MS. now, 1964, in the possession of Brigadier Hugh Mainwaring, Hafod-y-Coed, St. Asaph.)

The woods were cut down and the timber brought Mr. Thrale £4,000. See *Thraliana*, ed. Miss K. C. Balderston, i. 222 and 424.

Page 438, line 6. The 'Chapel of Lleweney' must be, as Sir J. E. Lloyd points out to me, the Carmelite Friary in the outskirts of Denbigh. It was founded towards the end of the thirteenth century by Sir John Salusbury of Llewenny, who died in 1289 and was buried in the Friary Church. Pennant's report that the church, which was in his time converted into a barn, was the only remaining building is inaccurate, as some of the claustral buildings still survive. The roof of the church was destroyed by fire in 1898. See the Royal Commission's *Inventory of the Ancient Monuments in Wales, Denbigh*, 1914, pp. 69-70, and Pennant, *Tour in Wales*, 1784, ii. 38.

Page 438, lines 10 ff. The parish church of Denbigh, Whitchurch, was ' for many years neglected and practically deserted, save for burials ' ; it was restored in 1845 and again in 1908, and is now once more the parish church. It contains an alabaster tomb, with effigies, of Sir John Salusbury of Llewenny (†1578) and his wife, and a mural monument, also in alabaster, to Humphrey Llwyd (1527-68), the antiquary.

See *ante*, v. 440, the Royal Commission's *Inventory of the Ancient Monuments in Wales, Denbigh*, 1914, pp. 42-3, and Pennant, *Tour in Wales*, 1784, ii. 27 ff.

Page 442, lines 18 ff. The cascade or waterfall was that at Diserth. Pennant, after giving the position of the church as lying ' in a picturesque and romantic bottom ', continues :

' A water-fall in the deep and rounded hollow of a rock, finely darkened with ivy, once gave additional beauty to this spot ; but of late the diverting of the waters to a mill, has robbed the place of this elegant variation.' *Tour in Wales*, 1784, ii, p. 6.

The other house, ' belonging to Mr. Lloyd ', which Johnson and his friends visited after leaving the Diserth waterfall was probably, as Sir J. E. Lloyd suggests to me, Pengwern. This mansion was the seat of Edward Lloyd, c. 1710-95, who was High Sheriff of Flintshire in 1768-9, and created a baronet in 1778. His first wife was Anna Maria, daughter and heiress of Evan Lloyd of Pengwern. The first Baron Mostyn was his grand-nephew and heir. G. E. C., *Compl. Baronetage*, v. 201 and J. Y. W. Lloyd, *History of . . . the Ancient Nobility of Powys Fadog*, v. 299.

Page 443, lines 10 ff. John Myddelton of Gwaynynog was born in November 1724; he matriculated from Oriel College, Oxford, 12 March

1742/3, but took no degree : he became a colonel in the militia in 1782 and died, without issue, on 8 Sept. 1792.

Gwaynynog, or, as it is often spelled, Gwaenynog, the family seat, is two miles south-west of Denbigh. Mrs. Thrale's description of the company she met there at dinner on 5 August differs from Johnson's. She says :

' Here I saw a company of genuine Welch folks, and cannot boast the elegance of the society. The women were vastly below the men in proportion, their manners were gross, and their language more contracted. The men, however, were not drunk nor the women inclined to disgrace themselves.' A. M. Broadley, *Dr. Johnson and Mrs. Thrale*, 1910, p. 189.

She added :

' Mr. Johnson's fame has penetrated *thus* far, and Mr. Myddleton said he had never before had so great a man under his roof, that he was perfectly sensible of the honour done him, etc.' *Ibid.* 190.

Mr. Myddelton invited the party to visit him on their return from the Lleyn peninsula and they made Gwaynynog their head-quarters from 29 August to 6 September : under the first-mentioned date Mrs. Thrale writes :

' We pushed forward for Gwenynnog, and got there in the close of the evening and were very kindly received. Mr. Myddelton is apparently pleased with Mr. Thrale's company, and proud of Mr. Johnson's. The lady too is agreeable enough.' *Ibid.* p. 205.

On the next day, 30 August, she records :

' This seems to be the only place where we have been received and treated with attention for our own value. At other places we have been taken in because it was fit to take us. . . . Here we are loved, esteemed, and honoured, and here I daresay we might spend the whole Winter if we would.' *Ibid.* p. 206.

There is other evidence of the hospitality of the squire and the natural beauty of the place. Pennant says in his *Tour in Wales* (1784, ii. 44) :

' From Denbigh I went to the hospitable house of Gwaenynog, about two miles distant, fronted by the most majestic oaks in our principality. The fine wooded dingles belonging to the demesne are extremely well worth visiting; they are most judiciously cut with walks by the owner, John Myddelton, esq ; and afford as beautiful scenery in their kind, as any we have to boast.'

Richard Twining is no less enthusiastic. Writing to his brother in 1785 he says :

' We breakfasted at Colonel Myddelton's, at Gwynanog. This is, altogether, better worth seeing than any place which I met with in Denbighshire. It is not so highly ornamented as Mr. Yorke's at Erthigg, but it is much more wild and picturesque, and contains a much greater variety of scene. . . . I could not help saying to Hughes, " I wish I could show my brother this spot ". Colonel Myddelton immediately turned round ; " Bring him next summer; I have plenty of beds and shall be heartily glad to see you both "*.' Selections from Papers of the Twining Family*, ed. R. Twining, 1887, p. 116.

Gwaynynog passed out of the Myddelton family in 1870, when the Reverend Robert Myddelton (1795–1876) sold it. See also Croker's *Boswell*, 1835, v. 211 note, and W. M. Myddelton, *Family of Myddelton* (1910).

Page 443, line 18. Evan Evans, 1731–88, was one of the earliest translators of Welsh poems into English. His important work, *Some Specimens of the Poetry of the Ancient Welsh Bards translated into English*, was published in 1764; parts of it were shown in manuscript to Gray, who based his imitations of Welsh poetry upon them. See *Correspondence of Gray*, ed. Toynbee and Whibley, iii. 1229–31, and E. D. Snyder, *Celtic Revival in English Literature*, 1923, pp. 19 ff. Evans, who left Oxford without a degree, took holy orders, but never rose above a curacy. His addiction to strong drink has been adduced as both the cause and effect of his failure to obtain preferment. Thomas Rees, writing in 1815, says :

' [Evans's] disappointment in his profession preyed considerably on his mind, and led him to seek an oblivion to his vexation in excesses which impaired his health and greatly limited his usefulness.' *South Wales*, 1815, p. 465 (Beauties of England and Wales, vol. xviii).

The anonymous editor of his *Specimens* (published at Llanidloes, c. 1862), who quotes the above passage, says (p. 141) :

' He was most averse to the appointment of English prelates to Welsh dioceses. That will partly account for his stationary position in the Establishment. His excessive love of the " wine-cup " may also have had something to do in preventing his appointment to a more lucrative position in the Church.'

See also *The Correspondence of Thomas Percy and Evan Evans*, edited by Aneirin Lewis (The Percy Letters, ed. D. Nichol Smith and Cleanth Brooks). Louisiana State Univ. Press, 1957.

Page 443, line 11 from foot. The Welsh grammar of David ap Rhees, or, more accurately, Siôn Dafydd Rhys, was published at London in 1592 under the title *Cambrobrytannicæ Cymraecæve linguæ institutiones et rudimenta*; it is a folio of some 300 pages. Robert Williams describes it as ' a work of deep learning ... it shews not only great labour, but a thorough knowledge of the language of which it treats, not merely of its grammatical rules, but the Welsh metres and their concatenations, which [Rhys] has taken astonishing trouble to explain and illustrate '. *Biogr. Dict. of Eminent Welshmen*, 1852, p. 447. Mr. Tom Parry points out that Rhys was greatly indebted to earlier Welsh grammarians, especially Gruffydd Roberts (1567), and that his endeavour to form a Welsh grammar which fitted the framework of Latin grammar was a cardinal error. *Y Llenor*, 1931, p. 40. The book is written in Latin and Welsh : the orthography of the Welsh was Rhys's own ; it was adopted by one or two authors, but was never established. Proposals for a new edition were made early in the nineteenth century, when a prospectus containing a list

… Appendix D … Page 447

of ' subscribers already received ' was issued by J. Evans of Carmarthen. See also W. J. Gruffydd, *Llenyddiaeth Cymru*, 1926, pp. 155 ff., and the *D.N.B.*

Johnson subscribed to *Gorchestion Beirdd Cymru*, a collection of Welsh poems, mostly of the fourteenth and fifteenth centuries, edited by Rhys Jones with the assistance of Evan Evans, and published at Shrewsbury in 1773. *Mod. Lang. Notes*, June 1921, p. 374.

Page 447, line 10 from foot. Mrs. Thrale confirms Johnson's account of the inn at Bangor, and adds to it :

' The accommodations at Bangor were very bad ; poor Mr. Johnson got only a share of some men's room, and the woman of the house proposed that he should sleep with Mr. Thrale and Queeney and I, who were all stuffed in one filthy room.' A. M. Broadley, *Dr. Johnson and Mrs. Thrale*, 1910, p. 196.

Dr. T. Richards, of the University Library, Bangor, suggests that the inn was The Mitre, now named The Castle, near the Cathedral.

Page 447, line 5 from foot. Baron Hill, the seat of the Bulkeley family, about a mile from Beaumaris, is described by Mrs. Thrale as ' a place of beautiful situation commanding the Castle, the streights, and the mountains, an assemblage scarcely to be mended even by the imagination '. A. M. Broadley, *Dr. Johnson and Mrs. Thrale*, 1910, p. 197. The original mansion was built in 1618 by Sir Richard Bulkeley (1533–1621): Pennant, writing in or shortly before 1784, says, ' the present seat has of late been wholly altered, with excellent taste, by its noble owner, by the advice of that elegant architect Mr. Samuel Wyat ' (*Tour in Wales*, ii. 253). The alterations were almost certainly made between Johnson's visit and Pennant's. The noble owner in Johnson's, and Pennant's, time was Thomas James, 7th Viscount Bulkeley of Cashel, in the peerage of Ireland, 1752–1822 ; he devised the estate to the eldest son of his uterine brother, Sir Richard Bulkeley Williams, who assumed the name of Bulkeley. Burke's *Dormant Peerages*, 1882, p. 80. The present owner, Sir R. H. Williams Bulkeley, tells me that the house was burnt down soon after his great-great-grandfather inherited it, and that he built its successor (now, 1964, an abandoned shell) on the same site about 1830–5.

Page 447, line 4 from foot. The headmaster of Beaumaris Grammar School at the time of Johnson's visit was the Reverend William Lloyd : he was presented to the mastership on 31 July 1774 and held it till 1778. John Williams, *David Hughes and his Free Grammar School at Beaumaris*, ed. V. Bowen, 1933, p. 26, and A. Ivor Pryce, *The Diocese of Bangor during Three Centuries*, 1929, p. 37. The statutes of the school at the time required the master to be a graduate of Oxford and Mr. Lloyd himself stated that he had met Johnson at University College. I have therefore no hesitation in identifying him with William Lloyd, the son of the Reverend William Lloyd, of Bangor, who matriculated at Oxford from University College on 21 Feb. 1766, aged 17. He took his first

Appendix D

degree in 1769, proceeded M.A. in 1773, and B.D. and D.D. in 1802. Foster, *Alumni Oxon.* 1888, iii. 865. He was ordained priest on 16 July 1775 (A. Ivor Pryce, *op. cit.* p. 114) and licensed to the curacies of Llandegfan and Llansadwrn. See also below.

Page 447, line 3 from foot. The late Registrar, Mr. A. Ivor Pryce (†1940), told me that Thomas Roberts, born *c.* 1698, was Notary Public from 1751 and Notary Public and Registrar of the Diocese of Bangor from 1754 till 1778, when he presumably died. The office of Registrar was at that time important, as the proving of wills, and other legal business, passed through the Diocesan Registry.

From Mrs. Thrale's diary it appears that Mr. Roberts put up the party at his house in Bangor the night of 19-20 August. She writes :

' As I was returning to breakfast at the Inn I spyed Mr. Thrale standing at a gentleman's door with the master of the house. He invited us in, lamented our ill accommodation, and promised us beds at his house for tonight. We accepted his kindness and he ordered his Boat to Sea, and accompanied us to Beaumaris, where he sent for the Schoolmaster to show us the curiosities of the place. The Schoolmaster claimed acquaintance with Mr. Johnson. . . . The gentleman was desirous of shewing Mr. Johnson his School, and so he did, and we rowed back to our good hospitable Mr. Roberts, whose Wife gave us her best tea, and lodged us in her best beds.' A. M. Broadley, *Dr. Johnson and Mrs. Thrale*, 1910, pp. 196-7.

Page 448, lines 22, 23. Mrs. Thrale says that the party landed at ' Llanver ' where Mrs. Hugh Griffith of Brynodol preferred to live :

' She entertained us chearfully, was sorry she was not at her other house (Brynodol), but insisted on our using that instead of an Inn when we went further into Llin, where no accommodation of a public kind could be hoped for. From this good lady's we rowed on to Carnarvon, where the guns were firing for the arrival of General Paoli, whom we soon saw perambulating the Town and Castle under the conduct of Sir Thomas Wynn. Paoli embraced Mr. Johnson and Sir Thomas invited us to dine with him to-morrow.' A. M. Broadley, *Dr. Johnson and Mrs. Thrale*, 1910, p. 198.

Sir Thomas Wynn, 1736-1807. was at this time Lord Lieutenant of Carnarvonshire and M.P. for the county ; he had succeeded his father in the baronetcy in the previous year and was created Baron Newborough, in the peerage of Ireland, in 1776. G. E. C., *Complete Peerage*, 1936, ix. 508. For his first wife see *ante*, v. 449, note 1.

Page 448, line 24. Mrs. Piozzi says, in a note printed by Croker, ' Lieutenant Troughton I do recollect, loquacious and intelligent he was. He wore a uniform, and belonged, I think, to a man of war.' Croker, commenting on this note, says :

' He was made a lieutenant in 1762, and died in 1786, in that rank ; he was on half-pay, and did not belong to any ship when he met Dr. Johnson, in 1774. It seems then that, even so late as this, half pay officers wore their uniform in the ordinary course of life.' Boswell's *Life*, ed. 1848, p. 422, note 2.

Mr. J. B. Smith, the Admiralty Librarian, informs me that Mr. Ellis Troughton was, at the age of 29 and after eight years' service in the Navy, appointed 5th Lieutenant of H.M.S. *Dublin* on 4 April 1759 ; he was on half-pay from October 1763 till March 1777, when he was appointed a lieutenant of H.M.S. *Conqueror*, in which he served till November 1778, being superseded abroad ; he was on half-pay from 21 June 1780 till his death on 7 April 1786.

Page 450, line 8. Humphrey Llwyd shows, in his ' De Mona Druidum Insula ', that the Mona of Tacitus, Pliny the Elder, and Dio Cassius was Anglesea and not the Isle of Man. This tract was originally written as a letter, dated 5 April 1568, to Abraham Ortelius, who published it in his *Theatrum Orbis Terrarum*, 1570 and subsequently; it was also appended to Sir John Price's *Historiæ Brytannicæ Defensio*, 1573, and reprinted by Moses Williams in the eighteenth century (*Humfredi Llwyd Armigeri, Britannicæ Descriptionis Commentariolum*, 1731). The statement, made by W. Rowlands (*Cambrian Bibliography*, 1869, p. 360) and repeated by the *D.N.B.* (s.v. H. Llwyd), that only six copies of Moses Williams's edition were printed, is a serious error ; in some copies, e.g. two in the Bodleian and two in the National Library of Wales, the names of forty-seven subscribers are given, and in a copy which belonged to Lewis Morris, now in the last-mentioned library, there is a note in his hand : ' There were but fourscore copies of this Book printed .' For Llwyd see T. M. Chotzen in *Trans. of the Cymmrodorion Soc.* 1937, pp. 129-44, F. J. North in *Arch. Camb.* 1937, pp. 11-63, and H. N. Jerman in the *National Library of Wales Journal*, 1940, p. 164.

Page 450, lines 9 ff. ' Llanerk ' is Johnson's spelling of Clynnog, usually styled Clynnog Fawr, nine and a half miles from Carnarvon. The remarkable parish church and the older chapel formerly adjacent to it are mentioned by John Leland, who travelled through Wales in or about the years 1536-9. He wrote :

' *Clunnok Vaur*, a Monasteri sumtime of White Monkes suppressid many Yeres ago. But the Original of this Monasteri was by S. Benow, of whom mention is made in S. Wenefrides Life. The Whit Monkes were of a newer Fundation. Guithin, Uncle to one of the Princes of North-Wales, was the first Giver of Clunnok Village and Place to Bennow. The Chirch that is now ther with Crosse Isles is almost as bigge as S. *Davides*, but it is of a new Worke. The old Chirch wher S. Bennow liyth is hard by the new. This *Clunnok* stondith almost on the Shore of the Maine Sea x. Miles above Cair Arvon toward the Counteri of Lline.' *Itinerary*, ed. Hearne, 1711, vol. v, p. 13.

He later describes the parish church as ' the fayrest Chirch yn al Cairarvonshire, as better then Bangor'. *Ibid*. p. 42. Pennant, nearly 250 years later, is even more enthusiastic :

' The church [of Clynnog] is the most magnificent structure of its kind in North Wales, built in the form of a cross ; the length from east to west is about a hundred and thirty-eight feet, from north to south seventy.' *Tour in Wales*, 1784, ii, p. 208.

Pennant's statement (*ibid.* p. 209) that nothing remained of the chapel but the covered cloister connecting it with the church is erroneous; much remained in a dilapidated condition in 1849: the chapel was extensively restored in 1856 and again in 1913. See *Archaeol. Camb.* vol. iv, 1849, pp. 118 ff.; ser. v, vol. xvii, 1900, pp. 174 ff.; ser. vi, vol. xiv, 1914, pp. 271 ff.; and H. H. Hughes and H. L. North, *Old Churches of Snowdonia*, 1924, pp. 262 ff.

The parson, whom Johnson failed to find, was the Reverend Richard Ellis. He matriculated at Oxford from Jesus College, 17 Dec. 1748, aged 17, took his first degree in 1752, and proceeded M.A. in 1755: the college presented him to the vicarage in 1768 and he held the living till his death in 1805. The late vicar, the Reverend John Davies (†1956), to whom I owe this information, told me that he hung the two bells and introduced new seating into the church.

Page 450, lines 13 ff. Bodvil or Bodvel, about two miles from Pwllheli on the Pwllheli–Nevin road, was the first home of Mrs. Thrale's parents and Mrs. Thrale's birth-place: it is to-day (1939) a farm-house. Mrs. Thrale's own description of her visit is given in her Welsh diary under date 23 August:

'My Master took me to Bodville where I saw the place which I first saw, and looked at the old pond with pleasure, though it is now dry. The walk of Sycamores is all cut away. . . . The present possessors of the house were very civil, and indulged all my silly curiosity, letting me look into all their hiding-places.' A. M. Broadley, *Dr. Johnson and Mrs. Thrale*, 1910, p. 201.

The exact date of her birth was 16 January 1741 (O.S.) and that of her baptism at Llannor Church 10 February following. Her record continues:

'We rode on then [after visiting Dick Lloyd's mistress at Tynewydd] to my Parish Church at Llanere, which is truly wretched, and so are its few inhabitants. We examined the register and found that I was baptized on the 10th of February 1742.' *Ibid.* p. 202.

The register of baptisms, now deposited in St. Peter's Church, Pwllheli, gives the correct year, 1741. Mrs. Thrale got the year of her birth wrong on other occasions. See *Thraliana*, ed. Miss K. C. Balderston, i. 3, note 1, and Mr. J. L. Clifford's *H. L. Piozzi*, 1941, pp. 8 ff.

Page 451, lines 5 ff. Mrs. Thrale records under date 23 August:

'From here [Bodvel] we wished to go to Tynewydd, where my poor old friend Dick Lloyd lived, who had played many a game of romps with me, and at draughts with my Father before I was seven years old. I did not remember the road to his house, though I used to go there often and beg milk, but then I walked, and now, as Mr. Johnson hates walking, and no carriage way could be found, we borrowed horses of the people at Bodvel and rode over to Tynewydd. There we found Poor Mr. Lloyd's mistress or maid, to whom he left his little all, and she shewed us where he had hung Queeney's print in the place of honour.' A. M. Broadley, *Dr. Johnson and Mrs. Thrale*, 1910, p. 202.

Appendix D

Richard Lloyd was the boon companion of John Salusbury, Mrs. Thrale's father, when the latter was living at Bodvel, and he acted, for many years, as his business agent in connexion with the tithes of Tydweiliog and Llangwnodl. There is, in the John Rylands Library, Manchester, a series of business letters from him to John Salusbury and his wife (*Eng. MS.* 599). He was High Sheriff of Carnarvonshire in 1760, and died in May 1771. John Jones (Myrddin Fardd), *Gleanings from God's Acre*, 1903, p. 149.

Page 452, lines 11 ff. Mrs. Thrale records under date 24 August her account of Cefn Amwlch and its squire :

'We went on to Kefnamwylloch and saw a man, in my mind, very respectable; he found the place a ruin, and it is now a very habitable house ; he found the demesne a waste ; he has divided it into fields and gardens, and has a hot-house and vinery [pinery *MS.*]. He gave us the first melon we have seen since we came from home. This is the Squire of Kefnamylloch, and he has possessed the estate but a year.' A. M. Broadley, *Dr. Johnson and Mrs. Thrale*, 1910, p. 203.

The squire was John Griffith, who was High Sheriff of Carnarvonshire in 1765 ; he died *s.p.* in 1794 at the age of 52, and bequeathed his estate to his cousin, Jane Wynne, of Voelas, who married the Hon. Charles Finch, second son of the third Earl of Aylesford. See John Edwards Griffith, *Pedigrees of Anglesey and Carnarvonshire Families* (Horncastle, priv. pr.), 1914, p. 169, Burke's *Landed Gentry*, 1886, ii. 2057. The estate is now, 1940, held by Col. J. C. Wynne Finch.

Page 453, line 19. Johnson and the Thrales probably, but not certainly, stayed at Chirk Castle ; they appear to have been entertained, not by the squire, Richard Myddelton (†1795), but by his chaplain. Mrs. Thrale's record of the visit is much fuller than Johnson's :

' From Wrexham we went on the 8th to Chirk Castle, but I must observe that Wrexham afforded us the best lodging we have had at any Inn since we set out. Chirk Castle is by far the most enviable dwelling I have yet ever seen, ancient and spacious, full of splendour and dignity, yet with every possible convenience for obscurity and retirement. Here we saw the best Library we have been shewn in Wales, and a ridiculous Chaplain whose conversation with Mr. Johnson made me ready to burst with laughing.' A. M. Broadley, *Dr. Johnson and Mrs. Thrale*, 1910, p. 208.

There is, however, at Chirk no record or tradition that Johnson ever stayed there. For Chirk Castle, see Pennant, *Tour in Wales*, 1784, i. 285 ff., and the Royal Commission's *Inventory of the Ancient Monuments of Wales*, Denbigh, 1914, pp. 32 ff.

Page 455, line 2. The library Johnson saw was that of Dr. John Taylor, 1704-66, the Cambridge classical scholar and University Librarian (see the *D.N.B.* and *ante*, iii. 318 and 524). He was a native of Shrewsbury and attended the grammar school there ; to it he left a portion of his collection of books. Hugh Owen, one of the historians of Shrewsbury, wrote of him :

Page 455   *Appendix D*

'His library at the time of his death was large and valuable. This, with the residue of his fortune, for the support of an exhibition at St. John's [Cambridge], he bequeathed to the school where he received his education ; reserving, however, to his friend and physician, Dr. Askew, all his MSS. and such of his printed books as contained his marginal annotations.' *Some Account of the Ancient and Present State of Shrewsbury*, 1808, p. 392.

The number of manuscripts and annotated books was apparently very great, but the bequest, which was received in 1767, added about 3,500 volumes to the school library. See J. Nichols, *Lit. Anecd.* iv. 511 and 513, G. W. Fisher, *Annals of Shrewsbury School*, 1899, p. 242, and an account of the school library by Mr. J. B. Oldham (to whom I owe my thanks) in *The Library*, 1935, xvi. 59.

The Library room, with the gallery (now removed) above it and the chapel below it, formed one wing of the school buildings ; when the school moved, in 1882, to Little Grange, it was used as a museum ; it is now (1939) an art gallery.

Page 455, line 12. The 'old tower' is the sole remaining fragment of the Norman castle of Bridgnorth ; it is 70 feet high and leans 13 or more degrees out of the perpendicular. The local authorities have carefully preserved it. See R. W. Eyton, *Antiq. of Shropshire*, 1854, i. 253 ff., and G. Bellett, *Antiq. of Bridgnorth*, 1856, p. 27.

ADDENDA

The extracts in the first two of the following notes are printed with the courteous permission of Yale University, Professor F. A. Pottle, and the McGraw-Hill Book Co., New York.

Page 383, line 13. The actual retort which Boswell out of filial piety forbore to mention was preserved by Malone. His note, now at Yale, is:

'At Auchinleck, when old Mr. Boswell pretended to recommend *Durham on the Galatians*, he concluded, "You may buy it at any time for half a crown or three shillings." *Johnson.* "Sir, it must be better recommended before I give half the money for it." ' Boswell's *Hebrides*, ed. Pottle and Bennett, 1962, p. 443.

Page 403, line 9. Sir John Dalrymple's sacrifice of a seven-year-old sheep seems to have been imaginary, but it nevertheless produced Johnson's Swiftian jest on Lady Dalrymple, repeated maliciously by Boswell who must have been, as Professor Pottle remarks, very loath to suppress it:

'Next morning at breakfast a scene truly ridiculous was exhibited. Sir John, who had boasted of his seven-year old sheep which he had killed on purpose for

596 Addenda

Dr. Johnson and which it was plain could not yet be all eat up, asked the Doctor whether he chose to have the *fore leg* or the *hind leg* to dinner, and having put the question, his lady voted *fore leg*. This contrivance failed, for it being explained to Dr. Johnson that in the Scottish dialect *fore leg* meant *shoulder* in opposition to what alone is in England called *leg*, he honestly said, 'I vote hind leg, to be sure.' He was certain of my vote, and Sir John who could not in decency deny his guest what he liked best, was obliged to join. Poor Lady Dalrymple appeared much disconcerted, and was an innocent victim to the censure of Dr. Johnson, who supposed she was unwilling to give us what was best. He said to me afterwards, "Sir, this is an odious woman. Were I Dalrymple, I'd go and entertain my friends at Edinburgh and leave her to herself. Did you observe her when we voted leg? Sir, she looked as if we had voted for roasting one of her children." The truth, as I afterwards discovered, was that Sir John was not accurate in his information. There was no seven-year old sheep killed, and no leg in the house. Accordingly none appeared, for which some foolish excuse was made.' Boswell's *Hebrides*, ed. Pottle and Bennett, 1962, pp. 450–1.

Professor Pottle describes this as 'the best piece of new Johnsoniana' recovered in his edition.

Page 538 (note on p. 214). Mr. J. C. Maxwell, of Balliol College, in a letter to Dr. R. W. Chapman, dated 14 Jan. 1947, suggests that the reading of the first edition of Sir George Mackenzie's *The Religious Stoic* is perfectly correct. I agree with him. See *O.E.D.*, s.v. *Engine* 3, and Sir William Craigie's *Dictionary of the Older Scottish Tongue*, s.v. *Engine* 2 b. and *Ingine* 4.

THE END OF THE FIFTH VOLUME